COMMENTARY ON THE WHOLE BIBLE, with its thorough, carefully composed and easily understood analyses, fills the void of doubt and lack of understanding. Lovingly prepared by a noted Bible scholar, the Commentary clarifies and enriches every section of the Holy Book.

Whether one selects a Psalm, a passage from Genesis, Ecclesiastes, or the Book of Revelation, he will find in this Commentary an interpretation that will give added meaning, increased inspiration—and heightened comfort to all who seek to understand the Word of God to its fullest.

COMMENTARY
on the
WHOLE BIBLE

•

JAMES M. GRAY

SPIRE BOOKS

FLEMING H. REVELL COMPANY
Old Tappan, New Jersey

ISBN 0-8007-8374-3

A SPIRE BOOK

This book was previously published under the
title *Christian Workers' Commentary on the Whole Bible,*
Copyright © 1953 Fleming H. Revell Company
All rights reserved
Printed in the United States of America
SPIRE BOOKS are published by Fleming H. Revell Company,
Old Tappan, New Jersey 07675, U.S.A.

THE AUTHOR'S EXPLANATION

"Whoever attempts it will find it far easier to write a long commentary than a brief one," says Jamieson, Faussett and Brown. This we believe. The Christian Workers' Commentary represents the labor of eight years in the use of such spare hours as could be found in an otherwise well-filled life, but had the plan permitted its expansion into a series of volumes instead of one, it might have been completed earlier.

HOW TO UNDERSTAND THE BIBLE.

Fundamental to any first-hand knowledge of the Bible is the reading of the Holy Book itself, and all the commentaries in the world can not be substituted for it. Moreover this Commentary is planned on the supposition that such reading will be done in connection with it.

And it should be done in an orderly and scientific way. One of the greatest marvels and most convincing evidences of the Divinity of the Bible is its unity. Although composed of sixty-six different books, and written by different authors at widely different times, yet it has a single plan and purpose in all its history, prophecy and doctrine both in the Old Testament and the New, and it is vital to its understanding that this be recognized in our approach to it.

In other words the serious student should not "start in anywhere" to read the Bible, unless it be as a member of a class whose teacher is capable of filling in the gaps. The Divine Author should be treated at least with the respect of a human author, and given an opportunity to interpret and explain Himself in the practical and orderly unveiling of his thought. No one would begin a volume on science, history or philosophy in the middle of it or towards the close, and still hope to be deeply interested in or clearly understand it, and why act on a different principle in coming to the Word of God?

THE PLAN OF THE COMMENTARY.

Begin where the Holy Spirit has indicated to begin, at Genesis, and follow the order of the books. As tallying with this, the reader or student of this Commentary will find that it does not usually refer a second time to subjects which it has already touched upon, and that the comments do not repeat themselves to any appreciable extent. One should examine the marginal references in his Bible as he proceeds, and then turn back to the first instance where the subject or event is treated to find the comment on it. For example in the case of the Psalms, when one has become acquainted with their general character and the method of arriving at their contents as illustrated in the treatment of a few at the beginning, he may be expected to be capable of analyzing most of the remainder for himself. After that the more difficult, some of the more familiar and popular, and those distinctively Messianic or Millennial are treated more at length, but others are omitted.

Moreover as the reading of the Bible should be done in an orderly and scientific way, so it should be done not in small detachments, but in large and generous portions. For example, in the Commentary, where the character of the contents will permit, its sections or divisions cover not merely a single chapter, but several chapters, and are designed to interest the reader in the broad outlines of revelation. In some instances where their outstanding importance calls for it, special attention is given to chapters, verses or even single words, but these are in the nature of great principles whose understanding carries one a long ways. Nor should beginners in the study of the Bible, and of these we are thinking, spend much time on isolated texts or be too curious about the difficulties and perplexities it presents, but rather seek a general and comprehensive knowledge of its contents as a whole, assured that in the light of such knowledge the difficulties and perplexities will be reduced to a minimum.

THE WAY TO USE IT.

The average layman has been kept in mind in the preparation of the Commentary, hoping that by its aid he might be interested not only to read but really study the Bible. He is advised to begin at the beginning and follow the wake of the Divine Author in the unveiling of His mind to men. First let him read the text in the Bible thoughtfully and prayerfully, and then the Commentary upon it. In the text of the latter are occasional questions, which he is advised to try to answer on the spot; while at the close of each section or division are other questions in the nature of a general review. The theme of the first section is "Creation of the World," and the Bible text is Genesis I. Let him read Genesis I, then the Commentary upon it, giving attention to the questions if any, in its text, and finally review the whole with the questions at the close. This process if pursued, will soon awaken enthusiasm in the study of the Bible, and ere long the sense of joy and strength in the mastery of its inspired contents.

AT THE FAMILY ALTAR.

It is hoped the Commentary may be welcomed at the family altar whose decay is so seriously to be deplored. To make the family altar interesting the element of instruction should be added to it—not too much at a time however, and not too deep. The head of the family after reading the Bible portion might read the Commentary upon it when necessary or desirable to do so, and then put the questions. Or if scarcity of time prevented in the morning, the Bible and the Commentary might be read then, and the questions passed around the family circle in the evening, or for that matter on the following morning. In such cases the prayer to follow will be saved from uniformity and formality.

ADULT BIBLE CLASSES.

But the author has especially considered the Adult Bible Class movement, and the desire so earnestly felt for a method of studying the Bible by "wholes" as some Sunday School leaders have expressed it, whole books and whole themes in their sequence being in mind. The Bible is a single revelation as we have said, with a beginning, continuation and end, and in our Adult Bible classes at least it should be studied in this way. The different books of the Bible, and the different parts of those books, fit into one another with such exactness that it can not properly be understood, much less thoroughly enjoyed, except as one thus approaches it, and patiently and systematically pursues the golden thread to its glorious end.

It is not essential, but very desirable that every member

7

of such a class possess a copy of the Commentary, and the intent is to publish it at a price making that permissive when compared with the cost of other "Lesson Helps" covering the whole Bible and extending over as long a period of study.

Beginning with Genesis I, let the teacher a week in advance, assign the lesson, which commonly should be a single section or division of the Commentary as indicated by the "Questions" at the close. Let him insist that the class read the Bible text as often as possible during the week and the Commentary afterward, and let him do the same. In many instances the explanation, questions and suggestions in the Commentary will be all the preparation he requires, and particularly as the class advances in the book, and the self-interpretative character of the Bible discloses itself. In the case of a wise and prayerful teacher such a preparation of himself and his class will make for a social conversational hour on the Lord's day, and one of the greatest pleasure and profit.

EXPOSITORY PREACHING.

Finally, although this is a layman's commentary, the pastor, and especially the younger men in the ministry and in the mission fields have not been forgotten in its preparation. The author believes in expository preaching as the staple of any pulpit, and in these pages the inexperienced will find such material, and it is hoped a stimulus to employ it.

A PERSONAL WORD.

Naturally in a work of this kind, many books have been consulted and many authors quoted, but except where they are mentioned in the text it has been thought unnecessary to particularly allude to them. Occasional references have been made to the author's "Synthetic Bible Studies," which has been drawn upon especially in the treatment of some of the Minor Prophets, and the Pastoral and General Epistles.

We have tried to avoid too great uniformity in the treatment of the different parts of the Bible by employing the narrative style in some cases and the more didactic in

8

others as circumstances indicated, and we trust the whole will be found readable and useful to all the classes of persons for whom it is intended.

Prayer has accompanied the study and explanation here given of every book of the inspired record, and with confidence it may be added that the Holy Spirit Who has helped in the compilation, will help in the study of it in the case of all who call upon Him for His aid.

We praise Him for the completion of the work, for the joy found in it all the way, for the new light it has brought to our own soul again and again, and for the assurance He has given that the labor will not be in vain.

JAMES M. GRAY.

ORDER OF THE BOOKS OF THE BIBLE

Old Testament

New Testament

FOREWORD

The Moody Bible Institute of Chicago is justly proud that for over thirty years it enjoyed the inspiring leadership of Dr. James M. Gray, the author of this book. Able as an executive, gifted as an editor, he was preeminent as a teacher. From the summer of 1892 (when he came to the Institute at Mr. Moody's request, as a special instructor) until he was translated into the Presence of the Lord on September 21, 1935, he was the incomparable, meticulous, Bible-believing, Spirit-filled teacher of the Word of God.

A contemporary has said of him, "He never failed to teach and expound the Bible itself, ever recognizing the fact that God's Word would not return unto Him void." Further, ". . . it was not only his marvelous knowledge and understanding of Scripture, but his full appreciation of the laws of pedagogy which made him a giant in the classroom. . . . The thoroughness and soundness of his teaching have ever been spoken of by the students in all of his classes." But, best of all, this teacher par excellence had the gift of leading his students into a joyous and voluntary decision to read and study the Holy Scriptures for themselves. Speaking of Dr. Gray's address on "How to Master the English Bible," a witness records, "It invariably resulted in many of his hearers' returning to their Bibles and studying them with a new zeal."

You will find that this book has the same quality.

It is not to be expected, of course, that a single-volume commentary will deal with every problem and answer every question; what multiple-volume commentary does that? Dr. Gray gives us here a single-volume commentary on the whole Bible, by chapters. It is practical, it is inspirational, it is filled with instruction, it will help mightily in the study of the Word. Read it with your soul well saturated with the Biblical passage under discussion.

Perhaps it will not be out of order to conclude this word of introduction with Dr. Gray's five rules for entering into the meaning and the spirit of the Word: (1) read; (2) read continuously; (3) read repeatedly; (4) read independently; (5) read prayerfully. Use this volume not as a crutch, but as the ripened instruction of a master teacher—instruction which will help you understand better the Word with which you are already acquainted.

WILLIAM CULBERTSON
President, Moody Bible Institute

GENESIS

CREATION OF THE WORLD

CHAPTER 1

1. Creation of Heaven and Earth, v. 1.

Here are three facts. What was done? Who did it? When did it occur?

There are two words that require explanation, "created" and "beginning." Does the former mean that heaven and earth were created out of nothing? The word ("bara," in Hebrew) does not necessarily mean that, but its peculiar use in this chapter suggests that it means that here. It occurs three times, here in v. 1, at the introduction of life on the fifth day, and at the creation of man on the sixth day. Elsewhere, where only transformations are meant, another word ("asah" in Hebrew) is used, translated "made." "Bara" (created) is thus reserved for marking the introduction of each of the three great spheres of existence—the world of matter, of animal life and of spirit, all three of which, though intimately associated, are distinct in essence, and constitute all the universe known to us. Professor Guyot adds that whenever the simple form of "bara" is used in the Bible it always refers to a work made by God and never by man. These considerations, with others, justify the statement that "created" here means created out of nothing.

But when was the "beginning"? The margin indicates a period about 4,000 years before Christ, but these marginal notes are not part of the divine text, but the work of uninspired minds and therefore open to debate. Should science ultimately determine on millions of years ago as the period of the creation there is nothing in this verse of the Bible it would contradict.

2. Making Day, vv. 2-5.

What was the condition of inert matter as represented in verse 2? The first verb "was" has sometimes been translated "became." Read it thus and you get the idea that originally the earth was otherwise than void and waste, but that some catastrophe took place resulting in that state. This means, if true, that a period elapsed between verses 1 and 2, long enough to account for the geological formations of which some scientists speak, and a race of pre-Adamite men of which others speculate. It suggests too that the earth as we now know it may not be much older than tradition places it. The word "earth" in this verse, however, must not be understood to mean our globe with its land and seas, which was not made till the third day, but simply matter in general, that is, the cosmic material out of which the Holy Spirit organized the whole universe, including the earth of to-day.

"And the Spirit of God moved upon the face of the waters." "Moved upon" means brooded over as a bird on its nest. "Waters" means not the oceans and seas as we know them, but the gaseous condition of the matter before spoken of. The Spirit of God moved "upon" the waters and not "inside of" them, showing that God is a personal Being separate from His work. As the result of this brooding, what appeared? We need not suppose that God spake just as a human being speaks, but the coming forth of light out of thick darkness would have seemed to a spectator as the effect of a divine command (Ps. 33:6-9). On the natural plane of things vibration is light or produces light, which illustrates the relation between the moving of the Spirit upon inert matter and the effect it produced.

"And God called the light day." The Hebrew word "yom," translated "day," is used in five different senses in the first two chapters of Genesis. Here it means light without reference to time. Later in the same verse it means the period covered by "the evening and the morning" mentioned, the exact duration of which we do not know. At verse 14 it stands for what we know as 24 hours, at verse 16 it means the light part of the day of 24 hours, and at 2:4 the whole period during which the heaven and the earth were created. All this bears on the question whether creation was wrought in 6 days of 24 hours or 6 day-periods of unknown length; and it will be seen that one does not necessarily contradict the Bible if he believes the latter. When we recall that days of 12 and 24 hours were altogether excluded before the appearance of the sun on the fourth day, the latter hypothesis receives the stronger confirmation.

3. Making Heaven, vv. 6-8.

What does God call forth in verse 6? "Firmament" might be translated by "expanse." What was it to divide? Notice that according to our definition of "waters" this means a separation of the gaseous matter into which light had now come. What did God call this expanse? "Heaven" here means not simply the atmosphere around the earth but the greater chamber of immensity where the sun, moon and stars are located. In connection with this read Psalm 148, and notice that there are "waters," that is, gaseous matter above the heaven of which this verse speaks, and that the "waters" below it include the clouds of our atmosphere as well as the oceans and seas we navigate.

4. Making Earth and Seas, vv. 9-13.

What command goes forth from God on the third day (v. 9)? What did He call the result(v. 10)? Heaven, or the firmament, had divided the cosmic or gaseous matter on the second day. Motion was now everywhere, and gravitation and chemical forces tended to concentrate this matter under the firmament around particular centres, one of which became our globe. A cooling process set in, shrinking and folding its surface into great wrinkles, the shrinking of some parts furnishing basins for oceans or seas and the projection of other parts bringing continents into view. Thus would astronomers and geologists comment on these verses.

But another work than the formation of the globe was accomplished on this day (vv. 11, 12). A principle superior to matter begins to govern its particles, and they assume new forms. What does the earth put forth? Which came first, the plant or the seed? "The plant is not yet life," says Guyot, "but the bridge between matter and life."

5. Making Lights, vv. 14-19.

What command went forth on the fourth day? For what six purposes were these lights made (v. 14, 15)? What discrimination is made between the two greater lights (v. 16)? Where were the lights placed (v. 17)? What special purpose of their making is emphasized in verses 17 and 18? It is well to keep in mind that light itself was made on the first day, and that these "lights" of the fourth day were (so to speak) light-holders. It is of course unnecessary to state how they divide the day from the night, and in what sense they are for signs and seasons, as every one knows the first result is secured by the daily rotation of the earth among them on its own axis, and the second by its annual revolution around the sun. It is presumable that originally their light was merged in that of the earth's own outer covering of light, and that as her luminous envelope disappeared they became visible, and she came to depend on them for both light and heat.

6. Creating Animal Life, vv. 20-25.

What is the command of verse 20? The "waters" here referred to are our oceans and seas. The Revised Version corrects the misapprehension that "fowl" came forth from the water. What word in verse 21 indicates that we have now entered on a new sphere of existence? What was the nature of the blessing on the fish and fowl (v. 22)? What was the further work of creation on this day (v. 24, 25)? It is interesting to note: (a) that this peopling of the water, the air and the land is in the precise order indicated by the science of geology; (b) that the plant life of the third day was the preparation for the animal life of the fifth day; (c) that the plant is now in the animal shaped into new forms, and subservient to higher functions than it could ever perform by itself; (d) that two powers which place the animal on a higher platform than the lower grades of existence are sensation, by which it perceives the world around it, and will, by which it reacts upon it. This is life, and is not the result of chemical elements left to themselves, but the effect of previously existing life. In other words, the Bible and science agree in declaring that "spontaneous generation is an untenable hypothesis," and life only begets life.

7. Creating Man, vv. 26-31.

What word in verse 26 suggests more than one person in the Godhead? What dignity is given to man above every other work of creation? What dignity in his position? What word in verse 27 shows that in his creation we have entered another new sphere of existence? What blessing is bestowed on man in verse 28? How does it differ from that bestowed on the lower animals? What provision has God made for the sustenance of man and beast? Note: (a) that the consultation in the Godhead regarding man's creation foreshadows the New Testament doctrine of the Trinity; (b) that the "image of God" may mean the trinity in man represented by body, soul and spirit (2:7; 1 Thess. 5:23), but especially that moral image suggested in Colossians 3:10; (c) that the dominion of man over the lower creation has in some measure been lost through sin, but will be restored again in Christ (Psalm 8) (d) that the creation of matter, of life and of man are three distinct creations out of nothing, and that God's action in them is direct, hence evolution from one into the other is impossible. There may be evolution within any one of these systems of existence considered by itself, but this is different from that other evolution which would make man the descendant of an ape and rule God out of the universe which He made.

Questions.

1. What does "create" probably mean in this chapter, and why do you think so?

2. When may "the beginning" have been?

3. What does "earth" mean in verse 2?

4. What word in verse 2 opposes pantheism by showing God to be a Person?

5. If the creation days were not limited to 24 hours, why do you think so?

6. What does "heaven" of the second day stand for?

7. What two works were accomplished on the third day?

8. What two powers in the animal define life?

9. Quote Colossians 3:10.

10. How would you distinguish between a rationalistic and a possibly Biblical evolution?

THE GARDEN OF EDEN

Chapter 2

1. God's Sabbath, vv. 1-3.

The first three verses of this chapter belong to the preceding as a summing up of its contents. Of what day do they treat? What did God do on that day? How did He regard it? These verses, in the light of the fourth commandment, seem to countenance the thought of creative days of 24 hours each, that is, God's Sabbath seems to be set over against man's Sabbath, but the two should not be confounded. The latter was made for man and fitted to his measure (Mark 2:27), and therefore while the proportion of time may in some sense be the same, yet the actual time may be different.

2. Man's Nature, vv. 4-7.

"The generations of" in verse 4, frequently repeated in this book, forms the dividing line between the various sections of it, or, as Dr. Urquhart puts it, "the heading of the various natural chapters into which the whole book was divided by its author. It refers not to what goes before but what comes after." In this case it is not the story of the heaven and the earth which we are to have repeated, but an account of the transactions of which they were to be the scene, the things which followed their creation.

Notice the new name of God used here, "LORD God." The first of these words printed in capitals translates the Hebrew "Jehovah," while the second translates "Elohim." Elohim is the far-off name, that which distinguishes God as creator, hence its uniform employment until now. But Jehovah is the near-by name which distinguishes God in relation with man, the covenant-making and covenant-keeping God, hence its employment here where man is to be especially considered. Later on when both Jehovah and Elohim are used in connection with human affairs, the former seems to be generally reserved for God's dealing with His own people as distinguished from the unbelieving nations.

Verse 5 should be read in the Revised Version, where a certain condition is described and the reason is given. What were the condition and the reason? What interesting fact of natural history is stated in verse 6? Especially interesting will it be to recall this when we reach the first mention of rain at the flood. Of what was the body of man formed? What did the LORD God do with the formation He had made? And what was the production of these two elements according to the last clause? Here is the starting-point of the psychology of the Bible, which seems to speak of man as a trichotomic being—having body, soul and spirit (compare 1 Thess. 5:23; Heb. 4:12). Tertullian, one of the early church fathers, used to call the flesh the body of the soul and the soul the body of the spirit, an opinion which has maintained among psychologists to the present. Others have called the body the seat of our sense-consciousness, the soul the seat of our self-consciousness, and the spirit the seat of our God-consciousness.

Before leaving this verse note: (a) that the word "formed" in Hebrew is practically the same as "potter" in Job 10:9; Jer. 18:1-6; Ro. 9:20, 21; (b) that the word for "ground" is "adamah," which means red earth, and that from it the proper name Adam is derived; (c) that the reference to the spiritual life which man received by God's in-breathing is that which is the common property of all men, and which should be distinguished from the new life in Christ Jesus which becomes the possession of those who, as fallen creatures, receive the Holy Spirit to dwell in them through faith in His name. For the common spiritual life see Job 32:8; Prov. 20:27; 1 Cor. 2:11; and for the life of the Holy Spirit in the believer see Ezek. 36:26, 27; Ps. 53; John 14:16, 17; 1 Cor. 6:19, etc.

3. The Garden Located, vv. 8-14.

What name is given to the locality of the garden? In which section of that locality was it planted? What expression in verse 9 shows God's consideration for beauty as well as utility? What two trees are particularly named? Where was the tree of life planted? What geographical feature of verse 10 accentuates the historical character of this narrative? Observe how this is further impressed by the facts which follow, viz: the names of the rivers, the countries through which they flow, and even the mineral deposits of the latter.

Note: (a) the use of the present tense in this description, showing that the readers of Moses' period knew the location; (b) it must have been an elevated district, as the source of mighty rivers; (c) it could not have been a very luxuriant or fruitful locality, else why the need of planting a garden, and where could there have been any serious hardship in the subsequent expulsion of Adam and Eve? It used to be thought that "Eden" was a Hebrew word meaning pleasure, but recent explorations in Assyria indicate that it may have been of Accadian origin meaning a plain, not a fertile plain as in a valley, but an elevated and sterile plain as a steppe or mountain desert. Putting these things together, the place that would come before the mind of an Oriental was the region of Armenia where the Euphrates and the Tigris (or Hiddekel) take their rise. There are two other rivers taking their rise in that region, the Kur and the Araxes, thence uniting and flowing into the Caspian Sea, but whether these are identical with the Pison and Gihon of the lesson can not yet be determined. Science now corroborates this location of Eden in so far as it teaches (a) that the human race has sprung from a common centre, and (b) that this centre is the table-land of central Asia.

4. The Moral Test, vv. 15-17.

For what practical purpose was man placed in the garden (v. 15)? What privilege was accorded him (v. 16)? And what prohibition was laid upon him (v. 17)? With what penalty? Some test must be given a free moral agent by which his determination either to obey or disobey God may be shown, and it pleased God, for reasons He has not been pleased to entirely reveal, to select this test. It was an easy one in the light of Adam's condition of sinlessness and the bountiful privileges otherwise bestowed upon him. "The forbidden tree was doubtless called the tree of the knowledge of good and evil because through the eating of it

mankind came to the experience of the value of goodness and of the infinite evil of sin."

The phrase "Thou shalt surely die" is translated a little differently in the margin. The nature of this death was two-fold. It was a spiritual death, for "in the day" Adam ate thereof he was cast out from the garden and cut off from the communion with God theretofore enjoyed. It was physical death, for in the end Adam returned unto the dust whence he was formed. It would seem from the ensuing record that it was his exclusion from "the tree of life in the midst of the garden" which ultimately resulted in death. "It seems to have existed to confer the gift of immortality, perhaps to counteract sickness, repel bodily ills of every kind, and keep the springs of activity and enjoyment preserved in abounding fulness."

5. Man's Helpmate, vv. 18-25.

What further evidence of God's consideration is in verse 18? What occurred as a preliminary to its expression (v. 19)? How does verse 20 illustrate the intelligence of Adam and in so far disprove the theory of man's ascent from a lower level than the present? Note the five steps on God's part before the helpmate is introduced to Adam (vv. 21, 22). How does Adam express his recognition of the helpmate? What name is given to her, by whom is it given, and why? Do you suppose verse 24 is the record of an expression of Adam, or a later one of Moses, the human author of this book? Of course, in either case, it is God speaking through the human agent, but which agent is it? (Compare also Ephesians 5:22-33, but especially verses 30, 31.) Speaking of the formation of Eve from Adam, one of the older commentators has remarked that "she was not made out of his head to surpass him, nor from his feet to be trampled on, but from his side to be equal to him, and near his heart to be dear to him." The last verse of the chapter indicates that "in their state of innocence modesty did not require clothing as a covering for shame, and that the climate of the garden did not require it for protection." Of God it is said (Ps. 104:2); "Thou coverest Thyself with light as with a garment," and some have thought that in man's state of innocency a similar shining may have served him in the same way, an outer light which he lost when sin robbed him of the inner one.

Questions.

1. What relation do the first three verses of chapter 2 bear to the preceding chapter?

2. What significance attaches to the phrase "the generations of"?

3. How would you distinguish the names of God in this lesson?

4. What is the nature of man, three-fold or two-fold?

5. Give some evidences of the historicity of Eden.

6. Where may it have been located, and what reasons are there for so thinking?

7. What made Adam's moral test an easy one?

8. Why was "the tree of the knowledge of good and evil" probably called by that name?

9. In what two ways was the penalty executed on Adam?

10. What shows that Adam was not a savage but rather the noblest type of the race?

INTRODUCTION OF SIN

CHAPTER 3

1. The Temptation, vv. 1-5.

That more than the serpent was present is suggested by the speech and reasoning powers displayed, but is rendered certain by a comparison of Rev. 12:9 and 20:2, where the serpent is identified with Satan. Some think the serpent originally stood upright and was very beautiful to look upon, which, if true, would contribute to its power over the woman and further explain why Satan employed it as his instrument. Nevertheless, that Satan

was the real tempter is additionally assured by John 8:44; 2 Cor. 11:3; 1 John 3:8 and 1 Tim. 2:14.

Read Satan's inquiry of the woman in the Revised Version, and perceive how it differs from the words of the prohibition (2:16). How does it prove Satan "a liar from the beginning," and how does it impugn God's wisdom and love? Do you think the woman made a mistake in parleying with Satan? And how does her language (v. 3) deflect from the truth? Does she also make God a harder master than He is, and thus has sin already entered her soul?

Notice that "gods" (v. 5) is translated "God" in the Revised Version. It was in seeking to be as God that Satan fell (1 Tim. 3:6), and he tries to drag man down by the same means. Compare the history of the Anti-Christ, Thess. 2:4.

2. The Fall, vv. 6, 7.

What three steps led to the open act of sin? How does 1 John 2:16 characterize these steps? Compare the temptation of Jesus for the use of the same method (Luke 4:1-13). How does the further conduct of the woman illustrate the progress and propagation of sin? Did any part of Satan's promise come true? What part failed? Our first parents came into the knowledge of good and evil by coming to know evil to which they had been strangers before, the moral effect on them being shame (compare 2:25). To quote another: "What the man and woman immediately acquired was the now predominant trait of self-consciousness. God-consciousness has been lost, and henceforth self-contemplation is to be the characteristic and bane of mankind, laying the foundation for those inner feelings or mental states comprehended under the term 'unhappiness, and for all the external strivings whereby effort is made to attain a better condition." What was the first of these efforts they made (v. 7, last clause)? And (to quote the same author again) "is not this act the germ of all subsequent human activities? Conscious of self and feeling the pressure of need, and no longer having a God to supply that need, man begins to invent and contrive" (Eccl. 7:29). Nor are these inventions of a material kind merely, but chiefly a spiritual kind, since their effort to cover themselves illustrates the futile attempts of the race to save itself from the eternal effects of sin by works of morality, penance and the like. What is the only covering that avails for the sinner (Ro. 3:22; 2 Cor. 5:21)?

3. The Trial, vv. 8-13.

"Voice" might be rendered by sound, and "cool" by wind. How does verse 8 indicate the character and degree of their shame? Do God's words (v. 9) express judgment only, or may they have expressed grace? If the latter, in what sense? Does Adam tell the exact truth (v. 10)? Was it merely shame or the sense of sin that drove him away? How does God's question (v. 11) suggest the kind of knowledge that had now come to Adam? Does verse 12 show a spirit of repentance or self-justification on his part? In the last analysis does he cast the blame on the woman or-God?

4. The Sentence on the Serpent, vv. 14, 15.

On which of the guilty does God first pass sentence? Has the curse of verse 14 been fulfilled? Compare Isaiah 65:25, and notice that even in the millennium when the curse is removed from all other cattle it will still remain on the serpent. But how does this curse suggest that previously the serpent did not crawl? (Naturalists describe the organism of the serpent as one of extreme degradation, and say that although it belongs to the latest creations of the animal kingdom, yet it represents a decided retrogression in the scale of being, thus corroborating the Biblical explanation of its condition.) Has the curse of verse 15 been fulfilled?

But we must not suppose the curse of verse 15 to be limited to the serpent, or else Satan were exempt. See by the marginal references that the seed of the serpent is placed by metonomy for that of Satan, and is identified as the wicked and unbelieving people of all the ages (Matt. 3:7; 13:38; 23:33; John 8:44; Acts 13:10; 1 John 3:8). In the same way the seed of the woman might be supposed to stand for the righteous and believing people in all the ages, and so it does in a certain sense, but very especially it stands for our Lord Jesus Christ, the Head and Representative of that people, the One through whom they believe and by whom they become righteous. He Himself is the seed of the woman, and they in Him (Is. 7:14; Matt. 1:18-25; Luke 1:31-35; Gal. 4:4, 5).

Observe how much this means to us. It is really a promise of a Redeemer and redemption, and being the first promise, it is that out of which all subsequent promises flow. The Bible refers to it again and again in one way and another, and we need to become well acquainted with it. Indeed the rest of the Bible is just a history of the fulfilment of this promise. The Bible is not a history of the world or even of man, but a history of the redemption of man from the sin into which he fell in the garden of Eden. This explains why the whole story of creation is summed up in one chapter of the Bible, and why so little is said about the history of the nations of the earth except Israel.

But in what sense is this a promise of redemption? On the supposition that Christ is the Seed of the woman, what will He do to Satan (v. 15)? When the serpent's head is bruised is not its power destroyed? (For the parallel see Heb. 2:14, 15; Rev. 20:1-3, 7-10.) But what will Satan do to Christ? How may Satan be said to have bruised Christ's heel? (For answer see Isaiah 50 and 53, Psalms 22 and 69, and the chapters of the Gospels which speak of Christ's sufferings and crucifixion.)

5. The Sentence on Adam and Eve, vv. 16-21.

What is the first feature of the sentence on the woman (v. 16, first clause)? With what chiefly will her sorrow be connected (second clause)? What second feature of her sentence is contained in the last clause?

For what is the man condemned? Does this show him less or more guilty than his wife? What curse precedes that on the man himself? And yet how is it shown that this too is a curse on the man? "Sorrow" is rendered toil in the Revised Version, and hence the curse on the ground entails the toil on the man. How does this curse on the ground express itself *from* the ground (v. 18)? (The necessaries of life must now be forced out of the earth which before might have spontaneously yielded them.) What will this condition of things force out of man (v. 19)? For how long must this normally continue? What part of man returns to the dust (Eccl. 12:7)? Naturalists corroborate the Bible testimony to the curse by explaining that thorns and thistles are an abortion in the vegetable world, the result of arrested development and imperfect growth. They disappear by cultivation and are transformed into branches, thus showing what their character may have been before the curse, and what it may be when through Christ the curse will have been removed (Rev. 22:1-5). How deeply significant the crown of thorns, the sign of the curse which Jesus bore for us!

6. The Penalty, vv. 22-24.

To whom do you suppose the Lord God said this? Who is meant by "us"? Did you notice the same plural pronoun in 1:26? The use of this is one of the earliest intimations of the Trinity more fully revealed in the New Testament. Indeed the earliest intimation is in the first verse of Scripture in the name God or (Hebrew) Elohim. This is a plural noun but associated with a singular verb, thus suggesting the idea of plurality in unity.

What reason is given for thrusting Adam and Eve out of Eden (v. 22)? Has it occurred to you that there was mercy in this act? Having obtained the knowledge of evil without the power of resisting it, would it not have added to their calamity if, by eating of the tree of life, they had rendered that condition everlasting?

What is the name of the mysterious beings placed on guard at the east of the garden? (v. 24). They seem to be the special guardians of God's majesty, the vindicators of God's broken law, a thought emphasized by their symbolical position over the mercy-seat in the tabernacle at a later period. "The flaming sword" has been translated by "shekinah," the name of the visible glory of God which rested on the mercy seat. May it be that we have here a representation of the mode of worship now established at Eden to show God's anger at sin, and to teach the mediation of a promised Saviour as the way of access to God? As later, so now God seems to say: "I will commune with thee from between the cherubim" (Ex. 25:10-22).

Questions.

1. How would you prove that Satan and not the serpent was the real tempter in Eden?.

2. In what way does the temptation of the second Adam (Christ) harmonize with this of the first Adam?

3. What does the making of the aprons of fig leaves illustrate?

4. How does natural history throw light on the curse pronounced on the serpent?

5. Who especially is meant by "the Seed of the woman"?

6. What is the Bible?"

7. What do naturalists say as to the nature of thorns and thistles?

8. With what two or three suggestions of the Trinity have we met thus far in our lessons?

9. Of what do the cherubim seem to be the vindicators, and what suggestions does this fact bring to mind?

10. How many questions in the

text of our lesson have you been able satisfactorily to answer?

THE STREAM OF HUMANITY DIVIDED

CHAPTERS 4-5

1. Two kinds of Worshippers, 4: 1-8.

What were the occupations of these brothers? What does the name of God in verse 3 bring to mind from our second lesson? We are not told how God showed respect for Abel's offering and disrespect for Cain's, but possibly, as on later occasions, fire may have come out from before the Lord (i.e., in this case from between the cherubim) to consume the one in token of its acceptance. A more important question is *why* God showed respect for it? Reading Hebrews 11:4 we see that "by faith" Abel offered his sacrifice. This means faith in some previous revelation or promise of God touching the way a guilty sinner might approach Him. Such a revelation was doubtless given in Genesis 3:21, which has been reserved for consideration until now.

Where did God obtain the "coats of skins" mentioned there except as some innocent animal (a lamb?) was slain for the purpose? In this circumstance doubtless is set before us in type the truth afterwards revealed that there is such a thing as a sinner's placing the life of another between his guilty soul and God (Heb. 9:22). Abel grasped this truth by faith, and submitted his will to God's testimony regarding it. Just what teaching he had concerning it we do not know, but the result shows that it was sufficient. He approached God in the revealed way, while Cain refused to do so. It is not that Cain's offering was not good of its kind, but before a man's offering is received the man himself must be received, and this is only possible on the ground of the atoning sacrifice and the shed blood of Jesus Christ to which Abel's offering pointed. See Matt. 20:28; John 14:6; Acts 4:12; Ro. 3:21, 25;

Heb. 11:11-14; 1 Peter 1:18-21; 1 John 1:7; Rev. 1:5, 6.

What was the effect on Cain (v. 5)? Notice that the question put to him "If thou doest well, shalt thou not be accepted?" might be rendered: "If thou doest well, shall it (thy countenance) not be lifted up?" When a man does ill he can not look God in the face. But the following sentence is equally interesting: "If thou doest not well, sin lieth (croucheth) at the door." The idea is that sin, like a hungry beast, is waiting to spring upon Cain if he be not wary. But another idea is possible. The word for "sin" being the same as for "sin-offering," it may be that God is calling Cain's attention to the fact that hope of acceptance remains if he will avail himself of the opportunity before him. The lamb, the sin-offering, is at hand, it lieth at the door,—why not humbly lay hold of it and present it as Abel did? What a beautiful illustration of the accessibility of Christ for every sinner! Does Cain accept or reject the invitation? What was the final outcome? (Read here 1 John 3:12.)

2. The First City Built, 4:9-18.

What sin did Cain add to murder (v. 9)? What additional curse is now laid upon the earth and upon Cain on account of his sin (vv. 11, 12)? How does the Revised Version translate "vagabond"? The explanation of the "mark" is unknown, but it may have been set upon Cain lest by his death the populating of the world would have been arrested at a time when it was almost uninhabited.

Verse 16 is significant—"Cain went out from the presence of the Lord." His parents were thrust out of the garden but were still in the presence of the Lord (see the last lesson concerning the cherubim and the flaming sword), but he is excluded further. This is the sinner's fate in time and eternity. He now lives in the world without God and without hope (Eph. 2:12), but even this will be exceeded in the day mentioned in 2 Thessalonians 1:7-10. which please read. In what land did Cain dwell, and what geographical relation to Eden did it bear? The meaning of "Nod" is wandering, and it is affecting to think of Cain, and every sinner unreconciled to God through Jesus Christ, as a wanderer in the land of wandering.

The next verse brings up a question often asked: Where did Cain get his wife? The answer is: From among his sisters; for although such are not named, there can be no doubt that daughters were born to Adam and Eve. Marriages of this character are repugnant now and unlawful (Lev. 18:9), but it was not so at the beginning, since otherwise the race could not have been propagated.

When it is now said that Cain "builded a city," we should not think of a modern metropolis but only a stockade perhaps, and yet it represents an aggregation of individuals for the promotion of mutual comfort and protection. During Cain's long lifetime it may have attained a prodigious size.

3. Products of Civilization, 4:19-24.

The posterity of Cain is now given till we reach the seventh from Adam, Lamech, whose history is narrated at length. Of what sin was he guilty in the light of revelation (Mal. 2:15)? "Adah" means ornament, and "Zillah" shade, and it is not unlikely that the sensuous charms of women now began to be unduly prominent. The suggestion of wealth and possessions is presented in verse 20, art comes into view with Jubal (see especially the Revised Version), and the mechanical sciences with Tubalcain. The cutting instruments speak of husbandry and agriculture, but also alas! of war and murder, preparing us for what follows in Lamech's history. The latter's words to his wives are in poetry, and breathe a spirit of boasting and revenge, showing how man's inventions in science and art were abused then as now.

These antediluvians, in the line of Cain at least, seem to have done everything to make their life in sin as comfortable as possible in contrast to any desire to be delivered from it in God's way.

4. Men of Faith, 4:25 to 5:24.

What is the name of the third son of Adam? While contemporaneous with Cain what indicates that he was younger? What is immediately predicated of his line (4:26)? Notice the capital letters in the name of God, and recall the Hebrew word for which it stands and the truth it illustrates. If now men began to call on the name of Jehovah, the God of promise and redemption, may it indicate that they had not been calling on Him for some time before? Does it then speak of a revival, and single out the Sethites from the line of Cain? In the same connection, notice that nothing is said of their building cities, or owning possessions, or developing the arts and sciences. Nor is mention made of polygamy among them, nor murder, nor revenge. Not that they may have been wholly free from these things, but that the absence of any record of them shows a testimony to their character as compared with the descendants of Cain. They were the men of faith as distinguished from the men of the world. Thus early was the stream of humanity divided.

Notice again the phrase "the generations of" and refer to what was said about it in an earlier lesson. Here it introduces the line of Seth as distinguished from Cain and for the purpose of leading up to the story of Noah, with whose history the next great event in the story of redemption is identified.

But first fasten attention on Noah's ancestor Enoch (5:18-24). This is not the same Enoch as in 4:17, but a descendant of Seth. What mark of faith is attached to his life-story (v. 22)? And what reward came to him thereby (v. 24)? How does Hebrews 11:5 explain this? The translation of Enoch into the next world is a type of the translation of the church at the second coming of Christ (1 Thess. 4:16, 17). Enoch was a prophet and spoke of that day (Jude 14). And notice finally that he was the seventh from Adam in the line of Seth, as Lamech was in the line of Cain. What a contrast between the two, between the people of the world and the people of God, the men of reason and the men of faith! What a contrast in their lives and in the end of their lives!

This lesson had better not close without some reference to the longevity of men in those days. It is singular that it is not spoken of in the line of Cain. May it be attributed to the godliness in that of Seth? Examine Psalm 91, especially the last verse, and consider also what Isaiah says (65:20) on the longevity of men in the millennium. Observe too, that this longevity was a means of preserving the knowledge of God in the earth, since tradition could thus be handed down for centuries from father to son.

Questions.

1. Can you recite Hebrews 11:4?

2. With what previous event may Abel's act of faith be connected?

3. If Abel walked by faith, by what did Cain walk?

4. What two constructions might be placed on the phrase—"Sin lieth at the door"?

5. What was the name of the oldest city in the world?

6. Who was the first polygamist?

7. Was primeval civilization based on holiness or sin?

8. What did men begin to do in the days of Seth?

9. Whose history shows death to be not inevitable?

10. What evidential value is found in the longevity of antediluvian man?

THE FIRST CLIMAX OF SIN

CHAPTERS 6-9

1. Degeneration, 6:1-8.

The results of civilization were morally downward instead of upward, even the Sethites becoming corrupted in time as seen in the fact that after Enoch's translation only Noah and his family were found faithful. Just as the translation of Enoch was a type of that of the church when Jesus comes, so the moral condition of the world after his translation is a type of that which shall prevail after the translation of the Church. See Luke 18:8; 2 Thess. 2; 2 Tim. 3; 2 Peter 3.

To return to Genesis 5:28 note that the Lamech there spoken of is not the descendant of Cain previously mentioned, but the son of Methuselah in the line of Seth. "Noah" means comfort, but how do Lamech's words testify of the sad experiences of men in those days on account of sin? What feature of sin is mentioned at the opening of chapter 6? Some think the Sethites are meant by "the sons of God," but others regard it as a reference to fallen angels who kept not their own principality, but left their proper habitation (Jude 6) and consorted with human beings. Pember's work, *"Earth's Earliest Ages,"* presents arguments for this view which are corroborated by such scientific facts as are given by Sir J. William Dawson in *The Meeting Place of Geology and History*. In consequence of this awful sin, to what determination does Jehovah come (v. 3)? But what respite, nevertheless, is He still willing to bestow?

Verse 4 is sadly interesting. The Hebrew for "giants" is *nephilim* (R. V.), which means fallen ones, and in the judgment of some refers to the "sons of God" or fallen angels of the preceding verses. A slightly different punctuation makes the verse read thus: "There were nephilim (fallen ones) in the earth in those days, and also after that." The "after that" seems to refer to Numbers 13:31-33, where in the report of the spies to Moses they speak of the men of Canaan as of "great stature," adding: "And there we saw the nephilim, the sons of Anak which come to the nephilim." This suggests that the culminating sin of the Canaanites was not different from that of the antediluvians. Observe further that the offspring of these sinful unions became the "mighty men which were of old, the men of renown," from which possibly the ancients obtained their ideas of the gods and demi-gods of which the classics treat.

How does verse 5 define the extent of the wickedness of these days? Of course, when Jehovah is spoken of as repenting (v. 6), the language is used in an accommodated sense. Jehovah never repents or changes His mind, but His dealings with men as governed by their conduct appear to them as if He did so. What now becomes His purpose? Who alone is excepted? What shows that even in this case it-is not of merit?

2. The Ark and Its Contents, 6:9 to 7:10.

Notice the phrase "the generations of," and recall the instruction about it in lesson 2. When Noah is spoken of as "just and perfect," that relative sense is used in which any man is just and perfect before God who believes His testimony and conforms his life to it. It is in this sense that every true believer on Jesus Christ is just and perfect. What two charges does God make against the earth (vv. 12 and 13)? What is Noah commanded (v. 14)? The measurement of the cubit is uncertain, the ordinary length being 18 inches, the sacred cubit twice that length, and the geometric, which some think may be meant, six times the common cubit. At the lowest calculation the ark was as large as some of our ocean liners. Notice "covenant" (v. 18), and connect it with the original promise of 3:15. Why was Noah to take two of every living thing into the ark (vv. 19, 20)? What else was he to take (v. 21)? Mention is made of the sevens of clean beasts (7:2), doubtless for the purpose of sacrifice in the ark and after departing from it. If inquiry be raised as to how so many animals could be accommodated in such a

space, it is to be remembered (1) that the ark in all its three stories contained probably 100,000 square feet of space; (2) perhaps the animals were not the totality of all the animals known in all the world, but those known to Noah; (3) that the distinct species of beasts and birds even in our own day have been calculated as not more than 300.

3. Duration and Extent of the Flood, 7:11 to 8:14.

When did the flood begin (v. 11)? What shows an uprising of the oceans and seas, occasioned perhaps by a subsiding of the land? How long did the rain continue? What suggests a rising of the water even after the rain ceased (vv. 17-19)? How long did it continue to rise (v. 24)? What circumstance mentioned in 2:5 may have given "a terrifying accompaniment" to the rain? When and where did the ark rest (8:4)? "Ararat" is rendered Armenia in 2 Kings 19:37 and Is. 37:38. (See Pratt's *Genesis* for an interesting dissertation on this subject.) What is the story of Noah's messengers (vv. 6-12)? How long did the flood last (v. 14)? A beautiful parallel is found in considering the ark as a type of Christ. All the waves of divine judgment passed over Him, and He put Himself judicially under the weight of all His peoples' sins. But He rose triumphantly from the grave to which that penalty had consigned Him. Nor did He thus rise for Himself only, but for all believers who are in Him by faith as was Noah and his family in the ark.

But did the flood actually occur? and did it cover the whole earth? are questions frequently asked. As to the first, the Word of God is all-sufficient to the man of faith, but it is pertinent to add that the event is corroborated by tradition and geology. As to the second, there may be a division of opinion even among those who accept the authority of Scripture. Chapter 7:19-23 seems to teach its universality, but whether this means universal according to the geography of

Noah or Moses or the geography of the present, is a question as to which Christians are divided.

4. God's Covenant with Noah, 8:20 to 9:19.

What did Noah do on leaving the ark (v. 20)? How does this verse bear on 7:2? What indicates the acceptance of his offering, and by its acceptance that of himself (v. 21)? What divine promise was associated with this acceptance? Of course, this does not mean that no further judgment is to be visited on the earth, as may be seen by 2 Thess. 1:7-10; 2 Peter 3:10-13, and Rev. 14 to 22.

Where, earlier, have we met the blessing now bestowed on Noah and his family (9:1)? What new power over the brute creation is now put into man's hands (v. 2)? If his dominion previously was that of love, of what was its nature to be henceforth? If his food previously was limited to herbs, to what is it now extended (v. 3)? But what limitation is put upon it, and why (v. 4)? To quote Pratt at this point: "We see here that from the times of the deluge the blood was constituted a most sacred thing, devoted exclusively to God, to make expiation on the altar of sacrifice for the sins of men (see Lev. 17:11-14). When the blood of the Lamb of God who taketh away the sin of the world had been shed, this prohibition ceased naturally, together with the reason for it. The apostles, nevertheless, as a concession to the scruples of the Jewish Christians, ordained its continuance (Acts 15:1-29), a concession which likewise of itself fell into disuse with the cessation of the occasion for it—the disappearance of Judaic Christianity."

To speak further of eating meat, some regard it as a lightening of the curse in that flesh was more easily obtained than the products of the soil, but others consider it as bearing on the intercourse with the spiritual beings previously spoken of. In this connection it is in point to remark that the votaries of spiritualism, theosophy and other occultisms are denied a meat diet on the ground that it interferes with their mysterious (and sinful) affinities.

What magisterial functions are now conferred on man, not previously exercised (vv. 5, 6)? Another remark of Pratt is pertinent here: "The death penalty has been abused in almost all the countries of the world, but this does not justify its abolition in cases of premeditated homicide; and unwillingness to apply to the criminal the pain of death ordained by God Himself, the Author of life, always tends to the increase of crime and gives loose rein to personal vengeance. The inviolability of human life means that the life of a human being is a thing so sacred that he who takes it without just cause must pay for it with his own in amends to outraged justice, both human and divine." Compare Numbers 35: 33.

What are the terms of the covenant now made with Noah (vv. 8-11)? And what token or seal does God set to it (vv. 12-17)? The rainbow may have been seen before, but God now employs it for a new purpose. And the token is not only for us, but also for every living thing, and for perpetual generations. And then, too, God looks upon it and remembers the covenant whether we do or not, our deliverance depending not on our seeing it. This calls to mind the promise of Exodus 12:13: "When *I* see the blood, I will pass over you."

Questions.

1. What was the result of the earliest civilization, morally considered?

2. What two applications have been given to the "sons of God" in Genesis 6?

3. What is the Hebrew for "giants," and its meaning?

4. How might be explained the large number of animals in the ark?

5. In what way may the ark be used as a type of Christ?

6. In what two ways is the story of the flood corroborated?

7. What two reasons have been given for the privilege of eating meat?

8. What element will be employed in the next destruction of the earth?

9. Have we Biblical authority and mandate for capital punishment?

10. What circumstances of special interest do you recall in connection with the rainbow?

THE ORIGIN OF THE NATIONS

Chapters 9:18-41

1. Noah's Prophecy, 9:18-29.

To which of the sons of Noah is attention called at the beginning of this section, and why (v. 18)? To what occupation did Noah apply himself after the flood (v. 38)? Of what sin was he guilty (v. 21)? Of what grosser sin was his son guilty (v. 22)? What curse did Noah pronounce on the line of Ham (v. 25)? Which particular line? Just why Canaan is selected one can not say. We only know that his father is not once mentioned in this chapter without him, for which God must have had a reason even if it is not revealed. One reason may be to emphasize that the curse rested upon Asiatics rather than Africans. Because certain of these latter are descendants of Ham, and are black, and have served as slaves, men have associated the curse with them, but the facts of the next chapter (10:15-19) are against that idea. The Hebrews or Israelites, the descendants of Shem, who were themselves slaves in Egypt for a while, afterwards enslaved the Canaanites (Joshua 9:23-27; 1 Kings 9:20-21), and this in part is a fulfillment of this prophecy. It is pertinent further that the Canaanites, like others in the line of Ham, the Babylonians, Egyptians and Africans, inherited the sensuous characteristics of their progenitor for which the judgments of God fell upon them later.

Passing over the blessing upon Shem, or rather the God of Shem, mention the three things prophesied of Japheth (v. 27). He is "enlarged" in the sense that the peoples of Europe sprung out of his loins, to say nothing of the Hindus and doubtless the Mongolians. He "dwells in the tents of Shem" in the sense at least that he partakes of the blessing of their religion, that of the Bible. Canaan is his "servant" in the sense doubtless in which the nations and tribes descendant from him are subject to the control of Europe.

2. The Nations, 10.

This chapter is more than a list of names of individuals. Several are names of families or nations, and make it the most important historical document in the world. You will see that the stream of the race divides according to the three sons of Noah. Whose division is first traced (v. 2)? What part of the world was settled by his offspring (v. 5)? This might read: "By these were the coast lands of the nations divided," and research indicates that the names of these sons and grandsons are identical with the ancient names of the countries bordering on the seas of northern and northwestern Europe. (Examine map number 1 in the back of your Bible). Whose offspring are next traced (v. 6)? A similar examination will show that these settled towards the south and southwest in the lands known to us as Palestine, Arabia, Egypt, Abyssinia, etc. Whose offspring are last named (v. 21)? What distinction is given to Shem in that verse? "Eber" is another form of the name Hebrew, and the distinction of Shem is that he was the ancestor of the Hebrews or the Israelites. His descendants settled rather in the south and southeast, Assyria, Persia, etc.

3. The First World-Monarchy, 10:8-12.

The verses relating to Nimrod call for attention. What describes the energy of his character? How does verse 9 show his fame to have descended even to Moses' time, the human author of Genesis? What political term is met with for the first time in verse 10? Attention to the map will show "the land of Shinar" identical with the region of Babylon in Asia, affording the interesting fact that this kingdom was thus founded by an Ethiopian. Verse 11 might read: "but of that land (i. e., Shinar) he went forth into Assyria," etc., indicating Nimrod to have been the inspiration of the first world-monarchy in the sense that he united under one head the beginnings both of Babylon and Assyria, proving him a mighty hunter of men as well as wild beasts. Rawlinson's *Origin of the Nations* will be found instructive in this connection. He says, in a word: "The Christian may with confidence defy his adversaries to point out any erroneous or impossible statements in the entire (10th) chapter, from its commencement to its close."

4. The Tower of Babel, 11.

The contents of this chapter seem to precede in time those of chapter 10. There we have the story of *how* the nations were divided, and here *why* they were divided. What was true of the race linguistically until this time (v. 1)? To what locality had they been chiefly attracted (v. 2)? What new mechanical science is now named (v. 3)? What twofold purpose was the outcome of this invention (v. 4)? What was the object in view? Is there a suggestion of opposition to the divine will in the last phrase of that verse? (Compare 9:1 and 1:28.) If we take verse 5 literally it suggests a theophany like that in chapter 18, but perhaps the writer is speaking in an accommodated sense. He means that God's mind was now fastened on this act of human disobedience and rebellion, for such is seems to be. Notice the divine soliloquizing in verse 6, and the reasoning it represents: (1) this people are united by the fact that they have but one language; (2) this union and sense of strength have led to their present undertaking; (3) success here will generate other schemes in opposition to My purposes

and to their disadvantage; therefore this must be frustrated. What was the divine plan of frustration (v. 7)? What was the result (v. 8)? What name was given this locality, and why (v. 9)? (Observe that Babylon and Babel are the same.)

"With this blow of the avenging rod of God came to an end the third experiment God was making with the apostate race. They had again turned their backs on God, making haste to caste into oblivion the terrible lesson of the flood; and so with the confusion of their speech God delivered them up to the lusts of their own hearts" (Pratt). (Read here Romans 1:28.)

Questions.

1. From which of Noah's sons did the Hebrews descend?

2. What peoples are the descendants of Japheth?

3. Who seemed to aspire after the first world monarchy?

4. What distinction in the account of the origin of the nations is seen as between chapters 10 and 11?

5. What came to an end at this period?

THE ORIGIN OF ISRAEL

Chapters 11:10-12:9

1. The Divine Purpose.

We have reached a fourth experiment in God's dealings with the apostate race, only this shall not ultimately be the failure the others proved. It should be understood, however, that in speaking of failure the reference is to man's part and not God's. Before the flood the sin of the race was atheism, outright denial of divine authority with the indulgence of sinful lusts it produced and the dissolution of moral and social bonds. But after the flood idolatry took its place—just how, or why, it is difficult to say—and long before Abram's time polytheism prevailed both in Chaldea and Egypt.

But God's purpose from the beginning was the redemption of

the race according to the promise of Genesis 3:15, and as incident thereto He will now call out a single individual from the corrupt mass, and make of him a nation. Special training and care shall be given to this individual and this nation that there may be in the earth (1) a repository for His truth to keep alive His name; (2) a channel through which "the Seed of the woman," the world's Redeemer, may come among men; and (3) a pedestal on which He Himself may be displayed in His character before the other nations of the world to the sanctifying of His name among them and their ultimate return to His sovereignty. Steady contemplation of this three-fold purpose in the call of Abram and the origin of Israel will prevent any charge of partiality against God for dealing with them differently from other peoples, and will help us to see that all His blessing of them has been for our sake, thus quickening our interest in all that is revealed concerning them.

Israel has thus far fulfilled only part of her original mission. She has retained the name and truth of God in the earth, and given birth to the Redeemer (though she crucified Him), but she has not sanctified God among the peoples by her behavior. For this she has been punished in the past, and is now scattered among the peoples in whose sight she denied Him; but the prophets are a unit that some day she shall be restored to her land again in a national capacity, and after passing through great tribulation, be found penitent and believing, clothed in her right mind and sitting at the feet of Jesus. Then she will take up the broken threads again, and begin anew to carry out the original plan of sanctifying God among the nations. She will witness for Jesus as her Messiah in the millennial age for the conversion of those nations and their obedience to His law. All this will be brought out gradually but plainly as we proceed through the prophets.

2. The Generations of Shem and Terah, 11:10-32.

"The generations of Shem and Terah" are the children who sprang from them, and furnished the descent of Abram and the Israelites. Which one of the sons of Shem was divinely chosen for this honor? (Compare v. 10 with 10:21.) What seven facts are stated of Haran (vv. 27-29)? Iscah, one of his daughters, not otherwise mentioned, is thought by some identical with her whom Abram married and whose name was changed to Sarai (my princess) after that event. Others, however, based on Abram's words (20:13) that Sarai was a daughter of Terah by a second wife, and thus his half-sister. Still others conjecture that of the supposed two wives of Terah, one was Haran's mother and the other Abram's, so that in marrying his niece, he was at liberty to speak of her as his sister, as in Egypt (12:19), in the same sense in which he could call Lot his brother though he was also his nephew (14:14).

"Haran," which is the name of a locality, called "Charran," in Acts 7:2-4, must not be confounded with the other word which is the name of Terah's son, since they are quite distinct. Notice the location of these places on the map, and observe that because of the desert of Arabia they had to travel first towards the northwest (about 650 miles) to the fords of the Euphrates, and then southwest (say 500 miles) to Hebron or Beersheba, which later on became Abram's favorite abode.

Ur must have been a city of great wealth and influence, so that Abram was brought up under circumstances of the highest civilization. Documents written in his day have recently been brought to light, in which his name is mentioned as borne by men of that land. And as a further mark of historicity, the name of the city itself, Ur of the Chaldees, or Ur-Kasdim, as the Hebrew puts it, was the peculiar form of its name in Abram's time, though subsequently it had another form. One more feature of interest is that it was the ancient seat of the worship of the Moon, and that Abram and all his family were undoubtedly idolaters, so that this call of God to him, like His call to us in Christ, was entirely of grace. In examining this point consult chapter 31:53; Joshua 24:2, 3, 14, 15.

3. Abram's Call and His Response, 12:1-9.

How does the King James Version indicate an earlier date for the call of Abram than that which chapter 12 narrates? How is this corroborated by Acts 7:2? Stephen, speaking of this call, indicates that God "was seen to Abraham," as if some visible manifestation was vouchsafed to him at the beginning. In what form this may have been we do not know, but sufficiently clear to have shown the patriarch the distinction between gods of wood and stone and the only true God.

What seven promises are given Abram to encourage his faith (vv. 2, 3)? God's authority could find fit expression only in a *nation* bound together under institutions of His own appointment, since many scattered family altars could not bear an adequate witness for His unity. Notice again that for Abram to become great and his offspring to develop into a great nation co-operation would be required on the part of his and their neighbors, hence to secure this God lays this curse and blessing upon their enemies and friends.

Have you located Shechem? How is Abram comforted at this place (v. 7)? What additional promise is now given him? This gift to his seed of the land should be strongly emphasized. It was, and is, Jehovah's land. Ezekiel speaks of it as the "middle, or navel, of the earth" (38:12, R. V.), and it is peculiarly situated geographically, commercially and politically, but especially historically and prophetically. It has been given to Israel as her *possession* forever, but not her *ownership*, as we shall learn by and by (Lev. 25:23). Moreover, so closely is Jehovah's purpose of redemption associated with the land as well as the people of Israel that when they are separated from it, as we shall see, they are separated from Him, and the lapse of time in their history is not considered until they are returned to their land again. In a word, they can never dwell elsewhere and be His people or fulfill their calling.

Questions.

1. How would you identify the three previous experiments with the race?

2. How would you distinguish between the sin of men before and following the flood?

3. What was the threefold purpose in the call of Abram and the nation of Israel?

4. How should the knowledge of this influence us?

5. How far has this purpose yet been realized?

6. Will it be entirely realized, and if so, when and how?

7. How might Abram's conduct in 12:19 be explained?

8. What outside proof have we of the historicity of these chapters?

9. What is God's peculiar relation to the land as well as the people of Israel?

10. Draw an outline map of Abram's journey from Ur to Haran and Shechem.

THE PROMISE RENEWED TO ABRAM

CHAPTERS 12:10-13

1. Abraham in Egypt, 12:10-20.

It is felt that Abram acted unadvisedly in taking this journey to Egypt, for which three reasons are assigned: (1) God could have provided for him in Canaan, notwithstanding the famine; (2) there was no command for him to leave Canaan, to which place God had definitely called him; (3) he fell into difficulty by going, and was obliged to employ subterfuge to escape it. Still these arguments are not convincing, and in the absence of direct rebuke from God we should withhold judgment.

Concerning the trial which Abram encountered, how did the last lesson justify in part, his subterfuge? What shows the unwisdom of it even on the natural plane of things (vv. 18-19)? How does his character suffer in comparison with that of Pharoah? Who interposed on his behalf, and how (v. 17)? How does this circumstance demonstrate that the true God has ways of making Himself known even to heathen peoples? How does it further demonstrate that the record itself is true?

2. Separation from Lot, 13:1-13.

If Abram has been out of fellowship with God during his Egyptian sojourn, how is that fellowship now restored (vv. 3, 4)? Have we any lesson here concerning our own backsliding? (Compare 1 John 1:9.) What shows the unselfishness and breadth of Abram's character in dealing with Lot (vv. 8, 9)? How does this show that Canaan at this time must have been largely depopulated? What principle governed Lot in his choice (vv. 10, 11)? How does the Revised Version render verse 12? Have you identified these localities on the map? What shows the unwisdom of Lot's choice (v. 13)? Read on this point 2 Corinthians 6:14 to 7:1.

3. The Promise Renewed to Abram, 13:14-18.

Does Abram suffer for his unselfishness? What advance does this renewal of the promise record so far as the land is concerned (v. 15)? So far as Abram's posterity is concerned? What two references to Abram's seed do verses 15 and 16 record? In what way may he be said to have taken possession of the land in advance (v. 17)? Have you identified Hebron? Abram by the Egyptian episode may have well felt he had forfeited the promise, if it had rested on his faithfulness, but instead it rested upon the faithfulness of God. How

kind, therefore, for God to have reassured His servant, unworthy as he was, and even to have given him a larger vision of what the promise meant!

Questions.

are rendered unnecessary in this case because of the number and nature of those in the text itself. Hereafter when omitted at the close of the lesson, it will be for this reason.

THE ABRAHAMIC COVENANT

Chapters 14, 15

1. The Confederated Kings, 14:1-12.

How does the Revised Version translate "nations" in verse 1? In what valley was the battle joined (3)? How is that valley now identified? Against what six peoples did Chedorlaomer and his confederates campaign in the fourteenth year (5-7)? You will find these peoples located on the east and south of the Dead Sea.

Who were victors in this case (10)? How did they reward themselves (11)? What gives us a special interest in this story (12)? Objectors have denied the historicity of it, but the monuments of Assyria, Babylonia and Egypt, with their inscriptions and paintings, confirm it. The names of some of these kings are given, and it would appear that Chedorlaomer was the general name of a line of Elamite kings corresponding to the several Pharaohs and Caesars of later times.

2. Abram's Exploit of Arms, 14: 13-24.

By what name was Abram distinguished among these heathen peoples (13)? What hint have we of his princely power (14)? What was the manner of his attack (15)? The motive for it (16)?

We are not surprised at Abram's meeting with the king of Sodom on his return, but what other king is named (18)? What office did he hold beside that of king? Was he a heathen like the others (19)? Who gave the tithes,

Abram or he? (Compare Heb. 7:6.)

Melchizedek seems to have been a king of Salem, later called Jerusalem, who like Job had not only retained the knowledge of the true God but also like him was in his own person a prince and a priest. (Compare Job 1:5-8; 29; 25.) Recent discoveries of correspondence of the Egyptian kings written at about the time of the Exodus refute the theory once held that Melchizedek was an imaginary character and that this incident never occurred. This correspondence includes letters of the king of Jerusalem, Ebed-Tob by name, which means "the servant of the Good One," who speaks of himself in the very phrases used by his predecessor Melchizedek (Heb. 7). The probability is that Melchizedek, like Chedorlaomer, was the common name of a race or dynasty of priest-kings ruling over that city. He is employed as a type of Christ in the 110th Psalm and in Hebrews 7.

How does the king of Sodom probably the successor to him who had been slain (10), express his gratitude to Abram (21)? What is Abram's response (22-24)? How does this response show that Melchizedek worshipped the same God? What elements of character does it show in Abram?

3. The Second Test and Reward of Faith, 15:1-6.

"After these things" Abram might have feared that the defeated warriors would return in force and overwhelm him, nor is it improbable that misgivings arose as to relinquishing the spoil he was entitled to as the conqueror. But God could deliver him from fear in the one case and make up to him the loss in the other. How does He express both ideas in verse 1?

But what burdens Abram heavier than either of these things (2)? God promised him a seed to inherit Canaan, which should be multiplied as the dust of the earth, yet he was going hence childless. He who should be pos-

sessor of his house under these circumstances would be Dammesek Eliezer (R. V.). Just how to explain this is difficult, but Eliezer was his steward, and oriental custom may have entailed the possessions of his master on such an one where no natural heir existed. We cannot explain this but would call attention to the reply of Jehovah, that it is not an adopted son he shall have but a supernatural one (4). And now what does Jehovah do to Abram (5)? And what does He ask Abram to do? And what does He then promise him? Was Abram's faith able to measure up to this stupendous declaration (6)? And in what did this faith of Abram result to him (v. 6, last clause)? These words,

"COUNTED IT TO HIM FOR RIGHTEOUSNESS,"

reveal a fact more important to Abram personally than the promise of a seed, except that the seed, considered as the forerunner and type of Christ, was the only ground at length on which Abram might be counted righteous. To understand these words is vital to an understanding of our own redemption, and an apprehension of the Gospel.

Abram was a sinner, born into a state of wrongness, but God now puts him by an act of grace into a state of rightness, not because of Abram's righteous character but on the ground of his belief in God's word. Nor does this righteous state into which he is brought make it true that thereafter he is without flaw in his character, for he is guilty of much. But he has a right standing before God, and because of it God can deal with him in time and eternity as He cannot deal with other men who do not have this standing. The significance of this to us is seen in Romans 4:23-25, which you are urged to read prayerfully.

The question is sometimes asked whether Abram—and for that matter, any Old Testament saint—was justified or made righteous just as we are in these days. The answer is yes, and no. They were made righteous just as we are in that Christ took away their guilt on the cross and wrought out a righteousness for them, but they were not made righteous just as we are in that they knew Christ as we do. Christ indeed said that Abram rejoiced to see His day, and he saw it and was glad (John 8:56), but this does not mean that he saw and understood what we now do of the Person and finished work of Christ.

The fact is this: God set a certain promise before Abram. He believed God's testimony concerning it and was counted righteous in consequence. God sets a certain promise before us, and if we believe God's testimony concerning it we are counted righteous in consequence. The promise to Abram was that of a natural seed; the promise to us is that of salvation through Jesus Christ, the anti-type of that seed. We have but to believe His testimony concerning Jesus Christ, as Abram believed it concerning the seed, to obtain the same standing before God forever. It is not our character that gives it to us, nor does our change of standing immediately produce a change of character, but this does not affect the standing, which is the important thing because the character grows out of it. The reward of the first test of faith brought Abram a country (Gen. 12), but that of the second brought him a better country, that is, a heavenly (Heb. 11:8-16).

4. The Covenant of God, 15:7-12, 17-21.

In what words does God now identify Himself and renew the promise of the land (7)? Is Abram altogether satisfied about the land (8)? What does God tell him to do (9)? What now happens to Abram (12)? What next takes place with reference to the sacrifice (17)? And in connection with this what does God do with Abram? How does He define the boundaries of His gift? We ought to say that "the river of Egypt," can hardly mean the

Nile, although some so regard it. Others think it is that wady or brook of Egypt lying at the southern limit of the land of Israel, referred to in Num. 34:5; Josh. 15:4, and Isaiah 27:12.

The strange incident recorded here is of symbolic importance. Men entered into covenant with one another in this way, that is, they would slay an animal, divide it into parts, walk up and down between them and thus solemnly seal the bond they had made. Afterward part of the victim would be offered in sacrifice to their gods, while the remainder would be eaten by the parties to the covenant. It was the highest form of an oath. God thus condescended to assure Abram, since the smoking furnace and burning lamp, passing between the pieces and doubtless consuming them, typified His presence and acceptance of the bond. Among men it takes two to make a covenant, but not so here. God is alone in this case, and asks of Abram nothing in return but the repose of confidence in His faithfulness. It is thus that God covenants with us in Christ. He gives, and we take. He promises, and we believe.

But dwelling on what Abram saw we passed over what he heard, and this is an essential part of God's covenant with him (13-16). What did He say would be true of Abram's seed for a while? It is a matter of dispute how these four hundred years are computed, but Anstey's Romance of Chronology says that Abraham's seed here means Isaac and his descendants from the time of the weaning of the former when he became his father's heir, to the date of the Exodus, which was precisely 400 years. What twofold promise is given Abram personally (15)? What particular reason does God give for the delay in possessing Canaan (16)? "The Amorite" here is the name used doubtless for all the inhabitants of Canaan, of which they were a chief nation and a very wicked one. The long-suffering of God will wait while they go on filling up the measure of their iniquity, but at last the sword of divine justice must fall. The same thing happens with sinners in general, and as another says, it ought to embitter the cup of their pleasures.

Questions.

1. What corroborative evidence of the historicity of Chapter 14 can you name?

2. Recall in detail what has been taught or suggested about Melchizedek.

3. How would you explain Genesis 15:6?

4. Can you repeat from memory Romans 4:23-25?

5. In a word, what is the significance of the transaction in 15:7-21?

THE TOKEN OF THE COVENANT

CHAPTERS 16, 17

Our lessons are grouping themselves around the great facts of Scripture as we proceed, and while we are omitting nothing essential, emphasis is laid on the strategic points. In this lesson the point is the token of the covenant God made with Abram, but there are other thoughts leading up to and giving occasion for it.

1. Sarai and Hagar, 16:1-6.

The incident we now approach is not creditable to Abram or his wife, but there is an explanation of it. At least ten years had elapsed since God promised a seed to Abram (compare 12:12 with 16:16), and yet the promise had not been realized. Abram had been a monogamist until now, but concubinage was the custom, and the idea impressed Sarai that the delay in the promise might mean a fulfillment of it in another way. Might it be that they should *help* God to fulfill it? A wise teacher has said that human expediency to give effect to divine promises continues still one of the most dangerous reefs on which the lives of God's people are wrecked. The result might have been foreseen so far as Hagar's treatment of Sarai is con-

cerned (4), but the latter's unfairness towards her husband does nothing to redeem her previous improper conduct. Abram's action (6) will be differently judged by different people, but seems consistent with the original purpose to accept of Hagar not as on equality of wifehood with Sarai, or even as his concubine, but as Lange puts it, "a supplementary concubine of his wife."

2. The Angel of the Lord, 16:7-14.

It is not "an angel" of the Lord here brought before us, but "The Angel," an expression always referring to the second Person of the Trinity. He assumes the divine prerogative at verse 10, and is identified as God at verse 13. It is no objection to say that it is only Hagar who thus identifies Him, not only because she must have had evidence of His identity, but because the inspired record in no way contradicts her. While this Angel is Jehovah, it is remarkable that in the name "Angel," which means "messenger" or "one sent," there is implied a distinction in the Godhead. There must be one who sends if there is one sent, and since the Father is never sent but always sends, the conclusion is that "The Angel of the Lord" must be God the Son.

Identify on the map "the way to Shur" (7), and observe that Hagar was departing in the direction of her own land. Ishmael means "God heareth." Why was he to be thus called (11)? What character and experience are prophesied of him (see R. V.)? Where was he to dwell? "In the presence of his brethren" seems to mean "over against" or "to the east of" his brethren.

3. The Covenant Renewed, 17:1-8.

Abram's disobedience or unbelief as illustrated in the matter of Hagar kept him out of fellowship with God for fourteen years or more. (Compare first verse of this chapter with the last of the preceding one.) What takes place after so long a time? With what new name does God introduce Himself?

The Hebrew here is "El Shaddai." "El" means might or power, and "Shaddai" means a shedder forth of bounty. The name represents God as the all-bountiful One, and comes as His revelation of Himself to Abram just when the latter needed to learn that the strength of God is made perfect in human weakness. Abram sought to obtain by his own energy what God only could give him, and having learned his lesson and being ready to give himself to God, God is ready to give Himself to Abram and make him fruitful. To quote Jukes here: "He puts something into Abram which at once changes him from Abram to Abraham—something of His own nature."

But what is required of Abram, however, before this (1)? He must be "perfect," not in the sense of sinlessness, impossible to mortal, but in that of doing the whole will of God as it is known to him. And on that condition what promise is renewed (2)? It is not as though the covenant of chapter 15 had been abrogated for "the gifts and calling of God are without repentance" (Ro. 11:29), but that now the first step is to be taken in its fulfillment. What new attitude, physically considered, is now assumed by Abram in his intercourse with God (3)? What new name is given him, and its meaning (5)? How does the promise of verse 5 read in the Revised Version?

Compare the promise as more fully outlined in verses 6 to 8 for features additional to those previously revealed. What does God say He will make of him? And what shall come out of him? Have either of these things been said before? What did God say He would establish, and with whom, and for how long? What is new here? A father of many nations indeed has God made Abraham, if we consider his offspring not only in the line of Isaac, but of Ishmael, to say nothing of the children born to

him by Keturah, subsequently to come before us.

These nations include the Jews, Arabians, Turks, Egyptians, Afghans, Moroccans, Algerians, and we know not how many more. But we are not to understand the covenant as established with all of these but only with the Jews of Israel, as descendants of Isaac. Isaac is the seed of Abraham in mind here, and of course his anti-type, Jesus Christ, is the seed ultimately in mind. Keeping this latter point in view, therefore, the seed includes more than Israel after the flesh, since it takes in all who believe on Jesus Christ, whether Jews or Gentiles (Gal. 3:29). Peculiar privileges belong to each, but their origin is the same.

4. The Covenant Token, 17:9-14.

It is in dispute whether circumcision was original with Abraham and his descendants, or had been a custom in other nations, though of course for other reasons in their case. Nevertheless, as Murphy reminds us, "the rainbow was chosen to be the sign of the covenant with Noah though it may have existed before, so the prior existence of circumcision does not render it less fit to be the sign of the covenant with Abraham, or less significant." And he adds: "It was the fit symbol of that removal of the old man and that renewal of nature which qualified Abraham to be the parent of the holy seed." To what extent was it to be carried out among the males? What was the penalty for its omission (14)? This cutting off of the people from the covenant did not mean physical death, but exclusion from all their blessings and salvation, an even more serious judgment, since in the end it denoted the endless destruction and total ruin of the man who despised God's covenant. To despise or reject the sign was to despise and reject the covenant itself (see verse 5, last clause). A serious thought for the professing Christian who neglects to observe both parts of the obligation in Romans 10:9, 10.

5. The Promise Concerning Sarah, 17:15-27.

How is the name of Sarai changed at this point (15)? God had never promised she should be a mother, and Ishmael, now thirteen years old, had doubtless been recognized through the whole encampment as his father's heir. But now what distinct promise does God give concerning her (16)? How is it received by Abraham (17)? This laughter of Abraham was the exultation of joy and not the smile of unbelief. In this connection note that Isaac means "laughter," and also that it is with him, and not Ishmael, that the covenant is to be established everlastingly.

Are you not pleased that Abraham should have thought of Ishmael as he did (18)? "Ishmael as an Arab of the desert, with his descendants, does not make much of a figure among the nations of the earth until we consider him as the ancestor of Mohammed. It is estimated that he holds one hundred and fifty millions of the inhabitants of the world subject to his spiritual sway, which indicates that Ishmael still lifts his head aloft among the great founders of empires, and in the moral sphere greater than them all."

Questions.

1. How do God's people sometimes wreck their lives, as illustrated in this lesson?

2. How does this lesson afford another foreshadowing of the doctrine of the Trinity?

3. Give the meaning of the name "Almighty God."

4. Name some of the nations proceeding from Abraham.

5. Whom does "the seed" of Abraham include?

6. How does this lesson impress us with the importance of confessing Christ?

7. Where in this lesson have we a kind of parallel to Luke 24:41?

8. What distinguished descendant of Ishmael can you name?

LOT'S AFTERMATH

CHAPTERS 18, 19

We have almost forgotten Lot, but he is not having a happy time in the land of his choice. The Sodomites have learned nothing by experience, and are increasing in iniquity and ripening for judgment. The facts in chapter 18 introduce the story of the climax in their case.

1. A Second Theophany, 18:1-15.

The word "Lord" in verse 1 is in capitals, another manifestation of the second Person of the Godhead as in the case of "the Angel of the Lord" in the last lesson. Compare also 13:18, and notice that Abraham is still at Hebron, about twenty miles south of Jerusalem, where he had settled perhaps twenty-five years prior to this time. We may judge this by the fact that when he had become separated from Lot the latter was unmarried, but now, as chapter 19 indicates, had a family including married daughters. Keep giving attention to the map in these historical studies, as it will be found increasingly beneficial as we proceed.

In what form does Jehovah seem to have appeared to Abraham (2)? How are the other two "men" identified? (19:1, R. V.) Abraham's action in running to meet and show hospitality to these travelers shows that he did not know their true nature, but yet there was something about them which he recognized as unusual. Notice, for example, his address in verse 3.

How does the speaker in verse 10 identify himself with Jehovah? What do you think of Sarah's laughter in verse 13 as compared with that of Abraham in the last lesson? In the light of the context does it express confidence or doubt (13-15)?

2. A Great Prayer, 18:16-33.

Abraham's prayer is the first prolonged supplication recorded in the Bible, and suggests several thoughts upon the subject. (1) *The duty and privilege of inter-*

cessory prayer, for Abraham was now asking for others, not himself. (2) *The source and inspiration of prayer,* which in this case is the revealed purpose of God concerning Sodom. He who knows God's purposes prays in harmony with them and thus finds abundant food for prayer; but to learn His purpose one must listen to His voice in His Word. (3) *The value of argument in prayer.* See how Abraham pleads the holy and just dealings of God! But to be possessed of arguments one needs to be familiar with what God is and what He says—another reason for searching His revealed Word. (4) *The right of importunity in prayer.* God is not displeased to have us press our cause, but expects us to do so, and frequently answers according to our earnestness. (5) *The efficacy of prayer,* for Abraham received his real desire, the deliverance of Lot, even though Sodom itself was not saved.

How is Jehovah discriminated from the two "men" at verses 16 and 17? What reason is given for His readiness to reveal His purpose to Abraham (18)? Read verse 19 in the Revised Version and observe that Abraham's faithfulness to God, resulting in the fulfillment of God's promise to him, was itself of grace. Jehovah says: "I have known him to that end," which is the same as saying: "The purpose I have in calling and blessing Abraham is to keep him faithful that I may bring upon him that which I have promised." Here is food for prayer surely, that God might know us as He knew Abraham; and perhaps one reason He revealed this dealing of His with Abraham is to stimulate us thus to plead.

How strangely verse 21 sounds, bringing to mind Genesis 11:5, the note on which please again read. Perhaps in this case the words were spoken by Jehovah in Abraham's hearing. They suggest His fairness in dealing with the wicked, for (speaking after the manner of men) He will not act on hearsay evidence, but learn the facts for Himself. He will send special messengers to report to Him, who, alas! obtain all the evidence they need. Does Jehovah Himself visit Sodom? What, in a sense, prevented Him?

3. The Sodom Mob, 19:1-11.

What leads to the belief that Lot did not recognize the nature of his visitors (2, 3)? (Compare Hebrews 13:2.) The following verses show that the Sodomites sought acquaintance with these supposed men for those vile purposes which have ever been associated with the name of their city. It was for this that Lot, at the risk of his life, came to their defense, for the duty of protecting a guest has always been accounted among orientals as the most sacred obligation. Lot's offer concerning his daughters is inexplicable, and yet it shows what Sodom had done for him. How does verse 9 show Lot's unpopularity with his neighbors? What suggests that he had testified against them? (Read here 2 Peter 2:6-9.) Who rescued Lot, and how (10)? What physical judgment was visited upon his antagonists (11)?

4. Lot's Escape, 19:12-26.

How does verse 12 illustrate our responsibility for the salvation of our relatives? And verse 14 the indifference with which they often hear our testimony? How does verse 16 illustrate the preventing grace of God to lost sinners? What elements of Lot's character are illustrated in verses 18-20? How does verse 30 show his folly a second time in selecting an abiding place? How do verses 21 and 22 show God's regard for the people of His choice, notwithstanding their unworthiness? The prophets of the Old and New Testaments speak of tribulation coming upon the earth at the close of this age such as was never seen before, but they speak also of the deliverance of the saints out of it and a removal of them by translation (1 Thess. 4:13-18) before the judgments fall (Rev. 3:10 to 7:14, etc.), and this dealing with Lot illustrates it in certain ways. By what means were Sodom and Gomorrah destroyed? "Overthrew," verse 25, indicating upheavals and submersions of the ground, perhaps the result of natural causes, but under divine control. The explosion of gas might account for it when the soil, soaked with bitumen, would easily convey the fire until all the cities were destroyed. It used to be thought that the Dead Sea covered the site of these cities, but this opinion is now contradicted.

What judgment befell Lot's wife, and why? Her motives for looking back are not hard to conceive and we need not dwell upon them now, but observe how Jesus applies this circumstance to the end of the age (Luke 17:31-33), and note that He thus not only warns us concerning that period but guarantees the authenticity of this whole story.

5. Origin of the Moabites and the Ammonites, 19:30-38.

It must not be supposed that the conduct of Lot's daughters recorded here is endorsed by God because of that fact. Its record is an incidental evidence of the truth of the Bible, for an imposter palming off a so-called revelation would have omitted such a circumstance reflecting upon them whom God in His mercy had separated unto Himself. The purpose of the record is doubtless to give us the origin of the Moabites and the Ammonites, who figure so largely at a later time as the implacable enemies of Israel, whose vile character is here foreshadowed. They ultimately met the fate at God's hands which their history deserved.

ABRAHAM AT GERAR

Chapters 20, 21

Why Abraham took the journey in verse 1 is not stated, but perhaps to better his pasturage, for he remained in the vicinity for some time (21:34). Why he employed the same subterfuge

about Sarah as before also is not stated except in a general way (12), but it resulted as it did then (2). The chapter illustrates *certain principles of God's dealings with different men*:

(1) Imputed righteousness, while instantaneously giving man a right standing before God, does not make that man instantaneously righteous in his own character. If it did, Abraham would not have been guilty of this falsehood, if it were such.

(2) God can reveal Himself to the heathen as clearly as to one of His own people. Abimelech had no doubt that he had received a revelation from the God of Abraham.

(3) The sin of a heathen is against God, no matter what religion he professes or what gods he worships—"I withheld thee from sinning against Me."

(4) God is the conservator of His own truth, and man cannot be trusted with it. Twice has He interposed against Abraham himself for the protection of his wife, in whom were deposited the hopes of the whole human race. These hopes would have been disappointed if Abraham had controlled them (Psalm 105:13-15).

(5) Natural graces of disposition are not a ground of acceptance with God. Abimelech commends himself to us by his expostulation with Abraham (9-10), his restoration of Sarah and his generous treatment of both (14-16), and yet it is Abraham (whose conduct suffers by comparison) and not Abimelech who has the privilege and power of intercession—"He is a prophet, and he shall pray for thee, and thou shalt live" (7).

(6) God deals with His own people, those to whom His righteousness is imputed, on a different principle from that on which He deals with others. Abraham suffers no punishment for this repeated offense, although in the course of his life he had his share of chastisements and corrections, but God is dealing with him not as a criminal be-

fore a judge, but as a child before a loving father.

Abraham and Abimelech in Covenant, 21:22-34.

The circumstance in this section belongs to that of the previous one, although it seems to have taken place at a later time and subsequent to the birth of Isaac. Notice how God blessed Abraham in such a way as to glorify Himself (22), and recall the teaching in an earlier lesson that this was His purpose in the whole history of Israel, which their disobedience at the present time has defeated. Abraham must have had much influence and power for Abimelech to have found it worth while to make a covenant with him (23), but his "kingdom" was very likely limited to the city of Gerar and the surrounding territory. Abraham takes advantage of the occasion to present a claim for damages, as we would say (25), and serious damages, too, when we reflect on the value of wells in an oriental country to the possessor of sheep and cattle. In verses 27-30 we have a repetition of the transaction in chapter 15. "Beersheba" means "the well of the oath." This now becomes the dwelling place of Abraham for some time (34). What new name is ascribed to God in this verse?

Questions.

1. How does this lesson teach that the ground of our righteousness is objective rather than subjective?

2. What encouragement does it afford in preaching the Gospel to the unsaved?

3. How does it illustrate God's faithfulness to His promises?

4. How does it exhibit the difference between the natural and the spiritual man?

5. Can you find here an illustration of Matthew 5:16?

FROM THE BIRTH OF ISAAC TO THE DEATH OF SARAH

Chapters 21-23

1. The Bondwoman and Her Son, 21.

There is little requiring explanation in this chapter, but verses 9-13 should not be passed without a look at Gal. 4:21-31. Christians are the spiritual seed of Abraham, and those who would supplement faith in Christ by the works of the law are the children of the bondwoman, who have no place with the children of the promise.

God, however, is not unmindful of Hagar and Ishmael, nor of His promise to Abraham concerning the latter. Although the blessing on the nation is not to flow down through them, yet they are not precluded from partaking of it when it comes. Abraham, there can be little doubt, followed the steps of Ishmael with deep interest, although at the moment appearances are not that way. He was probably included in the gifts spoken of at 25:6, while his presence at his father's obsequies (25:9) shows that the bond of affection between them was not broken.

We know little of Ishmael's subsequent life except that gathered from 25:12-18, but the presumption is that he afterward abandoned the religion of his father, since his descendants preserved no trace of it except the rite of circumcision.

2. Abraham's Hardest Test, 22.

The shock communicated to Abraham by this command may have been qualified by the fact that the sacrifice of human beings, and even one's own children, was not unknown to heathenism; but this could not have explained his patient obedience had it not been for that faith mentioned in Hebrews 11:17-19. He knew that God's honor and faithfulness were involved in the preservation or renewal of the life of Isaac, and reposed confidently in that fact. Indeed, there is reason to believe from verse 8 that he foresaw the very means by which God would interpose for his son.

That verse is a beautiful foreshadowing of the substitutionary work of Christ. Transpose the emphasis, and we learn (1) that God is the source or originator of our salvation through Christ— "*God* will Himself provide a lamb"; (2) that God had as much necessity for Christ as we, on the supposition that He purposed to redeem us—"God *will provide* Himself a lamb"; (3) that God is the provision as well as the provider—"God will provide *Himself*," i. e., He is the lamb!

Note two or three other interesting things: (1) that Solomon built the temple to Jehovah on Mt. Moriah (2 Chron. 3:1), and that the eternal Father afterward sacrificed His only begotten Son in the same place; (2) this circumstance of the sacrifice of the Son of God for the sins of men silences the charge of infidelity that it was barbarous for God to command Abraham to sacrifice Isaac. If it was not barbarous for God to sacrifice Christ, neither was it barbarous that it should have been prefigured in the history of Abraham; (3) Isaac himself becomes a notable type of Christ, especially in the meek and submissive spirit shown throughout, and when we remember that although called a "lad" he was presumably 25 years old at this time (compare here John 10:18).

What new name of God is suggested by this event (14)? This means "Jehovah will see" or "Jehovah will provide." How does God now further confirm His promise and covenant (16)? Note the marginal references to Ps. 105:9, Luke 1:73, Heb. 6:13, 14. What additional promise or prediction is now added to the original one (17)? The "gate" of ancient cities being the strongest part of the wall and the most stoutly defended, to possess it was to possess the city itself.

Do not pass this lesson without observing how Abraham showed his faith by his works (James 2:21-24). "All our righteous-

nesses are as filthy rags (Is. 64:6) as a ground of merit before God, but as the fruit of our faith obedience is of great price. Abraham's faith without the works of obedience would have been a lie, while his work without faith would, in this case, have been a sin. The virtue of this act consisted in the fact that he obeyed God."

3. The Cave of Machpelah, 23.

That Sarah should have died not in Beersheba but in Hebron, and that Abraham should have "come" to mourn for her, are facts which the record nowhere explains; but the chapter affords an insight into the customs of the orientals of this period. For "the children of Heth" compare 10:15, etc. It will be seen by verse 10 that these people were the Hittites whom Joshua (1:4) mentions as occupying a great territory in that day, of whom the Egyptian and Assyrian monuments speak as a cultured and powerful nation of antiquity, although until recently critics were disposed to say that they never existed because secular history had lost sight of them.

Let it not be supposed, however, that the courteous formality of this occasion meant that Ephron intended to give Abraham the field for nothing. It was the oriental way of raising the price, so that in the end Abraham paid many times its value. Four hundred shekels of silver were equal to about $240 of our money, the value of which at that time would be five or ten times as much.

Questions.

1. Give book and chapter of the New Testament which refer allegorically to Sarah and Hagar.

2. Give book and chapter which show Abraham's faith in the resurrection.

3. In what three ways does verse 8 of chapter 22 foreshadow the work of Christ?

4. What three events are associated with Mt. Moriah?

5. Give chapter and verse which speak of Abraham's fruit of faith.

FROM THE MARRIAGE OF ISAAC TO THE DEATH OF ABRAHAM

Chapters 24-25

Traveling facilities were limited in Abraham's time, so that communications between families separated by long distances were few and far between. But he seems to have gotten news from his brother's home sometime after the birth of Isaac, as recorded at the close of c. 22, a circumstance linking that chapter to the one we are now considering.

1. Selecting the Bride, 24:1-52.

Notice the preparation made by Abraham for Isaac's marriage (1-9), the oath he administers to his servant, the condition he exacts, the prohibition he places upon him, the assurances he gives him, the exemption he grants. It may not at first appear why Abraham is so solicitous that Isaac's wife shall be taken from his own people rather than the Canaanites, since both were idolaters. But the evil traits of the Canaanites, which afterwards caused them to be driven out of the land, must have been apparent to Abraham even then; moreover there may have been something in his people on the other side of the Euphrates making them more amenable to the purposes of God with reference to the coming Seed, in whom all the families of the earth should be blessed. But it is always to be kept in mind that Abraham was under the guidance of God, and that there was more than man's wisdom or foresight in this transaction.

Notice the preparation made by the servant for his journey (10-14), and observe that the gifts were a dowry for the expected bride, to be paid, however, in accordance with oriental custom, not to her but to her father. How does the servant show his knowledge of the true God? How does his prayer illustrate Prov. 3:5, 6? And yet there is another side to the matter, for it is ill-advised to leave the decisions of life to the arbitrament of signs, and grievous errors have arisen from accrediting God with the outcome of them. "When we have the Word of God, the Spirit of God and the providences of God for our guides, and the throne of grace open to our appeals, it is expected and doubtless salutary that we bear the responsibility of our own decisions in difficult places." Indeed, we are likely to show more reverence for and confidence in God's guidance in this way than in the other.

Notice the facts about Rebekah in vv. 15-28.

Notice the servant's faithfulness in vv. 29-52. Do we get a touch of Laban's character in vv. 30, 31? How does it impress you? How does the servant testify to Abraham and his son in vv. 35, 36? What is the result of the embassy so far as the father and brother of Rebekah are concerned? Which of the two seems to assume the more importance?

2. Accepting the Husband, 24:53-61.

Notice the additional gifts now presented to Rebekah. But who else are also remembered? What objection is interposed, by whom, and why? Who settles the question, and how? What blessing is pronounced upon her? Do you think it has been, or will be, fulfilled?

3. The Marriage Rite, 24:62-67.

Notice how Isaac is represented in v. 63. Was he thinking about his bride? Notice the action of Rebekah, which was an indication of the inferiority to men with which women were then regarded. It would have been improper for Rebekah to have approached her future husband either unveiled or riding, instead of walking. What title did the servant give to Isaac, and what report did he make to him? In what did the wedding ceremony consist? What must have been the significance to the whole camp in this act of Isaac in bringing Rebekah "into his mother Sarah's tent"? Did it not show that she had now come into that place of importance and authority thereto fore occupied by Sarah, and belonging by right to her, who was the recognized wife of the head of the clan?

4. The Symbolism of the Transaction.

We have, in this beautiful story, a striking type of the union between Christ and His bride, the Church;

(1) Abraham arranged the marriage for Isaac, and so the Father has made the marriage for Christ (Matt. 22:1, 2);

(2) The servant selected the bride, and so the Holy Spirit calls out the Church (1 Cor. 6:11; 12:3, 13);

(3) The plan of the servant was simply to tell who his master was, and how he had honored his son, and so the Holy Spirit takes the things of Christ and shows them unto us (John 15:26; 16:13-15).

See further the free agency of the bride in accepting Isaac, and the expression of her purpose in the words "I will go"; also, the separation from loved ones, but the compensation for all in anticipation.

Observe, as well, Isaac's coming out to meet her in the eventide, with its suggestion of Christ's return for His Church at the close of the present age (John 14:1-3); and even his leading Rebekah into his mother's tent, how it foreshadows the place of authority and glory the Church shall have when she reigns with Christ over the millennial earth. (Matt. 19:28; 1 Cor. 6:2; Col. 3:4; Rev. 20:4-6.)

5. The Death of Abraham, 25:1-10.

It is presumable that Abraham's relationship to Keturah was entered into sometime before the marriage of Isaac, and indeed it may have been before his birth. This seems probable, since v. 6, as well as 1 Chron. 1:32, speaks of her as his concubine, and not his wife. The occasion for the allusion to the matter is suggested by the servant's remark in the preceding chapter concerning the possessions of Isaac (compare 24:36 with 25:5). In other words, the gifts to the offspring of Keturah and the settlement of the latter in the east were matters that had been attended to before the marriage of Isaac and Rebekah.

Note the age of Abraham (7) and the way in which his departure from this life is designated (8), affording an intimation of the conscious and sentient condition of the dead while awaiting the resurrection of their bodies.

Questions.

1. What connection do you see between chapters 22 and 24?

2. Can you give any reasons for Abraham's solicitude about the wife of Isaac?

3. Can you quote from memory Proverbs 3:5, 6?

4. Can you name four or five features in which the marriage of Isaac and Rebekah symbolizes the union of Christ and His Church?

5. Recall three or four features in which Abraham's life-story illustrates Romans 4:20, last clause.

JACOB AND ESAU

CHAPTERS 25-27

1. The Defrauded Birthright, 25: 19-34.

As we read the introductory part of this chapter, we are impressed that many of the mothers of the notable men of the Bible were for a long while childless: Sarah, Rebekah, Rachel, and the mothers of Samson, Samuel and John the Baptist. Was this that their faith might be proved? We wonder, too, what is meant by the statement that Rebekah "went to inquire of Jehovah." There seems to have been some way, even in that early time, by which individuals could communicate with God. As Abraham was a prophet, and living not far from her, it has been suggested that she may have gone to inquire of the Lord through him.

In considering v. 23, be careful not to charge God with partiality in the choice of Jacob, and it will save us from so doing if we remember that (1) on the natural plane of things, if there be two nations one is likely to be stronger than the other; (2) God not only foresees this but has the right to pre-determine it, especially when the blessing of all the nations is involved therein; (3) this determination in the present case brought no hardship upon the weaker nation as such, nor did it prevent any of its individuals from receiving all the blessings of the life to come.

And yet this by no means justifies the meanness of Jacob, any more than the recklessness of Esau. Neither brother distinguishes himself in the transaction, while Jacob's conduct is only another illustration of an attempt to assist God in the fulfillment of His promises. Patience would have gotten him the birthright with honor to himself as well as glory to God.

2. History Repeating Itself, 26:1-33.

How much of this chapter reminds us of the previous one in the life of Abraham! There is little to be explained, but the facts should be noted.

The well called Rehoboth still remains strengthened with masonry of immense proportions and great antiquity. It is believed that it is the well which Isaac dug, although the country is now a desert in contrast to its fruitfulness in his time. We may add that at present there are two old wells in Beersheba, three hundred yards apart, and Dr. Edward Robinson, in *Biblical Researches,* gives his opinion that the larger may be the famous well of Abraham, while possibly the second may be that which Isaac dug when the former was stopped up by the Philistines. The locality still bears the same name, only in Arabic form.

3. The Defrauded Blessing, 27:1-40.

The closing verse of c. 26 gave us a further insight into Esau's character, qualifying our sympa-

thy for him. His purpose in marrying the daughters of the Canaanite princes was doubtless to increase his worldly importance, a circumstance opposed to the divine purpose in the separation of Abraham and his seed from the other nations. "If the descendants of Abraham were the daughters of the heathen Canaanites, they would soon lose the traditions of their family and every trace of their heavenly calling. As a matter of fact, this became true in the case of the descendants of Esau, who were always the enemies of Israel and figure in the prophets as the type of the enemies of God."

We can hardly believe, however, that Isaac was entirely without blame in this case. But who can justify Rebekah, to say nothing of Jacob? Surely the goodness of God is of grace, and these things show that He has a plan to carry out in which He is simply using men as He finds them, and subsequently conforming them to Himself as His sovereign will may determine.

Notice that the blessings of Isaac on Jacob were a formal transmission of the original promise of God to Abraham (28:29), which when once transmitted could not be recalled (34-38). Esau is blessed, but it is not THE blessing which he receives. Notice the differences between his blessing and that of Jacob. There is an intimation that Esau —that is, the nation that should spring from him—would at some time break from his brother's yoke, but later prophecies show that this freedom would be only for a season. In connection with Esau's conduct compare Hebrews 12:15-17.

Note in passing that Herod the Great, the last king of Judah, was a descendant of Esau, an Idumean on the side of both father and mother, a circumstance, which was the foundation for that irreconcilable hatred with which the Jews regarded him during his long reign.

4. Jacob's Flight, 26:41 to 28:22.

What was the cause of Jacob's

flight (27:41-45)? The excuse for it (27:46 to 28:5)? At what place is he next found (10)? What did he see in his dream? Whom did he see, and why? How did the speaker introduce Himself? Do you recognize the promise given him? What particular addendum of a personal character is attached (15)? What effect had this on Jacob? How did he express his feelings? What did he name the place? (Bethel means "The House of God.") Compare John 1:51; Heb. 1:14; Luke 15:10, and recall that the beautiful hymn, "Nearer, My God, to Thee," is based upon this impressive incident in Jacob's life. "For the pious servants of God this dream threw a flood of light upon the certainty of heaven, of which they had known little or nothing until that time, as well as the facile communication there might be between heaven and earth, and the profound interest which God and the holy angels felt in the affairs of men." What vow did Jacob offer? In the consideration of this vow, which was entirely voluntary on his part, observe that "if" does not necessarily express a doubt in his mind, since it might be translated "since," or "so then." It may be regarded as his acceptance of the divine promise, so that from that moment Jehovah did in some sense become his God, as well as He had been the God of Abraham and Isaac.

We are accustomed to speak of the selfish proposition of Jacob in v. 22, last clause. But before casting the mote out of his eye, should we not cast the beam out of our own? With all the knowledge of God we possess does our character shine brighter? Do we not still use the "if" in the face of the promises? And do we give even as much as a tenth of our possessions to Him, notwithstanding the richer blessings we enjoy? Is it not still true that He is dealing with us on the principle of grace, and not merit? God sometimes consents to call Himself by the name of "the God of Jacob." What unutterable comfort it should bring to us!

Questions.

1. On what grounds is God released from the charge of partiality in the choice of Jacob?

2. In what ways do Isaac's life and character differ from that of Abraham?

3. What name is sometimes given to Esau's descendants?

4. What is the meaning of Bethel?

5. How would you explain God's patience with Jacob?

JACOB AND LABAN

CHAPTERS 29-31

1. Their First Meeting, 29:1-14.

Jacob's journey to Haran, his mother's country, was first to the north and then the east, re-traversing the original course of his grandfather Abraham. As he nears its termination, his attention is attracted by the shepherds with their flocks around a well, whose mouth is covered with a stone. Inquiry reveals that they belong to Haran, and are acquainted with his uncle Laban. Rachel, his daughter and the keeper of his sheep, will be there presently, for her they are waiting, since their custom is not to remove the stone or water the flocks till all are gathered. Rachel appears, and it is a case of love at first sight on Jacob's part, if one may judge by his action in rolling the stone from the well and watering her sheep, to say nothing of the kiss he bestows upon her. As another observes, the morals of these simple folk were good, and the estimation in which they held the honor of women was high, for a young and beautiful girl like Rachel might expose herself to the hazards of pastoral life without risk. But among the ancient Greeks it was the custom for daughters of princes to perform this office, and even to-day among the Arabs unmarried women expose themselves without harm to the same class of dangers. The personal habits of people make a great difference in their national customs. (Pratt.)

Anstey shows that Jacob was 77 years of age at this time.

Rachel's enthusiasm in carrying the news to her father reminds us of her aunt, Rebekah, at an earlier time. Though Jacob calls himself her father's brother, we know after the oriental fashion he means his nephew. What a talk they had around the family hearth as he rehearsed the story of the mother he loved so truly since she left her home long before! A month has passed before they settle down again to prosaic things (14).

2. Their First Contract, 29:15 to 30:24.

The seven years Jacob serves for Rachel are a heavy burden in one sense, but a light one in another. But how he is deceived at the end of it, when he begins to reap what he had sown! All this is part of God's plan for his conviction, conversion, sanctification, and preparation for His great purpose on behalf of Israel and the whole world later on. Happily Jacob is not obliged to wait another seven years before marrying Rachel, but receives that part of his compensation in advance (27-28).

One cannot read this story without being impressed with the use God made of the envy of these sisters for the purpose of building up the house of Jacob and of Israel. We meet with some indelicate things here, but we should remember that these histories were written not from our point of view but in the style of the simple people of the past. It is desirable to familiarize ourselves with the names of the twelve sons of Jacob, since they become so prominent in the history of Israel and of the world. Notice who was the mother of Levi and of Judah, and also of Joseph (29:24-35; 30:24). The polygamy and concubinage spoken of are not only contrary to the Gospel, but not to be regarded as approved of God at any time (Mal. 2:14-15; Matt. 19:3-9), but in accordance with the customs of those times. In this connection it is notable that Isaac seems to have remained a monogamist.

3. Their Second Contract, 30:25 to 31:16.

As one reads the story of this section he feels little sympathy for Laban, who deserved the punishment he received, but wonders at Jacob's smartness until he reads his explanation (31:4-13), and learns that God interposed on his behalf, and prompted him in what he did. This is in fulfillment of the original promise of blessing and cursing, which was carried out in the later history of Israel, and will be very markedly fulfilled at the end of this age and throughout the millennium. There is a divine reason why the Jew of to-day holds the money bags of the world, and why he is such a factor in our commercial centers.

O, thou treacherous and crafty Laban, type of the Gentile oppressor of Israel in all time, dost thou think thou canst circumvent Jehovah by removing all the speckled goats and black sheep from thy flocks that Jacob may have none (vv. 34-36)? Place three day's journey between thyself and Jacob, but leave to Jacob God, and he will ask no more (31:5)!

It is interesting that Jacob has the sympathy of his wives in the issue between him and their father, and that they support him in his purpose to return to his own land. What was the inspiration and the encouragement of this purpose (13)?

4. Their Separation, 31:17-55.

What advantage of Laban did Jacob take at this juncture (19, 20)? What shows Jacob's wives to have been idolators at this time? How does this further indicate the divine patience and long-suffering? How does it indicate that God has a purpose of grace He is seeking in the earth independent of the conscious and willing co-operation of His creatures?

Look on the map and determine what river it was that Jacob crossed in going from Haran into Gilead (a distance of probably 350 miles). How does God interpose for Jacob (24)? Where have we seen a similar revelation of Himself to a heathen? Do you think Laban was sincere in v. 27? What teaching do we obtain of the responsibilities and hardships of the shepherd's life in vv. 38-40? Notice Jacob's testimony to God's great favor to him (42), and the distinction of faith in Jacob's oath as compared with that of Laban.

It is desirable to add that the names which Laban and Jacob gave to the locality of their covenant means the same thing in the Aramic and Hebrew tongues, "The heap of witness," while Mizpah means "The watch tower."

How does the conclusion of this story illustrate Proverbs 16:7?

Questions.

1. Rehearse the story of Jacob from the time of leaving home until he met Laban.

2. Try to recall the story he would have to tell Laban.

3. Give the substance of the references to Malachi and Matthew.

4. Of what is Laban a type in all the generations?

5. Memorize the last Scripture reference, with chapter and verse.

JACOB BECOMES ISRAEL

Chapters 32, 33

1. Meeting With the Angels, 32: 1, 2.

Filled with wonders is this lesson! The appearance of the angels, the divine wrestling, the transformation of Esau—how much we need the Holy Spirit to understand the meaning of these things!

Be sure to identify these places. Galeed or Mizpah of the preceding chapter, and Mahanaim, Peniel and the river Jabbok named in this, are all on the east of the Jordan, not far from what was known later as Ramoth-Gilead.

How condescending of God to send His angels to encourage Jacob at this crisis—such a man as Jacob! In the margin you will find that Mahanaim means "two heaps" or "two camps," with reference perhaps to the angels as one camp and the household of Jacob as the other.

2. Meeting With God, 32:3-32.

Where was Esau dwelling at this time (3)? What shows Jacob's fear of him (4-8)? What reason had he for the increase of this fear (6)? To whom did he appeal, and how (9-12)?

Study this prayer, the first of its kind in the Bible—that of Abraham was intercessory and of the nature of a dialogue, but this is a personal supplication. Its elements are adoration, confession, thanksgiving, petition and pleading. Discover these divisions for yourself and locate them in the verses.

How does Jacob plan to propitiate Esau (13)? What kind of present does he prepare for him (14-15)? How many droves in all do you think there were (16-20)? Can you picture these five droves separated and appearing before Esau's astonished eyes at intervals? Was not the plan well adapted from a human point of view to have the desired effect?

But the incident following shows that something must be done in Jacob's soul and then the propitiation of his brother will be brought about in another way. In this incident we have another theophany such as we have seen before, but in some respects more remarkable still. To think that Jehovah should not only appear in human form but wrestle as a man with a man! What is the meaning of it all?

For one thing it shows Jacob's dogged determination to have his own way—a kind of symbolic action illustrative of his whole career. What a schemer and planner he was from the time he defrauded Esau of his birthright until now! While wrestling with God he was in spirit wrestling with Esau probably, seeking in his own strength and by his own schemes to make peace with him, but he is to learn that his strength is made perfect in weakness. In God's plan and purpose he cannot prevail with men until he first prevails with God, and with God he cannot prevail until he ceases his own efforts and simply clings to Him for support and blessing. But this he will not do until God afflicts and makes it impossible for him to do otherwise. What a lesson for us! May God help us to translate it into our experience!

3. Meeting With Esau, 33.

The action of Esau, especially v. 4, seems to indicate a supernatural work on him, changing his mind toward Jacob. It is not the result of Jacob's plan so much as God's grace, whether Jacob realizes it as yet or not.

His caution (12-15) still shows a certain fear of Esau, and this is shown further by the fact that he does not follow him to Seir (14), but turns sharply to the east, locating in Succoth, and then in Shechem. Notice the altar he erects and the recognition of his own new name "God, the God of Israel."

Questions.

1. Have you identified the localities?

2. Have you analyzed Jacob's prayer?

3. Have you pictured in your mind his plan of propitiation of Esau?

4. Have you compared yourself with Jacob as a planner?

5. Have you learned his secret of prevailing with God?

JACOB AT THE HOMESTEAD—MEMOIRS OF ESAU

Chapters 34-36

1. The Wickedness of Jacob's Sons, 34.

In the last lesson Jacob's altar at Shechem proclaims God to be his God, but (as another says) it is evident he has not gotten the power of this name for he is walking in his own ways still, as his house at Succoth and his purchase at Shechem testify. So new sorrow and discipline must come.

Dinah represents the young women of to-day who want to see the world and have their fling. Her conduct was indiscreet, to say the least, and dearly did all concerned pay the consequences. One can feel only utter condemnation for the beastliness of Shechem, and yet the reparation he and his father offered to make was honorable (3-12), and dignifies them in comparison with Jacob's sons and many modern offenders of high repute.

No justification can be found for the criminality of Jacob's sons (18-29). That Jacob appreciated its enormity, not only his fear (30) but also his later loathing of it and his curse upon its instigators (49:5-7), show.

In our indignation we ask why did not God destroy these sons of Jacob instead of continuing His interest in them and even prospering them? In reply, remember that He did this not for their sake but for the world's sake, our sake. His plan of redemption for the world involved the preservation of Israel, and to have destroyed them would have been to destroy the root of the tree whose leaves ultimately would be for the healing of the nation. It is this that explains God's patience in later periods of Israel's history, and indeed His dealings with us; for His own name's sake He does many things, or refrains from doing them.

2. The Later Journeys of Jacob, 35.

God comes to Jacob's relief in directing him to what place? What marks this as a time of religious crisis in his family (2-4)? If he had forgotten God's house in building his own, God now leads him to a higher plane where he sees his obligation to build God's house first. What was done with all their emblems of idolatry? In what way does God put Jacob's fear upon his enemies (5)?

How further is God's goodness shown to Jacob (9)? What assurance is renewed to him (10)? What are the Hebrew words for "God Almighty," and their meaning (see Lesson 10)? What relation do you perceive between this name and the promise which follows? In what way does God transfer the original blessing to Jacob (11)? How does the language (v. 13) show that we have here another theophany?

Jacob seems to be gradually approaching the old homestead. What place is now reached, and what later name is given it (16-19)? What domestic events occurred here? It is interesting to note that the pillar erected to Rachel was in existence at the time of Moses, three hundred years later, according to the testimony of v. 20. It is mentioned again four hundred years afterward in 1 Samuel 10:2. "The Mohammedans still mark the site with a monument of solid masonry."

What interesting circumstance is mentioned in v. 27? How does v. 29 testify to the reconciliation of Jacob and Esau? In coming to the end of Isaac's life it is worth while to note that his blessing, unlike Jacob's, was uniform and unbroken, doubtless the recompense of the obedience with which his life began. Note also how God preserved him in life so that he did not give up his place as a witness of God's truth in the earth until Jacob, the son of promise, had returned and was made ready to fill that place. Attention had better be called as well to the phrase, "was gathered unto his people" (29), which was used of Abraham (25:7), and points to a belief even in those early days of a continued existence of men after death.

3. The Memoirs of Esau, 36.

We can spare but a paragraph or two for this chapter, which is inserted doubtless because of the natural relations between Jacob and Esau, and the subsequent relations of their respective descendants.

It is noticeable that the author takes pains to identify Esau with Edom, mentioning the fact a number of times. In the second place, we see from the origin of Esau's wives that "Canaanites" includes the Hittites, Hivites and Horites. In the third place, we

should not be misled by the word "dukes," which simply means "chiefs," or heads of families or clans. In the fourth place, the reference to Esau's dwelling in Mount Seir (6-8) seems to refer to a second departure into that country after the return of Jacob and the death of Isaac. Finally, the reference in v. 31 to the "kings that reigned in the land of Edom before there reigned any king over the children of Israel" seems to point to a later author than Moses, since there were no kings in Israel until hundreds of years after his death. The entire paragraph with a few variations is found again in 1 Chronicles 1:43-50, and some have thought that it was taken from thence and added to this chapter.

Questions.

1. Has Jacob yet become perfected?

2. Should we palliate wrong in those who stand in close relationship to God?

3. Can we give a reason for God's forbearance in the case of Jacob's sons?

4. Describe the religious crisis in Jacob's household at this time.

5. What corroborative evidence of the historicity of this lesson is found in modern times?

DISPENSATIONAL ASPECT OF JACOB'S HISTORY

Following F. W. Grant, in the *Numerical Bible*, the life of Jacob gives as its lesson the story of that discipline by which the Spirit of God brings us from weakness to power, from nature's strength to that wholesome weakness in which alone is strength. But for this, natural strength must be crippled, which is provided for in two ways: (1) in allowing us to realize the power of another nature (Esau), and (2) in the direct dealing of God with our souls.

To this also correspond the two names which distinguish the two parts of Jacob's life, before and after these experiences have done their work. He is Jacob in his methods, however, long after his heart is set upon divine things, and is only Israel when, his human strength broken down, he halts upon his thigh. These two names—Jacob and Israel—are applied all through the Scriptures in a very beautiful manner to the nation which sprang from him, and of which he is the representative throughout. But of course the effect of God's discipline upon them cannot be read in their history hitherto, and awaits the fulfillment of prophecy concerning them. Their past history has been that of Jacob, but it will yet be said of "Jacob and of Israel: What hath God wrought!" (Numbers 23:23).

Jacob's history divides itself into three parts—his early life in Canaan, his stay in Padan-aram, and his life again as restored to Canaan; just as the history of the nation dispensationally divides itself into their first occupation of the land, their present dispersion, and their future and perpetual enjoyment of it when God brings them back again.

We find a kind of parallel between the first part of Jacob's life and that of the nation in his dream at Bethel when he is just about to leave the land, as we compare that dream with the application which Christ makes of it to Himself (John 1:51). Christ, as the Son of man, secures to Israel the care and ministrations of Jehovah while the nation is outcast from their inheritance, and when they shall with Nathanael's faith confess Christ as Son of God and King of Israel, they shall have in a more blessed way than ever their "house of God" on earth.

In the same way Jacob's history at Padan-aram suggests a parallel with the nation as they are now scattered from their land, for during the twenty years of Jacob's exile he enjoyed no such revelations of God's presence as he did before. During that time God deals with him as He is now dealing with the nation, as one for whom He has a purpose of blessing only to be reached through disciplinary sorrow. Like his descendants he is multiplied

as the dust, while trampled into it. The nation to-day is enslaved, persecuted, and yet preserved in order to merge in the end of the age into that place of wealth and power of which all the prophets speak.

Jacob's return to his own land, in its application to the nation, brings us into the field of prophecy. For the nation, as well as for him, Peniel must prepare the way to Bethel. That the nation may not fall into the hands of their enemies, God, whose name is yet unknown to them, must take them into His own hand, crippling the human strength with which they contend with Him that in weakness they may hold Him fast for blessing. Thus, broken down in repentance and purged from idolatry, the nation will have their second Bethel when God will reveal to them His name so long hidden, and confirm to them the promise to their father Abraham.

Questions.

1. What is the great lesson of Jacob's life?

2. Divide his history in three parts, and apply it dispensationally.

3. Quote from memory John 1:51.

4. In what way does the Padan-aram experience foreshadow Israel's history to-day?

5. What event in Jacob's life foreshadows a similar one yet to follow in the history of Israel?

JOSEPH'S HISTORY

CHAPTERS 37-47

The general familiarity with these chapters warrants the grouping of them in one lesson, especially as there is little requiring explanation within our present scope.

1. Loved and Hated, 37.

It may seem foolish for Joseph to have made known his dreams to his brethren, and thus increase their enmity against him, but we should consider God's purpose in the matter, whether Joseph understood it or not. In the outcome it was important that they should know these dreams, which were really prophecies, in advance of their fulfillment for the sake of the moral effect upon them.

In this chapter it will be seen that the merchantmen are called both Ishmaelites and Midianites, both being in the company, perhaps, as their territories were contiguous in Arabia.

2. Sold Into Slavery, 39.

Note the faith and piety of Joseph as indicated in v. 9, in language unlike anything hitherto recorded of the patriarchs. Note too that according to v. 20 Potiphar must have doubted the truth of his wife's charge, or else he would probably have executed Joseph.

3. Falsely Imprisoned, 40.

This chapter is chiefly notable for the further evidence it gives of Joseph's intimate acquaintance with and faith in God, and the close dealings of God with him in the revelation of these things.

4. Exalted to the Throne, 41.

Note Pharaoh's testimony to Joseph's power with God (38), not that he himself knew the true God, but that he witnessed to the power Joseph had with the God he (Joseph) served. How does this incident in Joseph's life illustrate 1 Tim. 4:8, last clause?

The name given Joseph by Pharaoh merits attention notwithstanding the difficulty in its interpretation. The Revised Version spells it "Zaphenathpaneah," but it is not determined whether it is of Hebrew, Egyptian or Coptic derivation. If the first it may mean "Revealer of secrets"; if the second, "Bread of Life"; if the third, "Saviour of the world"; all bearing on the same thought and any of them both significant and appropriate.

5. Dealing with His Brethren, 42 to 44.

The details of these chapters show the purpose of Joseph to "multiply unlooked for events and complicate the situation for his brethren, both to awaken their conviction of wrongdoing in the past and an expectation of something still more mysterious, whether good or bad, in the future"—thus preparing them for the great revelation soon to be made.

In chapter 44:17, 18 the reference to the three days is important for its bearing on the death and resurrection of Christ. It will be well to note, for example, the vague way of the Hebrews in using the words. According to our usage, had Joseph's brethren been imprisoned three days it would not have been until the fourth day that he changed his plan, but instead of that they were shut up but two nights and the intermediate day, with parts of the first and third days. This was the time Jesus was in the grave, so that there is no more reason to accuse the Bible of inaccuracy or contradiction in the one case than in the other. (*Studies in Genesis,* in loco.)

6. Revealing Himself to His Brethren, 45.

Why was Pharaoh so pleased to have Jacob and his family settle in Egypt? To show appreciation of Joseph? Yes, and for other reasons. It was not merely three-score and six souls that constituted the whole encampment of Jacob, but between three and four thousand souls, if we count all their dependents, which was a valuable accession to any nation when we consider the character of the people.

And there may have been another reason still, if it be true that the reigning dynasty at this time was the Hyksos or Shepherd kings, i. e., Syrians or Asiatics who centuries before had invaded and seized upon the kingdom, and so were unpopular with the native races. It would be a great advantage to them to have so powerful an accession of Asiatics as Jacob's tribe represented, not only to increase their riches but to "give additional firmness to the throne against the discontent and disturbance of the native races."

7. Settling the Family in Goshen, 46 to 48.

Note the suitableness of Goshen as a place of settlement for the Israelites. In the first place, it afforded good pasturage and they were shepherds, but in some parts of it there was excellent tillage as well. In the next place, its location near the Isthmus of Suez,—made it easy to depart from later on when the necessity was so great. And last, but not least, it was a location where the least offense would be given to the native races, and there was reason for such offense because shepherds were held in abomination by them. Their subjugation by a shepherd race explains this in part, but there was another reason in that the Egyptians for religious reasons did not eat flesh. They worshipped the beasts which the Israelites ate and offered in sacrifice to God.

How long did Jacob live in Egypt (47:28)? What solemn promise did he extract from Joseph just prior to his death (29-31)? Do you think this expressed only the natural desire to be buried with his own people, or did it express faith in the divine promise that his seed should ultimately inherit Canaan?

Questions.

1. What name did Pharaoh give Joseph, and what are its possible meanings?

2. How does this lesson throw light on the period that Christ remained in the grave?

3. What probable dynasty of Pharaoh's is before us in this lesson?

4. Give some reasons for Pharaoh's satisfaction in welcoming the Israelites to Egypt.

5. What made Goshen a desirable locality for them?

TYPICAL AND DISPENSATIONAL ASPECTS OF JOSEPH'S HISTORY.

The life of Joseph more than any other patriarch suggests that of Christ and shadows forth the history of Israel as a nation.

1. The first view we have of him he is loved of his father and hated by his brethren, and there are three things for which his brethren hated him, namely: the love of his father for him, his separation from them in a moral sense, and his dreams in which his future supremacy is announced. There were the same things for which Christ was hated by his brethren after the flesh: (1) His Father's love; (2) His separation from them (John 15:17-25); and (3) the announcement of His future glory (Matt. 27:57-68).

2. Joseph is conspired against and sold, and it is his love-mission to his brethren, as sent by his father, that gives occasion for this. How like the history of our Saviour in His coming unto Israel! Joseph is cast into a pit at first, but instead of putting him to death his brethren sell him to the Ishmaelites. So the Jews, knowing it was not lawful for them to put any man to death, transferred Jesus to the Gentiles.

3. Joseph is a slave in the house of the Egyptian, but that house is greatly blessed of God because he is in it: a type of Christ's ministry to the world while He abode therein. And yet Joseph's goodness to the Egyptian did not avail in the face of false accusation, nor did that of Christ to the world. The former is cast into prison where again all things come under his hand, and so Christ descends into a darker prison-house where He manifests Himself as master of all there (Col. 2:15; 1 Peter 3:18-22).

4. Joseph's humiliation issues in exaltation; the parallel to which in Christ's case is as we see Him raised from the grave to the throne of glory. "God sent me before you to preserve life," said Joseph to his brethren, and Jesus at the right hand of God is ministering in the spiritual sense, to His brethren of Israel to whom He is as yet unknown.

5. But in connection with Joseph's exaltation he enters on a new relationship—that of mar-

riage with a Gentile woman, suggestive of the unique relationship of Christ to His church, composed chiefly of Gentile believers.

6. Now comes the time of famine which speaks of the period at the end of this age, a literal seven years as indicated by Daniel 9, when the church shall have been translated to meet her Lord in the air, and Israel will be preparing through trial to recognize and receive her rejected Lord.

Benjamin Blended with Joseph.

7. At this point Benjamin comes into view as blended with Joseph in the prototypal relation. To quote another: "We see how all at last is made to depend upon Benjamin. No one person could be a full type of Christ, and Benjamin is brought in to supplement what is lacking in Joseph. Benjamin means 'the son of my right hand,' and he represents the Messiah of power for whom the Jews have always been looking. But Benjamin, before he was called by his father the name which means 'the son of my right hand,' was named by his mother 'Benoni,' which means 'the son of my sorrow.' It was necessary for Christ to be the sufferer before He could be the conqueror. Christ, known to us as the rejected One, is now exalted and seated at the right hand of God, and He is the One whom Israel *does not know.* A Christ triumphant and reigning over the earth is the One for whom they have always looked; the Sufferer for whom they did not look but who must precede the Conqueror they have refused.

"But power does not lie with Benjamin for whom his brethren are looking, but with Joseph whom they have refused. As a conquering Messiah Christ has been prophesied to them, and as such He longs to display Himself in their behalf. This He cannot do without atonement for the sin that led them to their refusal of Him. For this they must be brought to repentance, and God sends them into an agony for their ideal Messiah that makes them ready to re-

ceive the true one. In the last great sorrow that shall overtake Israel as a nation this shall be accomplished. Before Him whom they do not know they shall plead for the Benjamin who has been lost to them, and in the agony of that hour, while they are still pleading for the ideal conquering Messiah, the heavens shall suddenly open and they shall be overwhelmed by a revelation of the Christ they refused (Zech. 12:10).

"The Conqueror and the Sufferer are one and the same blessed Person. The 'Lion' that prevails to open the book is the 'Lamb' that was slain."—*The Numerical Bible,* by F. W. Grant: *The Unfolding of the Ages,* by Ford C. Ottman.

CLOSE OF THE PATRIARCHAL AGE

CHAPTERS 48-50

With the history of Joseph, Genesis concludes what is called the patriarchal age. Yet there are two or three facts for consideration before passing to the next book.

1. The Life of Judah.

For example, Joseph's history was interrupted almost at the beginning by that of his brother Judah (c. 38). A shameful history is that of Judah, but recorded because of its bearing upon the genealogy of Jesus, since Tamar, prostitute though she were, became an ancestress of our blessed Lord (Matt. 1:3).

2. Jacob Blessing Joseph's Sons, 48.

Note the past and the future of Jacob's faith as enunciated in vv. 3 and 4: his adoption of the two sons of Joseph, and how in some sense they were to receive the blessing forfeited by Reuben and Simeon (see the following chapter, and compare 1 Chron. 5:1, 2). By the adoption of these two sons the tribes of Israel were enlarged to thirteen, but by a special divine arrangement, as we shall see subsequently, that of

Levi had no part in the division of the land of Canaan, and the nation was thus able to always preserve the original number, twelve.

Of the two sons of Joseph Jacob gave the pre-eminence to one contrary to the law of primogeniture and evidently by divine guidance, though for reasons we do not know. By and by we shall see a fulfillment of this predictive blessing in the pre-eminence of the tribe of Ephraim. Notice the form of blessing on these sons, a kind of credal expression of Jacob (vv. 15, 16). This is the earliest creed of the true faith on record, and suggests an example to us in these days when all sorts of people say they believe in God, meaning so many different things thereby. We should be careful that it be known in what God we believe, namely, "the God and Father of our Lord Jesus Christ," with all that the term implies. When in this blessing Jacob speaks of "the Angel" who redeemed him, he means Jehovah Himself, since (as we have learned) He is identical with the second Person of the Trinity. "Angel" means "the sent One," in which connection read Gal. 4:4, 5.

Note the triumphant faith of Jacob through this closing transaction of his career. His assurance of the fulfillment of God's promises to His people takes away the fear of death from him and leads him to regard those promises greater than all the worldly glories enjoyed by Joseph and his sons as princes of Egypt. Observe also that he disposes of that which God has promised him for his descendants with as much confidence, as he would dispose of an earthly estate.

3. Jacob's Prophecy of the Twelve Tribes, 49.

In accordance with the curse on Reuben (3, 4), his tribe never attained distinction in Israel. Simeon and Levi for the same reason were both divided and scattered in the later allotment of the land (5-7): see for the former,

Joshua 19:9; 2 Chron. 15:9 and 34:6, and for the latter Num. 35:7, 8 and Joshua 21:1-42. Levi's curse was turned into a blessing, doubtless because of their righteous conduct, as will be seen later. Compare Ex. 32:25 and Deut. 33:8-11.

The reason Judah obtained the pre-eminence (8-12) was not for his superior moral character (as we have seen) but for reasons known only to God. "Judah" means "praise," and as Grant says, it is striking to see in the history of Israel how when Judah came to power in the time of David, the worship of Jehovah revived. David who came to Judah was himself the sweet psalmist of Israel who has given to the saints of every generation songs of praise that never grow old.

It is in connection with Judah (10) that we have the clearest prophecy of the Redeemer since that of Eden (Gen. 3:15). His was to be the royal tribe, and the scepter should not depart from him nor the lawgiver (or the rulers' staff) from between his feet until Shiloh should come. Both Jews and Christians agree that Shiloh, "peace-maker," applies to Christ, in which regard it is noticeable that the tribe of Judah maintained at least the semblance of government in Israel until after the crucifixion, while since that time she has had no national existence. All agree in regarding this one of the strong evidences of the Messiahship of Jesus.

Zebulon, in fulfillment of the prediction in v. 13, dwelt on the Sea of Galilee, his border running back on the west and north to Sidon. Naphtali being contiguous. Their occupations and dangers as seamen made them courageous, and "they jeoparded their lives" in the battles of the Kingdom (1 Chron. 12:33-34). The territory of Issachar was one of the most fertile in Canaan, explaining their pacific and industrious life as predicted in vv. 14, 15. The language concerning Dan is difficult to understand (v. 16, 17), but Asher's territory like that of the two other tribes mentioned was one of the best in Israel and corresponded with the meaning of his name, "happy" or "fortunate." Of Naphtali we have spoken in connection with Zebulon. The tribe of Benjamin seems to have been always warlike and cruel in character.

The death of Jacob calls attention to the fact that his last days were not only his most tranquil but those in which we see the work of his conversion and sanctification carried to its culminating point.

4. The Burial of Jacob and the Death of Joseph, 50.

What period of time was devoted to the ceremonial worship for the grandees of Egypt (v. 3)? During this period Joseph was isolated from the court of Pharaoh, which accounts for his request of others (v. 4, 5).

How did Joseph's brethren exhibit needless fear on their return (15, 16)? Do you think they spoke the truth in alluding to their father, or was it a ruse on their part? How does the circumstance illustrate the power of a guilty conscience? How does Joseph's reply illustrate the kindness of God to us in Christ (21)? In what way does the circumstance suggest the ground of assurance for them who put their trust in Christ?

In what way did Joseph exhibit his faith in God's promise concerning Israel (24, 25)? Compare Heb. 11:22.

Questions.

1. Which of Joseph's sons received the pre-eminence in Jacob's blessing?

2. What important lesson is suggested by 48:15, 16?

3. In what way has the meaning of Judah's name been fulfilled in history?

4. Quote the prophecy of 49:10, and show its application to Christ.

5. State the typical and dispensational aspects of Joseph's history as given in the last lesson.

EXODUS

FROM THE DEATH OF JOSEPH TO THE CALL OF MOSES

CHAPTERS 1-2:22

In Exodus we have the deliverance of Israel out of Egypt and the establishment of their relationship with Jehovah their Deliverer.

It opens by rehearsing the names of Jacob's sons and the passing away of Joseph and his generation (1:1-6)—matters considered in Genesis. Then follows a statement of the numerical development of Israel. Count the adverbs, adjectives and nouns descriptive of it, and see how God has fulfilled already one part of His prediction to Abraham, Gen. 15:13, 14.

1. Analysis of Chapter 1.

What circumstance is mentioned in v. 8? What course does the king pursue towards Israel, and why (9-11)? What effect had this on the development of the people (12)? How further did the Egyptians oppress Israel (13, 14)? How was the execution of the last-named method of oppression subsequently extended (22)?

2. Definition, Explanation and Application.

(1) Exodus begins with "Now" which might be translated "And," suggesting that the book was not originally divided from Genesis as at present, but constituted a part of it. This is true of all the first five books of the Bible, which were originally one unbroken volume and known as "The Law" or "The Law of Moses" (Luke 16:31 24:44).

(2) "The new king * * * which knew not Joseph" means a new dynasty altogether, the result of some internal revolution or foreign conquest. If that of Joseph's day was a dynasty of shepherd kings from the East or the neighborhood of Canaan, we can understand their friendship for Joseph and his family outside of any special debt of gratitude they owed him; and for the same reason we can understand how the new regime might have been jealous and fearful of his clan in the event of a war with the people of that region (10). Perhaps, "more and mightier than we," is not to be taken in a literal but comparative sense.

(3) Notice concerning "the Hebrew midwives" that while the names of but two are given these may have been heads of schools of the obstetric art. "Stools" (16) might be translated "stones," and suggests a vessel of stone for holding water like a trough, the application being to the children rather than to the mothers. When a newborn child was laid in the trough for bathing may have been the time for the destruction of the male issue.

Verse 21 will be better understood if we know that "them" is masculine and refers not to the midwives but Israel. "The midwives feared God," and because of this they did not execute Pharaoh's orders, and those orders remaining unexecuted, God built up Israel. "He made them houses" refers doubtless to the way in which the Israelites begat children and their families grew. It was for this reason that the king now gave commandment to his people generally to engage in the destructive work.

3. Analysis of Chapter 2.

The story now descends from the general to the particular and the history of one family and one child is given. To which tribe did this family belong (1)? For the names of the father and mother, see 6:20. What measures were taken to preserve the child (3)? Compare Heb. 11:23 for evidence of a divine impulse in this action. What is the meaning of "Moses" (Hebrew—Mosheh, 10)? While Moses was to have the advantage of all the wisdom and learning of the Egyptian court (Acts 7:22), what arrangement is made for his instruction in the traditions of his fathers (7-9)?

Do you see any relation between this training of Moses and his action in vv. 11 and 12? May it have been that Moses was fired by a carnal desire to free his people at this time and in his own way? What led to his flight from Egypt (13, 14)? Were his fears well grounded (15)?

Identify Midian on the map, and from your studies in Genesis recall what Abrahamic stock had settled in that neighborhood. Is there anything in v. 15 and the following verses to recall an ancestor of Moses, and if so, which one?

4. Definition, Explanation and Application.

(1) It is probable the marriage of Moses' parents had taken place previous to the order for the destruction of the male children, for Aaron, the brother of Moses, was older than he and there is no intimation that his infancy was exposed to peril.

(2) Speaking of the wisdom and learning of the Egyptians, Dr. Murphy has a paragraph explaining it as follows:

"The annual overflow of the Nile, imparting a constant fertility to the soil, rendered Egypt preeminently an agricultural country. The necessity of marking the time of its rise led to the study of astronomy and chronology. To determine the right to which it rose in successive years and the boundaries of landed property liable to be obliterated by these waters, they were constrained to turn their attention to geometry. For the preservation of mathematical science and the recording of the observation needful for its practical application, the art of writing was essential; and the papyrus reed afforded the material for such records. In these circumstances the heavenly bodies, the Nile and the animals of their country became absorbing objects of attention and eventually of worship."

(3) This part of Moses' history should be studied in connection with Acts 7:20-29 and Heb. 11:23-27, where we have an inspired commentary on his actions and motives.

It would appear that he declined all the honor and preferment included in his relation by adoption to Pharaoh's daughter, and for all we know the throne of Egypt itself, in order to throw in his lot with the Hebrews, and this before the incident recorded in this lesson. And if this be so, no man except Jesus Christ ever made a choice more trying or redounding more to His credit; for it is to be remembered that the step was taken not in youth or old age, but at the grand climacteric of his life when he was forty years of age.

(4) The Midianites being descended from Abraham by Keturah, had doubtless to some degree preserved the worship of Jehovah so that Reuel (elsewhere called Jethro) may, like Melchisedec, have been a priest of the Most High God, and Moses in marrying his daughter was not entering into alliance with an idolator.

Questions.

1. What are the two main subjects of Exodus?

2. What is suggested as to the original form of the first five books of Moses?

3. How would you explain the opposition of the Egyptians?

4. Can you give the history of their learning and wisdom?

5. How do the events of this lesson exalt Moses?

THE CALL OF MOSES

CHAPTERS 2:23-4:28

The Egyptian records refer to Moses. To quote Prof. Kyle: "Rameses, said by many to be the Pharaoh of the Exodus, built a great monument on which he made an inscription naming the nobility who were present when it was erected. Toward the end of the list he mentions 'The ra-Moses, Child of the Lady and Priestess of the Sun God Ra.'" Note the peculiarity of the description. "The ra-Moses" means some distinguished ra-Moses, while the "Child of the Lady" describes a situation and relation not unlike that of Moses and Pharaoh's daughter. There are other corroborative data for which we have no space, and these are mentioned as a further hint concerning what archæology has to reveal on the historicity of the Old Testament.

1. The Burning Bush, 2:23-3:10.

Observe the prelude to the oratorio of power and grace the next chapter reveals, which is found in the language of the closing verses of the present chapter: "God heard," "God remembered," "God looked," "God had respect unto," or took knowledge of them. His spiritual apprehension is limited who finds nothing for his soul to feed upon in this.

Observe in the burning bush a type of Israel—afflicted but not consumed, because God was in the midst of her. Observe in Moses' action (3) an illustration of the purpose God has in a certain kind of miracle which He performs. This purpose is simply to arrest the attention of men to listen to His voice, that they may be convinced. Observe the name by which God reveals Himself (6), and the identity it establishes with Israel's past, awakening hope and confidence in Him as the God of promise.

What does God now propose to do for Israel (8)? Why (9)? How (10)? To what extent is Moses to be used, that is, shall he bring Israel out and *in*, or only *out* (10)?

2. The Great Name, 3:11-22.

It is not surprising that when Moses hesitates to accept His command (11), God should encourage him with a token (12), but is it not singular that the token shall not be realized upon until after the command has been fulfilled (same verse, last clause)? Did God mean that the burning bush was the token, or are we to suppose that the token was the event itself? In the latter case, it were as though God said: "Go, and try, and you shall find

in the trial and its result that I have sent you." The former view accords better with the Hebrew accents in the case and with our ordinary idea of a sign, but the latter is corroborated by later Scriptures, such as Isaiah 7:14.

Have we ever met with this name of God before (14)? It is the expression of what God is, the sum of His being and the greatest of all His names. A commentator paraphrases the verse thus: "If Israel shall ask: What are the nature and attributes of Him who hath sent thee to bring us out of Egypt? tell them it is the eternal, self-existent, immutable Being who only can say that He always will be what He always has been."

Compare Christ's words concerning Himself in John 8:58, and observe the identity of expression as well as the application of it made by the Jews, who understood Christ to appropriate this name to Himself.

Are you troubled about the ethics of vv. 21 and 22? If so, you will wish to know that "borrow" does not imply a promise of return but signifies simply to ask or demand (compare Ps. 2:8). The Israelites were but receiving at last the fair wages for their toil which their oppressors had denied them. They shall not be ashamed who wait for God.

3. Moses' Hesitancy and Distrust, 4:1-17.

Moses' long tutelage in Midian has developed caution. He is a different man from the one who slew the Egyptian in haste forty years before (1)! What is the first sign now given him (2-5)? The second (6-8)? Were these simply for his own assurance or that of Israel? What power was bestowed upon him with reference to a third sign? Doubtless there was an adaptedness of these signs to the purpose for which they were to be used in Egypt, but space will hardly permit a discussion of that feature.

In what does the backwardness of Moses approach the danger point of unbelief (10-13)? Light is thrown on the answer to this question if we reflect that v. 13 amounts to this: "Choose another, a better man to send." No wonder God was angered, and yet how does He express His patience (14-16)? Nevertheless, Moses may have forfeited a certain privilege because of his waywardness. Bush suggests as a rendering of v. 14: " 'Is not Aaron thy brother the Levite?' By which we may understand that in consequence of Moses' act the honor of the priesthood and of being the official head of the house of Levi was denied him and conferred on Aaron." If this be true, it teaches that "those who decline the labor and hazard connected with the call of God to a special service may lose a blessing of which they little dream."

4. The Start for Egypt, 4:18-28.

How is Moses encouraged (19)? What peculiar designation is given Israel (22)? You will recall the harmony between this and what we have learned as God's purpose in calling Israel for her great mission. She was favored beyond other nations not for her own sake but that of those nations to which she was to minister.

What mysterious incident occurred on this journey (24-26)? We do not know the meaning of this, but following we give the views of James G. Murphy in his commentary on Exodus:

"The Lord had charged Moses with a menace of the gravest kind to Pharaoh and it was well that Moses himself should feel acutely the pang of death in order to comprehend the meaning of this threat. It appears that his youngest son had not been circumcised through some fault of his; the neglect of which was a serious delinquency in one who was to be the leader and lawgiver of the holy people. It was therefore meet that the perfection of the divine holiness should be made known to him and that he should learn at this stage of his experience that God is in earnest when He speaks, and will perform what He has threatened. Hence the Lord sought to kill

him probably by some disease or sudden stroke. It is also probable from her promptitude in the matter that Zipporah was in some way the cause of the delay in circumcising the child. Her womanly tenderness shrunk from the painful operation, and her words seem to imply that it was her connection with Moses that had necessitated the bloody rite. It was doubtless a salutary and seasonable lesson to her as well as to Moses. The Lord, who sought to put the latter to death, remitted the penalty when the neglected duty had been performed."

Questions.

1. How does archeology testify to Moses in Egypt?

2. What is a purpose of God in certain miracles?

3. How would you define "I AM THAT I AM"?

4. Give an argument from John 8:58 for Christ's deity.

5. How would you explain the word "borrow" (3:21, 22)?

6. How does Murphy explain 4:24-26?

MOSES AND AARON IN EGYPT

CHAPTERS 4:29-6

1. Before Israel, 4:29-31.

What is the first step taken by Moses and Aaron on their return (29)? What "signs" are referred to in v. 30? (For answer compare 4:1-9.) How did the people receive their message (31)? What effect was produced on the people by God's compassion?

2. Before Pharaoh, 5:1-23.

How does Moses limit his demand (v. 1 compared with 3:18)? Do you think it was necessary to tell Pharaoh the complete purpose of God with reference to His people? In replying to this question, however, it is well to know that "a three days journey" would take them clear out of Egypt, and that therefore there was no deceit in what Moses said. And by making this smallest demand upon Pharaoh did it not give him the least possible occasion to harden his heart?

How does he express his contempt of the demand (2)? What charge does he lay against God's messages (4)? What new hardships are imposed on Israel (5-14)?

By whom are the messengers now reproached (19-21)? These "officers" seem to have been Israelites placed over their brethren in subordination to the Egyptian "taskmasters." Their Hebrew name, "shoterim," is defined as referring to managers who kept account of matters under their charge. What is the effect of this reproach on Moses, and how is his dejection expressed (22-23)?

3. Before the Lord, 6:1-13.

We receive a stirring impression of the encouragement this interview must have brought to Moses if we consider the several declarations of God about Himself and His purposes thus (vv. 1-8):

I am the Lord.

I appeared unto Abraham, unto Isaac and unto Jacob.

I have established My covenant with them to give them the land of Canaan.

I have heard the groaning of the children of Israel.

I have remembered My covenant.

I will bring you out from under the burden of the Egyptians.

I will redeem you with a stretched out arm.

I will take you to Me for a people.

I will be to you a God.

I will bring you in unto the land.

I will give it you for an heritage.

I am the Lord.

What do you suppose God means in v. 3? Of course the literal name "Jehovah" was known to the fathers, but its complete import was unknown. The name denotes not only the eternal existence of God but that unchangeable truth and omnipotent power which give fulfillment to His

promises. The fathers had received the promises but had not yet enjoyed them. Now, however, God was about to do what He had decreed, and the following verses which speak of this are explanatory of the name. It were as though He said:

"I am Jehovah, for I am now to do what I have declared to be My purpose." Compare, for further illustration of this name, Ex. 7:5, Ezek. 28:22.

How is the renewal of Moses' message received by the people, and why (9)?

4. Genealogical Record, 6:14-27.

The design of this record just here is to establish the lineage of Moses and Aaron because of their prominence and importance in the coming history of the nation (26-27).

THE PLAGUES OF EGYPT: AN INTRODUCTORY STUDY

Chapters 7:1-13

1. Import of the Event.

Murphy reminds us that "to understand the import of this conflict we need to recall that for the first time since the dispersion of the nations (Genesis 11) the opposition between God and Satan in the history of mankind is coming out into broad daylight.

"This nation for the time being represents all heathendom, which is the kingdom of the prince of darkness, and the battle to be fought is the model and type of all future warfare between the Seed of the woman and the seed of the serpent. Hence it rises to a transcendent importance in the ways of God with man, and holds a place even in the preface to the Ten Commandments (20:2)."

2. The Rod and the Serpent.

There are at least three ways to account for what these sorcerers are said to have done, and the suggestions apply similarly to their later performances with the water and the frogs.

(1) One may deny that they did it, for the Hebrew will admit

of this rendering in v. 12: "They cast down every man his rod that they might become serpents, but Aaron's rod swallowed up their rods." In other words, their rods were not changed at all, and were lost into the bargain.

(2) One may say that by some feat of juggling an optical delusion was effected by which it appeared that their rods were changed.

(3) One may accept the text on its face and say that they actually did the things by the power of Satan. This is the simplest view, harmonizing with the deep import to Satan of the whole transaction and with what we subsequently learn of his interference in the affairs of men and nations and the "lying wonders" he enables the former to perform (2 Thess. 2:9).

In this last case, the superiority of God's power over Satan is seen in that Moses' rod swallowed up those of the magicians, and hence Pharaoh was in so far inexcusable in not acknowledging his omnipotence.

3. Hardening of Pharaoh's Heart.

In the story the "hardening" of Pharaoh's heart is spoken of nineteen times, in eleven of which God is said to have done the hardening, in three Pharaoh is said to have done it, and in five it is simply announced as being done.

From this it is plain that no inscrutable omnipotence bore down on Pharaoh to make him go against his will, but that without such constraint he freely resisted God's command.

In Bates' *Alleged Discrepancies*, from which the above paragraph is taken, it is explained that Pharaoh by his conduct put himself under the operation of that law according to which a man's heart becomes harder the longer he resists divine mercy. Inasmuch as Pharaoh himself resisted he hardened his own heart, but inasmuch as God ordained the law it may be said that God hardened it.

But while thus seeking to explain this awful circumstance, let us not try to eliminate divine sovereignty from it, nor neutralize the inspired interpretation of Romans 9:14-22.

God did not say: "Go to now, I will by a personal impact on Pharaoh's mind and subjugating control of his faculties, harden him." Nevertheless, Pharaoh did not hold out against God because God *could* not subdue him, but because He "had great ends to accomplish in permitting him to prolong his obstinacy."

The story, and especially Paul's inspired comment on it, should have a strong effect in bringing any sober-minded sinner to his knees before God.

4. The Order and Progress of the Plagues.

There were ten plagues in all, and it will be found that there was a kind of order and progress in their arrangement, going from the external to the internal and from the mediate to the immediate hand of God.

Divided first into nine and one, the one standing out from the others in the awful loss of the first born, the nine again are arranged in threes. This arrangement is marked by the way, the place and the time in which they are announced to the king, or the abruptness of their coming without announcement; by their effect on him, and on the magicians, and in other ways, leading to the conclusion that there was "a deeper order of nature and reason out of which they sprung."

Speaking of their effect, it will be seen that at the third the magicians acknowledge the finger of God, at the sixth they can no longer stand before Moses, and at the ninth Pharaoh refuses to see his face further.

Finally, the first three fall alike on the Hebrews and the Egyptians, but the last seven are reserved for the latter alone.

Examine 2 Tim. 3:8-9, and observe that the two names mentioned there may be those of the leaders of the magicians, traditional names probably, and preserved in documents since lost. They represented Satan much as

Moses represented God, and their defeat was an impressive demonstration of the supremacy of the God of the Hebrews.

5. The Miraculous in the Plagues.

There are two kinds of miracles, absolute and providential, the latter those which are not so miraculous in themselves as in the circumstances of their performance. Such were these plagues, for in their character they were the natural phenomena of the land, only that in these instances they came at an unusual season, in an unusual degree, and in immediate response to Moses' command.

Also they were particularly humiliating to the Egyptians because they reflected on the power and dignity of their gods. The Nile was their patron god, and to have its waters turned into blood and become a torment to them was dishonoring to that divinity. Another of their gods was represented by a frog's head. They also worshiped flies, reared temples in honor of the ox and the cow, and idolized the sun which was turned into darkness to them. How strange that they should not have been awakened by these things!

Questions.

1. What gives great significance to the events of this lesson and those immediately following?

2. In what three ways may we account for the acts of the sorcerers?

3. How would you explain the hardening of Pharaoh's heart?

4. Discriminate between the two classes of miracles.

5. Why were the plagues peculiarly humiliating to Egypt?

THE PLAGUES IN DETAIL

CHAPTERS 7:14-10:29

1. First Group, 7:4 to 8:19.

(1) The river turned into blood (7:14-25). How far did this plague extend over the waters of Egypt (19)? If this were literally so, it may be asked where did the magicians find material on which to work with their enchantments (22)? Is the answer suggested in v. 24? May they have dug up water from the ground for this purpose? If so, we can imagine the limited scale of their performance in contrast with that of Moses.

In connection with this miracle it should be known that commonly the Nile begins to rise about the end of June and attains its highest point at the end of September. It assumes a greenish hue at first, and becomes disagreeable to the taste and unwholesome. Then it becomes red and turbid for two or three weeks, although fit for use when red. The miraculous is seen here: (a) because it occurred in the winter, as we have not now time to prove; (b) the water was not merely reddened but turned into blood; (c) the fish died, which was not the case under the other circumstances; (d) the river stank and became offensive, while in the other case it was fit for use when red; (e) the stroke was arrested at the end of seven days, but ordinarily the redness lasted three weeks; (f) the change was brought on instantly at the command of Moses before the eyes of Pharaoh (Murphy).

(2) The frogs, 8:1-15. Frogs abound in Egypt, but "miracles are not the less supernatural because their products are natural objects, previously well known." That this visitation was miraculous is seen in that the frogs came at the word of command, and at an unusual time, and in an unusual degree and magnified form. "Frogs are not usually spawned, transformed into tadpoles, and then into frogs and spread over a country in a few moments."

What different effect on Pharaoh has this plague from the previous one (8)? It is difficult to understand the meaning of Moses' words: "Glory over me" (9), unless we take them in the sense of "appoint unto me a time, etc." As one of the older commentators suggests: "Moses experiences so much joy at Pharaoh's apparent relenting that he willingly gives him the honor of appointing the time when he should entreat the Lord for the removal of the plagues."

(3) The lice, 8:16-19. In other cases the water produced the cause of torture, whence does this arise (16)? What made this plague more aggravating than the former ones (17)? To what conclusion do the magicians come in this case (19)? Do you think they meant it was a judgment from Jehovah, or only a providential event? With which of these two possible opinions does Pharaoh's action seem to agree?

2. Second Group, 8:29 to 9:12.

(1) The flies, 8:20-32. What preliminary is omitted here that was observed in the other cases (compare v. 16, first part, for example)? How does this teach that the true wonder-worker is not tied to any particular mode of introducing his wonders? What distinction is now put between the Egyptians and the Hebrews? Why were the first three plagues permitted to fall upon the latter? Was it to help detach them from that land of their birth? How did this division between the two people emphasize the fact that the judgments were coming from the God of the Hebrews?

What further effect has this plague on the king (25)? Which is he willing to concede, the time or the place for sacrifice? Why will not Moses conform to his plan (26)? The Egyptians worshipped animals, like the cow and the sheep, and should the Hebrews offer them in sacrifice it would be an abomination in their eyes and bring serious consequence upon the offerers. Moreover, to do so in Egypt would, in some way, be an abomination to the Lord as well, and hence could not be considered.

What permission is now given the Hebrews (28)? What admonition to Pharaoh (29)? Was the latter heeded (32)?

(2) The Murrain, 7:1-7. Note that "cattle in the *field*" are specified. Some cattle among the Egyptians were stall-fed, and these seem to have been exempt (compare v. 19). What interesting investigation is the king led to make at this time, and with what confirmatory result (7)?

(3) The boils, 9:8-12. It is to be noted that the uncleanness resulting from such an attack would be particularly severe on a people who, like the Egyptians, made personal cleanliness a part of their religion.

3. Third Group, 9:13 to 10:29.

(1) The hail, 9:13-35. Read carefully vv. 14-17 of the section and observe the insight which God gives into the theory of His administration (Murphy). It is instructive, corrective and punitive, but never destructive of moral agents. He might have smitten Pharaoh and his people as easily as their cattle, annihilating them and thus removing all opposition to His demands, but such is not His way in dealing with His rational creatures. He approaches them with love, reason and justice, and only when they fail will He have recourse to correction, and finally punishment. Pharaoh will be an example of these things to all succeeding generations. It was for this God "raised him up" instead of striking him down.

How even yet does God remember mercy and leave an opening for faith (19-21)?

(2) The locusts, 10:1-20. What effect are the plagues beginning to have on the Egyptian generally (7)? What expression in the verse indicates the terrible devastation that must have already taken place? To what further extent is the king now prepared to yield (8-11)? What in the last verse shows his spirit in the premises? How does this plague finally affect him (16-17)? But does he yet surrender?

(3) The darkness, 10:21-29. What an object lesson is in v. 23. Not only for Pharaoh and Egypt is this so, but for us in a spiritual sense. The world is in darkness even until now, but Christ is the light of the world, and where He dwells is no darkness at all. What a text for a sermon, especially if treated in the light of its awful context!

How much further is Pharaoh willing to assent to Moses' demand (24)? But on what does the latter still insist (25, 26)? What "reckless madness" takes possession of the king? What is there ominous in the reply of Moses to him (29)? Is it not strange in this connection that Pharaoh never attempted to destroy the lives of Moses and Aaron? What better evidence could we have of the divine protection that accompanied them than this? And how it proves also the limitations of Satan's power (compare Job 1 and 2).

There is an awful significance in the plague of darkness, since the sun was a leading object of adoration with the Egyptians (under the name of Osiris), of which the king himself was the representative, entitling him in some sense to divine honors. Thus all the forms of Egyptian will-worship have been covered with shame and confusion in these nine plagues (Murphy).

Questions.

1. What should the sorcerers have done to demonstrate superiority to Moses?
2. Prove the supernatural character of what Moses did.
3. What spiritual lessons are suggested in this lesson?
4. What light is here thrown on God's administration of the universe?
5. In what particular was there divine restraint on Pharaoh?

THE PASSOVER

CHAPTERS 11–12:36

At the close of the 10th chapter Moses declares Pharaoh shall see his face no more, while in the 11th he is present with him again. Therefore with the exception of the first three verses of c. 11 the remainder must be a continuation of c. 10.

Let us consider it thus, taking up the questions in vv. 1-3 in connection with c. 12.

1. The Last Plague Announced, 11:4-10.

Hitherto God plagued Egypt mediately, but how was this plague to be distinguished (4)? Why was this plague harder to be borne than if the whole nation had been consumed? By what proverbial expression is the security of the Hebrews assured (7)?

How does v. 8 indicate that Moses has ceased to speak in God's name and is now speaking in his own name? Is he not, nevertheless, speaking representatively? How do the last two verses show that Pharaoh's disobedience is not a divine defeat?

2. The Passover Instituted, 12:1-13.

What new appointment of time distinguishes this event (2)? The year formerly began in the month of Tisri, corresponding to our September 15 to October 15, but what had formerly been the seventh month now becomes the first. This month was known as Nisan. The original order of the months continued so far as ordinary affairs were concerned, but the solemnities observed in honor of God began henceforth with Nisan.

What were the Hebrews to do (3)? When? According to what measurement or proportion? Israel was divided into twelve tribes, these again into families and the families into "houses," the last named being composed of particular individuals. According to Josephus, the Jewish historian, a paschal company consisted of not less than ten members, although sometimes there were as many as twenty. In this company they were free to include everyone capable of eating as much as the size of an olive.

In what two ways was the lamb to be distinguished (5)? What liberty was there in its selection? A male was accounted more excellent than a female (Malachi 1:14), and during its first year not only would its flesh be more tender and grateful but in that period it would best represent the idea of harmlessness and simplicity (1 Peter 1:19).

How long should the lamb be kept before slaying (6)? At what time should all the lambs be killed simultaneously? The "evening" here means sometime between the time of the sun's beginning to decline and that of its setting, say about 3:00 p. m. For the typical application to Christ, compare John 19:19 and Matthew 26:46.

What should be done with the blood (7)? How was the flesh to be cooked and eaten (8)? "As the sacrificing of the lamb is a symbol of the redemption by which the death penalty due by one is paid by another, so the eating of it is a figure of the participation in pardon, acceptance and full blessedness consequent on the atonement being made and the law being satisfied."

Both the roasting and eating of it with unleavened bread was for greater expedition in leaving the land that night. They would have time neither to boil the one nor wait for the yeast to rise in the other. And yet doubtless there is a moral or typical side to this matter as well, for since the paschal lamb and all pertaining to it foreshadow the person and work of our Redeemer, the roasting of the flesh may suggest the extremity of His sufferings under the fire of God's wrath, while the absence of leaven from the bread finds a spiritual application in such a passage as 1 Cor. 5:7-8. Leaven is a mass of sour dough in which decomposition has set in, and is therefore a symbol of corruption. Hence, unleavened bread is the emblem of purity and life becoming those who have exercised faith in God, the blessed fruit of a new nature (Murphy).

What other regulations accompanied this institution (9, 10)? It would appear from this that the lamb was to be roasted whole and entire, excepting doubtless the intestinal canal. There was to be no breaking of its bones (John 19:33). This "was strikingly expressive of the unity of the sacrifice, of the salvation it pre-figured, and the people who partook of it (Ps. 34:20; 1 Cor. 10:17). Nothing should remain of the lamb lest it should be put to a superstitious use, and also to prevent putrefaction, for it was not meet that anything offered to God should see corruption (Ps. 16:10)."

In what attitude were the people to be (11)? And why?

What did God say He would do (12)? Note the reference to "the gods of Egypt" in this verse. There is a Jewish tradition that the idols were actually demolished on that night, but from a figurative point of view, "what could be a more signal infliction upon these gods than the complete exposure of their importance to aid their worshippers in a time of need?"

By what means should the Hebrews experience immunity from this destruction (13)? Note the words: *When I see the blood I will pass over you.* It was not their character that saved them, neither the mercy of God in the abstract, nor their faith and obedience considered as a meritorious act, but the actual sprinkling of the blood upon the door posts. Without this they would not have been in the will of God, and His mercy could not have been operative towards them. No matter the degree or intelligence of their faith which led to the sprinkling of the blood, it was the latter divinely-ordained token which was the means of their deliverance.

The bearing of this on our redemption through the atonement of Christ should be prayerfully considered. The Hebrews were sinners in the general sense as well as the Egyptians, and God might justly have punished them by taking away the life of the first-born, but He was pleased to show them mercy for reasons considered in earlier lessons and to accept the life of a lamb as a substitute for their life. This blood was a signal of this, and all who acted on the command of God and relied on His protection were secure from the stroke of the avenger.

Nothing could more strikingly

set before us the truth about the application of Christ's blood to our guilty conscience as a means of deliverance from the wrath to come (Rom. 3:24-25; Eph. 1:7). It is not our character, neither the mercy of God towards us in the abstract nor the strength or intelligence of our faith, but the application of the blood to our souls that saves. Do not pass this lesson without satisfying yourself that this has become true of you, and that you have by faith displayed the token (Act 4:27).

As the paschal lamb is the type of our Redeemer, so the Passover itself is a type of our redemption through Him; for an outline of which see the author's *Synthetic Bible Studies.*

3. The Passover Commemorated, 12:14-20.

(1) The feast of unleavened bread (15) was a distinct ordinance from the Passover, commencing on the day after the killing and eating of the lamb, the 15th of Nisan. Of course in the first instance it could not have been observed until they left Egypt.

(2) The "cutting off" from Israel meant not necessarily physical death but excommunication from the society and privileges of the chosen people.

(3) Note the "holy convocation" for the public worship of God in connection with this feast (16). Doubtless the people of a neighborhood thus came together for praise and prayer, and some think that even from an early period portions of the written Word may have been read and expounded. This convocation, it is thought, was the origin of the synagogue, a term which originally denoted the assembly, and was doubtless at first held in the open air.

(4) The word "stranger" here doubtless means the Gentile proselyte in contrast with a native Israelite.

4. The Stroke Falls, 12:29-36.

We need not dwell on the awful horror of this night, but should not fail to recognize God's righteous retribution in it. The Egyptians who had slain the Hebrew children now see their own die. Four score years had passed since the persecution began, but God visits the iniquity of the fathers upon the children unto the third and fourth generation (Bush).

A further word on vv. 35 and 36. When the Orientals attend their sacred festivals they put on their best jewels, thinking it is a disgrace to appear otherwise before their gods. It is said nothing is more common than to see poor people adorned on such occasions with borrowed ornaments.

It is notable that the Egyptians lent their jewels to the Hebrews because the Lord gave them favor in their sight. The rank and file of the Egyptians may in the end have sympathized with the afflicted Hebrews, or else for their own safety they were so anxious to have them go as to offer them an inducement. In this connection read again 11:3, and see the reverence and awe inspired among the Egyptians by Moses' miracles.

Nor should we conclude this lesson without consulting Ezekiel 39:10, where we see that the Jews will spoil the Gentiles a second time, in that day when God with a high hand shall restore them to their own land at the end of the present age.

Questions.

1. Name the first month of the Jewish religious year.

2. State what the slaying and eating of the paschal lamb prefigure.

3. What does leaven symbolize?

4. Show the parallel between the cause of the Hebrews' deliverance and that of our eternal redemption.

5. What reasons may have influenced the Egyptians to give their jewels to the Hebrews?

THE PILLAR OF CLOUD

CHAPTERS 12:37—13:17

1. The First Stage of the Journey, 12:37-51.

How did the Hebrews get from Goshen to Rameses? Perhaps Rameses was in the land of Goshen or it was a name used here in the sense of the general locality rather than the specific city which the Hebrews helped to build (1:11). Compare Genesis 47:11. "Succoth" is not capable of identification, but since the word means "tents" or "places for tents" some think it specifies a camping spot en route.

Note the number of the men, which, multiplied by four to allow for families, gives an aggregate of 2,400,000 souls in all, without counting "the mixed multitude" of the next verse. Some of these latter may have been the poorer Egyptians and some foreign slaves of both Egyptians and Hebrews.

Note the time named in v. 40 and the exactitude of the fulfillment of prophecy mentioned in v. 41, a date which is to be reckoned from the time Abraham received the promise (Gen. 15:13), which makes just 430 years.

2. The First-born Set Apart, 13:1-16.

We can see a reason for the command in v. 1 when we recall the preservation of their first-born in Egypt. Doubtless it was to keep alive the memory of that event as well as to express their gratitude for it. "All things belong to God by right of creation: the Israelites by right of redemption; the first-born of Israel by right of passing over them in the judgment upon Egypt."

Moses immediately communicates this command to the people. Note that the month "Abib" (4) is the Hebrew for the Chaldaic "Nisan" previously mentioned.

By what figurative language does he impress the people with the duty of remembering all God's goodness to them (8, 9)? We thus see the duty of parental instruction enjoined, and are impressed by the fact that "the history of the ways of God with men is a trust to be conveyed faithfully from father to son."

By what two words in v. 12 is "sanctify" of v. 2 explained? Note that the "firstlings" of the clean beasts as subsequently explained, calves, lambs and kids, were dedicated to God and used in sacrifice, but those of the unclean were redeemed. How (13)? And if not redeemed, then what? What about the first-born of man? The law concerning this will be met with later (Numbers 18:16). Of course this regulation was to come into force when Israel should reach Canaan (11). As Murphy remarks, "the residence of Israel for forty years in the wilderness was in consequence of their unbelief and is not here contemplated. Here it is presumed they were to pass immediately through the wilderness into the Promised Land, with the exception of a year in the peninsula of Sinai for which special provision is made later on (Numbers 3)."

3. The Second Stage of the Journey, 13:17-22.

Do not neglect the map in this study, since it is at least approximately correct. Why were not the Hebrews permitted to go the near way (17)? Could not God have delivered them from the Philistines as well as from the Egyptians? How then does this illustrate the principle that God makes no unnecessary displays of miraculous power?

By what route were they led (18)? At its northern extremity the Red Sea separates into two minor gulfs which enclose the peninsula of Sinai. The western gulf is called Suez, which is the one they crossed. Its varied width is about thirty miles, narrowing very much at its northern extremity, and its varied depth about twelve fathoms, with a sandy bottom.

The word "harnessed" in this verse is unusual. According to its derivation it means "by five in a rank," but we can only explain it

on the supposition that in some
way the men went up marshalled
in orderly array, the better to
protect the women and children
of the company as well as their
cattle and other possessions.

What special command does
Moses execute (19)? Compare
Acts 7:16.

What is the name of their next
camping place (20)? In what supernatural way were they guided
(21)?

We have not now the pillar of
fire and cloud, but we have the
Word of God, which is a lamp to
our feet and a light to our path.

Excursus on the Pillar of Cloud.

Dr. Bush has an interesting ex-
cursus on the pillar of cloud,
from which a few paragraphs are
taken:

The Hebrew root "amad" signifies "to stand" and imports an
upright, standing mass of cloud
resembling a column in a building. It appears from Ps. 105:39
that it was spread at the base so
as to cover as with a canopy the
whole host of Israel, shading
them from the heat. The height, if
it bore any proportion to its base,
must have been immense, as the
encampment covered a space
(say) of twelve square miles. It is
evident from Deut. 31:15 that it
was the habitation of the divine
presence from which oracles
were proclaimed to the people.

For further allusion to its use
as a guiding signal see Ps. 78:14;
Neh. 9:12; and observe also its
re-appearance in the millennial
age (Is. 4:5; Rev. 7:15, 16).

Some think the whole mass
was opaque by day and luminous
by night, while others believe
there was a rending at night of
the outer, dark body of the cloud
and consequent disclosure of an
interior splendor enveloped from
view during the day.

This unwrapped splendor appearing at night was presumably
"the glory of the Lord" which occasionally appeared by day when
God would express displeasure
towards His people or impress
them with His majesty, as at Sinai
(Ex. 16:10; Num. 16:40). In

other words, taken as a whole,
this pillar was intended to serve
as the shekinah or visible representative of Jehovah dwelling in
the midst of His people.

Compare now Ex. 14:19 and
observe that the pillar of cloud is
called in the same verse "the
angel of God." The term "Angel"
is used in Scripture to denote
various kinds of agency, personal
and impersonal, but "THE Angel
of God" (as we have learned) is
a phrase descriptive of the second
Person of the Trinity, Jehovah-
Jesus. There is reason to believe,
therefore, that this cloud was in
some sense a manifestation of
His presence to Israel. See further, Ex. 23:20-23; Is. 63:8, 9. As
Bush says: "To all practical purposes it was the Angel of Jehovah, and they were to look up to
that sublime and awful column
as a visible embodiment of their
covenant with God, as an ever-
present witness, and feel as if a
thousand eyes were looking out
of the midst of it upon them,
from which not even their slightest word or deed could be hidden. Through the whole tenor of
the Mosaic narrative this is to be
understood as associated with the
title 'Lord' or 'the Angel of the
Lord.' "

It was this visible symbol, too,
which was their oracle or means
of communication with Jehovah,
the WORD of the ancient economy,
both in the course of their wilderness journey and when afterwards it was removed into the
Most Holy Place of the Tabernacle and Temple. See Ex. 33:9-
11; Ps. 99:6, 7. Compare also
John 1:1-14, where the glory of
the WORD incarnate is referred to,
"not that intrinsic moral glory
that distinguished His character
always, but rather that special
and overwhelming display of
glory of which Peter, James and
John were eye-witnesses on the
Mount of Transfiguration, when
there was a temporary laying
aside of the veil of His flesh and
disclosure of the indwelling shekinah, the glory of His Godhead." A preintimation indeed of
that glory in which He shall appear when He comes "a second

time, without sin, unto salvation."

What a wonderful theme of study we have in this pillar of cloud!

Questions.

1. In what two ways may the location Rameses be understood?

2. How does this lesson illustrate God's conservation of the miraculous?

3. Of what was the pillar of cloud a symbol?

4. Show its fitness for this purpose.

5. What takes its place for God's people to-day?

THE HORSE AND ITS RIDER OVERTHROWN

CHAPTERS 14-15:21

1. Through the Red Sea, 14.

What was the command now given to Moses (2)? From Etham, their present stopping place, the next step was of great importance. That town was near the head of the Red Sea at the border of the wilderness of Arabia and the limit of the three days' journey for which they had applied to Pharaoh. Would they remain there and offer their sacrifices as proposed, or continue their journey and endeavor to leave the country of the Egyptians altogether? The latter people were watching them with keen eyes, doubtless. What must have been the surprise of all when this command began to be obeyed. The natural way to leave the country was by the north and around the head of the Red Sea, but Pi-hahiroth was in a southeasterly direction and would "entangle" them in the land.

A study of the map will add to the interest of the lesson even though all the localities are not absolutely identified. It is clear, that in their new station the Israelites had the mountains on the west and south and the sea on the east. As Pharaoh would follow them from the northwest it would seem at first as though they must become his easy prey,

being in a snare from which it was impossible to escape.

What, however, is the divine purpose in this movement (3, 4)? How did the Hebrews behave in face of the new peril that now seemed to confront them (10-12)? Point out their fear, unbelief, injustice, selfishness, cowardice and ingratitude. How does Moses' character shine in comparison (13, 14)? Point out his meekness, forbearance, composure, faith.

How does v. 15 indicate that there is a time for all things, even prayer? How does v. 16 attest the authority of Moses before the people as an instrument of God? In what way do the next two verses illustrate that the providences of God have a two-fold aspect as between sinners and saints? By what method were the waters of the sea divided (21)? Compare here Ps. 77:16-20. "A strong northeast wind has always had much influence on the ebb of the tide in the Red Sea, but such an annual occurence only drives out the old body of water further from the shore. It does not divide the waters or make them 'a wall' on each side of the dry ground, or leave space for the passage of a large multitude, or happen precisely at the moment when escape from a foe makes it convenient for the leader of a people to wave over the water a rod of power." In other words, this was a supernatural event, a miracle of divine power.

Do you suppose the Egyptians really knew they were walking into the bed of the sea (23)? May not the supernatural darkness of the pillar of cloud have kept them in ignorance of this? If so, what a fearful discovery they made subsequently!

No wonder that in view of the present and the past the Egyptians declared that the Lord fought for Israel.

Notice the closing phrase of v. 30: "Israel saw the Egyptians dead upon the sea shore," and compare Ezekiel 32:4 which speaks of the latter judgment on the same people, and Rev. 19:17, 18, referring to that which shall fall upon the ungodly nations at the close of this age.

What effect had this awful judgment upon Israel?

2. The Song of Victory, 15:1-21.

Compare the circumstances of this chapter with Rev. 15:2, 3 and see the likeness of the two events.

This is the most ancient of songs, whose poetical merits are of the first order, which we might suppose to be the case since it was given by divine inspiration.

A remarkable feature of the song is that almost all its verbs are in the future tense, carrying the implication "that what happened on this occasion to God's enemies would happen in like manner in all future time so far as utter discomfiture and signal perdition were concerned."

What is the prediction of vv. 14-18? Compare Joshua 2:9-11 for an illustration of its fulfillment.

Who is once more introduced into the history at v. 20? Observe that the dancing mentioned was that of women alone, the method being to follow the leader, imitating her steps and if she sings to make up the chorus. The song was probably sung alternately by the men and women ranged in two bands, Moses leading the one and Miriam the other; or possibly the men sung the song and the women joined in the chorus of v. 21 after every period of five verses and at the end of the whole:

"Sing ye to the Lord,
For He hath triumphed
    gloriously,
The Horse and his rider hath
    He thrown into the sea."

Observe the new name of God found in this song (2), and note that it occurs for the first time after the signs and wonders in the land of Egypt, just as the other name occurred *before* these events. This leads to the supposition that Jehovah is the name of God on His prophetic side and Jah His name on His historic side. As the first denotes Him

who *is about to* manifest His being, so the second denotes Him who *has* manifested His being.

Questions.

1. Have you sought to identify Etham and Pi-hahiroth on the map?

2. Prove the miraculous nature of the event at the Red Sea.

3. How does it and its attendant circumstances bear on the literalness of later earthly judgments?

4. Has the song of victory prophetic value, and how?

5. What is the meaning of the name "Jah"?

THE TYPICAL ASPECT OF ISRAEL'S VICTORY

Paul speaking of the early history of Israel says (1 Cor. 10:11): "Now these things happened unto them by way of example (or, as types), and they were written for our admonition, upon whom the ends of the ages are come."

We have already spoken of the value of Grant's *Numerical Bible* as bearing on the symbolic application to be made of these things, and from him we quote the substance of this lesson.

At the Red Sea the question is no longer one between the Israelites and God. That was the status represented in the Passover, but the question now is between Israel and her enemy. The question with God had been settled in the Passover, and forever settled. They had been redeemed from bondage and had come into a new relationship to God in which He was pledged to certain things on their behalf.

The question now raised was the old question of servitude to Pharaoh or of liberty. This question God Himself now takes up on their behalf, and they find Him with them in a more manifest way than they had ever found Him as yet. From the very moment of the Passover God was with them, but it is the experience at the Red Sea that makes them understand how truly He is with them.

Epistle to the Romans Compared.

The situation suggests the doctrinal part of Romans, in the first eight chapters of the epistle. If we consider the first half of this part, that is, down to the middle of the 5th chapter, it sets before us the teaching concerning our redemption through the blood of Christ and what it effects for us. We see that through the righteousness of God which this redemption declares, there has been provided for us in Christ a place of assured shelter. We are justified by His blood, and this justification reaches on in its effects to the final judgment of the world. Judgment for us is rolled away forever! Our standing before God is now of grace, our hope is now of glory, and we are enabled to glory, even in tribulations because all things are working together for our good.

All this may be called the Passover truth, for like the Israelites we are now sheltered from judgment, feeding upon the Lamb, and equipped for our journey.

But at this point the truth set before us in Romans 5:12 becomes operative. That is the question of the experience of the new life. It suggests itself in the words: "What then, shall we continue in sin that grace may abound? Shall we sin because we are not under the law but under grace?" And finally, when the discovery of the hopeless evil and weakness of our old nature is made, we cry: "O wretched man that I am, who shall deliver me from this body of death!"

Israel's Bondage and the Christian's Sin.

Who can but think of Israel's bondage in Egypt here, and of the divine method of deliverance? Did Israel's bondage to Pharaoh cease on the night of the Passover? In one sense it did. There was a breaking of chains and a real start. God was now with them and could never allow His claim to them to be cancelled, for He had redeemed them to Himself. The enemy never could regain possession of His people. But when we pass from God's point of view to that of the people themselves we find them losing their confidence and trembling again before their old tyrant in such fear that even the actual presence of God with them in the pillar of cloud could not remove. Shut up between the desert and the sea with Pharaoh in full pursuit, their cry is that of unbelieving despair. The controversy between them and their old enemy had to be taken up afresh by God in their behalf, and now to be ended forever. God interferes and fights for them, and they do nothing but stand still and see the salvation of the Lord.

It is so with the soul who has found shelter under the blood of Christ and seen the judgment of God removed from him. The question of deliverance from "the law of sin" is settled for him, but he does not always come at once into the realization of it. In other words the first teaching of holiness is this, that in me as a believer in Christ, that is, in my old nature, there is no good thing. In order to have strength, in other words, we must learn the lesson of thorough and continual weakness.

What the Red Sea Means.

At first, when salvation is new and one has seen death turned into life through faith in a risen Saviour, it may seem as if sin could no more put shackles on the soul. But as yet there is little knowledge of the old self, and full deliverance from it is not known until this has been realized, that is, until the Red Sea is reached and Egypt is left behind forever. How many have begun to follow God in the way of holiness until He has led them where they had to cry and cry again that they cannot do the things that they would! Progress seems impossible, and hence they would stop here and imagine they must after all serve Pharaoh with the best grace they can. They are at peace with God through the blood of Christ, yet so far as the sin which is within them is concerned they expect no special deliverance. "With the mind they serve the law of God, but with the flesh the law of sin."

Such as these do not see that after all it is only the border of Egypt they have reached, and that where all progress seems to have stopped God is at hand to give them so great a deliverance from their enemy that their hearts shall sing aloud forever.

God Our Deliverer.

Now look at the type again. Observe that God does not lead Israel up against Pharaoh. In other words, He does not strengthen their arm by His own to bring salvation to them, but rather they had to "stand still" and see His *salvation*. God does not call us to fight against the flesh and subdue it, nor does He point or lead in that direction at all. The sea divides, and a channel is made for His people to pass through. In other words, Christ's precious death is for us so that we are dead in Him and are no longer "in the flesh." His death has ended our history before God. In Him we have passed through death untouched, dry-shod, and are now beyond it.

There is a sense, of course, in which this is not a matter of attainment on our part, and yet there is another sense in which it is. It is ours already the moment we receive Christ, and yet we are to apprehend it as ours. All this was true of Israel on the night of the Passover, and yet it was some little time after the Passover before they really came to know and enjoy its blessedness.

Faith is thus the principle of sanctification as it is of justification or the new nature. Faith is turning from myself to God and His Son Jesus Christ. By faith I pass through the sea to take my new position outside of my old nature altogether, and when I look back I find that my enemies are buried in the waters. Privileged to turn away from self, the conflict and the distress are over. In Christ is my place, in Him I find a satisfying object lifting me out of the old sphere of things in which the lust of the flesh finds what it seeks. In Him the new na-

ture expands and develops and bears fruit. The fruit of the Spirit needs to be ripened in the Son. The least degree of occupation with Christ is glory. No wonder that they who know it should, like the Israelites, sing a song of victory!

PROVISION IN THE WILDERNESS

CHAPTERS 15:22-16

As we have entered upon a new sphere of Israel's history it may be well again to briefly call attention to the way in which archaeological data corroborate it. These data are already so numerous, and every decade is bringing so many more to the front, that one hardly knows what to quote.

The flight of the Hebrews is not mentioned on any of the monuments of Egypt but there is a reason for that, since this escape of slaves meant a defeat of Pharaoh's purposes, and monarchs are not in the habit of recording their defeats. And again, such migrations are not infrequent in lands of shepherds and nomads. The route of the Exodus, however, is now known beyond all reasonable doubt. The Pharaoh of the Exodus is thought to be Menephtah II, whose mummy has been discovered with those of Rameses II and Seti I, all of whom were connected with the history of the Hebrews in Egypt.

The real character of the Wilderness is now known as never before, and is described as a rolling plain dotted with ridges, low terraces and knolls, and containing sufficient shrubs and herbs to give pasturage to the camels of the Bedouin. Water courses, dry in summer, and called by the Arabs wadys, cross the plain and in some cases are as much as a mile wide. The traveler occasionally discovers charming spots like the Elim of this lesson. All these things help us to understand how the Israelites found sustenance through the Wilderness during wandering.

1. Healing and Refreshing in the Wilderness of Shur, 15:22-27.

By what general name was the section of the country known which is now entered (22)? What is their first stopping-place (23)?

How was the people's instability displayed at this crisis (24)? How was the difficulty remedied (25)? Some one may ask the difference between a "statute" and an "ordinance" as named in v. 25. The first is a fixed decree, and the second an injunction accompanied with an intimation of the good and evil consequences of obedience and disobedience. When it is said that God "proved them" it means that this experience tested the qualities of their hearts and whether they had faith and patience or not.

The Lord Our Healer

What comforting words are these: "I am the Lord that healeth thee!" How shall they be taken? Do they mean that as He had healed the waters of Marah so would He heal them? Or have they a significance in the past tense, that is, had the bitter waters sickened them, and in healing the waters does the Lord mean that He had really healed them? There cannot be any doubt, in either case that physical healing is referred to, and that God declares Himself the healer.

But observe that the waters being the illustration, God uses *means* in healing. This is not to say that He never heals otherwise, but only that it is going too far to say that the use of means necessarily excludes the thought of God as the healer.

Nor should we omit another lesson, namely, the relation of sin and disease. If they hearkened unto God and did right, He would put none of these diseases on them. The converse therefore would be true, that either directly or indirectly God puts diseases upon men who disobey Him.

What location is next reached, and what distinguishes it (27)? Elim is identified with a place now called Wady Ghurendel, a few miles from Marah, a place fringed with trees and shrubbery, forming a charming oasis. Here the people seem to have remained, judging by the next chapter, for the space of three weeks, resting and preparing themselves for the journey to follow.

2. Bread From Heaven in the Wilderness of Sin, 16.

Where did they now come, and how long after leaving Egypt (1)? The word "Sin" here is supposed to mean "clay" although some give it the meaning of "bush" or "thorn."

What new ground of complaint arises (2, 3)? How does the Lord propose to meet it (4, 5)? Where did we find the word "prove" in this same connection before?

What warning is given the people in v. 7? What further intimation of God's provision for their immediate need in v. 8? How is the warning realized in v. 10?

What was the provision in v. 13? It was natural for quails to be found in the region of Arabia at certain seasons of the year, but the miracle consisted in bringing them there at this particular time and in sufficient numbers for the supply of so many people, and also in announcing their arrival beforehand.

How is the deposit of the dew described (14)? Did the people clearly know its nature? It would appear then that they simply gave it the first name which suggested itself, for there is a certain scanty product of nature called "manna" to which this seemed to bear a resemblance. Does Moses reject the name? How does he explain the nature and origin of the substance, however? "The natural manna is gathered early in June, a month later than the present time, and in small quantities, but this supernatural manna was gathered every day, Sabbaths excepted, throughout the whole year, and in quantities sufficient for the main support of a nation and during a period of forty years."

How were the people to gather it (16)? How was their covetousness in the matter curtailed (18)? How was their pride leveled (19)?

Had Moses revealed all the details to them at first (22)? What provision is made for the Sabbath (23-26)? What rebuke is necessary concerning this (27-30)? What further description of the manna is given (31)? What arrangement is made for a memorial of this miracle (32-36)? How does Hebrews 9:4 interpret the character of the vessel in which the omerful of manna was laid up? The phrase "before the Lord" is how explained in v. 34? And how is this in turn explained in the verse just referred to in Hebrews? Must not then the act of Aaron in v. 35 have been performed at a later time, although recorded here?

The Sabbath: God's Gift to Man

The Sabbath, according to v. 29, was a gift of God to man; how precious the thought! And think of Jesus' comment upon it. "The Sabbath was made for man, not man for the Sabbath." Man is doomed to labor in his fallen state, but how could his weariness have been endured without a periodical recurrence of relief from it? How much he needs this leisure for himself, and for fellowship with God and with his fellowmen!

It is interesting to know that the Israelite was at liberty to go abroad for any purpose accordant with the Sabbath (Lev. 23:3; Acts 15:21), and that works of necessity or mercy that could not be put off until the next day were not regarded as a breach thereof (Matt. 12:1-13; Mark 2:23-28). There seems to have been no limit to the distance to be walked on the Sabbath beyond that of convenience, the Rabbinical rule of later times being an addition of man rather than a command of God (Murphy).

What a happy world this would be if men would only obey God, and the land be permitted to keep her Sabbaths!

Questions.

1. How does archaeology contribute to the interest of this lesson?

2. What three things about physical healing are here taught?

3. State the miraculous feature in the incident of the quails.

4. Do the same concerning the manna.

5. What have we learned about the Sabbath?

EVENTS AT REPHIDIM

CHAPTERS 17-18

1. Water Out of the Rock, 17:1-7.

What is the next stopping place (1)? What do you suppose is meant by "the commandment of the Lord" in this verse?

Rephidim is a wide-spreading plain at the northern base of the cluster of mountains to which the general name of Horeb was given. What made it unfit for an encampment? How does this show that God sometimes guides His people into trouble? Are distress and difficulty an indication that believers are not in the will of God?

How did the people express impatience and lack of faith (2, 3)? How does Moses act in comparison (4)? What does God command him to do (5, 6)? Were the elders to go with him as *witnesses?* Did the Lord stand on the rock in the pillar of cloud? How must the people have felt when the water came rushing down the valley towards them? Which prevailed, gratitude or shame? What names were given this place, and why (7)? Bush remarks that the people may not have uttered the very words here ascribed to them, but that such was the language of their conduct, and he applies the circumstance to Matthew 12:37, saying that Christ will judge men by the actions which have the force of words.

2. Amalek Conquered and Cursed, 17:8-16.

The Amalekites were a nomadic people living in the north of

this peninsula, and to the south of the Philistine country (Gen. 14:7), who came out of their way to attack Israel, approaching them in the rear where they were the more defenseless. (Compare Deut. 25:18.)

As the Amalekites were descendants of Esau, hereditary hate may have prompted this attack. Then also the thought of loot is to be considered, for they probably knew the wealth Israel brought out of Egypt. But their strongest hostility was aroused by the fact that Israel was to take possession of Canaan, into which their territory penetrated (Judges 5:14; 12:15). At all events, it is with them that Gentile antagonism to God's peculiar nation is seen to begin as soon as the latter's political independence is established. Their action therefore was a virtual defiance of Him who had so lately destroyed the Egyptians, a fact which explains His resentment as shown in the sequel.

Who now comes into the forefront, and what is he directed of Moses to do (9)? The word "Joshua" means "saviour," the Greek of which is "Jesus."

What new personage is before us in v. 10? For a little of his genealogy see 1 Chronicles 2:9-20. What was the significance of the transaction in v. 11? Do you suppose Moses held the rod of God in his hand? And if he did, was it not merely as an indication and accompaniment of prayer? Where in the incident do we find an emblem of the value of united and common prayer? What lesson is taught by the combination of the rod in the hand of Moses and the sword in the hand of Joshua? Which, however, assumes the more importance, Moses' prayer or Joshua's sword?

How does God emphasize the significance of this battle (14)? We have not met with the word "write" before, but where with the word "book" (Gen. 5:1)? There is the definite article before "book" in the original indicating that a book, and doubtless this particular book, was well known. Can you imagine a reason for

this matter being rehearsed to Joshua? For the subsequent fate of Amalek read Deut. 25:19; 1 Samuel 15 30; 2 Samuel 1:1; 8.12.

How is this victory commemorated on the spot (15)? Have we met with any other "altar" since we ended the history of Jacob? Does not this then mark a new epoch in the affairs of Israel? "Jehovah-nissi" means "Jehovah my banner" (compare Ps. 20:5-7), and expresses thanks to God for the past and confidence in Him for the future. Perhaps it was suggested by the lifting up of the rod of God as a banner or standard in this action.

The last verse of the chapter is obscure.

3. A Visit from Jethro, 18.

It is felt that the visit here recorded, with the events growing out of it, took place at a later time, and after Israel had arrived at Sinai, but is related here either not to interfere with the main narrative, or for some other unxplained cause.

It is a story of mutual affection and esteem, but one is not more impressed by it than by the importance God attaches to such chapters in our lives by causing it to be recorded for our learning and example.

Note that Jethro was one of those outside of Israel by whom the tradition of the true God was retained, and who gave glory to Him for His mighty works.

The incident (13-26) needs little comment, but there are a few things worth noticing. One is the practical wisdom in it (18); another, the qualification for the choice of these sub-rulers, ability, godly fear, truthfulness, incorruptness (21); a third, the circumstance that this advice is given in submission to God (23); and a fourth, that the selection was by the people and the appointment by Moses (Deut. 1:9, 13); a fifth, that God did not disdain to permit Moses to be taught through another man, and he one not of the commonwealth of Israel. It is remarkable, as another says, that the rudiments of the Jewish polity were thus suggested by a stranger and a Midianite. There is food for reflection here in the ways of God in teaching His own people wisdom.

PREPARATION FOR RECEIVING THE LAW

CHAPTER 19

The Exodus includes two concurring elements in the moral history of the people—their redemption and their renovation. It is worthy of notice, that God did not give Israel the law first and then say: "I will redeem you if you will obey it," but that He redeemed them first and gave them the law afterwards.

1. The Arrival at Sinai, 19:1, 2.
"In the third month—the same day." These words lead to the belief that the first day of the third (lunar) month is meant, just 45 days (as we can easily recall) from their departure out of Egypt. To these, quoting Bush, let us add the day on which Moses went up to God (3), the day after when he returned the answer of the people to God (7, 8), and the three days more named (10, 11), and we have just fifty days from the passover to the giving of the law. Hence the feast kept in later times to celebrate this event was called Pentecost, which means fiftieth day. And it is interesting that it was at this very feast the Holy Spirit was given to the disciples of Christ (Acts 2:1-4) to enable them to communicate to all men the new covenant of the Gospel.

The text of v. 2 in the King James version makes a distinction between the "desert" and the "wilderness" of Sinai, but there seems to be no good reason for this. "Sinai" denotes a particular mountain of that name, while "Horeb" denotes the range of which Sinai is a part. The wilderness of Sinai would seem to be the plains and wadys in its immediate neighborhood, including the mountain itself, and perhaps coextensive with the term Horeb.

2. The Divine Exordium, 19:3-9.
When it is said "Moses went up unto God," remember the pillar of cloud in which in a sense the divine Presence abode, and which now rested doubtless on the summit of the mountain. Evidently Moses did not ascend the mountain at this time, but simply approached it.

By what two names are the people designated in v. 3? Which points to their natural and which their spiritual derivation (Gen. 32:23-33)?

With what three words in v. 4 does God call them as witnesses to the fidelity of His promises? What beautiful figure of speech does He use expressive of His care for them? (Compare v. 4 with Deut. 32:11, 12.) Also examine Rev. 12:14, where His care for them in their coming tribulation at the end of this age is spoken of in similar terms. The parent eagle in teaching its nestlings to fly "sweeps gently past them perched on the ledge of a rock, and when one, venturing to follow, begins to sink with dropping wing, she glides underneath it and bears it aloft again."

But what is expected of them as the result of this grace? And what promise is bestowed upon them in this contingency (5)? And how will their preciousness to God find expression in their service (6)?

Note (1) that while all the inhabitants of the earth belong to God by right of creation and general benefaction. Israel belonged to Him by special grace and covenant; (2) that while they themselves were to be objects of priestly intercession and kingly protection they were also to be elevated into the dignity and authority of performing priestly functions and dispensing royal favors to others; (3) that as a qualification for all this they were to be a holy nation.

3. The People's Pledge, 19:7-9.
By "the elders of the people" (v. 7) is meant the leaders and principal men of the different tribes. How is the Lord's command received by them (8)?

While this is commendable, yet in the sequel how much better if they had asked God's help to enable them to obey and to appreciate His goodness! How little they knew themselves, and how well they represent us in the earlier stages of our new experiences in Christ!

What does God now promise to Moses personally (9)? To what end? And why was it necessary? Had not God given evidence of His divine commission in the sign of the rod and the serpent? Yes, but this was only before the elders of the people. And had He not given evidence in the miracles of judgment upon Egypt? Yes, but many of these were not before all the people. So now they are to have a general and personal attestation which should last forever. Observe our Saviour's recognition of this authority of Moses in Luke 16:31, and compare a similar recognition of His own authority in 2 Peter 1:16-18.

4. The People's Purification, 19: 10-14.

We can see the propriety of this command, but should remember that there is no virtue in external washings and other abstinences, except as they symbolize and impress us with the obligation of inner holiness and separation on the part of those who are to hold intercourse with God.

What was the Lord now about to do (11)? And with reference thereto what warning is promulgated (12)? What should happen to the man or beast overstepping these bounds (13)? The word "it" in the first clause of the verse refers to the man or beast. That is, no one should cross the bounds, even to go after it (the man or beast) to drag it back or punish it, but from a distance it should be stoned or shot. What a commentary on presumptuous sin!

By the "trumpet" is meant a supernatural one to be heard from the mountain. The people were to "come up to the mount" in that they were to draw nigh to it, but no nearer than the bounds already prescribed.

5. The Phenomena on the Mount, 19:16-25.

Describe the impressive phenomena of vv. 16 and 18, and their effects on the people. Never until the close of this age and the coming of our Lord will anything like this be seen or heard again. Compare 2 Thess. 1:6-10, and the language of the Apocalypse, for example, cc. 4 and 5.

How did God speak to Moses (19)? Doubtless this means by "an audible and articulate form of word." What seems to have been impending on the part of the people, judging by v. 21? How is God's attention to details (if one may so say), and how is His mercy manifested here?

Who can be meant by "priests" in v. 22, since the Aaronic priesthood was not yet instituted? The common answer is the firstborn or eldest son in every household. This seems to be suggested by the patriarchal history as one of the privileges connected with the birthright. Compare also 24:5.

Who was to come up into the mountain with Moses when the latter returned (24)? We shall see the reason for this later when Aaron is invested with the priesthood, for it was fitting that there should be put upon him that distinction which would inspire respect for him on the part of the people.

Questions.

1. What have we learned about the day, or feast, of Pentecost?

2. What have we learned of the priestly character of Israel?

3. Can you quote Luke 16:31?

4. Name one or two illustrations here of God's grace to us in Christ.

5. Have you examined the Scripture references in this lesson?

THE FIRST TABLE OF THE LAW

Chapter 20 1-11

We have now reached the most remarkable event in the history of Israel until this time, and one of the most remarkable in the history of the world.

While it has primary reference to Israel, still it affects the whole race for time and eternity, since the moral law is "the expression of God's will, the reflection of His nature, and the immutable standard of right for His ac countable creatures" everywhere and always.

These remarks apply particularly to the ten commandments, but the special enactments which follow them pertain for the most part only to Israel

1. The Division of the Commandments.

The commandments have generally been divided into two "tables": the first including the first four commandments embracing our duty to God, and the second the last six embracing our duty to man (Matt. 22:37-40).

The Roman Catholic Church has a different arrangement from the Protestant, making but one commandment of the first two, and in order to maintain the number ten dividing the last into two. The result is that some of their devotional books omit altogether the last half of the first commandment, or what we call the second, which forbids idolatry. Their motive for doing this, to any who are familiar with the worship of that Church, is easily discerned.

2. The Preface, vv. 1, 2.

What is meant by "God spake?" Compare Deut. 5:12, 13, 32, 33, and the conclusion seems irresistible that, as was stated in a preceding lesson, they refer to an articulate voice.

Notice the authority by which He speaks: "I am the Lord" (Jehovah), the self-existent, independent, eternal fountain of all being, who has the right to give law to all the creatures He has made. Notice the restriction to the Israelites: "*thy* God," not only by creation but by covenant relationship and by the great redemption He has wrought in their behalf: "Which have brought thee out, etc."

How inexcusable their disobedience under these new circumstances! And ours also, who as Christians have been redeemed by Christ from a bondage infinitely worse, and at a cost unspeakable!

3. First Commandment, v. 3.

"None other gods before Me" means as antagonists in My eyes, "as casting a shade over My eternal being and incommunicable glory in the eye of the worshipper."

The primary reference is to the idols the heathen worshipped, not that they really worshipped the idols, but the gods supposedly represented by them. Nor yet are we to imagine these were real gods, for there is none other God save One, but rather demons (Lev. 17:7; Deut. 32:17; Psalm 106:37; 1 Cor. 10:19, 20).

How awful to think that even now, professing Christians worship demons through Spiritism, clairvoyance, palmistry and related occultisms (Deut. 18:9-22)!

Moreover, in the application of this and all the commandments, we should remember that they lay their prohibitions not on the outer conduct merely but the inner actings of the spirit. See Christ's Sermon on the Mount (Matt. 5:20-48) and Paul in Romans 7:7-11. Hence there may be idolatry without idols in the vulgar sense, and also without worshipping demons in any form. "Whosoever seeks happiness in the creature instead of the Creator, violates this commandment."

4. Second Commandment, vv. 4-6.

A "graven image" is made of wood, stone or metal; a "likeness" is a picture of any kind as distinguished therefrom. The "water under the earth" means "lower in level" than the earth.

Was any manifestation of God seen at Sinai (Deut. 4:12, 15)? The Israelites were not to make these things. What command was laid upon them when others made them?

What warning is contained in this commandment? Is God "jealous" in the sense of passion, or as expressing the feeling of a holy Being against evil (Deut. 32:21, etc.)?

How does this commandment show the responsibility of parents? Do you suppose this responsibility is limited to this sin? Did not Israel at this time have a striking illustration of it in Egypt? Had not their persecution by that people begun just four generations before, and was not the nation now reaping what had been then sown?

"Unto the third and fourth generations of them that hate Me." Here two thoughts suggest themselves: (1) there is no difference between forsaking God and hating Him; (2) it is only them that hate Him, i. e., follow in the footsteps of their fathers, who will be visited with the punishment (Ezek. 18:20). Perhaps also a third thought is pertinent, viz: that this warning only applies to the temporal effects of sin and not its eternal consequences, hence a son who turns to God, although he may through the working of divinely-ordained laws of nature suffer physical consequences here, will be spared eternal consequences hereafter.

"Mercy unto thousands of generations" the Revised Version reads. See also Deut. 7:9. Of this also Israel had an illustration before their eyes, as they were now gathering the mercy destined for them in the faithfulness of their father Abraham who lived a thousand years before.

"Of them that love Me and keep My commandments." Behold what is meant by loving God, viz: keeping His commandments; a declaration which "gives a new character to the whole decalogue, which thus becomes not a mere negative law of righteousness, but a positive law of love!"

Let us not conclude these reflections without remarking how far the Greek, Roman, and even some of the Protestant churches have fallen in this regard.

From the use of crosses and relics as aiding their bodily senses and quickening devotion, it has been easy to advance to altars, images and pictures not only of the Holy Ghost and Christ but of the Virgin, and the saints and martyrs without number, until at last these objects have themselves become, at least to the ignorant, actual objects of worship. And what superstition, profanation and mockery have grown out of it all! And shall not a jealous God visit for these things?

5. Third Commandment, v. 7.

The "name" of God is that by which He makes Himself known, the expression of His Godhead: hence to take that name "in vain" is to violate His essence.

The word for "vain" signifies what is false as well as vain, so that all false swearing or perjury which would make God a witness to a lie, as well as all light or frivolous uses of His name or attributes in conversation, are here prohibited.

This does not mean judicial oaths, however, which, as we see by Christ and His apostles, may be acts of worship in which we solemnly call God to witness to the truth (Jer. 4:2).

But what of blasphemy and profanity by which some interlard their speech, using such expressions as "God," "Lord," "Christ," "the Lord knows." "O heavens!" "My goodness!" and the like (Matt. 5:33-37)?

God "will not hold him guiltless" that does these things. Look at Psalm 139:20, and see who they are that take His name in vain, and then read Mal. 3:5.

The third commandment, is of the same gravity as the two preceding, guarding the deity of God as those do His unity and spirituality (Murphy).

6. Fourth Commandment, vv. 8-11.

How does the first word here indicate an earlier origin than Sinai for the institution of the Sabbath? How early was that origin? How does this show that the Sabbath is an obligation for all men, Christians as well as Jews?

But "remember" points not simply to an act of memory but a commemoration of the event. Lev. 23:3 and Num. 28:9, 10 confirms this.

But it is the "Sabbath" day and not necessarily the seventh day that is to be remembered. This means one day of rest after every six, but not according to any particular method of computing the septenary cycle. Though the Jewish Sabbath was kept on Saturday, Christians are in accord with the spirit of the commandment in keeping Sunday enriching the original idea of the day of rest by including that of the new creation when our Redeemer rose from the dead.

How does God provide for our hallowing of this day, and what is His definition of such hallowing? When He says: "Six days shalt thou labor and do all thy work," is it an injunction merely, or may it be considered as a permission? Some think there is a difference between "labor" and "work," the latter term being the more inclusive as involving the management of affairs and correspondence to the word "business."

How is the equality of husband and wife recognized in the wording of this commandment (10)? The responsibility of parents and employers? The rights and privileges of employees? The proper treatment of the lower animals? To what further extent did the obligation of the Israelite extend? Has this any bearing on the present obligation of our nation to compel an observance of the Sabbath on the part of our alien population?

Is anything more than secular or servile work intended in this prohibition? Did not Jesus both by precept and example give liberty for works of love, piety and necessity? (Mark 2:23-28; John 5:16, 17).

What historical reason is assigned for this commandment (11)? And what additional in Deut. 5:15? We thus see that God's authority over and His loving care for us combine to press upon us the obligation of the Sabbath day to say nothing of its advantage to us along physical and other material lines. And thus its observance becomes the characteristic of those who believe in a historical revelation, and worship God as Creator and Redeemer.

Questions.

1. Can you recite Matthew 22:37-40?

2. To what demonolatry are some professing Christians addicted?

3. Can you recite Ezekiel 18:20?

4. How do we show love to God?

5. Are you breaking the third commandment in ordinary conversation?

6. What two meanings should be attached to "Remember" in the fourth commandment?

7. Are the Sabbath and the seventh day necessarily identical?

8. To what do we bear testimony in observing the Sabbath?

SECOND TABLE OF THE LAW

CHAPTER 20:12-26

1. Fifth Commandment, v. 12.

To "honor" means to regard with respect and loving fear. What reasons there are for it on the part of children toward their parents, who are under God the author of their existence, and their teachers, benefactors and rulers!

What promise is attached to this commandment? For a comment see Deut. 5:16. Although this promise applies primarily to Israel in Canaan, as we see from Ezek. 22:7-15, yet its principle is true in God's moral government everywhere.

The child who honors its parents—of course wise and true parents are assumed—gains the experience of the latter which makes for a good, and with necessary exceptions, a long life.

2. Sixth Commandment, v. 13.

The reference here is to the unlawful taking of life by suicide or homicide, but not to capital punishment for capital crimes (see Gen. 9:6), nor the taking of life in self-defense or lawful war. It forbids all violence, passion, lust, intemperance in eating or drinking, and any other habit which tends to shorten life. So far as the more spiritual import is concerned it interdicts envy, revenge, hatred, malice or sinful anger, all that provokes to wrath or murder. See Matthew 5:21-26, 38-48; 1 John 3:15-17.

3. Seventh Commandment, v. 14.

The Hebrew word for "adultery" refers to the unlawful act taking place between man and woman where either or both are married, thus differing from another word commonly translated "fornication" and where the same act is referred to between unmarried persons.

Nevertheless, as the sanctity of the marriage relation is the object aimed at it prohibits everything contrary to the spirit of that institution in thought, word or deed. See Matt. 5:27-32. We may therefore include not only lustful looks, motions and verbal insinuations, but modes of dress, pictures, statues, books, theatrical displays, etc., which provoke the passions and incite to the unlawful act.

Sins of this character are more frequently forbidden in Scripture and more fearfully threatened than any other, and they are the cause of more shame, crime, misery and death. Moreover, they have one striking characteristic, viz: that "you cannot think or talk about them without being more or less excited and led into temptation." How continually need we be praying the prayer of the Psalmist—19:12.

4. Eighth Commandment, v. 15.

As the sixth commandment secures the right of our neighbor's life, and the seventh the right of his family, so this secures the right of his property. The essence of dishonesty is the possessing ourselves of that which rightfully belongs to another, for which there is a variety of ways besides putting our hands into his money-drawer—fraudulent bargains, contraction of debts which we know we shall be unable to pay, cornering the market, graft, usury, evading taxes, false weights and measures, etc.

And as in the previous cases, so here also, the command reaches beyond outward acts to the spirit of them, and includes inordinate love for the world and the things that are in the world, living beyond our means, idleness, and everything that leads up to theft. This commandment may be regarded as the most comprehensive of all.

5. Ninth Commandment, v. 16.

This has primary reference to testimony in courts of law (see Deut. 19:16-19), and differs from the three preceding in that it deals with words rather than deeds.

But, as in those cases, it has a larger import and prohibits everything in our dealings with one another not according to truth. Compare Lev. 19:16; Prov. 19:9; Psalm 15:2; Col. 3:9.

Among some of these things might be named exaggeration in speech, polite equivocations, flattering compliments, and of course all classes of slander, backbiting, and imputations of evil where no evil is.

It is usually felt, however, that there is a distinction between telling a lie and concealing the truth or a part of the truth from those who have no right to demand it. The one is always wrong, the other sometimes may be right.

6. Tenth Commandment, v. 17.

"Covet" means to earnestly desire or long after, a feeling not sinful in itself, but which becomes so under particular circumstances. Its sinfulness appears in longing for anything unlawful, or longing for that which is lawful to an inordinate degree. A passing wish to have anything our neighbor possesses may be innocent, but to long for it excessively is prohibited.

The reason for the prohibition is that such longing begets a grudging, discontented and envious spirit, which leads often to injustice and violence. The case of David who coveted Uriah's wife and finally caused him to be slain is in point.

From deeds and words the decalogue has thus come to deal with the thoughts and intents of the heart, the fountain head of sin; and that it reaches deep into the interior of human life, read Paul's words in Romans 7:7-14.

These words are worthy of careful consideration. On one occasion he said that "touching the righteousness which is in the law" he was blameless (Phil. 3:6). A wonderful thing for a man of his honesty and introspection to say! How then may we explain the fact that near the end of his life he testifies that he is the chief of sinners (1 Tim. 1:15)? The explanation is found in these words in Romans. Meditating upon the tenth commandment he observed that it had to do not with the body but the mind, and from this he argued that the other commandments were regnant in the same mental area. Thus taught by the Spirit he perceived that so far from being blameless he had daily transgressed the principles of the decalogue even though he had never done outwardly the things condemned. The law did for him what God intends it to do for all of us. It killed him, slaying his self-righteousness and taking the life out of his self-confidence. As he thus lay hopeless in the dust of his earthliness it led him to Christ the Saviour of the lost (Gal. 3:24).—*Dean Hart.*

Questions.

1. What does "honor" mean in the fifth commandment?
2. What sins are most frequently forbidden and threatened in Scripture?
3. How may "covet" be qualified?
4. Which commandment has most to do with the mind?
5. Can you quote Galatians 3:24?

THE CIVIL CODE

CHAPTERS 21-24

The ten commandments constitute the moral law, a perfect rule of duty for all men and everywhere. But the "judgments" (v. 1) that follow are an application of those commandments to Israel in the peculiar circumstances of their history at that time and when they should inhabit Canaan. The ten commandments, let us say, represent the constitution of the United States, and the "judgments" the legislative enactments based thereon by Congress.

The three chapters now entered upon have certain natural divisions, corresponding, though not in exact order, with the last seven commandments of the decalogue:

1. Laws of Servitude, 21:1-11.

This division refers to the duties of masters and servants, and is a natural expansion of the 5th commandment, the master being substituted for the parent.

It is slavery of a certain kind that is here dealt with, for it was common in those days when for centuries the rights of man had been beclouded by sin, and in the absence of a divine revelation. Heavenly reforms sometimes move slowly, and it was not God's purpose to immediately do away with this feature of social life, but to regulate, elevate in any other way. Compare Lev. 25:93 and Deut. 15:12.

Vv. 4-6. We can see the advantage of the wife and children remaining with the master in this case, since he doubtless was best able to support them. Moreover, he had rights in the case which should not be violated. But what provision is made for a happy solution of the problem? Behold in this servant whose ear is bored an affecting type of the willing obedience of the Lord Jesus Christ (Ps. 40:6-8)!

Vv. 7-11. If the maid-servant should not please her master in the sense that he espouse her, in what two ways are her rights guarded (8)? What acknowledged position would she have did she become the espoused of his son (9)? And how are the rights of this poor maiden guarded in this case as well (10, 11)? We are not to suppose that this law instituted either polygamy or concubinage, but finding it in existence it was permitted until the period was ripe for its extermination (Matt. 19:1-9).

2. Laws of Personal Security, 21: 12-32.

This section is an expansion of the 6th commandment.

Vv. 12-14. What distinction is made between premeditated and unpremeditated murder? See Numbers 35:9-32.

Vv. 23-25. This law of retaliation has been misunderstood as though it encouraged revenge, but it refers to the administration of justice at the hand of the magistrate (6).

3. Laws of Property, 21:33 to 22: 15.

This section is an expansion of the 8th commandment.

"Breaking up" (22:2) should read as in the Revised Version "breaking in," which makes the sense plain.

"Judge" all through these chapters is translated "God" in the Revised Version. Israel is a theocracy. Its supreme ruler is God. The magistrates represent and speak directly for Him. Thus will it be again in the millennium.

4. Laws of Conjugal Fidelity, 22: 16-31.

This is an expansion of the 7th commandment, and yet its subject matter is miscellaneous. Murphy gives a unity to the verses by supposing the relation between God and His people to be symbolized by that of husband and wife, God being the avowed

guardian and representative of the stranger, the widow and the orphan.

V. 28. The word "gods" should be "God," and it will be seen from the context that reviling rulers is regarded as reviling God (compare Ro. 13:1-7).

V. 29. "Liquors" has been rendered "the trickling juice of the vine."

Some things in this section are more fully explained in later Scriptures.

5. Laws of Veracity, 23:1-9.

This corresponds to the 9th commandment.

V. 3 means that one is not to countenance or favor a poor man in his cause just because he is poor, if the cause be unrighteous. Compare Lev. 19:15.

6. Laws of Set Times, 23:10-19.

This corresponds to the 4th commandment.

What was the law for the land in the seventh year (11)? For what purpose was the spontaneous growth of that year to be used? How did the divine Legislator provide against an emergency of famine (Lev. 25:20-22)?

Note the moral advantages resulting from the observance of this law: (1) a check on avarice, (2) a stimulant to brotherly kindness and compassion, (3) a demonstration of human equality, (4) a cultivation of prudence and economy, (5) a sense of constant dependence upon God.

What are the three annual feasts (14-16)? Murphy compares them with the three elements of salvation: the passover with the atonement, pentecost with the new birth, the ingathering with pardon and its accompanying plentitude of blessing. What obligation is attached to these festivals?

V. 19, last sentence, is difficult, although the command itself is plain. It is in connection with sacrifice (18)—has it therefore a symbolic meaning? Or was it to prevent the slaying and eating of the kid at too early a period? Or does the application bear simply on a barbarous and cruel action?

7. Laws of Pity, 23:20-33.

This is allied to the 10th commandment because of its reference to the service of Jehovah alone, who estimates the motive of men.

Whom have we seen to be meant by "the Angel" (20)? In what way have we seen His presence hitherto displayed? On what commission is He now sent? What shows His authority? Power? Dignity (21)? What are the blessings of obedience (22-27)? What precaution would God take in bringing them into possession of the land (28-30)? What final warning is given (32-33)?

8. Ratifying the Covenant, 24.

At the beginning of this chapter we are introduced to the two sons of Aaron, soon to be associated with him in the priesthood and to have a sad ending nevertheless. With what words do the people accept the obligations imposed upon them (3)? What kind of an altar presumably did Moses build (v. 4 compared with 20:24-26)?

What provision is made for the careful transmission of the law (4)? What name is given to the book thus written (7)? By what solemn act is the covenant ratified (8)? Compare the marginal reference.

What sublime experience was granted to these representatives of Israel on the mount (10)? What this means, in the absence of further record, who can say! Why may we judge that they did not see the "face" of God (33:20-23)? Or any "similitude" of Him (Deut. 4:15)? What description is given of that which they *did* see?

How was God's mercy shown to them on this occasion (11)? How is their escape from death expressed in the last clause? Is not this escape explained by the covenant relationship with God into which they had now come? Was this relationship grounded on their keeping of the law or on the blood of propitiation that had been shed and sprinkled upon the people? What did this typify

(Ro. 3:19-25)? Compare also Hebrews 10:16-20.

What final seal to the authority of the law is now given (12)? What two individuals are here seen for a second time with Moses (13, 14)? What grandeur on the mount is now described (15-17)? What new event in Moses' experience (18)? The reason for this new event will come before us in the succeeding lesson.

Questions.

1. What distinction is suggested between "commandments" and "judgments"?

2. What beautiful type of our Lord Jesus Christ does this lesson contain?

3. What testimony to Israel's theocratic status?

4. How are the rights of the rich guarded as well as of the poor?

5. What witness have we here to an early written revelation?

THE PATTERN IN THE MOUNT

CHAPTER 25:1-9

We have now reached in the revelation of the tabernacle the most important step in the history of grace yet met with in Holy Scripture.

There are several reasons for believing this:

1. The unusual preparation required on man's part for its reception. (See the preceding chapter, vv. 9-18).

2. The large space occupied by its recital—13 chapters in all.

3. The particularity of detail seen throughout.

An Object Lesson

To quote Prof. W. G. Moorehead:

The tabernacle was "a divine object-lesson; an embodied prophecy of good things to come; a witness to the grace and saving power of God. It taught salvation through propitiation, forgiveness and blood-shedding. Access to God and worship it disclosed; the holiness of God; the sinfulness of man; the reconciliation which in due time should be affected, are all clearly set forth by the tabernacle and its rites."

Seven chapters are given to the specifications of the tabernacle, and six to its construction; while in between the two is the record of the unbelief and apostasy of the people in the matter of the golden calf.

Of the seven chapters of specification, three are occupied with the tabernacle itself, three with the priesthood, and one with the arrangement for carrying the whole into effect.

Our present lesson deals with the tabernacle itself.

The Offering of the People, vv. 1-9.

On what principle was this offering to be presented (2)? What three metals are specified (3)? Three colors (4)?

What vegetable textile is mentioned, and what animal (4)? What two kinds of skins (5)? The badger here spoken of is thought to be not the animal commonly known by that name among us, but some other animal equally well-known in Arabia.

What species of wood is named (5)? This is supposed to be the acacia, abundant in Moses' day.

The oil (6) was from the olive, the spices are more particularly indicated (30:23, 24); the precious stones (28:15-21), as also the ephod and breastplate in the same chapter.

What name is given to the building in verse 8, and for what purpose is it to be? The fulfilment of this purpose was in the visible cloud of glory which overshadowed the tabernacle when completed, and rested upon the mercyseat in the Most Holy place.

As to the name "sanctuary," it denotes especially the holiness of the place. What other name is given it in verse 9? This simply means a dwelling, and is sometimes used in an indefinite way for the curtains, the frame-work or the entire structure.

"Tent" is the name given to it in the following chapter; and at other places "the tent of meeting," having reference to the meeting of God with His people (29:42, 43); or the tent or tabernacle "of testimony" (Num. 2:50, 53), as designating the place where God declared His will, and especially testified against the sins of His people, by His holy law which, within the ark, witnessed to the covenant they had entered into at Sinai.

According to what design was the sanctuary to be erected (9)? Thus we see it was a type of God's dwelling place in the heaven of heavens, a fact that profoundly impresses us with its significance in every detail.

We do not know how the pattern or type was shown to Moses in the mount, whether by a visible model, or vision presented to his mind, but we know it was in some sense a copy of heavenly things, and that hence Moses was allowed no liberty in constructing it.

Archæological Discoveries.

Archæology has shown an analogy between the tabernacle service and the ritualistic practice of some of the heathen nations, but this is not to be interpreted as imitation or adoption on Moses' part.

There is a similitude in the modes of worship fundamental in the human race, and Moses may have been used of God to cull out the truth from this mass of wrong and falsehood.

A parallel is that of the "Code of Hammurabi," a Chaldean monarch, hundreds of years before Moses, who in this "code" gave laws to his people corresponding to those in the previous chapters.

The critics used to argue that the Mosaic code could not be of so early a date as Moses since it presupposed too advanced a civilization on the part of the people for whom it was intended. When, however, this code of Hammurabi was discovered, their tune was changed, and they exclaimed: "Ah! Moses copied after Hammurabi."

The truth rather is that just

suggested about the tabernacle. Hammurabi's code is based upon fundamental principles of law in the constitution of the race, albeit commingled with many grotesque fancies in consequence of the fall. These fundamental principles, however, are, in their origin, divine, and in the code of Moses we find them separated from the false by the hand of their heavenly originator.

Questions.

1. What three reasons show the importance attached to this theme?

2. What names are given to the tabernacle, and what are their meanings?

3. How may the "pattern" have been revealed to Moses?

4. How would you explain the similarity of the tabernacle service to the rituals of heathen nations?

5. What is the "Code of Hammurabi," and what light does it throw on Moses' writings?

THE TABERNACLE AND ITS FURNITURE

CHAPTERS 25:10-27:21

1. The Ark of the Testimony, 25: 10-16.

Notice the kind of wood and the dimensions (10). The "cubit" measures from the elbow to the tip of the middle finger, and is variously estimated from 18 to 21 inches, usually 18. How was it to be overlaid (11)? The "crown of gold" meant a rim or moulding. The "four rings" (12) were attached to the four "corners," in the sense of the four feet of the ark. The "staves" or poles were used in carrying it (14). What was to be placed in the ark (16)? The "testimony" means the ten commandments. (Compare 24: 12)

2. The Mercy-Seat, 25:17-22.

Notice its material and dimensions (17). What was to be placed at either end (18)? "Even of the mercy-seat," should be rendered "out of" or "of one piece with the mercy-seat"; i. e.,

they were not separate attachments from it. What was to be the attitude and position of the cherubim (20)? This was the attitude of observant attention, while they seemed to guard with their wings the place of the manifestation of the divine glory. Where was the mercy-seat to be placed (21)? This does not mean that it was merely the cover of the ark, but a separate article, composing with the ark a unity "not so much in outward as in inward design."

What promise is connected with the mercy-seat (22)?

These two articles, the ark and the mercy-seat, were the only objects, (and they appeared as one), in the Holy of Holies, or the Most Holy place of the tabernacle; and about them, or rather about it, the whole service of worship centered.

The "ark" was God's throne (Ps. 80:1, R. V.), but it was a throne of grace (Heb. 4:16). The "mercy-seat" means "the place of propitiation," and here the blood of the sin-offering was sprinkled on the day of atonement, and satisfaction was rendered to the divine claims on the people represented by the law in the ark of the testimony (Ps. 85:9, 10).

What the mercy-seat did symbolically for Israel, Christ has accomplished perfectly for all who will believe on Him (Ro. 3:25; 1 John 2:1, 2).

3. The Table of Shewbread, 25: 23-30.

This table was to have not only a "crown" or rim, but also a "border" with a crown or rim (24, 25), the distinction between which is difficult to make.

Observe the appurtenances of the table (29). The dishes were to hold the shewbread (30, compared with Lev. 24:5, 6); the bowls were for frankincense (Lev. 24:7). "Covers" is, in the Revised Version, "flagons" or vessels for wine, used in drink-offerings (Num. 15:1-12). The shewbread consisted of 12 cakes (Lev. 24:5, 6), corresponding to the twelve tribes of Israel, and is sometimes called the "presence-bread," or the "bread of the face."

At certain times the priests, who represented the whole of Israel, ate this shewbread from off the table. As the table is the Lord's and in the Lord's house, here we have the idea of hospitality based upon friendship. We see the family of God regaled by Him at His paternal board, which speaks of perfect reconciliation and communion with Him, and helps to explain the phrase, "the bread of the face." That is, man is represented as face to face with God in fellowship through atonement for sin. (See Gen. 14:18-20.)

Furthermore, whatever the "bread of the face" was for Israel in old times, Jesus Christ is now for His people. In and through Him we have communion with the Father (1 John 1:3), and He is the true Bread which sustains us in our new life (John 6:31-58).

4. The Golden Candlestick, 25:31-40.

"His bowls, his knops, his flowers," refers to the ornaments on the branches of the candlestick, and which were to be all of one piece. The seven lamps rest on the flowers at the extremities of the stems. The latter part of verse 37 means that the candlestick shall be so set up (on the south side of the tabernacle, 40:24) as to throw light upon the table opposite. It was the only light in the tabernacle, the home or dwelling place of God.

According to Zech. 4, the candlestick is a type of Israel, and according to Revelation 1, a type of the church. Oil is the symbol of the Holy Spirit, and light typifies God (1 John 1:5), and Christ (John 8:12; 2 Cor. 4:6). The typical significance of the whole in its present position is difficult, but may appear as we proceed.

Note that as the ark and mercy-seat were to be placed in the Most Holy place, the table and candlestick were to be placed in the Holy place, i. e., outside the veil separating the two, of which later.

5. The Curtains, 26:1-14.

After revealing the above-mentioned pieces of furniture, attention is turned to the curtains.

To begin with the inner curtains, they were to be of what number, material, in colors, design, length and breadth (1, 2)?

Five were to be sewed together in one piece and five in another (3). These two halves were to be connected by loops of blue fastened with golden clasps (4-6), the whole to cover the top, sides and western end of the tabernacle, and correspond to the papering of our modern dwellings.

Of what material were the outer curtains to be made (7)? How many in number? Do they differ in length or breadth from the inner curtains. (8)? How was the sixth curtain to be used (9, 12)? Of what material were the clasps to be in this case (11)? How many outside "coverings" were to be made (14)? "Badger" is translated "seal" or "porpoise" in the Revised Version.

6. The Framework, 26:15-30.

Notice the material, length and breadth of the boards (16). How many "tenons" to each board? "Set in order," means "mortised." Of what material were the "sockets" for these tenons (19)? The word "sides" (22) should be translated "back part." The sockets probably rested on the ground as nothing is said of sleepers under them.

How were the boards braced together (26-28)? How were the boards and bars overlaid (29)? What a costly edifice it must have been! Some have calculated it as reaching $1,500,000.

7. The Vail, 26:31-35.

The vail for the Most Holy place, and the hanging or screen for the door of the Holy place (36, 37) require no comment here. The typical significance of the former will come before us in its proper place.

8. The Brazen Altar, 27:1-8.

We are now in the outer court. Notice the material, size, height and shape of this altar. The "horns," or the parts of the corner-posts projecting above the upper surface of the altar, were to be of one piece with it (R. V.), and the whole was to be overlaid with brass to protect from fire and weather, whence its name "the brazen altar" (2). Upon this altar the burnt-offerings were presented.

Questions.

1. What is the meaning of "testimony" in the lesson?

2. What is the meaning of "mercy-seat"?

3. What is the meaning of "the bread of the face"?

4. Of what are the candlestick and the oil types?

5. What is an estimate of the cost of the tabernacle in our money?

THE PRIESTLY GARMENTS

Chapters 28:1-43

The abrupt termination of the directions for the tabernacle at the close of the preceding chapter is remarkable; especially as the subject is taken up again at chapter 30. There must be some reason why the intervening chapters are occupied with the priesthood.

Some see in this the symbolism of a deep fact. God has in grace come out from His throne in the Holy of Holies through the way He has prepared for Himself in the table of shewbread and the candlestick, to meet man in his sin at the brazen altar. And now man is to be brought back through the way God has Himself come, to the place of communion with Him before His throne. The priesthood is necessary for this, and ere the way is itself shown the arrangements for the priesthood are completed.

As soon we reach the altar, in other words, we feel the need of the priest (which means mediator or advocate), who is to officiate thereat. From God he comes to man, authorized to invite man to return to God with penitence, confession and faith, and to make for him the propitiatory sacrifice to that end.

The garments of the priests as well as the details of their consecration are specified in this and the next chapter, because they are symbolical of their standing and office before God, as well as types of Him of whom Aaron and the Aaronic priesthood are the shadows. (See Hebrews, particularly chapters 5 to 10.)

What family is chosen for the priesthood (1)? What provision has God made for the preparation of their clothing (3)? What are the number and names of the garments (4)? Notice the correspondence of color and texture of material to those of the inner curtains already named (5). It will be seen later that three of these garments are peculiar to the high priest—the first three, and that he wears the rest in common with the other priests. There is this further exception, however, that whereas he dons a mitre, they only have bonnets or turbans (40). It might be advisable to say here that while the high priest typifies Christ, the priests, his sons, typify believers on Christ, or the church.

1. The Ephod, vv. 6-12.

The ephod was a shoulder-piece covering the back and reaching under the arms, kept in place by the two shoulder-straps (7) and the belt around the waist (8), leaving the breast uncovered. The gold was beaten into thin pieces, cut into wire and interwoven with colored threads.

What two precious stones belonged to the ephod? What was graved on them? How were they set? Where were they placed, and why (9-12)? These indicate that God was to have Israel in perpetual remembrance through the mediation and representation of the high priest. The shoulder, moreover, is symbolical of power, so that the high priest thus arrayed became a beautiful suggestion of Him whose everlasting arms are underneath His people

(Deut. 33:27). This ephod was the upper-most garment and worn outside the blue robe whose description follows.

2. The Breastplate, vv. 13-30.

What name is given to the breastplate (15)? Its shape and size (16)? What precious stones should it contain (17-20)? What graving upon them (21)? What was the significance of this latter (29)? This "breastplate of judgment" represents the high priest as the spokesman of God, at the same time that he is the affectionate intercessor for Israel—for each tribe and each member of it.

3. Urim and Thummim, v. 30.

Urim and Thummim are thought to be the sum of the twelve precious stones attached to the breastplate. That is, the twelve stones are Urim and Thummim, which means "the lights and the perfections." Lights as to their brilliancy, and perfections as to their hardness and absence from flaws.

"They represent the light and the right that are in the high priest for the enlightenment and reconciliation of those who come unto God by him. He exercises the functions of teaching and sacrificing in their behalf, as the type of the great High Priest.

"The import of Urim and Thummim dawned on the Israelite as he saw the high priest making an offering on the altar for the sins of the people, thus rendering them imputatively perfect, and then returning oracular answers from God out of the Most Holy place to the reverent inquirer.

"But we have no ground for supposing that God conveyed verbal messages to the high priests by illuminating any letters on the stones, as some have fancied. In other words there is nothing concealed nor mystical about this transaction after the manner of the heathen temples and priesthoods, nor anything in the nature of a charm as in an amulet. God indicated the light and the perfection which He

vouchsafed to His people by means of these stones, but that light and perfection did not reside in the stones in any way."—Murphy.

4. The Robe, vv. 31-36.

How does verse 31 show that this robe belong to the ephod in some way? What shows it to have been entirely woven, and without seam (32)? "Habergeon" means "a coat of mail." How was the base to be trimmed (33, 34)? The significance of this (35)?

It would appear from the last words of this verse that the wearing of this robe on the part of the high priest while ministering, was necessary to insure him from death. It becomes therefore a type of that robe of Christ's righteousness which is the only security of eternal life for human kind (Isa. 61:10). The sound of the bells testified that "the mail of proof had been put on, and the dread of death removed." It must have been a constant source of comfort and encouragement to the high priest as he stood alone in the Holy of Holies in the presence of the awful glory of Jehovah. Every slightest movement he made brought the assurance from the bells that all was well.

5. The Crown, vv. 36-38.

More is revealed about the plate on the mitre (or turban) than the mitre itself. What is this plate called in 39:30? By the names on the precious stones the high priest is shown to be the representative of the people, and by what in this case is he shown to be the representative of God? For what does this holiness thus qualify him (38)?

The ephod, the breastplate, and the golden crown combined present us symbolically with the three-fold office of our great High Priest, Jesus Christ. "In the ephod the priestly office is obvious, in the breastplate the prophetic comes into the view, and in the crown the kingly makes its appearance, although the priestly discloses and maintains itself throughout."

6. The Common Garments, vv. 39-43.

In these verses we have directions for the garments common to all the priests including the high priest.

The coat was to be woven in chequer work as intimated in the Revised Version. It seems to have been provided with sleeves and to have reached to the feet. The mitre, or turban, was of the same material, and was wrapped around the head. The girdle was wound twice around the body it is said, and tied in front with the ends hanging down to the feet. Note the difference between this girdle going around the waist and holding the coat in place, and the "curious" or cunningly-woven girdle of verse 8, which fastened the ephod. Notice also that the head-gear of the priests is not called a "mitre" but a "bonnet," evidently different somewhat in shape and appearance. The linen breeches are described in verses 42 and 43. They do not seem to have belonged to the official dress of the priests, but to have been prescribed for the sake of propriety in other respects.

Questions.

1. Why may chapters 28 and 29 be a parenthesis in the revelation of the Tabernacle?

2. What New Testament book treats of the typical character of the priesthood?

3. What typical distinction seems to exist between the common priests and the high priest?

4. What may be the significance of Urim and Thummin?

5. What did the robe and the bells signify?

THE INIQUITY OF THE HOLY THINGS

In the last lesson attention was called to the phrase at the head of this lesson found in 28:38.

The significance of the expression, both for Israel and for Christians, and the widely-prevailing ignorance on the subject of which it treats, is the justification for a special lesson in the way of an addendum to it.

The following is from William R. Nicholson, D.D., bishop in the Reformed Episcopal Church.

These words, "the iniquity of the holy things," are only part of a sentence, their connection being that Aaron the high priest should *bear* the iniquity of the holy things. Of course, the bearing of this iniquity means the atoning for it.

But we are startled by the repellency of the idea. How strange to hear of the iniquity of what is holy!

The "holy things" are described in the context as the sacrifices and offerings of Israel. Whatever they presented to God in worship were holy in the sense that they were consecrated to and appointed by Him. And yet these things themselves had iniquity. When the worshiper brought his bleeding victim as an offering for his sins his very act of bringing it had in it additional sin which required to be atoned for.

And the truth with regard to Israel is the same with ourselves. We were by nature children of wrath, and now, although as believers on our Lord Jesus Christ we are regenerated by His Spirit, still in our flesh there dwelleth no good thing (Ro. 7:18; 8:7). The consequence is that we entail our sin upon whatever we attempt to do. We worship God, even in the way of His own appointment, and yet the sin in us imparts to that worship the imperfection of its sinfulness and therefore the sin of imperfection. We pray, and our act of prayer has iniquity in it. We sing God's praises, we read His Word, we come into His house, we kneel at the sacrament and at each and all there is sin, for they have the imperfection and defilement of our sinfulness. Indeed, we trust in Jesus for the pardon of our sins as the Israelite brought his bleeding victim to the altar, and yet the very act of trust is sinfully done and needs for itself the divine pardon.

God's People Are Meant.

Notice that "the iniquity of the holy things" was affirmed of Israel, the type of the true people of God, and not unregenerate men.

When they assembled at the Tabernacle they did so as the redeemed of God. The blood of the paschal lamb had been sprinkled upon their houses in Egypt. Sheltered beneath it from the curse which had devastated that land, they had gone forth from its bondage and terror, and were now brought nigh to God in His own house of communion. They were even supplied by His hand with all holy gifts which they were now permitted to offer to Him.

They represent real Christians, therefore, true believers in Jesus Christ, delivered out of the condemnation of the world, and having received through His blood the forgiveness of sin, made nigh to God in the privilege of worship and the joy of fellowship.

There is therefore iniquity in *our* holy things. In every act of our worship there are imperfection and defilement, because there is present in that act the old evil nature along with the new. We need therefore to be forgiven for every duty we perform, for every sorrow for sin we feel, for every hope we cherish, and for all the love we enjoy.

Bishop Beveridge said: "I cannot pray but I sin; I cannot hear or preach a sermon but I sin; I cannot give alms or receive the sacrament but I sin; no, I cannot so much as confess my sins but my very confessions are still aggravations of them; my repentance needs to be repented of; my tears want washing; and the very washing of my tears needs still to be washed over again with the blood of my Redeemer."

The Proof.

That the meaning of these words is not exaggerated may be seen in that the same truth is taught again in the 16th of Leviticus, where we meet with a description of the annual Day of Atonement.

In the present text the high priest is *directed* to bear the iniquity of the holy things, but in that chapter he is represented as actually bearing them. He is attired in his holy garments, his forehead glittering with "Holiness to the Lord," and actually sprinkling the blood of sacrifice to cleanse the uncleanness of the worshipers, to make atonement for the holy sanctuary itself, for the altar on which the sacrifices are offered (for these things were polluted by the very presence of sinners), for the priests who offered the sacrifices, and for all the people accustomed there to worship.

Once a year regularly and solemnly the great truth of this text was recognized and enforced. Every day in the year, to say nothing of extra sessions, the blood of atonement was offered for pardon and acceptance, but the acts of offering had iniquity in them and needed themselves to be specifically sprinkled with the atoning blood. This was done on this annual day, the greatest of all the occasions of expiation.

Moreover, the New Testament is full of this teaching of the iniquity of our holy things. It speaks to us concerning it in those words of Paul throughout the 7th of Romans, and in his words to the Philippians where he speaks of discarding his own righteousness, even that which belonged to him as a Christian (3:1-15). Indeed, it speaks to us in all that is said in the New Testament concerning the sanctification which comes to believers through faith in the blood of Christ.

A Three-Fold Application.

The application of this truth is wide-reaching.

(1) In the first place, it enhances our appreciation of our Saviour and the value of His merits for us. It helps us to see how deeply we need Him, and how great is the sovereign mercy and the boundless grace of God towards us in Him.

The high priest in the tabernacle typifies Him, and the service he rendered for Israel, even in the iniquity of their holy things, typifies the service Christ has rendered and is rendering for us in a like case. For if there is iniquity in our holy things, thank God there is also atonement for it accomplished, and full, and of instant efficacy (1 John 2:1, 2)!

(2) In the second place, it opens our eyes and broadens our vision as to the relative meanings of sin and holiness. In the light of this text, what Christian can question—much less deny—the application to him at all times of the words of the apostle John: "If we say we have no sin we deceive ourselves, and the truth is not in us" (1 John 1:8)?

Who can talk about sinless perfection in the light of this truth? And how professions of the eradication of evil shrink into worthlessness, and themselves become sin in its shadow! So deeply indeed is the truth of this text imbedded, as a living principle, in the experience of true and enlightened Christians, that the more devoted they are the more it is felt.

It is indeed a test of our nearness to God to have a Christian conscience so cultivated as to appreciate our daily and hourly need, and at the same time our daily and hourly completeness only in Christ. This is the way to feast upon Him richly. If our faith, considered as an act, does itself require to have blood sprinkled upon it, then as we appreciate that fact shall our faith itself sink down more and more upon Christ for all that He is to us, and rest upon Him with the very rest of heaven.

(3) It furnishes a momentous warning to the unbeliever and the unregenerate man. If there is no such thing as even a Christian's self-righteousness, if there is no such thing as a Christian's purchasing to himself the divine favor even by such life-long goodness as that of Paul, how impossible must all this be to the man who has not received Christ at all! If no Christian who is himself personally accepted in Christ can put forth one act which does not need forgiveness, what can he do to commend himself to God who is unwashed in redeeming blood, and on whom even now abideth His condemnation?

With regard to any dependence on one's own righteousness it becomes us all to say, Christian or non-Christian, with the patriarch Job: "If I wash myself with snow water, and make my hands never so clean, yet shalt Thou plunge me into the ditch, and mine own clothes shall make me to be abhorred!"

"The iniquity of the holy things"!

What Jesus is, and that alone,
  Is faith's delightful plea;
Which never deals with *sinful* self
  Nor *righteous* self in me.

Questions.

1. Where is the phrase found which is the title of this lesson?

2. Of whom is this iniquity affirmed, the world's people or God's people?

3. On what great day in Israel was this solemnly enforced?

4. What New Testament Scripture shows that there is atonement in Christ for such iniquity?

5. What erroneous doctrine does this truth contradict?

6. To whom is it a solemn warning?

THE CONSECRATION OF THE PRIESTS

CHAPTER 29

1. The Ceremony in Outline. vv. 1-9.

What animals were required for sacrifice, and what qualification must they have (1)? What offerings accompanied them (2)? Where was the place of ceremony (4)? What was the preliminary act?

This washing of the bodies of the priests typified the cleanness of the whole man in a moral and spiritual sense, which, while it was true of Aaron only ceremonially, was true absolutely of the Lord Jesus Christ, whom he set forth and pre-figured.

What followed the washing (5, 6)? What followed the investure of the clothing (7)?

This holy anointing oil, for which (as we shall see) God

Himself gave the prescription, was the emblem of the gift and grace of the Holy Spirit communicated to the priesthood for their service. At the same time it should be borne in mind that the service accomplished by them in a symbolical sense was accomplished actually by Christ for His people, who was anointed of the Holy Spirit to that end (Luke 4:16, 21; Acts 4:27; 10:38).

For how long was the office to remain in Aaron's family (9)? This means of course to the end of the Levitical economy (Heb. 7:11-19).

"Consecrate" in v. 9 means "to fill the hands," and signifies "the placing of the sacrifices in their hands, in the offering of which they are not only sanctified but instituted into their office."

2. The Sin-Offering, vv. 10-14.

What was the nature of this offering (10)? Where presented? How were Aaron and his sons to identify themselves with it? What was to be done to it (11)? How was its blood to be used (12)? Which of its parts should be burned on the altar (13)? Which without the camp, and why (14)?

The presentation of this offering was to remove the legal disqualifications from Aaron and his sons on account of sin. The life which is in the blood of the animal makes atonement for their life, which like the lives of all of us was forfeited through sin. This is not to say that there was any intrinsic virtue in the blood of a bull, but as we shall be told by and by it is typical of the blood of the Son of God, which is efficacious in the cleansing from all sin (1 John 1:7).

The details of these offerings come before us in Leviticus, where they are commanded for the people as they are here for the priests.

3. The Burnt-offering, vv. 15-18.

The nature of this offering (15)? Observe the same act of identification as before. What distinction do you see in the use of the blood (16)? What was to be done with the flesh of this offering as distinguished from the other (18)? And before it was burnt, what (17)? What did it then become (18)?

Sin is not named in connection with this offering as in the other case. There God's judgment is executed on the victim as charged with the sin of the offence, but here God's satisfaction with the offerer is expressed as based on the previous putting away of his sin and the presentation of himself for acceptance and worship.

4. The Peace-offering, vv. 19-28.

These two rams bear a close relation to one another, and are to be considered theoretically as one. What is done with the blood here (20)? Touching the person with the blood symbolizes the purging of that person from his guilt.

What further ceremony follows (21)? This symbolizes "the outward and legal and the inward and moral purification essential to the priestly office."

What is this ram called (22)? How is the idea of consecration expressed in v. 24? Here Aaron and his sons "take the first step in offering and are at the same time initiated into the priestly office."

Moses who initiates them is to "wave" these offerings, doubtless by taking hold of their hands thus filled, and moving them back and forth. The significance of this is difficult to determine. The forward movement toward the altar might indicate the dedication of the offering to the Lord, and the backward movement a transference of it again to the priest as his share, only that in this case the offerings are not afterward consumed by the priests but are burned on the altar (25). We await more light.

What parts of this ram are assigned as the portion of the priest (27)? Observe that a "wave" and a "heave" offering are both mentioned here, the motion of one being horizontal and the other vertical. It is "heaved" in token of being offered unto God, and then, accepted by Him, it is assigned to His representative on earth, the priest (28). To what class of offering does this heave offering belong?

"Peace offering" in this verse is translated in the Septuagint Version, "a sacrifice of salvation," and is an acknowledgment of salvation already received as expressed through the sin and burnt offering previously presented and accepted, and which invariably preceded it in the Levitical ceremonial. (Compare Ro. 5.) As indicative of this it was essentially a *communion* feast. God's portion was burned on the altar, but of the remainder the priest and the offerer (as we shall see later) each had a part.

5. The Daily Burnt-offering, vv. 38–46.

What was its nature (38)? How many times a day? What offering accompanied it (40, 41)? How would God show His reconciliation and communion with them on the ground of this offering (42)? This intercourse promised to the people would come, through the high priest. How should the Tabernacle be hallowed? In what other language is the same idea expressed (45)? Of what should this be to them an assurance (46)? This manifestation of His presence was the shekinah glory, successor in a sense to the pillar of cloud.

Aaron a Type of Christ.

This is an appropriate place for a further word concerning the typical relation of the Aaronic priesthood to Jesus Christ.

That priesthood is set before us in two sections. Aaron, the high priest, the true type of Christ, and his sons, consecrated to the office in virtue of their relation to him. These latter who ministered at the altar of sacrifice and in the Holy Place, but never in the Most Holy, do not so much typify Christ as believers on Christ, who with Him constitute the royal and priestly family of which He is the head.

Aaron is a type of Christ in his person, since what he was ceremonially and symbolically the Lord Jesus is intrinsically and divinely. Although as to His hu-

manity He descended from a long line of impure ancestors, yet He brought no stain of sin into the world with Him, nor contracted any while here (Heb. 7:26).

The high priest, however, was a type of Christ not only in his person but in his office and functions. The Epistle to the Hebrews will amply assure us of this. It will be seen indeed that it is in virtue of Christ's priestly office that the Aaronic was ever instituted. In other words, Christ's priesthood reflects backward and gives to that of Aaron all the efficacy and meaning it possessed.

Aaron was Israel's representative before God, and in his priestly character he stood for the whole nation. As God was pleased with him so was He pleased with the nation. All his official acts were reckoned as having been done by the people here represented. All of which we know to be true of Jesus Christ as the representative of them that believe on Him. He died for them, and they died in Him (2 Cor. 5:14). They are raised in Him, quickened and seated with Him in the heavenlies (Eph. 2:5, 6). As Aaron bore the tribes into the Most Holy place so Jesus Christ bears His people into God's presence (Heb. 10:19-22). The chief duty of the human priest was to reconcile men to God by offering an atonement for their sins, effected by sacrifice. What Aaron thus did for Israel in the type Jesus has done for His people actually (Heb. 8:3; 9:12; 10:10).

It is furthermore an element of the priestly office to make intercession on behalf of those whom it represents. This was done for Israel by the sprinkling of the blood on the mercy seat and the offering of incense on the golden altar, of which we shall learn in the next lesson. In the same way the New Testament combines Christ's intercession for us with His sacrificial death (Heb. 7:25; 9:24; 1 John 2:1, 2; Ro. 8:33, 34).

To allude to a feature of the *consecration* of Aaron and his sons, we find something particularly suggestive in their anointing. Aaron was anointed before the bloody sacrifices were offered, while his sons were not anointed until afterward. And so, long before the cross, Jesus was anointed with the Holy Spirit (John 1:33, 34), but the disciples, who are the anti-types of the sons of Aaron, did not receive that anointing until after Jesus was glorified (John 7:39, R. V.; Acts 2).

Moreover, Aaron received a greater unction than his sons, the holy oil being poured upon his head and running down upon his beard, even to the skirts of his garments (Psalm 133). Compare John 3:34, (Heb. 1:9).

These are hints of the typology of the Aaronic priesthood, of which we shall be learning more as we proceed, and from which we shall be gaining richer apprehensions of the person and work of our Lord Jesus Christ on our behalf. For thus these things have been written for our learning.

Questions.

1. Whom do the ordinary priests typify?

2. In what three ways did Aaron typify Christ?

3. What were two chief duties of the priest?

4. What New Testament epistle treats especially of Christ's priesthood?

5. Can you quote 1 John 2:1, 2?

THE WORK FULLY REVEALED AND THE WORKMEN CHOSEN

Chapters 30-31

1. The Altar of Incense, vv. 1-10.

Of what material and for what purpose was it made (1)? Its size and shape (2)? Its furnishings (3)? The means for its removal (4, 5)? Its location (6)? How often and at what time was the incense to be offered (7, 8)? What prohibition was placed on its use (9)? How does v. 10 bear on "the iniquity of the holy things"?

Although no sacrifice was offered on the altar of incense yet the worship there was acceptable only because of the sacrifice previously made at the brazen altar. These two altars were connected as one by the fact that the live coals which consumed the sacrifice on the brazen altar also burned the incense before the altar of incense.

This incense symbolized prayer, thanksgiving and obedience accepted through the intercession of the high priest. The offerer of the sacrifice, having been reconciled to God at the brazen altar and cleansed or sanctified as shadowed forth by the laver, soon to be spoken of, is here at the altar of incense seen to be accepted of God and adoring Him in consequence.

See Ps. 141:2; 1 Tim. 2:8, and especially Rev. 5:8; 8:3, 4.

The fact that the altar was "before the Lord" is significant. Although the veil interposed between it and the ark, nevertheless God speaks of it as if nothing intervened, thus showing its intimate relation to the ark, the mercy seat and the divine presence. So prayer brings us into closest communion with our heavenly Father.

We have spoken of the relation of the two altars, the significance of which lies in the fact that in the brazen altar we have Christ typified in His atoning sacrifice, and in the incense of the golden altar we have Him typified in His intercession. The latter is thus seen to be bound up with and finding its efficacy in the former. Compare Ro. 8:34; Heb. 9:25. Efficaciousness in prayer, therefore, is always in conjunction with the work of Christ for us. In Rev. 8 incense was offered with the prayers of the saints. It is the incense, therefore, typifying Christ's intercession, which makes the prayers of the saints acceptable to God.

2. Support of the Worship, vv. 11-16.

The numbering here referred to took place as recorded in Numbers 1:3. What accompanied the numbering, and how did it become a testimony of their actual condition of guilt before God (12)? What penalty attached to failure in this case? Amount of ransom (13)? (The approximate value of the shekel was 60 cents.) Upon whom did the obligation rest, and upon what scale (14, 15)? For what purpose was the money used (16)?

3. The Laver, vv. 17-21.

What next was to be made, of what material and for what purpose (18)? Where placed? What parts of the priests' persons were to be washed (19)? (Notice the word "thereat," indicating probably that water was removed from the laver into a smaller vessel for this purpose.) When (20)? What penalty attached to a failure to comply (21)?

This washing symbolized the soul purity of those who might approach God. See John 3:5; Eph. 5:25, 26; Titus 3:5.

The laver represents not the regeneration of the believer in Christ so much as it does his daily renewal in Christ. As Moorehead says, there is a bath which requires no repetition, being accomplished once for all (John 13:10, R. V.). Regeneration is never repeated (1 Cor. 6:11, R. V.). But the believer comes into daily contact with the world's defilement, and is polluted by his own remaining corruption. How is he to be kept clean? How is interrupted communion to be re-established? By washing the disciples' feet Christ gave an illustration of the way in which this might be done. This act was a type of His intercession on our behalf continually (John 13:1-17; 1 John 2:1).

This purpose is set before us in the laver, for Aaron and his sons were bathed upon their entrance on the priest's office, which acts were not to be repeated in the same way or for the same purpose. Their acceptance and consecration in that sense were final and complete from the beginning. But each time they entered the sanctuary to perform their office they must wash their hands and feet. It was for this the laver was provided.

So at the altar our sin is judged and forgiven, and at the laver our sin is washed away from our persons. Jesus Christ in His atoning death and prevailing intercession is the glorious anti-type of both.

4. Bezaleel and Aholiab, vv. 31: 1-11.

These are two of the most interesting of the secondary characters in the Old Testament.

They who did the mechanical work on the Tabernacle and the garments of the high priests— work so sacred and important in God's eyes—must have had the consciousness of His being very near to them, and they to Him. Humanly speaking, what a nervous strain must have been their experience continually! Yet how did God provide against this, and at the same time for the perfect execution of His will (3)?

Note the lesson here of the way God provides for the execution of His will and His work in the spiritual realm. Whom he chooses He anoints and equips in every necessity for His work. That these two men had the natural gifts for such employment were not enough, but these gifts must be imbued with power from on high.

Oh that every preacher, teacher and Christian worker might appreciate this, and put himself in that attitude before God where he might attain the equipment!

5. The Sabbath Law, vv. 12-17.

Why do you suppose his reference to the Sabbath is found here? Was it to prevent even so holy a work as the building of the tabernacle to be done on that day?

What does God call the Sabbath in v. 12? What is meant by the closing words of v. 17? God does not require "rest and refreshment" as we do, but may He not experience "delight from the accomplishment of His work and the contemplation of its excellence?"

6. The End of Moses' Mission on the Mount, v. 18.

Note this verse and compare it with 24:12. How sacred the words: "written with the finger of God!" Certainly no material finger is referred to, but there was a putting forth of power for the purpose which effected the result just the same.

Questions.

1. What truth is illustrated in the order in which this revelation is given?

2. What does the altar of incense symbolize?

3. The significance of the two altars?

4. The symbolism of the laver? And the anointing oil?

5. How does God provide for the execution of His work?

THE BREACH MADE AND REPAIRED

Chapters 32-33:6

Moses for forty days has been absent in the mount, and to the people it seemed long. Had they forgotten the awe-inspired sights and sounds they had seen and heard? Had all the sublime and stirring events of the months since they departed from Egypt been obliterated from their memory? How can we explain the folly into which they now fell? If we can not explain it, let us ask our own hearts if we know anything like it.

1. The Molten Calf, 32:1-6.

What demand was made of Aaron (1)? How was their sinful impatience shown? How does the phrase: "who shall go before us," indicate the cause of their impatience? Describe Aaron's guilt (2-5). Does this appear to have been a violation of the first or the second commandment?

The idol was probably a piece of wood carved into the shape of a calf, and overlaid with melted gold. The model was the bull worshipped by the Egyptians. The last words of v. 6 refer to unclean practices associated with such worship among the heathen.

2. Divine Wrath, 32:7-14.

By the use of what pronoun in v. 7 does God renounce leadership of the people? What test of loyalty is put to Moses in v. 10? How does he apparently ignore God's rejection of the people in v. 11? Notice the two strong arguments he presents in his expostulation (12, 13). One is God's honor in the sight of Egypt, and the other His honor in the keeping of his original promise to Israel. But does Moses excuse the sin of the people? When it says: "the Lord repented," does it mean that He had changeable feelings like a man? Or should we say, rather that He acted on His unchangeable principle, always to show mercy to the penitent?

3. Swift Punishment, 32:15-29.

Joshua in all probability had been awaiting Moses on the mount outside the cloud that enveloped him, and therefore had not heard the communication about the idolatrous worship. This doubtless explains the conversation in vv. 17 and 18.

Observe what Moses did: (1) He broke the two tablets of testimony, doubtless as emblematic of the breach the sin of the people had made in their covenant with God; (2) he destroyed the image, grinding it into powder and casting it in the brook from which they were supplied with drink; then did they experience in a physical sense the bitter results of their infatuation; (3) he rebuked Aaron, whose act was inexcusable (compare Deut. 9:15-21); (4) he judged the people through the instrumentality of the sons of Levi.

"Fill your hand" (29) means, as in a previous lesson, "consecrate yourselves this day unto the Lord." If it seems strange that the Levites met no effective resistance in their righteously indictive work, an explanation may be found in that many sympathized with them and disapproved of the sin committed. Perhaps also there were many indifferent ones, who simply had been led astray by strong and wicked leaders. Then, consider the weakening effect of a conscience stricken by the sense of sin, which must have followed Moses' words and actions.

4. Potent Intercession, 32:30 to 33:6.

Instant destruction had been stayed, but full pardon had not been obtained, hence Moses' action in these verses.

Note the impassionate form of entreaty in v. 32. The consequences if God will not forgive their sin are unutterable. He does not name them. He feels that he could not live or enjoy the blessings of eternity if this were not done. Compare Paul's words concerning the same people (Ro. 9:1-5).

What can he mean by "the book Thou hast written"? How interesting that phrase thus early in the history of revelation! The Israelites were familiar with a register of families. Did Moses grasp by faith that such a register of the saints was to be found above?

What divine principle concerning sin and sinners is laid down in v. 33? (Compare Ezekiel 17:19-23.)

What command, promise and warning are found in v. 34? How does v. 35 show that God assumes the responsibility for what Moses and the Levites did? And how does it show that the people were held responsible for what Aaron did?

For "My Angel" of v. 34 compare 23:20, and recall the previous instruction that He possesses the attributes and prerogatives of God. Subsequent revelation will conclusively show Him to be the second Person of the Trinty.

The last clause of this verse shows that while "the intercessor has prevailed, he has not yet heard the word of full remission." The breach is repaired, but the relationship with God is not yet what it was before. The next lesson shows how that is brought about.

THE COVENANT RENEWED

CHAPTERS 32:7-34

1. Moses Separated Unto God, 33:7-11.

The tabernacle, or tent, here referred to (7), was that of Moses, as the Tabernacle of the Lord had not yet been erected. As the Lord would no longer manifest Himself among the people, it was necessary thus to become separated from them if Moses was to enjoy such intercourse. (Compare 2 Cor. 6:14-18.) "The tabernacle of the Congregation" is rendered in the Revised Version, "the tent of meeting," i. e., the place where the Lord met Moses and others who in penitence and faith gathered with him there.

In what now familiar way did the Lord manifest His presence with Moses (9)? What effect had this upon the people (10)? How is the Lord's loving kindness towards Moses expressed in v. 11? Compared with v. 20 it will be seen that Moses did not behold the divine essence, but only such a vision of God's face as it is possible for men to look upon and live.

2. Moses' Interview with God, 33:12-23.

What information does he seek (12)? And what argument does he use to obtain it? Observe further that he also wants to know God's "way," i. e., His way of salvation and leading for the people (13). Moreover, he would know God Himself better, to the end that he might obtain more grace. Increasing grace always accompanies increasing knowledge of God (2 Peter 1:2). Observe the holy boldness with which he declines to relieve the Lord of the responsibility for the people He has chosen. He begs Him to consider that they are still His, and that He cannot thus break His covenant. What startling faith! And how God honors it! "The Angel" that shall go with them is the Angel of His presence (Is. 63:9).

And what greater boon does Moses ask (18)? Murphy has an excellent paragraph on this verse, quoted here in full:

"To show mercy and yet do justly, to magnify grace and holiness at the same time, to bestow a perpetuity of blessing on a people wavering now and again into disobedience, was a problem that seemed to task the highest intelligence, to transcend the ordinary ways of providence, and call into exercise some inner and higher reaches of the eternal mind. Moved by a wish to do his duty with intelligence, Moses desires some insight into this mystery. Feeling that it touches the very center of the divine nature, involves the sublimest manifestations of His glory, his last and grandest petition is: 'Show me now Thy glory.' "

And from this point of view what is God's glory (10)? An expansion of this thought is found in the next chapter. What necessary limitation must be laid upon Moses in the answer to his request (20)? The "face" of God means doubtless His essential self, the sight of which would be irresistible or insupportable to a finite being tainted with guilt as man is. But His "back" is His averted self, that mediate manifestation which a man may see and still live (23).

3. Moses' Vision of the Glory of God, 34:1-10.

Moses now returns to the mount (2). What is he to prepare and take with him (1)? Who prepared the former tables which Moses broke? (Compare 31:18.) What prohibition is laid upon him in this instance (3)?

Note carefully the proclamation of God's glory in seven characteristics, "three pairs referring to His mercy and a single one affirming His justice" (6, 7).

If God "will by no means clear the guilty," how can He at the same time forgive "iniquity, transgression and sin"? Only as the guilt falls on a voluntary and accepted substitute. A substitute accepted by God in the first instance, and humbly and penitently received by the sinner when revealed to him. It is this which gives meaning to all the Levitical sacrifices of which we are soon to learn more and which typify the person and work of Him whom God had in mind from all eternity as the bearer of human guilt—His Son, Jesus Christ, our Lord.

How is Moses affected by what he sees and hears (8)? In what terms does he repeat his intercession for the people (9)? How does he identify himself with them?

Is Moses' prayer heard, and the covenant fully renewed (10)? What promise accompanies it?

4. Moses' Face Reflecting the Vision of God, 34:11-35.

The first part of this section is occupied with the repetition and enforcement of certain admonitions; (a) concerning entangling alliances with the idolatrous nations of Canaan (11-17), and (b) concerning the observance of the feasts (18-26). Note especially the obligation imposed on the males in v. 23, and the provision for their comfort in the promises in v. 24, last half. Note further the second command to Moses to "write" what he had heard (27). This writing doubtless includes the record of his present interview with God, but from Deut. 10:4 we learn that it was God Himself who wrote the ten commandments again on the two tables which Moses had prepared.

How is Moses' appearance described in v. 29? The word "shone" might be rendered "sent forth beams" or "horns," which explains why some of the old artists show Moses with horns of light. How did this extraordinary lustre affect the people (30)? How is the word "till" of v. 33 translated in the Revised Version? What a conspicuous sign this was of Moses' acceptance with God and his authority over the people! And how it must have demonstrated to the latter their utter unpreparedness as yet for any higher manifestations of the divine glory than what they had already received. Compare 2 Cor. 3:7-18, in the Revised Version.

THE TABERNACLE ERECTED

Chapters 35-40

The closing chapters of this book give in detail the execution of the plan of the Tabernacle previously revealed. In the first we are told of the offerings the people made for the work, in the next four the progress of the building is recorded, and in the last we have the completion and acceptance of the whole on God's part.

Note (1) that an important principle in the gifts was the willingness of those who gave (35:5); (2) the women contributed as well as the men (35:22); (3) their liberality exceeded the necessity (36:5, 6); (4) the sum total was very large (38:24-29), so large, that although the people were laborers in Egypt for the most part, yet they must have had much wealth. We should remember, too, the contribution the Egyptians made to them as they departed.

When was the Tabernacle to be set up (40:1, 2)? How long was this after they had left Egypt (5:17)? In what manner did God set His seal of approval on the work (40:34)? What indicates that the cloud now rested permanently on the Tabernacle (40:36)?

LEVITICUS

INTRODUCTORY

1. The Place and Plan of the Book.

How does the opening verse of this book show its close connection with the preceding book? This connection is seen among all the books of the Pentateuch, and not only shows that they are placed in proper order for an intelligent grasp of their history and meaning, but also that their spiritual use and purpose should be apprehended in the same order.

As Hubert Brooke suggests, they form the A B C of religious knowledge. Genesis represents the first lesson of man's lost estate, Exodus unfolds the second step of the divine redemption and way of salvation, while Leviticus provides the immediate consequence of those two steps in the revelation of God's way of holiness and communion.

Mr. Brooke truly says that the practical purpose of Leviticus can never be tested in any life unless the lessons of Genesis and Exodus have been mastered. Only as we learn that we are lost souls do we desire redemption, which is the central topic of Exodus following the revelation of the former in Genesis. And so is the next step as personal as these two. When the lesson of Exodus is experienced, when God's redemption is yours, and you thus are His, then only are you prepared for the lesson of Leviticus. This book is entirely occupied with the condition of those who are redeemed and brought nigh to God, and for all others it is a closed book so far as its spiritual apprehension is concerned.

2. The Divine Authority of the Book.

How does the first verse show the divine authority of what follows? And also the human authorship?

There are twenty-seven chapters in this book, and in these chapters a similar formula to that employed in v. 1 recurs fifty-four times. How does this strengthen the claim of the Mosaic authorship of Leviticus? In deed, while all Scripture is given by inspiration of God yet this portion of it records more of the exact words of God than any other in the Bible.

Of course it is not necessary to affirm that Moses wrote absolutely every word as we now have it, and we may admit that different sections of the book may have been combined in their present form by inspired men at a later day. But nevertheless in a true and proper sense Moses is the human author. Observe how Christ corroborates this statement in Matt. 8:4, compared with Leviticus 14:3, 10; and John 7:22, 23 compared with Leviticus 12:3.

3. The Meaning of the Book for Israel.

It is not to be supposed that Israel understood the full significance of Leviticus as we understand it. Its meaning or purpose for them was, as Kellogg says, "to furnish a code of laws for their well-being, physical, moral and spiritual, and to prepare them for the coming of the Messiah."

If Israel was to be a blessing to all the other nations, as we have seen, then Israel must for this purpose be separated from all the other nations. This separation was to be effected by a revelation to her of the holiness of God, and this revelation is made in the system of sacrifices which Leviticus reveals, as well as in the precepts of the law, and the enactment of penalties.

The way Israel was to be prepared for the Messiah was by suggesting to her the thought of redemptive mercy to be revealed, which was suggested by the conviction that the blood of bulls and goats never could remove sin (Heb. 10:4). In the interpretation of this book we are always to distinguish between its historical intention for Israel and its typical meaning for us.

4. The Meaning of the Book for Us.

This book is of great value to Christians, containing five distinct revelations of the first importance, Kellogg defines them: (a) the character of God; (b) the fundamental conditions of true religion; (c) the principles that should guide human legislators; (d) the work of Christ; (e) the prophecies in types of things to come in the kingdom of Christ.

It reveals the character of God by showing us His holiness, His intolerance of sin, and His mercy to the penitent.

It teaches us the fundamental truths of true religion by showing the need of a mediator with a propitiatory sacrifice for (Heb. 9:22).

It reveals the right principles of human legislation concerning civil government and religion, capital and labor, landholding, the social evil and cognate matters.

It reveals the work of Christ by exhibiting the way of salvation through atonement, and showing the present and future position of the believer in His name. In this book Christ is the offerer of sacrifice, He is the offering, and He the priest or mediator who presents the offering. Thus, as Jukes affirms, Leviticus reveals the work of Christ differently from any other Old Testament book.

How wonderful as we thus think of Christ in this threefold way! As the offerer He is the one who became man to meet God's requirements. As the offering He is the victim in His character and work, by which atonement was made for man. As the priest He is the officially appointed intercessor who brings man to God.

Finally, this book reveals things to come in the kingdom of Christ by showing us in the Day of Atonement (c. 16) a type of the entering into the heavens of our great High Priest. In the feast of trumpets we have His coming again and the ingathering of the full harvest of redemption. In the sabbatic and jubilee years we have foreshadowed the millennial blessing which follows His second coming.

5. The Outline of the Book

Leviticus might be called the book of the laws—not law, but laws. The whole of the Pentateuch (the first five books of the Bible) is called "The Book of the Law." But Leviticus is distinctly the book of the laws, in that it gives laws in detail for the government of the priests in the regulation of the morals and worship of the people.

With this thought in mind, the following is a suggested outline of the book:

1. The law of the offerings, 1 to 7.

2. The law of the priests, 8 to 10.

3. The law of purity, 11 to 15.

4. The law of the Day of Atonement, 16.

5. The law of holiness, 17 to 22.

6. The law of the feasts, 23.

7. The law of the sabbatic year and the jubilee, 25.—*Synthetic Bible Studies.*

Questions.

1. State the spiritual and evangelical relations of the first three books of the Bible.

2. To what class of persons does the spiritual teaching of Leviticus apply?

3. What distinction has this book with reference to the doctrine of inspiration?

4. What was its historical application to Israel?

5. How was God's holiness impressed on the nation?

6. How was she prepared for the coming of the Messiah?

7. What distinctive value has this book for Christians?

8. How does it reveal Christ?

9. How does it reveal things to come?

10. Can you name the seven great "laws" it contains.

THE BURNT OFFERING

CHAPTER 1

There are five offerings in cc. 1 to 7, and these five include all the offerings and sacrifices referred to in the history of Israel. It will simplify matters if we remember this. Sometimes offerings are presented for the priest himself, sometimes for the nation, a ruler of the nation, or a common individual; sometimes the offering is a bullock, sometimes a sheep, a goat, a turtle dove, or a pigeon; but in any case, it is always one of these five offerings. In c. 7, for example, reference is made to offerings for vows, thanksgiving offerings and voluntary offerings, but these are all simply different aspects of one of the five, namely, the trespass offering.

It should not be supposed, that these offerings in themselves satisfied God (Heb. 10:4), but their importance lay in what they symbolized, namely, the person and work of the Lord Jesus Christ.

These five offerings, again, may be divided into three kinds. The first two (that is, the burnt and the meal offerings) are forms of dedication by which the surrender of the offerer to God's perfect service is expressed. The third (the peace offering) is really an offering of thanksgiving by which the offerer expresses his praise to God and communion with Him. The last two (the sin and the trespass offerings) are those of expiation, and deal with the removal of sin and pardon of its guilt.

The order in which these five are revealed here is not that in which Israel presented them, but in their actual use the sin and trespass offerings came first. Then in the consciousness that sin was put away and pardon secured through those offerings the burnt and meal offerings followed, by which their desire to devote themselves to God wholly for His service was expressed. Lastly, in the peace of a cleansed conscience and a surrendered life the peace offering was presented, expressing fellowship and communion with God. See 2 Chron. 29:21-31 for an illustration of the order in which the offerings were presented. (*Hubert Brooke.*)

The Burnt Offering

Which offering is first referred to (3)? It is probably called the burnt offering from a Hebrew word which means "that which ascends." It is distinguished from the other offerings, in that the whole of it was consumed upon the altar, and none of it was eaten by either the offerer or the priest. The typical significance of this, to quote Kellogg, is as follows: (a) it acknowledged God's claim for the perfect services and entire devotedness of the offerer; (b) it acknowledged that the offerer was destitute of that service and devotedness, and hence presented a substitute in his stead; (c) it acknowledged that the absence of this service and devotedness involved guilt and deserved death, hence the slaying of the substitute; (d) it acknowledged that because no such service and devotedness was found in the offerer he needed an offering to be wholly accepted in his place as a sweet savor to God.

How is the acknowledgment of (d) expressed in the first specification of the burnt offering (3)? What class of victim is referred to here? O what sex and quality must it be? We thus see that God claims the best as to strength, energy and perfectness (compare Mal. 1:8, 13). Christ is the only and absolutely perfect One.

What other kinds of victims might be used in the burnt offerings (10, 14)? It is difficult to say why these varieties were permitted. Some think they represent consideration for the poor who might be unable to present those more costly; others say they represent different aspects of Christ, as (for example) service in the case of the bullock, submission in the case of the lamb, mourning innocence in the case of the dove: while others that they represent different degrees of faith or apprehension of Christ on the part of believers, some being more feeble than others in their apprehension of Christ, having only a partial recognition of what He has done or what He is to them.

The Ritual of the Burnt Offering.

Seven features constitute the ritual of the burnt offering, as follows:

The presentation, v. 3.

The laying on of hands, v. 4.

The slaying of the victim, v. 5

The sprinkling of the blood, v. 5.

The separating of the pieces, v. 6.

The washing of the pieces, v. 9.

The burning of the whole, v. 9.

Concerning the presentation, who was obliged to make it (2)? That the offerer should do this was doubtless to represent his individual confession of his need, his individual acceptance of God's way of salvation, and his individual recognition of the excellency of his offering. The Revised Version adds a thought to v. 3 namely, that the offerer is to present his offering in order that *he may be accepted.* In other words, it is not enough for a man to praise God, or even seek to serve Him, until he first is accepted before God, and for this acceptance of himself he requires a propitiatory offering. God is thus satisfied by the perfectness in the offering. In the sin offering the atonement is for sin and not acceptance, but here in the burnt offering the worshiper comes without sin. That, therefore, which he offers is received as a sweet savor by the Lord (Eph. 5:2), and on the ground of it the service of the offerer is received. Note, where the offering was to be presented, namely, at the door of the Tabernacle. This not only to guard against idolatry in groves, or to compel men to worship as God appointed, but to provide for publicity. See Matt. 10:32; Ro. 10:9, 10.

The laying on of hands (4) is instructive. The act implied the identification of the offerer with the offering not only, but also the transfer to it of his obligation of guilt to it as his substitute. What expression in this verse proves that the offering was in his stead? Compare Lev. 16:21; Numbers 8-11, R. V.; 1 Peter 1:24.

Who should kill the victim, the offerer or the priest (5)? The fact that the offerer did this signifies each individual's responsibility for his own sin.

But who sprinkled the blood? That the priest should do this shows us Jesus presenting our offering of Himself before God.

The flaying and cutting were done by the offerer (6). Some would say that this was to render the parts more convenient for burning, but others that it signifies a minute appreciation on the part of the offerer of the excellency of his offering. The application of this to the believer on Christ is clear.

The burning of the whole is important, since it signifies the ascending of the offering in consecration to God, and His acceptance of it (9:24). As He taught the Israelites that complete consecration to God is essential to right worship, so He teaches us that Christ represented us in perfect consecration and surrender (John 17:19; Ro. 5:19; Heb. 10:5-10). He died that we might not die, but it does not follow that since He was consecrated for us we need not be consecrated. This will be referred to later, but just now examine Ro. 12:1.

Questions.

1. How many offerings are included in "the Law of the Offerings"?

2. What do they symbolize?

3. Name them, and describe their meaning.

4. In what order did Israel present them?

5. What spiritual acknowledgments were involved in the burnt offering?

6. Name the seven features of its ritual.

7. State the spiritual significance of the presentation.

8. Do the same for the laying on of hands.

9. Who killed the victim, and what did it signify?

10. What was signified by the burning?

THE MEAL AND PEACE OFFERINGS

CHAPTERS 2-3

The Meal Offering, c. 2.

We call the second offering the "meal" instead of the meat offering, following the Revised Version. The burnt and meal offerings really belong together. They are both offerings of consecration, and when the one was presented the other followed as a kind of appendage (see Lev. 23:12, 13, 18; Num. 28:7-15; Judges 13:19; Ezra 7:17; etc.)

We have seen that the burnt offering was entirely consumed upon the altar as expressive of the entire consecration of the one who offered it, and God's acceptance of it as a sweet savor to Him. In this it typifies Christ who is the only perfect life of consecration, and who has been accepted by God on behalf of all who put their faith in Him. This aspect of the sacrifice of Christ is indicated in Eph. 5:2 and John 6:38.

The meal offering, composed mainly of fine flour, is generally taken to represent a consecrated life in its use for mankind, since flour is the universal food of man. It is a fact that God habitually uses for His service among men the lives and powers of those who are truly dedicated to Him, and this seems expressed in the fact that the burnt offering always had the meal offering attached to it. Our Lord's life represents this consecration in such places as Matt. 10:28 and Acts 10:38, and is a consecration to God for the service of mankind, which He offered and God accepted on behalf of all who put their faith in Him.

Varieties in the Offering.

It will be seen that there are certain varieties of the meal offering. The first is referred to in vv. 1-3, whose substance was fine flour, oil and frankincense. What parts and portion of the offering was to be taken out by the offerer to be presented unto the Lord (2)? To whom did the remainder belong for their use (3)?

The second is referred to in vv. 4-10, and contains the same substance except the frankincense, the distinction being that the offering is baked in the oven, or in a pan, and the priest rather than the offerer removes the Lord's portion.

The third is alluded to in vv. 14-16, and consists of what substance? How was it to be prepared? What is included in this class which was omitted from the second class?

In vv. 11-13 reference is made to articles that were prohibited from the meal offering, and one was particularly prescribed. Name those prohibited, and that prescribed? Leaven and honey represent decay and corruption, the first-named being the type of evil recognized as such, and the second, evil that is unrecognized because it has earthy sweetness in it. Both kinds of evil were absent in Jesus Christ, and the perfection of the type necessitates their absence in it. As to salt, it is the symbol of incorruption (Matt. 5:13; Mark 9:50).

Taking the offering as a whole, it may be said to symbolize His fulfilment on our behalf of the second table of the law, just as the burnt offering symbolizes His fulfilment on our behalf of the first table. Of course, in fulfilling the first He fulfilled the second, but in the burnt offering the one thought predominates and in the meal offering the other thought. To quote Moorehead: "In the burnt offering Christ is, representatively, man satisfying God and giving Him what belongs to Him, while in the meal offering He is, representatively, man satisfying man and giving him what belongs to him as an offering to the Lord. The burnt offering represents His life Godward, and the meal offering His life manward."

The Peace Offering, c. 3.

The data for the law of the peace offering are found by comparing c. 3 with the following passages: 7:11-34; 19:5-8; 22:21-25. We put them all together, in this lesson that the student may obtain a complete view of the whole. There are certain features of this offering which differ from the others:

(1) The objects offered. The peace offering might be a female (1), the explanation for which may be that the effects of the atonement are contemplated rather than the act itself. Furthermore, no turtle dove or pigeon was permitted, the explanation for which may be that as the offering was connected with a sacrificial meal of which several partook, a small bird would be insufficient.

(2) The Lord's portion consisted chiefly of the fat (3-5), the richest portion, symbolizing that the best belongs to Him. Kellogg calls attention to the fact that the eating of the fat of all animals was not prohibited, but only those used in sacrifice, and in these only when they were being so used. The prohibition of the eating of blood, however, applied to all animals and always (17:10-12). The peace offering was to be consumed *upon* the burn offering (5), thus symbolizing that the peace it typified was grounded upon the fact of atonement and acceptance on the part of the offerer. The peace offering usually followed the meal offering (see the details in the dedication of Aaron, c. 8, and those of the Day of Atonement, c. 16).

(3) By turning to 7:28-34 it will be seen that certain parts of the peace offering belonged to the priests. The waving of these parts back and forth, and the heaving of them up and down, were a token of their dedication to God first and their being received back again from Him by the priests.

By comparison of 7:15, 22:29-30 and parallel places, it will be seen that the offerer himself had for his portion all that remained. It also will be seen that he was at liberty to invite his friends to the feast, which must always be eaten at the sanctuary and which was an occasion of joy (Deut. 12:4-7, 17, 18). The only condition for partaking of the feast was that of ceremonial cleanness (7:20, 21).

The Significance of the Offering.

The meaning of "peace" in this case includes not only tranquility of mind based on a cessation of hostilities (that is, a mere negative peace), but positive joy and prosperity. Quoting Moorehead, three propositions define it: "Peace *with* God, Ro. 5:1; the peace *of* God, Phil. 4:7; and peace *from* God, 1 Cor. 1:3, conceived of as flowing into our hearts."

The feast, therefore, is an expression of friendship and fellowship growing out of the fact that the breach between man and God has been healed by His grace. The Israelite, who represents the Christian saint, is seen to be enjoying a feast with God, where God Himself is the host rather than the offerer. God first accepts the victim in expiation of sin and then gives it back for the worshiper to feast upon with Himself. Moreover, the feast is held in God's house, not in that of the offerer, emphasizing the fact that God is the host. Of course Christ is the offering represented here, whose blood is shed for our guilt and to bring us into reconciled relation with God, and who Himself then becomes the meat by which we who are reconciled are thereafter sustained (John 6:51-58).

Keep in mind that this is a *joint* repast in which all three partake. God, the priest and the offerer. It therefore represents our fellowship with the Father, and with His Son Jesus Christ (1 John 1:3). Remember also that cleanness is the condition (1 John 1:9). An Israelite might remain such and be unclean, but he could hold no feast and enjoy no communion with God while in that condition. The application to Christians is very plain (1 Peter 1:13-16).

Questions.

1. By what name is the first of these offerings known in the King James Version?

2. Give the distinction between the burnt and meal offering as to the scope of consecration.

3. What do honey and leaven symbolize?

4. Where was the peace offering consumed and why?

5. What did the waving and heaving mean?

6. What is the meaning of peace in this case?

7. What is the idea of the peace offering?

8. Can you quote 1 John 1:3?

SIN AND TREASPASS OFFERINGS

CHAPTERS 4-7

The Sin Offering.

The data for the sin offering will be found in 4:1-35, 5:1-13 and 6:24-30.

1. As to the *name* of this offering, it will be seen that "sin" is mentioned here for the first time in connection with the law of the offerings. The *idea* of sin is included in the others, but it was not the predominating idea as it is here. There was atonement for sin in the other offerings, but rather for sin in man's nature than the actual transgression in his life, while here the latter is brought into view. In Hebrew the same word applies for "sin" and "sin offering" as though the two were completely identified, or as though the offering were so charged with sin as to itself become sin. In this connection read Ro. 8:3, 2 Cor. 5:21 and Gal. 3:14 to see how this was also true in our substitute, Jesus Christ. Another matter of interest is that while the preceding offerings were all known more or less in other nations and before the time of Moses, this offering is entirely new and original with Israel. This shows that Israel enters on a new stage of existence in the sense that as a nation she has a truer conception of sin and the need of expiation than the other nations that received no special revelation from God.

For evidence that the other offerings existed before Moses and were not confined to Israel compare Gen. 31:54; Ex. 18:12; 32:6, 1 Cor. 10:6, etc. Kellogg, remarks that this should strengthen our faith as showing man's natural sense of spiritual need and desire for fellowship with God, and also as pointing back to an original revelation from God to man on the whole subject. God thus seems to have based the Mosaic ordinances upon His earlier revelations to man, correcting them where they had been corrupted, and adding to them where it was necessary to the progress of revealed truth.

2. Passing from the name of this offering to its *nature*, what kind of sin is referred to in 4:2? This shows that while ignorance might palliate it could not remove the guilt of sin; sin is sinful whether it be recognized by the sinner or not, and requires atonement just the same. Compare Ps. 19:12; 1 Cor. 4:4, R. V.

3. Observe the *different sections* of this law. What class of persons are first referred to in (3-12)? After the priests, who are mentioned (13-21)? The congregation of Israel means the nation. What is the third class specified (22-26)? The fourth class (4:27 to 5:13)? In c. 5 prescriptions were made for the common people (a) as to the nature of the offense (1-5) and (b) as to the nature of the offerings (6-13). In regard to these the higher the rank of the offerer the more costly must be his offering, expressing that guilt is proportionate to privilege (compare 1 Kings 11:9; James 3:1). Note the responsibility for sin on the part of whole communities (compare here Ps. 2; Rev. 2 and 3). It is just as important to note also that no one can be overlooked, however obscure. God demands from and provides an offering for the poorest and the neediest (5:11-13).

4. In this offering, where was the victim to be burned (12-21)? To make the burning without the camp more distinct from that of the altar, another Hebrew word is used (compare in this case Heb. 13:10-13). The burning on the altar symbolizes the full surrender to and the acceptance by God of the offerer, while the burning without the camp sym-

bolizes the sacrifice for the sin of the world on the part of Him who was "despised and rejected of men."

The Trespass Offering.

1. The facts associated with the trespass offering are found in 5:14 to 6:7 and 7:1-10. It is hard to distinguish between the sin and trespass offerings because they almost necessarily overlap. "Trespass" means an invasion of the rights of others (compare Josh. 7:1; 2 Chron. 28:20-22) and there are those who distinguish between the two offerings by saying that the sin offering represents sin as a principle, and the trespass offering sin as an act. Penalty is prominent in the first, and reparation or restitution in the second. Both find their fulfilment in Christ, who not only bore the penalty of but redressed every claim which God had upon the sinner.

The trespass offering had reference only to the sin of an individual and not the nation, as only an individual perhaps could make reparation. The victim in this case was the same for the poor as for the rich, a ram of the flock, indicating possibly that the obligation to repair the wrong cannot be modified to suit the condition of the offerer. Furthermore, notice that anything unjustly taken must not only be restored but a fifth must be added. In other words, no advantage must be gained by the trespass. Thus if the sin offering called for faith the trespass offering called for repentance. It is blessed to know that in our Lord Jesus Christ both God and man received back more than they lost.

2. There appear to be *two distinct sections* of this law of trespass offering. The first refers to trespass in the holy things of the Lord (5:14-19), and the second to trespass on the rights of man (6:1-7). By the "holy things of the Lord" are meant—the eating unwittingly of the flesh of the firstling of one's cattle, or using one's tithe or any part of it for himself (compare Mal. 3:8, 10). The trespass on the rights of man

included embezzlement, robbery, fraud, falsehood, etc. The order of proceeding in the latter instance was : (a) to confess the wrong, (b) to make restitution and add one fifth, (3) to bring the guilt offering to God.

How comforting to know that Christ is the great antitype of all these offerings so far as we are concerned, that is, we who have believed on Him as our Saviour and confessed Him as our Lord!

He is our burnt and meal offering in the sense that He is our righteousness. In Him we are fully surrendered to and accepted by God. He is our peace offering in the sense that in Him our life is in perfect fellowship with God. He is our sin offering, the One who has fully borne our sin, expiating our guilt. Finally, He is our trespass offering, rendering perfect satisfaction unto God and making reparation for all our offences against Him in the completest and to the fullest extent.

Questions.

1. What view of sin is emphasized in the sin offering?

2. What peculiarity lies in the Hebrew word in this case?

3. What peculiarity is found in the history of the offering itself?

4. Is sin which is unrecognized sinful?

5. What is symbolized by "burning without the camp"?

6. Define the word "trespass."

7. Distinguish the sin and trespass offering.

8. For what spiritual exercise did the trespass offering especially call?

9. Describe how Christ is represented by these offerings.

10. Have you received Him as your substitute Saviour?

THE OTHER SIDE OF THE OFFERINGS

CHAPTERS 4-7

In the lessons on the offerings we have seen what Christ is to us and what He has done for us as symbolized in them, but before we pass from the subject it might be well to touch on the response which the work of Christ should awaken in our hearts.

In Brooke's *Studies in Leviticus* he quotes the following collect from the liturgy of the Church of England:

"Almighty God, who hast given Thine only Son to be unto us both a sacrifice for sin and also an example of godly life, give us grace that we may always most thankfully receive that His inestimable benefit, and also daily endeavor ourselves to follow the blessed steps of His most holy life."

This expresses the two ways in which the lessons from the offerings should be applied by Christians.

We need to "always most thankfully receive His inestimable benefit." In other words, we must by faith accept Christ as our five-fold offering, on the basis of which alone we are saved and have our standing before God. Morning by morning as we awaken let it be with the consciousness that in the burnt offering and meat offering of Christ we are accepted and blessed of God, that in His peace offering we have the right to commune with Him, that through His sin and trespass offering every defect is remedied and every fault will find pardon.

But then let us remember that we should "also daily receive ourselves to follow the blessed steps of His most holy life." After we have accepted Him and represented Him to God as our sacrifice by faith, then we can follow His example. But we are not in a position to do this before. If He is our example, as the author we are quoting says, then we may expect to find Him so in relation to each form of offering or sacrifice in which He has been revealed to us.

He is our burnt offering, a perfect dedication to God, but are we not also bidden in Him to present our bodies a living sacrifice, holy, acceptable unto God, which is our reasonable service (Ro. 12:1)? He is our meal offering, presented to God for the service of man, but we too are

"every one of us to please his neighbor for his good to edification" (Ro. 15:2). He is our peace offering, making and maintaining peace between God and us, but we are to be peacemakers, not in the sense in which He alone is our peacemaker but in that human sense in which we can bring man and man together and so be called "the children of God." He is our sin and trespass offering, and in this too we may follow His example. It is impossible that we should make atonement for sin as He did, but there is a sense in which we may "bear one another's burdens and so fulfill the law of Christ" (Gal. 6:2).

In other words, our lives are to reflect what we have received and are receiving from Christ, a surrendered will, a loving walk, a life of blessing, a heart of compassion, a spirit of patience. So, "with open face beholding as in a glass the glory of the Lord, we are changed into the same image from glory to glory as by the Spirit of the Lord" (2 Cor. 3:18).

STRANGE FIRE AND ITS CONSEQUENCES

Chapters 8-9

In an earlier lesson the present chapters were outlined as "The Law of the Priests," though we might better have said, "The Law of the Consecration of the Priests." And yet in either case the phrase must be used in an accommodated sense, since we are not here dealing with the law itself but with the initial execution of the law in the consecration of Aaron and his sons. The law itself was considered in the Book of Exodus, for which reason we may pass over cc. 8 and 9 of the present lesson, the contents of which were sufficiently dealt with at that time.

The Aaronic Line.

Before taking up c. 10, however, let us consider the history of the priesthood which begins here.

The priesthood was originally appointed to remain in Aaron's family through all generations, and no other could intrude into that office. Aaron was succeeded by Eleazar, his elder surviving son after the death of Nadab and Abihu, and the priesthood continued in his family through seven generations, until the time of Eli, named in the earlier chapters of First Samuel.

Because of the wickedness of Eli's sons the priesthood was removed from that branch of the family and given to the descendants of Ithamar, Aaron's other son; but in the time of Solomon it returned again to the line of Eleazar (1 Kings 2:27), in whose line it continued until the Babylonian captivity.

After the return of the Jews from captivity Joshua, the first high priest, was of the same family, but subsequent to his time the appointment became uncertain and irregular, and after Israel became a Roman province no regard was paid to this part of the original institution. As a matter of fact, the office became so desecrated in the corruption of later times, that it was often sold to the highest bidder, whether of the family of Aaron or not. This was the case a long while before the coming of Christ (Bush).

What part the Aaronic line will play on the future return of the Jews to their land and their form of worship we cannot say, but there is reason to believe that in the millennial age God may restore it for the execution of His purposes through Israel in that dispensation.

1. The Evil Conduct of Aaron's Sons, 10:1-7.

Resuming here the text of the lesson, what was it that Nadab and Abihu did (1)? What was the immediate consequence (2)? How did Moses explain this awful circumstance (3)? and what was its effect on Aaron? What prohibition of mourning was laid on him and his remaining sons (6)? and what further command, and why (7)?

"To understand the death of Aaron's sons, notice the last verse of c. 9, which speaks of the sacri-

fice on the brazen altar in the outer court and holy fire from the Lord consuming it. It was this fire that consumed the sacrifice, which should have been employed in the censers to burn the incense before the Lord. Nadab and Abihu neglected this, and offered strange fire, and were instantly slain."

This looks like a terrible punishment for a slight offence. But the offence was not slight. It was a flagrant disobedience of a plain command, several commands, in short. Not only did they disobey in the matter of the fire (16:12), but also in performing an office which belonged only to the high priest, for, as some think, they went into the holy of holies. And two went in where only one was permitted. Furthermore, the offence was committed at a critical moment in the history of the people, at the beginning of their covenant relationship with God. It suggests a somewhat similar occurrence in the opening era of the Church, Acts 5:1, 3. In both cases a signal manifestation of the divine displeasure was necessary for the sake of impressing the lesson upon the whole nation in the one case and the whole Church in the other.

It need not be supposed that this punishment involved the eternal loss of the souls of these men. That question need not be raised in this connection. It was a case of God's judging in the midst of His people, not a case of His actings among "them that are without." It affords a solemn warning, however, to any within the visible church who would depart in worship from the plain revelation of God, and to any without who would seek to approach Him in some other way than the prescribed one (John 14:6; Acts 4:12).

2. The Prohibition of Strong Drink, 10:8-11.

From what are the priests to be prohibited, and when (10, 11)? To quote Kellogg: "It is natural to infer from this that the offence of Aaron's sons was occasioned by strong drink such as made it possible for impulse to get the better of judgment, from which we learn that it is not enough for the Christian to abstain from what is in its own nature sinful, but also from that which may heedlessly become an occasion of sin."

3. The Renewed Warning, 10:12-20.

The substance of these verses has been considered in a previous lesson, but in view of the occurrence of this day Moses is moved to renew the charge to Aaron and his sons upon the matter.

The explanation of the closing verses seems to be like this: On this day of special privilege when they had performed their priestly duties for the first time, God's name had been profaned by the will-worship of Nadab and Abihu, and the wrath of God had broken out against them and their father's house. Could it then be the will of God that a house in which such guilt was found should yet partake of the holy things in the sanctuary? In other words, Aaron and his remaining sons had been so awakened in their consciences as to the holiness of God and their own inborn evil that they associated themselves with Nadab and Abihu as under the displeasure of God. Thus, although they had disobeyed the law in the letter (16-18) yet their offence grew out of a misunderstanding and showed how deeply they had been moved by the judgment that had fallen upon them (Kellogg). What was the result of their explanation upon the spirit of Moses (20)?

Questions.

1. Can you rehearse the history of the priesthood to the time of the capitivity?

2. What do you know about it subsequent thereto?

3. What do you understand by the "strange fire"?

4. What was the real nature of the offence of Aaron's sons?

5. What may have been the extent of their punishment?

6. What lessons does it teach us?

7. How do Aaron and his remaining family express a sense of their own responsibility for the offence of Nadab and Abihu?

WHAT TO EAT AND WHAT NOT TO EAT

CHAPTER 11

We begin at this chapter the consideration of that section of the book previously designated as "The Law of the Clean and Unclean."

Let us gather the facts by a series of questions, and then seek to learn what they mean. Read the verses and answer the questions, for that is the only way to approach a mastery of the lesson.

How is "beasts" translated in the R. V.? What creatures might Israel eat (3)? What exceptions were made (4-7)? How far did the prohibition extend (8)?

Of sea creatures what might be eaten (9)? How should others of them be regarded (12)? What were abominations among the fowls (13-20)? What might they eat of the fowls (21-22)?

And of the creeping creatures what were unclean (29-31)? How far did the uncleanness extend (32-35)? What exception in the case (36-37)? What reason is given for these prohibitions (44-45)?

Explanation and Application.

The laws are to be explained:

(1) On *hygienic* grounds, and as making for the physical well-being of the people. As a matter of fact, the Hebrews have always been marked by an immunity from sickness and especially infectious diseases as compared with other races.

This does not mean, however, that all nations are still subject to these laws. They were given to a people few in number, living in a small country, and under certain climatic conditions. But what is unwholesome as food in one part of the world may be the opposite in another, and hence when the Jewish religion is merged in the

Christian, and become world-wide these laws are abrogated (Acts 10:9-15; Gal. 4:1-3; Col. 2:20-22). The individual Christian is now left at liberty to exercise an enlightened judgment, under the law of love to Christ.

(2) On *spiritual* grounds, and as engraving on the mind an idea of holiness. From this point of view they are to be looked upon as the earlier laws touching the offerings and the priests. Each particular is so ordered as to reflect purity on all the rest, converging ray upon ray to bring out the great conception of what holiness is. Without these laws the world does not know the nature of holiness. It is an abstract quality which has no place in the thought of man except as derived from the outward separations, washings and consecrations of the Mosaic ritual. Holiness is not "wholeness" nor "entireness" merely, but an idea which signifies separation, higher qualities than common, devotion to sacred purposes, and then ultimately, wholeness in the sense of the moral purity—*Joseph A. Seiss, in Holy Types.*

This holiness has to do with the *body*, and through it with the soul. There is, therefore, no religion in neglecting the body and ignoring the requirements for its health. To do this is to sin and to come short of the law of holiness (1 Cor. 6:20, R. V.; 10:31).

(3) On *dispensational* grounds, and as preparing the nation for its share in the redemptive work of the earth. To execute its mission Israel must be kept distinct from other nations, "fenced in and barricaded against inroads of idolatry," which was accomplished by this system of religious dietetics. The difference between them was thus ever-present to their minds, touching at almost every point of every day life. Other peoples, like the Mohammedans have had such distinctions more or less, and it is stated that wherever they have been rigidly enforced as a part of a religious system the people in question have never changed their religion. We all know how it has been a wall of exclusion to the orthodox Jews which has withstood all the changes of these more than three millenniums.

(4) On *symbolic* grounds the flesh of certain animals being forbidden because typifying by their character certain sins and vices, while others, permitted as food, typified certain moral virtues. Hence the law was a "perpetual acted allegory" reminding Israel to abstain from these sins in the one case, and to practise those virtues in the other.

"The beastliness of sin" is a common expression, and God has suggested it in these laws. The sinner—and we are all sinners by nature—is unclean, filthy, disagreeable, noxious, *brutish.* Thank God, that although our uncleanness is intense, mercy holds out to us, and indicates typically in this chapter, a means of complete and eternal deliverance!

Questions.

1. Name four grounds on which the laws in this chapter may be explained.

2. Are these laws binding on us all in the same sense?

3. How have they worked out practically in the history of the Hebrews?

4. What is Scriptural holiness?

5. Quote 1 Corinthians 6:20 in the Revised Version.

SIN AT THE FOUNTAINHEAD

Chapter 12

What period of uncleanness followed the birth of a male (2)? What transaction in his life took place on the 8th day (3)? How long was the period of the mother's purification (4)? What difference was there as to these two periods in the case of a female child (5)? What was required of the mother at the close of this period (6)? The reason for it (7)? How does v. 8, compare with Luke 2:24, point to the lowly condition of the mother of

Jesus as well as to her own need of a Saviour?

Explanation and Application.

The great principles underlying this chapter will come before us more definitely in chapter 15. The theme is the same there as here, and indeed throughout the whole section, viz: sin and its only remedy. Here, however, we have sin at its source, humanly speaking. Sin is not merely something which man takes outside of himself, but something which is a part of him. It belongs not to his nature as God made him, but to his nature as fallen and transmitted from Adam. Sin is here seen mingling with the transmission of life and tainting the vital forces as they descend from parent to child, and from generation to generation (Ps. 57:5). It is this awful truth that forms the subject of this chapter.

The mere physical uncleanness spoken of is not the real thing, but only ceremonial and typical. In other words, the regulations laid down are not for women everywhere and always, but as a figure for the time then present.

They impose a special legal disability on the woman because she was first in the transgression of Eden (1 Tim. 2:24), and show us that we all have come of sinful mothers and hence are ourselves sinful (Job 14:4). "In the birth of a child," says Kellogg, "the original curse against the woman is regarded by the law as reaching its fullest expression, for now by means of those powers given her for good and blessing she can bring into the world only the child of sin."

The Meaning of Circumcision.

We have learned that circumcision was not original with the Hebrews, being practiced by other nations in warm climates for hygienic reasons; but God adopted and constituted it in Abraham "a symbol of an analagous spiritual fact, viz: the purification of sin at its fountainhead, the cleansing of the evil nature with which we all are born." Read Col. 2:10, 11, the meaning of which is that there is no need of ritual circumcision for believers on Christ as they have the spiritual substance of it in Christ. Their circumcision is not made with hands, but is a spiritual thing, a real thing. It is "the putting off of the body of the flesh," the realization of that which the other symbolized. Not of the putting off of a part, but the nature itself. It took place when we were "buried with Him in the baptism," i.e., the baptism of the Holy Ghost, by which we were made one with Him so thoroughly that in God's sight we lay in the same grave, having died on Calvary in Him.

The Eighth Day.

The "eighth day" will be often met as we proceed, and needs to be recognized in its symbolic and prophetic significance.

The old creation was finished in six days with a following Sabbath, rendering six the number of the old creation as under imperfection and sin. But the eighth day, which is the first of a new week, appears everywhere in Scripture as symbolizing the new creation in which all things shall be restored in the redemption through the second Adam.

The thought finds its fullest expression in the resurrection of Christ as the Firstborn from the dead, the Beginning and the Lord of the new creation, who rose from the dead on the first day, on the day after the seventh, the eighth day.

This gives the key to the use of the number eight in the Mosaic symbolism.

With good reason, therefore, was circumcision ordered for the eighth day, as it symbolized the putting off of the old nature and the putting on of a new and purified nature in Christ (2 Cor. 5:17, R. V., margin).—*Hubert Brooke.*

Questions.

1. What is sin?
2. Quote Job 14:4.
3. What Christian fact is symbolized by circumcision?

4. What does the 8th day symbolize in Scripture?

5. Quote 2 Corinthians 5:17 in the Revised Version.

THE TYPICAL DISEASE

Chapters 13, 14

Here we have what appears like a treatise on leprosy, but it is not introduced simply for medical purposes. There were other diseases more serious, but this is singled out and made the subject of special regulations because of its typical character. It is a parable of sin, drawn by the divine hand, "of the workings, developments and effects of inborn depravity."

The disease is diagnosed under four heads: (1) leprosy rising spontaneously (1:17); (2) rising out of a boil (18:24); (3) out of a burn (24:28); (4) on the head or beard.

To take the first class: What symptoms are named in v. 2? Who is to deal with the case? How is the diagnosis to be confirmed (3)? In cases of doubt what must be done with the suspect (4-8)? What are the symptoms of an advanced case (9-11)? What further condition showed that it was not a genuine case of leprosy (12, 13)? What was necessary to prove its genuineness (14-17)?

What requirements were made of the leper (45, 46)? According to this, "he is to assume all the ordinary signs of mourning for the dead; he is to regard himself, and all others are to regard him, as dead. He is to be a continual mourner at his own funeral."

One might suppose the reason for this to be hygienic, and because of the contagious nature of the disease, but Kellogg finds it still deeper.

It is one of the principles of divine teaching that death is always connected with legal uncleanness. It is so connected because it is the extreme manifestation of the presence of sin in the race and of God's wrath against it. But all disease is a forerunner of death, an incipient dying, and thus a manifestation of the presence of sin working in the body through death.

Now it would be impracticable to have a law that *all* disease should render the sick person ceremonially unclean, but in order to keep the connection between the two, sin and disease, continually before Israel this one ailment which is a kind of living image of death was selected from all the others for the purpose. "It is the supreme type of sin, as seen by God."

Typical Features.

These are the typical features:

(1) Its extreme loathsomeness.

(2) Its insignificant and often even imperceptible beginning.

(3) Its progressiveness in the body.

(4) Sooner or later it affects the whole man.

(5) Its victim in process of time becomes insensible to his condition.

(6) It is hereditary in its nature.

(7) It is incurable by human means.

(8) It excludes from the fellowship of the holy people, and hence the fellowship of God.

1. The Cleansing of the Leper, 14:1-32.

Although leprosy was incurable by human remedies, yet it did not always continue for life. Sometimes, being sent as a special judgment from God, as in the case of Miriam, it ceased with the repentance and forgiveness of the offender. Indeed, the Jews generally looked upon it as a judgment, and its very name means "a stroke of the Lord." We know also of lepers healed by divine power in the Saviour's time and prior thereto.

In this connection it is noticeable that the regulations in this chapter were not for the *cure* of the leper but for his ceremonial cleansing *after* the cure, which agrees with Matt. 8:1-4. For this reason Seiss thinks these rites illustrate the nature of sanctification rather than justification, although the latter is also implied.

2. Leprosy in Garments and Houses, 13:47-59; 14:33-57.

It seems strange to read of disease in garments and houses? And yet Moses, by inspiration of God, was only a few thousand years ahead of the science of today which speaks so familiarly of germs, and bacilli, and other things of which the fathers never dreamed!

We now know that minute parasitic forms of vegetable life may exist and propagate themselves in other places besides the tissues of the human body. We are acquainted with mould and mildew, and know it to imply unhealthy conditions, and the leprosy in the present case may border thereon, though it be not the same thing.

The provision in these verses therefore was in the first place sanitary, and teaches how God cares not only for the souls but for the bodies of men and all their material surroundings.

But in the second place it was spiritual as in the other instances, teaching that the curse of sin and death was not only upon man but his environment; that sacrificial cleansing was as needful for the one as the other; that the atonement of Christ covered in some mysterious way not only animate but inanimate creation as well. Read Romans 8:18-23, and Peter 3:10-13.

Questions.

1. Of what is leprosy a type?
2. Name its typical features.
3. What is absolutely incurable?
4. What scientific fact in this lesson goes to prove the inspiration of the book?
5. Have you read the New Testament Scriptures referred to above?

THE GREAT DAY OF ATONEMENT

Chapter 16

When was the law of this chapter revealed to Moses (1)? This has led some to think that the chapter is misplaced and that it should follow chapter 10, an idea strengthened by the fact of its cutting into the middle of these laws concerning the clean and the unclean.

What prohibition is laid upon Aaron, and with what penalty (2)? Is there a suggestion here that the disobedience of Nadab and Abihu was aggravated by their entering into the Holy of Holies when they should not have done so?

With what sacrifices was Aaron to appear (3), and in what apparel (4)? What further ceremonial precaution must he take?

What is the offering for the people on this occasion (5-7)? What peculiarity is mentioned in this case (8-10)? What is the ceremony connected with the scape-goat (20-26)?

In what month, and on what day of the month were these ceremonies to occur (29)? What kind of a day was this to be (31)?

The Significance of It All.

This Day of Atonement was the most important in the whole Mosaic system of sacrifices, for then the idea of the removal of sin received its highest expression.

To illustrate: It must be that countless sins were committed by the people collectively and individually of which they were unaware, and which were not covered by any of the daily offerings. If, then, there were not some great act of atonement covering everything to the fullest extent, the sacrificial system had fallen short. To meet this the law of the Day of Atonement was instituted.

On this day atonement was made for Aaron and his house (6); the holy place and the tabernacle (15-17); the altar and the outer court (18, 19); and the whole congregation of Israel (20-22, 33); and this "for all their iniquities, and all their transgressions, even all their sins" (21); i. e., unknown to every one except God (compare Hebrews 9:7-9).

Notice further among other things, (1) that only the high

priest could officiate on this day (17); and (2) that he could do so only after certain specific preparations, among them the bathing of himself, the laying aside of the "garments for glory and beauty" and the donning of a vesture of unadorned white; (3) that he entered the Holy of Holies sprinkling the blood even on the mercy seat in that secret place where no other Israelite might tread. All these things impress us that the sin offering on this day, more than any other, symbolizes in the most perfect way the one offering of Christ who now appears in the presence of God for us.

The Scapegoat.

The significance of the scapegoat is difficult to determine. The Revised Version translates the word by the name "Azazel," whose meaning is not clear. Either it is a name of an evil spirit conceived of as dwelling in the wilderness, or else an abstract noun meaning "removal" or "dismissal," as indicated in the margin of the Revised Version.

If we take it in the latter sense, then the scapegoat may be regarded as bearing away all the iniquities of Israel, which are symbolically laid upon him, into a solitary place where they are forever away from the presence of God and the camp of his people. Thus, to quote Kellogg, as the killing and sprinkling of the first goat set forth the *means* of reconciliation with God, so the sending away of the second sets forth the *effect* of that sacrifice in the complete removal of those sins as already indicated (compare Ps. 103:12; Micah 7:19).

If, however, the word is taken as the name of a person, then the understanding would seem like this: Satan has a certain power over man because of man's sin (Heb. 2:14, 15; 1 Jo. 5:19, R. V.; Rev. 12:10). To this evil one, the adversary of God's people in all ages, the live goat was symbolically sent bearing on him the sins of Israel. These sins are considered as having been forgiven by God, by which it is symbolically announced to Satan that the

foundation of his power over Israel is gone. His accusations are now no longer in place, for the whole question of Israel's sin has been met and settled in the atoning blood.

Questions.

1. What makes the Day of Atonement the most important in the Mosaic system?

2. Can you quote verse 21?

3. How does the Revised Version translate "scapegoat?"

4. If the word be an abstract noun, how would you understand its meaning?

5. If the name of a person, how?

ABOMINATIONS UNTO THE LORD

CHAPTERS 17-19

The underlying thought of this section is in the words of 18:1-5. Israel is redeemed and separated unto God, therefore she is to live consistently with that fact in all her ways. She is not to do after the heathen peoples round about her.

1. The Question of Eating, c. 17.

It looks as though the opening injunction of this chapter touched once more upon the ceremonial and recurred to a matter considered under the offerings. But in that case the design was to prevent idolatry in connection with worship, and here to prevent it in connection with the preparation of food. It is to be remembered also, that these regulations were for the tent life in the wilderness, and were afterward repealed in Deut. 12:15-24, ere entering upon the settled habitation of Canaan.

The reasons for the prohibition of blood are clearly stated. It was the life of the flesh, and the symbol of that life which was substituted for the guilty in making atonement.

As to the first, modern science is illustrating its wisdom in teaching that the germs of infectious disease circulate in the blood. As to the second, the relation of the blood to the forgiveness of sins was thus always kept prominently before the mind of the people. There is a great lesson in this thought for us as well as them.

2. The Question of Chastity, c. 18.

All sexual relationship is prohibited as between a man and his mother; step-mother; sister; grand-daughter; step-sister; aunt; daughter-in-law; sister-in-law; a woman and her daughter or her grand-daughter; a wife's sister (while the wife is living); a woman at the time specified in v. 19; a neighbor's wife; another man; a beast. The Canaanites did these things, which explains their expulsion from their land; and these things were also common with the Egyptians among whom the Israelites had lived.

A few comments follow: For example, the law forbidding such relationship with a brother's wife (16), is qualified in Deut. 25:5-10, so far as to permit marriage with the widow of a deceased brother when the latter died without children, in order to perpetuate his family.

The reference to "Molech" in v. 21, grows out of the connection between some of the licentious practices just mentioned and the worship of the heathen god (compare 2 Kings 17:31; Jer. 7:31; 19:5). In that worship children were slain like beasts and offered in sacrifice to their god.

3. Contents of Chapter 19.

It is difficult to generalize in chapter 19, which seems to contain repetitions of laws already dealt with in other connections.

Among these reference is again made to the Sabbath; the making of molten images; the eating of peace offerings; gleaning of the harvest for the poor; theft, perjury, oppression; the treatment of the blind and deaf; fairness in judgment; talebearing; revenge; hybridity; carnal connection with bondwomen; uncircumcised fruit; enchantment; physical marks of idolatry; honoring the aged, etc.

The first three have to do with

reverence for God. The next series, having regard to the poor, was not only a protest against natural selfishness, but an intimation that the land did not belong to the human occupant but to God, and that its husbandman was merely His steward.

In several verses following, God still speaks on behalf of the weak and defenseless, but ere long balances the subject by showing that the rich are no more to be wronged than the poor.

Reaching the middle of the chapter, the commands concerning hybridity among cattle and in the vegetable kingdom are sufficiently clear, but that about the mingling of stuffs in our garments is not. Perhaps this whole section of laws is to cultivate reverence for the order established in nature by God, nature itself being a manifestation of God. In this case the precept about garments would be a symbolic reminder of the duty to a large class who did not so frequently come in contact with the other reminders referred to.

In verses 20-22 we come upon what seems a divine approval of concubinage and slavery, but we are to remember the explanation of it in Matt. 19:8.

The "uncircumcised" fruit (23-25) is as interesting a feature as any in the chapter. The explanation is in the law that the first-fruit always belongs to God. But it must be a *perfect* offering as well as the first-fruit, and this is not usually true of the fruit of a young tree. During the first three years of its life it is regarded as analogous to the life of a child uncircumcised or unconsecrated to the Lord. It is not until the fourth that its fruit becomes sufficiently perfected to offer unto God, and not until after that is it to be partaken of by the Israelite himself.

The reference to the trimming of the hair and beard is explained by the fact that among heathen peoples to do so visibly marks one as of a certain religion or the worshiper of a certain god. Today certain orders in the Roman Catholic Church are indicated in this manner. But the Israelite was not only to worship God alone, but to avoid even the appearance of worshiping another.

Questions.

1. To what do the contents of these chapters relate?

2. Why was "blood" prohibited in eating?

3. In what way does God claim ownership of the land of Israel?

4. How does He defend the rich as well as the poor?

5. Can you quote Matthew 19:8?

6. What is the meaning of "uncircumcised" fruit?

7. To what does the trimming of the hair and beard refer?

NEW TESTAMENT APPLICATION

Before pursuing these lessons further we would pause, to point out their application to the Christian, and how he should make use of them for his spiritual advancement and God's glory in this sinful world.

Brooke will once more be our guide:

In chapters 1 to 10 there is revealed what God is, and does, and gives to His people, but in chapters 11 to 22 we have what His people should be and do for Him. The first half of these latter chapters, 11 to 16, show that the life of God's people is to be *clean*, while the second half, chapter 17 to practically the close of the book, shows how it is to be holy. There is a difference between the two ideas represented by "clean" and "holy" (2 Cor. 7:1).

(1) The word "clean," together with "unclean," "purify" and their derivatives, comes from two Hebrew roots, occurring in the 6th chapter over 164 times, thus showing the emphasis God puts upon the thought they express, and impressing us with the fact that a line of separation must be drawn between those who are God's people through redemption by the blood, and those who are not.

(2) But we are taught that only God Himself can indicate what this line of separation is. Only He can say what is fit and what unfit for His people to think, and be, and do. This is New Testament as well as Old Testament teaching (Phil. 1:9-11), and means much more than the broad distinction between right and wrong. The people of the world know what these distinctions are, and for worldly reasons endeavor more or less to maintain them; but the people of God know the mind of God, and are expected to follow it in details of which the world is ignorant.

(3) We learn how communion with God may be hindered or promoted by things otherwise exceedingly small, like eating and drinking (1 Cor. 10:31), the way we dress, or keep our dwellings, the physical condition of our bodies, and the like. Indeed there are many questions of casuistry, which the full-grown Christian recognizes as essential in order to walk with God, of which other people know nothing. Compare (Deut. 14:21; 1 Cor. 2:14; 10:23; Eph. 5:17; 2 Tim. 2:4).

The Christian cannot say: "I may do this for others do it." The "others" may not be redeemed and separated unto God, and hence he must leave the doubtful things to them "who claim not royal birth," and "come out from among them and be separate" (2 Cor. 6:17, 18).

(4) Our author distinguishes between the first half of this section of the book, chapters 11 to 16, and the latter half, 17 to 22, by speaking of the latter as presenting on the *positive* what the former presents on the *negative* side. In illustrating the thought from the New Testament point of view he uses 2 Cor. 7:1.

"Having therefore these promises, dearly beloved, let us cleanse ourselves from all filthiness of the flesh and spirit, perfecting holiness in the fear of God."

The two phrases "cleanse" and "perfecting holiness" are in different tenses in the Greek. The former is in the aorist, and marks a definite action, something done once for all; but the latter is in the present tense, and implies a continuous line of conduct. When we are bidden to "cleanse ourselves" it means that everything marked by God as unclean is to be at once and forever put away; but when we are bidden to be perfect in holiness a life-long course of action and conduct is in mind.

Brooke helps us to understand this by his definition of "holiness," which in its primary sense does not mean supereminent piety but "the relationship existing between God and a consecrated thing." It is in this sense we read of a holy day, a holy place, or a holy animal.

(5) But as soon as this title is given to anyone or anything, the power of it is supposed to begin to work, that is, it immediately demands altered usage or conduct harmonizing with the new relationship to God into which it is brought. As applied to human beings, it is an instant summons to a new line of conduct, and thus passes into the meaning of practical piety. He uses this illustration: If one were rebuking a peer for unworthy conduct he might say: "You are a nobleman; *you ought to be a noble man.*" In this sense Paul uses it in 1 Cor. 5:7: "Purge out the old leaven, that ye may be a new lump, *even as ye are unleavened.*"

(6) These chapters therefore (17 to 22), bring into startling prominence the breadth and depth of the idea of holiness as God conceives of it. It concerns the table of God's people, the home, and all their social and business relationships.

It is only as we realize this idea of holiness, and how far we are separated from it by our old nature, that we can appreciate the typical significance of the Day of Atonement and the place its revelation occupies in this book (chapter 16). The other chapters preceding and following that revelation raised the question, Who can be clean before God? We perceive that, notwithstanding what provisions we make or precautions we take, we can never be sure that no spot of uncleanness remains, or that the conditions for communion with God are fulfilled. Only God can be sure of this, or make us sure, but that assurance is what chapter 16 in its typical aspect is intended to provide.

Once a year, and on that day, "all the iniquities of Israel, and all their transgressions, in all their sins" were completely removed, and atonement made for every uncleanness. The prototype of this we find in the person and work of our blessed Lord, whose grace is sufficient for us, and whose blood cleanseth us from all sin.

Questions.

1. Why is the standard of righteousness for God's people different from that of the world?

2. Name some of the little things which may affect the saint's communion with God.

3. Quote 2 Corinthians 7:1.

4. How would you define "holiness"?

5. Quote 1 Corinthians 5:7.

PENALTIES FOR PEOPLE AND PRIESTS

CHAPTERS 20-22

The 20th chapter is of deep interest as showing what infinite wisdom, and love has considered a just punishment for certain crimes. These crimes are still committed in civilized communities but a different view of their treatment seems to exist. Are human governments in modern times wiser, and better than this theocracy, where Jehovah ruled? Are the weaknesses of our democracies explained by their indifferences to the code here exhibited?

Why does not this code obtain in Christian nations, since God has revealed it and such nations are supposed to serve God?

The answer is, that no nation on earth is a God-governed nation, as Israel was, and shall again be in the millennial age. The laws of so-called Christian nations are man-made, not God-made. They may bear a likeness of relationship to these laws of God, but only as they grow out of a necessity of human experience. No nation has ever set itself the task of finding out God's mind with reference to this or that penalty, and squaring its legislation accordingly. Hence the lawlessness we see on every hand, and the injustice; hence the teaching of the prophets that the present order of things shall end in a grand catastrophe, and God shall set up His own kingdom on the earth over which His Son shall reign.

Outline of the Chapter.

The first section (1-6), relates to the giving of seed to Molech, and consulting with familiar spirits, or what we call Spiritualism. With Spiritualism might be included other occultisms, such as fortune-telling, clairvoyance, palmistry and the like.

A second section (7, 8), consists of a command to sanctification of life and obedience to God.

A third (9-16) enumerates other cases for which death was ordered, some of them very unnatural crimes.

A fourth (17-21), names offenses for which a lesser penalty is prescribed.

A fifth (22-26), consists of a concluding exhortation against disobedience enforced by the impending punishment of the Canaanites, and the goodness of God to them (Israel).

For what crimes is death ordained as a penalty (2-5, 10, 12, 13, 14, 15, 16, 27)? What manner of death is ordained (2)? In the case of certain crimes is any difference made between the sexes (10, 11, 12, 14, 15, 16)? In what instance were the bodies of the criminals to be burnt after death (14)?

In the case of the lesser penalties, which offense demanded the most public excommunication (17)?

The Principles Involved.

Certain "reformers" claim that the primary, if not the sole, object of the punishment of crime is the reformation of the individual. How does such a theory square with this divine precedent? Had reformation been the chief thought in God's mind, would He have ordained the death penalty with such unqualified severity?

How does verse 3 show that the intention of the punishment is to satisfy the outraged holiness of God? How does verse 12 show that it is to preserve the natural order of the human family? How does verse 14 show that it is for the moral benefit of the race?

The multiplication of murders and crimes against the family in these days may be explained by the laxity of the laws, or the indisposition of the people to enforce them. "Where God pronounces the death penalty, man apologizes for the crime, then lightens the penalty, then abolishes it, and at last legalizes the offense. This modern drift bodes no good, and in the end can only bring disaster to the family and the state."

1. Holiness of the Priests, c. 21, 22.

We pass over chapters 21 and 22 with a remark or two, as they treat of the same subject as the preceding chapter except as it applies to the priests. While all Israel, as Kellogg says, was called to be a priestly nation and holy to Jehovah in life and service, "this sanctity was represented in degrees successively higher in each of its three divisions, the people, the priest, and the high priests," like the three-fold division of the tabernacle, the outer court, the holy place, and the Holy of Holies.

The principle still holds good, in that special privileges place him who enjoys them under special obligations to holiness of life. Christians, in other words, should not merely be equally correct in life with the best men of the world, but more—they should be holy. And within the Church, those who occupy official positions or who are otherwise elevated above their fellows, are under the more stringent obligations of life and work.

Questions.

1. What kind of government was that of Israel?

2. How would you account for much of the disorder and lawlessness in so-called Christian nations?

3. What will bring this to an end?

4. Have you tried to answer the Questions asked under the head of "Principles Involved"?

5. What peculiar obligation of conduct lies upon Christians, and why?

FEASTS OF THE LORD

Chapter 23

There is nothing more affecting in all this legislation than the provision God makes for the physical happiness and the temporal welfare of His people. He wants them to rejoice if only they rejoice in Him. (Phil. 4:4). This chapter sets this forth.

Compare the Revised Version and observe that the word in verse 2 is "set feasts," or, "appointed seasons."

Why are they called "set feasts *of the Lord*"? Is it not because He appointed them and because He would be glorified in them? What other title do they receive (2)? When "holy convocations" are mentioned we think of public gatherings at the tabernacle, or, later on, at the temple; but these were commanded only for the three occasions, the passover in the spring, and the feast of weeks (Pentecost), and atonement in the autumn (Exodus 34:22). Probably, therefore, the other convocations were local gatherings crystallized afterwards in the weekly synagogue.

1. The Weekly Sabbath, v. 3.

What is the first feast mentioned (3)? Although the weekly Sabbath is included among these appointed seasons, yet it is distinguished from them by the fresh heading of verse 4, and by verses 37 and 38. It is indeed an appointed season, but dating from the creation of man, and not here first prescribed. It is in this sense a kind of germ of all the other appointed seasons.

How is the sanctity of the weekly Sabbath expressed in the Revised Version? What was prohibited on this day? Did this prohibition extend only to outside work, or what we would call in our day business affairs?

Do you remember what was taught previously about the two reasons for the weekly Sabbath? A memorial of God's rest in creation it was, and yet also a memorial of redemption (Exodus 31:13; Deut. 5:15). While the redemption specifically in mind is the Jews' deliverance from Egypt, yet it is a type of our spiritual deliverance from sin through Christ.

The original Sabbath rest of God, in which man participated, was marked by sin, so that the whole creation became "subjected to vanity" (Romans 8:20). God could not rest in this state of things, and began a work of new creation. The object of this is the restoration of that Sabbath rest which thus was interrupted; hence, the weekly Sabbath looked forward as well as backward.

2. The Passover and Unleavened Bread, vv. 4-8.

The feasts of the passover and unleavened bread we met in Exodus, but here we learn how the latter shall begin and end with a holy convocation, and be characterized by the omission of "servile work." This last seems to refer to labor in the field and otherwise, outside of the home.

The spiritual meaning of these two feasts we have considered. Through the slaying of the lamb and sprinkling of its blood Israel secured deliverance from Egypt, and by eating its flesh strength for the journey before them. The unleavened bread, however, had more than an historic reference. Leaven is the type of evil or moral corruption and its removal signifies that the redeemed nation must be a holy and separate people.

3. The Sheaf of the Firstfruits, vv. 9-14.

In connection with the two

feasts just named, what further ceremony is established (10, 11)? With this what offering should be presented (12, 13)? What prohibitions are entailed (14)?

We have here a preliminary feast of the harvest. The waiving of the sheaf of the first-fruits indicates that the whole harvest to follow belonged and was consecrated to God. Until this action was taken they were not at liberty to use the harvest.

In this we have another symbol. Israel is God's firstborn among the nations (Exodus 4:22), of the redeemed earth. She is the earnest of the redemption of all these nations—the beginning of the world's harvest, which shall be realized in the millennial age.

And the idea is not exhausted yet, as we judge by 1 Cor. 5:7, 8. Christ our passover was sacrificed for us, and the sheaf of the firstfruits in His resurrection was presented unto God as a type of the resurrection of all His people (1 Cor. 15:20).

4. Pentecost, or the Feast of Weeks, vv. 15-21.

How long after the presentation of the sheaf of the firstfruits came the next feast (15, 16)? What should be offered on this day (17-20)? With what should these loaves be baked (17)? What was the design of this offering (17)? Because this feast came on the fiftieth day after the presentation of the sheaf of the firstfruits, it is called the Feast of Pentecost, from the Greek numeral meaning fifty; and the Feast of Weeks, because it followed seven weeks after that of the sheaf.

The former festival marked the beginning of the harvest with the first sheaf of barley, and this, the completion of the grain harvest, with the reaping of the wheat. In the former the sheaf was presented as it came from the field, but in this the offering was of the grain as prepared for food. Why it might be baked with leaven we do not know.

Speaking of the typical aspect of this feast, and comparing it with the Passover, there God was seen to be the Redeemer of Israel, here He is seen to be her preserver.

Comparing it with the sheaf of the firstfruits, there we see a type of Christ's resurrection as "the firstfruits of them that sleep," but here a type of the descent of the Holy Ghost on the day of Pentecost when "the church of the firstborn" was formed as the beginning of the great ingathering of the whole number of the elect. (Acts 2:1-4; Col. 1:18, James 1:18).

As compared with the weekly Sabbath, this feast, in celebrating the rest after the labors of the harvest, became a type of the great rest to follow the harvest at the end of this age (Matt. 13:39).

5. The Feast of Trumpets, vv. 23-28.

We have seen that the Feast of the Sabbath on the seventh day of each week was a germ of the whole series of septenary feasts. The Feast of Pentecost on the seventh week, and now the Feast of Trumpets at the beginning of the seventh month carry forward the idea. Spring, summer and autumn each has its feast. This seventh month, corresponding to that period of our year from the middle of September to the middle of October was the great month of the Jewish year in that three great events occurred in it—the Feast of Trumpets, the great Day of Atonement, and the Feast of Tabernacles.

The blowing of trumpets was an announcement from God to His people that the great glad month had come, the month of atonement and of the greatest festivity of the year resulting from that atonement, and the earthly blessing accompanying it.

On other occasions trumpets were blown only by the priests and at the central sanctuary, but in this case they were blown by everyone who would throughout the whole land.

How reconciled we could be to the noises preceding New Year's Day, or the 4th of July, or

Thanksgiving Day, if only the blowing of the horns were an act of worship in recognition of the goodness and faithfulness of God!

6. The Day of Atonement, vv. 26-32.

The Day of Atonement has been considered in chapter 16. Coming at this season of the year it demonstrated the complete rest brought in, both for God and His people, through the expiation of their guilt.

How were the people on this day to express penitence for their guilt (27)? (Cp. Is. 58:3-7; Zech. 7:5.) What penalty followed the absence of such penitence (29)?

How do these great truths of sin, repentence, expiation, rest, apply to the people of all ages?

7. The Feast of Tabernacles, vv. 33-43.

This is the greatest of the feasts. When did it begin, what is it called, and how long did it last? On what two days were "holy convocations" called?

What reference to the complete harvest is found in this enactment (39)? With what unusual feature was this feast to be celebrated (40)? What did the dwelling in booths commemorate (42, 43)? As the passover typified our redemption through Christ, the unleavened bread our feeding upon Him for strength, the first sheaf His restoration from the dead, Pentecost, the descent of the Holy Ghost, or the spiritual ingathering of the first fruits of the world's harvest in the formation of the church, so the Feast of Tabernacles is thought to typify the completion of that harvest in the final ingathering of the elect at the end of the age. Then all that are Christ's shall either rise from the dead or be translated to meet Him in the air at the second coming (1 Thess. 4:13-18).

The eighth day after the feast is a type of that new week ushered in by the millennial age, when the earth and all that is therein shall experience the rest promised to the people of God (Zech. 14: 16; 21).

Questions.

1. Quote Phil. 4:4.
2. What feast may be said to be the "germ" of all the others?
3. To what does the weekly rest day look forward?
4. Of what is "leaven" always the type in Scripture?
5. Of what is the sheaf of the firstfruits the type?
6. Of what is the Feast of Weeks the type as compared with that of the firstfruits?
7. What was the great month of the Jewish year, and why?
8. Give the name, history and typical significance of the greatest of the feasts.

THE SABBATIC AND JUBILEE YEARS

CHAPTER 25

Considering the limited scope of this work, we pass over chapter 24, to give more attention to the subject of the present chapter, which is closely connected with that of the "feasts" or "appointed seasons."

The Sabbatic Year.

It deals first with the Sabbatic year (1-7). From what were the Israelites prohibited in the seventh year (4)? How much further did the prohibition extend (5)? But while there should be no sowing, pruning or reaping for the year, nevertheless were all the spontaneous produce of the land to be a waste (6, 7)? What may have been God's object in this law?

Agricultural science recognizes that a periodic rest of land is of advantage, particularly where it is difficult to obtain fertilizers in adequate amount. But there must have been a deeper reason here, and we wonder whether the enactment was not intended as a discipline in faith towards God, teaching the Israelite that man does not live by bread alone (Cp. vv. 20-22; with Deut. 8:3). Then may not another thought have been to impress him that his right to the soil and its produce came from God? We can see also how such an enactment would curb selfishness and covetousness, and place the rich and the poor periodically on the same level. It has, of course, some symbolical and typical aspects as well, which will be considered later.

The Jubilee Year.

The chapter deals in the next place with the Jubilee year (8-12). In what month, and on what day did it begin (9)? What name was given to this day? By what ceremony was it introduced? What was the proclamation on this day (10)? Was it also a Sabbath for the land (11)? Then, did two Sabbath years come in immediate succession?

A question may arise as to how a new year could begin in the seventh month. But the answer is that Israel had two kinds of years. What might be called its religious year, began with the Feast of the Passover in the spring (Exodus 12), while its civil year began with the day of atonement in the fall.

Liberty Proclaimed.

One feature of the "liberty" of the Jubilee year concerned the redemption of the land (vv. 12-17, 23, 24). In that year what must be returned to every man who had suffered a loss of it (13)? What was the basis of value in the purchase and sale of land (15. 16)? Since the possession must revert to the original holder in the year of Jubilee, it had only just so much value as there were years and crops intervening between the time it left his hand and the next Jubilee. What was the purpose or effect of this law (17)? What was its basis, or in other words, why could not the land be sold in perpetuity, but must be returned to its first holder (23)?

Observe from this that in Israel, under the theocracy, there was no such thing as either private or communal ownership of the land. The owner was Jehovah, and all any man could buy

or sell was the right to its produce, and that only for a limited time.

The Kinsman Redeemer.

The law of the kinsman redeemer is an interesting feature of this subject (25-28).

If one for reasons of poverty was obliged to sell his land, whose duty was it to redeem it for him did his circumstances permit (25)? Might the original possessor himself redeem it (26)? Observe that the basis of price (27) was that referred to above. Observe also, that if it could not be redeemed in either case, then it must return to him at the Jubilee (28).

Exceptional Cases.

The exception as to walled cities is peculiar (29-34). If a man sold a dwelling there, might he ever get it back again (29)? If the opportunity was not availed of, what then (30)? Did this apply to other than walled cities (31)? Was there any exception as to the owners of dwellings in walled cities (32)?

The reason for exempting houses in walled cities seems to be that there was no land here which might be used agriculturally for man's support. In the case of unwalled towns or villages it was otherwise, hence the exception there. The inhabitants of such towns or villages were the cultivators of the soil, and their houses belonged to their farms. The case of the Levites is explained by the fact that according to the divine command, earlier recorded, they had no other possession than their houses.

The Question of Slavery.

The question of slavery comes again before us in this chapter (vv. 39-55).

What kind of a slave is referred to in v. 39, voluntary or involuntary? A Hebrew or an alien? What difference must be made in his case? How did the Jubilee year affect him (40, 41)?

What other kind of slave is allowed for in vv. 44, 45?

Provided that a Hebrew sold

himself to an alien, what then (vv. 47-49)?

We wonder at Jehovah permitting slavery. But if we carefully considered the laws governing it in Israel, we must have seen how different it was from modern slavery, how just and equitable, and even how desirable for those whose circumstances made it necessary. We shall see also that these laws had such an educational power as to altogether banish slavery from the Hebrew people.

The Typical and Symbolical Aspect.

The Sabbatic year and Jubilee year are the last two members of the Sabbatic system of septenary periods all of which have a typical significance. Each brings out some aspect of redemption through Christ, and all combined form a progressive revelation in type of the results of Christ's work for the world.

These last two periods began on the great Day of Atonement in which all Israel was to afflict their souls in penitence for sin; and on that day they both began when the high priest came out from within the veil, where, from the time of offering the sin-offering, he had been hidden from the sight of Israel. Both also were ushered in with a trumpet blast. We have in both a type of the final repentance of Israel in the latter days, and their re-establishment in their own land, of which all the prophets speak. The earlier restoration from their Babylonian captivity was doubtless prefigured here as well; and yet the ultimate reference must be to that event still in the future vs. 11:11.

The World Fulfilment.

The type, however, reaches beyond Israel and includes the whole earth. See Peter's reference in Acts 3:19-21, where Jesus Christ the heavenly High Priest shall come forth and when the last trumpet shall sound and He shall appear "the second time without sin unto salvation" (Heb. 9:28; Rom. 8:19-22).

Questions.

1. Name four practical reasons for the Sabbatic year.

2. When did the civil year of Israel begin?

3. Who owned the land of Israel?

4. Can you explain the exemption of "walled cities"?

5. What effect has God's law about slavery had upon that institution among the Hebrews?

6. On what day of the year did the Sabbatic and Jubilee years begin?

7. Of what are both these years a type?

8. How far beyond Israel's history does the type of the Jubilee year extend?

THE GREAT PROPHECY

Chapter 26

This chapter opens with injunctions (vv. 1 and 2), which practically cover the first table of the law, and then follow (1), promises of blessing in the case of obedience (3-13); (2), warnings of judgment in case of disobedience (14-39); and (3), a prophecy of ultimate repentance and restoration to divine favor in the latter days.

The Promised Blessings. vv. 3-13.

These blessings include (1), fruitful seasons (3-5); (2), internal security (6-8); (3), multiplication of numbers and the increased harvest necessary to support them (9-10), and (4), the abiding presence of God with them (11-12). All these promises are based on and grow out of their original redemption from Egypt and God's covenant with them at that time (13).

Warnings of Judgment. vv. 14-39.

The judgments are first spoken of in general terms, and include physical disease, bereavement, famine, conquest and dispersion (14-17).

Then there follow, as Kellogg shows, four series of warnings, each conditioned on the supposition that they did not repent as the result of the preceding experiences. Each series is prefaced by the formula, "*I will punish you seven times more for your sins*" (vv. 18, 21, 24, 28). The thought is that each new display of impenitence on Israel's part shall be marked by increasing severity. Notice (1), that the rains will be withheld (19-20); (2), wild beasts will destroy their children and cattle (22); (3), war, pestilence and famine shall follow (25-26); (4), all these calamities will come upon them with increasing terror, so that they shall eat the flesh of their sons and daughters, and their city shall become waste and their land desolate to that extent that their enemies shall be astonished at it. Moreover, they will be scattered among the Gentile peoples (29-33).

The importance of this prophecy is that all the later prophecies concerning the judgments upon Israel are a kind of application of it to the later conditions. It is also an epitome of Israel's history from the death of Joshua, say, until the present time.

This chapter, is of great importance as proof of the divine origin of the Bible. We have here an evidence of foreknowledge, and therefore, of the inspiration of the Holy Spirit, which cannot be gainsaid.

Repentance and Restoration. vv. 40-46.

The word "If" at the beginning of verse 40 is in the R. V. "And." It thus becomes a positive statement of God that Israel shall confess her iniquity and be humbled before Him; and that in consequence, the Lord will remember His covenant with Jacob (42).

These words had a partial fulfilment in the return from the Babylonian captivity, but this did not exhaust the prophecy. Israel again forgot Jehovah and committed her greatest sin in crucifying her Messiah. As the result her people are now scattered among the nations, and her land is desolate. Nevertheless, God's covenant with her fathers is not forgotten. The promises to her were renewed after the return from Babylon with reference to events that shall take place in her history at the end of this age (Zechariah 12:8-14 and 13:1). See also Paul's epistle to the Romans (chapter 11:2 and 25:29).

Observe that the promises for the future pertain to the land as well as the people of Israel (42). Compare Luke 21:24. The inference is clear that Israel shall not only be restored to God in repentance through faith in her Messiah, but she shall also be restored to Palestine, whose fruitfulness will be greater than ever.

Questions.

1. Give a general outline of this chapter.

2. What blessings are promised on Israel's obedience?

3. How does this chapter prove the divinity of the Bible?

4. How does verse 40 become a positive statement?

5. Have you read Romans 11?

VOWS AND TITHES

CHAPTER 27

We have in this closing chapter a supplement to the whole book. Hitherto we dealt with obligations and duties resting on all Israelites alike, but now we come to vows of an additional and voluntary character. (Deut. 23:22.)

Persons Might be Vowed. vv. 1-8.

The thought is, that persons might be vowed for service in the sanctuary; but since service could not be found for so large a number, and especially for young children, who might be vowed, there might be a money equivalent for them. This equivalent, which was to be paid into the treasury of the sanctuary, was determined by the labor value of the person vowed as based on sex and age. It was always low enough not to burden the poor.

Domestic Animals Might be Vowed. vv. 9-13.

If the animal were suitable for sacrifice, it might be accepted for the service, but if otherwise, the priest must set a price on it for which it might be sold by the owner and the money placed in the treasury. In this case one-fifth more was to be added to the price, as a check perhaps, on rashness in vowing.

Exclusions from Vow. vv. 26-33.

Houses and fields might be vowed (14-25), upon the same principles as the foregoing. But three kinds of property could not be vowed, the firstlings of the beasts (26); a "devoted thing," in the sense of an accursed thing like the property in Jericho, (28, 29 compared with Joshua 7:17); and "the tithe of the land" (30).

The reason for these prohibitions was that these things already belonged to God and hence their human possessors had no right to them.

There is a serious matter here in the devotement or accursing of human beings, but we postpone its consideration till we meet with a conspicuous application of the principle at a later period.

Law of the Tithe.

The "tithe" was one of the things belonging to God in any event, and which could not be voluntarily vowed.

This is specially interesting as raising the question whether the tithe is binding upon Christians at the present time. In our judgment it is not; but that does not mean that Christians may give according to impulse or caprice, since the New Testament lays down the principle of giving a fixed portion of our income to the Lord as He hath prospered us. (1 Cor. 16:1, 2; 2 Cor. 8:7-9).

It is customary under the Gospel to leave much to the individual conscience regarding the details of worship and conduct, which, under the Mosaic law was regulated by rule. Paul gives the explanation in Galatians 4: 1-5.

Christian Vows.

Has a vow of any kind a place in the practical life of Christians? It seems not forbidden in the New Testament, but neither is it approved.

As Kellogg says, "the true conception of Christian life and duty leaves no room for a promise to God of what is not due, inasmuch as through the transcendent obligation of grateful love to Him for our redemption," everything is due. (2 Cor. 5:14, 15.)

The question is not speculative, since it constitutes one of the distinctions between Romanism and Protestantism. The Romish theory of works of supererogation comes in here, and closely associated with it, the doctrine of purgatory. Here is the germ of the celibate life of the clergy, of sisterhoods and monasticism, the tendency of which is towards legalism on the one hand and moral declension on the other. (Gal. 4:9; Col. 2:16-23).

Questions.

1. What particular kind of vows is dealt with here?
2. For what service were persons vowed?
3. What properties could not be vowed, and why?
4. Quote 1 Corinthians 16:1-2.
5. Is a vow normal in the Christian life?

LAW OF THE TITHE
(Abridged from "The Expositor's Bible.")

The "tithe" or the dedication of the tenth of one's possessions to God, is a practice of antiquity, and a question arises as to whether the obligation is still resting upon those who would serve God in this dispensation? An answer was given in the last lesson, but it is desirable to enlarge upon it.

While we hear nothing of the tithe in the first Christian centuries, it came into practice in the 4th century, and later on was established as a law of the church for some centuries.

The modern spirit has become more and more averse to it, until under the present voluntaryism it has seemed likely to disappear altogether.

In consequence of this there

has been a revival of interest in it of late as necessary for the maintenance and extension of the church, those who would revive it holding that the principle is still binding on the Christian.

In settling the question, it is to be remembered that the moral obligation is one thing and the legal another. Morally it is our duty to set apart for God a fixed proportion of our income, but the precise proportion is a subject on which the New Testament is silent. For the moral obligation see 1 Corinthians 16: 1, 2, where no reference is made to the legal obligation. If the tithe had been still binding as to the letter, this would have been the place for the apostle to have mentioned it.

As a matter of fact, it is commonly found in the New Testament, that the individual is left at liberty regarding the details of worship and conduct as compared with conditions under the Mosaic law. (Gal. 4:1-5.)

One author however, calls attention to a matter of importance not commonly considered in the discussion of this subject. For example, the people of Israel were under a theocratic government, where God Himself ruled, where the whole system of law was divinely instituted and supposed to be divinely executed. When thus carried out this system would have prevented excessive accumulation of wealth in the hands of individuals, as we have seen in the consideration of earlier chapters of this book. There would thus have been secured an equal distribution of property, such as the world has never seen, and doubtless never will until the millennium. Under such circumstances it would have been possible to exact a certain proportion of income for sacred purposes with a certainty that it would have worked with perfect fairness to all.

But with us it is different. Wealth is unequally distributed in our economy, and no law of the tithe could be made to work as in Israel. To the poor it would be a heavy burden, and to the rich a tax so small as to amount to exemption. The poor man would sometimes be required to take bread out of the mouths of wife and children, while the millionaire would still have thousands to spend in luxuries. The latter might often more easily give nine-tenths of his income than the former one-twentieth.

While, therefore, the law of the tithe would not seem to be binding upon us as to the letter, let us not forget that from the moral point of view it is still in force. It forbids the Christian to give simply according to impulse or caprice. He is to lay by in store as the Lord hath prospered him. Let there be systematic giving to the Lord's work under the law of a fixed proportion of gifts to income, and under the inspiration of the memory of God's grace to us (2 Cor. 7:9), and the Lord's treasury will never be empty, nor will the Lord Himself be robbed of His due.

Questions.

1. Is the "tithe" a Biblical conception only?

2. What is the difference between the moral and legal obligation in this matter?

3. Why could the tithe operate successfully in Israel?

4. Why not in our system of political economy?

5. What obligation of giving rests on Christians?

NUMBERS

NUMBER AND ORDER OF THE TRIBES

CHAPTERS 1-4

A secondary name for Numbers might be "The Book of the Journeyings" since it gives the story of Israel from Sinai to the arrival on the border of Canaan. Examine verse 1 and perceive that the time covered by Exodus and Leviticus was not more than fourteen months, while that of Numbers is over thirty-eight years. You will doubtless find a map in the back of your Bible which will aid in mastering this book. The journey will be seen to be first northwest as far as Kadesh, then south to the fork of the Red Sea, and finally northwest as before, around the land of Edom to Moab.

We will keep this geographical outline in mind, considering first the principal events at Sinai before they start, then what occurred between Sinai and Kadesh, and finally between Kadesh and Moab.

"The Book of the Murmurings."

The book might be called the book of the "murmurings" as well as "journeyings," for it is pervaded with a spirit of disobedience and rebellion against God, justifying the abstract given of the period in Psalm 95:10.

While annals of many powerful nations of this period are entirely forgotten, these of a comparative handful of people are preserved and that too, notwithstanding their ungrateful spirit, because of the relation they bear to the redemption of the world through Jesus Christ. This accounts for the Divine long-suffering towards them, and all the exhibitions of Divine love the book contains. We have rehearsed this before, but it is well to keep it in mind as we pursue our studies. Read also 1 Cor. 10, to discover how their history is a kind of object lesson illustrating God's dealings with us in a spiritual sense. (Synthetic Bible Studies.)

1. The Tribes Numbered, c. 1.

What was Moses commanded to do, and when was he commanded to do it (1, 2)? What people were thus to be numbered, and why (2, 3)? Comparing 4 and 16, what description is given of the "heads" of houses who were to be with Moses and Aaron in this matter?

"Renowned" means them that were called out of the different tribes for leadership; and "princes" stands for the same thing. These were usually the oldest son in each tribe after the manner of the nomads of the East today.

On what basis was the numbering conducted (18)? This reference to "pedigrees" is important, as showing the care taken about genealogies. This was to keep the Aaronic order intact, but especially as a provision for tracing the descent of the Messiah through Judah.

Which tribe was the most numerous (27)? Can you recall how this fulfills Jacob's prophecy (Gen. 49)? What prophecy of his is fulfilled in verses 32-35? What was the sum of the enrolment (46)? What an increase from the seventy-five who went down into Egypt 215 years before! And yet this did not include the women and children, nor the old men, nor the tribe of Levi! It is estimated there were two and a half millions in all.

About the Levites. What direction is given concerning them (47-49)? What were they to do, and where were they to camp, and why (50-53)?

2. The Tribes Arranged, c. 2.

What was the rallying point for each family in the camp (2)? We do not know the colors or forms of these ensigns, but possibly they were copied after Egypt minus their idolatrous symbols, and were of a fan-like form made of feathers, shawls, etc. and lifted on long poles. Some think they were symbols borrowed from Jacob's blessing on the tribes, and that Judah's ensign was a lion, Benjamin's a wolf, and so on. Perhaps the color was determined by the precious stone representing the tribe in the high priest's breastplate.

Were the tribes, other than the Levites, allowed to pitch their tents near the tabernacle (2)? Which tribes took the lead on the march (3-9)? What seems to have formed the central company (17)?

3. The Levites' Service, cc. 3, 4.

What genealogy is given at the opening of this chapter (1-4)? What shows the subordination of the rest of the Levites to the family of Aaron (6, 7)? Give the history of the choice of this tribe in verses 12, 13. Who chose them? In substitution for whom? On what ground were the latter taken by the Lord?

On what different principle were the Levites numbered from the other tribes (15)? Can you give a reason for this? Name the three sub-divisions of this tribe (17). What was the particular place and charge of each (23, 25, 26; 29, 31; 35, 36, 37)? Who was Eleazar and what official position had he (32)? Compare 1 Kings 4:4; 2 Kings 25:18. What location was assigned Moses and the family of Aaron (38)?

Why was a new reckoning of all the males to be made (40-46)? How much was the ransom money (47)? (A shekel was about equal to 60 cents.)

What was the age limit of Levitical service (4:3)? Compare 8:23-26. What precautions were necessary in the case of the Kohathites (15)? Compare also 17-20. What carrying work was assigned the Gershonites (24-26)? Which of the sons of Aaron had the immediate charge of them (28)? What was assigned the Merarites (31, 32)? What word in verse 32 indicates that an inventory was kept of all the little things that nothing might be lost? What a lesson this teaches as to God's regard for the details of

His service, and His interest in trivial things. What a strong light it flashes on the meaning of obedience.

Questions.

1. What three-fold geographical division of Numbers might be made?

2. What secondary name might be given to the book; and why?

3. Interpret "renowned" and "princes."

4. How many Israelites in the gross are supposed to have come out of Egypt?

5. Give an illustration of obedience in this lesson.

OTHER PRELIMINARIES

CHAPTERS 5:1-9:14

What command is given Moses in chapter 5:1-4?

What is the next command, and where has this previously been treated (5:5-10)? It must not be supposed that such repetitions are *merely* such. There is always a reason for the repetition which the context will commonly disclose.

1. The Trial of Jealousy, 5:11-31.

The trial of jealousy, contains some new features to which attention should be called. As usual, get the facts in mind by a process of questioning, before attempting to generalize / upon them.

The law provides for jealousy in a husband whether he has good ground for it or not (12-14). What is he to do under the circumstances (15)? What preparations shall the priest make (16-18)? Then follows the adjuration of the woman and her assent to it (22), and after this the actual test of her conduct (27, 28).

The law was given, as a discouragement to conjugal unfaithfulness on the part of a wife, and as a protection from the consequences of a wrong suspicion on the part of her husband.

"From the earliest times, the jealousy of Eastern people has established ordeals for the detection and punishment of suspected unchastity in wives. And it has been thought that the Israelites being biased in favor of such usages, this law was incorporated to free it from the idolatrous rites which the heathens had blended with it. Viewed in this light, its sanction by Divine authority in a corrected form exhibits a proof at once of the wisdom and condescension of God."—*Bible Commentary.*

2. The Law of the Nazarite, c. 6.

This chapter is new in some respects. It concerns the vow of the "Nazarite," from a Hebrew word which means, to separate. This was a voluntary consecration of the person such as we studied about under "vows" in a former lesson. He has a strong impulse towards a holy life, and renounces certain worldly occupations and pleasures to that end, for a given period.

What is the first thing marking his separation (3, 4)? The second (5)? The third (6-8)? Suppose the vow in this last respect were accidentally violated (9-12)? After the period of the vow is terminated, what is the procedure (13-20)?

The reasons for these restrictions are obvious. Wine inflames the passions and creates a taste for undue indulgences. As a shaven head was a sign of uncleanness (Lev. 14:8, 9), so the long hair symbolized the purity he professes. It kept him in remembrance of his vow also, and acted as a stimulus for others to imitate his piety. Contact with a dead body, as we have seen, disqualified for God's service, hence his avoidance of it.

3. The Aaronic Blessing.

Observe the doctrine of the Trinity foreshadowed in the three-fold repetition of the Name "LORD" or JEHOVAH—three Persons and yet but one God. Observe their respective offices. The Father will bless and keep us; the Son will be gracious unto us; the Spirit will give us peace. Observe the last verse. It is not the name of man that is put upon them, not even Moses' name nor Aaron's, but God's own Name, "*I will bless them.*"

4. The Princes' Offerings, c. 7.

Who were these princes (2)? What was the first offering they brought (3)? Why were none given the Kohathites (9)? (Compare for a violation of this rule 2 Samuel 6:6-13). What other offerings did they present and for what purpose (84-88)? What shows the voluntary nature of these offerings (5)?

There are two or three practical lessons here. In the first place, an example to wealthy Christians to generously support and further the work of the Lord. Secondly, an encouragement to believe that while in the great matters of worship and church government we should adhere faithfully to what God has revealed, yet in minor details liberty may be left to the means and convenience of the people. Moses would not have accepted and used these gifts, but God relieved his embarrassment, from which we infer that other things may be done without a special warrant if they are in the right direction, and in general harmony with God's will.

Where were the wagons obtained? Did they bring them from Egypt, or did Hebrew artisans construct them in the wilderness? The latter inquiry suggests that some of the offerings in this chapter may not have come entirely from the individual "prince," but have represented the general contributions of the tribe.

5. The Lamps and the Levites, c. 8.

The last verse of the preceding chapter seems to belong to the present one. What great honor was accorded Moses? Though standing outside the vail he could hear the voice of God within (Exod. 25:22). Compare John 14:21.

What is now communicated to Moses (1-4)?

"It was Aaron's duty, as the servant of God, to light His house, which, being without windows, required the aid of lights. (2 Peter 1-19.) And the course he was ordered to follow was first to light the middle lamp from the altar fire, and then the other lamps from each other—a course symbolical of all the light of heavenly truth derived from Christ, and diffused by his ministers throughout the world."—*Bible Commentary.*

6. Consecrating the Levites.

What cleansing process was ordained (6, 7)? What offerings required (8)? Who were to lay their hands on the Levites (10)? Perhaps some of the first-born did this, thus indicating the substitution of the Levites in their place.

What was the next step in their consecration (11)? The word for "offer" in this verse is "wave," and the probability is that some such motion was made by the Levites in token of their giving themselves to God and then being given back again to the nation for His service. (Compare verses 14-19.)

What seeming contradiction is there between verses 24 and 4:3? The probable explanation is that at the earlier age they entered on their work as probationers and at the later as fully equipped servitors. At the age of fifty were they to entirely cease labor, or is there an intimation in verse 26 that lighter tasks were assigned them?

7. A New Passover Law, 9:1-14.

What is the command in verses 1-5? It may seem strange that any command should be given in this case, till we recall that Israel was still in the wilderness, and the institution of the Passover only implied its being observed in Canaan (Exodus 12:25). To have it observed under present conditions required a special command.

But the circumstance is spoken of here to introduce the case next referred to (1-14). What is that case (6-8)? What special provision is made for it (9-11)?

Questions.

1. What reasons can you give for the law of jealousy?

2. How are Divine wisdom and condescension shown in that law?

3. Give your conception of a Nazarite.

4. Explain the restraints he was to observe.

5. Learn by heart the Aaronic benediction.

6. What precious doctrine does it unfold?

7. What practical lessons are taught by chapter 7?

8. What is symbolized by the lighting of the lamps?

SINAI TO PARAN

CHAPTERS 9:15-10:36

The people had been at Sinai for about a year (compare Exod. 19:1). They were refreshed after their Egyptian servitude. The law had been given, the tabernacle erected, and the means and method of approach to God had been revealed. Thus had they entered on a course of moral and religious training which inspired them with a conviction of their high destiny, and prepared them to begin their journey to the promised land.

The events of this lesson revolve around the intial step of this journey, and include the following:

(1) Directions about the guiding cloud (9:15-23).

(2) Directions about the trumpets (10:1-10).

(3) Record of the first three days (11-28).

(4) Moses' request to Hobab (29-32).

(5) Moses' prayer (33-36).

The Cloud.

We have sufficiently considered the subject of the cloud (Exod. 13).

Of what was it the signal (17)? To what was its action equivalent (18)? What indicates their strict obedience to this signal (22, 23)?

The Trumpets.

The Egyptian trumpets which called their votaries to the temples were short and curved like ram's horns, but these of Moses, to judge by those represented on the arch of Titus, were long and straight, very much like our own.

Of what, and how were they to be made (2)? What was their purpose (2, 3)? How many different calls were represented (4-7)? To whom was the use of the trumpets restricted (8)?

Observe verse 9, and compare chapter 31:6 and 2 Chronicles 113:12. The sounding of the trumpets on the eve of battle was a solemn and religious act, animating the hearts of those engaged in a righteous cause, it was a promise also, that God would be aroused to aid with His presence in the battle.

Hobab, the Brother-in-Law.

Probably this relative of Moses remained during a part of their encampment at Sinai, but it was natural that as they started north, he should like to remain in his own neighborhood and with his own people.

But why Moses should have importuned him to remain with them as a guide when they had the "cloud" for that purpose, is a question. The answer seems to be that the cloud showed the general route, but did not point out minutely where pasture, shade and water were to be obtained, and which were often hid in obscure spots by the shifting sand. Then too, detachments of the Israelites may have been sent off from the main body. Hobab meant more to them than a single individual, for he was doubtless, prince of a clan, and hence could render considerable service.

Notice the motive Moses places before him (29), and the reward he promises him (32), and yet, it does not influence him favorably, if we may so interpret Judges 1:16, and 1 Samuel 15:6.

Preachers will find a text for a gospel sermon in these words of Moses. They are:

(1) A confession: "We are journeying";

(2) An invitation: "Come thou with us";

(3) A promise: "We will do thee good";

(4) A testimony: "The Lord hath spoken good concerning Israel."

Questions.

1. About how long had Israel remained at Sinai?

2. What five events are included in this lesson?

3. How would you interpret the trumpets on the eve of battle?

4. How explain Moses' request of Hobab?

5. Can you give a homiletic outline of Numbers 10:29?

MURMURING AND SEDITION

CHAPTERS 11-12

1. A Complaining People, 11:1-3.

Fatigue of travel, desolate physical surroundings, disappointment at the length of the journey and other things brought about discontent. The Revised Version says the people began to speak "evil in the ears of the Lord."

What is represented as the effect on the Lord (1)? How was it expressed by Him? What shows the locality in which this "murmuring" chiefly occurred? The nature of the "fire" is not stated, and there is some question whether it was an external burning, as in the case of Nadab and Abihu, or an internal one in the nature of a consuming fever, though the circumstances favor the first view. The allusion to the extremities of the camp, put with that to the "mixed multitude" of verse 4, indicates to some that the discontent originated among the Egyptian followers of Israel, however it may have been participated in by the latter ultimately (4). In their distress to whom did the people resort, and with what result (2)?

2. Heavenly Provision, 11:4-9.

For what did the people long (5), and what did they loathe (6)? How is it described, and how prepared or used (7-9)? "The resemblance of the manna to coriander seed was not in the color but in the size and figure; and from its comparison to be-dellium, which is either a drop of white gum or a white pearl, we are enabled to form a better idea of it. Moreover, it is evident, from the process of baking into cakes, that it could not have been the natural manna of the Arabian desert, for that is too gummy to admit of being ground into meal. In taste it is said (Exodus 16:31) to have been like 'wafers made with honey,' and here to have the taste of fresh oil. The discrepancy in these statements is only apparent; for in the former the manna is described in its raw state; in the latter after it was ground or baked. The minute description given here of its nature and use, was designed to show the great sinfulness of the people in being dissatisfied with such excellent food, furnished so plentifully and gratuitously."—*Bible Commentary.*

3. Aid for Moses, 11:10-30.

Who now is complaining, and why (11-15)? We can sympathize with Moses, but can we justify him? How does God answer him (16-17)? The Jews believe this to be the origin of the Sanhedrin, the highest court in Israel, so often named in the New Testament, and yet it may have been only a temporary expedient.

When God said, "I will come down" He doubtless meant not by a visible local descent, but by the tokens of His divine operations (17). By the "Spirit" is meant the Holy Spirit, only His person is not referred to but His gifts or influences (Joel 2:28, John 7:39). Some of the heavenly-bestowed qualities of leadership which had been given Moses would in like manner be distributed to them.

What relief is promised the people (18)? How does the language show, that the blessing would turn into a curse (19, 20). How does even Moses show incredulity in this (21, 22)? And how is he rebuked (23)?

4. The Plague of Quails, 11:31-34.

These quails (v. 31) were on their migratory way from Egypt, when the wind drove them into the camp. When the text says they fell over the camp "about a day's journey," it means, that there was a countless number of them. When it says they fell about "two cubits high," the statement is that the level of their flight was two cubits above the earth. Being exhausted with their journey they could fly no higher, and so were easily caught.

How swiftly did the punishment fall on the people (33)? "The probability is that their stomachs, having been long inured to manna (a light food) were not prepared to so sudden a change of regimen of which they seem to have partaken to so intemperate a degree as to produce a general surfeit. On a former occasion their murmurs for flesh were raised (Ex. 16) because they were in want of food. Here they proceeded, not from necessity, but lustful desire; and their sin, in the righteous judgment of God, was made to carry its own punishment."

Kibroth-hattaavah means, "the grave of lust" (see margin), which indicates that the deaths were confined to those who indulged immoderately.

5. Miriam and Aaron's sedition, c. 12.

What was the occasion of this sedition (1)? Judging by the order of the names, who may have been the leader in it? What testimony is borne to Moses (3)? May this obervation have been made because Moses took no notice of the reproaches of his relatives, leaving his vindication to God? Have we any other instance of an inspired penman eulogizing himself when circumstances seemed to demand it (2 Cor. 11:5; 12:11, 12)?

What shows that the divine interposition on Moses' behalf was open as well as immediate (4, 5)? How does God indicate a difference of degree in the gift and authority of His servants (6-8)?

"Mouth to mouth" means without an interpreter or visionary symbols and "dark speeches," without parables or similitude. The "similitude" of the Lord" cannot mean His face or essence (Ex. 33:20; John 1:18; Col. 1.15) but some evidence of His presence of another character (Ex. 33:2; 34:5).

What punishment fell on Miriam (10)? Why not on Aaron? Perhaps because his offense was not so great, or because leprosy would have interrupted or dishonored the holy service he performed.

How did Aaron express penitence (11)? How did Moses show a conciliatory spirit (13)? Nevertheless what continued humiliation must his sister endure (14, 15)?

Questions.

1. In what two ways may the "fire" of chapter 11:1 be interpreted?

2. What shows the supernatural character of the manna of verse 8?

3. Why was it so minutely described?

4. What deep spiritual lesson is suggested in verse 25?

5. How would you interpret the phrase "two cubits high" of verse 31?

6. What is the physical explanation of the plague, verse 33?

7. How would you harmonize verse 8 with other Scriptures?

8. Why was not Aaron punished as well as Miriam?

THE CRISIS AT KADESH-BARNEA

CHAPTERS 13-14

The unbelief exhibited at Kadesh-barnea, and the divine comment on it invest the transaction with great significance. The people had faith to sprinkle the blood of atonement (Ex. 12:28), and to come out of Egypt (type of the world), but had not faith to enter their Canaan rest. Therefore, through redeemed, they "grieved" Jehovah for forty years. Compare the chapters of

this lesson with Deut. 1.19-40; 1 Cor. 10:1-5; Heb. 3.12-19; 4:3-11.

Outline of the Chapters.

In the lesson we have:

(1) God's command to Moses and his execution of it (13: 1-20).

(2) The work of the spies (21-25).

(3) Their report to Moses, Aaron and the congregation (26-33).

(4) The effect on the congregation (14: 1-10).

(5) Jehovah's threat (11, 12).

(6) Moses' intercession (13-19).

(7) Jehovah's answer and decree of chastisement (20-38).

(8) The presumption and punishment of the people (39-45).

Matters to be Noted.

(1) By comparing Deut. 1:23, it will be seen that the proposition about the spies came from the people themselves, God granting their request both as a trial and punishment of their unbelief. Led by the pillar of fire and cloud they might have entered and conquered the land without any reconnaissance of it.

(2) Kadesh (13:26) is usually identified with Kadesh-barnea mentioned in 32:8, and since the researches of Henry Clay Trumbull (1884) there has been little doubt about it.

(3) According to Neh. 9:17, the unbelief of the people actually went the length of nominating a "captain" to lead them back to Egypt, demonstrating the wisdom of the decree that debarred that generation from entering the promised land.

(4) Remember the two witnesses for God (14:6), often referred to afterwards, and reflect on the arguments they present (7-9). If Jehovah's word be true as to the land, may we not believe it as to His ability to bring us in? By what divine interposition only were the lives of these witnesses preserved (10)?

(5) Moses' intercession is another of the great prayers of the Bible. See the boldness of his

faith in the arguments he employs. For whose honor is he most concerned (13-16)? What promise does he quote (17, 18)? Where in previous lessons was this commented on? What precedent does Moses rely upon (19)?

(6) Do not pass by the prophecy of v. 21. How much of human hopes are wrapped up in these words! Primarily they mean that the report of God's doings at that time would spread over all the land magnifying His name, but their ultimate application is to the millennium and beyond, as we shall see.

(7) How perverse the conduct of the Israelites, who, shortly before, were afraid that, though God was with them, they could not get possession of the land; yet now they act still more foolishly in supposing that, though God were not with them, they could expel the inhabitants by their unaided efforts. The consequences were such as might have been anticipated.

Questions.

1. Give the outline of this lesson by chapters.

2. With what other location is Kadesh identified, and on whose authority chiefly?

3. Have you read Neh. 9:17?

4. Name the two faithful witnesses for God, chapter 14:6.

5. Name two great prayers of the Bible.

6. How would you interpret the prophecy of verse 21?

7. What illustrates the foolishness of Israel at this crisis?

THE WILDERNESS WANDERINGS

Chapters 15-20

"The wilderness was part of the necessary discipline of the redeemed people, but this was not true of the years of wandering. The Red Sea, Marah, Elim, Sinai were God's ways in Israel's development and have their counterpart in christian experience; but from Kadesh-barnea to the Jordan all is for warning, and not imitation (1 Cor. 10: 1-11; Heb.

3:17-19). There is a present rest of God, of which the Sabbath and Canaan were types into which believers may and therefore *should* immediately enter by faith, but alas, too many christians never enter into it, and in a spiritual sense their carcasses fall in the wilderness. It is remarkable, that just when the people are turning in unbelief *from* the land, *God* should be giving directions (as in c. 15) for their conduct when they should enter it; but this is grace, and illustrates God's purpose in human redemption always."—*Scofield Bible.* It is not for anything in us that God has redeemed us in His Son, but for the magnifying of His own Name, and hence he has the same reason for keeping us saved to the end that He has for saving us at the beginning. Read here Ro. 11:29 and Phil. 1:6.

The Chief Events

The chief events of this section are the rebellion of Korah and his associates (16, 17), the death of Miriam and Aaron (20), and the miracle at Meribah (20), interspersed with particular laws and regulations of a Levitical chapter (15, 18, 19).

1. The Laws and Regulations, c. 15.

(1.) Note that the sin of ignorance needs to be atoned for as well as other sins (15:22-29), and God in His grace has provided for it. Christians who talk about possessing sinless perfection need forgiveness for such talk, for it is sin.

(2.) Note the difference between ignorant and presumptuous sins, and the illustration furnished of the latter (30-36), compare also Ps. 19:12,13.

The law of the Sabbath was plain, and this transgression of it very aggravated. Remember in the punishing that Jehovah was acting not only as Israel's God, but King. Israel was a theocracy, whose Sovereign was Jehovah, which is not true of any other nation. This offense was not only a violation of a divine command in the ordinary sense, but a violation of the law of the realm. It was as Sovereign that God gave this order to execute the man.

2. The Great Rebellion, cc. 16, 17.

Who were its chief leaders (1)? How many joined, and who were they (2)? What was their grievance and their argument (3)? What test is proposed by Moses (5-7)? How does he describe the ambition of Korah (8-11)? What indicates that the rebellion of the other leaders was instigated by jealousy of the supremacy of Moses (12-14)?

How is God's wrath expressed (21)? And His punishment (32-35)? What exhibition of popular passion follows (42)? Its punishment (49)? How does Aaron's action (48) typify Christ?

This controversy required a decisive settlement, for which reason, as we see in the next chapter, a miracle was wrought. In a word, what was that miracle?

3. The Ordinance of the Red Heifer, c. 19.

Among the regulations of this section that of the red heifer stands out with peculiar distinctness.

Was the heifer to be presented by an individual or the whole congregation (2)? This indicates that it was to be used for the general good. What must be its color? Just why is not known, unless it be in opposition to the superstition of the Egyptians who sacrificed red bulls and oxen, but never red heifers or cows which were sacred to their goddess Isis.

What ritualistic action of the priest showed that he was presenting an expiatory sacrifice (3, 4)? How does v. 6 suggest the ordinance for cleansing the lepers? (Lev. 14: 4-7.)

The subsequent verses of the chapter show the uses to which this "water of separation" was to be applied. For example, in case of a death.—"As in every family which sustained a bereavement, the members of the household became defiled, so an immense population, where instances of mortality and other cases of uncleanness would be daily occurring, the water of separation must have been in constant requisition."

We need to remember that the defilement here to be remedied as, in some other cases we have met with, implied no moral guilt but had only a ceremonial and typical significance. It was part of that system which God would teach Israel, and through Israel the whole world, the essential nature of holiness.

4. The Miracle at Meribah, c. 20.

If you compare v. 1 with vv. 22 and 23, and then chapter 33:38, you will see that between the last verse of the preceding and the first verse of this chapter "there is a long and undescribed interval of 37 years." In other words, "in this book only the most important incidents are recorded, and these are confined chiefly to the first and second and the last years of the wanderings in the wilderness."

Where were the people now (1)? This was their second arrival there after an interval of 38 years (compare Deut. 2:16). The old generation had nearly all died, and the new was now encamped here with the view of soon entering Canaan.

We need not suppose that during all this time the people moved about in a compact mass without any employment or object, but that their life was similar to nomads generally.

What event occurred at Kadesh at this time (1)? What physical necessity arose (2)? How did the people deport themselves (3-5)? Where as usual, did their leaders take refuge (6)? What were they commanded to do (8)? What "rod" is meant (compare 17:10)? How is the hasty and passionate conduct of Moses illustrated (10)? Compare Ps. 106:33. He had been directed to *speak* to the rock, but what did he do? How were the leaders rebuked (12)?

Contrast this miracle with the one in Ex. 17:5-7. The rock in both instances typified Christ (1 Cor. 10:4); but Christ once smitten, needs not to be smitten (crucified) again. Moses' act not only displayed impatience and perhaps vain glory, but (in type) made of none effect one of the most vital doctrines of grace. The believer from whom the divine blessing has been withheld through sin needs not another sacrifice. It is for him to *confess* his sins according to 1 John 1:9, and receive cleansing and forgiveness. This is the symbolism of speaking to the rock instead of smiting it a second time.

Questions.

1. How do the wanderings of Israel differ from their experience in the wilderness from a Scriptural point of view?

2. Give the chief events of this lesson?

3. Is ignorance counted a sin?

4. How did Israel in its government differ from every other nation?

5. State from memory what you know about the ordinance of the red heifer.

6. Do the same of the miracle at Meribah.

THE JOURNEY RENEWED

Chapters 20: 14-21:35

1. Preparation for the Journey, 20:14-29.

Israel prepared to renew the journey, what now does Moses do (14-18)? In what spirit does Edom meet this request (18:20)? For the reason Israel was not permitted to force a passage through Edom, see Deut. 2:1-8.

What event in Israel's history takes place at this juncture (23-28)? In what sense was this a chastisement on Aaron (24)? Who succeeded him (26:28)? (Note the manner in which this incident is used in Is. 22:20-25). Compare Heb. 7:23-25. A tomb has been erected near the spot where Aaron was buried.

2. Fightings and Fears, c. 21.

What event is narrated in the opening of chapter 21? We wonder why this discomfiture of Israel at the first was permitted,

but perhaps to teach them the lesson of their weakness and of dependence solely upon God (Ps. 44: 1-8). The phrase "utterly destroy" (2) might be rendered by "devote." In what earlier lesson was this subject of devotement considered?

What prolongation of their journey was necessitated by Edom's refusal (4)? What effect had this on the people? What previous cause of murmuring was renewed (5)? What chastisement followed (6)? What effect had it (7)? How did God provide for their deliverance (8:9)? In what way did this show that the deliverance was not the effect of nature or art, but of God's power and grace? How is it used in the New Testament as a type of our salvation from sin through Christ? (See John 3:14, 15.) How did this "brazen serpent" subsequently become a snare to Israel? (See 2 Kings 18: 1-4.) "That part of the desert where the Israelites now were—near the head of the gulf of Akaba—is infested with reptiles of various kinds, particularly lizards, which raise themselves in the air, and swing from branches; and scorpions which lying among long grass, are particularly dangerous to the bare-legged, sandaled people of the East. The species that caused so great mortality amongst the Israelites cannot be ascertained. They are said to have been fiery, either from their bright color, or the inflammation their bite occasioned."—*Bible Commentary.*

In studying the verses that follow it will be desirable to have a good map.

Note what is said (14) about the book of "The Wars of the Lord" as indicating a writing of some sort of which we have little record. The words following to the end of verse 16 are apparently a quotation from this book, and presumably inserted to decide the position of Aaron.

What discovery was made near this point, and how was it celebrated (17, 18)? What country did the Israelites now obtain by right of conquest (21-32)?

Questions.

1. How does this lesson teach that trials sometimes come for our good?

2. Quote John 3:15, 16.

3. Why is "fiery" used of the serpents?

4. What ancient historical writing is quoted in this lesson?

BALAAM AND HIS PROPHECIES

CHAPTERS 22-24

1. The Historical Setting, c. 22.

In what neighborhood are the Israelites now camped (1)? Where is this located? Who was the king of this people (4)? What effect on him was wrought by Israel's victories over his neighbors (2-4)?- What plan of defense other than war does he adopt (5, 6)?

Balaam's History and Character.

Balaam is a mystery. He comes from Mesopotamia where the knowledge of the true God lingered after it had been lost in the other parts of the known world. He is one of the group containing Melchizedek and Job, who testified that although Jehovah was now revealing Himself peculiarly to the Hebrews, yet He had not left Himself without witnesses in the other nations.

Not only Balaam's history but His character is a mystery, some thinking him a saint, and others a charlatan. Probably he was between the two, worshiping God ostensibly and yet serving himself where the temptation was strong, as it seems to have been in this case.

Examine v. 13 as an illustration where his answer conceals the reason for the divine prohibition while it shows a willingness to go if only he could get permission.

When that permission is obtained (20), it is an instance where God gave up a man to his own lust without approving it (22), while he proposed to overrule the wrong desire for the furtherance of His own will. It is one thing to serve God and an-

other to *willingly* serve Him. For the ultimate fate of Balaam, compare c. 31:8, and for inspired comments on his character, 2 Peter 2:16 and Jude 11.

The Dumb Ass Speaking.

Some say that verses 22-35 represent merely a version and not an actual occurrence, but this seems inadmissible in the middle of a plain history. That the ass may have been uttering sounds like a parrot, without understanding them is probable, but the tenor of Peter's language strengthens the conviction that we are dealing with an external act.

But why does not the prophet show astonishment at the phenomenon? He may have done so, without a record of it being made, or the lack of it may be explained by the engrossment of his mind with the prospect of gain, for Peter speaks of "the madness of the prophet."

2. The Disappointed King, c. 23.

Balak prepared these altars and offered these sacrifices (23: 1-3) in honor of Baal, the god of his country, but in whose honor did Balaam intend them (4)? And yet how is his superstition mingled with the true worship? Compare 2 Kings 18:22; Isa. 17:8; Jer. 11:13; Hosea 8:11.

How does the prophet express the truth that no charms or demoniacal power can avail against God's purposes (8)? How does verse 9, last part, harmonize with what we have learned about Israel previously? (Compare Ex. 19:5; Lev. 20:24 and Deut. 33:28). How does the prophecy show not only Israel's separateness but greatness (10)? Do you recall Gen. 13:16 and 38:14?

When Balaam says, "Let me die the death of the righteous," he is still referring to Israel. The Hebrew word for "righteous" is Jeshurun, another name for the Israelites. And the prophet's meaning is that as they were blessed above others, not only in life but in death, because of their knowledge of the true God, he desired to have a part with them.

But his desire was not very strong, in which he represents a large class in the world who wish for the salvation of Christ, and yet never accept it by receiving and confessing Him.

God's Unchangeable Grace.

In the second prophecy (18-24), how is the unchangeable purpose of God's grace expressed (19)? Compare how this principle in Israel's case still maintains, and applies to believers on Jesus Christ in this dispensation. The following will aid: 1 Sam. 15:29; Mal 3:6; Ro. 11:29; Titus 1:2; Heb. 13:8; James 1:17, etc.

How does verse 21 show that this divine purpose toward Israel is one of grace? Does it say that there was no iniquity in Israel, or simply that God took no cognizance of it? But does His noncognizance of it mean that He never chastised Israel for it? On the contrary, we have seen Him chastising Israel continually as she has provoked it. What then *do* these words mean?

They mean that God neither has seen, nor shall see any iniquity in Israel that shall cause Him to change His original promise to Abraham and discard them as a nation from the place of privilege He has intended for them. This promise to Abraham is based on His original promise of the redemption of man in Gen. 3:15. This promise is unalterable, and depends not on man's goodness, but on God's truth and honor and grace. That is not to say that it has no effect on human character, and that mankind never will become good as the result of it, but only that its source is heavenly love and not earthly conduct. John 6:37-40; Ro. 4: 4-8; 8: 28-39; Eph. 2:1-10; 1 Peter 1: 3-9; 1 John 5: 9-13.

3. The Great Prophecy, c. 24.

At what conviction has the prophet now arrived, and with what effect on his conduct (24:1)? What was the feeling in his heart, do you suppose? Look at Deuteronomy 23:5 for an answer. One wonders why God should use such a man as a prophet of good for His people, but before He ordained a regular line of prophets, He was pleased to reveal His will instrumentally through various persons.

Christians are sometimes solicitous to be "anointed for service," as though that were the highest or only fruit of the new life. But while not disparaging the aim but encouraging it in its proper place, let us be humbled by the thought that God can get service out of bad as well as good men when He pleases. There is a higher aim for the Christian, and that is to "walk worthily of the Lord unto all pleasing" (Col. 1:10). When one is doing that he is not likely to come short in service.

The prophecy of Balaam is arranged as poetry in the Revised Version. "The redundant imagery of verses 5 to 7, depicts the humble origin, rapid progress and great prosperity of Israel."

With what king and kingdom is Israel compared (7)? The Amalekites are meant, the most powerful of the desert tribes, a common title for whose kings was "Agag," like "Pharaoh" or "Caesar."

What does Balaam say of the future of Israel (8)? With what effect on Balak (10, 11)? How does the next prophecy particularize (14)? Who do you suppose is the ultimate fulfilment of the word "him" in verse 17? It may mean the nation of Israel, but doubtless it is identical with the "star" and the "sceptre" of the same verse, whose application is Christ. That is not to say that the prophet knew this, but only that the event proves it. He only saw some great one coming out of Israel, not knowing whom, but we know whom in the light of the New Testament. Compare Gen. 49:10; Ps. 110; Matt. 2:2. Of course, David was an approximate fulfilment of the words, and did the things referred to in verses 17 and 18, but in the completest sense the reference is to Christ, and especially at His second coming, see Is. 59:20; Ro. 11:25-29.

What other national fate is

predicted as well as Amalek (21)? What great nation would ultimately deport the Kenites (22)? What ultimately would be its history (24)? "Chittim" or "Kittim" is an earlier name for Greece and some of the other western lands bordering on the Mediterranean, particularly Italy. What finally would become of the conqueror of Assyria (24)?

Compare for some of the fulfilments of these prophecies Ex. 17:14; 1 Sam. 15:1; Judges 1:16; 4:11, 16, 17; 2 Kings 15:29; Dan. 2:36-45; 5: 7, 3, etc. The Assyrians were overthrown by the Greeks under Alexander and his successors, and afterwards by the Romans who conquered the Greeks. The Romans, however, are yet to be overthrown with the son of perdition at their head, by the second coming of Christ to set up His kingdom on the earth through restored Israel. Some of these things we shall learn more about later on, but in the meantime what a sweep there is in this vision of Balaam! Little did he know the meaning of it all!

Questions.

1. With what group of men may Balaam be classed and why?

2. What is your impression of his character?

3. What two ways are there of serving God?

4. What shows the unusual incident of the ass historical?

5. What is the explanation of 23:21?

6. What is a higher aim for a saint than merely service?

7. Give the common title of the kings of Amalek.

8. Apply the words of 24:17 and tell why.

9. What territory is defined by "Chittim"?

10. What is the sweep of Balaam's prophecy?

BALAAM'S SCHEME AND ITS CONSEQUENCES

CHAPTERS 25-31

We are not through with the "hireling" prophet. We find him referred to in three places in the New Testament. 2 Peter 2:15 speaks of his "way," Jude 11 of his "error" and Rev. 2:14 of his "doctrine."

His *way* is that which characterizes all false teachers, viz: making a market of their gifts. His *error* lay in failing to see the principle of the vicarious atonement by which God can be just and yet the justifier of believing sinners (Ro. 3:26). In other words, he felt that a holy God must curse such a people as Israel, knowing only a natural morality. His *doctrine*, which concerns us more particularly just now, refers to his teaching Balak to corrupt the people whom he could not curse (compare 25:1-3 with 31:16).—*Scofield Bible*.

1. Harlotry and Idolatry, c. 25.

Into what sin did the people fall (1)? This fall in morality was soon followed by what fall in religion (2, 3)? Baal was a general name for "lord" and "peer" for a mount in Moab. The real name of this lord of the mount was Chemosh, whose worship was celebrated by the grossest obscenity.

What punishment fell on them (4, 5)? Capital punishment in Israel meant that the victim was first stoned to death or otherwise slain, and then gibbeted. "The heads of the people" means the chief leaders in the outrage.

Verse 6 speaks of a flagitious act in connection with this disgraceful conduct, promptly revenged by whom (7)? What reward to him follows (12, 13)? What judgment had come to Israel (8)? What judgment does God order upon the Midianites (17, 18)?

2. Second Numbering, c. 26.

What new command is now given Moses (1 2)? The probability is that the plague just mentioned had swept away the last of the older generation and hence the census.

This census was necessary to preserve the distinction of families in connection with the distribution of Canaan soon to take place.

By comparing the numbers with those of chapter 1, it will be seen that divine judgments had reduced the ranks of some of the tribes which had been particularly disobedient, while others had been increased so that Israel still continued about the same in numbers at the close of this period of thirty-eight years as at the beginning. What was the total diminution?

Before passing to the next chapter observe verse 64 and note that its statement must not be considered absolute. For, besides Caleb and Joshua, there were alive at this time Eleazar and Ithamar, and in all probability a number of Levites, who had no participation in the defections in the wilderness. The tribe of Levi, having neither sent a spy into Canaan, nor being included in the enumeration at Sinai, must be regarded as not coming within the range of the sentence; and therefore would exhibit a spectacle not witnessed in the other tribes of many in their ranks above sixty years of age—*Bible Commentary*.

3. A Brief Glance at Chapters 27 to 30.

We pass over the request of the daughters of Zelophehad (27:1-11), the injunction to Moses (12-14), and the ordination of Joshua (15-23), as requiring no explanation under the circumstances. The same may be said about the offerings (chapter 28) whose repetition was necessary doubtless because a new generation had sprung up since their enactment, and because the people would soon be settled in the land where they could be observed.

4. The Midianites Judged, and Balaam Slain, c. 31.

What is practically the last command Moses received from God (1, 2)?

The Midianites, as may be recalled, were descendants of the marriage of Abraham with Keturah, and occupied the east and the south-east of Moab. They were the chief actors in the plot to seduce Israel into idolatry, by which it was hoped Jehovah would withdraw His blessing from them and permit their enemies to triumph. Were the plan successful it would mean in so far the defeat of God's purpose for the redemption of the nations through the instrumentality of Israel as we have already learned. An understanding of this fact is necessary to preserve this chapter from misinterpretation.

A Religious War.

Who were to be avenged according to Jehovah (2)? And who according to Moses (3)? How interesting to perceive here another illustration of the identification of God with His people! They have the same cause, the same friends, and the same enemies. Compare Acts 9: 4, 5.

And note another circumstance equally strange as the world considers things; viz: the preparation for death enjoined upon Moses! Were these Midianites his own enemies merely, one would expect him to be exhorted to forgive them and thus "die in peace with all the world." But being God's enemies, the most appropriate close of his earthly career would be to execute God's judgment upon them.

Are there not lessons here for the peace advocates of this century? While sympathizing with them in many things, yet if they expect wars to cease until God has had a final settlement with the wicked nations of the earth, they are yet in the primary class of Bible instruction.

"Some Things Hard to be Understood."

The faith of some will stumble at things in this record, but a deeper knowledge of God makes all plain, and our duty is to trust Him until that knowledge comes.

(1) The slaying of the males (7), was in accordance with the divine principle in all such cases, as shown in Deuteronomy 20:13. In this instance, however, the destruction seems to have been only partial, if we may judge by

Judges 6:1 and the following verses. Perhaps this is explained by the circumstance that only those families were slain who were in the neighborhood of the Hebrew camp or had been accomplices in the plot. Many may have saved themselves by flight.

(2) The slaying of Balaam (8) raises a question when we compare the statement with chapter 24:25. Perhaps he changed his plan about returning home after starting, and remained among the Midianites for the evil purpose already spoken of; or, learning that Israel had fallen into the snare laid, he may have returned to demand his reward from Midian. His judgment was just in consideration of his sin in the light of special revelations received from God.

(3) The killing of the women and children (14-18) will stagger us till we remember that Moses' wrath was not an ebullition of temper, but an expression of enlightened regard for the will of God, and the highest interests of Israel. By their conduct the women had forfeited all claims to other treatment, especially in view of the sacred character of this war. As to the male children, it is to be remembered that a war of extermination required their destruction. We will deal with this subject more fully when we come to the broader illustration in the destruction of the Canaanites in Joshua.

(4) Observe the declaration in verses 48-50, especially the last clause of 49. Here we have an astonishing miracle witnessing to the interposition of God in this whole matter, and in so far silencing every objection raised on the ground of cruelty and injustice. Compare here the opening verses of Psalm 44, and other similar places. These judgments of God on sin and disobedience should open our eyes to its nature, should cause us to tremble at the fear of it, and adore the grace which has given such guilty souls as we a sin bearer in Jesus Christ.

Questions.

1. How is Balaam spoken of in the New Testament, and by whom?

2. Define the meaning of Baalpeor.

3. Define capital punishment in Israel.

4. What was the need for this census?

5. Which tribe had the most of the older men at this time, and why?

6. Who were the Midianites, and where were they located?

7. What justifies their punishment?

8. What comment on the universal peace theory does this lesson contain?

9. What particular circumstance shows God's approval on the extermination of these enemies?

GETTING READY FOR CANAAN

CHAPTERS 32-34

1. Reuben and Gad's Choice, c. 32.

What was their choice of possessions, and on what ground was it made (1-5)? What suspicion of their motive possessed Moses (6-15)? What assurance is given him (16-19)? How is the matter closed (20-27)? What charge does Moses transmit to his successors (28-32)?

2. Review of the Journey, c. 33.

The following from the *Bible Commentary* is useful: "This chapter may be said to form the winding-up of the history of the travels of the Israelites, for the following chapters relate to matters connected with the occupation and division of the land.

"As several apparent discrepancies will be discovered on comparing the records here with Exodus, and the occasional notices of places in Deuteronomy, it is probable that this itinerary comprises a list of only the most important stations in their journeys; those where they formed prolonged encampments, and whence they dispersed their flocks and herds to pasture on the plains till the surrounding herbage was exhausted. The catalogue extends from their departure out of Egypt to their arrival on the plains of Moab."

At whose authorization was this record made (2)? Thus was established the truth of history, thus a memorial of God's marvelous work on Israel's behalf preserved for all generations.

For additional light on verses 3 and 4, consult the Revised Version.

"As there are no less than eighteen stations inserted between Hazeroth and Kadesh, and only eleven days were spent in performing that journey (Deut. 1:2) the record here must refer to a different visit to Kadesh. The first was when they left Sinai in the second month (c. 1:2; c. 13:20), and were in Kadesh in August (Deut. 1:45), and 'abode many days' in it, and murmuring at the report of the spies, were commanded to return into the desert 'by the way of the Red Sea.' The arrival at Kadesh, mentioned in this catalogue, corresponds to the second sojourn at that place, being the first month, or April (c. 20:1).

"Between the two visits there intervened a period of 38 years, during which they wandered hither and thither, often returning to the same spots, as the pastoral necessities of their flocks required."

When did Aaron die, and at what age (38, 39)? What command is renewed to Moses (50-53)? What warning accompanies it (55, 56)?

3. The Boundaries, c. 34.

It is difficult to trace these boundary lines on the map, especially those on the south, and students must be referred to Bible dictionaries on the subject.

In the meantime, it is clear that Israel never entered on the possession of all this territory, even in the golden era of David and Solomon. That they will do so in the millennial age there can be no doubt.

Questions.

1. How would you explain certain discrepancies between these chapters and other parts of the Pentateuch?

2. How is the truth of this history established?

3. What explanation might be given of the 18 stations and only 11 journeys?

4. Has Israel ever entered on possession of all her territory?

5. Is she likely to do so?

THE CITIES OF THE LEVITES AND CITIES OF REFUGE

Chapter 35

We may conclude our exposition of Numbers with this chapter, as the final one contains no difficulties not dealt with in previous lessons, or that are not explained in the text itself.

1. The Cities of the Levites, vv. 1-5.

"As the Levites were to have no domain like the other tribes, they were to be distributed throughout the land in certain cities appropriated to their use; and these cities were to be surrounded by extensive suburbs.

"There is an apparent discrepancy between vv. 4 and 5 with regard to the extent of these suburbs; but the statements refer to different things—the one to the extent of the suburbs from the walls of the city, the other to the space of 2,000 cubits from their extremity.

"In point of fact, there was an extent of ground, amounting to 3,000 cubits, measured from the wall of the city. One thousand were probably occupied with outhouses for the accommodation of shepherds and other servants, with gardens, or oliveyards. And these, which were portioned out to different families (1 Chron. 6:60), might be sold by one Levite to another, but not to any individual of another tribe (Jer. 32: 7). The other two thousand cubits remained a common for the pasturing of cattle (Lev. 25:34)."—*Bible Commentary.*

2. The Cities of Refuge, vv. 6-29.

The remarks which follow, taken from the same source as the preceding, will furnish a general introduction to an analysis of the text:

"The practice of Goelism—i.e., of the nearest relation of an individual who was killed being bound to demand satisfaction from the author of his death, existed from a remote antiquity (Gen. 4:14; 27:45).

"It seems to have been an established usage in the age of Moses; and, although in a rude state of society it is a natural principle of criminal jurisprudence, it is liable to great abuses. The chief of the evils inseparable from it are, that the kinsman, who is bound to execute justice, will often be precipitate, little disposed, in the heat of passion, to discriminate between the premeditated purpose of the assassin and the misfortune of the unintentional homicide.

"Moreover, it had a tendency not only to foster a vindicative spirit, but, in case of the Goel being unsuccessful in finding his victim, to transmit animosities and feuds against his descendants from one generation to another. This is exemplified among the Arabs in the present day.

The Humane Object.

"This practice of Goelism obtained among the Hebrews to such an extent that it was not expedient to abolish it; and Moses, while sanctioning its continuance, was directed to make special regulations, which tended to prevent the consequences of personal vengeance, and at the same time, to afford an accused person time and means of proving his innocence.

"This was the humane end contemplated in the institution of cities of refuge. There were to be six, three on the east of Jordan, both because the territory there was equal in length, though not in breadth, to Canaan, and because it might be more convenient for some to take refuge across the border. They were appointed for the benefit, not of the Israelites only, but of all resident strangers."

Analysis of the Text.

How many of these cities were there (6)? For whom appointed? From among what other cities? What important qualification is made in verse 11? And what further one in verse 12? How were these cities arranged with reference to the Jordan (14)? "On this side Jordan" should be rendered *beyond Jordan*, and the idea is that three were specially for the accommodation of those tribes which so recently had elected to stay on the east side of the river. Was this refuge limited to the Israelites (15)?

The Avenger of Blood.

What three cases of premeditated murder are mentioned in verses 16-18? What three in verses 20 and 21? What name is given him whose duty it was to slay the murderer (19)? The word "revenger" or *avenger* (see v. 12), is the translation of the Hebrew word *Gaal* from which comes *Goelism*. It means a kinsman, the nearest of kin. It was he, only, who could perform this office.

In the case of premeditated murder was there any escape for the guilty? But in the case of unpremeditated murder what protection did these cities provide (22-24)? What was the method of operation (24, 25)? What condition was necessary for the man-slayer to observe (26-28)? "Once having reached the nearest city, for one or other of them was within a day's journey of all parts of the land, he was secure. But he had to 'abide in it.' His confinement was a wise rule, designed to show the sanctity of human blood in God's sight, as well as to protect the man-slayer himself, whose presence in society might have provoked the passions of the deceased's relatives. But the period of his release from confinement was not until the death of the high priest. That was a season of public affliction, when private sorrows were overlooked under a sense of the national calamity, and when the death of so eminent a servant of God naturally led all to serious consideration about their own mortality."

We meet this subject again in Deuteronomy 19 and Joshua 20, all of the passages put together furnishing rich material for a Bible reading or a sermon on the cities of refuge as

A Type of Christ.

They are a type:

(1) In their *origin*, since they were divinely ordained.

(2) In their *necessity*, for without them there was no hope for the pursued.

(3) In their *accessibility*, for being on both sides of the Jordan, and within a day's journey of all parts of the land, they might be easily reached.

(4) In their *security*, for the man-slayer once received within their walls could not be assailed.

(5) In their *applicability*, for they were designed for all, Jew and Gentile, friend and alien, without distinction.

Any able to use such an outline will not need to be reminded of the New Testament Scriptures which parallel the different divisions. In working out the details it might be well to show that like our salvation in Christ, the value of these cities of refuge was limited to those that remained in them. "Abide in Me."

Also, point the contrast, that whereas they were restricted to the innocent man-slayer, Christ receives the guilty. The man-slayer had to be judged first, we believers are already judged, condemned, and yet free in Christ.

It is proper to say also that the "avenger of blood" or the kinsman redeemer is a beautiful type of Christ, some think more fitting than the cities of refuge themselves, but of this we shall speak in the next lesson.

Questions.

1. How is the supposed discrepancy between verses 4 and 5 explained?

2. What is meant by the word "Goelism"?

3. Of what is "Gaal" or "Goel" the translation?

4. What is the meaning of the word?

5. To what abuses was Goelism liable?

6. In what ways was the Mosaic legislation intended to restrain them?

7. Where were the cities of refuge located with reference to the Jordan, and why?

8. How comprehensive were their benefits?

9. Why should the man-slayer be *confined* in them?

10. In how many ways may they be considered typical of Christ?

THE KINSMAN REDEEMER

In fulfillment of the promise in the last lesson there is here a consideration of the kinsman redeemer as a type of Christ, being an abridgment from the Rev. Henry Melvill, D.D., an eloquent English university preacher of an earlier generation. Our object is not only to open up the subject to those who have never considered it, but also to furnish material for a Gospel sermon to those who have opportunities in that direction.

Great Truths Taught by Common Things.

Melvill begins by speaking of the close connection between the Jewish and Christian dispensations as we have discovered in our study of the Pentateuch. We have seen this especially in regard to redemption, the redeemer under the law being the type of the Redeemer under the Gospel. There may be no distinct allusions to Christ, but whenever you meet with a transaction of redemption, either of land or of a person, the matter is so ordered as to be typical of the person and work of Christ. Thus the Jews were taught even through the common dealings of life the great spiritual deliverance that was wrought out in the fullness of time.

There are three conditions marked in the Old Testament as requiring the interposition of a redeemer:

(1) If there had been a forfeiture of an inheritance, a loss of personal liberty, or the shedding of blood. In each it was enjoined that the Goel or redeemer should interfere on behalf of the distressed individual. Moreover, the occasions which necessitated the interference of the Goel, and the manner in which it was conducted bear so close a likeness to the Gospel redeemer that we can scarcely doubt it to have been the purpose of the Holy Spirit to keep the scheme of human redemption always before Israel.

The Forfeiture of an Inheritance.

To begin with the forfeiture of an inheritance alluded to in the twenty-fifth chapter of Leviticus. If an Israelite had become poor, and sold some of his possessions, the Goel was directed, if possible, to redeem the land. In that case it became the property of the Goel until the year of jubilee, when it returned to the original proprietor. The forfeited possession might be redeemed by the latter at any time were he able to pay the price of it; but were he not, then only the Goel could redeem it for him, and if he did or could not do so, no stranger might interfere, the possession must remain unredeemed.

We see the typical character of this transaction indicated first in the fact that only a kinsman could fill the office of Goel. Some other individual might be ready to render aid, but had he the rights of the closest kinsmanship? If not, the law refused to allow his interposition. In laying down this principle, God taught that He who should arise as the Goel or Redeemer of a lost world, must be bone of our bone, and flesh of our flesh. No angel could redeem us. (Hebrews 10 to 18.)

In the next place, if you wish to describe man's natural condition and the change effected in it by the work of Christ, where can you obtain a better illustration than from the directions of this law in regard to a forfeited inheritance? Who is the Israelite that has grown poor and alienated himself from the possession of his fathers if it be not the sinner originally made in the image of God, and who has destroyed that image by an act of rebellion? An eternity of happiness was our possession, but we threw it away, bringing upon ourselves the curse of death of body and soul. We became poor, and who shall measure our spiritual poverty? Have we a solitary fraction of our own to pay for our redemption? Therefore the inheritance must be forfeited forever, unless a kinsman redeemer shall arise. God has provided this redeemer in a man, and yet infinitely more than a man, the God-man Christ Jesus.

But furthermore, as in the case of the impoverished Israelite, what Christ had redeemed He has not instantly restored. The year of jubilee has not yet come for us, but with a mightier trumpet peal than could be heard upon the mountains of Israel shall that jubilee year be introduced. The resurrection and glorifying of our bodies will be their completion for entrance on the fulness of the purchased possession.

The Loss of Personal Liberty.

To pass now to the second instance of redemption where there has been a loss of personal liberty, and where all that has been spoken of in regard to the forfeiture of an inheritance applies with only a slight change. The same chapter shows that for the discharge of a debt or the procurement of subsistence an Israelite might sell himself either to another Israelite or a stranger. Should he become the servant of an Israelite, there was no right of redemption, but he must remain in the house of his master till the jubilee. But should he become the servant of a stranger and cause arise for the interposition of the Goel the law ran: "After that he is sold he may be redeemed again; one of his brethren may redeem him." If he were able to redeem himself he might do so but were the ability lacking then his kinsman must interpose, no stranger could discharge the office.

Observe that the Goel had no right to interfere unless the Israelite had sold himself to a stranger. The reason is that if his master was an Israelite like himself, then he had not become separated from God's people and the exigency had not arisen for his redemption in the same sense. It were only when the master were a stranger that the serving became typical of man's bondage to Satan. It was in such a case only that we find the illustration of the New Testament, saying that the servant of sin has been "made captive by Satan at his will."

Thank God in such a case the sinner need not languish forever in bondage. The chain need not be eternal, for there advances his kinsman, made of a woman, made under the law, and in the likeness of sinful flesh, to pay down the price of redemption and to bid the prisoner come forth into the glorious liberty of the children of God.

The Shedding of Blood.

The third case of redemption, where there had been the shedding of blood, differs from the two already examined.

This is referred to in the thirty-fifth of Numbers, and in connection with the appointment of the cities of refuge.

The King James translation speaks only of the "avenger of blood," but the original is Goel or the kinsman redeemer. You will recall that the latter must pursue the murderer and take vengeance if he overtake him before reaching the city of refuge. But if the Goel were not at hand to follow him no stranger had the right to do so. This feature of the Goel therefore stands out as prominently here as in the other instances.

It is the common idea that the cities of refuge were typical of Christ and the murderer was the human race pursued by the justice of God. Of course, there is some fidelity in this figure, and under certain limitations it may be considered as a type, but still it remains that the standing type of Christ under the Mosaic law

was the Goel, or kinsman redeemer. It is for this reason we seek the figure of Christ, not in the cities of refuge, but in the avenger of blood.

For example, those who were really guilty fled in vain to the city and must be delivered up to the punishment due their crime. Who can find in this any emblem of the flying of sinners for refuge to Christ?

On the other hand, observe that the human race, created deathless, was slain by Satan when he moved our first parents to the act prohibited in the words "in the day that thou doest it, thou shalt surely die." It was with reference to this slaughter of mankind that Christ said of him: "He was a murderer from the beginning." It was through Satan that death, whether of body or soul, gained footing in this creation, and we count it therefore proper to describe him as the great man-slayer.

Our Nearest of Kin.

But who pursued the murderer? Who took on him the vengeance which drew the wonder of the universe and "through death destroyed him that had the power of death"? Who but the kinsman redeemer? Who but that "seed of the woman" predicted to bruise the serpent's head? Though Satan for a while may be permitted to roam over this creation, there has been gained a mastery over him which has reduced him into the bond-slave of our kinsman. And the latter is only reserving the full taking of vengeance until the year of jubilee arrives, when the enemy will be hurled into the lake of fire forever and ever.

Finally, we should not suppose that in pleading for the typical character of the Goel we plead for the existence of a figure hidden from the men of the old dispensation. When Job exclaims: "I know that my redeemer liveth," what he really says is, "I know that my Goel, my kinsman, liveth." And if the saints among the Jews could describe Christ as the Goel, would they not naturally turn to the offices of the Goel that they might ascertain the offices of Christ?

Who is there that is not the kinsman of Christ, since that kinsmanship resulted in His taking human nature upon Him? It is enough to be a man to know oneself Christ's kinsman. He tasted death for every man. He redeemed every man's inheritance. He regained every man's liberty. He avenged every man's blood. Will anyone put from him through unbelief the benefits of His interposition? "If ye will not believe, surely ye shall not be established."

This is the glorious Gospel of the Son of God, and nothing but unbelief can exclude the poorest, the meanest, the wickedest among men from a full and free share in the perfect redemption.

Questions.

1. What great truth were the Jews taught even in the common duties of life?

2. What three conditions in the Old Testament required the interposition of a redeemer?

3. What relation must this redeemer bear to the distressed person?

4. Could any other person act in this capacity?

5. What great principle of our redemption is illustrated in this case?

6. How long might the Goel retain a redeemed possession, and what does this illustrate?

7. Why, in the second case, might not the Goel interpose unless an Israelite had sold himself to a stranger?

8. Can you quote Job 19:25-27?

DEUTERONOMY

NOTE

There were fewer lessons in Numbers in proportion to its length than in the previous books, and the same will be true of Deuteronomy and some others. The reason is because of the lesser comparative importance of these books, and because of the repetitions they contain.

It would be serious, however, both to the understanding of the Bible and the spiritual life of those following these lessons if the books referred to should be omitted in the course of study. They are part of the revelation of God's will, and have their value in our coming to know Him, and in the moulding of our character and our training for service.

How to Utilize the Lessons.

But how shall the teachers of Bible classes utilize such lessons? Let not their length discourage them, but let that feature be seized upon as a precious opportunity to get their classes feeding on the Word of God in large portions, and drinking from the fountain of life in copious draughts. The experience to many will be new, but that will give it freshness. At the same time the task will be easy, simply to *read* and not necessarily to *study* the assigned chapters. The interest is likely to increase with the reading, until the variety afforded by such lessons over those briefer in space and more closely analytic in character will be anticipated with pleasure.

A Method Suggested.

The author would recommend this method: Announce to the class that the next lesson will be on such or such a general theme, and cover so many chapters. As it has few difficulties of any kind, or covers matters treated previously, the class are asked merely to read the text carefully and in a prayerful spirit. But they are asked to read it several times, if possible make it their daily reading for the intervening week. Then when they come together in the class they will begin to discuss its contents as familiar with it, having something to communicate worth while.

The teacher or leader of the class will always find a basis or starting point for such discussions in the questions and annotations furnished in the Commentary.

REVIEW OF ISRAEL'S HISTORY

CHAPTERS 1-3

A book has been written by Canon Bernard entitled, "The Progress of Doctrine in the New Testament," in which he shows not only that the contents of its books are inspired, but their arrangement and order as well.

The same might be said of the Old Testament, especially of the Pentateuch. To illustrate, the purpose of the Bible is to give the history of redemption through a special seed. In Genesis we have the election of that seed (Abraham), in Exodus their redemption, in Leviticus their worship, in Numbers their walk and warfare, and in Deuteronomy their final preparation for the experience towards which all has been directed. (C. H. M.)

The Book of Review.

A secondary name for Deuteronomy might be "The Book of Review." The word comes from two Greek words, *deuter*, "second," and *nomos*, "law," the second law, or the repetition of the law. And yet when it comes to reviewing the law it adds certain things not mentioned previously (see 29:1).

The one great lesson it contains is that of obedience grounded on a known and recognized relationship to God through redemption.

The Divisions of the Book.

1. Review of the History, 1-3;
2. Review of the Law, 4-11; 3. In-

structions and Warnings, 12-27;
4. Prophecy of Israel's Future,
28-30; 5. Moses' Final Counsels,
31; 6. Moses' Song and Blessing,
32-33; 7. Moses' death, 34.

Review of the History.

"This side Jordan" (v. 1), is in
the Revised Version "beyond Jordan," and means the east side,
where Moses and the people now
were. How long is the direct journey from Horeb (or Sinai) to
Kadesh-Barnea (2)? The allusion
is doubtless to remind the people
of their sin, which prolonged this
journey from eleven days to forty
years.

What is the first great fact of
the review (5-8)? The second
(11-18)? What do you recall
about this second fact from our
previous studies? What is the
third fact (19-46)? What do you
recall about this? What is the
fourth (2:1-8)? The fifth (9-12)?
Is there anything in vv. 10-12 to
suggest an addition by a later
hand than Moses'?

Note to the Student.

It is hardly necessary to analyze the chapter further. Every
student who has pursued the
course thus far will be able to do
it for himself, after receiving the
suggestions above. If there are
any beginning to study the Commentary now for the first time, let
them examine the marginal references in their Bible for the places
where the facts are first mentioned in Numbers, and it will be
easy to compare the instruction
given upon it in the previous lessons.

This may be a good place to
again state that the object of this
Commentary is to assist the
reader to *study* the Bible. It has
little value for those who eat only
predigested food. There are better helps of that kind at hand,
and more are scarcely called for.

The author also has in mind
leaders of adult Bible classes who
are looking for suggestions more
than anything else, and to whom
it is hoped the Commentary may
be a blessing.

An Explanation or Two.

While further questions on the
text of this lesson are hardly necessary, there are some things calling for explanation.

For example, chapter 2:4 says:
"The children of Esau shall be
afraid of you," which seems contradictory to Num. 20:14. But
the solution is that in the former
instance the Israelites were on
their western frontier where the
Edomites were strong, while now
they were on the eastern, where
they were weak.

It may be asked why they
should be necessitated to buy
food of the Edomites, when the
manna, still continued to be
given them. The reply is, that
there was no prohibition against
eating other food, if they did not
have an inordinate desire for it.

A reasonable explanation of
other seeming contradictions may
be found, but the student must be
referred to larger commentaries,
and a good many of them, if he
wishes to learn everything that
can be learned. Many things
must be taken for granted in
these lessons, but if we only get
well acquainted with those that
are explained we shall be in a fair
way to master the rest.

Og and His Bedstead.

But what about the giant Og
and his bedstead? He was the
only remnant in the transjordanic
country (Joshua 15:14) of a gigantic race, supposed to be the
most ancient inhabitants of Palestine.

Although beds in the east are
with the common people a simple
mattress, yet bedsteads were not
unknown among the great. Taking a cubit at half a yard, the bedstead of Og would measure thirteen and one-half feet, and as
beds are usually a little larger
than the persons who occupy
them, the stature of the Amorite
king may be estimated at about
eleven or twelve feet.

But how did the bedstead come
to be "in Rabbath, of the children of Ammon"? Perhaps on
the eve of the engagement they
conveyed it to Rabbath for safety. This is so unlikely, however,

that some take the Hebrew word "bedstead" to mean "coffin," and think that the king having been wounded in battle, fled to Rabbath, where he died and was buried, and that here we have the size of his coffin.

Questions.

1. How far may the inspiration of the Scriptures have extended, and how is it illustrated in the Pentateuch?

2. What is the meaning of "Deuteronomy"?

3. Name the seven divisions of the book.

4. On which side of the Jordan was this book written?

5. How would you explain the allusion to the bedstead of Og?

REVIEW OF THE LAWS

Chapters 4-6

1. The Lessons of Sinai, c. 4.

What makes a nation wise and understanding (6)? What makes a nation great (7, 8)? What obligation does one generation owe the next (9)? Of all the divine commandments, which are the most important (10-13)? Of these ten, which one is particularly emphasized (15-28)? How is God's merciful character illustrated in one connection with these commandments (29-31)? What expression in v. 31 gives a peculiar interest to this promise just now? On what divine action does the hope of Israel rest (31, last clause)?

2. The Mosaic Covenant, cc. 5, 6.

By "all Israel" (1) may be meant a. general assembly of the people, or possibly only the elders, as their representatives. "The Lord made not this covenant with our fathers, but with us" (3), means not with our fathers only, but also with us, their successors. "The Lord talketh with you face to face" (4), means not in a corporeal or visible form, but in a free and familiar manner.

What comment is added to the fourth commandment in this review (15)? What expression of mingled desire and disappointment is attributed to God in connection with the original giving of the law (29)? What is the sum of the commandments (6:4, 5)? In what particular do these words testify to the divine nature? How do verses 6-9 amplify the thought in chapter 4:9 previously referred to? As suggested by the verses following, how were the people to keep their religion in mind through the avenue of their eye? What provision was made for its inculcation in the young?

Jewish Phylacteries.

The following quotation is interesting as bearing upon the Jewish phylacteries: "It is probable that Moses used the phraseology in the seventh verse in a figurative way, to signify earnest and frequent instruction; and perhaps the eighth verse is to be taken in the same sense also. But as the Israelites interpreted it literally, many suppose that a reference was made to a superstitious custom of the Egyptians, who wore jewels and trinkets on the forehead and arm, inscribed with words and sentences, as amulets to protect them from danger.

"These, it has been conjectured, Moses intended to supersede by substituting sentences of the law; and so the Hebrews understood him, for they have always considered the wearing of the tephilim or frontlets a permanent obligation.

"The form was as follows: Four pieces of parchment, inscribed, the first with Exod. 13: 2-10; the second with Exod. 13: 11-16; the third with Deut. 6: 1-8; and the fourth with Deut. 11: 18-21, were enclosed in a square case or box of tough skin, on the side of which was placed the Hebrew letter *shin*, and bound round the forehead with a thong or ribbon. When designed for the arms, these four texts were written on one slip of parchment, which, as well as the ink, was carefully prepared for the purpose.

"With regard to the other usage supposed to be alluded to, the Egyptians had the lintels and imposts of their door and gates inscribed with sentences indicative of a favorable omen, which is still the case; the front doors of houses—in Cairo, for instance—are painted red, white and green, bearing inscribed upon them sentences from the Koran, the Mohammedan bible.

"Moses designed to turn this custom to a better account, and ordered that, instead of the former superstitious inscriptions, should be written the words of God."

Questions.

1. What three allusions are explained under the head of the "Mosaic Covenant"?

2. What is the history of the Jewish phylacteries?

3. Describe the phylacteries.

4. What was the Mosaic design in their use?

WARNINGS AND EXHORTATIONS

Chapters 7-11

1. Obedience, c. 7.

What were the names of the seven nations of Canaan to be cast out for their iniquity (1)? Who would cast them out, and in what manner is the supernatural character of the act emphasized? Nevertheless, what illustrates the divine use of means (2)? What command is laid on the Israelites in the premises (2, 3)? And why (4)? To what extent should their zeal be exhibited, and why (5, 6)? What shows the choice of Israel to be of grace and not debt (7, 8)?

What shows the blessing of Israel to be grounded on obedience (9-12)? How is the temporal and material character of the blessing illustrated (13-15)? How are the people encouraged (17-21)? What shows God's very particular care for them (22, 23)?

2. Gratitude, c. 8.

What shows that Israel was too small a people to occupy the land at first (1)? Notice in the verses following (2, 3), how their experiences in the wilderness were intended to teach obedience as well

as impress them with the goodness of God. What miraculous occurrence is noted in verse 4? Compare 29:5.

What attractive features of the land are named (7-9)? All accounts speak of the natural beauty and fertility of Palestine, and its great capabilities when properly developed. To be among its brooks, and hills and valleys after passing through the desert, can be appreciated by those who have entered California after crossing the plains.

For the plenteousness of the wheat and barley of Palestine see Matt. 13: 8; but these products of the northern regions were equalled by the fruits of the south. "Honey" is often used indeterminately to signify a syrup of dates or grapes, which was esteemed a great luxury in the east. "Iron" was found in the mountains of Lebanon. The "brass" was not the alloy brass, but copper ore. Compare 1 Chron. 22:3; 29:2-7; Isa. 60:17.

After mentioning these instances of God's goodness, what arguments are founded upon them in the closing verses? Note the appropriateness of this chapter to be read on Thanksgiving day, and other national holidays.

3. Humility, cc. 9-11.

Notice the description of the Canaanitish cities in v. 1. They are called "great" because of the space they covered. Unlike our cities, the houses stood far apart, with gardens and fields intervening. They were usually fenced, sometimes as high as forty feet, with burnt or sun-dried bricks. It would not be much to demolish such a wall in our day, but such engineering skill was then unknown. Nevertheless, would any obstacle prevent their taking possession?

Would the victory be theirs, or God's? And would He give it to them on the ground of merit (4)? What would move Him in the premises (4, 5)? How does Moses dissuade the people from any idea of their own righteousness (see the remainder of the chapter)? The plainness of Moses' speech and the submission of the people is a strong evidence of the truth of the history. An impostor would have operated on opposite lines.

What instances of unfaithfulness does Moses name? For answer note vv. 12-21, 22, 23. The reference to his humiliation in the last-named verse does not apply to a third experience of the kind, but is a fuller description of the second named in v. 18.

The Bible Commentary has the following on "the brook that descended out of the mount" (21): "Though the Israelites were supplied with water from this rock when they were stationed at Rephidim (Wady Feiran), there is nothing in the narrative which should lead us to suppose that the rock was in the immediate neighborhood of that place (see on Exod. 17:5, 6). The water of this rock was probably the brook that descended from the mount. The water may have flowed many miles from the rock, as the winter torrents do now through the wadys of Arabia Petraea (Ps. 78:15, 16). And the rock may have been smitten at such a height, and at a spot bearing such a relation to the Sinaitic valleys, as to furnish supplies of water during the journey from Horeb by the way of Mount Seir and Kadesh-Barnea (c. 1:1, 2). On this supposition new light is cast on the language of the apostle, when he speaks of 'the rock following' the Israelites (1 Cor. 10:4)."

The general subject of chapter 9 is extended into chapters 10 and 11.

In chapter 10 note, in verse 4, that it was not Moses who wrote the words on the tables of stone, but God Himself. A professor in one of our universities is quoted as making light of this by inquiring whether God is supposed to have turned stone mason and chiselled these words with His own hand. We can afford to treat such remarks with silence, remembering the words of Scripture that some professing themselves to be wise have become fools (Rom. 1:22).

Note in v. 5, a minute circumstance, the mention of which at the time attests the truth of the record.

Note that vv. 6-9 seem to be inserted out of their place, the explanation of which no one knows. The address of Moses is resumed again at v. 10.

With v. 16 compare Rom. 2:25, 29 for its New Testament application to the Jew, and Col. 2:11, to the Christian.

In chapter 11 there is little requiring particular notice. The blessing and the curse (26-32) will be referred to in a later chapter, but just here it may be mentioned that "most signally is the execution of the curse seen in the present sterility of Palestine."

Questions.

1. What were the wilderness experiences intended to teach Israel?

2. What were the chief products of northern and southern Palestine, respectively?

3. Why were the cities of Canaan called "great"?

4. What evidence of its truth does this record contain?

5. Can you quote 1 Cor. 10:4?

CONDITIONS OF BLESSING IN THE LAND

CHAPTERS 12-16

1. Places of Worship, c. 12.

In Canaan, what were the Israelites to destroy and how thoroughly was the work to be done (1-3)? What contrast were they to place between themselves and the heathen in public worship (4-7)? Did this apply to the same extent in the wilderness, and if not, why not (8-14)? What exception was made as to their private and domestic affairs (15, 16)? What were they not at liberty to eat in their own homes (17-19)? Against what snare were they to be on their guard (29-32)?

In explanation of the foregoing it should be observed that no mention is made of heathen temples in Canaan at this time, and doubtless none were in existence. The places chosen for worship were the mountain tops, or groves, in order to direct attention toward heaven and secure retirement.

Note that while God promises to choose a place for the worship of Himself in the land, yet He does not divulge it in advance. Was this to prevent the Canaanites from concentrating their opposition there, or to prevent a course of strife among the Israelites themselves?

Notice from v. 12 that while the males only were commanded to appear before God at the annual feasts (i. e. at Jerusalem), yet the women were at liberty to accompany them.

The heathen believed in local deities who expected their dues from all who came to inhabit the country they protected.

This explains the caution in the closing verses of the chapter.

2. False Prophets, c. 13.

How were they to regard the teachings of false prophets (1-3)? How were they to deal with the prophets themselves (5)? Did it make any difference even if the wonders of the prophet had a show of reality? Does God ever permit such wonders to be done by false prophets, and if so, for what purpose? How are God's people to be preserved from temptations (4)? Compare Isaiah 7:19, 20, and 1 John 4: 1-6. The student will see the bearing of this upon the false teachings of the present day, such as Theosophy, the New Thought, Spiritualism, Christian Science, and anything else, no matter how fair it appears, that is not in accord with the Gospel (see Gal. 1:8).

In the case of these false teachers should it make any difference if they were friends or relations (6-11)? Suppose a whole city should have been led away into idolatry thus, what then (12-16)? Might this action be taken hastily, or only after investigation?

The Jews appeal to this chapter as justifying their crucifixion of Jesus Christ, but it is replied that "to Him gave all the prophets witness." He had all the characteristics of the *true* prophet and was the fulfilment of all that had been written in the Scriptures concerning the Coming One. Moreover so far from alienating the people from Jehovah and His worship. He honored Him by observing His worship, and the purpose of His life was to fulfil the law and the prophets and put away the reproach of sin.

3. Dietary Matters, c. 14.

This chapter is taken up chiefly with dietary matters, but before they are touched upon what prohibition is laid in vv. 1, 2, and for what cause ? It was an idolatrous practice on certain occasions (1 Kings 18:28; Jer. 16:6, 41:5), to make cuttings on the face and other parts of the body with the finger nails or sharp instruments. To make a large bare space between the eyebrows was another such custom in honor of the dead. This was referred to in Lev. 19. These usages, were degrading, and inconsistent with the people of God (1 Thess. 4:13).

Coming to the dietary matters, the student must be referred to what was said in earlier lessons, particularly in Leviticus.

No misunderstanding of verse 21 should be allowed as though what was not good enough in the physical sense for the Jew might do for the Gentile. The explanation has been shown previously, that it was for ceremonial and spiritual reasons.

4. The Sabbatic Year, c. 15.

The subject of this chapter has been dealt with in Exodus and Leviticus (see the marginal references in your Bible), but there are a few features calling for particular notice.

(1) The first matter is release from debt in the Sabbatic year (1-11). At this time what is every creditor obliged to do, and why (2)? It is not necessary to suppose that this was an absolute discharge of the debt, but a suspension of payment for the period named; and this, because in that period there was a suspen-

sion of agricultural labor which might have made it a hardship to pay a debt. We have seen that the underlying idea of the Sabbatic year was to impress all with the fact that they held their property from God, and that supreme gratitude was due to Him.

From whom might such civil rights and privileges be withheld (3)? What further qualifying thought is in v. 4? This seems to mean that in the case of well-to-do Israelites debts might be collected even in the Sabbatic year. But some think the words should be: "In order that there may be no poor among you," which would preclude any exception.

What promise does God renew unto Israel (6)? Remember that this is to be literally fulfilled unto Israel in that day when, obedient and penitent, they shall return unto God and Jesus as their Messiah.

Read carefully vv. 7-11, and observe the detail with which God as the theocratic King of His people would watch over their welfare. The foregoing law of release might prevent some covetous Hebrew from lending to the poor, hence the warning and the promise.

(2) The second matter is release from slavery. For the former treatment see Lev. 25. What provision is made for enabling such an one to regain his original status in society (13-14)? For the ceremony of the awlboring see the chapter before mentioned. The meaning of verse 18 seems to be that such a servant is entitled to double wages because his service was more advantageous on the ground that he was serving "without wages and for a length of time, while hired servants were commonly engaged only by the year."

5. The Feasts, c. 16.

There is nothing in this chapter calling for particular attention. Students will find the feasts treated of in Exodus and Leviticus where they are first brought before us. See the marginal references in your Bibles for these places.

Questions.

1. Why were groves or mountains chosen by the heathen as places of worship?

2. Why presumably did not God reveal His intended place of worship?

3. Have you examined the New Testament references in this lesson?

4. What argument offsets the present Jewish appeal to chapter 13?

5. How would you explain 14:21?

6. Does 15:2 contemplate an absolute discharge of debt?

7. When will the promise of 15:6 be fulfilled?

8. Give the probable meaning of 15:18.

9. Are you observing the marginal references in your Bible?

FURTHER CONDITIONS OF BLESSING

CHAPTERS 17-20

1. The Judge and the King, c. 17.

In the preceding chapter, v. 18, provision was made for judges and other officers of the civil law. They were to hold court in the *gates* of the cities, the place of ingress and egress, for the cities were walled. This idea of judges sitting in the gates still lingers in the Orient and gives significance to the Mohammedan terms "Ottoman Porté" and "Sublime Porte."

Review the preceding chapter and observe the charge laid on these judges to be just, straight, impartial and of clean hands. Then compare the present chapter, vv. 2-13, and note the method of procedure in the courts.

What is the offense here treated of (2, 3)? How should they guard against hasty judgment (11)? What was the punishment in such cases (5)? The extent of the testimony (6)? Who were the executioners of the penalty (7)? (Compare Acts 7:58.) The object of this requirement "was to deter the witnesses from rash charges and to give a public assurance that the crime had met its due punishment."

Verses 8-13 are explained by the *Bible Commentary* thus: "In all cases where there was difficulty in giving decision, the local magistrates were to submit them to the Sanhedrin—the supreme council, composed partly of civil and partly of ecclesiastical persons. 'The priests and Levites' should be 'the priests—the Levites'; and who, as forming one body, are called 'the judge.' Their sittings were in the neighborhood of the sanctuary, because in emergencies the high priest had to consult God by Urim (Num. 27:21). From their judgment there was no appeal; and if a person were so perverse as to refuse' obedience, his conduct was to be punished as a capital crime."

What prophecy is made in v. 14 (compare 1 Sam. 8:7)? What prohibition is laid on them in the matter (15)? What prohibitions are laid upon the king himself (16, 17)? (Compare 2 Sam. 8:4; 1 Kings 16:26; 2 Chron. 1:16; Isa. 31:3.) Can you name a king who violated both these prohibitions? What command is laid upon the king, and why (18-20)?

2. The Messianic Prophecy, c. 18.

This chapter is one of the most important in the Mosaic legislation.

After touching on the Levitical dues elsewhere considered, abominations are dealt with which, under other names, are ripe in our own time exposing those under their influence to the divine curse.

Note the things warned against in vv. 10, 11; the relation they bore to the cursing of Canaan, 12; and the obligation resting upon Israel, and on us, to have nothing to do with them. (Compare the marginal references for former allusions to these matters.)

The modern names of some of these are fortune telling, clairvoyance, astrology, mesmerism, palmistry, spiritualism and the like, all associated more or less with demonolatry, and although practiced sometimes by professing Christians, as much of an abomination unto God as they ever were. Verse 13 shows the reason. To be "perfect (or sincere) with the Lord thy God," means to worship, and serve Him implicitly and without the intrusion of another god. But they who consult fortune tellers, mediums, etc., do so to be guided or comforted by what they reveal. And since that which they reveal, when it is fact and not fraud, comes through demoniac channels and from the powers of darkness, it is really worshiping and serving Satan when the lips are professing to worship and serve God.

The Israelites might plead that since Moses was to leave them before they entered Canaan, and they would be without a mediator between them and Jehovah, it might be necessary to cultivate these who were regarded as the gods of the land.

How is such a plea met before it could be advanced (15)? Had they ever sought a mediator (16, 17)? How does this show that the successor to Moses, here referred to, was to have all his power and authority? What was the nature of that authority (18)? And power (19)? How might they be satisfied as to the divinity of such a prophet (21, 22)?

This prophet, the immediate successor of Moses, we know to have been Joshua, but it is evident from John 1:45, Acts 3:22, 23 and other places that ultimately it is Jesus Christ.

What a solemn obligation is thus placed upon all Christians to hearken to Jesus Christ, and how awful the consequences to those who while in lip they confess Him, do in heart and in life deny Him? (Compare Heb. 10:28-31.)

3. Landmarks and Warfare, cc. 19-20.

The first part of chapter 19 deals with the cities of refuge which we considered in our concluding lesson in Numbers. The only other matter claiming special attention is that of landmarks (14). Palestine in this respect was the same then as now. Gardens and vineyards were surrounded by hedges or walls, but tilled fields were marked by a little trench or a simple stone placed at certain intervals, hence a dishonest person could easily fill the trench and remove the stones. Thus he would enlarge his own field by stealing part of his neighbor's.

The oft repeated question, "Is war ever justifiable?" is answered in this chapter. In a world of sin war must needs be. It is one of God's methods of punishing sin in the present time. As the theocratic King of Israel He expected war and made ample provision for it, a consideration which should aid us in determining another question about the future retribution of the sinner. Thoughtless and ignorant men say He is too good to punish. But the fact is that He punishes because He *is* so good. As long as sin exists punishment must exist, and since Jesus Christ teaches that there is such a thing as eternal sin (Mark 3:29, R. V.), we may expect, alas! eternal punishment.

What words of encouragement are to be addressed to the army and by what officials (1-4)? The presence of the priest in this case rather than an army officer is explained by the fact that in a theocratic government everything is done directly by God through His delegated ministers, and these were the priests.

On what principles was the army to be sifted, or rather, what were the grounds of exemption from army service (5-8)? The answer is:

(1) The dedication of a new house which, as in all Oriental countries still, was an important event, and celebrated by festive and religious ceremonies (Neh. 12:27); in this case there was exemption for a year.

(2) The planting of a vineyard. The fruit of the first three years being declared unfit for use, and the first-fruits being producible only on the fourth, the exemption in this case lasted at least four years.

(3) The betrothal of a wife, which was a considerable time before marriage. It was deemed a hardship to leave a house unfinished, a new property half cultivated, and a recently contracted marriage; and the exemptions in these cases were founded on the principle that a man's heart being engrossed with something at a distance, he would not be enthusiastic in the public service.

(4) The fourth ground of exemption was cowardice. From the composition of the Israelitish army, which was an irregular militia, all above 20 years were liable to serve, many, totally unfit for war, must have been called to the field; and it was therefore a prudential arrangement to rid the army of such unwarlike elements —persons who could render no efficient service, and the contagion of whose craven spirit might lead to panic and defeat."—*Bible Commentary.*

The same authority thus comments on the following verses of this chapter:

"With the cities of those people which God doth give thee" in Canaan, it was to be a war of utter extermination. (vv. 17, 18). But when on a just occasion they went against other nations, they were first to make a proclamation of peace, in which case, if followed by a surrender, the people would become dependent, and in the relation of tributaries. The conquered nations would then receive the highest blessings from alliance with the chosen people; they would be brought to the knowledge of Israel's God and of Israel's worship, as well as a participation of Israel's privileges. But if the besieged city, or nation, refused to be taken, a massacre was to be made of the males, while the women and children were to be preserved and kindly treated (vv. 13, 14). By this means a provision was made for a useful connection being established between the captors and the captives; and Israel, even through her conquest, would prove a blessing to the nation.

In a protracted seige, wood would be required, both for military work and for fuel, but fruit bearing trees were to be carefully spared. In countries like India, where the people live much more on fruit than we do, the destruction of a fruit tree is a sort of sacrilege.

Questions.

1. What significance attaches to the Oriental use of the word "Porte"?

2. What was the later name of the Jewish Supreme Court, and of whom was it composed?

3. Give modern names to some of the abominations mentioned in chapter 18.

4. Explain v. 13 of that chapter.

5. How can you prove the application of verses 15-22 to Jesus Christ?

6. Why the need of landmarks in Palestine?

7. What evidence of future retribution is suggested by the legislation concerning warfare?

8. Can you name the grounds and give the reasons for exemption from army service?

9. How does this lesson magnify God's attributes of righteousness and holiness?

10. Do you think God can ever overlook sin?

11. What provision has He made for satisfying Himself on the question of sin?

DIVERS REGULATIONS

Chapters 21-22

In these chapters are a number of matters which, for want of a better title, we class as above.

1. Expiation of Innocent Blood, c. 21:1-9.

These ceremonies showed the sanctity associated with human life. The "rough valley" of verse 4 is in the Revised Version "running water," and the whole was calculated to lead to the discovery of criminals and repress crime.

2. Female Captives, vv. 10-14.

These regulations were to improve the usages of the nations concerning the capture of females in war. A month was the period of mourning among the Jews, and the details of v. 4 were the signs of grief which the captive must be permitted to manifest for the loss of her parents and old associates now the same as dead. The delay was an act of humanity and kindness. How further were these virtues to be manifested (14)? We should ever remember, that we are comparing conditions not with our present ideas of social and domestic obligations, which are what they are because of the later teachings of the Bible, but with those existing in the days of Moses.

3. Right of the First-born, vv. 15-17.

In this case it is presupposed that the first wife was dead at the time referred to. The opening of verse 15 should be: "If a man *have had* two wives." In other words, the legislation does not touch a man who has two wives at the same time, for polygamy, while tolerated under the Mosaic law, was never legalized.

4. Prodigal Sons, vv. 18-21.

This law was qualified by the fact that the consent of both parents was necessary to its execution.

5. Common Humanities, c. 22:1-12.

"Brother" in v. 1 comprehends not only relatives, but neighbors or even strangers which should stand in need of such justice and charity.

The command of vv. 6, 7 needs reenforcement to-day in certain quarters. Birds serve important uses in nature, and the extirpation of a species is productive of evils. The mother bird should be left for propagation, but the young occasionally might be taken as a check on too rapid an increase.

There is a lesson in the prohibitions of vv. 9-11, to which reference has been made in Leviticus; but touching v. 10: "An ox and ass being of different species, and different characters, cannot associate comfortably, nor unite cheerfully in drawing a plough or a wagon. The ass being smaller and his step shorter, there must be an unequal and irregular draught. Besides, the ass, from feeding on poisonous weeds, has a foetid breath, which its yoke-fellow seeks to avoid, not only as offensive, but producing leanness, or, if long continued, death; and hence it has been observed to hold away its head from the ass, and to pull only with one shoulder."—*Bible Commentary*.

6. Sexual Matters, vv. 13-30.

On these verses Horne says: "The regulations might be imperatively needful in the then situation of the Israelites; and yet, it is not necessary that we should curiously inquire into them. So far was it from being unworthy of God to leave such things upon record, that the enactments must heighten our admiration of His wisdom and goodness in the management of a people so perverse and so given to irregular passions.

"Nor is it a better argument that the Scriptures were not written by inspiration to object that this passage, and others of a like nature, tend to corrupt the imagination, than it is to say that the sun was not created by God, because its light may be abused by men as an assistant in committing crimes."

Questions.

1. What was the intended effect of the legislation about innocent blood?

2. With what conditions should this legislation be compared?

3. Was polygamy legalized by Moses?

4. How is the severity of the legislation about the "prodigal son" qualified?

5. How does this lesson illustrate the divine care for the comfort of animal life?

6. How would you reply in general terms to arguments against the contents of vv. 13-20?

DIVERS REGULATIONS—
CONTINUED

CHAPTERS 23-26

1. Public Privileges, c. 23:1-9.

The privileges referred to here are doubtless honors in the state and perhaps, in the case of foreigners, incorporation with Israel by marriage. Eunuchs and bastards were denied these privileges (1, 2), and also members of what Gentile nations (3)? What caused the latter prohibition (4-6)? Such passages as Neh. 13:1; Ruth 4:10, and 2 Kings 10:2, show that there were some exceptions to this prohibition, although it may be that it excluded males, but not females.

What other two nations were exempt from this rule, and on what grounds (7, 8)?

2. Bodily Uncleanness and Other Details, vv. 10-25.

Verse 13, should be translated as in the Revised Version, "thou shalt have a paddle (marg. or *shovel*) among thy weapons," which explains the meaning of the direction. Think of it in the light of the following verse, and remember the words of Wesley, that "cleanliness is next to godliness." There is a sense indeed, in which it *is* godliness, and the man who honors his Creator and Redeemer will see to it that himself and his surroundings are ever in a wholesome and sanitary condition. These directions have reference to camp life when engaged in war (9), but how much more obligatory in ordinary living.

Verses 15 and 16 refer to slaves who run away from tyrannical masters, or for deliverance from heathenism, and they afforded a ground for the action of Northern abolitionists who aided runaway slaves prior to our civil war.

As to verses 19 and 20, the Israelites lived in a simple state of society, and were encouraged to lend to each other without hope of gain. But the case was different with foreigners, who, engaged in trade and commerce, borrowed to enlarge their capital, and might reasonably be expected to pay interest on loans. Besides, the distinction was conducive to keeping the Israelites separate from the rest of the world.

3. Marriage and Divorce, c. 24: 1-5.

Divorce seems to have become known to the Hebrews in Egypt, and was tolerated by the Mosaic laws for the reason indicated in Matt. 19:3-9. But it was restricted by two conditions. What was the first (1)? And the second (4)? Because of increasing laxity in these matters to-day, we ought to familiarize ourselves with these two passages of Scripture, and especially the words of Christ.

4. Consideration for the Poor, vv. 6-22.

Why was a creditor not at liberty to take either the mill (R. V.), or the upper millstone as a pledge for debt (6)? Corn was ground every morning for that day's consumption, and if either were taken it would be depriving a man of his necessary provision.

According to verses 10 and 11, how were a borrower's feelings to be considered?

Verses 12 and 13 are explained by the fact that the cloak of a poor man was commonly all the covering he had to wrap himself in when he retired for the night.

What beneficient provision for the poor is made in verses 19-22, and why?

5. Justice in Law and in Trade, c. 25.

The bastinado was common to Egypt, but God through Moses here introduces two important restrictions (1-3):

First, the punishment should be inflicted in presence of the judge, instead of in private by some heartless official;

Second, the maximum amount should be forty stripes, instead of the arbitrary will of the magistrate. The Egyptian, like Turkish and Chinese rulers, often applied the stick till they caused death or lameness for life. In later times, when the Jews were exceedingly scrupulous in adhering to the letter of the law, and, for fear of miscalculation, were desirous of keeping within the prescribed limit, the scourge was formed of three cords, terminating in leathern thongs, and thirteen strokes of this counted thirty-nine (2 Cor. 11:24).

The usage concerning a childless widow existed before this time (Gen. 38), but the law now made it obligatory on younger brothers or the nearest kinsman to marry the widow (Ruth 4:4, Matt. 22:25). The reason for this was not only to perpetuate the name but also preserve the property in the family and tribe.

The reference to Amalek's deed (17-19) is not mentioned in Exod. 17, where the battle is recorded, but as it was a daring defiance of God, this command against them went forth. (See 1 Sam. 15.)

6. The Laws of Tithing, c. 26.

The regulations here considered, like almost all the foregoing, were for observance, not in the wilderness, but in Canaan after they should enter it (1). What were they then to do? Where were they to go (2)? What were they to say (3)? After the priest's acceptance of the basket and its contents, what was the next feature in this ritual (5-10)? In what spirit should this be done (11)?

This is not so much a question of tithing, i. e., the giving of one-tenth, as a general acknowledgment that all belongs to God as represented by the basket of first fruits and the confession and thanksgiving.

The actual tithing is referred to in the verses following (12-15). There were really two tithings. Ther first was appropriated to the Levites (Num. 18:21); and the second, the tenth of what remained, was brought to Jerusalem, in kind or in money value. In the latter case, the money was used to purchase materials for the offerings and their thanksgiving feast (Deut. 14:22,23). This was done for two years together, but on the third year (Deut.

14:28, 29) the thanksgiving was to be eaten at home and distribution to be made among the poor.

1. Name the six leading subjects of this lesson.

2. What two restrictions on divorce are given

3 How would you explain 24.12, 13?

4 What light can you throw on 2 Cor. 11 24?

5 Who should marry a childless widow, and why?

PROPHECY OF ISRAEL'S FUTURE

Chapters 27-28

As we approach the conclusion of this book we come to its most important part from a prophetical point of view—indeed the present lesson contains (chapter 28), a foreview of Israel's history to the end of the present age, in some respects unparalleled in the Bible, although touched upon in Leviticus (26) as we saw.

1. Stones for the Law and Stones for an Altar, c. 27:1 -8.

What should they do when they crossed the Jordan (2)? How should they cover these stones to obtain a writing surface or to render them more conspicuous? What was to be written on them (3)? (It is a question whether the decalogue is here meant or the blessings and cursings that follow.) Where were they to be set up (4)? Rocks and stones are seen in the Far East today with inscriptions in paint or plaster thousands of years old.

Besides these stones for the law, what others are commanded. and for what purpose (5)? Were these to be hewn or unhewn? The probability is that this pile was to be a pedestal for the other stones containing the law, as well as a place for sacrifice. What religious ceremonies were to be observed there (6,7)? The burnt offerings were part of the "worship for sinful men," while the peace offerings were connected with the

"festivities of a reconciled people." Hence we have here, "the law which condemned and the typical expiation—the two great principles of revealed religion."

2. Mount Gerizim and Mount Ebal, vv. 11-26.

These rug.. n Samaria, the peaks being near Shechem, rising to about 800 feet, and separated by a valley about 500 yards wide.

On Mount Gerizim (now Jebel-et-Tur) were the descendants of Rachel and Leah, the two principal wives of Jacob, and to them was assigned the office of pronouncing the benedictions; while on the twin hill of Ebal (now Imad-el-Deen) were the posterity of the two secondary wives, Zilpah and Bilhah, with those of Reuben. who had lost the primogeniture, and Zebulun, son of Leah; to them was commited the duty of pronouncing the maledictions (see Judge. 9:7). Amid the silent expectations of the assembly, the priests, standing round the ark in the valley, said aloud, looking to Gerizim, "Blessed is the man that maketh not any graven image," when the people ranged on that hill responded, 'Amen" then turning round to Ebal, they cried, "Cursed is the man that maketh any graven image"; to which those that covered the ridge answered, "Amen." The same course at every pause was followed with all the blessings and curses (see Josh. 8:33, 34).

"These curses are given in the form of a declaration, not a wish, as the words should be rendered, 'cursed is he' and not 'Cursed be he.' "—*Bible Commentary*.

3. The Great Prophecy, c. 28

This chapter seems a continuation of the former, the blessings and cursings being enumerated more at length. Here the whole destiny of Israel is laid out before them as the result of their obedience or disobedience

What comprehensive blessing is promised in verse 1? Observe that the lesser blessings following go to make up this great one

These include every kind of material prosperity (2-6); the confusion of their national enemies (7); and the independent power of Israel (12, 13). Moreover, all this shall tend to the glory of Jehovah before the nations (9, 10).

The curses are the counterpart of the blessings (15-19). "Sword," verse 22, is in some ancient versions "drought"; which agrees better with the figurative expressions of the two following verses.

The history of the Jews for the past 2,500 years has been a minute fulfilment of this prophecy, but it may be said to be divided into three periods, marked off by the Babylonian and Roman captivities and their present scattered and distressed condition.

(1) The Babylonian captivity comes into view at verse 36, say, to the close of verse 48.

(2) The Roman captivity, begins at verse 49, continuing to verse 64. The Romans "came from afar"; their ensign was an "eagle"; their "tongue" was not understood; they were of a "fierce countenance." i. e., bold, implacable; they left neither "corn, wine nor oil," but strewed devastation everywhere. They successfully besieged the fortified cities, even Jerusalem being razed to the ground. So terrific was the suffering from famine (verses 53-57), that parental affection was extinguished, and delicate and refined women ate the flesh of their own children. For the details we are indebted to Josephus.

(3) The present scattered and distressed condition of Israel is depicted, beginning at verse 64, for an account of whose fulfilment it is only necessary to keep one's eye on the daily press. Well, therefore, may we ask, with Bishop Newton, "What stronger proof can we desire of the divine legislation of Moses?"

Questions.

1. What is the sweep of the great prophecy in this lesson?

2. Describe Mounts Gerizim and Ebal.

3. What three things are included in the blessings?

4. Into what three periods is the fulfilment of the curses divided?

5. Who is a distinguished uninspired historian of the Jews?

THE PALESTINIAN COVENANT

CHAPTERS 29-30

The subject of these chapters is new and exceedingly important, containing what is called the Palestinian covenant.

Following the Scofield Bible, note that while the land was unconditionally given to Abraham and his seed in what we call the Abrahamic covenant (Gen. 13:15; 15:7), it was under another and conditional one that Israel ultimately entered the land under Joshua. It is this covenant that is recorded in the present chapters.

This was utterly violated by the nation, for which reason the latter was first disrupted (1 Kings 12), and then altogether cast out of the land (2 Kings 17:1-8; 24:1; 25:11). But this covenant unconditionally promises a national restoration of Israel yet to be accomplished, in accordance with the original promise to Abraham (Gen. 15:18). It will be then, and not till then, that Israel will possess the whole land. This she has never done hitherto.

The Need of Eye Salve.

The first of these chapters is simply an introduction to the covenant fully declared in the following one. We would not pause in its consideration were it not for the spiritual truth of verse 4, which we would emphasize.

Great as the events were which the Israelites had seen in Egypt and in the wilderness, yet, they had made no lasting impression on them. The reason was that they lacked the divine wisdom to apprehend them.

Do not pass this verse without comparing the passages in the Old and New Testaments, which throw light upon it. These are indicated in the margin of your Bible, such as Isa. 6:9, 10; 63:17;

Matt. 16:17; John 8:43; Acts 28:26, 27; 1 Cor. 2:9-14; Eph. 1:15-23; 4:18; 2 Thess. 2:11, 12; 1 Peter 1:10-12; Rev. 2:29; 3:18.

The Terms of the Covenant, c. 30.

The Scofield Bible analyzes the Palestinian covenant into seven parts, as follows:

Verse 1. Dispersion for disobedience. Compare c. 28:63-68 and Gen. 15:18.

" 2. Future repentance while in dispersion.

" 3. Return of the Lord (compare Amos 9:9-14; Acts 15:14-17).

" 5. Restoration to the land (compare Isa. 11:11, 12; Jer. 23:3-8; Ezek. 37:21-25).

" 6. National conversion (compare Hos. 2:14-16; Rom. 11:26, 27).

" 7. Judgment on Israel's oppressors (compare Isa. 14:1, 2; Joel 3:1-8; Matt. 25:31-46).

" 9. National prosperity (compare Amos 9:11-14).

We are not to suppose that the promises were fulfilled by Israel's restoration from the Babylonian captivity. It will be recalled that she was not then scattered "among all the nations" or "unto the utmost parts of heaven." Moreover, when God recalled them from Babylon, they were not all brought back nor multiplied above their fathers (5), nor were their hearts circumcised to love the Lord (6).

It may be said that there was a foreshadowing of the ultimate fulfilment of the prophecy at that time, but nothing more. The complete accomplishment is yet to come. Israel is yet to be converted to Jesus Christ as her Messiah, and returned to her land in accordance with what all the prophets teach.

Questions.

1. Name and distinguish between the two covenants mentioned.

2. How many of the Scripture references have you examined under the paragraph "The Need of Eye Salve"?

3. Name the seven features of the Palestinian covenant.

4. Why was not the restoration from Babylon the fulfilment of these promises?

5. When will they be fulfilled?

THE CLOSE OF MOSES' LIFE

Chapters 31:1-32:43

1. Encouragement, 31:1-8.

The law has been rehearsed and Moses' exhortation is drawing to a conclusion. Several days may have been occupied in the review covered by Deuteronomy thus far. And now, Israel, by its leaders, having been gathered together at the place of meeting, Moses is apprising them of his departure.

Though advanced in years (2), was he conscious of mental or physical decay (34:7)? Can you perceive a reason for the mention of this fact? Has it any bearing on the truth and virility of the divine messages Moses was chosen to communicate? What indicates that it was by revelation he knew of his approaching separation? Name three or four elements of the encouragement Moses gives Israel in verses 3-6.

2. Responsibility, vv. 9-13.

What provision was made for the perpetuity of the law (9)? Note the allusion to the bearing of the ark by the priests, which they did on extraordinary occasions (Joshua 3:3-8; 1 Chron. 15:11, 12), although commonly it was borne by the Levites.

While the people were to be instructed in the law in their homes, what public rehearsal of it was here provided for (10-11)? We appreciate how this guaranteed the preservation of the sacred oracles from generation to generation, and can thank God for remembering *us* in this obligation upon them.

3. Prediction, vv. 14-30.

In what language is the infidelity of Israel foretold (16)? What would cause this apostasy? What consequence would follow (17, 18)? When God says, "I will forsake them," "I will hide My face," etc., He refers to that withdrawal of His protection as symbolized by the cloud of glory, the shekinah. This never appeared in the second temple, i. e., after the Babylonian captivity, and, "its non-appearance was a prelude of 'all the evils that came upon them, because their God was not among them.'"

Where was the book of the law placed (26)? In the Revised Version "in" is "by." It is thought that it was deposited in a receptacle by the side of the ark which contained nothing but the tables of stone (1 Kings 8:9). But some, guided by Hebrews 9:4, believe it was placed within, and that this was the copy found in the time of Josiah (2 Kings 22:8).

4. Inspiration, 32:1–43.

In verse 19 of the preceding chapter Moses is commanded to write a song and teach it to Israel, and get them singing it as a witness for God against them in the day of their unfaithfulness.

"National songs take deep hold of the memories and have a powerful influence in stirring the deepest feelings of a people," and because of this God causes this song to be composed, and is indeed Himself the composer of it. In the Revised Version the whole chapter down to verse 44 is arranged as poetry.

(1) After the exordium (1), notice the comparison of the divine instruction to what gentle, useful and beautiful feature of nature (2)? What gives this instruction this character (3)? Point out the seven attributes of God indicated in the ascription of praise that follows (3, 4). Notice that these attributes constitute the proclamation of His name. Preachers and Christian workers will find the outline of a rich discourse here.

(2) After the exordium we come to an indictment of the people (5, 6). It is predictive as indicating what they would do in the future, and yet also a historic record of what they had already done. These verses, especially 5, are clearer in the Revised Version.

(3) The indictment leads to a reminiscence of God's goodness to them, to deepen their repentence in that day as it shall quicken their gratitude (7-14).

With verse 8, compare Acts 17:26, 27 in the light of chapter 2:5-9 of the present book, and Genesis 10:5, and observe that God has from the beginning reserved Palestine for this people, through whom He would show forth His wonders to the other nations. And admirably suited is the locality for the purpose. In Ezekiel it is described as "the middle of the earth," and as from a common center the glad tidings were, and shall be, "wafted to every part of the globe."

Notice the figure in verses 11 and 12. When the eaglets are sufficiently grown, the mother bird at first supports them on the tip of her wing, encouraging and aiding their feeble efforts to higher flight.

(4) This reminiscence of God's goodness is followed by another indictment, fuller than the former, and showing the aggravation of the people's sin.

"Jeshurun" is a poetic name for Israel. Notice the reference to "demons" of verse 17 (R. V.), and observe that such beings exist and are the real objects of the worship of false religions.

(5) This second indictment is followed by an announcement of punishment (19-28). Note the allusion to the calling out of the Gentiles into the Church in verse 21 (third clause). What are God's arrows (23)? See for answer the following verses—famine, pestilence, wild beasts, the sword, fear, captivity, etc. Why would He not altogether destroy such a faithless people (26, 27)?

(6) The announcement of punishment leads to a promise of forgiveness and restoration in the latter time (29-43). When will the Lord lift His hand from off His people (36)? How shall He

afflict them who afflicted Israel (41)? What shows that the day of Israel's blessing will be that of the whole earth (43)? Compare Psalm 65.

THE BLESSING AND THE END

CHAPTERS 32, 44-34:12

After Moses ended his song (32:44) he exhorted the people in language familiar to us (45-47), and then the voice of the Lord was heard to what purport (49, 50)? And why (51)? Can you recall the details referred to in that verse? If not, look up the story again as indicated in the margin of your Bible. What grace does God show Moses, notwithstanding his disobedience (52)? Does Moses complain at his disappointment? On the contrary, what does he now do, as indicated in the next chapter?

1. Blessing the Tribes, c. 33.

Notice the sublime exordium (2, 3). From what object of nature is the metaphor borrowed? Why does he describe the law as "fiery"? (Compare again Ex. 19:16-18). Nevertheless, in what spirit had the law been given (3)? What shows the law to have been a great privilege to as well as a great obligation upon Israel (4)?

Which tribe is first blessed (6)? Reuben, as we saw in Genesis 49, was denied the right of primogeniture, and yet he was to hold rank as one of the tribes of Israel. Observe the reward of Levi (8-11) for their zeal in supporting Moses at the time of Israel's idolatry (Ex. 32:26-28). What indicates their impariality in executing judgment at that time (9)?

Read the beautiful words expressive of Benjamin's blessing (12). Historically it means that the land of this tribe was located near the temple. "Between his shoulders" might be rendered "on his borders," and means that Mt. Moriah, the site of the temple, lay in the territory of Benjamin, although Mt. Zion, on which Jerusalem itself stood, was in Judah.

How does the language of Joseph's blessing (13-17) show that his territory would be diversified in beauty and rich in productions?

What shows that Zebulun's progeny would be sailors and traders, while that of Issachar would be landsmen (18)? And yet would not the latter traffic in the things the Zebulunites would bring home with them (19)?

Do you remember on which side of the Jordan Gad was located, and why? May this explain the reference (20) to the enlargement of his borders? What expression (21) may refer to his having been settled in his territory by Moses himself, and before the conquest by Joshua?

What is said of Dan (22)? His original settlement was in the south, but these quarters being limited, he suddenly leaped, made an irruption, and established a colony in the north.

Which tribe semed to have no occasion for murmuring with their assignment (23)? And which was a close second (24, 25)? Is there anything to indicate that Asher's soil may have been particularly adapted to the olive? Were there any minerals in his rocky coast?

Do not omit the map in the back of your Bible, entitled, "Canaan in Its Division among the Tribes," which will aid you in fastening the details on your minds.

2. Moses' Death, c. 34.

This chapter seems to have been written after the death of Moses, and his been regarded as a kind of introduction to Joshua.

Travelers say that no miraculous powers were necessary to be communicated to Moses to discern what is here recorded (1-3), and that any one could see the same from that elevation, the climate being very "subtle and free from vapor."

What distinction had Moses in his death above all other men (6)? While the concealment of Moses' tomb seems wise to prevent its becoming the resort of superstitious pilgrims, yet that there was a deeper reason for it seems clear from Jude 9. What that was we may not at present know, and yet there are hints about it which will be considered later on.

What eulogium does inspiration pronounce upon Moses (10-12)?

JOSHUA

THE DESTRUCTION OF THE CANAANITES—INTRODUCTORY

At the close of the Pentateuch we left the Israelites at Moab, where, after the death of Moses and the investiture of Joshua as his successor, the people were to cross the Jordan and take possession of Canaan.

But before entering upon the study of Joshua, a few words should be said as to the justification of such a course.

The substance of what follows is from Kellogg's *Leviticus,* but before quoting him we should like to state our own feeling in the premises.

Among men it is not a wrongful thing on the part of a landlord to eject a tenant who has not only failed to pay his rent, being able to do so, but also injured the property for which the rent was due.

This was the situation with the Canaanites, magnified a thousand-fold, in their rebellion and oppositon to the true God.

Therefore the justice and holiness of God, without which the respect of His creatures could not be commanded, made necessary just such a judgment as that which befell this people, and will befall every other people who equally defy Him. His sovereignity requires it, and the well-being of His creatures who serve and trust Him require it.

Canaan Accursed.

Kellogg connects the accursing of Canaan with what he had said on "The Law of the Ban" (Lev. 27:28, 29), to which attention was called when we were studying that book. He says in substance:

(1) It is imperative to remember that *we have before us not the government of man but of God, a true theocracy.* It is obvious that if fallible men may be granted power to condemn men to death for the sake of the public good, much more must this

right be conceded to the righteous and infallible King of kings, who was the political head of the Israelitish nation, if that expression may be allowed. Further, if this right of God be admitted, it is plain that He may delegate its execution to human agents.

(2) The only question now remaining concerns *the justice of the exercise of this right in particular cases.* It is possible that men might sometimes apply this law without divine authority, a situation we are not required to defend any more than the infliction of capital punishment in America sometimes by lynch law. As to its execution in the case of the Canaanites, however, it is not so difficult to find justification. Indeed, when the facts are known, this destruction cannot be regarded as irreconcilable with the moral perfections attributed to the Supreme Being.

(3) The discoveries of recent years have let in light upon *the state of society in Canaan at this date,* and warrant us in saying that in the history of our race it would be hard to point to any civilized community which has sunken to such a depth of moral pollution. Leviticus gives many dark hints of these things, such as the worship of Molech, the cult of Ashtoreth, the moral sacrifice required of every female, and other things into which one cannot go. Indeed, if the holy and righteous God had *not* commanded these depraved communities to be extirpated His omission to do so would have been harder to reconcile with His character.

(4) It must be noted that *these corrupt communities were in no obscure corner of the world, but on one of its chief highways.* The Phoenicians more than any people of that time were the navigators and travelers of the age, so that from Canaan this moral pestilence was carried hither and thither and, worse than the "black death," to the very extremities of the known world. Have

we then so good reason to call in question the righteousness of the law which ordains that no person thus accursed should be ransomed, but be put to death? Rather are we inclined to see here not only a vindication of the righteousness of God but a manifestation of His mercy, not merely to Israel, but to the whole human race of that age who, because of this infection of moral evil, had otherwise sunk to such depravity as to have required a second deluge for the cleansing of the world. Read Psalms 62:12 and 136:17-22, where God's mercy is shown in His judgment upon the wicked and their iniquity.

(5) Nor can we leave this matter without noting *the solemn suggestion it contains*, that there may be in the universe persons who, despite the redemption of grace, are irredeemable and hopelessly obdurate. Persons for whom nothing remains but the "eternal fire which is prepared for the devil and his angels" (Matt. 25:41). And this because God's mercy endureth forever.

Questions.

1. What is the nature of the book of Joshua?

2. What made necessary this judgment on the Canaanites?

3. What is a theocracy?

4. What do we know of society in Canaan?

5. What geographical relation did Canaan bear to the world?

6. Have you read the quotations from the Psalms?

7. What bearing has this lesson on future retribution?

JOSHUA IN COMMAND

Chapters 1, 2

This book might have for a secondary name, "The Book of Conquest and Division," with reference to the events it records. The marginal chronology indicates that it covered a period of about 25 years, but we have seen that this chronology is not part of the inspired text, and is not to be taken as absolute authority. It is

safer to say that we do not know how long a period may have been covered by these events. According to Martin Anstey's "The Romance of Chronology," 7 years elapsed from the entry into Canaan to the division of the land.

The book is a record of a military campaign, and criticisms of it from that point of view have placed Joshua in the first rank of military leaders.

1. The Call of Joshua, 1:1-9.

(1) Here note that "the Lord spake unto Joshua" (v. 1), just how we do not know, but as He may have spoken unto Moses out of the cloud of glory, or by Urim and Thummin (Num. 27:21).

(2) Note the renewal of the promise of the land which had been given to Moses and to Abraham (vv. 2-4), and with this a reassurance of the divine support to Joshua as it had been with his predecessor.

Observe the reference to the Hittites. They were the dominant nation of Canaan and rivals of Egypt, and to merely human eyes it seemed preposterous that Israel could dispossess them, but, "Is anything too hard for the Lord?" Notwithstanding the greatness of the Hittites secular history has known nothing about them until recently, and archaeological discoveries revealing their record have been one of the triumphs of the past century and one of the strongest evidences to the historicity of the Old Testament.

(3) Only one condition is required of Joshua for the fulfilment of these promises—strength and courage. But his strength and courage is not physical, but the moral quality found in obedience to God. And even this is narrowed to one thing—the observance of the written law, knowledge of and meditation upon which will produce this virtue within him (vv. 6-9). Thus God provides our requirements and rewards us for exercising them!

2. The Preparation of the People, 1:10-18.

The "victuals" in verse 11 could scarcely have been the

manna, which would have spoiled in the keeping, but the corn, cattle, etc., which may have been gotten in the enemies' country through which they had passed.

The reference to the two and a half tribes (vv. 12-16) recalls their wish to Moses and his consent that they might locate east of the Jordan for the sake of their flocks; *provided*, that leaving their families for the time being, the men of war should cross the river and aid in the conquest of the land (Num. 32:1-42).

The point that strikes one here is the relation of faith and works in the execution of God's plans by His people. Why should these tribes be required to cross the Jordan since in one sense they were not necessary? Could not God have conquered Canaan without them? But God does not work miracles unnecessarily, and what man himself can do, consistently with the divine glory, he is obligated to do, a principle which has a wide sphere of application

3. The Reconnoitering of Jericho, c. 2.

(1) We cannot pass by Rahab's falsehood (vv. 1-7), which we must not suppose God endorsed, notwithstanding the commendations she received in Hebrews 11:31 and James 2:25. It is her faith that is spoken of in those instances, but God was no more pleased with her lie than her unchastity. Lying is a common vice among the heathen, and Rahab probably had no consciousness of its moral guilt.

(2) Rahab's faith was very simple (vv. 8-14). Like the heathen round about, she believed that each nation had its own god, and that some gods were stronger than others. The God of the Hebrews seemed the strongest of all, for she had heard what He had done for them (v. 10). Her city could not stand before such a God and hence she surrendered at once. The other inhabitants of Jericho from the king down had the same evidence as she, but did not act on it. In other words she had faith and they had not. There was fear mingled with her faith,

and ignorance, and superstition, and selfishness, but God overlooked these things.

In the same way we are not expected to have a perfectly intelligent faith in our Lord Jesus Christ before we can be saved, nor must we know the whole Bible, or be able to explain its great mysteries. Do we apprehend our danger, and are we disposed to fly to the refuge He offers, that is all.

(3) Every Christian is impressed with the symbolism of the red cord in the window (vv. 15-22). It forces itself upon us in the light of all the Bible teaches about the blood of Jesus Christ and the token of our salvation from the more awful destruction than that awaiting Jericho. It was Rahab's sign of the covenant the men had made with her. It was her mark of identification as one to be saved in the day of calamity. And it was that which her deliveries required as the condition of the fulfilment of their pledge. The story affords many points of resemblance to that of our redemption through Christ, and will repay a study as a basis for a Bible reading or address.

Questions.

1. Give a secondary name to this book.

2. How has Joshua been estimated?

3. What can you say about the Hittites?

4. What gives moral courage to men?

5. Give an illustration of how God uses second causes.

6. Does God commend men for bad deeds?

7. Describe the nature of Rahab's faith?

JORDAN CROSSED

CHAPTERS 3-5

1. Preparation of the People, 3: 1-13.

The events in this section are the removal to Shittim and the encampment there (v. 1); directions about the leadership of the priests (vv. 2-4); sanctification of the people (v. 5); encouragement of Joshua (vv. 7-8); encouragement of the people (vv. 9-13).

There is little requiring explanation, but notice in v. 4 the care God took for the people's guidance and the occasion for it. And do not forget the obedience required if the guidance were to prove effectual. All these things have their spiritual lessons and were "written for our examples."

Notice in v. 5 the forerunner of divine wonders. When we sanctify ourselves by putting away all known sin, God does wonders among us. Notice the demand for faith, "tomorrow" He will do it.

Notice in v. 7 how God removes all apprehension from Joshua so far as the allegiance of the people is concerned. They will follow him because God will put His honor upon him as upon his predecessor. When God calls a man into His service He equips him for it, and makes it so plain that His people recognize it and submit themselves to his leadership (cp. 4:14).

Notice in vv. 9-13 that presumably the people had no knowledge how they were to cross the river till just before the event. These words of Joshua therefore, with the miraculous result, must have greatly confirmed their faith in Jehovah as unlike the idols of the nations round about.

2. The Division of the Waters, 3:14-17.

What play for the imagination here: "As the feet of the priests were dipped in the brim (brink) of the water"! Not a minute before, but just then "the waters which came down from above stood and rose up upon an heap." Read the comment in Psalm 114.

All the more marvelous because it was the time that Jordan overflowed its banks (v. 15), i. e. about our April or May, the period of the early harvest in that land. The river about Jericho is ordinarily only about 150 to 180 feet across, but at this time it was twice as broad, as well as deep and rapid.

The city of Adam beside Zaretan (v. 16) is about 30 miles north. There the river suddenly stayed and the waters gathered into a heap. From that point downward being no longer supplied from above, they began to fail, and hurrying towards the Dead Sea were swallowed up. The river-bed for miles was dry, it has a pebbly bottom there, and people "passed over right against Jericho."

3. The Memorial Stones, 4:1-9.

Observe that v. 2 is a repetition of 3:12, indicating that these 12 men had been chosen previously for this service, though only now had they been made acquainted with its nature. That nature is described in the verses following. Verses 19 and 20 show where the stones were placed.

Observe their purpose (vv. 6-7). A common mode in earlier times of remembering remarkable events. No inscription need have been placed upon them, as tradition would hand down the story from age to age.

Observe that another set of stones was set up elsewhere (v. 9). "Unto this day" means when the record was made in the book, which may have been in Joshua's own time and by him, or at a later time by some other hand.

4. The Circumcision and the Passover, 5:2-12.

The reason for this circumcision is in vv. 2-7, but the moral effect of it is stated in v. 9.

The observance of the Passover at the time fixed by the law (v. 10, see marginal references) was another evidence that the national existence was re-commenced, and it was appropriate that the manna should cease at this time and the new chapter of their history begin with a new dietetic regimen.

"The old corn of the land" seems to mean that found in the storehouses of Gilgal and its neighborhood on which they levied. The fact that the manna ceased at this time when they no longer needed it, is a further proof of its miraculous provision in the wilderness.

5. The Lord of Hosts, vv. 13-15.

This occurrence is another of the theophanies, a subject on which we have commented. "Theophany" means a manifestation of God to men by actual appearance. It might be called a "Christophany" or manifestation of Christ, for all such appearances in the Old Testament were those of the Second Person of the Trinity.

We are impressed with the intrepidity of Joshua, suggesting a supernatural enduement of courage (v. 13). We are impressed, too, with the warlike appearance and the warlike declaration of his divine visitor. As before stated, men ask in ignorance whether war is ever justifiable? Let them remember that the Lord is a God of war, and that until His enemies are subdued war will never end. In the present instance everything betokens heaven's approval of this war of invasion. Only a weak apprehension of sin, and of the divine character, can argue otherwise.

Observe the evidences of the deity of this Person—His name, His acceptance of worship, His command and the reason for it. The place of His appearance was Gilgal, part of accursed Canaan, and yet His presence made it holy (v. 15).

Questions.

1. Name the events in the first section of this lesson.

2. At what period of the year was the Jordan crossed?

3. How far north of the crossing did the flow of the river cease?

4. How many sets of memorial stones were there?

5. What further evidence of the "manna" does this lesson afford?

6. What is the meaning of "theophany"?

7. How is the deity of this "Captain" proven?

JERICHO AND AI

CHAPTERS 6-8

1. Divine Orders, 6:1-5.

These verses should not be separated from the foregoing by a chapter division, since it is evident that the orders here received by Joshua were given by the Captain of the Lord's host previously described. Observe another proof of His deity in the words, "I have given into thine hand Jericho."

The mode by which Joshua was to proceed (vv. 3-5) calls for no explanation. What had been his own preparations for the attack on the city? Was he meditating upon them when the "Captain of the Lord's host" met him? Nevertheless he surrenders to the divine will, and implicitly obeys.

But it was not Joshua merely, but the whole nation which was to be taught great lessons about God in this transaction. And are not the same lessons applicable to us? Behold divine omnipotence, and the power of faith and obedience on our part in laying hold of it!

God could have destroyed the walls of Jericho in the twinkling of an eye, and without any such precedure on Israel's part, but the circuits they were to make and the length of time involved had value in arresting attention and deepening the impression upon them and their enemy. What if the latter had repented as did Nineveh at a later time?

2. Human Obedience, vv. 8-16.

The record in these verses is the fulfilment in detail of the foregoing decree. "Passed on before the Lord" (v. 8) refers to the ark of the covenant, the symbol of His presence, which was carried in the procession.

It is supposed that, at least upon the seventh day, only the fighting men engaged in the march, it being almost inconceivable that two millions of people more or less, young and old, could have compassed the city seven times in one day.

But what a trial of faith this was! No battlement raised, no foundation undermined, no sword drawn, no spear pointed, no javelin hurled, no axe swung, no stroke given—they must "walk and not faint," that was all.

3. Promised Results, vv. 17-27.

The first three verses appear somewhat out of place in the record—a command in the midst of a historic recital, but the subject to which they refer is familiar to those who have studied the previous lessons (see Deut. 7:2, 20-17 and other places).

If we conceive of Joshua as pronouncing this curse we must remember it was done by divine command, while on the reasonableness of the curse itself, we should consider what was said in the introductory lesson. The sin of Jericho was aggravated by their closing their eyes to the miracle at the crossing of the Jordan. God might have swept them away by famine or pestilence, but "mercy was mingled with judgment in employing the sword, for while it was directed against one place, time was afforded for others to repent."

"By faith the walls of Jericho fell down" (Heb 11:30). Faith did not do the work of a battering ram, but it put Israel in an attitude toward God where He might work for them who required no outward agencies. It is the same kind of faith that saves the sinner and sanctifies and builds up the saint.

Rahab's deliverance (vv. 22-25) speaks for itself. She and all her kindred were left "without the camp," doubtless for fear of its ceremonial defilement. The remark that "she dwelleth in Israel even unto this day" shows that the book must have been written within a reasonable date after the event.

The curse on the rebuilding of the city (v. 26) reads in the Revised Version: "Cursed be the man . . . . . . with the loss of his first-born shall he lay the foundation, and with the loss of his youngest son shall he set up the gates thereof." For the fulfilment of this curse see 1 Kings 16:34.

4. Sin and Its Consequences, c. 7.

The sin is named in v. 1, and the consequences to Israel in vv. 2-5 in language which needs no commentary. The effect on Joshua is equally intelligible (vv. 6-9), but one is not more impressed with his humiliation and alarm than his jealousy for the divine honor (v. 9, last clause).

The divine interpretation of the situation (vv. 10-15) is of the deepest interest to every generation of God's people. Israel had sinned, transgressed the covenant concerning Jericho, and dissembled besides by hiding the stolen articles. The whole nation had not done so, but the sin of a part was that of the whole (James 2:10).

The curse of Jericho now rested on Israel itself (v. 12), and could only be removed by the punishment of the offender who is soon discovered (vv. 16-18), and confesses his crime (vv. 19-21).

The retribution seems severe (vv. 22-26), but not in the light of the offence if we judge of it as God did, and who is wise if he set up another standard? Observe that it is not said positively that Achan's sons and daughters were stoned, although c. 22:20 witnesses that he did not perish alone. They may have been brought out only as witnesses to his punishment, but if it also fell on them then they must in some way have been partakers of his sin. (Read Deut. 24:16.) "The valley of Achor" means "the valley of troubling."

5. Defeat Turned to Victory, 8: 1-29.

Why was Joshua to "take all the people of war" with him in this case, say 600,000, when the whole population of Ai was only 12,000 (v. 25)? Was it as a rebuke for their self-confidence before (7:3)? Was it to inspire courage after the memory of their former repulse? Or was it, that the division of the spoil now to be allowed (v. 2) might be shared amongst all as a reward for their former obedience and a stimulus to further exertions (Deut. 6:10)?

The campaign outlined in vv. 3-13 is common in modern warfare, but apparently unsuspected by the Aites. Observe that the people of Bethel were confederate with the Aites.

6. The Altar on Mt. Ebal, vv. 30-35.

For the history of this altar compare Deut. 27, a command the Israelites presumably could not obey until this victory, since Ebal was 20 miles beyond and through a hostile country.

Questions.

1. What spiritual lessons are taught us in the fall of Jericho?

2. How was the sin of Jericho aggravated?

3. What expression shows an early origin of this book?

4. In whose reign was Jericho rebuilt?

5. Can you quote James 2:10?

6. What does "Achor" mean?

7. Name three possible reasons why all the men of war were to advance against Ai.

8. With what sacred event is this period of the campaign brought to an end?

CONQUEST OF THE SOUTH

CHAPTERS 9, 10

1. The Compact with the Gibeonites, c. 9.

Verses 1 and 2 are a general statement, telling how the kings of the surrounding nations felt in view of Israel's victories, and what they planned to do about it. The narrative then ends in order to describe the method of the Gibeonites, which differed from the others. We must again refer the student to the map in the back of his Bible, for details as to the location of these nations.

Gibeon will be discovered a little to the west, perhaps southwest, of Jericho. It was of the Hivites (v. 7), and seemed to represent a democracy more than a monarchical form of government (v. 11).

"They did work wilily" and

caught Joshua and his associates by guile, vv. 4-15. "Wine-bottles" is in the R. V. "wine-skins," for bottles were made of the skins of animals, goats for example, and when they were old or much used they were liable to be rent.

Notice in v. 7 that the Israelites were a little on their guard. "Suppose you really dwell here in Canaan," they said, "we are not at liberty to enter into a covenant with you" (cp. Exod. 23:34; 34:12; Deut. 7:2). One would have asked counsel of the Lord, but this they disobediently failed to do (v. 14).

Joshua now comes into the coloquy (v. 8), but even he is guilty of the same oversight. And yet, as another suggests, if they had sought divine guidance, perhaps "they would not have been forbidden to connect themselves with any Canaanites who renounced idolatry and worshipped the true God." Rahab is in point. "At least no fault was found with them for making this league with the Gibeonites: while the violation of it later was punished (2 Sam. 21).

"Hewers of wood and drawers of water" (v. 21) were the menials who performed the lowest offices in the sanctuary (called "Nethinim" in 1 Chron. 9:2 and Ezra 2:43). But notwithstanding the chastisement of the Gibeonites in this respect, their relationship to Israel brought them into the possession of great religious privileges (see Psalm 84:10).

2. The Great Battle with the Kings, c. 10.

The story now seems to return to the opening of c. 9. The kings are exercised by the compact between Israel and Gibeon, for the latter is a strong power. To be opposed by Israel was serious, but Israel and Gibeon united were a greater menace (vv. 1-5).

Gibeon's extremity is Joshua's opportunity (vv. 6, 7), but he receives new encouragement from God for this, the heaviest undertaking in which he has engaged. Everything about this conflict is supernatural, which if we keep in mind will remove the strangeness of the miracle in vv. 12-14. For example, observe vv. 10 and 11.

"Beth-horon" (v. 10) means the "house of caves," and as throwing light on the record, the following from Dr. Robinson will be interesting:

"There were two contiguous villages of that name, upper and nether. Upper Beth-horon was nearer Gibeon, about ten miles distant, and approached by a gradual ascent through a long and precipitous ravine. This was the first stage of the flight. The fugitives had crossed the high ridge of upper Beth-horon, and were in flight down the descent to Beth-horon the nether. The road between the two is so rocky that there is a path made by steps cut into the rock.

"Down this path Joshua continued his rout. Here the Lord interposed, assisting by means of a storm, which burst with such fury that 'they were more which died with hailstones, than they whom the children of Israel slew with the sword.

"The oriental hailstorm is a terrific agent; the hailstones are masses of ice, large as walnuts, and sometimes as two fists; their size, and the violence with which they fall, make them injurious to property, and often fatal to life. The miraculous feature of this tempest, which fell on the Amorite army, *was the preservation of the Israelites from its destructive ravages.*"

Sun and Moon Stand Still.

In the New Testament we are taught to pray in the Holy Ghost, and that the Holy Ghost prays in us (Jude 20; Rom. 8:26). "The effectual fervent prayer of the righteous man" of which James speaks (5:16), would seem to be the prayer "energized" in the believer by the Holy Ghost himself, the prayer He prays in the man according to the will of God. May we explain Joshua's prayer in v. 12 this way?

It is as follows that the *Bible Commentary* speaks of this event:

"The inspired author here breaks off the thread of his history of this miraculous victory, to introduce a quotation from an ancient poem, in which the mighty acts of that day were commemorated. The passage, which is parenthetical, contains a poetical description of the victory which was miraculously gained by the help of God, and forms an extract from "the book of Jasher," i.e., "the upright"—an anthology, or collection of national songs, in honor of renowned and pious heroes.

"The language of a poem is not to be literally interpreted, and therefore, when the sun and moon are personified, and represented as standing still, the explanation is that the light of the sun and moon was supernaturally prolonged by the laws of refraction and reflection that ordinarily cause the sun to appear above the horizon, when it is in reality below it. Gibeon (a hill) was now at the back of the Israelites, and the height would soon have intercepted the rays of the setting sun. The valley of Ajalon (stags) was before them, and so near that it was sometimes called 'the valley of Gibeon' (Isa. 28:21).

"It would seem from v. 14 that the command of Joshua was in reality a prayer to God for this miracle; and that, although the prayers of men like Moses often prevailed with God, never was there so astonishing a display of divine power in behalf of his people as in answer to the prayer of Joshua. Verse 15 is the end of the quotation from Jasher; and it is necessary, to notice this, as the fact described in it is recorded in due course, and the same words, by the sacred historian, v. 43."

Questions.

1. What geographical relation did Gibeon bear to Jericho?

2. How does c. 9:11 indicate that Gibeon may not have been a petty kingdom like the other cities?

3. Are you familiar with the story in 2 Sam. 21?

4. Name the supernatural phenomena associated with the battle of Beth-horon.

5. Can you quote Romans 8:26?

6. What do you know about the book of Jasher?

CONQUEST OF THE NORTH

CHAPTERS 11, 12

Owing to the length of the last lesson no comment was made on the latter half of the previous chapter. But it will be seen that vv. 16-27 gave an account of the final destruction of the five kings in the confederacy against Gibeon.

The map will show Makkedah (16) to the west of Gibeon, near the sea and in what we know as the Philistine country. In a cave the kings hid and were imprisoned by Joshua until the rout of the warriors was complete (17-21), when they were slain (22-27).

Then in a rapid survey (28-42) we get the record of the campaign through the South as far as Goshen, including victories over Libnah, Lachish, Gezer, Eglon, Hebron, Debir, Kadish-Barnea and Gaza. "All these kings and their land did Joshua take at one time, because the Lord God of Israel fought for Israel" (42). It was the conquest of the whole Southern Canaan, leaving Israel free to turn attention to the North, the later Galilee region, whose conquest begins in chapter 11.

1. The Battle of Lake Merom, c. 11.

As the decisive battle in the South seems to have been at Beth-horon, that in the North seems to have been at Merom (5). Let the student trace the localities on the map if he wishes to have his interest kindled, and the facts fastened on his mind.

Notice that horses and chariots appear for the first time and it was for this reason the battle was attempted to be fought on the shores of Lake Merom, where there could be free play for such a force.

Emphasis is laid upon the great numbers of the enemy engaged in this encounter (4). Josephus in his *Wars of the Jews* gives 300,000 infantry, 10,000 cavalry and 20,000 war-chariots. If true, a formidable host was this in every way, and Israel may well have been dispirited at the knowledge of it, but God comes with timely encouragement (6), which He makes good (7, 8).

Inquiry may be raised as to why they should destroy the horses and chariots (9), and not keep them for subsequent use, but Psalm 20: 7-9 is a sufficient answer. What a flood of meaning is thrown on such expressions by an event like this! Then, too, not only was Israel to trust in the Lord independent of such means, but to be neither a traveling nor trading, but rather an agricultural people, which would not require accessions like these.

The following verses in this chapter give a survey of the completed conquest of the North as in the former case of the South (10-14), and after recapitulating the Southern campaign, the story reaches a conclusion at verse 23.

2. Recapitulation, c. 12.

We give but little space to this chapter. In vv. 1-6 we have an account of the kings overcome and the cities taken by Moses on the east of Jordan, and the distribution of their land to the two and a half tribe (see Num. 21:31, Deut. 2:36, 3:3-16).

Following this we have a record of the 31 kings overcome by Joshua on the west of Jordan in the two campaigns, already dwelt upon.

Questions.

1. What was the decisive battle in the conquest of Southern Canaan?

2. Reply to a similar question about Northern Canaan.

3. Have you located Makkedah and the waters of Merom on the map?

4. Can you quote Psalm 20:7?

5. How many kings were overcome by Joshua in his campaign west of the Jordan?

SPIRITUAL TEACHINGS AND TYPES

Having come to a natural division of this book, we pause to consider some of its spiritual teachings and types.

1. For example, take Joshua himself, who is a type of Christ as the "Captain of our salvation" (Heb 2:10, 11). It is interesting that "Joshua" is a combination of Jehoshua, which means Jehovah-Saviour. The more important points in the typical relation of Joshua to Christ are indicated in the *Scofield Reference Bibles:*

"(1) He comes after Moses. Compare John 1:17; Rom. 8:3, 4; 10: 4, 5; Heb. 7:18, 19; Gal. 3:23-25.

"(2) He leads to victory. Compare Rom. 8:37; 2 Cor. 1:10; 2 Cor. 2:14.

"(3) He is our advocate when we have suffered defeat. Compare Joshua 7:5-9; 1 John 2:1.

"(4) He allots our portions. Compare Eph. 1:11, 14; 4:8-11."

2. We have already spoken of Rahab as illustrating the history of redemption, but going into the subject more minutely we mention the following:

(1) She lived in a condemned city, and we live in a condemned world.

(2) Her character was bad, and we all are sinners.

(3) She believed in the power of God for her deliverance, and we are justified by faith.

(4) She received a promise for her faith to rest upon, and God has said that whosoever shall call upon His name shall be saved.

(5) She displayed a token and seal of her faith in the scarlet cord, and we believe with the heart unto righteousness, but "with the mouth confession is made unto salvation."

(6) Her deliverance was sure and complete, and "there is therefore now no condemnation to them that are in Christ Jesus."

All these can be wrought out into a helpful discourse by a selection of the New Testament passages called for by the different divisions.

3. The crossing of the Jordan has always seemed an impressive type of the intercessory work of Christ on behalf of His people. The priests standing in the river-bed until every member of the host passed over, brings to mind Heb. 7:25.

To other teachers the passage of the Jordan is an impressive type of our death with Christ. Compare Rom. 6:1-11; Eph. 2:5, 6; Col. 3:1-3.

4. "The twelve stones taken out of Jordan and erected by Joshua in Gilgal, and the other twelve left in Jordan to be overwhelmed by its waters, are memorials marking the distinction between Christ's death under judgment in the believer's place, and the believer's perfect deliverance from judgment."

For the first-named consider Psa. 42:7; Psa. 88:7; John 12:31-33. For the second, one has a large variety of New Testament passages which will readily come to the mind.

5. The Rev. F. B. Meyer speaks of the significance of the vision of the Captain of the Lord's hosts:

"We sometimes feel lonely and discouraged. The hosts with which we are accustomed to co-operate are resting quietly in their tents. No one seems able to enter into our anxieties and plans. Our Jerichos are so formidable—the neglected parish; the empty church; the hardened congregation; the godless household. How can we ever capture these and hand them over to the Lord?

"We summon all our wit and energy to solve the problem. We study the methods of others, put forth herculean exertions and questionable methods, borrowed from the world. But still we are disappointed, and have gone forth alone, confessing our helplessness, and then it is that we have seen the Captain of the Lord's host. He will undertake our cause, and marshal His troops and win the day.

"But we must be holy. 'Put off thy shoes from off thy feet, for the place whereon thou standest is holy ground.' We must put off the old man, with his affections and lusts, and cleanse ourselves from all filthiness of the flesh and spirit. Cleanness rather than cleverness is the prime condition of successful service. It is only out of such a heart that the faith can spring which is able to wield the forces of the unseen and spiritual and divine."

6. The author mentioned above uses the story of the Valley of Achor for a chapter on sin, from which the following is taken, which might be easily filled up for a Gospel address:

"(1) We should grieve more for sin than its results. Joshua smarted from the disgrace inflicted upon his people and the consequences which would ensue when the tidings were noised abroad. He was dreading the discovery more than the misdoing. But with God it was not so, and never is so. It is our sin in itself that presses Him down, as a cart groans beneath its load.

"(2) We should sumbit ourselves to the judgment of God. 'Get thee up; wherefore liest thou thus upon thy face?' It were as though God said, 'Instead of grieving for the effect, grieve for the cause.' In searching the cause of our failures we must be willing to know the worst. And that we may know the worst God traces our sin back through its genealogy, just as He did in this case.

"(3) We should hold no parley with discovered sin. God never reveals an evil which He does not require us to remove. When this is done the Valley of Achor becomes 'the door of hope' (Hos. 2:15).

7. "And the land rested from war" 11:23. In the use of this text Mr. Meyer compares the rest experienced by Israel in Canaan with the rest the believer may share in Christ:

"(1) There is the rest of reconciliation. The soul no longer works up towards the cross to obtain justification, but is assured that all needed to be done has been done by Jesus Christ on our behalf.

"(2) There is the rest of assured victory. When we realize all that Jesus has done, we see

that Satan is a conquered foe, and that his weapon cannot reach a life hidden in God.

"(3) There is the rest of a surrendered will. When our wills move off the pivot of self on to the pivot of God, our lives become concentric with the life of God, and our feet keep step to the music of His divine purpose.

"(4) There is the rest of unbroken fellowship. As Jesus is one with the Father, so we become one with Him, and through Him one with the blessed trinity. Truly 'our fellowship is with the Father and with His Son Jesus Christ.'

"(5) There is the rest of perfect love. When we enter into the life of the ascended Jesus, we find that our hearts become pervaded with the love of God, and there is no longer the yearning and bitterness of unsatisfied desire. We hunger no more, neither thirst any more.

"(6) There is the rest of the holy heart. It is not occupied with inbred lust nor tossed to and fro on seething passion. The flesh is crucified, the self-principle quelled, and the empire of the Holy Saviour is supreme."

Questions.

1. Have you compared the New Testament Scriptures with reference to the typical character of Joshua?

2. Can you give from memory the points in which the story of Rahab illustrates that of our redemption?

3. In what two ways may the crossing of the Jordan be used symbolically?

4. What symbolical distinction is there between the two mounds of memorial stones?

5. To what spiritual use might you put the reference to Israel's rest in the land?

DIVISION OF THE LAND

CHAPTERS 13-19

Seven chapters make a long lesson from one point of view but not from another, as the subject-matter will not require the same attention as in other cases. It is about the division of the land among the tribes, and we will touch on the principal points by chapters.

Chapter 13. Although the warfare of extermination had been carried on for some time, some think seven years, yet it was not entirely completed (1). The Lord therefore stirs Joshua to portion out the territory among the tribes, that each may continue to work in its own neighborhood after he has departed. He died at 110 (24:29), from which it may be gathered that he was now past 100.

There follows an account of the land unappropriated which includes, as a first division, the country of the Philistines on the southwest, and that of the Geshurites bordering on it and further south (comp. 1 Sam. 27:8). A second division is that of the Canaanites near by the Sidonians, in what we know as Upper Galilee. A third the land of the Giblites on the Mediterranean north of Sidon (2-6).

This sketch of the unconquered territory finished, the directions for allotment are taken up (7), but not until a record is made of the boundaries of the two and a half tribes on the East of Jordan which Moses alloted them in his lifetime (8-33).

The distribution was by *lot* (6), as announced in Num. 33:54, a system which accomplished two purposes, (1) the prevention of partiality on the part of the leaders, and (2) the acknowledgment of God's rights in the disposal of His and not their property. The lot seems to have been used only in determining the general locality where a tribe should be settled, the actual extent of the settlement being otherwise determined (Num. 26:54). The control of God in the whole matter is seen in that each tribe received the possession predicted by Jacob and also Moses (comp. Gen. 49 and Deut. 33).

Chapter 14. At this point the allotment begins on the west of the Jordan. Nine and a half tribes only are mentioned (2), because the other two and a half. Reuben, Gad and half of the tribe of Manasseh, were provided for on the east.

It is to be remembered that the Levites were to have no allotment as the others (3), but only certain cities with their suburbs. To make up the even number of the 12 tribes, Joseph's inheritance had been multiplied by two, and Ephraim and Manasseh, his sons, each represented a separate tribe (4). This covers vv. 1-5 of this chapter. From v. 6 to the end we have the story of Caleb's choice and allotment of Hebron. See Num. 14:24, and Deut. 1:36.

Chapter 15. This gives the borders of the tribe of Judah, whose possession was large because of its preeminence over the other tribes.

Caleb's possession is within Judah, and in connection with it is the story of his daughter's dowry (16-19). She married Othniel the brave, the first successor to Joshua in the time of the Judges.

The last verse is interesting because of the subsequent history of the Jebusites and Jerusalem in David's day. If Judah could not drive out the Jebusites it was not for lack of power, but faith. But O, how fatal to them as to other tribes with a similar history, that they should have neglected the divine command to drive out the idolators. All the sufferings of Israel for hundreds of years arose from that neglect.

Chapter 17. This describing the lot of Manasseh is interesting for two things. The first is the apportionment made to the daughters of Zelophehad (3-6) according to the command of God through Moses (Num. 27:1-11). And the second, Joshua's rebuke of the unbelief of Ephraim (14, 15). There was the spirit of patriotism in this sarcasm.

Chapter 18. The first verse of this is the most important, testifying to the setting up of the tabernacle at Shiloh whither the camp had now removed. By the camp is meant the remainder of the tribes after the departure of those receiving their allotments (2). Look up Shiloh and identify its location about 25 miles north of Jerusalem.

The importance of this is its bearing on certain questions of the "higher criticism." The view of the rationalistic critics is that the Pentateuch was written much later than the period commonly supposed. That instead of its contents being revealed by God they were conceived by the priests and palmed off on the people as the work of Moses, to bolster up their power. According to this the tabernacle and its worship were of comparatively late origin, a hypothesis shaken by the circumstances recorded here. The tabernacle seems to have remained at Shiloh for a long period, probably more than 300 years, if we may judge by the reference to the ark in 1 Sam. 4:11.

Verse 3 of this chapter is an unhappy revelation of the feeling in Israel at this time. Perhaps the people loved ease, perhaps they perferred a nomadic life, but for some cause they were slow to avail themselves of their opportunities to do the will of God.

If Canaan be a type of Christ and the privileges of the risen life in Him, what a rebuke these words convey to many a Christian heart! How foolish we are, and how ungrateful to God to be satisfied with present attainments when there is so much more and so much better ahead.

And do we say, "O, that our Joshua would stir us up to possess the land?" Is He not doing it? Do we not hear the rebuke of the still small voice?

Let us get back to the Word of God and its great and precious promises. Let us "arise and go through the land and describe it," that a holy passion may be quickened to possess it.

Joshua's directions to the 21 land surveyors in vv. 4-9 give rise to the question as to where, or how, the latter obtained their knowledge, for the task was no simple one. Had they been taught geometry in Egypt? What light this throws upon the civilization of the Hebrews at this time.

Chapter 19. The feature in this chapter is the allotment of Joshua recorded in the last two verses. Notice when it was done (49), and by whose authority and decree (50). There is no record of this decree, but it probably had a similar history to that in the case of Caleb (14:9).

"So they made an end of dividing the country."

Questions.

1. About how long a period was covered by the campaign of conquest in Canaan?

2. Was the conquest entirely completed by Joshua?

3. What advantages were there in the distribution by lot?

4. How was the providence of God shown in the distribution?

5. What was the character of the allotment for the tribe of Levi?

6. Of what sin of neglect were the tribes guilty?

7. What was the root cause of this sin?

8. Where was the tabernacle set up in Joshua's time, and how long presumably did it remain there?

9. What bearing has this circumstance upon the science of Biblical criticism in these days?

10. What important spiritual analogy de we find in chapter 18?

SPECIAL CITIES AND THE ALTAR OF WITNESS

CHAPTERS 20-22

1. The Cities of Refuge, c. 20.

The decree concerning the cities of refuge was considered in its place. It will be well, however, again to notice that they were not instituted to shield criminals but innocent murderers. Whether innocent or guilty though, the murdered had an asylum until his case could be heard by the authorities (v. 6). If innocent he was permitted to remain in the city, immune from the legal avenger, until the death of the high priest. When this occurred he was free to return to his home town, and the rights of the avenger ceased (v. 6).

Observe the symbolical character of the high priest in this particular. How the man-slayer, desirous of his liberty, must have calculated the probabilities of his death, and wondered whether, after all, it would antedate his own! But what a type it is of the Mediator of the new covenant who by means of death has secured redemption and deliverance for all that believe on Him (Heb. 9:15-17).

2. The Cities of the Levites, c. 21.

In the distribution of these there is nothing more remarkable than the allotment of the priests (vv. 9-19), in which all the cities falling to them were located within the territories of Judah and Benjamin. Simeon indeed is named (v. 9), but an earlier chapter showed that this tribe had received part of the territory of Judah which had proven too large for them.

Behold, the providence of God! At a later period there is a revolt among the tribes (1 Kings 12), and they separate themselves on the north to form the kingdom of Israel, while two on the south remain loyal to the Davidic and Messianic line, retaining the temple worship and Aaronic priesthood intact, and these two are Judah and Benjamin!

3. The Altar of Witness, c. 22.

Notice the commendation Joshua is enabled to give the men of war of the two and a half tribes, who for a probable period of seven years, had separated themselves from their families and flocks in fulfilment of their pledge, to assist in the conquest of the land and the settlement of the tribes on the other side of the Jordan (vv. 1-4).

Note the warning and benediction he bestows upon them (vv. 5, 6), and the share of the spoil they carry back, and the purpose of it (v. 8).

But soon a misunderstanding arises. Note its cause (v. 10); the commotion it occasioned among the tribes on the west (vv. 11, 12); the wise counsels that

prevailed (vv. 13, 14); the conference held with the supposed offenders (vv. 15-20); the explanation offered (vv. 21-29), and the satisfaction experienced (vv. 30-34).

Questions.

1. In what parts of the Pentateuch are the cities of refuge referred to?

2. What type of Christ, not heretofore mentioned in these lessons, is found in the record concerning them?

3. What providence is seen in the lot of the priests?

4. Can you give the history of the altar of witness?

5. What name was given it, and why?

RENEWAL OF THE COVENANT AND DEATH OF JOSHUA

CHAPTERS 23-24

1. The Gathering at Shiloh, c. 23.

"A long time after that the Lord had given rest unto Israel," refers to a period elapsing after the distribution of the land. We do not know how long it was, but Joshua is old and his departure is near (v. 1).

This is a gathering of the leaders presumably at Shiloh, where the central place of worship was (v. 2).

It is an occasion to exhort the people to faithfulness in their obligations to God, the address of Joshua falling into three parts: (1) He recalls past blessings (vv. 3, 4); (2) He rehearses promises yet to be fulfilled (vv. 5-11); (3) He renews the warnings in the event of disobedience (vv. 12-16).

Under the second head, he applies almost the same words to Israel that the Lord spake to him at the beginning (v. 6). Courage is necessary to drive out the enemy, but it consists in doing the will of God. The enemy will vanish if they do this. Moreover the will of God is their separation from the nations which constitute the enemy, and especially the worship of their gods. How aptly this fits in with the obligations of the Christian. The world is our enemy, but "this is the victory that overcometh the world, even our faith" (1 John 5:4). That is, as we believe God and obey Him in the Gospel of His Son, He subdues our enemy and the world loses its power over us. "The Lord your God, He it is that fighteth for you" (v. 10).

Under the third head, note verses 12 and 13, which serve as a text, alas! for the whole story of the book of Judges which follows this.

2. The Gathering at Shechem, c. 24.

Just why this gathering was held at Shechem instead of Shiloh is not revealed, but it may have been because this was the locality between Mounts Gerizim and Ebal, where the covenant had been ratified on their entrance into the land (see chapter 8). It may have been desired to give the present occasion the impressiveness of that memory, and of other events which had taken place there (see Gen. 12:6, 7; 33:18-20; 35:2-4).

(1) God's past blessings are once more rehearsed (vv. 2-13); (2) The covenant solemnly renewed (vv. 14-25); (3) The words written and the witness recorded (vv. 26-28). It is a wondrous recital of God's grace towards Israel that verses 2 to 13 contain. And it was grace towards all the world, too, when we consider the purpose of Israel in the redemption of the latter. Let not these verses be passed over hastily.

Grace precedes service on our part, but service follows grace, hence the obligations in verses 14-25. Notice Joshua's example (v. 15), and the all too prompt vow of the people. Joshua seems to doubt them (vv. 19, 20), but they reiterate their allegiance (vv. 21-24), and the scene closes.

Note the existence of "the book of the law of God" in Joshua's time and his own addition to it (v. 26), as a historical fact

bearing upon the science of Biblical criticism in our time. This testifies to the early origin of the Pentateuch and points to Moses as the author.

Archaeological Corroboration of Joshua.

Before concluding our lessons in Joshua it will be stimulating to faith to speak of the new light thrown on Canaan during Joshua's time by the excavation work in southern Palestine under Prof. Sellin.

He tells us that the foundations of the walls built by the Canaanites around their cities can easily be traced. During their occupation by the Israelites these walls were repaired or "pointed," and as the Canaanites used polygonal stones and the Israelites four-sided ones, the archaeologist is enabled to exactly define the portions of the walls of Israelitish origin.

The ruins of the walls of Jericho are well preserved, and the remnants of house walls over six feet high. The houses of the Israelites were small, and the difference between those occupied by the common people and the princes is largely one of the number of rooms.

These discoveries bear on the religious conditions of the people and their development. Under the high altars in the groves, vessels, armulets, and idols, made of clay and bronze, were found. The inscriptions point to the offering of newborn children in these vessels as a votive offering to the goddess, Astarte. Professor Sellin says that the exact truthfulness of the Biblical records receives emphatic corroboration from these discoveries.

Speaking of the walls of Jericho again, a well-defined citadel was unearthed upon the northern boundary having two sturdy towers upon its flanks, one of them with an area of 40x16 feet. The inner wall was about 26 feet high and afforded protection to various apartments and offices for military and domestic uses. In and about the citadel were remains of the older Canaanite time which preceded the siege of Joshua.

It is doubtful whether the towers existed in Joshua's time, although they seemed to have preceded the reign of Ahab, during which Hiel of Bethel rebuilt the city. Referring to this rebuilding, Professor Vincent speaks of a gap observed by explorers between the early Canaanite remains and those of the Jewish monarchy, and he sees in this a corroboration of the fact that Jericho lay in ruins for several centuries between its destruction at the hands of Joshua and its rebuilding under Ahab.

Of course the material of these discoveries needs sifting and collocating, and some conclusions may receive modification, but nevertheless they are of great value and likely to become increasingly so.

Questions.

1. What was the central place of worship in Joshua's time?

2. Can you quote 1 John 5:4?

3. Name some events that have made Shechem memorable in the history of Israel.

4. What evidence of the Mosaic origin of the Pentateuch does this book afford?

5. How does archaeological science corroborate the historicity of this book?

JUDGES

INTRODUCTION

The story of Judges is something like this: While Joshua and the elders of his generation lived —those who had personally known the wonders of Jehovah— the people continued in measurable obedience to the divine law. But when these died and another generation came on the scene there began a decline.

The way had been made easy for this by their failure through unbelief to drive out all the Canaanites from amongst them, as was related in Joshua.

The proximity of these heathen acted like leaven in the dough. Israel intermarried with them contrary to the divine decree, and was led into idolatry thereby. This weakened their power so that from conquerors they were changed into the conquered. Turning their back upon God, He, in a sense, turned His back upon them, and allowed them to be taken captive and sorely oppressed.

In their distress they would repent and cry for mercy, when He would deliver them through a leader miraculously endued, and called a judge. As long as this judge lived they would be held in obedience again, but on his decease a relapse into sin followed and the same round of experience was repeated.

An Inspired Summary.

The story of the book is practically outlined for us in chapter 2, verses 6 to 19, which takes the place of a summary, and suggests as the spiritual outline of its contents these four words:

Sin.
Punishment.
Repentance.
Deliverance.

General History of the Period.

There are twelve judges named in the book unless we count Abimelech and Barak in the number, which would make fourteen. Abimelech was a conspirator and

usurper (c. 9) and is not usually counted a judge, as he was not of divine appointment. Barak was associated with Deborah and the honor of the judgeship is assigned to her rather than him.

It will stimulate interest in the book to read it through in advance, and if possible at a single reading, as far as the close of chapter 16, where the real history of the judges concludes. Use a sheet of paper and record the name of each judge and that of the nation from which he delivered Israel. You will find these nations were Mesopotamia, Moab, Philistia, Canaan, Midian and Ammon.

Now examine the map, or a Bible dictionary and see where these nations were located on the north, east, south and west of Israel. This will raise the question as to whether the whole of Israel was in captivity to each of these nations at different times, or only those tribes which were in closest proximity to each.

If the latter be our conclusion, as seems likely, a second question arises as to whether each judge ruled over the whole of Israel at any time, or only so many of the tribes as he delivered from bondage? The latter seems the more probable, and gives a different conception of the history of the period from that commonly understood. It indicates, that the periods of these judges were not necessarily successive, and that two or more may have been ruling at the same time in different parts of the land. It was this unsatisfactory state of things that was instrumental in moving the people to demand a king.

The Chronology of the Book.

As was stated above, the history of the judges so far as this book is concerned ends at chapter 16, the remaining chapters being supplementary. The dates given at the beginning of the book and at chapter 16 indicate the period covered to be about 300 years, to which might be added the time of Eli, if not Samuel, both of whom judged Israel, and whose story is found in the next book but one.

But even with these additions the period does not approximate that named in Acts 13:20, "about the space of 450 years until Samuel the prophet."

A perfectly satisfactory explanation of this disagreement cannot as yet be given, but a suggestion is that there is a divine chronology distinct from the human, whose centre seems to be Israel. It is important to note, that God does not count time in the history of Israel while she is absent from her own land, or dominated by, or in captivity to, other nations.

The most striking illustration of this is in the present age. Nineteen hundred years in round numbers have elapsed since Jerusalem was destroyed by Titus and the Jews became scattered among the Gentiles, but the briefest mention is made of them in prophecy in all this time. When we reach the prophets we shall see that they break off their references to Israel at the time of this dispersion, and take it up again at their restoration at the end of this age, just as though no time had intervened. It is on this principle only that one can understand the meaning of the seventy weeks in Daniel 9.

Many minor illustrations of this are found in the Old Testament. Of Israel's thirty-eight years in the wilderness, when they were out of touch with God through disobedience, we are told almost nothing. "Abram listened to Sarah concerning Hagar, which was a suggestion of the flesh, and we find a blank in his life of thirteen years, see Gen. 16:16; 17:1. In the same way we may be able to explain this apparent discrepancy between the chronology in Judges and that in the Acts.

For example, during the captivities in Judges, the nation lost successively, 8, 18, 20, 7, 18 and 40 years, a total of 111 years (see Judges 3:8; 3:14; 4:3; 6:1; 10:8; 13:1). Add to these 111 years 200 during which they were said

to have had rest, 136 during which they were ruled by judges, and the 3 years of Abimelech's usurpation, and you have precisely 450.

In the same way some would explain the seeming discrepancy between 1 Kings 6:1 and this passage in Acts. All of which is interesting and will be found more so as we come to other illustrations of the principle in later books.

Questions.

1. Give in a sentence or two the story of Judges.

2. How do you explain the spiritual decline of Israel during this period?

3. Give from memory a spiritual outline of the book.

4. How many judges are named in the book?

5. What reason is there to believe that the servitudes mentioned did not always extend over the whole of Israel at one time?

6. How does divine chronology seem to differ from the human?

7. On what principle only can we understand the meaning of the seventy weeks in Daniel 9?

8. Apply this principle to the apparent discrepancy between the chronology in Judges and Paul's reference to the period.

JOSHUA TO SHAMGAR

CHAPTERS 1-3

1. Judah's Incomplete Victory, c. 1:1-20.

After the death of Joshua the question of which tribe should lead in the subsequent campaign was answered by the Lord in the choice of Judah (vv. 1, 2), which was in accordance with the divine prophecy through Jacob (Gen. 49:8). Doubtless the inquiry was made by Urim and Thummim on the breastplate of the high priest, to which reference was made in Exodus.

Judah invites the co-operation of Simeon because the territory of the latter was contiguous and intermixed with Judah (v. 3).

These tribes are guilty of barbarity in the case of Adonibezek

(vv. 5-7), but it is not to be supposed that God commended this action. It was, however, in accordance with the warfare in that day, and even the heathen king admitted the justification of the act in his case.

The defeat in verse 19 is explained not by the lack of power in the case of Judah, but by unbelief.

2. Similar Experiences of the Other Tribes, vv. 21-36.

Judah's example of unbelief is followed by all the tribes named in the conclusion of this chapter, Benjamin, Ephraim (the house of Joseph), Manasseh, Zebulun, Asher and Naphtali. Note particularly verse 21 in comparison with verse 8. The border of the two tribes, Judah and Benjamin, seems to have run through Jerusalem, and while the first named expelled the heathen from their part of the city, the latter were unable to do so and, this city did not fully come into possession of Israel until David's time.

3. Divine Warning, c. 2:1-5.

The Revised Version indicates by the definite article before "angel," in verse 1, that He who came from Gilgal to Bochim to warn Israel was the Angel of the Covenant, who appeared in Human form as the Captain of the Lord's host to Joshua. In other words, the Second Person of the Trinity. It was a serious indictment He laid against them and an awful penalty He announced (vv. 1-3). No wonder the people wept, but would to God their sorrow had been to better purpose. The result shows how temporary it was and how little confidence may be put in tears for sin, which do not mean amendment of life.

4. The Summary of the Book, vv. 6-23.

We called attention to these verses in the preceding lesson as giving an outline of the whole story of Judges. Verses 6-10 are copied from Joshua 24, and inserted here to explain the warn-

ing preceding. The following verses should be read with care, because they give the key, not only to Judges, but to 1 Samuel, and the whole of this period of Israel until the monarchy.

In explanation of verse 16 the Bible Commentary speaks of the judges as God's vicegerents in the government of Israel, He Himself being the supreme ruler. As we shall see, there was no regular unbroken succession of judges, but individuals prompted by the Spirit of God were from time to time aroused and empowered to achieve deliverance. They were without pomp or emolument, and had no power to make laws. In a special sense, however, they were executors of the law and avengers of crimes, especially that of idolatry.

5. Othniel, the First Judge, c. 3:1-11.

After enumerating the nations left in the land unconquered, and the reason for permitting them to remain, the story takes up the first general apostasy of Israel and the rule of the first judge. Notice in verses 1-4 the interacting of divine sovereignty and human responsibility. We have seen the reason why these nations were not exterminated from the human point of view to be a lack of faith, but from the divine point of view there was another reason. God permits these nations to remain, as a school for Israel in the art of war (v. 2), and, as an instrument for their discipline in divine things (v. 4).

From intermarrying with these nations the Israelites soon came to serve their gods (vv. 6-7). When therefore they turned their back upon Jehovah, He, in a sense, turned His back upon them, so that they were compelled to serve the Mesopotamians eight years (v. 8). Distress followed sin and repentance resulted from distress. Whereupon God raised up a deliverer in Othniel, whose history has been spoken of before (vv. 9, 10). No details are given of this war, though it must have been a serious struggle. Othniel is victorious and rules Israel in peace for forty years (v. 11).

6. Ehud, the Second Judge, vv. 12-30.

When Israel again fell into sin, God's scourge against them was the Moabites, who joined their earlier enemies, the Amorites and Amalekites, in a successful conquest for eighteen years (v. 14), when distress and repentance are again followed by deliverance.

It makes the blood run cold to read what Ehud did, but we must remember that he was not a murderer but a warrior, and the world has always made a distinction between these two. His act was not one of personal revenge, but patriotic and religious fervor. Moreover, while he was doing God's service in the general sense of that term, his deed is nowhere approved in Scripture. This last remark suggests an important qualification, to which attention has been called before, and which should be applied in instances of a similar character in the Bible record. Lange calls attention to the further fact that a shadow seems to hang over the official career of this man, for his name is not praised in Israel, neither is it said anywhere that the Spirit of the Lord was upon him, nor that he judged Israel. These omissions may be without significance, but are they not noticeable?

7. Shamgar, the Third Judge, v. 31.

The notice of this judgeship is brief and limited to a conflict with the Philistines. The "ox goad" with which he slew 600 men is as an implement eight feet long and about six inches in circumference. At one end it has a sharp prong for driving cattle, and at another a small iron paddye for removing the clay which encumbers the plow in working. Such an instrument wielded by a strong man would do great execution.

Questions.

1. What tribe takes the lead after Joshua's death?
2. What heathen people inhabited Jerusalem?
3. Name a theophany in this lesson.
4. What illustration of divine sovereignty and human responsibility does it contain?
5. Do you know the location of Mesopotamia?
6. Is God necessarily responsible for the atrocities named in this lesson?
7. What can you say about the story of Shamgar?

THE PERIOD OF DEBORAH

CHAPTERS 4-5

1. The Servitude to Canaan, c. 4.

We met before with "Jabin king of Canaan, that reigned in Hazor" (see Joshua 11), but this seems to have been a second of the name who built a new capitol on the ruins of the former one. The Israelites failed to exterminate these enemies on the north, who had now become strong enough to visit them with the severest oppression they had yet experienced, and which lasted twenty years, (v. 3).

Deborah's appearance on the scene (v. 4) is remarkable, who stands out uniquely in the sacred history of her nation. There was no predecessor and no successor like her. The palm tree under which she dwelt (v. 5) may mean the open-air court where justice was administered during her judgeship.

While a judge, she was not a military leader, hence the call for Barak to rally Naphtali and Zebulon which were in proximity to the enemy and suffered the heaviest oppression (v. 6). This was not her call, but God's call communicated in some special way to her, and it was God, and not Barak, who was to deliver the enemy into their hands (v. 7).

Barak's reply may not have been such an evidence of weakness as it appears, since the presence of the prophetess would encourage the troops and add sanction to the conflict (v. 8). Nevertheless, it met with rebuke

(v. 9) and an ultimate disappointment very humiliating to a conqueror.

Notice that this was the Lord's battle, and not man's (v. 15), as we have seen so many times in the history of Israel. That the panic was caused in a supernatural way is seen in chapter 5:20.

Jael's Savage Deed.

No apology can be made for the action of Jael the Kenite woman of vv. 17-21. Her house was at peace with the Canaanites. She had invited the fugitive into her dwelling. She had given him the special protection of the women's apartment, always sacred to the Oriental, and she had come upon him unawares with probably one of the pins with which the tent ropes are fastened to the ground. She was the meanest of maddest murderers.

It must not be supposed that although her action was foreknown to God it was sanctioned by Him; neither that because Deborah praises it in her song (c. 5), therefore she is pronouncing a eulogy on the moral character of the woman.

The following is the manner in which *The Expositor's Bible* refers to it:

"Jael is no blameless heroine, neither is she a demon. Deborah, who understands her, reads clearly the rapid thoughts, the swift decision, the unscrupulous act, and sees, behind all the purpose of serving Israel. The praise of Jael is therefore with knowledge, but she herself would not have done the thing she praises.

"Not here can the moral be found that the end justifies the means, or that we may do evil with good intent, which never was a Bible doctrine, and never can be. On the contrary, we find it written clearly that the end does not justify the means.

"Rightly does Christian society affirm that a human being in any extremity common to men, is to be succored without inquiry whether he is good or bad.

"Law is to be of no private, sudden, unconsidered administration. Only in the most solemn and orderly way is the trial of the worst malefactor to be gone about, sentence passed, justice executed. To have reached this understanding of law with regard to all accused and suspected persons is one of the great gains of the Christian period.

"We need not look for anything like the ideal of justice in the age of the Judges; deeds were done then and honestly praised which we must condemn. They were meant to bring about good, but the sum of human violence was increased by them, and more work made for the reformer of after times."

While quoting the above with approval, in the main, yet the author feels obliged to close the subject by alluding to what he has said in *Synthetic Bible Studies* (page 40), that these are questions too deep for his soul to fathom, and he would be careful not to be found replying against God.

2. Deborah's Song, c. 5.

The words of this chapter appear in better form in the Revised Version, where they are arranged as poetry.

The song begins with a reference to God's interposition on behalf of His people by a storm (vv. 4, 5). Then the condition of the people is depicted (vv. 6, 7) and their apostasy from God (v. 8). This latter was the cause of their affliction (same verse).

Praise is spoken for the tribal leaders and especially for God in the help rendered in extremity (v. 9), and all the great and wealthy are urged to join in it (vv. 10, 11).

At v. 12, Deborah bestirs herself to greater flights of fancy, and Barak is urged to parade his prisoners in triumph. Then follows an account of the tribes of Israel which assisted in the conflict, Ephraim, who dwelt near the Amalekites, Benjamin, Zebulon, Issachar. Reuben is reproached for abiding among the sheepfolds, and Gad, Dan and Asher for not leaving their ships to assist in the fight. Zebulon and

Naphtali are again especially commended (vv. 14-18).

The battle is described. Jabin seems to have been reinforced by other kings, who joined him without any money recompense (v. 19). The storm helped Israel, swelling the river so that the enemy were sunk in the quicksands, or washed into the sea (vv. 20, 21).

The story of Jael's action follows in vv. 24-27. "Butter" in v. 25 seems to refer to curdled milk. From Jael a transition is made to the mother of Sisera, the Canaanitish commander, who is looking through the window wondering why her son is so long in returning from the battle. Her companions help her to the answer by suggesting that the victors have waited to divide the prey (vv. 28-30).

The song concludes with an invocation to Jehovah in v. 31.

The land now rested for forty years.

It is to be remembered that this was a song of Deborah, and not a song of God. The record of the song is inspired by God, and in that sense is part of His Word, but it is not to be supposed that the Spirit of God indicted it, as is true of some other parts of Holy Writ.

A parallel has been found in the history of Oliver Cromwell, in whose letter after the storming of Bristol he ascribes the victory to God, saying: "They that have been employed in this service know that faith and prayer obtained this service for you. God hath put the sword in the parliament's hands for the terror of evil-doers, and the praise of them that do well."

This may have been true, and yet God should not be held accountable for everything that Cromwell did or said with reference to that action.

Questions.

1. To what part of Canaan is our attention called in this lesson?

2. Which tribes seemed to have taken the lead in this conflict?

3. Name some evidences of supernatural interposition.

4. Is Jael's action justifiable?

5. Of what does this lesson speak as one of the gains of Christian teaching?

6. Make an analysis of Deborah's song.

7. Where does inspiration terminate in this case, in the thoughts of Deborah or in the record of her thoughts?

8. Where has a parallel been found in modern history?

GIDEON AND THE MIDIANITES

CHAPTERS 6-8

The old story of sin and suffering is repeated after the death of Deborah.

The Midianites occupied territory on the south and east, contiguous to Moab, and were wandering herdsmen like the modern Bedouins, who, in connection with the Amalekites, harassed Israel at every opportunity with the results indicated in c. 6:1-6.

God sends a prophet to His people in this case before He sends a Saviour (vv. 7-10), for they must be brought to repentance before deliverance can be vouchsafed.

1. Gideon Called, c. 6:11-24.

"An angel of the Lord" (v. 11), should read "The angel," for the context shows this to be another manifestation of the Second Person of the Trinity. Study the context for evidences of this. Observe Gideon's consciousness of it, the angel's assumption of it (vv. 14 and 16), and its final demonstration (vv. 21-23). Note Gideon's modesty and diffidence (v. 15), suggesting Moses at the burning bush. His request for a sign (v. 17) is neither wrong nor unreasonable as the event shows. Although the acceptance of his sacrifice meant the acceptance of himself (v. 21), yet so deep-seated is fear in the heart because of sin (v. 22), that a special assurance from Jehovah is needed to restore his peace after he had become conscious of the Divine Presence (v. 23).

2. The Ensign Raised, c. 6:25-32.

Immediately upon his call Gideon enters upon service (v. 25). The "second bullock" of his father is named probably because the first had been stolen by the enemy. The father was an idolator like all the rest, it would appear, and the altar on his ground may have been one for public use. Secrecy is necessary in destroying this altar (v. 27), as the commotion following evidences (vv. 28-30). Joash's defense of his son suggests Elijah on Mt. Carmel (1 Kings 18), and, in another sense, Gamaliel before the Sanhedrin (Acts 5), or the town clerk at Ephesus (Acts 19).

3. The Battle Arrayed, c. 6:32-40.

"The Spirit of the Lord came upon Gideon" (v. 34). The margin of the Revised Version says, "The Spirit of the Lord clothed Himself with Gideon," an Old Testament way of speaking of the filling of the Spirit of which the New Testament so often speaks in connection with Christian experience (see Eph. 5:18). No wonder that Gideon could "do exploits" (Dan. 11:32), under such circumstances. This explains the gathering of the people to Gideon's standard (v. 35).

And yet Gideon's weak faith calls for another sign—two of them indeed (vv. 36-39)—for he has reached a second crisis in his career, and God condescends to manifest it (vv. 38, 40).

4. The Victory Won, c. 7:1-23.

This must be God's victory and not man's, therefore, although 32,000 men (v. 3) were few enough against an army "as grasshoppers for multitude" (c. 6:5), they must be reduced still further. For the first test (v. 3), compare Deut. 20:8, the second (vv. 4-7) was unique. Wandering tribes in Asia, when in haste, do not stoop deliberately on their knees to drink water, but only bend forward to bring their hand in contact with the stream, and throw up the water rapidly and with great expertness into their mouths. The Israelites who chose to do so on this occasion were the earnest and energetic ones fitted for the expedition God now had in mind.

What a trial of faith to attack an overwhelming force with only 300 men! No wonder Gideon needed another sign to reassure him for the engagement, which God now vouchsafed to him.

Observe the expression in v. 9: "Arise, get thee *down* unto the host." The latter were in the valley and attention to this is of importance to understand something of what follows. The dream and its interpretation in their effect on Gideon require no explanation. They were God's way of animating the little band of Israelites and they had such result.

But if the smallness of the army is astonishing, what shall we say of the foolishness of their armament (v. 16-18)? Compare 1 Cor. 1:18-31. The pitchers concealed the lamps, which were what we call torches, and being earthenware were easily broken, the 300 men were divided into three bands that they might seem to be surrounding the camp. Suddenly, in the darkness and stillness of the night, a loud echo of trumpets is heard, followed by a mighty shout from every side; a blaze encircles the camp, and the sleepers started from their rest and supernaturally alarmed as they doubtless were, run tumultuously hither and thither, not knowing friend from foe, and soon precipitately flee (vv. 19-22). "The men of Israel" who pursued after them, were either the 10,000 or the 32,000 who had lingered near the scene and were now ready to join in the fight when everything appeared so hopeful.

5. The Campaign Extended, c. 8:1-21.

Verses 1-4 require little comment, but should not be passed over without observing Gideon's modesty and greatness in soothing the wounded pride of

Ephraim (compare Prov. 15:1 and Phil. 2:4).

"The men of Succoth" (v. 5) and those of Penuel (v. 8), were of the tribe of Gad, but one would hardly think they were of Israel at all by the way they acted in this case. They were afraid of the Midianitish kings, and doubted Gideon's ability to overcome them. Verse 14 shows that it was the chief men of these places that had treated him thus, and whom he now returns to punish. "He *taught* the men" (v. 16) means according to the margin that he "threshed" them. The method was placing thorns and briers on the naked body and pressing them down by heavy implements of some kind. Cruel torture, but we can say nothing more about it than in the cases of cruelty mentioned earlier.

The Midianitish kings had slain Gideons brothers (vv. 18, 19), and it was his duty as nearest of kin to take requital, although he offered the honor to his son (v. 20). Jether failing in the premises, Gideon acted the part (v. 21).

6. End of Gideon's Life, c. 8: 22-32.

The tribes would have made Gideon king (v. 22) had not the latter showed his loyalty to God, and to them also by declining the offer (v. 23). He would be judge, but Jehovah must be King. And yet he made a mistake, though not intentionally perhaps, in what follows (v. 24-27). In other words, there seems no reason to believe that he had idolatry in view in what he did, although after his decease it worked that way (v. 33). What he had in mind apparently was an ephod for his use as a civil magistrate as in David's case later (1 Chron. 15:27).

Questions.

1. Where were the Midianites located with reference to Israel?

2. How many signs in all does God grant Gideon?

3. To what tribe did "the men of Succoth" belong?

4. Give two or three illustrations of Gideon's modesty.

5. How long did he judge Israel?

GIDEON TO JAIR

Chapters 9-10:5

1. Abimelech's Usurpation, c. 9: 1-6.

The close of the last lesson shows idolatry creeping into Israel, the fruit of which is reaped in the years following. God is forgotten and Gideon also (8:34, 35), the meaning of the last verse being interpreted by the story of Abimelech.

This Abimelech fraternized with his nearest of kin, the relatives of his mother's side (vv. 1-3), a striking instance, as one says, of the evils of polygamy, where one son of a father has connections and interests totally alien to his brethren. Contrast the verses just alluded to with 8:22, 23 and observe the difference in spirit and motive between father and son.

What is meant by the allusion to the "one stone" in v. 5 on which Abimelech slew his brothers, it is difficult to say. Some think he dashed them from one rock, and others that the stone was the pagan altar on which their lives were sacrificed.

2. Jotham's Parable, c. 9:7-21.

The reason Jotham, the youngest son of Gideon, was spared from the general slaughter is given in v. 5. The spot chosen for his proclamation was the public place of Shechem, and "the parable drawn from the rivalry of the various trees was appropriate to the foliage in the valley below." With a little exertion of voice it is said he could easily be heard in the city.

Someone may ask an explanation of v. 13, and in what sense wine could be said to "cheer" God? Jotham not being present to explain the expression, we are at a loss for it is not God who is here speaking, but man, whose word God is causing to be recorded. Wine was sometimes used in sacrifices as was oil. The latter is said to "honor" God (v. 9), and perhaps in the same sense it is meant that wine cheered Him.

Note the malediction Jotham pronounces on Abimelech and Shechem (v. 20), and the fulfillment we reach at the close of chapter 9. Thus would it appear that Jotham was in this case a prophet and minister of God.

3. Gaal's Conspiracy, c. 9:22-49.

The combination of Abimelech's usurpation and Shechem's idolatry did not work well, for by and by God sent a judgment upon them (vv. 22-25). Gaal, who, some think, represented the original Canaanites of the locality, took advantage of the feeling against Abimelech and raised an insurrection (vv. 26-29). Zebul, the ruler of the city, is loyal, and informs on him (vv. 30-33) with the result following (vv. 34-40). Subsequently Shechem itself is destroyed (vv. 41-45), and the people who took refuge in the stronghold consumed with fire (vv. 46-49).

4. Abimelech's Death, c. 9:59-57.

A subsequent campaign against Thebez, now called Tubas, was not so successful (vv. 50-55), and Abimelech like Sisera, came to his end at the hand of a woman. Thus his evil deeds met their reward (56-57).

5. The Judgeships of Tola and Jair, c. 10:1-5.

Not much is said about these two judges, and yet together they ruled forty-five years. As foreign aggression is not spoken of, the probability is that the "defense" or saving of Israel referred to was from internal dissension or usurpation like that of Abimelech. For this cause they have sometimes been called "civil" judges.

Something of the magnificence of the second of the two may be gathered from v. 4. To ride on an ass is characteristic of royalty in those times, and if each of these sons did that, and each had his

own city to rule, Jair's possessions were extensive. "Havothjair," interpreted, means "the towns of Jair."

It will be interesting to compare Num. 32:41, Deut. 3:14 and 1 Chron. 2:22 for the story of an earlier Jair, but although the two have points of unusual similarity they were evidently different persons.

Questions.

1. What is the spiritual condition of Israel following Gideon's death?

2. Give the history of Abimelech's rise to power.

3. Recite Jotham's parable and give its application.

4. What shows Jotham to have been a prophet?

5. Give the history of Shechem's destruction.

6. With what earlier military captain may Abimelech be compared in his death?

7. What characteristic has sometimes been given the judgeships of Tola and Jair, and why?

8. What is the meaning of "Havothjair"?

9. Have you compared the histories of the two Jairs?

JEPHTHAH AND HIS VOW

CHAPTERS 10: 6-12: 7

1. Oppression East and West, 10:6-18.

The story of these verses suggests that preceding the deliverance of Gideon's time (chapter 6). There seem, indeed, to have been no such widespread idolatry and iniquity in Israel before, and for 18 years the nation suffered at the hands of the Ammonites on the east and the Philistines on the west (v. 8). The Ammonites were very bold and pressed their conquests across the Jordan (v. 9).

The repentance of Israel (v. 10) seems to have been genuine for there is no cloaking of their sin, and yet Jehovah would put in the plow deeper (vv. 11-14). Just how the communication of these verses was made the record says not. It may have been gathered in substance from the providences in the case, or it may have come directly through the high priest; probably the latter. Nevertheless, when they are ripe for mercy the mercy comes (vv. 15-16).The ripeness is shown in their putting away sin, and making their backs bare for the punishment, whatever it may be, "Do anything you will to us, O Lord, but send deliverance." When the sinner in the present dispensation gets into this place of surrender, help through Christ is not long delayed. Compare the close of Romans 7 with the opening verses of the next chapter in that epistle.

2. Jephthah the Deliverer, 11:1-11.

Jephthah was low-born and had a hard time of it (vv. 1-3). He was at the head of a band of outlaws, with a history not unlike David at one time; but he was a gallant leader and his innings have come at last (vv. 4-11). Notice that Jephthah was not without a knowledge of God as shown in verses 9 and 11, so that with all His roving habits and his life of plundering on his enemies, the Ammonites perhaps, he may have been more godly and loyal than the people who cast him out.

3. The Ambassage to Ammon, 11:12-28.

The record of these verses is self-explanatory, and is noticeable, first, for Ammon's false assumption based on an untrue interpretation of history (vv. 12, 13); second, Jephthah's acquaintance with Israel's past, pointing to the accuracy with which the records were kept, notwithstanding the long period of turmoil since Moses' day (vv. 14-22); and third, his abounding faith in Jehovah's power in the premises (vv. 23-27).

4. Jephthah's Vow, 11:29-40.

The vow of Jephthah is celebrated for its awfulness and, like others, we have tried to explain it in some other than its literal sense, but the effort has not brought satisfaction. We can understand why he made it, because it was a custom with heathen chieftains on the eve of battle to promise their gods oblations or booty; and also because vows were practiced by the Israelites and approved of God, as we saw in Leviticus 27 and other scriptures, although, of course, not vows of this kind. Jephthah lived beyond the Jordan, far from the tabernacle, and on the borders of a heathen country, where human sacrifices were common. It was, too, a time of great spiritual declension in Israel. All these things are to be considered, and yet why did he do it, and why did God permit it, abhorrent to Him as it must have been, if it absolutely occurred? We might as well ask the old question, Why did God permit sin? We can say nothing in answer, but simply wait. There are many mysteries to try our faith and patience. One thing is certain, it furnishes an awful lesson against rash and hasty vows.

It is but just to add that the other view of this matter is that Jephtha consecrates his daughter to a life of virginal service. This indeed would have been a serious sacrifice to him as it ended his hopes as the head of his line, inasmuch as she was his only child. It also deprived her of the crown of motherhood. Verses 39 and 40 are thought to offer justification of this latter view.

5. Close of Jephthah's Career, 12:1-7.

Ephraim shows the same jealous spirit in this case as in the earlier time of Gideon. They wanted the glory without earning it, and, although Jephthah dealt with them almost as tactfully as his predecessor, the issue was different (vv. 1-3).

Verse 6 shows the test by which the escaping Ephraimite was discovered. "Shibboleth" means a stream, and "sibboleth" a burden. The appropriateness in the demand that they pronounce the first word is that they were trying to pass the fords of Jordan. The Ephraimites had a dialect peculiarity that identified them anywhere.

Questions.

1. How long was Israel in bondage at this time and to what peoples?

2. How does she testify her sincere repentance?

3. Have you examined the passages in Romans?

4. Give the early history of Jephthah.

5. Give evidences of his reverence for Jehovah.

6. Give the story of Jephthah's debate with Ammon.

7. Give the story of his vow.

8. Give the story of the word "shibboleth."

SAMSON THE NAZARITE

Chapters 13-16

The close of chapter 12 furnishes the history of three other civil judges, and then we reach that of another warrior as picturesque as Gideon or Jephthah. And Sampson's life is so full of inconsistencies and mysteries considered from the divine standpoint, that again we can only wait the explanations until we shall know as we are known.

1. The Promised Son, c. 13.

Here is another theophany for "the angel of the Lord" is none other than Jehovah—Jesus.

The beginning of this captivity to the Philistines is recorded in chapter 10:6, apparently, when the historian digresses to speak of the probably simultaneous captivity to the Ammonites on the east and here returns to the south again.

"Zorah" (v. 2) was in the tribe of Dan on the border of Judah, and hence approximate to the Philistine country. For the law of the Nazarite, compare Numbers 6. Manoah and his wife were of faith and piety remarkable for these times, as illustrated in the former's prayer (v. 8). Verse 16 identifies the angel with Jehovah. The word "secret" (v. 18) is, in the revised version, "wonderful," and harmonizes with the name of Christ in Isa. 9:6. "Wondrously" (v. 19) is the same word.

The angel's words (v. 16) are similar to those of our Lord in Matthew 19:17, and spoken for the same reason, viz: to instruct Manoah that the viands must be offered, not to a human prophet or an ordinary angel, but to the Lord Himself.

While both husband and wife had faith, the latter seemed to possess the better spiritual understanding, as judged by vv. 22, 23. She was able to draw a logical inference, and her words offer a suggestions on *God's Love— Proven by His Work."*

Text for a Gospel Sermon

His manifestation in the flesh of Jesus Christ, His sacrifice and resurrection from the dead, and His revelations in the written Word, to follow the outline of v. 23, are all so many evidences of His purpose to eternally save them that believe.

2. Sweet from the Strong, c. 14.

The key to this chapter has been put thus: "Jehovah by retributive proceedings, was about to destroy the Philistine power, and the means he chose was not an army but the miraculous prowess of this single-handed champion. In such circumstances the provocation to hostilities could only spring out of a private quarrel, and this marriage seems to have been suggested to Samson as the way to bring it about." See v. 4 as authority for this line of thought.

In the East parents negotiated the marriages of their sons, and the Israelites were not commanded against intermarrying with the Philistines as they were not of the accursed nations.

It may not be that Samson loved this woman so much, as that he found her well-suited for his purpose, which may explain the last clause of v. 3.

Observe that it was by the Spirit of the Lord, i. e., through superhuman courage and strength, he was enabled to slay the lion (v. 6), an incidental circumstance by which with others of the kind, he was gradually trained to trust in God for greater and more public work.

The bees are clean creatures, and time enough must have elapsed for the sun and the birds of prey to have put the lion's carcas in fit condition for their use (vv. 8, 9). The thirty companions (v. 11) were to honor Samson, and yet the outcome shows that they were there with ulterior motives also. "Sheets" (v. 12) means linen garments. "If ye had not plowed with my heifer" (v. 18) means if ye had not used my wife to deceive me. There must have been some reason why Samson went to Ashkelon (v. 19), and it is thought the men of that city were particularly hostile to Israel. Verse 20, compared with the first two verses of the next chapter, indicates base treachery to Samson, which might well arouse just resentment.

3. The Hill of the Jawbone, c. 15.

Samson now feels that he has a reason for revenge (v. 3), which (with assistance perhaps) he executes in vv. 4, 5. The margin of the Revised Version translates "foxes" by jackals, a cross between a wolf and a fox, which prowl in packs. Two of these were tied together, tail by tail, a slow fire brand being fastened between each pair. The brand lighted, they were started down the hillside into cornfields, and, of course, nothing could stop them as they ran widely here and there.

The remainder of the chapter calls for little explanation, except to say that the slaughter accomplished by the jawbone of the ass must have been, like the breaking of the cords that bound Samson, a supernatural act.

4. The Pillars of the Temple, c. 16.

The event at Gaza is discreditable to Samson both on account of his sinful conduct and the careless exposure of his life to his enemies, but God is still pleased to continue His power toward him (v. 3).

The event with Delilah is equally discreditable and he pays the penalty for it (v. 21). Of course Samson's strength did not lie in his hair, but in God (v. 17), and in the consecration of his life to Him as symbolized by the growth of his hair. He broke his Nazarite vow by cutting it and in that sense cut himself off from God. The loss of spiritual power to the Christian is always accompanied by grinding in the prison-house of sin.

But how merciful God was to Samson that on his repentance, as evidenced in the growth of his hair again, He should have vouchsafed power to Him once more, albeit it was to use him further as an executioner (vv. 22-30). It is important to bear this latter point in mind, to relieve Samson of the charge of suicide. He put forth his strength against the pillars of the temple in the exercise of his office as a public magistrate, and his death was that of a martyr to his country's cause. His prayer was doubtless a silent one, but the fact that God revealed it and caused it to be recorded is an evidence that it was heard and approved.

As we dwell on the biographies of these judges, so reprehensible, and yet so used of God, we see the great distinction between a holy life and simply power for service. There are Christians seeking the latter who appear indifferent to the former, but for the individual in eternity it is the former that counts and not the latter. God may use any man, but it is only the holy man who seeks to do His will who pleases Him. Let our ambition be not to do great things so much as to be acceptable to Christ when He comes (2 Cor. 5:9). Samson, like Jephthah, is honored for his faith in God (Heb. 11:32), and it was great, but he could never be honored for anything else.

Questions.

1. Name the three judges referred to in the close of chapter 12.

2. Define the law of the Nazarite.

3. Quote Isaiah 9:6.

4. Quote Matthew 19:17 and explain it.

5. Quote Judges 13:23 and expound it, giving topics and divisions.

6. State the key to chapter 14.

7. What is the meaning of "sheets" in 14:12?

8. Describe the burning of the Philistine cornfields.

9. Where lay Samson's strength?

10. Was Samson a suicide?

11. Which is preferable, and why, power for service or a holy life?

12. Quote 2 Cor. 5:9.

APPENDIX TO THE BOOK

CHAPTERS 17-21

The chapters concluding the book, give in detail certain incidents at various periods during the preceding history, when the whole nation was disordered and corrupt, and "every man did that which was right in his own eyes."

1. A Man-made Priest, c. 17.

Chapter 17 tells of Micah who established a sanctuary of his own in imitation of the tabernacle. Of course it was contrary to the law and evinced ignorance and superstition, although the motive may not have been bad.

2. Origin of the City of Dan, c. 18.

Chapter 18 carries the story further and shows how Micah lost his tabernacle, and his priest obtained a broader field. The Danites wanted more territory and dispatched five men to search out a good place (vv. 1, 2). By accident they discovered Micah's self-made "priest" and sought counsel of him, which was as ambiguous as the heathen oracles (vv. 3-6). Nevertheless they come to a town called Laish, which seems a desirable and easy prey, and which they persuade the men of war of their tribe to advance upon (vv. 7-12). Passing through Micah's town on their errand, they impress his priest into their service (13-21), and, although Micah and his fellow townsmen pursue them, it is without avail (vv. 22-26). They overcome Laish at the end, build their city there and call it Dan. They also continue their idolatrous worship introduced by Micah's priest, down to the captivity (vv. 27-31).

3. An Awful Deed and an Awful Retribution, cc. 19-21.

Chapters 19 to 21 tell an awful story of lust, civil war and pillage fearfully illustrative of a world without God.

A Levite, after the manner of those days, married a secondary wife who proved unfaithful. Returning to her father's house at Bethlehem, he followed her to persuade her to come back (19:1-4). After a few days they start on their journey accompanied by a servant, lodging the first night at Gibeah (19:5-21). Here wicked men abuse the concubine until she dies; her husband, his servant and his host acting so discreditably as to be almost unbelievable, were it not for the sacred record of the fact (19:22-28).

Subsequently her husband took a remarkable way of obtaining redress, explicable only on the absence of regular government among the tribes. He divided the corpse into 12 pieces and distributed them with the story of the wrong among all the tribes, so that the latter came together saying: "There was no such deed done nor seen from the day that the children of Israel came up out of the land of Egypt unto this day; consider of it, take advice, and speak your minds" (19:29, 30).

The result was a conference of the tribes at Mizpeh (20:1). The phrase "unto the Lord" is possibly explained by the circumstance that Mizpeh was near Shiloh, the place of the tabernacle, and that the leaders went there to consult Jehovah, if haply He would reveal His mind at this crisis, through the high priest.

The Levite is now given an opportunity to state his case formally, in which he inferentially lodges a complaint against the whole tribe of Benjamin, as Gibeah was in its territory (20:4-7).

The decision is to punish that city (20:8-11), but first to demand that the perpetrators of the crime be surrendered for execution, which Benjamin, through pride or some other reason, refuses to do (20:12-13). Internecine war follows, in which the Benjamites are at first successful, but in the end succumb to the greater numbers and the strategy of the united tribes (20:14-48).

Humbling Experiences and Their Cause.

But why, if the united tribes asked counsel of the Lord, and acted on it were they so unsuccessful at first, and why did they suffer so heavily? Perhaps they did not seek it early enough. Their own plans seem to have been formed first, and all they sought of the Lord was to name their leader (20:18). It was their disasters that seemed to bring them to their senses and to the Lord, in real earnestness, and then the tables were turned (20:20-28).

It is notable that Phineas, the grandson of Aaron, was their high priest, indicating the time to be not long after Joshua's death.

Folly upon Folly.

All that was left of Benjamin was 600 men (20:47), for it appears that all the women and children were slain. Now, the other tribes had sworn that they would not give their daughters to the Benjamites for wives, and the result was that the whole of that tribe was likely to become extinct —another illustration of a rash vow.

Ashamed of their folly, they repented of it, but not to the extent of taking back their vows (21:1-8). Instead of this, having discovered that none of the men of Jabesh-gilead had gathered to the battle, they determined to destroy its inhabitants, with the exception of the unmarried women, and give the latter to the Benjamites (21:8-15).

But there were not enough of these to suffice. Therefore, they decided upon the expedient of permitting 200 more to be stolen by the Benjamites from the other tribes under the circumstances narrated in chapter 21: 16-23.

No wonder the book closes with the refrain heard several times before, "In those days there was no king in Israel; every man did that which was right in his own eyes."

Questions.

1. What designation might be given to the closing chapters of the book?

2. Did these events come presumably after the last judgship, or before?

3. State the history of the city of Dan.

4. What was the occasion of the war between Benjamin and the other tribes?

5. What means were taken to perpetuate Benjamin?

6. How is the disorder in Israel explained?

7. Was a divine or human king required the more?

RUTH

BACK TO THE HOMELAND

CHAPTERS 1-2

Chapter 1.

This beautiful story is an event occurring during the Judges (c. 1:1), but separated from the former to give prominence to the genealogical record with which it concludes (c. 4:18-22), showing Ruth an ancestress of David, and hence of Jesus Christ.

The story is so simply told as to render necessary but the briefest comments.

Elimelech and his family are called "Ephrathites of Bethlehem-judah" (c. 1:2) for the reason that Ephrath was orginally the name of Bethlehem (Gen. 35:19; 48:7; Mic. 5:2), and also because there was a Bethlehem in Zebulun as well as Judah (Joshua 19:15).

The marrying of Moabitish women by the sons of Elimelech was contrary to the Mosaic law (Deut. 7:3; 23:3), but such disobedience was common in those times, as we have seen.

Why Naomi should not have encouraged her daughters-in-law to return with her (v. 8) is explained by the thought that they would fare better in material things in their own land and among their own people. Her piety was not of the depth to make her feel that the spiritual benefits of Israel would offset these advantages.

The utterances of Naomi in verses 11-13 are explained by the ancient custom (Gen. 38:11), sanctioned by the law of Moses. (Deut. 25:5), requiring a younger son to marry the widow of a deceased brother.

Naomi seems not to have been a cheerful person (vv. 13, 20, 21), but were we in her circumstances perhaps we would not have felt differently. And then she may have had reason to believe her affliction a divine chastisement upon her household.

Chapter 2:1-17.

Verse 2 reminds us of Lev. 19:9, 10, and Deut. 24:19-21, giving the right to the poor and to strangers to glean after the reapers; but we are not to suppose that Ruth purposely selected the field of Boaz, or that she had knowledge at this time of her relationship to him.

Reaping was done by women (v. 8), but the gathering and threshing was the work of men. How beautifully Boaz' character shows in these verses! His greeting to the reapers, his interest in his relatives, his attention and generosity toward them, and his confidence in Jehovah. What poetry of faith in the expression, "The Lord God of Israel, under whose wings thou are come to trust!" (v. 12.)

Verses 18-23.

Naomi recognizes the relationship of Boaz, and the phrase, "one of our next kinsmen," might be rendered, "one of them that hath the right to redeem for us." (Lev. 25:25.) This "right to redeem" carried with it the duty to protect them, to purchase their tribal lands, and in this case to marry Ruth and maintain the family name. Naomi's advice to Ruth, therefore, can readily be understood and appreciated (v. 22).

Questions.

1. During what period did the history of Boaz and Ruth occur?

2. What gives special prominence to the Book of Ruth?

3. What was the original name of Bethlehem, and how many towns of that name were in Israel?

4. What law was violated by the sons of Elimelech?

5. What was involved in the kinsman's right of redemption?

A BLESSED BRIDE

CHAPTERS 3-4

Chapter 3:1, 2.

The "rest" Naomi would secure for Ruth is that of a husband and a home.

Threshing-floors were commonly on the field where the grain was reaped, the process consisting in throwing it against the evening wind, the farmer remaining all night on the field for that purpose as well as to protect his property.

Verses 3-6.

The indelicacy of these verses is removed by the fact that it was the custom thus to remind a kinsman of his duty in such a case. The openness of the location is also to be kept in mind, together with the circumstance that orientals sleep by night in the clothing worn during the day, reclining simply upon a cloak or rug. Servants frequently sleep in the same tent with their master, lying crosswise at his feet, and if a covering be needed are allowed to draw the skirt of his covering over them.

Verses 7-18.

Spreading a skirt over one is in the East a symbol of protection, and in the case of a man's doing it for a woman equivalent to a marriage contract.

Rising while it was still dark, Ruth could without immodesty remove the veil from her face to receive in it the generous gift of barley for her and her mother-in-law. The word "veil" might be rendered "apron" or "sheet," which in the case of poorer women, was linen or cotton and wrapped around the head so as almost entirely to conceal the face.

Note Boaz testimony to Ruth's character from one point of view (v. 11), and Naomi's testimony to his from another (v. 18).

Chapter 4:1-8.

The "gate" was something like the town hall with us, where all the legal business was transacted. It was a building with a cover but without walls, and a place which everybody passed by. It was easy to find a jury of 10 men there any time; and as soon as the kinsman came in sight whose duty it was first to redeem before Boaz, calling him to wait, the case was entered upon with simplicity and informality (vv. 1-4). (For the law governing this matter, see Lev. 25:25.)

The kinsman was disposed to take the land until he learned that he must take Ruth with it when he changed his mind (vv. 4-6). (For the law, see Deut. 25:25.) How it would have marred his inheritance to have married Ruth is not clear (v. 6), except it be that a son born to him by her could not have carried his name but that of his brother, or possibly her Moabitish nationality alarmed him because of its contrariness to the Mosaic law. Boaz believes that the law is suspended in Ruth's case, who has become a proselyte to the Jewish faith, but the other kinsman does not.

"The shoe symbolized a possession which one had, and could tread with his feet at pleasure. Hence when the kinsman pulled off his shoe and gave it to Boaz, he surrendered to him all claims to the possession which would have been his under other circumstances."—*Cassel.*

Verses 9-17.

Verses 11, 12 seem to be a bridal benediction. Rachel and Leah had been greatly blessed with offspring and Pharez was honored as an ancestor of the Bethlehemites (v. 18).

The blessing of Ruth is regarded as that of Naomi as well (v. 14), for in the former's child her house will be raised up again. This is set forth in the name, Obed, which means "one that serves," i.e., one that serves Naomi.

In the conclusion of this verse we have the words in which the whole book reaches its culmination, the completion of the blessing pronounced on Ruth by Boaz (c. 2:18). "Thus the coming of the King is prepared for, on whom the Lord had determined to confirm the dominion over His people for evermore. And the converted Moabitess, who entered as a worthy member into the commonwealth of God's people, became the mother of David and of Christ."—*Gerlach.*

Speaking of the genealogical question itself, there is an interval of 380 years between Solomon and David (vv. 20-22). Whole generations are omitted evidently and only leading characters are named.

Questions.

1. Describe an Eastern threshing floor, and the process of threshing.

2. How would you explain the indelicacy in verses 3 to 6?

3. How did Boaz testify to Ruth's character?

4. With what may the gate of an oriental city be compared?

5. For what reasons may the nearer kinsman have declined to purchase this land?

6. What did the shoe symbolize?

1 SAMUEL

THE BIRTH AND DEDICATION OF SAMUEL

CHAPTERS 1-2:11

1. A Sorrowful Wife, c. 1.

Like Ruth, the opening of First Samuel deals with events in the time of the Judges, and is the book of transition from that period to the monarchy.

Verses 1-8. Though there is difficulty in locating the city named in verse 1, yet it appears that Elkanah was a native of Bethlehem-judah like Elimelech (see the first lesson in Ruth). He was a Levite, as we see by I Chron. 6:33, 34, and if it is surprising that he should have practiced polygamy (v. 2), we must remember the moral condition of the people at this time, but not imagine that God approved it.

Verses 4 and 5 suggest a situation not unlike that of Jacob and Rachel and Leah (Gen. 29:15-35). The latter of the verses is rendered in the Septuagint: "But unto Hannah he gave a single portion, because she had no child; howbeit Elkanah loved Hannah." It will be recalled from Lev. 3:7 and Deut. 12:12 that the offerer received back the greater part of the peace-offerings, which he and his family might eat at a social feast in connection with the act of worship, and it is to this that "portion" alludes. The "adversary" (v. 6) is translated "rival" in the Revised Version and refers to Peninnah.

Verses 9-18. What a beautiful illustration of Psalm 50:15 is found in these verses! As Hannah was the wife of a Levite, a son would in any event have belonged to the Lord (v. 11), but if this one was to be a Nazarite from his birth (Num. 6:5; Judges 13:5) it meant that his residence and service in the sanctuary must begin at an earlier period than usual.

Eli's words in verse 17 were spoken by the Holy Spirit through him whether he were aware of it or not. And Hannah seemed to understand them as a divine answer to her prayer (v. 18).

2. A Joyous Mother, 2:1-11.

Hannah's song will recall that of Mary in Luke 1:46-55, and must not be regarded simply as a natural song of thanksgiving, although it came from Hannah's heart. It was a prophecy of the Holy Spirit within her, making her joy to overflow in praise for those greater blessings in Christ of which the whole race will partake, and of which Samuel's birth was an earnest and pledge.

Study the words carefully, and see how they pass over all the intermediate steps of the development of the kingdom of God, and point to the final goal when the dominion is extended over the ends of the earth.

Doctrinally considered, the song expresses joy in the power of God (v. 1); it praises Him for His holiness and faithfulness, which is as firm as a rock (v. 2); it extols His providence in His omniscience and omnipotence in dealing with the strong and the weak, the rich and the poor, the high and the low, the godly and ungodly (vv. 3-8); and finally, it bears prophetic testimony to His victory at the end and the establishment of His Kingdom on the earth through Jesus Christ (vv. 9, 10.)

Questions.

1. How may this book be characterized?

2. To what tribe did Elkanah belong?

3. Can you quote from memory Psalm 50:15?

4. Have you read the law of the Nazarite in Numbers 6:5?

5. What was the nature of Hannah's song?

6. State its scope in a sentence or two.

7. Give a theological or doctrinal exposition of the song.

ELI AND HIS SONS

CHAPTERS 2: 12-36

After leaving their son with Eli in Shiloh, Elkanah and his wife returned home (v. 11). Then follows an account of how "Samuel ministered before the Lord" (vv. 18, 19), and how he grew in favor with God and man (v. 26).

In the meantime other blessings had come to Hannah (vv. 20, 21), a confirmation of the divine principle, "Them that honor Me, I will honor" (v. 30).

But what ministry could a child have wrought in the sanctuary? It is difficult to say, but he may have played upon the cymbals or lighted the lamps, or performed other simple tasks.

Priestly Graft, vv. 12-17.

But the burden of this lesson is the wickedness of Eli's sons, over against whom the life of Samuel is placed by contrast.

The explanation of verses 13-16 seems like this: When worshipers presented a peace-offering it was brought to the priest, who caused the Lord's portion to be burnt on the altar, and whose further duty was to cause the other portions for himself and the offerer to be sodden. The priests were entitled to the breasts and shoulders of the animal (Ex. 29:27; Lev. 7:31, 32), but Eli's sons demanded more, and even seized upon it before the waving and heaving before the Lord took place (Lev. 7:34). They added also the offence of taking up with their fork whatever portion they wanted while it was still raw, in order to have it roasted. The injustice of this must have been revolting to devout worshipers.

A Powerless Remonstrance, vv. 22-25.

But wicked as this was, the offence in verse 22 was more rank. The women referred to are mentioned in Ex. 38:8, but what their duties were in the sanctuary is not told. (Compare Luke 2:36, 37.)

Eli's old age (v. 22) is named not as an excuse but as an explanation of his weakness. He seems to have been an over-indulgent father, whose duty set before him in Deut. 21: 18-21, was not performed. Love triumphed over justice with the usual evil consequences to other people. It is only God who holds the balance evenly.

A Good Gospel Text.

God must be the judge when man fails (v. 25, last part), but it was not His fore-ordination but their wilful sin which was to cause the destruction of these sons.

Pastors will find a text for a Gospel discourse in the former part of this verse, "If a man sin against the LORD, who shall entreat for him?" The idea is that when men sin against men, God, through appointed human agents, restores the disturbed relations by composing the strife; but when men sin against God, who is there to arrange the matter? As Wordsworth puts it, "A man may intercede with God for the remission of a penalty due for injury to himself, but who shall entreat for one who has outraged the majesty of God?" Who, save Him Who is Himself God, and yet made Himself of no reputation that He might take upon Him our sins, and suffer in our stead?

The Punishment of Eli and His House, vv. 27-36.

Eli is held directly responsible for the conduct of his sons (v. 29). Notice that God can change His mind when it is conditioned on the conduct of His people (v. 30). Notice further, the prophecies upon Eli and his house.

1. "I will cut off thine arm and the arm of thy father's house" (v. 31). This meant that the high priesthood would be taken from the line of Ithamar, to which Eli belonged, and restored to that of Eleazar, from which it had been taken previously.

2. "There shall not be an old man in thy house," a circumstance which lowered the respectability of a family in Israel.

3. "Thou shalt see an enemy in

my habitation" (v. 32), or as the Revised Version expresses it, "Thou shalt behold the affliction of my habitation."

Eli would not personally live to see these things in detail, but he would see enough to assure him that the rest was coming (v. 34).

But God would take care of His own, and fulfil all His promises, as indicated in verse 35, which seems like a prophecy of Christ. The following verse somewhat qualifies this application, but perhaps the prophecy finds a partial fulfilment in Samuel and Zadok (of whom we shall learn later on), and a complete and final one in Christ, which would meet the difficulty.

Questions.

1. What blessing came to Hannah as her reward?

2. What ministry could a child exercise in the sanctuary?

3. Explain the nature of the priestly graft?

4. What was Eli's fault as a father?

5. What chastisement came upon him?

ELI'S DEATH AND THE LOSS OF THE ARK

Chapters 3-6

1. God Speaks to Samuel, c. 3.

"The word of the Lord was precious (or rare) in those days" (v. 1), is introductory to the record that it was now heard in the case of Samuel. It was Israel's sin that hid God's face from them and caused His voice to be silent so long,—only twice heard during the period of the Judges (Judges 4:4; 6:8)—but He was again to be gracious unto them in this respect, and a new epoch was to open in their history.

How God spake to Samuel we are not informed, but His voice in earlier times was heard in a literal sense, and there is no good reason to doubt that it was here. Of course, God is not a man with physical organs, but who shall say that He who made man's voice is not able Himself to be heard and understood by man?

It is touching that the "man" to whom God chose to reveal Himself was a boy, and yet by this time perhaps quite a lad. How interesting that He is willing to reveal Himself to such an instrument! How it should encourage the ambition of a boy.

The revelation God gives to Samuel concerning Eli is a repetition of that of the "man of God" of the preceding lesson (2:27). And the meekness with which the old priest takes it is an evidence that his personal character was good, notwithstanding his conduct as regards his sons.

2. A Crisis in Israel, c. 4.

Verse 3 furnishes another illustration of the low spiritual state of Israel at this time, and how little removed they were from their pagan neighbors. To trust in the ark of the covenant instead of the God it symbolized was scarcely different from the worship of the idols of the Philistines. It is significant that the elders and the priests were the leaders in this folly (v. 4). Their fathers had carried the ark at Jericho, but there was a reason for it then, and God had commended it, but how different now.

What judgment fell on Israel for this! And surely as we read the chapter to the end, we can understand the prophecy, "Thou shalt behold the affliction of my habitation."

But notice how the character of Samuel as a prophet is being established (3:19-21). How sad that he had not been consulted in the case of the ark. If he had been, what a different story might have been written for Israel!

3. The Ark Among the Philistines, cc. 5, 6.

This lesson will not be too long if we add the story of the ark among the Philistines, especially as there is little requiring explanation.

"Dagon" was a heathen god represented by a human bust joined to the belly and tail of a fish. The details of verses 3 and 4 of chapter 6 show the manner in which God was pleased to demonstrate His superiority over this heathen god, so called. "Unto this day" (v. 5) means the date when the story was recorded, probably the later years of Samuel's life.

"Emerods" is vulgarly known as piles, which the Philistines regarded as a judgment upon them (vv. 6-12). Thank-offerings were made to heathen gods for recovery from illness in the form of metal images of the diseased parts of the body, (still true in some Roman Catholic countries and in India), which accounts for the advice of the priests and diviners (6:1-6). Note especially verse 6, and the witness it bears that written records or tradition had kept some knowledge of the true God before the minds of these nations contiguous to Israel in all these years.

The lowing of the cattle for their young, notwithstanding that they did not turn back to recover them, shows that God was controlling their steps in another direction (vv. 10-12).

The judgment that fell on the Bethshemites (v. 19), was calculated to impress Israel anew with the sacredness attaching to the worship of Jehovah, but there seems to be an error in the translation here. Bethshemesh was only a village, and it seems unlikely that 50,070 men could have been slain there; but there is no explanation of the difficulty of which we know.

Questions.

1. Why was not God's voice heard for so long in Israel?

2. What stimulus to the spiritual life of a boy does this lesson contain?

3. Give an illustration of Eli's goodness of character.

4. What was the nature of Israel's sin in carrying the ark into the battle?

5. Tell the story of the discomfiture of the Philistines because of the ark.

6. Describe the sacrilege of the Bethshemites.

PASSING OF THE JUDGESHIP

CHAPTERS 7-10:16

1. A National Revival and Its Results, c. 7.

In our last we left the ark in care of the men of Kirjathjearim, which means "the city of woods," and is located near Bethshemesh and northwest of Jerusalem. Why the ark was not brought to Shiloh is not stated, but only that it remained in the city before-named twenty years. It would appear from 2 Samuel 6, and 1 Chronicles 13, that it remained there longer, but that period had elapsed when the event of this chapter began.

That event was a revival. "Israel lamented after the Lord" (v. 2), because they were suffering the consequences of His averted face, which included the oppression of the Philistines.

Samuel tells them how to find relief (v. 3). "Ashtaroth" was a goddess of the Sidonians, whose worship was popular in other lands, and which the Greeks and Romans knew by the name "Astarte." The worship was licentiousness under the guise of religion. Baal and Ashtaroth are named together, and taken by some to represent the sun and the moon, and by others the male and female powers of reproduction. "Asherah" translated in the King James Version "grove," was really an idol-symbol of the goddess.

The people listened to Samuel and gathered to Mizpah (v. 6). This refers to a public meeting for the observance of religious ceremonies, one of which was fasting, and another the pouring out of water before the LORD as a token, of their need of purification of which it was an emblem. Samuel seems to have begun his duties as a judge or civil magistrate at this time, having only exercised the office of prophet and teacher theretofore.

The enemy is quick to discern danger, for a return of Israel to God means a return to power, and hence they spring upon them while unprepared (v. 7). But Samuel's intercession is effective (vv. 8-10), and Israel so follows up the advantage gained by the supernatural interposition that the Philistines never fully recovered the blow all the days of Samuel's judgeship.

Observe in verse 16 that Samuel was a "circuit" judge. As later we read of "schools of the prophets" in the places named in that verse, some think that Samuel was the founder of them at this time.

2. The Demand for a King, c. 8.

This chapter presents no difficulties. Observe how history repeats itself in the case of Samuel and his sons as compared with his predecessor (vv. 1-5). Samuel's displeasure may have been in part personal, but chiefly because of the dishonor done to God and the injury that would be wrought by such a revolution to the people themselves (v. 6). God will grant them a king in His anger (vv. 7-9, compare Hos. 13:10, 11), and tells them what kind of a ruler they will have (vv. 9-18).

3. Seeking for Asses and Finding a Kingdom, cc. 9:1-10:16.

The drama in this chapter and the next disposes itself into five scenes:

We have first the country lad seeking his father's asses (9:3-5). Like the cattle on our western plains they were allowed to roam at will during the grazing season and were brought home at its close.

Secondly, there is the meeting with the prophet (9:6-21). That he should have been consulted on so trifling a matter, and that it should have been thought proper to offer him so insignificant a present as "the fourth part of a shekel of silver," perhaps 15 cents of our money, seems strange to us; but probably we appreciate Samuel's greatness better than his contemporaries. Moreover oriental ideas are different from ours.

It was probably the peace offering that was to be presented on this occasion, which under special circumstances seems to have been permissible at a distance from the sanctuary.

"Now the Lord had told Samuel in his ear a day before" (v. 15). How intimate this expression! In the 103d Psalm it is written that God "made known His *ways* unto Moses, His *acts* unto the children of Israel" and here He is honoring Samuel in the same way. His acts are what men see, His ways are the reason and foreknowledge of them, and to them that fear Him such secrets are still given (1 Cor. 2:9-12).

"Samuel's words to Saul in verse 20 are "a covered and indirect promise of the royal dignity that awaited him."

Thirdly, the introduction to the people (9:22-24). The things here recorded were intended to show honor to the young man, and in so far prepare the people to receive him as king. For example, his being received into the apartment assigned to the special guests, and given a high seat among them (v. 22): and his being offered the choicest portion of the feast (v. 24). The words "that which is left" should be rendered "that which is reserved."

Fourthly, the communion on the housetop (9:25-26). Oriental houses being low and flat-roofed, the roof offered the most desirable place for quiet conversation and rest in the cool of the day. Here the prophet instructed Saul in the way of the kingdom, pointing out to him, perhaps, the religious decline of the people, and the need of a leader obedient to God.

Fifthly, the anointing with oil (9:27-10:1), which was the ancient ceremony of investing with the royal office. This was followed by predictions of what should be met by Saul on the way home, which, as they came to pass, by testifying to Samuel's authority as a prophet, would confirm Saul's reliance upon what he had declared concerning himself.

Questions.

1. Have you looked up the location of Kirjath-jearim?

2. What does "Ashtaroth" stand for?

3. In what sense was Samuel a "circuit" judge, and what institution may have grown out of that fact?

4. How would you expound Psalm 103:7?

5. In what manner does Samuel distinguish Saul at this feast?

6. What was the significance of the anointing with oil?

7. How was Samuel's authority certified to Saul?

SAUL CONFIRMED AS KING

CHAPTERS 10: 17-12:25

1. The Peasant Becomes a Prince.

There was one verse in the last lesson (10:6) we should think of more fully. When Samuel said the Spirit of the Lord would come upon Saul and he would be turned into another man, it is not necessary to suppose it meant his regeneration. There is a question as to whether Saul ever was regenerated, for his life-story would not lead us to believe he was.

The Spirit of the Lord coming *on* a man is one thing, and the Spirit of the Lord coming *into* a man is another. He comes on a man for service, He comes in him for salvation. We saw Him coming on Balaam, enabling him to prophesy, although the event shows that Balaam was not in fellowhip with God, and so it may have been with Saul, and so it may be with any man. Service should not be our first desire, but salvation.

Saul had been a farmer's son, with no training for a monarch's throne, but the Spirit of God "rushed" upon him, as the word means, and endowed him to act in a manner far superior to his previous character and habits. "Instead of the simplicity of a peasant he now displayed the wisdom and energy of a prince.

2. The Choice of the Lot, 10:17-27.

The event here is an illustration of the relation of the divine sovereignty to human free agency. It was God's purpose that Saul should be king as indicated in His earlier selection of him and yet, so far as we can see, the people who were ignorant of this were perfectly free in their casting of the lot. So in the case of our salvation. "No man cometh to the Father but by me" (John 14:16), and yet, "whosoever will may take of the water of life freely" (Rev. 22:17).

Note, that the "Magna Charta" of the kingdom was laid up "before the Lord," placed with the other sacred records for safe-keeping and transmission, a circumstance to which attention has been called on earlier occasions as bearing upon the history of the text of Scripture.

That is a beautiful expression in verse 26, showing how God provided for the suite of the new sovereign and the dignity of the kingly state. These men feared God and honored the king (1 Peter 2:17). There were others, however (v. 27), but Saul in his treatment of them showed himself a king.

3. The Selection Confirmed, c. 11.

This chapter divides itself into two parts: Saul's victory over the Ammonites (vv. 1-11), and the effect upon the people in reference to himself (vv. 12-15). It contains no difficulties, but it ought to be stated that the demand of the Ammonites (v. 1) was based upon a supposed right of original possession in Gilead (read Judges 11).

Notice that no appeal was sent to Saul personally for aid, indicating that the people generally had not accepted him as king. But God had chosen and equipped him, which was sufficient (vv. 6-8).

Do not pass this by without observing God's sovereignty in the deliverance of His own. The men of Jabesh-Gilead are not looking to Him but to the people

—to some *man* who may help them. And yet their only hope is in God. And when He helps them it is through the instrument they have ignored. Moreover, it is His Spirit that does the work. Where otherwise could Saul have obtained the boldness to act as he did? And even then, would the people have had confidence to follow Him had not the Lord put His fear upon them?

What a lesson for our churches and missionary boards! How the magnitude of their work oppresses them in these days; how feeble the results in comparison with the effort and the size of the need. Why not turn to the God of Israel instead of wearing ourselves out with our own planning? Why not expect Him to carry on His work in His own way and His own time? The Spirit of God may fall upon any man He pleases, and His fear upon the people when He will, and then a revival comes and great is the accomplishment. Let us turn to Him in continual, humble and expectant prayer if we want to put the Ammonites to shame.

There is nothing so successful as success, and the enthusiasm of the people for Saul now is so strong, that with difficulty are they restrained from summary vengeance on those who would not follow him theretofore (vv. 12, 13). But Saul once more shows the strong reserve of a king, and is fully confirmed in the kingdom.

4. The Challenge of the Old Leader, c. 12.

The people have no charge to lay against Samuel (vv. 1-15), but he has one to lay against them, not for himself but for God. It was wrong and ungrateful for them to have desired a human king, yet they might be spared many of the unhappy consequences of that act if, even now, they would fear the Lord and serve Him (vv. 13-15).

It was needful that there should be a sign of the authority by which he spake. A thunderstorm in itself was not a miracle, but coming from a clear sky, in an unusual time of the year, and at the word of the prophet made it so (vv. 16-19).

Notice the testimony to the divine faithfulness and consistency in verse 22. How ever-recurring it is in Holy Scripture! And notice the cause of it, it hath "pleased" Him to do so. No desert on the part of His people, but just His own gracious pleasure (compare Eph. 1:4-6, 11, 12). This is humbling but assuring. If He pleases to save, He will save. And He pleases to save all who put their trust in His Son. It is the mark of the regenerated man that he submits to the Lord's pleasure always. It brings him pleasure to do so.

But do not lose the lesson of what Samuel says in verse 23. He would consider it calamitous for him to neglect the office of intercessor. Could a parent think more of his child than he of this nation? What an example for pastors! What an example for every Christian! (Eph. 6:17, 18.)

Questions.

1. How might one explain the reference to the Spirit of the Lord coming upon Saul in chapter 10:6?

2. Which should be our first desire, salvation or service, and why?

3. What theological problem is illustrated in the choice of the lot?

4. What circumstance bears on the history of the sacred text?

5. How is God's sovereignty in salvation further illustrated in this question?

6. What made the thunderstorm in this case supernatural?

7. What lesson about prayer did we learn from Samuel?

THE MONARCHY ON ITS WAY

CHAPTERS 13-14

The period covered by these chapters is doubtless of some length, whose history is summed up in the closing verses of the second (47-52). But there are special features reported in detail which constitute the substance of the lesson.

1. The Rendezvous at Gilgal, 13: 1-4.

Saul's plan seems to have been not a large standing army but a small bodyguard, divided between him and his son (v. 2), for the purpose of harassing the enemy in detachments.

"Garrison" (v. 3), is rendered by some "pillar" or "flag-staff." In any event Jonathan's act was a signal for battle, and the hosts gather (vv. 3, 4).

2. Saul Weighed in the Balance and Found Wanting, vv. 5-14.

Some regard "30,000 chariots" (v. 5), as a textual error, and that it should be "3,000." But the Israelites act as though there were 30,000 (vv. 6, 7), and even Saul loses his balance (v. 9). Had he withheld his hand until the end of the seventh day Samuel would have appeared, whose delay doubtless was providentially ordered to test the king's character.

The king failed. He had no right to intrude into the priest's office. It showed a lack of faith and obedience, and a desire to get glory to himself rather than God. Moreover, under rebuke he showed no humility or penitence, but a self-justifying spirit (vv. 11, 12), that led to his rejection from the kingdom and the prophecy of a successor of another type (vv. 13, 14).

3. "A Trembling of God," 14: 15-18.

The closing verses of chapter 13 depict the awful condition into which Israel had fallen under the mastery of the Philistines. They were totally disarmed. With the exception of a "file" for sharpening their smaller instruments of husbandry, there were weapons in the hands of none except the two named.

It is clear from this that what follows at the opening of the next chapter was supernatural. Verse 6 shows Jonathan's faith, superincluded doubtless by a special enduement of the Holy Spirit. Otherwise his conduct would have been rashness. The thought is further strengthened by the earthquake in verse 15, which contributed to the panic in the enemy's camp. "There was a trembling in the host," is in the margin, "a trembling of God," i. e. a trembling which He produced.

4. Zeal Without Wisdom, 14:19-46.

Ecclesiastes says there is "a time to every purpose under the heaven" (3:1), and Saul thought there was a time to cease praying and begin acting, for God had heard his prayer and was answering it (v. 19). The deserters were all coming back and the Lord was giving victory (vv. 21-23).

But the king had laid a foolish obligation on his soldiers, and a foolish vow upon himself (vv. 24-30). It was a case of zeal without wisdom as his son points out, and it came near costing him the loss of his son, but for the intervention of the people (vv. 36-45).

When Jonathan speaks of the honey "enlightening" his eyes (v. 29), it is another way of referring to the refreshment experienced by eating it.

The event in verse 32 took place at the end of the day's battle, when the obligation about eating being removed, the hungry soldiers could wait neither to cook their meat nor properly slay their animals. The stone Saul commanded to be brought (v. 33), was to slaughter the animals upon in accordance with the Levitical law about the blood, and seems afterward to have been used for an altar of worship.

Questions.
1. What, do some think, "garrison" means in this lesson?
2. What was the character of Saul's failure in this case?
3. What shows the extent of Israel's subjection to the Philistines?
4. How would you explain Jonathan's action in verse 6?

5. Tell the story of Saul's foolishness in this battle.

6. What is the meaning of "enlightening" in verse 29?

THE MAN AFTER GOD'S OWN HEART

CHAPTERS 15-16:13

1. Another Commission for Samuel, 15:1-9.

How long a time elapsed since the last chapter is indeterminable. Saul's victory seems to have driven the Philistines out of Israel's territory, and to have been followed by successful sallies against other enemies.

He had been warned of God that because of his presumption at Gilgal (c. 13), the kingdom would be taken from him and given to another; but God seems willing to allow him another chance, or at least another test of his quality to be His vice-gerent in Israel before executing His purpose (v. 1).

For an explanation of verse 2 look up Ex. 17:8-14; Num. 24:20; Deut. 25:17-19. We have seen the reason for God's anger against such nations as Amalek in that they represented the powers of darkness, and sought as the instruments of Satan to frustrate His purpose of redemption of the world through Israel.

2. Saul's Rejection from the Kingdom, 15:10-31.

This part of the chapter requires little comment. Notice Saul's falsehood (v. 13), and his self-justifying spirit (vv. 15, 21). Notice the principle in verse 22, and the final rejection of him in verse 23. Nor is his repentance sincere, inasmuch as he is still trying to excuse himself (v. 24), and desires to make a good showing before the people (v. 30).

God's Repenting and Not Repenting.

Here is a seeming contradiction which needs a word of explanation. Twice is it said that it repented the Lord that He made Saul king (vv. 11, 35), and in another place that "He is not a man that He should repent" (v. 20). In the last case "repent" is to be taken in the positive sense that God's decrees are unchangeable, which is necessary to be believed of the divine nature. But in the former case it is to be taken in the figurative sense, as explaining in terms capable of human understanding why He was about to act as He did.

He intends to alter His purpose with reference to Saul because of the latter's wickedness. It would not have been altered but for this, and yet He foreknew in choosing Saul that this would take place. In the larger sense, He did not repent or change His mind at all, while in the narrower sense He did. But since the narrower was included in the larger, it is to be regarded as part of His original decree, from which point of view God did not repent, but carried out His purpose as from the beginning.

3. The Choice of David, 16:1-13.

When in chapter 13 it was said that the Lord sought Him a man after His own heart, the reference was to David. But it is not to be supposed that David was a perfect man in the natural and moral sense, for we know to the contrary. It will be found, however, that while he was a sinner like Saul, he was a regenerated sinner while Saul was not, so far as man can judge. With all his sin, David, loved God supremely, and his underlying motive was to do His will. His history, checkered as it is, establishes this fact, and the sense in which he was a man after God's own heart is seen by a comparison of his history with that of Saul.

There is nothing of difficulty in the section of Scripture now under consideration.

Questions.

1. How extensive does the conquest of the Philistines seem to have been?

2. What further opportunity does God afford Saul?

3. Have you refreshed your memory concerning the history of the Amalekites?

4. Have you located them on the map?

5. Can you quote the principle in verse 22?

6. What indicates the insincerity of Saul?

7. How would you explain the apparent contradiction about God's repenting?

8. In what sense could David be said to be a man after God's heart?

DAVID BEFORE SAUL

CHAPTERS 16: 14-18:4

1. As a Minstrel, 16:14-23.

When it is said that "the Spirit of the Lord departed from Saul" (v. 14), we have a further illustration of the distinction between the Spirit coming on a man and the Spirit dwelling within him. In the latter case we do not think of His departing from him (John 14:16; Rom. 11:29), but in the former He may do so for more than one reason, but especially when the man through disobedience has placed himself outside the pale where God cares to use him. As to "an evil Spirit from the Lord" troubling him, we are to regard it as a judgment upon him (see Judges 9:23; 1 Kings 22:15-23; Job 1 and 2; 1 Cor. 5:1-5), in consequence of which he became "jealous, irritable, vindictive and subject to morbid melancholy." The ancients believed music had an influence in healing such disorders (v. 23).

It is easy to see why this providence came in the way of David (vv. 18-22), when we consider how it may have prepared him for his future position by acquainting him with the ways of the court and the business of government.

We are interested in the description of the young man David, by one who knew him well (v. 18). The word "servants" is "young men" in the Revised Version, indicating that it may have been one of his former chums. But how could David have been a "man of war"? If not on the battle field as yet, nevertheless in his conflicts with wild

beasts (17:34, et seq.), which demonstrated that he had the soldier in him when the time came.

2. As a Champion, 17:1-54.

This story is so familiar as to require little comment. The event occurred, according to the chronology in the margin of our Bibles, almost a quarter of a century after the victory over the Philistines at Michmash (c. 14), and when the old time enemy of Israel had again become bold. The place (Shocoh) seems to have been a town in the western section of the territory of Judah.

There is no explanation of David's prowess in the presence of this strong enemy (vv. 26, 32), save the supernatural enduement of God. It was not the temporal reward that moved him, but the desire that God be magnified. This is discovered in the faith evidenced in verse 37. His success had been God's success rather than his own and would continue so to be (v. 45). And yet works wrought with his faith, since he took not only his staff but *five* stones, not one alone. If one failed he had others (v. 40). Surely the description of him was true, he was "prudent in matters."

But why should David have brought the giant's head to Jerusalem (v. 54)? Probably because it was the nearest city, and hence the appropriate place of deposit for such a trophy. We learned (Joshua 15:63 and Judges 1:21) that the Jebusites possessed this city, but probably that means only the fortress on Mount Zion, while the rest was in Israel's hands.

3. As a Courtier, 17:53-18:4.

We are not surprised to find David a favorite at Saul's court after this, but we are surprised that he does not identify him (vv. 55-58). In explanation, remember Saul's mental condition at times, as well as the fact that time had elapsed since David's minstrel days, and the ruddy youth may have changed into the bearded man. And as to Abner, he may have been absent from court when David had been there.

In the next chapter (18), we have the beginning of a friendship that has gone into history as one of the most beautiful among men.

Jonathan and David were doubtless nearly of an age and, although the former had taken no notice of the minstrel, the heroic though modest warrior had commanded his admiration and affection at once, and "he loved him as his own soul" (v. 3).

"To receive any part of the dress worn by a sovereign or his eldest son and heir, is deemed in the East the highest honor which can be conferred on a subject." (cf. v. 4 with Esther 6:8).

Questions.

1. How are we to regard the saying that "an evil Spirit from the Lord" troubled Saul?

2. Have you read 1 Corinthians 5: 1-5?

3. How is David described in verse 18?

4. Where was Shocoh?

5. What was David's motive in the conflict with Goliath?

6. What do you know about the Jebusites and Jerusalem?

7. How would you explain Saul's failure to identify David the second time?

DAVID AND JONATHAN

CHAPTERS 18:5-20:42

1. Jealousy and Fear, c. 18.

Jonathan's love for David is put to a serious test, but is found genuine.

On the homeward march from the victory over the Philistines, the women of Israel, following oriental custom, met the warriors and accompanied them along the road, singing and dancing. But their joy outran their judgment, so that they praised David more than their king. A better man than Saul could scarcely have resisted the temptation to envy, sinful as it was (vv. 6-9).

No . wonder his malady returned and made him a murderer

in his heart (vv. 10-11). When it is said "he prophesied," it cannot be that he was the mouthpiece of God, but as the term denotes, one under the influence of either a good or bad spirit, the probability is he was in a kind of frenzy. In religious meetings, where some have professed miraculous tongues, a similar phenomenon has been witnessed. There has been prophesying, and some have supposed it was God speaking; but events have proven otherwise, for there are evil spirits in the universe as well as good, and, if possible, they would "deceive the very elect."

Saul would give David a military commission, but he would no longer retain him at the court (vv. 12, 13). The latter had merited the king's eldest daughter in marriage (17:25); but this is now forgotten and, like Jacob with Laban, he must do something more to obtain her. Nor is this enough (vv. 17-19). Another snare is set for him in the case of the younger daughter (vv. 20-25), for to slay an hundred Philistines, in order to their circumcision, meant a hazard that might easily have resulted in his death.

No wonder Saul was afraid of him (v. 29), for supernatural power was exerted on his behalf continually, and nothing could prevent his accession to the throne. Of course the wisdom of his behavior, the self-control he showed in the face of danger, at Saul's hands, was equally the gift of God.

2. The Strategy of Love, c. 19.

The story of this chapter is plain. For the incident of verse 12, compare Joshua 2:15. Michal's subterfuge (v. 17) is justifiable though its recital in the record is not necessarily a divine approval of it. Endeavor to find Ramah on the map, northeast of Jerusalem and a little south of Bethel. The meaning of "prophesied" in verse 20, may be similar to that expressed above concerning Saul, and yet it is more likely "that the influence of the sacred exercises produced such an effect upon them that they were unable to discharge their commission, and were led by a resistless impulse to join in praising God." "Stripping off his clothes" (v. 24) is to be understood of his armor and outer robes, as he lay in a state of trance.

3. The Faithful Friend, c. 20.

The beginning of a new moon was celebrated by sacrifices and feasting at which all the family were expected to be present (v. 5). But David's excuse for visiting his old home was a good one, since a "yearly sacrifice" seemed more important than a monthly one (v. 6).

Notice the renewal of the covenant between Jonathan and David at this time, and the projection of its terms beyond the lifetime of the former who, with a prophet's eye, saw the outcome of the struggle in which his father and his friend were engaged (vv. 12-17).

"Clean" (v. 26), has reference to some ceremonial law such as was studied in Leviticus. The reproach of Jonathan's mother (v. 30) was not a reflection upon her character necessarily, but a stronger way of insulting the son than to fling a charge against him personally. The phrase has been rendered "thou son of perverse rebellion," with the reference to "woman" omitted. The last expression of the verse is an oriental way of saying that the son's conduct would bring shame on the mother.

"Artillery" (v. 40) is "weapons" in the Revised Version. The French "artillerie" signifies "archery," a term still used in England of an association of archers who long since disused bows and arrows.

The closing verses are an affecting conclusion of a chapter in the lives of two of the best and greatest men who ever lived

Questions.

1. What mistake did the Hebrew women make?
2. What is meant by "prophesied" in Saul's case?
3. What illustration of Saul's

perfidy toward David does this lesson contain?
4. Did Saul's fear of David arise from natural or supernatural causes?
5. Have you identified "Ramah"?
6. What indicates Jonathan's conviction that David, rather than he, would ascend the throne?
7. What does "artillery" mean?

DAVID IN EXILE

CHAPTERS 21-24

1. Deceiving the Priest, c. 21.

Nob was northeast of Jerusalem and about five miles from Gibeah. David's unexpected presence there, and alone, caused alarm (v. 1). His falsehood was unnecessary and wrong (v. 2), and is not commended of God (Psa. 119:29). "Hallowed bread" (v. 4) was the shew-bread in the tabernacle, of which we studied in Exodus and Leviticus. It was removed the day before the Sabbath when it became lawful for the priests to use it (Lev. 24:9). David might have it under the circumstances, if only he and his companions (supposed to be elsewhere) had complied with a requirement of the Levitical law. (Compare vv. 4 and 5 with Ex. 19:15.)

The last clause of verse 5 is in the margin thus: "especially when this day there is other sanctified in the vessel." The idea is that it was the Sabbath, and the new bread having been put on the table, there was no risk in giving David of the old. (Compare 22:10 with Matt. 12:3, Mark 2:25 and Luke 6:3).

Doeg, the Edomite, was a proselyte of the Jewish religion and perhaps detained at Nob because of the law forbidding journeys on the Sabbath (v. 7).

David's going down to the Philistines at Gath (vv. 10-15) is unaccountable, except as he may have had special divine guidance. He was no longer safe in his own country. Go somewhere he must, and Philistia was the less of two evils.

2. Leading the Outlaws, c. 22.

The cave of Adullam (v. 1) has been identified as the present Dier-Dubbon, on the border of the Philistine plain and about six miles southwest from Bethlehem. It is a location of natural pits or vaults, some of them 15 to 20 feet deep.

It was undesirable for David to dwell in hiding if innocent, and if he desired to commend himself to the people as Saul's successor, hence God's advice (v. 5).

Saul's motive in seeking to arouse Benjamin against David of the tribe of Judah is not hard to find (vv. 6-8), but it is notable that the Edomite is the first to respond (vv. 9, 10).

Abimelech, whom Doeg gets into trouble, is innocent of wrong against the king. David seemed faithful; he was the king's son-in-law; why should he not aid him when he asked, seeing he knew nothing of the trouble (vv. 14, 15)?

But his plea is in vain, though only the Edomite would lift his hand against him (vv. 16-19). Compare Psalm 52: 1-3, and note that this slaughter of the priests was a fulfilment of the prophecy against Eli in an earlier lesson.

3. Defending a City, c. 23.

Keilah was southwest from Jerusalem and near the Philistine country, though not far from the wooded district of Hareth where David had located himself (22:5). The event now recorded seems to have occurred prior to the destruction of Nob, as we judge by comparing verse 6 with the closing verses of the preceding chapter.

How David inquired of the Lord (v. 2) is not stated, but is suggested by verse 8. We have seen what the "ephod" was, and know from Exodus 28: 26-30 that it contained the breastplate of the high priest in which was the mysterious "Urim and Thummim" by means of which God was pleased to communicate with His people (Num. 27: 21).

It will be interesting to read Psalm 31, which David is supposed to have written and which remarkably tallies with his experiences here.

4. Befriending the King, c. 24.

Engedi will be found southeast of Keilah on the Dead Sea.

The diversion in Saul's pursuit of David caused by the attack of the Philistines (23:27-29) has come to an end, and he is seeking him again.

"To cover his feet" (v. 5) means to go to sleep.

Notice David's wonderful self-restraint and the motive for it (vv. 4-6), which affords another illustration of his being "a man after God's own heart." (Read Psa. 142.)

The chapter affords a striking illustration of heaping coals of fire on an enemy's head and the promised result of overcoming evil with good (Rom. 12:20, 21). But alas! the evil did not stay overcome, nor, if we may judge by the last verse, does David expect it will.

Questions.

1. Can you identify Nob, Hareth, Keilah and Engedi on the map?

2. What is the meaning of "hallowed bread"?

3. What prophecy did the slaying of Abimelech's family fulfil?

4. Describe the "ephod."

5. Have you read Psalms 31, 52 and 142?

MORE BROKEN PROMISES

CHAPTERS 25-27

1. David and Abigail, c. 25.

The romance of this chapter has a setting like this: The "Wilderness of Paran" on the south was a common pasture like our prairies, and for this reason open to marauders from among the Arabs.

David and his men must have been a protection to their countrymen from such incursions, and in the habit of receiving practical acknowledgments of their service.

Nabal was a rich sheep owner who must have been indebted to

them, and "good business," to say nothing of gratitude, should have induced him to contribute to David's need without asking, and his refusal to do so was a violation of established custom.

This does not justify David's blood-thirsty action, but explains it.

The "bottles of wine" (v. 18) were goatskins holding a large quantity.

The "bundle of life" (v. 29) is a poetic expression alluding to the security of the person to whom it is applied.

The last phrase of verses 22 and 34 should be rendered "any man child."

When Nabal's "heart died" (v. 37), it means that he fainted at the thought of his narrow escape, the shock ultimately ending his life (v. 38).

David's taking Abigail to wife was in accordance with eastern custom. He was the head of a clan, Abigail seemed to recognize him as the successor of Saul (v. 30), and such an one fancying a woman for his wife had a right to command her submission to his will. Abigail seems to have been very willing, however.

Polygamy was wrong, (v. 44), but, because of the condition of the times, God seems to have permitted it (Matt. 19: 3-9).

2. David and Abner, c. 26.

Why David returns to Hachilah (see 23:19) is not clear, especially when he was near his old enemies, the Ziphites.

"Within the trench" (v. 7), means "within the place of the wagons" (see Revised Version). The encampment was a circle, the wagons and the men lining it, and the place of the leader being in the center. "His bolster" is the same as "his head."

In explanation of verse 13 we are told that the air of Palestine enables the voice to be heard at a great distance. (Compare Judges 9:7).

David's heroic strategy gave good ground for his sarcastic inquiry of Abner (vv. 14-16).

Saul repents again and makes more promises; but he has broken so many hitherto that David's confidence is not restored (v. 25).

3. David and Achish, c. 27.

David's resolution (v. 1) was probably wrong (see 22:5), but God over-ruled it for good by making it contribute to the final destruction of Saul.

"Achish" seems to have been another than he named in the earlier chapter, and there is likelihood that he invited David into his territory. Perhaps it was good policy to do so in view of the feud between David and Saul, and his warlike purposes toward the latter.

Ziklag belonged orginally to Canaan and was given to Israel, but never conquered or occupied by the latter. It was far in the south on the border of Philistia, just northeast of Beersheba.

"Road" (v. 10) should be rendered "raid." David deceives Achish in what he says, for instead of destroying the king's enemies, he really did away with the king's allies and engaged in an awful slaughter to conceal the fact (vv. 11, 12).

As in other cases we must not suppose God endorses this because it is in the record or because it was done by one of His servants.

Some of ourselves are in point. Though redeemed by the blood of Christ, and indwelt by God's Spirit, what unsatisfactory instruments do we make in His service, and how often we bring dishonor on His name. Yet He loves and bears with us and, though He chastens, still uses us.

It is one of the proofs of the credibility of the Bible that it tells us the whole truth about a man. If it were false it would be covering over the defects of its heroes; but as it is, both the Old and New Testaments never compromise the facts for the sake of a good appearance. And very grateful we should be therefor.

Questions.

1. How may Nabal have become indebted to David?

2. How would you explain David's polygamous relations with Abigail?

3. Do you know where Paran, Hachilah, Ziph and Ziklag are located?

4. What was the name of Saul's chief captain?

5. Name a strong, incidental proof of the Bible, suggested in this lesson.

SAUL'S CAREER ENDED

CHAPTERS 28-31

1. Calamity Foretold, c. 28.

This chapter is important and illustrates again the deceptive character of Saul. Having professedly put the necromancers out of Israel in obedience to the divine command (Lev. 19:31; 20:27; Deut. 18:10, 11), he no sooner finds himself in straits than he seeks out one of them for his aid.

Two questions arise. Did Samuel really come forth from the dead, and was it the woman's power that brought him forth? To the first we answer yes, on the evidence of verses 12 to 16, and to the second, no. The woman was surprised to see Samuel and affrighted (v. 12), which is proof that she was not a factor in the matter, and that God brought up Samuel to rebuke Saul.

Two other questions follow. Is it possible for human beings to talk with the dead, or lawful to do so? We answer no in both cases. Spiritualistic mediums may have intercourse with demons who by their superior knowledge personate the dead, but they are not permitted of God to bring back the dead themselves. On the other hand God may be at liberty to do what He would not permit His creatures to do.

How are we to understand the words "Tomorrow shalt thou be with me." Was not Samuel one who feared God and Saul the opposite? How then could the future life of both be located in the same place? The answer is that the Jews regarded the place of the dead as composed of two realms, one for the righteous and one for the unrighteous. Saul might be with Samuel in that he was among the dead, and yet not in the sense that he was in the company of the righteous dead.

2. The Evil in Operation, cc. 29, 30.

There is no apology for David's hypocrisy in this chapter, but the situation in which he found himself was the result of the unbelief that led him to leave the land of his fathers and throw in his lot with the Philistines (27:1).

Achish, shows up better than he in this transaction, for he seemed to have confidence in David (28:1, 2). And had it not been for the shrewder judgment of his princes (29:3-5), David would have been found playing the traitor to him later, for it is unlikely he would have fought for him against his own kith and kin.

Chapter 30 may be included in this division because it still has to do with David. There is nothing in it requiring explanation except the observation in verse 6, "that David encouraged himself in the Lord his God." How he did it, and what encouragement he received is indicated in verses 7, 8, but why God would be willing to encourage such a man puzzles us, till again we think of ourselves. The best of us are unbelieving, mean, and hypocritical at times, and yet God's patience waits, and does not destroy and cast away. The reason is that God's love for us terminates on His own glory. He is doing these things for His Name's sake. His honor is at stake in the execution of His purposes and the fulfilling of His will. He had great plans for Israel and the world through David. And He is not measuring us by what we now are, but by what He sees us to be when the work of grace is perfected in us in the ages to come. David becomes a different man even before his earthly career is ended, and we find something of the same transformation in his career as in that of his progenitor, the supplanted Jacob who became Israel, the prince who prevailed with God (Gen. 32:28).

3. The End Reached, c. 31.

We need not comment on the events of this chapter which tell their own story, but the following from *Illustrations of Scripture*, by Hackett, will be quickening to faith:

"I venture to affirm that he who compares the Bible account of this battle with the regions around Gilboah, has the same sort of evidence that it relates what is true as a person would have concerning the battles of Saratoga, Yorktown and Waterloo, should he compare their histories with the localities where they occurred.

"Some of the most celebrated battle fields of Grecian and Roman history corresponds but imperfectly with the descriptions of ancient writers. The writers may be trustworthy, but the villages they mentioned have changed their names or entirely disappeared. In some cases convulsions of nature have altered streams, or disturbed landmarks between hills and valleys. But Saul's battle ground remains mapped out on the face of the country, almost as distinctly as if it occurred in our time, and yet it occurred in an age more remote than the founding of Rome, or the siege of Troy."

Questions.

1. How does chapter 28 illustrate hypocrisy?

2. What reason is there to doubt that the woman's power brought forth Samuel?

3. What is the nature of mediumistic power, and how is it limited?

4. How did the Jews regard the place of the dead?

5. Describe the equivocal position in which David finds himself in chapter 29, and explain it.

6. What is the secret of God's long suffering patience with His people?

7. How do present facts substantiate the story of the battle?

2 SAMUEL

DAVID MADE KING

CHAPTERS 1-5:5

1. Lamenting the Dead, c. 1.

Surely the harshness and gentleness of David are strangely blended in this chapter. That one should so lament an enemy and slay the man who professed to murder him surpasses ordinary thought; but David was built on a large mould. Of course the Amalekite lied to David, for the inspired record of the death of Saul in the preceding book must be regarded as correct.

Observe the motive governing David: "Wast thou not afraid* * * * to destroy the LORD'S anointed?" (v. 14). It is his zeal for God that moves him, and furnishes the key to his whole life, notwithstanding his defects and iniquities. This is the thing which distinguishes him from Saul, and gives him the right to the peculiar appellation attached to him.

The obscurity of verse 18 is perhaps explained thus: The *use* of the bow," might be rendered "the *song* of the bow," and doubtless refers to the song which follows (vv. 19-27), and which David composed, after the manner of the times, on the death of Saul and Jonathan. "The book of Jasher," or "the book of the upright," is mentioned in Joshua (10:13), and seems to have been a compilation of sacred poems not otherwise known to us.

2. War Between the Houses, cc. 2:1-3:6.

The leading facts of this section are: David's anointing as king over Judah, his own tribe (v. 4), including his tactful commendation of the men of Jabesh-Gilead (vv. 4-7). David was a diplomat as well as a warrior. Second, the succession of Ish-bosheth to the throne left vacant by his father, Saul (vv. 8-10). Third, the earliest battle between the opposing forces, precipitated by the failure of the duel to settle the question between them (vv. 12-

17). "Hel-Kath-hazzurim" means "the field of strong men" (see the margin), appropriately named from the deed of valor wrought that day. Fourth, the remarkable armistice (vv. 18-32). Evidently if Abner had not asked for a stay, Joab would have put it into execution the next day, and for the same reason (vv. 25-28). The great value of Asahel is graphically expressed in the words *"nineteen men and Asahel"* (v. 30). He was more than merely a twentieth. God needs such men in His service. Can He count on us?

3. David Comes Into His Own, cc. 3:6-5:5.

The circumstances leading up to David's ascendancy are as follows:

(a) Abner's indignity to the memory of Saul, and Ish-bosheth's protest against it (3:7-11);

(b) The former's league in consequence with David (vv. 12-21);

(c) The murder of Ish-bosheth (4:1-12);

(d) The anointing to the office of king (5:1-5).

The intervening verses (3:22-4:27) tell their own story of jealousy and murder. It was a dastardly act of Joab, and Abner seems to have been all through the better man, although Joab was valiant and loyal to his king. Note, however, the curse David puts upon him (3:28, 29), notwithstanding that he continued to use him as his chieftain. David was a noble soul, and his sincere lament for Abner won him the hearts of Israel (vv. 31-39).

Questions.

1. Where in this lesson is there an illustration of the difference between the truth of the record and that which the record contains?

2. What illustrates David's personal loyalty to God?

3. What can be told about "The Book of Jasher"?

4. How long did David reign over Judah alone?

5. How long over Israel and Judah?

6. In how many instances are the wisdom and tact of David shown in this lesson?

"GOING AND GROWING"

CHAPTERS 5: 6-7: 29

1. Conquering Foes, c. 5.

The title of this lesson is the literal rendering of verse 10, "David went on and grew great." The margin reads, "going and growing."

First, he overcame the inhabitants of Jerusalem known as the Jebusites and, capturing the city, made it his capital (vv. 6-9). The parallel passage in First Chronicles 11:4-9, will show the two accounts to complement and confirm one another, Samuel being the more biographic and analistic and Chronicles the more historical.—*Lange.*

The reference to the "blind and the lame" may mean that the Jebusites felt themselves so strongly fortified on Mount Zion, that in derision they put such persons on the wall as defenders —even then David could not take the citadel, they thought.

This is the first time "Zion" is referred to (v. 7), and it is well to identify it as the southwest hill of Jerusalem, the older and higher part of the city. It was here that later David brought the ark of the covenant, from which time the hill became sacred. After the building of the temple by Solomon on Mount Moriah, a different eminence, and the transfer of the ark thither, the name "Zion" was extended to comprehend it also (Isa. 8:18; Joel 3:17; Mic. 4:7). Often it is used, however, for the whole of Jerusalem (2 Kings 19:21), occasionally for the Jewish system of religion (Psa. 126:1), and once, at least, for heaven (Heb. 12:22).

David next overcomes the Philistines (vv. 17-25). Note the supernatural interposition in verses 23, 24. "The sound of a going," means probably the sound of

human steps as of an advancing army, the symbol of Jehovah's approach in power. "Thou shalt bestir thyself," means, "Be sharp!" "Rush quickly!"

Thus victory comes from the Lord, (1) when it is humbly asked for according to His will and word; (2) when the battle is undertaken in His name and for His cause; (3) when it is fought in obedience to His directions and guidance.

But observe, as Matthew Henry says, that "though God promises to go before them, yet David must bestir himself and be ready to pursue the victory." God's gace must quicken our endeavors (Phil. 2:12, 13).

Broadus calls the chapter "King David's first year of sunshine." After years of darkness, he now gains a new crown, a new capital, a new palace, a new victory over an old enemy, and in them all a new proof of God's favor.

2. Installing the Ark, c. 6.

The first attempt to bring up the ark is unsuccessful (vv. 1-11) because of the sacreligious act of Uzzah (Num. 4:14, 15; 7:9; 18:3); but the motive of David's heart was laudable, and unlike anything we read of Saul.

"Baale of Judah" is another name for Kirjath-jearim (1 Sam. 6:21; Joshua 15:60).

The second attempt was successful (vv. 11-19), because the Levitcal law was obeyed (see 1 Chron. 15:1-14), an incidental evidence that this law had been recorded, though overlooked. This, so far, answers the destructive criticism which would relegate the Pentateuch to a later period than David.

There may have been too much abandon in David's dancing (v. 16), but the spirit of Michal's criticism (v. 20) was not God-glorifying, for David's rebuke of her seemed to have the divine sanction (v. 23). See 1 Chron. 16, the Psalm composed on this occasion.

3. The Messianic Covenant, c. 7.

We have here one of the most

important chapters in the Old Testament, ranking in Messianic significance with Gen. 3, 12 and 49, and Deut. 18. The seed of the woman, who was to come in the line of Abraham and Judah, is now seen to belong to the family of Jesse; and the prophet like unto Moses is to be also a king on the throne of his father David.

A great honor for David is now to be revealed. He has a lofty motive in desiring to build a temple for the ark, and Nathan, not taking counsel of the Lord, is disposed to favor it, until differently informed (vv. 1-17).

In these words of the Lord by Nathan observe the promise of Israel's future prosperity and peace—still future (vv. 10, 11). Observe further that the "house" God promises to build for David (vv. 11, 13), is neither a material nor a spiritual one, but, as distinguished from either, a political one. It is a house in the sense of an earthly kingdom to be set up in his son. But it is clear that the son is not merely Solomon who immediately succeeded to the throne, but the Lord Jesus Christ, of whom, in a limited sense, Solomon is a type. The word "forever" in verse 13 forshadows this, but the first sentence of verse 14 compared with Hebrews 1:8, settles it.

In this connection Bishop Horsley's and Adam Clarke's translation of the latter part of that verse is interesting and significant: "When iniquity is laid upon Him, I will chasten Him with the rod of men"—a parallel to Isaiah 53 concerning the suffering Messiah.

David's adoration and thanksgiving at the revelation of this great truth is beautiful (vv. 18-29). Its humility, faith, and gratitude reach a sublimity unequaled since Moses.

He seemed to have recognized by faith the Messianic character of Nathan's words, if we may judge by Horsley's and Clarke's translation of verse 19: "O Lord God, Thou hast spoken of Thy servant's house for a great while to come, and hast regarded me in the arrangement about the MAN that is to be from above, O God, Jehovah." (See the author's *Synthetic Bible Studies*.

Questions.

1. From what do we obtain the title of this lesson?

2. What other book of the Old Testament parallels Second Samuel?

3. Give the meaning of "Zion" in the Bible.

4. When may victory be expected from the Lord?

5. What makes this David's "year of sunshine"?

6. How was the ark brought up the second time?

7. What makes chaper 7 so important?

8. What kind of a house does God promise David?

9. How would you prove the Messianic character of this promise?

10. Which, to you, is the best verse in chapter 7?

VICTORY EVERYWHERE

CHAPTERS 8-10

1. Introductory Words.

The title to this lesson is from the phrase, twice repeated in chapter 8, "And the LORD preserved David whithersoever he went", which the Revised Version renders, "And the LORD gave victory to David whithersoever he went."

The Lord's Battle.

It is important to keep in mind that the LORD gave the victory and that it was not David's prowess that won it. Neither did his character merit it. God has a purpose concerning the redemption of the race in which He is using Israel, and what He is now doing through David is part of the program. We have seen this before, but we must never lose sight of it.

Of course David is, in his heart, submitted to the will of God, and one whom God, for that reason, delights to use; but still it is God working and not David.

God also is responsbile for what follows in the punishment

and destruction of the nations. That is not to say that He approves of all of David's acts in detail, far from it indeed; but the great outlined plan or policy is His, a fact that should make the careless pause to think.

War's Cruelties.

There are things David does which are cruel in our eyes; but remember it is war we are considering and, as one of our own generals said, "War is hell," i. e., a taste of hell on earth. The barbarities of the present are in accordance with the thinking of our time. A milder age, a millenial state, will look back at the wars of the twentieth century with the horror that we now contemplate some of the history of the Bible.

Foreshadowing Coming Judgments.

But worse things are coming on the earth before those days, as we judge by the book of Revelation. The God who is judging and punishing the people of David's period is the same who will be judging and punishing when the Antichrist is potent in the earth.

Little is said about these things in current preaching and teaching. It is unpopular to talk of sin and judgment, and death and hell; but these things are in the Bible, and we have no right to believe what we like and turn a deaf ear to what we do not like. He is the faithful witness for God, and the faithful friend of his fellowmen, who warns them truthfully of the wrath to come.

2. Details of the Story, c. 8.

"Metheg-ammah" (v. 1) is identical with "Gath and her towns" (1 Chron. 18:1). Be careful to examine the map for these localities, as it will aid in mastering the lesson; and remember that light will be thrown upon the text here and there by comparing the parallel record in 1 Chronicles.

The "line" (v. 2), is explained by a custom of Eastern kings to make their prisoners lie on the ground, while they determine by lot, or a measuring line, who

should be spared as slaves and who should be slain.

"To recover his borders" (v. 3), may refer to David's purpose to get possession of all the dominion God promised his fathers (Gen. 15:18; Num. 24:17). Horses were forbidden Israel either in war or agriculture, and perhaps it was an act of disobedience for David even to save 100 for his kingly retinue.

Verse 15 shows that while David was much in war yet he also reigned well at home. He had a strong cabinet (vv. 16-18). An explanation of the two priests (v. 17) is that the former had been put in office by Saul, while David had exalted the latter. But now that David was supreme a compromise seems to have been effected, and Zadok exercised his office at Gibeon (1 Chron. 16:39) while Abiathar did the same at Jerusalem.

3. An Illustration of Grace, c. 9.

We need not dwell on chapters 9 and 10, but the Christian worker will discover a fine illustration of grace and a good outline for a sermon in that of Mephibosheth:

(a) He had nothing to commend him to David.

(b) David not only forgives and delivers him from the dread of retribution, but restores him to a good position in the kingdom.

(c) He did this for the sake of another, Jonathan.

(d) Mephibosheth served David faithfully all his days.

Questions.

1. From what is the title of this lesson obtained?

2. Why is God working for and through David?

3. How would you explain some of David's acts?

4. To what future event do David's victories point?

5. How would you explain the contemporary priests?

6. Can you tell the story of Mephibosheth from memory, and point out some of its spiritual lessons?

DAVID'S GREAT SIN

Chapters 11-12

1. God's Estimate of David's Sin, 12:1-14.

Why the incident in this lesson should be designated "David's great sin," when he committed so many which the popular mind might consider more serious, can only be answered by the divine estimate of it. Jehovah regarded nothing David had done as comparable in its iniquity with this. Nathan's address to David shows this, the chastisement that followed David through the rest of his life shows it, and David's own feelings revealed in Psalms 51, 32 and 103, which he is supposed to have written on his repentance for this sin, bear a similar testimony.

2. Uriah's Character, 11:6-17.

David's sin is scarcely more conspicuous in the picture than Uriah's self-restraint, patriotism and general nobility of character; and this, whether or not we regard him as having a suspicion of the king's motives in the premises and the reason for them.

3. Forgiveness Consistent with Chastisement, 12:10-14.

The king's indignation at the offender in the parable (12:1-6) is an illustration of a common fact that when men are most indulgent to their own sins they are most ready to condemn those of others. The judgment pronounced upon David shows it possible for a saint to be restored to God's favor, while at the same time the divine abhorrence of sin must be shown in bitter results in the present time. David lost four sons after this, and other evils came upon him. (Compare 1 Cor. 5:1-5; 11:28-32).

4. David's Faith and Ours, 12: 15-23.

David's remark in verse 23 may be taken as an intimation of the belief of a future life and the immortality of the soul; and yet David's faith could not have been as deep or broad as that vouchsafed to the believer in these days. When the child of a saint now passes hence, it is not for the latter to say that he shall not return to him for, according to 1 Thes. 4:13-18, Jesus may return before the saint dies and bring the loved ones with Him.

5. Explanatory Words, 12:26-31.

The concluding verses of chapter 12 require explanation. For example, as throwing light on Joab's words in verses 27 and 28, it would seem that Rabbah, which had been besieged for a long period, was divided into two parts, a lower and an upper town divided by a stream. The first had been taken by Joab, but the second, the more important of the two, must be taken by David in person if the latter were to get the honor for it. Now-a-days kings gain victories by their generals, but in earlier times it could not be done by proxy. This was a great city, and should it fall to Joab's arms it would have been named in his honor to David's humiliation.

The torture (v. 31) is another illustration of the horrors of war in that day, and is justified by some as an act of retributive justice on a people infamous for their cruelties (1 Sam. 2:2; Amos 1:13), but there is a happier explanation. The word "under" used three times, is by others translated "to," as referring not to their being slain in this manner, but being subjected to this kind of slavery. And so when it says he "made them pass through the brickkiln," with a slight change it would read, he "made them labor at the brickkiln."

Questions.

1. What three facts show the awfulness of this sin of David?

2. How does this lesson distinguish between forgiveness and chastisement?

3. Have you read 1 Thess. 4:13-18?

4. How might chapter 12:31 be rendered?

5. Try to memorize Psalm 51 and 103.

"O, ABSALOM, MY SON, MY SON!"

CHAPTERS 13-18

1. Lust, Murder and Deceit, c. 13.

In the preceding lesson judgments were foretold as coming on David, and we are entering on that part of his career when the prediction is fulfilled in earnest.

The foulness of this chapter we would not dwell upon more than we can help. Tamar of course, while sister to Absalom, was half-sister to Amnon, the two young men being sons of David by different wives.

"A garment of divers colours" (v. 18) might be rendered "a long garment with sleeves."

"Geshur," whither Absalom fled, was in the north near Syria and the country of his maternal ancestors (2 Sam. 3:3), for no refuge could have been given him in Israel (Num. 35:21).

2. A Strategem Well Meant, c. 14.

Joab could not be charged with lack of love and loyalty to his king, as the story of this chapter shows. He knows the struggle in David's heart between his love for his son and his desire to respect the law in the case of murderers. Therefore he concocts the scheme of this woman by whose supposititious case the king is brought to see that there may be a higher justice in ignoring a lower one. As Absalom was the light of Israel in the sense that on the death of Amnon he was heir to the kingdom, David would be doing nothing more in pardoning him than he had agreed to do in the case of this widow's son (vv. 13-17). But David's action was wrong nevertheless. See Gen 9:6, Deut. 18:18, etc.

Let not the beautiful words of verse 14 escape attention. How they suggest the love of God for us in Jesus Christ! He was the means devised that we might not be banished from His presence.

3. Love Ill-requited, c. 15.

Absalom had rather be free in Geshur than a prisoner in Jerusalem, and Joab is forced, after two years, to make an effort to bring him and his father together, which succeeds (14:21-33).

But Absalom is as mean in spirit as he is noble in appearance. His father has reigned too long to suit him and, availing himself of certain causes of complaint, and using the arts of the demagog, he raises a formidable insurrection to put himself on the throne (vv. 1-12).

The word "forty" (v. 7) is thought to be an error, and some versions have "four." With the reference to Ahithophel (v. 12), compare Psalms 41 and 55, and for the further experience of David, see Psalm 3.

The foreigners named in verses 18-22 were doubtless special guards David kept about him since the days of his exile among the Philistines.

The rest of the chapter is a striking illustration of how David combined piety with statesman-like leadership. He was still "behaving himself wisely" as in the days of his youth.

4. Kissing the Rod that Smites, cc. 16, 17.

Ziba was a liar seeking favor with the king he foresaw would return to power (16:1-4), and Shimei a cowardly avenger of his supposed wrongs who imagines David's days are numbered. Nursing his wrath a long while, now at a safe distance he displays it (vv. 5-14). But David kisses the rod that smites him. He sees the hand of God in it all and worhips His will (vv. 10-12). Happy the penitent in such a case who can exclaim with Elizabeth Prentiss:

"Let sorrow do its work,
    Send grief and pain;
Sweet are Thy messengers,
    Sweet their refrain,
When they can sing with me,
More love, O Christ, to Thee,
    More love to Thee."

Ahithophel, highly esteemed as a counsellor recommends, in verses 20-23, that which to Absalom would be like burning his bridges behind him and which would compel every man in Israel to determine whose side he was on. There could be no reconciliation between father and son after this indignity.

The contents of chapter 17 carry their explanation on their face. Ahithophel's counsel is wise to seize David's person before he can gather a formidable army (vv. 1-4), but the Lord defeats it through Hushai (vv. 5-14). (Compare 1 Cor. 1:27, 28). Hushai doubts whether his counsel will be taken, which explains his efforts to get the news to David (vv. 15-22); but Ahithophel, finding that it is taken, commits suicide foreseeing David's victory and his retribution as the result (v. 23).

5. How Fathers Love, c. 18.

The praises of a mother's love are often sung, but this chapter teaches us that a father's can be just as passionate and unreasoning (v. 5). Joab's act (vv. 14, 15) seems to have been justified by all the circumstances, for there could be no peace in Israel and Absalom alive. His death spared many lives. The manner of his burial, expressing loathing and abhorrence of him (v. 17), was different from what he had expected for himself (v. 18).

The heartrending cry of David (v. 33) seems to pierce all space from that day to this, and we hear it ringing in our ears even now.

Questions.

1. Have you refreshed your mind on the Levitical law concerning murder?

2. Can you quote 2 Samuel 14:14?

3. How does Absalom bring Joab to terms?

4. Memorize Psalm 3.

5. How does this experience in David's life bring out his piety?

6. Have you examined 1 Corinthians 1:27, 28?

7. What lessons, if any, does this lesson present to you?

BRINGING BACK THE KING

Chapter 19

1. An Over-Zealous Servant, 19: 1-8.

Joab was to David what Bismarck was to King William. He had the same iron in his blood, but sometimes, like the latter, he overdid things. The kaiser was glad to be rid of Bismarck, and Joab's conduct toward David is preparing the way for his successor. Those were too strong words he used in verse 7, and show the power he assumed over the army.

2. A Backward People, vv. 9-15.

Judah, the king's tribe, should have taken the initiative for his return, and the priests should have stirred them to it. It is disappointing that it was otherwise and perhaps explains David's adroitness in choosing Amasa to supersede Joab, who persuades the people to act as one man.

We can hardly pass the event without speaking of its parallel in the case of?

"Great David's Greater Son."

Why is His Church so silent about His coming back again? One would think He was not wanted back by the little that is said about it. And yet He has promised to come—"This same Jesus"—and to bring His reward with Him! Who can tell whether, if we spake one to another about it, we might not begin to act in such a manner as to hasten His coming? Will it be necessary for Him to cast away the present leaders of His Church and call to His aid some Amasa with the power to bow the hearts of His people toward Him as the heart of one man?

Why say ye not a word of bringing back the king?

Why speak ye not of Jesus and His reign?

Why tell ye of His kingdom and of its glories sing?

But nothing of His coming back again?

3. A Lenient Sovereign, vv. 16-40.

We wonder David should have been so forbearing to Shimei (vv. 16-23) when we consider the latter's conduct in the last lesson; and on the other hand we are surprised that Mephibosheth should not have had more cordial treatment (vv. 24-30). The meaning of verse 29 is not clear.

4. A Jealous Outbreak, 19:41-20:26.

The closing verses of chapter 19 exhibit the beginning of that tribal dissension which ultimately led to the dismemberment of the kingdom.

Nothing is known of Sheba (20:1, 2), but he was of much influence among the adherents of the former dynasty of Saul.

Amasa seems to have been unequal to rallying the army and Abishai is called into the service, to the further affront of Joab. But the last named joins in the battle and doubtless with the wicked intention he afterward executes (v. 10). His influence with the army is seen in that, even under these circumstances, the warriors rally around him and are led to victory (vv. 11-23). David is obliged to reinstate him, and the conclusion of the chapter shows the whole government reestablished in its wonted course.

5. A Wrong Avenged, 21:1-14.

Joshua had made a covenant with the Gibeonites (Joshua 9:3-27). But Saul, for political reasons, had violated its terms (v. 2)—just under what circumstances there is no record. It was a case of national guilt and received at God's hands a national punishment (v. 1). Awful was the atonement rendered and yet it might have been more severe. Moreover, God permitted, and indeed directed it (vv. 3-9), and the Judge of all the earth shall do right (Gen. 18-25). Let the circumstance teach us to fear God and hate sin.

"Michal, the daughter of Saul" (v. 8) should be "Michal's sister," or else, the two sons were adopted and brought up by her though born of her sister.

6. An Epoch Reached, 21:15-22.

David is beginning to feel his years and, in this war, he might have lost his life but for the interference of a stronger hand (vv. 15-17). He must no more go out to battle. He, as king, is the "light," of Israel, and must not run into danger lest he be quenched.

Philistia was prolific in giants, but the Lord was with His people to overcome them (vv. 18-22).

Questions.

1. What late historic character does Joab suggest?

2. How does David seek ineffectually to rid himself of Joab?

3. Quote Acts 1:11 and connect it with this lesson.

4. What arouses Israel's jealousy of Judah?

5. What were the natural relations of Joab to Amasa and Abishai?

6. Relate the story of the first part of chapter 21 in your own words.

7. What lessons does it teach?

8. What epoch, physical and historical, has David reached?

MINGLED EXPERIENCE

CHAPTERS 22-24

1. The Grateful Retrospect, c. 22.

The title of this section is that which Spurgeon gives the psalm which constitutes it. The psalm is numbered 18 in the book of Psalms, and will be found to contain variations in the text. A common explanation of these is that David sung it, or caused it to be sung, often, and hence revised it for final use in the tabernacle.

The second and forty-ninth verses of the psalm are quoted in the New Testament as the words of Jesus Christ (Rom. 15:9 and Heb. 2:13), which gives it a right to be classed as a Messianic psalm. Such psalms are those in which the psalmist is either referring to the Messiah, or in which the latter, by His Spirit, is speaking in the first person through the psalmist. There is a sense, therefore, in which all through this psalm we may think of Jesus as referring to His own sorrows while on the earth, His deliverance from His enemies, and His triumphs over opposition.

To speak of the psalm more in detail, verse 1 gives its occasion; verses 2 and 4, its theme; 5 to 19 speak poetically of the deliverances obtained through the power of God; 20 to 28, the reason for them as based on the psalmist's righteousness; 29 to 43, the preparation and girding the psalmist himself received; and 44 to 51 mingle praise for the past and prophecy for the future.

It is the fourth division, 20 to 28 more than any other, that makes it difficult to apply the psalm to David except in a highly poetical sense, and which gives it a Messianic significance.

2. The Last Words, 23:1-7.

What is meant by the first sentence of this chapter is difficult to say. It reads like a note of some editor and may mean that the verses following, although poetical, are not part of the preceding song.

The whole section is reminiscent and expressive of trust in God. The second verse is a strong testimony to the divine inspiration of David's words.

David's house had not been what it should have been (v. 5), yet God's covenant was sure, and for His own Name's sake it would be carried forward until the Messiah should sit upon the throne. He was David's desire and salvation.

3. A Catalogue of the Mighty, 23:8-39.

David's great human helpers are here designated and short sketches given of them. Space will not permit any enlarged commentary on the text, nor is it necessary. But note the supernatural character of their achievements—"the Lord wrought a great victory" (v. 12).

There were three classes of these men. The first consisted of

the first three named, verses 8 to 17; the second, of the next three, Abishai, Benaiah and Asahel, apparently, 18 to 24; and the third of the last thirty, of whom, it would appear, Asahel was chief.

4. Numbering the People, 24:1 -9.

When this took place is not easy to determine, but it is disappointing to note that it was a testing of David's character in which he failed.

"He" before "moved" in verse 1, refers to Satan, as will be seen from 1 Chronicles 21:3, and shows that although God does not tempt any man (Jas. 1:13), yet, sometimes He permits the adversary of souls to do it. In this case He withdrew His supporting grace and the king fell (vv. 3, 4).

How long did it take to obtain this census, and what was its report (vv. 8, 9)?

There is an apparent discrepancy between the record here and 1 Chronicles 21, which, however, can be explained.

Samuel says, "there were in Israel 800,000 valiant men"; while Chronicles says, "And all they of Israel were a thousand thousand and an hundred thousand men that drew sword"— 300,000 more. The words in the second case, "all they of Israel," suggests the key to the difficulty. Chronicles gives the full number of the military belonging to Israel, while Samuel omits the special guards of the king and the princes who were in actual service as militia, and which were just 300,000.

In like manner, Samuel says, "The men of Judah were 500,000 men," while Chronicles records that "Judah was 470,000 that drew sword." The difference is explained by the army of observation on the frontiers of Philistia (2 Sam. 6:1, 2) which were not included by the author of Chronicles, though they were by the author of Samuel. In this case the first-named does not say "all they of Judah," as he had of Israel.

5. A Choice of Chastisement, vv. 10-25.

God graciously leads David to repentance (v. 10), but He can by no means clear the guilty (vv. 11, 12), yet mercy mingles with justice (vv. 13, 14).

Note the difference between David's spirit in verse 17, and that of Saul in corresponding circumstances (1 Sam. 15:15). And do not overlook Araunah's kingly generosity on the one hand (v. 23), or David's conscientiousness on the other (v. 24). Of course, "Ornan" in Chronicles is only another pronunciation of Araunah in Samuel.

Observe from 1 Chronicles 21:28-22:5, that the threshing floor subsequently became the site of Solomon's temple.

Questions.

1. In what part of the Bible are the contents of chapter 22 again found?

2. How may the variations be explained?

3. What are "Messianic" psalms?

4. Give a proof of verbal inspiration in this lesson.

5. What shows the supernatural character of the achievements of David's worthies?

6. Quote James 1:13.

7. How might the discrepancy in the census be explained?

8. How famous did Araunah's threshing-floor become?

FIRST KINGS

THE CORONATION OF SOLOMON

CHAPTERS 1-2

1. The Occasion for It, 1:10.

The incident in the first four verses is recorded not for itself, but because of what grew out of it in Adonijah's case (2:13-25). It was a custom in the Orient, and still is, to do this for hygienic reasons on the supposition "that the inhalation of young breath will give new vigor to a worn-out frame." The event shows that Abishag was made a concubine or secondary wife to the king (2:22).

Adonijah, doubtless, felt some justification for his conduct in that he was now the eldest son of David (2 Sam. 3:4), and no public intimation had been made as to the successor on the throne. Moreover, his father seems to have indulged him in certain liberties (v. 6).

For the history of Zadok and Benaiah see 2 Samuel, 8:17; 15:24; 21:53 and 8:18; 20:23. With Nathan we have met (2 Sam. 7). There was something ominous in the omission of these men from Adonijah's feast (v. 10).

2. The Way of Procedure, 1:11-40.

Bathsheba was a capable woman, for it is inferred from verse 17 that she had great influence with the king. Nathan must have known of the promise spoken of and been aware of its harmony with the divine will to explain his action (vv. 11-27).

3. The Earliest Results, 1:41-2:46.

(4) Adonijah (1:50-53, 2:13-25). The four corners of the altar of burnt offering to which sacrifices were bound, were symbols of salvation and considered as a sanctuary for all except certain classes of offenders (Ex. 21:14). Adonijah's offense was rebellion, but he is spared on the conditions

named. Unhappily, however, he violates them and, apparently instigated by Joab and Abiathar (v. 22), adopts a course which, according to eastern ideas, was of dangerous consequence to the state.

(2) Abiathar (vv. 26, 27). The punishment of the priest follows that of the usurper. (Note the fulfilment of 1 Samuel 2:30).

(3) Joab (vv. 28-34). The crimes of this military leader merited death, according to the divine law (Num. 35:33), which would have been visited upon him earlier, no doubt, had it not been for his power with the army. Compare David's words in 2 Samuel 3:28, 29.

(4) Shimei (vv. 36-46). By the death of this man all the leaders of factions inimical to Solomon were cut off, which explains the last sentence of the chapter.

Questions.

1. What relation presumably did Abishag sustain to David?

2. Had Adonijah any apparent ground for his action?

3. What shows a plot in his case?

4. How does chapter 1:15-31 indicate the dignity associated with the human sovereignty of Israel at this time?

5. How did Adonijah show his heart unchanged?

6. In what line of the priesthood did Abiathar come?

7. In what sense did Solomon's kingdom come to be established at this period?

SOLOMON'S GREATNESS AND WISDOM

CHAPTERS 3-5

1. His Egyptian Alliance, c. 3:1-4.

It is disappointing at the beginning to speak of that which betokens neither greatness nor wisdom on Solomon's part, looking at it from the highest point of view. This marriage with a heathen wife was contrary to the law of God (Ex. 34:16); and while it was entered into for political reasons, and to strengthen Israel's hands, yet in the end it weakened them, as Israel came to trust in Pharaoh more than Jehovah.

And yet Solomon loved the LORD, and served Him with the limitations named in these verses, and the LORD was longsuffering toward him as with his father David.

Some think that since Solomon was not divinely rebuked for marrying this princess, as he was later for marrying other foreigners, she may have consented to become a proselyte to the Jewish religion. It is interesting also that the Song of Songs and the 45th Psalm were probably composed in her honor, although both, in the mind of the Holy Spirit, had a typical reference to the relation of Jehovah to Israel, or Christ to His Church, or both.

The "high places" in verse 2, were altars erected on natural or artificial eminences, on the theory that the worshipper was thus brought nearer the Deity. They had been prohibited by Moses because of their association with idolatry (Lev. 17:3, 4, etc); but, as the temple was not yet built in Israel and the tabernacle was moved about from place to place, they seem to have been tolerated without special rebuke from God.

2. His Noble Request, vv. 5-15.

Observe that the wisdom Solomon desired was not of the heavenly but the earthly kind (v. 9). Noble it was, and yet Solomon might have had something still more worth while had he sought it. How does God's answer illustrate Ephesians 3:20?

Solomon's expression "I am but a little child" (v. 7) is not to be taken in the sense of years but experience. He was probably twenty at this period.

3. His State and Retinue, c. 4:1-28.

How do verses 11 and 15 indicate that this chapter is dealing with a later period in Solomon's reign?

Observe the development of the kingdom at this time as indicated by these officials. The word "priest" (v. 2), it is thought, should be rendered "prince," so that Azariah was probably prime minister; then follow three secretaries of state (?), a historiographer, a military commander in chief, a high priest, provincial governors (?), a confidential adviser, a steward or chamberlain, a state treasurer or collector of customs, etc. (vv. 2-6).

Afterward local revenue officers are named, for the taxes raised were in the products of the soil rather than money. These were put in store cities in the different localities until required at the palace (vv. 7-21). Compare chapter 9:19.

The "provision" in verses 22 and 23 refers to the tables of the guests, etc., as well as his private board.

4. His Fame, vv. 28-34.

This exceeded that of the Chaldeans or Persians, or Egyptians, renowned as the last named were for all kinds of learning (v. 30). There were none of his contemporaries he did not excel (v. 31). He was author of wise sayings and songs by the thousands (v. 32). He was a master of forestry and arboriculture, of zoology, and ornithology and ichthology, so that kings as well as lesser people came to listen to and confer with him.

5. His Friends, c. 5.

Among the kings who came to pay court was Hiram of Tyre, who, whether he was the Hiram of David's time, or his son or grandson, it is difficult to say. This results in a contract for the building of the temple, in which the skilled workmen of Tyre are yoked with the commoner laborers of Israel (v. 6). Advantages are to be reciprocated (v. 9). Compare chapter 9:20, also 2 Chronicles 2:17, 18 and 8:7-9 from which we gather who were the laborers Solomon laid tribute upon for this work. The stones in verses 17 and 18 are still seen in the lower foundations of the site of the ancient temple.

Questions.

1. Have you read the 45th Psalm?

2. What does the Song of Songs typify?

3. Why were altars built on high places?

4. Quote Ephesians 3:30.

5. Name from memory the offices in Solomon's kingdom.

6. Name some of the branches of Solomon's learning.

7. For what arts or trades were the Phoenicians (or Tyrians) noted?

8. What do you recall of the dealings between Hiram and David?

BUILDING THE TEMPLE

CHAPTERS 6, 7

1. The Work in Outline, c. 6:1-14.

Note the particularities as to date, dimensions and general appearance (vv. 1-4), on which space will not permit extended comment. As to the size of the cubit, the question as to whether the elevation is external or internal, the description and purpose of the windows, for example students must be referred to Bible dictionaries.

The chambers (vv. 5-10) on three sides of the temple seem to have been three stories high, each wider than that beneath it, with a winding stairway on the interior leading to the middle and upper stories.

Travelers speak of a quarry near Jerusalem from which the stones are likely to have come. There is evidence too, that they were dressed there as the text says (v. 7), for other stones like them in size and substance are found in the remains.

The communication of the LORD to Solomon is significant of encouragement and warning. When He speaks of dwelling among His people it has the same meaning as when He used the words in the wilderness. The visible glory resting over the mercy

seat in the most holy place was the token of His presence. It remained there while the nation served Him, and that meant that He was protecting and blessing them.

2. The Details, vv. 15-38.

Verse 15 reveals that the walls were sheathed with cedar and the floor planked with fir or cypress; thus the stone was entirely hidden. The walls were carved in relief with foliage and flowers (v. 18) and cherubim and palm trees (v. 29). But the whole was overlaid with gold (v. 22).

Comparing the first and last verses of the chapter, how long was the temple in building? In round numbers how does the last verse reckon it?

3. Solomon's Own Palace, c. 7: 1-12.

Perhaps the longer time occupied in building this is explained by the fact that its completion was not so urgent or important as the temple, and that the same preparation for it had not been made in advance (v. 1).

In the Revised Version verse 2 begins: "For he built the house of the forest of Lebanon." This indicates that it is still his own house which is referred to, the material for which came from the same locality as that for the temple.

The edifice seems to have been oblong (v. 2), with a front porch used as a judgment hall (vv. 6, 7). There was also a large hall in the center, on one side of which were the king's apartments and on the other those of the queen (v. 8). Compare Esth. 2:3, 9.

The phrase in verse 12, "the inner court of the house of the LORD," should read as in the Revised Version, "like as the inner court," etc. The meaning is that, in the palace as in the temple, the same rows of hewn stones and cedar beams formed the wall.

4. The Foreign Craftsman and His Work, vv. 13-51.

This "Hiram" was not the king of Tyre, but another man of that country by the same name, and evidently a genius in metal work (v. 14).

Tyrians and other Phoenicians were not only great workers in timber (v. 6), but renowned the world over for the art in which he so greatly excelled.

But Hiram had Jewish blood in him too (v. 14). Here he is said to be of the tribe of Naphtali on his mother's side, while 2 Chronicles 2:14 speaks of her as of Dan; but she may have belonged to the first named while living in Dan.

Hiram's work, consisted, first, of the pillars of the temple and their capitols, the latter beautifully ornamented, and which were named as, they were set up. For the meaning of these names see the margin of your Bible (vv. 15-22).

Next came the "molten sea," (vv. 23-26), which was not the same as the brazen laver of the tabernacle, as will be seen by comparing 2 Chronicles 4: 1-6, especially verse 6.

Then "the ten bases of brass," (vv. 27-39), which, according to verse 38, were for the support of the brazen lavers. And these in turn were for the washing of the sacrifices (see 2 Chronicles 1, as above).

Hiram also made what other things (v. 40)? What locality was selected for the furnaces, and why? (For answer to the last half of this question compare the margin with the text of the verse). The reference here is to bronze rather than what we know as brass.

Observe in verse 51 that in addition to the furnishings which Solomon made for the temple and which were modeled after those in the tabernacle of the wilderness, he also deposited therein the sacred articles "which David his father had dedicated," though they probably were not used.

Questions.

1. What archaeological evidence is borne to the historical character of this narrative?

2. How does God encourage and warn Solomon?

3. Why may a longer period have been taken in building the palace than the temple?

4. For what were the people on the north of Palestine noted?

5. How would you harmonize verse 14 with the corresponding reference in 2 Chronicles?

6. What do the words "Jachin" and "Boaz" mean?

7. For what use was "the molten sea"?

DEDICATION OF THE TEMPLE

CHAPTERS 8, 9

1. The Time, 8:1, 2.

Since the temple was completed in the eighth month of the previous year (6:38) and not dedicated until the seventh of the following, how shall we explain the interval? The reason usually assigned is that the king waited for the feast of tabernacles in the fall when one of the greatest assemblies took place, and for this purpose the most appropriate.

2. The Grand Procession, vv. 3-9.

Observe who were the leading actors (v. 3). Also what articles they carried (v. 4). The "tabernacle" means the old tabernacle of the wilderness, which had been located at Gibeon and was now to be preserved in the temple at Jerusalem.

Notice the sacrificing on the march (v. 5). Notice that it was the original ark of the covenant that was placed in the most holy place of the temple (v. 6). "The wings of the cherubim" mean those that Solomon caused to be placed there, and larger than those of Moses' time which were firmly attached to the ark itself (Ex. 37:7, 8). The staves at the end of the ark were drawn out to be seen in the holy place, but not beyond it (v. 8). This was to guide the high priest on the day of atonement, that he might be able to enter the most holy place in the thick darkness (Ex. 25:15).

Note what the ark contained (v. 9), and compare Hebrew 9:4. This last Scripture should be understood as teaching that the things it names were placed *by* and not *in* the ark. (See Ex. 16.33; Num. 17:10).

3. The Divine Acceptance of the Work, vv. 10, 11.

It is only necessary to compare these verses with Exodus 40:34, to see the significance of this act of Jehovah. He thus established Himself in Israel and took His seat on the throne of His glory. What satisfaction it must have brought to Solomon, and indeed all the faithful in Israel. What a reward for their endeavors! Oh, if they had only been faithful thereafter, that the LORD might never have departed from them! What a different story this world would have had to tell.

But how glad we should be that that glory is coming back to Israel, and the world is at length to be blessed thereby. Let us pray for the peace of Jerusalem. They shall prosper that love her (Psa. 122.6).

4. Solomon's Blessing, vv. 12-21.

Just what is meant by the "thick darkness" (v. 12) is not easy to determine unless it is the cloud and pillar of fire of earlier days which indicated Jehovah's presence. The rest of the words of Solomon's blessing, however, are plain.

5. The Prayer and Benediction, v. 22-61.

For the place where the king stood and knelt see 2 Chronicles 6:13.

How strange that the king should have thus ministered and not the high priest! But it was lawful for him to minister *about* holy things though he might not minister *in* them.

After the ascription of praise to Jehovah (vv. 22-30), the prayer contains seven petitions or references to as many occasions when His interposing mercy might be required. Let the student discover them (vv. 31-53).

The chapter closes with an account of the surpassing number of sacrifices presented and the re-joicings of the people for the goodness of God.

6. Jehovah's Response, 9:1-9.

If the words of this vision are studied carefully they will be found to contain an answer to all Solomon's petitions.

Verses 7-9, however, are a prophecy finding a sad fulfillment in our time because of Israel's unfaithfulness. Their location in the record at this point leads up to the story of the king's worldly ambitions which were the beginning of the nation's decline.

7. The Compensation of the King of Tyre, vv. 10-14.

For the twenty years that Hiram the king aided Solomon (v. 10), the latter gave him twenty cities, a city a year. Doubtless they were adjacent to his territory and were those which never had been conquered by Israel and were still inhabited by Canaanites.

These cities being unacceptable to him (vv. 12, 13), he was recompensed in some other way, and Solomon took control of them in his own hands and peopled them with Israelites (2 Chron. 8:2).

8. The Levy, vv. 15-25.

The dedication of the temple seems to close at verse 25, for which reason the preceding verses about the levy are included in this lesson, though their exact bearing upon it may not appear at first sight. Perhaps the connection is discovered by going back to chapter 5:13 and the following verses.

However, the reason for the levy of both men and money is clear from the many great works Solomon undertook as indicated in this chapter. Observe that the people levied upon (vv. 20-22) were the Canaanites who had not been subdued or exterminated at the conquest. (See 2 Chron. 2:18). As prisoners of war they did the drudgery, while the men of Israel had the more honorable employment.

Questions.

1. At what period of the year did this ceremony occur?

2. What evidence have we that the Mosaic tabernacle had been preserved all this time?

3. Have you read Hebrews 9:4, and if so, how would you explain it?

4. How did God indicate His acceptance of the work?

5. Memorize Psalm 122.

6. How would you explain the ministering of the king on this occasion?

7. Name the subjects of the seven petitions of Solomon's prayer.

8. Why did Solomon make levies of men and money at this time?

9. Who were especially levied upon, and why?

10. With what general statement of Solomon's religious spirit does the lesson close?

CLOSE OF SOLOMON'S REIGN

Chapters 9:26-11:43

1. Wisdom and Wealth, 9:26-10: 29.

A look at map No. 5, at the back of your Bible, will identify the locality of verse 26, whence Solomon, with the assistance of Hiram, extended his influence by sea. "Ophir" (v. 28) has been regarded as a general name for all the territory on the south and in the neighborhood of the inland seas. A "talent" is not easy to estimate but, on the supposition of some that a talent of gold represented about $30,000, we have here a contribution of between $12,000,000 and $14,000,000. In our day not so much, but in that day a tremendous fortune.

One result of expansion by the sea was the visitors it brought, as illustrated by the Queen of Sheba, whose country cannot be identified except in a general way as indicated by our Lord (Matt. 12:42, Luke 11:31). A query arises as to whether verse 9 means that she was really converted to Jehovah as the result of what she saw and heard.

The "targets" or shields of verse 16, usually made of wood and covered with leather, were weapons of defense for the palace. (See 14:26).

"Tarshish" (v. 22) is a general term for the west, as Ophir was for the south, and points to Solomon's commercial ventures across the Mediterranean.

Verse 26 shows him departing from the commandment of God about horses and chariots (Deut. 17:16), and at a wholesale rate, judging by verses 28 and 29 in the Revised Version.

2. Voluptuousness and Idolatry, 11:1-8.

What had become of Solomon's wisdom? The answer is, that the wisdom he had was of the earthly rather than the heavenly kind. It was sufficient to keep the city but not to keep his heart. It helped him rule the kingdom but not his own spirit. Was Solomon really regenerated, who can tell? (Compare Prov. 31:1-3 and Eccles. 4:13).

The princesses were daughters of tributary kings taken as hostages perhaps, or to strengthen Solomon's hands in the political sense; but the concubines were secondary wives not having the same recognition in the kingdom.

Compare 2 Kings 23:13 for the name given to that part of Olivet on which Solomon built the temples for the false gods. These he had been induced to worship through the influence of his harem. God alone knows what loathsome wickedness this may have introduced into Israel.

3. Chastisement and Sorrow, 11: 9-43.

What aggravated Solomon's offence (vv. 9, 10)? What judgment is threatened (v. 11)? But what mercy is shown and why (v. 12)? To what extent was the kingdom to be rent from Solomon (v. 13)? The significance of this is that in the line of David that "greater than Solomon" was to come of whom we learned in 2 Samuel 11. (Compare also vv. 35 and 36.) We shall see later that not only was Judah left to Solomon's son, but Benjamin and Levi as well, three tribes, although here named as one. Many individuals and families in the other tribes in addition stayed with him for religious reasons. (See 12:17 and 2 Chron. 11:12, 13.)

Who was the first rod of God's anger raised against Solomon (v. 14)? And the second (vv. 23-25)? And the third (v. 26)?

This last was the most formidable because of the internal commotion he aroused. He came first into notice as a mechanical engineer in charge of some of Solomon's many works (vv. 27, 28); but God had chosen him for a higher task, the knowledge of which seems to have turned his head (vv. 29-31). He could not wait patiently for God to remove Solomon as David did in the case of Saul, but began to take matters into his own hand with the consequences in verse 40.

Observe the name of the book of record from which the inspired compiler of 1 Kings may have obtained his data (v. 41), and compare with it the statement in 2 Chronicles 9:29.

Questions.

1. Has your Bible any maps?
2. What can you recall of Hiram's history?
3. What two geographic names having a general application are given here?
4. How much value may have been represented by a talent of gold?
5. Have you a copy of the Revised Version?
6. How would you discriminate in the case of Solomon's wisdom?
7. Have you compared the Scripture references in this lesson?
8. What name was given that part of Olivet on which Solomon built the idol temples?
9. Name the three tribes that remained loyal to the house of David?
10. Name the three human scourges of Solomon towards the close of his life?
11. What prophet is named in this lesson?
12. What data may the compiler of Kings have had to draw upon?

EARLY DAYS OF THE TWO KINGDOMS

CHAPTERS 12-14

1. Cause of the Division, 12:1-25.

Verses 2-4 look as though there were a preconcerted purpose to revolt, and yet who can tell what a different history might have followed had the new king heeded wiser counsel?

Note the reason of the protest, which was not Solomon's idolatry and the heathenism he introduced, but their pecuniary burdens; their civil oppression, rather than their religious wrongs. It is still so, and political reform looks only on the surface and never takes into account the root of difficulties. Had Solomon kept true to God the people would not have been oppressed; but the latter were blinded as to this because they had become partakers of his sins. They, too, loved the heathen worship and only murmured at its cost.

And yet there was an overruling cause why Rehoboam hearkened to the younger men, for God had intended to inflict punishment (v. 15).

Rehoboam seems to have been incredulous as to the reality of the revolt; but if so, what event opened his eyes (v. 18)? What action is now taken by him (v. 21), and why is it brought to a standstill (vv. 23-25)?

2. Jeroboam's Folly, vv. 26-33.

To "build" Shechem and Penuel meant probably to fortify them as protection from attack (v. 25).

Had Jeroboam ground for thinking as is recorded in verses 26 and 27? (Compare 11:37, 38.) He had become familiar with calf worship in Egypt (v. 28), but in any event Solomon himself had prepared the people thus to be led astray.

Notice that it was for political reasons Jeroboam did this (v. 27). He had no intention of throwing off the yoke of Jehovah altogether, but was foolish enough to think He could be worshipped in one way as well as another. Why was he compelled to make priests "from among all the people" (Revised Version)? (Compare again 2 Chron. 11 12, 13.) What change did he make as to the time of the feast of tabernacles? (Compare v. 32 with Lev. 23:33, 34.) Where did he get the idea (v. 33)?

3. A Preliminary Warning, c. 13.

The story of this chapter, although containing supernatural wonders, is in the recital and meaning very plain. Jeroboam has his chance to repent and turn to the Lord if he will, but his heart is set to do evil.

No one knows the name of the prophet (v. 1) who, although a "man of God," acted so unworthily as to be denied the honor of its record. Note the prophecy he uttered and compare its fulfillment, over 300 years later, in 2 Kings 23:15, 16. This has been cited as one of the most remarkable prophecies in Holy Writ, "whose definiteness and minuteness stand in marked contrast to the obscure oracles of the heathen." What sign was given to its ultimate fulfilment (v. 3)? What personal judgment fell on the king and why (v. 4)? Do you think he was genuine in his invitation (v. 7)?

And the prophet referred to in the subsequent verses, if he were ever a servant of the Lord, surely he was a castaway now (1 Cor. 9:27)? What a warning his conduct brings before Christian workers to-day! Could his motive have been to curry favor with the King? How many supernatural events can be counted in verses 20-29? (Compare 2 Kings 23:15-18.)

4. A Final Judgment, 14:1-20.

Taking verses 1 and 2 together, how do they reveal Jeroboam's hypocrisy, political caution, fear and ignorance?

The Lord's commendation of David as contrasted with Jeroboam (v. 8) is to be considered in the light of the pure worship the former maintained in accordance with the divine law. It does not mean that David never sinned, although, of course, even in that he differed from Jeroboam because he repented of his sin. The phrase in verse 10 refers to "a man child" and is so rendered in the Revised Version.

What "good" was found in Abijah (v. 13) is not stated, but doubtless he was not in sympathy with all his father's wickedness and idolatry.

Note the earliest prediction of the captivity of Israel by the Assyrians as compared with 2 Kings 17:6).

5. Rehoboam's Iniquity and its Result, vv. 21-31.

What allusion in verse 21 furnishes a hint as to the reason of Rehoboam's apostasy (vv. 22-24)? What judgment falls on him and his people (vv. 25, 26)?

We should not misunderstand "the book of the chronicles" (v. 29), as meaning the book of the Old Testament bearing that name, but only one of the customary records of the kings. Neither should we imagine verse 30 to be a contradiction of chapter 12:21-24, as the former (v. 30) may refer to skirmishes in contrast with an aggressive war of conquest.

Questions.

1. Were the people of Israel any more religious and God-fearing than their first king?

2. Rehearse the story of God's relation to the division of the kingdom.

3. Did Jeroboam outwardly break the first or second commandment?

4. What king of Judah was named by the Lord over 300 years before his birth?

5. Quote 1 Corinthians 9:27.

ASA OF JUDAH TO AHAB OF ISRAEL

CHAPTERS 15-16

1. Abijam's Brief Reign in Judah, 15:1-8.

This commentary will permit but the briefest treatment of the less important reigns of Judah and Israel, that more attention may be given to the others.

"Abijam" is called "Abijah" in 2 Chronicles 12:16.

Verse 5, referring to David, is to be taken in the comparative sense spoken of in the lesson preceding.

Verse 6 is a mistake, as some copies of the text read "Abijam" for "Rehoboam."

Since Abijam began to reign in the eighteenth year of Jeroboam (v. 1), and was succeeded by Asa in the twentieth (v. 9), how could it be that he reigned three years (v. 2)? The answer is that parts of years among the Hebrews were counted as whole years.

2. Asa's Long Reign, vv. 9-24.

It would appear by comparing verse 10 with verse 2 that "Maachah" was really the grandmother of this king who, for some reason, is named instead of his immediate ancestress. She seems to have been the queen dowager (v. 13).

Asa's character, good in the main (vv. 11-15), suffers a decline later as indicated in his alliance with Benhadad of Syria against Baasha of Israel (vv. 17-21). Why not trust God instead? Had the lessons of the past been lost upon him?

The student is reminded of the necessity of studying the history of these kings in the light of 2 Chronicles. Much interest is added to the story of Asa by the parallel places in chapters 14-16 of that book.

3. Nadab's Brief Reign, vv. 25-31.

There is little said of this king, but verses 27-30 should be noted as a fulfilment of the prediction of chapter 14:10, 11.

4. Baasha's Long Reign, v. 33-16:6.

Note the name of the prophet here (16:1), who must not be confused with a king of the same name who appears subsequently. Note that *God* exalted Baasha over Israel (v. 2), though from the human side he appeared to take the kingdom by his own force. Note that God still calls Israel His "people" (v. 2), though they have dealt so wickedly towards Him. There were still faithful worshippers among them, and He is still sending prophets to them and working miracles on their behalf. Oh, the long-suffering of God! Note finally, that, although God had decreed the death of Jeroboam's house, He had not authorized Baasha as His executive, and hence the latter is punished for murder (v. 7).

5. Zimri the Suicide, vv. 8-20.

Of Elah, the immediate successor of Baasha, nothing need be said except that his death begins to fulfil the prediction of verse 3 which culminated as recorded in verses 12 and 13. It was a time of revelry and bloodshed; the army, as is usual in such periods, dictated its own terms (v. 16).

6. Omri and the New Capital, vv. 21-28.

After four years of civil war Omri is established on the throne and, the royal residence at Tirzah having been destroyed by fire, he selects Samaria for a new capital (v. 24). Observe why it was called by that name. Dean Stanley, speaks of the admirable position of this city as paralleled nowhere in the country for "strength, beauty and fertility." Locate it on the map.

7. The Wicked Ahab, vv. 29-34.

Note the iniquitous distinction of this man (v. 30). If Jeroboam broke the second commandment which forbade images, Ahab went further and broke the rest by throwing off even the outward semblance of worshipping Jehovah (v. 31).

The beginning of his gross offence was his marriage. Ethbaal, the father of Jezebel, was originally the priest of the heathen goddess Ashtaroth, or Astarte, whose worship was loathsome in its licentiousness. By murdering the king of the Zidonians (Tyre) he seized the throne and thus became a successor of the noted Hiram.

The worship of Baal and of Astarte were practically one and the same, Baal representing the male principle in the cult and Astarte the female.

In reading verse 31 refresh the mind by a reference to the curse against Jericho in Judges 6:26. Jericho is referred to prior to this time, i.e. in David's day (2 Sam. 10:5) as though it were inhabited, which makes these verses the more difficult to understand. But some think that the curse of Joshua referred not so much to dwelling in the city as to the re-building of its walls for defense.

Questions.

1. How did the Hebrews sometimes count years?

2. What book should be read in connection with 2 Kings?

3. How does this lesson show God's patience towards Israel?

4. What city had been the capital of Israel prior to Omri's time?

5. How did Ahab's wickedness exceed that of Jeroboam?

6. What was the relation between the worship of Baal and that of Ashtaroth?

7. Tell the story of the cursing of Jericho by Joshua.

ELIJAH AND AHAB

CHAPTERS 17-19

1. Elijah in Hiding, 17:1-24.
Nothing is known of Elijah's previous history, not even why he is called the "Tishbite" (v. 1) except, as suggested in the Septuagint translation, that the town of Tishbeh is meant, which was in the Gilead region east of the Jordan. A comparison of Deuteronomy 11:16, 17 shows that the judgment he announces (v. 1) was threatened by Jehovah for such iniquity as that now prevail-

ing; but of course the divine impulse must have come upon him to apply it in this instance.

His hiding "by the brook Cherith" (v. 3) was necessary to preserve him from the wrath of Ahab when his words were fulfilled. His being fed by "the ravens" (v. 4) will raise no question in the minds of any who accept the supernatural in the Bible, and for those who do not this commentary can have little value. The theory of some that the Hebrew word translated "ravens" might be rendered "Arabians," and that he was normally provided for by passing merchants of that region, is not generally accepted by evangelical scholars and would be only less a miracle than the accepted text.

Zarephath, or Sarepta, was in the country whence Jezebel had come, and which was visited by the famine also. The cause of Elijah's removal there is stated in verses 7-9, but there was a deeper reason in the new testings that were to come to him for the strengthening of his faith in view of the climax later on. Nevertheless, we are not to forget the lesson God had to teach the widow also, and to us through her. See Christ's testimony in Luke 4:25, 26.

2. Meeting with Ahab, 18:1-46.
"The third year" is spoken of here, while James says (v. 17) "three years and six months," a discrepancy which may be explained by saying that the drought had been experienced six months (the time between the early and latter rains in March and October respectively) before Ahab realized the situation and became incensed against the prophet.

Fire was the element over which Baal was supposed to preside, which explains verse 24. Observe the simplicity and faith of Elijah's prayer (vv. 36, 37). His command (v. 40) was justified as a magistrate of God (Deut. 13:5, and 18:20.)

Description of Mt. Carmel.
"The natural features of Mt.

Carmel exactly correspond with the details of this narrative. The conspicuous summit, 1,635 feet above the sea, presents an esplanade spacious enough for the king and the priests of Baal to stand on the one side, and Elijah on the other.

"It is a rocky soil, on which there is abundance of loose stones to furnish the twelve of which the altar was built—a bed of thick earth in which a trench could be dug; and yet the earth not so loose that the water poured into it would be absorbed.

"Two hundred and fifty feet beneath the plateau there is a perennial fountain which might not have been accessible to the people, and whence, therefore, even in that season of drought, Elijah could procure those supplies of water which he poured over the altar.

"The distance between this spring and the site of the altar is so short as to make it perfectly possible to go thrice thither and back again: whereas, it must have been impossible *once* in an afternoon, to fetch water from the sea.

"The summit is 1,000 feet above the Kishon, which nowhere runs from the sea so close to the base of the mount as just beneath El-Mohhraka; so that the priests of Baal could, in a few minutes, be taken down "to the brook and slain there."—*Jamieson, Faussett and Brown.*

3. The Results Following, 19:1-21.

There seems to be no explanation of Elijah's flight (vv. 1-4) except the natural one of great depression following great spiritual exaltation. God could have preserved him from this had He so willed, but it is good for all of us to know that we are but flesh (Jas. 5:17) and "that we have this treasure in earthen vessels" (2 Cor. 4:7).

We are impressed with the condescension of God in the supernatural provision for Elijah's physical needs of which he himself had thought nothing (vv.

5-8); and the no less condescension in instructing and continuing to use him as indicated in the subsequent verses.

The exhibition of divine power (vv. 11-13) had the effect of restoring the prophet to a spiritual equilibrium where he could listen to further commands (vv. 15-17) and receive the rebuke his conduct merited (v. 18). It is notable that the three persons he is to anoint are all to be employed, though in different ways, as God's instruments of judgment upon idolatrous Israel. The 7,000 mentioned is not to be taken literally, but as meaning a certain complete number of faithful ones of whom God was cognizant though the prophet was not.

Elisha was one of these (v. 19) who had doubtless been educated in the schools of the prophets of which we shall hear more, and who recognized the falling of his master's mantle upon him as his divine call.

When Elijah says: "What have I done to thee" (v. 20)? he seems to mean: "Do not disregard it. Bid thy loved ones farewell, but remain faithful to thy call."

Questions.

1. Have you read Deuteronomy 11: 16, 17?

2. Have you located Zarephath?

3. Can you give the context of Luke 4:25, 26?

4. Can you quote Elijah's prayer on Mt. Carmel?

5. Name seven particulars in which the natural features of Mt. Carmel correspond with this narrative.

6. How shall we explain God's actings towards Elijah at Horeb?

7. How explain the 7,000?

8. How does verse 15 show God's power over heathen nations as well as Israel?

CLOSE OF AHAB'S REIGN

CHAPTERS 20-22

1. His Dealing with Ben-hadad, c. 20.

Among the remarkable chapters of this book the present

stands out distinctively, but we shall be unable to give it the consideration it should have if we forget God's purpose in dealing with Israel. It has been reiterated that He is using that people as an instrument in the redemption of mankind, and especially as a witness to Himself before the nations. This explains everything in their history, and to ignore it is to make that history like a tale of the Arabian Nights. We should remember also that what is written is ofttimes the barest outline of what was said and done, and while we are by no means to fill in what we please, yet the omissions should have a qualifying influence in our understanding of the record.

"Ben-hadad" means the son of Hadad, and is a general title for the Kings of Syria of that period, like the Pharaohs of Egypt or the Caesars of Rome. He was a descendant of the king met with in Baasha's reign (15:20). The thirty-two kings with him (v. 1) were petty tributary princes, rulers over cities in his neighborhood.

His claim for tribute (v. 3) would have been acceded to had he not overreached himself, (vv. 5, 6), and had not frightened Ahab been encouraged by his subjects (vv. 7-11).

What an evidence we have of God's goodness and providential purpose in Israel in verse 13! Wine and panic explain the victory from the human side, but God's interposition from the divine side (vv. 19-21).

If this victory was great, that of the succeeding year was greater (vv. 22-30). Note the relative size of the armies (v. 27), and the giving way of the walls under the weight of those who there made a stand against Israel.

Ahab's clemency to Ben-hadad (vv. 31-34) was a repetition of Saul's disloyalty to God in the case of Agag (1 Sam. 15) and explains the circumstance following (vv. 35-43). The parabolic manner of the prophet in announcing Ahab's judgment suggests Nathan's dealing with David (2 Sam. 12).

2. His Dealings with Naboth, c. 21.

Note that Naboth's refusal to Ahab was not disregard for him, nor for selfish reasons, but from obedience to God. (Compare verse 3 with Lev. 25; 23; Num. 36:78.) "Sons of Belial" (v. 10) means "ungodly men."

For the fulfilment of verse 19 compare the next chapter, verses 37 and 38. The phrase, "sold thyself to work evil" means that he allowed evil to get the mastery over him. (Compare Rom. 7:11.) For the fulfilment of verse 23 compare 2 Kings 9:30-37. Note God's mercy to the penitent (vv. 27-29) and compare 2 Kings 9:21-26.

3. His Dealings with Jehoshaphat, c. 22.

Verse 3 indicates that Ben-hadad had not fulfilled the covenant with Ahab he had been so ready to make (compare 20:34).

Jehoshaphat, king of Judah, has not been met with before, but a history of his reign is found in the concluding verses of the chapter. He is a striking Old Testament type of the New Testament Christian who forms entangling alliances with the world, but more is said concerning him in 2 Chronicles 18.

Note the piety of Jehoshaphat (v. 15), and observe that a good man is sometimes found voluntarily in bad company.

Micaiah (v. 9) was in prison because of his faithful testimony to God against Ahab. Zedekiah was one of the false prophets (v. 11), but what worship he represented, now that Baalism had been discredited, is difficult to say; but certainly not that of Jehovah.

Observe the temptation placed before Micaiah and the manner in which he met it (vv. 13, 14). His words in verse 15 are ironical, but those of verse 17 are a prediction of the defeat that followed. It is he who speaks in verses 19-23, for a commentary on which see 1 Samuel 18, and also the first two chapters of Job. With verses 24 and 25 compare Jeremiah 20:1-6.

Observe that Jehoshaphat's "unholy alliance" nearly cost him his life (vv. 30-33), but it taught him a lesson (v. 49).

Questions.

1. In what light are we to interpret the marvelous transactions in this book?

2. Who was Ben-hadad?

3. How does this lesson illustrate the cowardice and the courage of Ahab?

4. How does it illustrate the goodness and mercy of God?

5. How many of the marginal references have you examined?

6. What is the meaning of "sons of Belial"?

7. Of what is Jehoshaphat a type, and why?

8. With what prophet may Micaiah be compared?

SECOND KINGS

ELIJAH'S TRANSLATION

CHAPTERS 1-2

1. His Last Commission, c. 1.

The story of Ahaziah's reign in the last chapter of First Kings, and the first verse of this lesson is a close link between the two books. It indicates that the death of Ahab and the accession of his son gave occasion to the Moabites for this uprising, the first since their conquest by David (2 Sam. 8:2).

"Baalzebub" (v. 2) "the lord of the fly" was the name under which the sun-god Baal was worshipped at Ekron, the city of the Philistines lying nearest to Ahaziah's capitol, Samaria. Probably the name comes from the supposition that he produced the flies and was consequently able to protect against them as a pest. The name is not to be confounded with "Beelzebub" of Matthew 10, although there may be a relation between the two. Observe the phrase at the beginning of verse 3, and recall that we have learnt about the Christophanies of the Old Testament. In verses 9-12 Elijah, as the representative of God, is speaking in judgment against malefactors, for such the soldiers and the king behind them must be regarded. Had Elijah been apprehended of them it would have meant his death and a victory of the kingdom of darkness over the kingdom of light. How the fire came down and consumed the soldiers is not stated.

2. His Last Journey, 2:1-11.

The localities in the first five verses—Gilgal, Bethel, Jericho, were doubtless where schools of the prophets had been established, as far back as Samuel's time. (1 Sam. 7:15-17.) These schools were for the training of godly youth in the law of God and the experience of a holy life. Elisha seems to have been among them while Elijah was their head at this period (v. 3). The awesome event about to transpire seems to have been revealed to them to some extent, explaining their communications to Elisha as well as his determination not to separate from Elijah till the end. The latter's indisposition to have himself accompanied is difficult to explain, some attributing it to his purpose of testing the fidelity of Elisha as qualifying him for his succession.

Of what earlier events does verse 8 remind you? How would you interpret Elisha's request in verse 9? Shall we say that it refers to Deuteronomy 21:17, where the law of the first-born is recorded? Elisha would have Elijah regard him as a first-born son, and give him, as compared with the other sons of the prophets, a richer measure of his prophetic spirit. He did not ask twice as much of the Holy Spirit as Elijah had which even on natural grounds Elijah could not have granted him. It is as a prophet that Elijah replies in verse 10. The translation in verse 11 suggests that of Enoch, that of Christ Himself, and that of the Church yet to occur. (Gen. 6:24; Heb. 11:5; Acts 1:9; 1 Thess. 4:17.)

3. His Last Token, vv. 12-18.

Elisha's expression (v. 12) means that Elijah had been the true defense of Israel rather than its military strength in chariots and horsemen. That defense was seen in his combating of idolatry which was Israel's real and only enemy. How otherwise does Elisha express his grief in this verse?

Compare the reference to Elijah's mantle (v. 13) I Kings 19:19, and observe that its possession by Elisha is a token that his petition is answered and he has been endued for the prophetic office.

Is his question (v. 14) an expression of doubt or a prayer of faith? What does the result show (v. 15)?

The desire of the sons of the prophets (v. 16) is difficult to explain on the supposition that they had any clear idea that Elijah had gone into heaven. "Into heaven," might be rendered "toward heaven," and it may be questioned whether the prophet really went into heaven. "In My Father's house are many mansions," and Elijah, for the time being, may have been located at some other happy stopping place.

4. His Successor's Inaugural, vv. 19-25.

The concluding verses furnish two other tokens of Elisha's official character and power which may be considered in this lesson.

Of course it was neither the new cruse nor the salt that healed the water and made it usable and fructifying to the ground (vv. 19-21), but the power of God. They were symbols. The new cruse was necessary because every vessel used for a religious act in the service of Jehovah must be as yet unused, i.e., uncontaminated. The salt was a type of the purifying and restoring power which God would put forth on the spring.

The second evidence of Elisha's power (vv. 23-24), has its difficulties. "Little children" in the margin of the Revised Version is "young lads," and there is good authority for so considering it.

In Lange it is suggested that the young people recognized him as a prophet and opponent of the popular idolatrous worship whose principal seat was at Bethel. Therefore they called to him in mockery, "What dost thou want here among us?"

The epithet "bald head" was a standing insult for old or reverend people whether they were bald or not. It was not so much scorn of Elisha as of Jehovah Himself. (Compare Exodus 16: 8, Acts 5:4, etc.)

She-bears are ravenous, but how two could tear forty-two young people must remain a mystery for the present.

Questions.

1. What is the meaning of "Baalzebub"?
2. Who commissioned Elijah in this case?

3. How many illustrations of swift judgment on sin does this lesson contain?
4. What may be understood by "the schools of the prophets"?
5. How has Elijah's desire to be alone been interpreted?
6. How do you understand Elisha's request of Elijah?
7. Of how many "translations" does the Bible speak?
8. What is the meaning of the "chariots of Israel and the horsemen thereof"?
9. Why did Elisha use means in healing the waters?
10. How would you try to explain the cursing of the children?

ELISHA'S MINISTRY BEGINS

CHAPTERS 3-5

1. Maneuvering an Army, c. 3.

The incident about Mesha (vv. 4, 5) is interesting from the point of view of Biblical criticism. This is the only time he is mentioned in Sacred Writ and his name does not appear in profane history. For this cause objectors to the Bible have demanded proof of his existence at the time named. Also, was Moab noted for its wool? Was it tributary to Israel at this period? Did this rebellion occur? etc.

It was impossible to answer these questions outside of the Bible until about forty years ago when the "Moabite Stone" was discovered, on which an inscription by Mesha recorded all these facts.

What earlier alliance does this between Judah and Israel recall (v. 7)? What earlier situation does Jehoshaphat's inquiry recall (v. 11)? Note the outward respect, at least, which the three kings pay to Jehovah's prophet (v. 12).

Why Elisha calls for the minstrel (v. 15) is not clear, except as a way of quieting his mind in the midst of turbulent scenes of battle, and so preparing him in the physical sense, to listen to God's voice. In our own experience we see the value of worshipful hymns as we approach the throne of grace.

How water came "by the way of Edom" (v. 20), may be explained by a shower or cloudburst. The water was reddened by flowing through the red earth of Edom, an effect heightened by the red light of the morning sun (v. 22).

The act of the king of Moab (v. 27) was not exceptional, but his thought in presenting the sacrifice upon the wall was probably that the besiegers beholding it might fear the heathen divinity to whom it was offered. He would now be appeased, presumptively in favor of his subjects, and it would go hard with their opponents. The meaning of "indignation against Israel" is obscure. Some understand it as indignation the Israelites themselves felt at this act so abominable in their sight, and which made them prefer to renounce further possession of Moab than to pursue the conflict. Or it may mean that God's wrath fell upon them for returning home with their work of judgment half done.

2. Ministering to Individuals, c. 4.

Notice the contrast between a poor woman (vv. 1-7) and a rich one in the verses following. Both have needs which only God can supply, and He is as ready to show His power in the one case as in the other, and His prophet makes no distinction between them in his ministry.

In the story of the Shunamite notice that out of modesty and respect, when the prophet calls her (v. 15), "She stood in the door." "It is well" (vv. 23, 26), is not to be understood as prevaricating, but as wishing to be let alone for the present.

The prophet's staff (v. 29) was the badge of prophetic office. Recall Moses' rod which was the symbol of divine power. It seems an error for Elisha to have dispatched his servant on this commission, but prophets are not infallible except where they speak or write by inspiration of God. (Compare Nathan in 2 Samuel 7.) In his desire to hasten matters, hoping the child was not quite dead, he hurries his servant hence; but he has to learn that he can not delegate God's grace and power according to his own will.

How does Elisha's action (vv. 33-35) compare with Elijah's under similar circumstances? The miracle that follows corresponds closely with that in chapter 2 verses 19 to 22, and may be understood in the same way. The concluding miracles of the chapter suggest Christ's multiplication of the loaves and fishes; but the difference is that here there was no multiplication, but the men were satisfied with the little each received. It was a miracle wrought on the men rather than the food.

3. Magnifying His Office, c. 5.

That is a noticeable phrase in verse 1, "by him the Lord had given deliverance unto Syria," which shows that the inspired annalist regards Jehovah as the God of the whole earth without whose providence even the heathen nations gained no victories.

Observe God using "the weak things of the world" in the case of the little maid (v. 2), whose testimony influences the general, and the kings of Syria and Israel, to say nothing of the prophet, and is handed down as a force for righteousness and truth for thirty centuries!

Both kings misunderstood the situation, however, he of Israel being without excuse. It is this that gives Elisha the opportunity to magnify his office (v. 8), which he does again in the case of Naaman (v. 10). The Syrian's greatness made no difference, he must be healed like any other leper, solely by the power and grace of God. The prophet's humility and disinterestedness are established by his reply in verses 15 and 16.

Naaman's request for earth (v. 17) was not superstition but reverence. His request in verse 18 indicates a tender conscience rather than a compromising spirit, or the prophet could hardly have bidden him "go in peace."

Questions.

1. Give the story of Mesha and its value as evidence of the truth of the Bible.

2. What three kings were in this combination against Moab?

3. Why, probably, was the king's son offered on the wall of the city?

4. What lessons may be drawn from Elisha's treatment of the two women?

5. What lesson was Elisha to learn from Gehazi's failure?

6. How does the miracle of the food differ from that in the gospels?

7. How does Elisha magnify his office in the case of Naaman?

8. In what two ways is Naaman's conversion established?

ELISHA AND THE SYRIAN INVASION

CHAPTERS 6-8

1. The Stratagem at Dothan, 6:8-23.

The incident in verses 1 to 7 seems an interpolation; and some think it belongs at chapter 4:38 in connection with the two miracles, having a somewhat similar occasion. "Swim" (v. 6) is in the Hebrew the same as "float," and the idea seems to be that by throwing the stick into the water the iron was caused to come to the surface where the young man could get it.

It is difficult to say when the event of verse 8 occurred, but it is assumed in the reign of Jehoram, with which we have been dealing since Elisha's ministry began. At a time when the Syrians were intending to encamp at a particular spot, and attack the Israelites as they passed by, the prophet gave warning to Jehoram, which enabled the latter to station troops in the threatened position and frustrate their plans (vv. 8-10). (Lange.)

This disconcerted the Syrian king, and, learning the truth of the matter, he tried to get hold of Elisha (vv. 11-14).

The "servant" of verse 15, is not Gehazi. To "open the eyes" (v. 17) meant to give that soul-vision which the bodily members can never behold. The "horses and chariots of fire" were the symbols of Jehovah's presence and might. "Blindness" (v. 18) is not absolute loss of sight, but an inability to recognize the prophet.

Elisha's words (v. 19) are not an untruth, as his real residence was Samaria; and in the end he led them to himself, not to harm them, but repay evil with good (vv. 21-23). His inquiry of the king (v. 22) presents difficulty, but probably means "could'st thou be justified in slaying with sword and bow these whom thou hast taken captive?" (See Deut. 20:10-13.)

2. The Famine in Samaria, 6:24-7:20.

An interval of some time must be considered since the close of verse 23. The famine caused by the siege was intense as gathered by the price paid for the meanest food (v. 25). "Dove's dung" is understood by some as an insignificant species of pease resembling it.

The king's putting the blame on the prophet (vv. 30, 31) recalls what episode in Elijah's time? Had Elisha advised against the surrender of the city, or did the king think he might have put an end to the distress in some other way? Verse 33 suggests that the king, who had doubtless followed his messengers, had repented of his threat against Elisha, but nevertheless had lost hope in Jehovah.

This brings forth the new promise of 8:1, 2. The remainder of the chapter presents no difficulties, but we should note the fulfilled prediction in verses 19 and 20.

3. The End of Ben-hadad's Reign, 8:1-15.

The event referred to (vv. 1-6) doubtless took place sometime before this, as the records of Elisha's ministry are not arranged chronologically. Compare 4:38 for the period. Gehazi's appearance (vv. 4, 5) further strengthens the thought that it was before his offence and punishment by leprosy.

The event that follows is tragical indeed (vv. 7-15). Hazael, though not related to Benhadad, had been the divine choice as his successor (1 Kings 19:15). When Elisha says the king may recover, yet he shall surely die, he is telling the exact truth, as verse 15 portrays. Had Hazael not murdered him he would have lived. It was Elisha who looked at Hazael until the latter was ashamed, as he might well have been (v. 11).

Questions.

1. Give in your words the story leading up to the event at Dothan.

2. How would you harmonize the prophet's words to the Syrian soldiers?

3. What striking prediction is fulfilled in this lesson?

4. What allusion in 4:38 leads to the supposition that the opening of this lesson refers to that period?

5. How would you harmonize Elisha's words about Ben-hadad?

THE OVER-ZEALOUS JEHU

Chapters 8:25-9:37

1. Preliminary Events, 8:25-29.

The last lesson should have spoken of the chronological difficulties in the history of the kings of Israel. (Compare especially 8:16 with 1:17.) But all our space will permit is to say that all such difficulties are satisfactorily solved, without doing violence to the text, in "The Romance of Chronology," by Anstey; who in turn quotes Dr. John Lightfoot, of the 17th Century, Beecher's Dated Events of the Old Testament, and The Companion Bible, published by the Oxford Press.

The story of blood and awful judgment from God begins at 8·25, where Ahaziah succeeds Jehoram as king of Israel. This is not the earlier Ahaziah of Israel (1 Kings 22: 51) any more than the two Jorams or Jehorams were the same persons, of whom we studied in the last lesson. He is called Jehoahaz in 2 Chronicles 21:17, and in 22:2, he is said to have been forty-two when he began to reign. This, is an intentional variation intended to teach a divine truth. On its face it makes him 2 years older than his father, but it should read, "a son of 42 years was Ahaziah when he began to reign, * * * and his mother's name was Athaliah, the daughter of Omri."

To quote Anstey "The Holy Spirit will not have him for a son of David. He is an imp of the house of wicked Omri, and as such a son of 42 years, which was exactly the age of that dynasty." Compare Ps. 109: 13-15. Note, too, that this interpretation is confirmed by Matthew (1:8), who omits him from the Kings of Judah, saying that Jehoram his father begat Uzziah, his great, great grandson, the fourth in the direct line of descent. Compare here Exod. 20:5.

Like his father, he was a wicked man (9:16-18), and the fruit of his grandfather, Jehoshaphat's, compromising attitude towards Israel. (Compare 9:18.) The reference to his mother (v. 26) is not contradictory, as "daughter" may sometimes be rendered "granddaughter" in translating the Hebrew. He was closely affiliated with his uncle, king of Israel (vv. 28, 29), and this led ultimately to his unnatural death in the next chapter.

2. Jehu Anointed and Proclaimed King, 9:1-13.

Elijah received the commission from God to anoint Jehu (1 Kings 19:16), but he was fulfilling it in his successor, as the latter was doing so in the representative of the school of the prophets whom he sent on the divine errand (vv. 1, 2). Jehu's father is not the Jehoshaphat of Judah (1 Kings 22:4).

This Jehu is a military commander in Israel, perhaps next to the king and, as the sequel shows, a bold and popular one. He is now in the company of his fellow-captains near the scene of battle where Joram left them when he went to Jezreel wounded. These captains recognize the validity of his anointing and by laying their garments on the steps for him to mount on, do him obeisance as they sound the trumpets of proclamation (vv. 11-13).

3. His Conspiracy Against Joram, vv. 14-16.

The army is not informed of what is transpiring (v. 15), but Jehu and a few followers advance upon Jezreel and the king (v. 16). The latter thinks he is bringing news of the battle after he had left (vv. 17-21), but he is soon undeceived (vv. 22-23). "The whoredoms of thy mother" (Jezebel) doubtless meant her idolatry with Baal. "The Lord laid this burden upon him" (v. 25), means "the Lord uttered this prophecy against him." (See 1 Kings 21.) Be not deceived by the thought that Jehu is doing all this out of zeal for God, as the sequel shows that zeal for Jehu was the stronger motive.

4. The Murder of Ahaziah and Jezebel, vv. 27-37.

2 Chronicles 22:8 gives other details of Ahaziah's death which, for want of light, are difficult to reconcile with the record, and which therefore must be passed over. Another difficulty is the discrepancy as to the date when he began to reign, whether it was the eleventh year to Joram (v. 29) or the twelfth as stated previously (8:25); but the explanation may be that he reigned with his father for one year before the latter's death. The probable reason for this is in 2 Chronicles 21, the last verse.

For the significance of Jezebel's challenge to Jehu (v. 31) see 1 Kings 16:9.

5. The Slaughter of the Families of Ahab and Ahaziah, 10:1-14.

The "70 sons" of Ahab (v. 1) mean doubtless his grandsons and all who might have any pretense to the throne. Jehu asks the men in authority at the capital (Samaria) and the summer pal-

ace (Jezreel) to place any of these on the throne, and rally to his support if they chose (vv. 2, 3); but they are afraid to do so, and instead surrender to Jehu (vv. 4, 5). Then he bids them go further (vv. 6, 7); and subsequently uses their deed as an argument before the people that the leaders are on his side, and that the word of the Lord is fulfilled in his accession (vv. 8-10). The slaughter of the relatives of Ahaziah follows (vv. 12-14).

6. The Destruction of the Prophets of Baal, vv. 15-28.

Of Jehonadab we read in Jeremiah 34. He seems to have been an honorable man in Israel, a worshipper of the true God, whose presence with Jehu contributed to the latter's influence with the people (vv. 15, 16). This part of our story shows that, although Baal's worship received a serious setback in the days of Elijah, yet it had been restored to practically its former power in the kingdom (vv. 18-28).

Jehu's real character is shown in verse 29, in the face of which one is astonished to read verse 30. But God was dealing with him as one who was hired for what he did. Had his heart been right with God his kingdom might have been established for generations, but as it was he could not complain.

God now begins His final work in Israel (vv. 32-33). The time is coming when the axe will fall at the root of the tree and the whole nation be carried away for its iniquity; but intimations of this are sent to warn and, if possible, bring them to repentance.

Questions.

1. Can the chronological difficulties be solved in the history of the Kings of Judah?

2. How would you explain the difficulty as to the age of Ahaziah?

3. What kings of similar names are met with in Israel and Judah?

4. What have you learned of Jehu's history?

5. What are the circumstances

under which he is proclaimed king?

6. What prophecies are fulfilled in this lesson?

7. What are some of the difficulties found in it?

8. What record has Jehonadab in Jeremiah?

9. How is Jehu's real character revealed?

ANOTHER CENTURY OF ISRAEL AND JUDAH

Chapters 11-14

1. Joash of Judah, Chapters 11 and 12.

The chief events of this reign are the rescue of the infant kings from the murderous grandmother (11:1-3); the *coup d'etat* of the high priest by which he was raised to the throne (vv. 4-16); the reforms of the high priest as regent of the kingdom (vv. 17-21); the repairing of the temple by the king (12:1-16); the surrender to the Syrians (vv. 17, 18), and the king's assassination (vv. 19-21).

Be careful to read the parallel chapters in 2 Chronicles (22-24), which add details, though at this distance it may be impossible to reconcile all the minor differences.

2. Jehoahaz of Israel, 13:1-9.

This reign is notable not for what man did but what God did, as indicated in verse four. That His compassion was awakened towards such a people commands the wonder even of the spiritually enlightened—a wonder which the sacred narrator Himself expresses in the parenthetic verses (vv. 5, 6). "Saviour" or delivered is used in a military sense, as in Judges. He did not appear in Jehoahaz's time but in that of his successors Jehoash and Jeroboam II.

3. Jehoash of Israel, vv. 10-25.

We need not speak further of the chronological difficulty here (v. 10 compared with v. 1), which we can not solve, but pass on to the preliminary fulfillment of the promised "saviour" (v. 5), found in verses 14 to 25.

Jehoash, or Joash (v. 14), is in sore distress by reason of the affliction in verse three, and sufficiently penitent to implore Jehovah through His prophet (v. 14). The symbolism of the subsequent verses (15-19) is plain. "Take bow and arrows" means, arm thyself for war against the Syrians. "The arrow of the Lord's deliverance" means that the victory would come from God. The second part of the action was an enhancement of it, and showed the king to lack that zeal and persevering trust in God that would have brought the complete destruction of his enemy (note verse 25).

The extraordinary event in verse 21 is to be accepted just as it is, but it is useless to speculate on the cause or the object of it.

4. Amaziah of Judah, 14:1-20.

An interesting event is the challenge Amaziah sends to Jehoash, the manner in which it is received, and the outcome of it (vv. 8-14). It is worthy of remark that he met death in the same way as his father whose murder he had been so prompt to avenge (vv. 19, 20).

5. Jerobam II of Israel, vv. 23-29.

Now God fully redeems His promise to give a "saviour" to Israel (13:5). Observe the long reign of this king—the longest in the annals of Israel (v. 23). Observe his remarkable victories (v. 25). Observe the reference to Jonah who seems in succession to Elisha, and lived probably contemporaneously with Jehoash or even Jehoahaz. It may have been through him that God gave the promise to that king to which we have made reference. The close of his reign marks about a century from the beginning of that of Joash of Judah.

Another circumstance of interest is that Amos and Hosea both lived and prophesied in this reign (see the opening verses of their prophecies).

Questions.

1. Name the first reigning queen of Judah.

2. Name the high priest who placed Joash on the throne.

3. How old was Joash when he began to reign?

4. What good work marked his reign?

5. Under what circumstances did he die?

6. Who was the "saviour" intended, 13:5?

7. In whose reign did Elisha die?

8. What nation was the constant enemy of Israel in those days?

9. Name some events making the reign of Jeroboam II the "golden age" of Israel.

10. Name three prophets of his period whose written works have come down to us.

THE ASSYRIAN CAPTIVITY

CHAPTERS 15-17

1. Azariah of Judah, 15:1-7.

This king is called "Uzziah" in verses 13 and 30, and in 2 Chronicles 26. Read the last-named chapter for an enlargement of his history and an explanation of certain features not given here. Note his long reign, his generally good character, the cause of his failure, and the circumstance that his son reigned with him jointly for a short period.

2. Israel's New Enemy, vv. 8-31.

Zachariah is the last of the line of Jehu, in whom the prophecy of 10:30 is fulfilled (v. 12). Shallum is a usurper only permitted to reign how long (v. 13)? Menahem comes into power in the same way as he, although he reigned a reasonably long period (v. 17). It was in his time that the new enemy of Israel appeared in Assyria, a strong nation of the East reaching out after world domination (vv. 19, 20).

Pekahiah, his son and successor, reigns but briefly (vv. 23-26), when another conspiracy costs him his life. Pekah's reign is prolonged for twenty years (v. 27), but Israel's days as a nation

are numbered, and Assyria is weakening her on every side. The first deportation of her people takes place in this reign (v. 29).

3. Jotham and Ahaz of Judah, v. 32-16:20.

Jotham was in the main a good king, but like all his predecessors since Solomon, either unwilling or unable to uproot idolatry (v. 35) or cause the nation to serve Jehovah with a perfect heart. How ominous in consequence, the words of verse 37.

But no king of Judah thus far had the preeminence in wickedness of Jotham's successor (16:3, 4). And yet God bore with him for the sake of His promise to the fathers. For a commentary on verse 5 to 9 read the contemporaneous prophet Isaiah, chapter seven.

Ahaz need not have turned for aid to Assyria had he trusted God; but now that he has done so, that nation has obtained a hold on Judah which practically is never loosed.

Note verses 10-18 and Ahaz's interest in the idolatry practiced among the Assyrians. This is the first time it comes into view, as it will be recalled that the worship of Baal and Ashtoreth was introduced by Jezebel from the Phoenicians or Zidonians. Something of what it meant may be gathered from the horrible reference in verse three, the actual significance of which it is difficult to determine. Is it possible that children were burned alive as offerings to the gods? There are those who maintain such to have been the case.

4. The End of Israel, c. 17.

The first half of this chapter is a sad review of Israel's iniquity and the justification of the divine punishment (vv. 6-23). It was surer and safer for their conqueror to carry them away (v. 6), than to place governors over them in their own land. These latter they might not obey, or they might refuse to pay tribute to them, involving ceaseless war to keep them in subjection. Moreover the policy had the advantage that other conquered peoples could be transplanted to the vacated territory with like results (v. 24).

With these foreigners in the land of Israel begins the history of the "Samaritans," of whom we hear in the gospels (see John 4). Note the character of their religion (vv. 33-41).

It was not promised that Israel, as a separate kingdom would be restored again, and therefore God permitted her cities to be occupied with other peoples, but it was not so with Judah and for a good reason, as we shall see later. Of course when Judah was restored after the Babylonian captivity many Israelites returned with her, but these did not constitute the kingdom of Israel. Finally, in the last days when the Jews shall once more occupy and control Palestine, they will not represent two kingdoms, but one united people (Isa. 11:11-16; Hos. 1:10, 11).

This lesson should not close without mentioning the importance of knowing something about Assyria, with which great people many of the following lessons deal. Any Outline History of the World will furnish some information, and encyclopedia articles are valuable, but Rawlinson's "Five Great Monarchies of the Ancient World" or Lenormant's "Manual of the Ancient History of the East" are recommended to those who can lay their hands upon them. Local librarians will give further help.

Questions.

1. By what other name is Azariah known?

2. Why was he smitten with leprosy?

3. Locate Assyria on the map.

4. Name the wickedest king of Judah thus far.

5. What prophet whose written words have come down to us was contemporaneous with him?

6. What evil religious distinction is associated with his name?

7. How is it shown that the fall of Israel came as a judgment of God?

8. Is it right therefore to measure the history of Israel by the standard of any other ancient people?

9. What was Assyria's object in their deportation?

10. Do you suppose "lions" were purposely sent in to slay the Samaritans (v. 25), or may they have increased in number and boldness while the land was for a while desolate?

11. Nevertheless, if the latter be true, was not the circumstance a divine punishment?

12. How does this lesson show that the heathen nations believed in localized gods?

13. From what we know of the worship of Israel before the captivity, what is the probability that any returned "priest" could teach the Samaritans about the true God (v. 27)?

JUDAH UNDER HEZEKIAH

CHAPTERS 18-20

1. A Summary of the Reign, 18: 1-8.

For a more extensive history of this good reign compare not only 2 Chronicles 29-32, but also Isaiah 36-39. In the first eight verses we have the usual summary like that of Ahaz (16:1-4), after which follows in detail the chief events of the reign. The summary contains the age and period of the king (vv. 1, 2); his attitude toward the true worship (vv. 3, 4); a reference to the spirit animating his life and conduct (vv. 5, 6), and in consequence the successes attained over foreign enemies (vv. 7, 8).

Note his enviable distinction (v. 5) and the cause of it (v. 4).

2. Sennacherib's Invasion, vv. 13-35.

The intervening verses (9-12) recapitulating Israel's captivity are inserted doubtless for the sake of contrast. Had the kings of Israel been as faithful to Jehovah as this king of Judah was, that calamity would not have overtaken them as it did not overtake him.

Sennacherib is on a tour of conquest against Egypt, Assyria's great rival for world dominion, and takes in Jerusalem *en route*. At first Hezekiah is disposed to make terms (vv. 13-16), which Sennacherib accepts and then wantonly disregards. While he proceeds on Egypt he detaches a force to attack Jerusalem (v. 17).

The language of Rabshakeh is insulting throughout. His claim to be acting for Jehovah (v. 25) is pure assumption as the event shows. Eliakim's protest (v. 26) was a blunder in that it encouraged him to greater boldness in seeking to influence the rank and file (vv. 28-35).

3. The Appeal to Jehovah, 19:1-37.

Rabshakeh did not commence the siege immediately, but joined the main army again at Libnah (v. 18), to which place Sennacherib retired on the approach of the Egyptian king (v. 9).

Another attempt is made to move Hezekiah by a letter, but as before he had appealed to Jehovah through the prophet, he now does so directly through his own prayer (vv. 14-19), and is answered through the prophet (vv. 20-34).

This answer contains (1), a rebuke of Sennacherib's boast (vv. 21-24); (2), a refutation of his self-assertion (vv. 25-28); (3), an encouragement to Judah and Hezekiah (vv. 29-31); and (4), the divine decree in regard to the crisis (vv. 32-34).

The execution of the decree brings to mind such modern parallels as the destruction of the Spanish armada by the storm, and the breaking up of the French army before Moscow when in one memorable night, 20,000 horses perished of frost.—Lange.

4. Hezekiah's Sickness and Recovery, 20:1-11.

It seemed to the king that he must have displeased God to be cut off in early manhood (see Prov. 10:27), hence his words (v. 3).

Figs were the ordinary remedy for boils (v. 7) but the prophet did not order their application until he was assured of the divine help. It was God, and not the figs that healed, just as is always the case in every remedy for bodily ills.

It does not seem wrong for Hezekiah to ask a sign in view of Isaiah's words to Ahaz (Isa. 7:11).

The reversal of the shadow on the sundial (v. 11) only can be regarded either as a miracle or myth, and as far as the true believer in the Bible is concerned, the former is accepted without seeking impossible explanations.

5. An Unholy Alliance, vv. 12-21.

Babylon at this time was trying to free herself from Assyrian supremacy, and when Sennacherib suffered so serious a calamity seemed an opportune moment for a forward movement. This doubtless reveals the reason for this embassy to Hezekiah with whom it was hoped to form an alliance. It also explains the latters' object in showing them his riches and strength (v. 13), which was not only a political blunder but an act of unbelief towards God. Hence the rebuke (vv. 16-18). Instead of help from Babylon that nation would at length prove Judah's ruin. This would not be on account of Hezekiah's fault alone, but because the whole nation had incurred guilt similar to his, and would continue to do so even in a greater degree.

Questions.

1. Have you read the parallel Scriptures in this case?

2. Rehearse the four outline facts constituting the summary of this reign.

3. What special form of idolatry is here mentioned?

4. What two strong nations were rivals for world-dominion at this time?

5. Analyze Jehovah's answer to Sennacherib's boast.

6. What practical lessons are here taught about divine healing?

7. Give what appears to be the true reason for the Babylonian embassy.

JUDAH UNDER JOSIAH

Chapters 21-23

1. His Immediate Predecessors, 21:1-26.

Manasseh's history shows that a good father does not always make a good son. The summary of his reign (vv. 1-9) ranks him with Ahaz, as the two wickedest kings Judah had known. Note that the same punishment which had fallen on Israel is soon to overtake Judah (v. 13), and this notwithstanding Manasseh's "humbleness," as indicated in 2 Chronicles 33:11-19.

The brief reign of Amon (vv. 19-26) was in character a continuation of that of his father, and marks the lowest period in the history of the nation until that time.

2. His Restoration of the True Worship, c. 22.

The youth of Josiah suggests that he may have been under a regency at first as in the case of Joash (12:3) though there is no mention of it. The temple had not been repaired since that king, 250 years before, which explains certain things in this chapter, especially when the wickedness and idolatry of some of the intervening reigns are considered.

"The book of the law" (v. 8) is regarded by scholars as the Pentateuch, which during the apostasy had been lost to public knowledge except as a tradition. Some of the older rabbis held that it was the original manuscript of Moses. Another theory is that Manasseh had ordered all copies to be destroyed, but that some faithful priest had concealed this copy until now.

Jeremiah and Zephaniah were prophets contemporaneous with Josiah, but the reason Huldah was inquired of, and not they, is probably because she "dwelt in Jerusalem" (v. 14), where the others may not have been at this time.

3. His Extension of the Reform Movement, c. 23.

It will be noticed that after the king had put an end to all illegal worship in Judah, he extended the reform, or the revival, to the former kingdom of Israel, where that worship had originally arisen (23:15-20).

Observe from verses 26 and 27 that God has not changed His purpose concerning the removal of Judah, which proves that, although in this reign the law was kept externally, yet the nation was by no means converted.

4. His Death and the Succession, vv. 29-37.

The story of Josiah's death (vv. 29, 30) is more fully related in 2 Chronicles. One reason he marched against Pharaoh was that although the latter's objective was Assyria, yet he was trespassing on Jewish soil to attain it.

Jehoahaz, whom the people preferred as his successor (v. 30), was a younger son, but he was soon deposed by the Egyptians, who placed his brother on the throne, making him their vassal (vv. 34, 35).

Questions.

1. How long did Manasseh reign?

2. What chastisement befell him during his lifetime, and why?

3. What effect had this upon his spirit?

4. What decree is now uttered against Judah?

5. What earlier king of Judah does Josiah suggest?

6. Name two or three parallel incidents in their histories.

7. How would you explain the loss of the book of the law?

8. With what is this book identified?

9. What two prophets, whose books have come down to us, were contemporaneous with this reign?

10. Did Josiah die a natural death?

THE BABYLONIAN CAPTIVITY

CHAPTERS 24–25

1. The Last of the Kings, c. 24.

In the previous lesson we left Judah tributary to Egypt, which had been victorious at Megiddo. This lasted, five years, when Babylon, now master of her old-time enemy Assyria, and eager to cross swords with Egypt for world-supremacy, came up against her, and compelled allegiance.

After three years Jehoiakim revolted (v. 1), and for the remainder of his reign was harassed by bands of enemies (v. 2) perhaps incited by the king of Babylon, himself too much occupied in other directions to attack Judah in person.

After he has defeated Egypt, however (v. 7), he turns his attention to Judah. Jehoiakim is dead and his son, Jehoiachim, is on the throne (v. 8). The latter is taken captive, and with him many of the best people of the land (vv. 12-16), among them Ezekiel, as we learn from the book bearing his name. (The prophet Daniel, with others, had been carried away by the same king on an earlier advance against Jehoiakim.)

Nebuchadnezzar shows the same consideration as the king of Egypt in placing another of the royal family instead of a stranger on the throne (v. 17), but his confidence is misplaced and the end comes. The whole situation is of God, and the execution of His judgment upon the unholy people (v. 20).

2. The Death Agony, 25:1-21.

For a comment on this chapter, read Jeremiah and Ezekiel. Jeremiah 21, 27, 32, 34, 37, 40 and 41 cover this period pretty thoroughly and also the first twenty-four chapters of Ezekiel.

3. The Remnant Left in the Land, vv. 22-26.

Gedaliah, whom the king of Babylon made governor over the few people remaining was, like his father, a friend of Jeremiah and joined with him in advising Zedekiah to surrender. Had this counsel prevailed, Judah would not have been plucked up out of her land. All this will be seen when Jeremiah is reached. This was known to Nebuchadnezzar, however, and explains his choice of Gedaliah, as well as the treachery of the people towards him, notwithstanding his oath (vv. 24, 25). Read Jeremiah 40 to 44.

4. The Favored Captive, vv. 27-30.

This closing incident carries its explanation on its face. The Babylonian king was the son and successor of Nebuchadnezzar. The grace bestowed on Jehoiachin is difficult to account for, except on some personal ground, especially as he is preferred before the other captive kings, who were retained at the court to inhance its triumph and glory.

In conclusion let it again be emphasized that the fall of Judah was God's judgment upon his faithlessness as a witness to Him. All the prophets testify to this. But, let it also be noted that it was His purpose that Judah should be restored after a period (70 years, Jeremiah 25:12). Her land was not populated by other peoples, a striking fulfillment of prophecy in itself. She must needs give birth to the Messiah there as the prophets had foretold, and so, when her captivity brought her to her senses she repented, and returned to Jehovah with a sincerity she had not before.

Questions.

1. In whose reign was Judah tributary, first to Egypt and then to Babylon?

2. What two later kings of Judah reigned but three months each?

3. In whose reigns were Ezekiel and Daniel taken captive?

4. What additional light on the period have you gathered from Jeremiah?

5. In what respect does Judah's captivity differ from that of Israel?

FIRST CHRONICLES

GENEALOGIES AND PEDIGREES

CHAPTERS 1-9

1. Introductory.

With this begins the study of those historical books of the Old Testament written shortly after the return from the Babylonian captivity, the remainder of the series including 2 Chronicles, Ezra, Nehemiah, and Esther.

"Chronicles" means "diaries" or "journals," and the books give a recapitulation of sacred history from the time of Adam, in which the earlier books of the Old Testament are drawn upon and occasionally supplemented. The Holy Spirit, who is the real Author, has a right to do this when the occasion calls for it.

The closest relation exists between the Chronicles and Kings. The last-named were written, it is thought, by Jeremiah, and the first-named by a priest or Levite. Kings must have been compiled shortly after the people went into exile, Chronicles after their return. Kings deal more with the inner spiritual condition of things, Chronicles with the external modes of worship.

There are differences in the two records here and there. Not only are genealogies differently grouped, but names of places are changed, speeches of persons are presented from dissimilar aspects, religious festivals have more than one description given them, and things of that kind; but there is no contradiction not explainable by the changes incident to time, the later writer's point of view, the object in mind, negligent transcribing and the like.

Why Chronicles were written is difficult to say, but there must have been some good reason for going over the ground again, "some new aspect of the history to signalize, and some new lesson to convey to the people of God on returning from the captivity." What these things may be must appear as we proceed.

2. Subdivisions.

The first nine chapters contain the genealogies of the patriarchs, the twelve tribes, and the inhabitants of Jerusalem till the beginning of the kingdom, the purpose being to connect David, the great forerunner of the Messiah, as well as the priests and Levites of his time with the antediluvian patriarchs. They have been subdivided as follows:

(1) The Patriarchs from Adam to Jacob and Esau, with the descendants of the latter till the era of the Edomite kings, c. 1.

At first these names may not seem of importance to us, but we remember that the Holy Spirit caused them to be written and that is enough. And "when we know how to awaken them from their sleep, they do not remain so dead as they at first appear, but revive the most important traditions of the ancient nations and families, like the petrifactions and mountain strata of the earth, which rightly questioned, tell the history of long vanished ages."

(2) The Sons of Jacob, or the Generations of Judah till David, with the Latter's Posterity till Elioenai and His Seven Sons, 2:1-4:23.

In this we discover a biographic gem in the story of Jabez and his prayer (c. 4:9, 10) of whom we are told nothing further. Verse 10 has homiletic value in the three things for which Jabez prayed and which he received—prosperity, power, and protection.

Another homiletic suggestion is in the words, "There they dwelt with the king for his work" (v. 23). These potters "that dwelt among plants and hedges," may have been artistic craftsmen adjacent to the royal gardens at Jerusalem, not merely in the reign of one king but all of them. Remains of these potteries have been found in recent times.

(3) The Descendants of Simeon and the Tribes East of the Jordan till the Assyrian Captivity, 4:24-5:26.

This division is interesting, as it records two conquests or migrations of the Simeonites (4:38-43), and corroborates what we learned earlier about the small size of this tribe (compare 5:27 with Numbers 1-4 and Joshua 19:1-9.) In the same way compare the reference to Reuben, Joseph and Judah, chapter 5:1, 2, with the earlier account in Genesis 49. Nor should we permit such an inspired comment as chapter 5:20 to escape us.

(4) The Levites and Their Locations, 6:1-81.

This division may be broken up, thus: The sons of Levi (vv. 1-3); the priests down to the captivity (vv. 4-15); the families of Gershom, Merari and Kohath (vv. 16-48); the office of Aaron and his line unto Ahimaaz (vv. 49-53); the cities of the priests and the Levites (vv. 54-81).

(5) The Remaining Tribes, cc. 7-8.

These tribes include Issachar (7:1-5); Benjamin (vv. 6-12); Naphtali (v. 13); Manasseh (vv. 14-19); Ephraim (vv. 20-29), Asher (vv. 30-40); the chief men of Benjamin (8:1-32); the house of Saul (vv. 33-40).

Two tribes are omitted, Dan and Zebulon, but why, no one can determine. In the case of Dan, perhaps, it is judicial punishment because of their early and almost total fall into idolatry. They are omitted again in the list of Revelation 8. Zebulon's omission is more difficult to explain. It was a small tribe, especially just before and after the exile, but it was the tribe whose territory included Nazareth where Jesus dwelt.

(6) The Inhabitants of Jerusalem Till the Times of the Kings, c. 9.

Questions.

1. Name the post-exilian historical books.

2. Give the scope and general contents of the books of Chronicles.

3. Contrast Kings and Chronicles as to their history and character.

4. What are some of the points of difference between Kings and Chronicles, and how are they explained?

5. Give the contents of 1 Chronicles 1-9 in outline.

6. What can you recall of the history of Jabez?

7. Which two tribes are altogether omitted from these genealogies?

DAVID'S REIGN

CHAPTERS 10-29

1. The Downfall of Saul, c. 10.

In reading this chapter with whose general contents we became familiar in 1 Samuel 31, it is important to note the inspired comment at its close (vv. 13, 14).

2. David's Heroes, cc. 11, 12.

In the history of David in this book, the writer dwells chiefly on its prosperous side, passing over the rest as lightly as possible. His annointing at Hebron (vv. 1-3), reveals nothing of what we learned earlier of the rival kingdom of the house of Saul, and the seven years before his exaltation over all Israel. Again, in the list of warriors (11:10-47), there is an omission of Joab's treachery and barbarous conduct in the cases of Abner, Uriah and Absalom.

Chapter 12 contains a supplemental list of braves who attached themselves to David earlier, and during the days of Saul, and of whom we have no record until now.

3. David's Victories and Festivals, cc. 13-16.

These begin with the bringing up of the ark as far as the house of Obededom (c. 13). Then follows the account of battles with the Philistines (c. 14), which occupies a different position from that in 2 Samuel 5, the reason for which can only be conjectured. After this the ark is brought up to Jerusalem (cc. 15, 16), the record being more detailed than in Samuel. Note, for example, the preparation and act of transfer. A tent is erected, (15:1) possibly in the vicinity of the palace, after the model of the old tabernacle. Then a consultation is held (v. 2), the representative men are assembled (v. 3), the bearers chosen (vv. 12-15), the singers appointed (vv. 16-24). Then the act itself, with its rejoicings, sacrifices and distribution of gifts (15:25-16:3). Then the initial service and the psalm of thanksgiving (vv. 4-36).

Another thus analyzes the eight strophes of this psalm: The first, summons to praise (vv. 8-11); the second, to think on the wonders and judgments of the Lord (vv. 12-14); the third, to think of the covenant made with the fathers (vv. 15-18); the fourth, gives the reasons to remember this covenant (vv. 19-22); the fifth, affirms that all the world shall concur in the greatness and glory of God (vv. 23-27); the sixth, all nations shall worship Him (vv. 28-30); the seventh, the inanimate creation will exult before Him (vv. 31-33); the eighth, closes with a repeated summons to praise and prayer (vv. 34-36).

4. David and The Temple, cc. 17-22.

Except as to its location the record in chapter 17 is in substance the same as in 2 Samuel 7. The "group of war reports," cc. 18-20, runs parallel to four sections in 2 Samuel which in that case are separated from one another by other matters. The story of the plague following the census (c. 21), contains some deviations from that in Samuel, as for example, its position in the record, the fact that the offence was instigated by Satan, that Benjamin and Levi were not numbered, and that the threshing-floor was thereafter the constant place of sacrifice by David. These things are additions and not contradictions. As to the last named, the words in verse 28, "At that time * * * he sacrificed there," have been rendered by Luther and others, "was wont to offer there," meaning that he did

it repeatedly, frequently. In an earlier lesson it was stated that this threshing-floor subsequently became the site of Solomon's temple.

After the episode represented by these chapters the author returns to the subject of the temple (c. 22), speaking of David's preparation of the materials (vv. 1-5), his charge to Solomon (vv. 6-16), and finally his appeal to the princes to assist (vv. 17-19).

5. The Temple and Military Officers, cc. 23-27.

The opening comment of this section gives the reason for what follows. David was old and felt the need of putting things in readiness for his son (v. 1). There are two things that concern him chiefly, the worship of God and the strengthening of the kingdom, and it is significant that the worship of God receives attention first.

The chapters arrange themselves thus: Chapter 23 deals with the Levites, their number and classification for work; 24 does the same for the priests, except that the closing verses refer again to the Levites; 25 speaks of the singers; 26 of the porters, treasurers and other business officers; and 27 of the army, including its divisions and commanders.

6. David's Last Directions and Death, cc. 28, 29.

The last directions of David concern the building of the temple where all the princes, the captains, the courtiers and the heroes are addressed (vv. 1, 2), and Solomon in their presence is invested with power and authority as his successor (vv. 5-21).

Note the words in verse 12. "And the pattern of all that he had by the Spirit." We use a capital "S" believing the Holy Spirit to be intended, and that the words should be read in the light of verse 19, "All this, the LORD made me understand in writing by His hand upon me, even all the works of this pattern." Are we not to understand, difficult as the words may be, that as God revealed the original of the temple to Moses in the wilderness when He revealed the tabernacle, so now also He controlled and directed David when the time came for the actual erection of the temple?

Do not pass chapter 29 carelessly. Note David's example of giving (vv. 3-5), and the lever it affords to make an appeal to others. See the working of the Spirit of God among the people in the gladness of it all (v. 9), a fact David recognizes and for which he praises God, verse 10 and the following.

When it says "they made Solomon king the second time" (v. 22), it is in contrast with 23:1. In that case the first proclamation was made, but now the actual anointing took place. (Compare 1 Kings 1:32 and the following verses.)

Questions.

1. What book gives the fuller history of Saul?

2. How would you compare the history of David's reign in 1 Chronicles with that in the earlier books?

3. What explains the successful transfer of the ark in this instance, as compared with the earlier attempt?

4. Have you read the psalm contained in this lesson, and noted its analysis?

5. What evidence of the personality of Satan does this lesson contain?

6. How does it show David's loyalty to God?

7. What may explain David's particularity as to the details of the temple?

SECOND CHRONICLES

SOLOMON'S REIGN

CHAPTERS 1-9

1 His Prayer and Its Answer, 1: 1-3,

With verses three and four compare 1 Chronicles 16, and especially verses 37-40. The tabernacle at Gibeon was the legal place for worship, but the threshing-floor on Mt. Moriah was chosen by David for the reason given (1 Chron. 21:29). A comparison with the corresponding place in 1 Kings will show how this account is abbreviated as the matter was not necessary to the author's purpose.

2. His Power and Wealth, 1:14-17.

This record is given in Kings near the close of the reign, but inserted here as a proof of the instant fulfillment of God's promise.

3. His Erection and Dedication of the Temple, cc. 2-7.

"Huram" is the same with whom we have previously met. The two houses (2:1) are the temple and Solomon's palace. The description of the temple here differs in several particulars from that in Kings. For example, this is more particular as to the plan of the building but less so as to the time when it began; this speaks of the arrangement of the building and its furnishings in an unbroken narrative, but that has two interruptions; this arranges the objects differently and describes with more fulness in some cases, etc. But remember what has been said about the Holy Spirit as the real author of Scripture, and His right to use such liberty to emphasize certain facts or impress certain lessons as He desires. This does not take into account errors of copyists to which reference also has been made.

Here the location of the temple is named for the first time (3:1), (compare Gen. 22:2). "Moriah" means "land of the appearing of the Lord." Note the reference to the brazen scaffold (4:13) not given in Kings, the additional words at the close of Solomon's prayer (vv. 40-42), and the fuller account of the divine acceptance of the temple (7:1-10).

The large number of oxen and sheep offered in sacrifice is astounding (7:5), but Josephus in his *"Wars of the Jews"* says that even in Roman times, 256,000 passover lambs were slain at Jerusalem within a few hours. A current commentator reminds us that these colossal offerings and festivals are no more astonishing to us than the magnitude of our steam or railway trade, or as modern warfare would be astonishing to the ancients.

4. His Earthly End, cc. 8, 9.

In the first of these chapters we have brief notes of events recorded more at length in 1 Kings, for example: the building of certain cities, the palace for the daughter of the Egyptian king, the navigation of Ophir, etc. The comments upon these in that book occupy as much space as seems relatively necessary.

In the next chapter the story of the Queen of Sheba is very much as in 1 Kings.

Questions.

1. Where was the tabernacle of Moses at this period?

2. Who is the real author of this book, and how does that fact bear on the differences in its record as compared with 1 Kings?

3. How may other differences be explained?

4. Tell what you know of the history of Mt. Moriah.

5. Give a later parallel to the large number of sacrifices at the dedication of the temple.

REHOBOAM AND JEHOSHAPHAT

CHAPTERS 10-20

1. Rehoboam, cc. 10-12.

The story of the rejected counsel of the older men and what came of it (c. 10) is practically as in 1 Kings 12, and furnishes an illustration of the relation of divine sovereignty to human free agency.

The fortification of Judah's cities against Israel (c. 11) was dwelt upon in the earlier books, as well as the return of the priests and Levites to Jerusalem.

Rehoboam's "wise" action (v. 23) is to be taken in the political sense. He thus gave his sons and grandsons something to do, each having a measure of independence, and being kept sufficiently apart from the others to lessen the likelihood of a cabal against the heir to the kingdom.

How long did Rehoboam remain faithful to God (11:17 and 12:1)? What punishment was inflicted for his infidelity (vv. 2-4)? How is God's goodness shown to him (v. 5), and with what result (vv. 6-8)? Note verse eight carefully. How much better to serve God than His enemies, but what bitter experience is necessary to teach this lesson (vv. 9-12). Note the reference of the heathen mother of Rehoboam (v. 13), and the reason for its record (v. 14), as showing her baneful influence on her son.

Speaking of the punishment which befell Rehoboam and Judah from Egypt, it is interesting that its record is found to-day on the walls of the Egyptian palace at Karnak. Carved nearly three millenniums ago, it is there still an impressive corroboration of Holy Writ.

2. Abijah and Asa, cc. 13-16.

These kings may be coupled, as the record of the first-named is brief. Verse two of chapter 13 does not contradict verse 20 of chapter 11, since "Michaiah" and "Maachah" are the same, and as "the daughter of Uriel," she was the grand-daughter of Absalom.

Such general statements are common in the Hebrew text, and it is impossible to consider each of them.

The numbers in verse three are immense, but compare 1 Chronicles 21:5. The harangue of Abijah (vv. 4-12), except in its character and terms, suggests that of the Assyrian commander before Jerusalem (2 Kings 18), and seems to have been a custom in ancient warfare. What advantage is taken of this dalay (vv. 13, 14)? What prevented a rout of Judah (v. 15)? How terrific was Israel's punishment (v. 17)? What was its effect in the subsequent history of Abijah's reign (v. 20)?

How far did this victory show its effect in Asa's reign (14:1)? What was his religious character (vv. 2-5)? For certain qualifications of these words compare the latter half of chapter 16. The statement in verse eight is to be taken in our sense of militia rather than a standing army. Great as was this force, what could it have accomplished against the Ethiopians (v. 9) but for God (vv. 11-14)? Which of his successors does Asa, in his faith, suggest? How is he further encouraged (15:1, 2)?

Note the story of a typical revival. Its need appears in verses 3-6, a people without God in the sense that they were without the teaching of His Word in power (v. 3), and therefore without peace (v. 5) and in affliction (v. 6). Its progress is set before us in verse eight — courage, repentance, prayers. Its results (vv. 9-15)—the gathering of the people (vv. 9, 10), their offerings (v. 11), renewal of their convenant (v. 13), joy and peace (v. 15). Its cause is revealed in the opening of the chapter as (1) the Spirit of God (2) the man of God, (3) the Word of God, (4) the work of God (vv. 1, 2 and 7). O, that history would repeat itself in our day; or rather that God would once more pour out His Holy Spirit upon some prophet through whom His word would have potency as of old!

It is a mystery that Asa with

such an experience should act as in chapter 16, except as we recognize the same inconsistency in ourselves. Sin makes fools of us all. As there is some confusion in the chronology here, however, it is uncertain just when this even occurred. (Compare verse one with 1 Kings 15:33.)

It is not a sin in itself to seek a physician's aid (v. 12), but an Egyptian physician such as Asa consulted doubtless used demoniacal charms and incantations forbidden by the law of God. It is the same now. An honest physician who heals in accordance with the well understood principles of therapy may be consulted by any Christian without sin; but it is different with a "New Thought" healer, a palmist, a hypnotist, a spiritualist, a Christian Scientist, or other practitioner whose underlying philosophy is paganish and contrary to the Gospel.

The "very great burning" (v. 14) is supposed to refer to the cremation of the corpse, a custom which prevailed at that time among the Hebrews (compare 21:19, also 1 Samuel 31:12, Jer. 34:5 and Amos 6:10).

3. Jehoshaphat, cc. 17-20.

The story of this reign opens with the customary characterization of the king, which as we know from the book of Kings, was commendable, resulting in the divine blessing (17:1-6). But in verses 7 to 11 something of special interest is recorded. The word "to" before each of the names should be omitted, for it was the princes themselves who were sent on this godly mission— "the first practical measure adopted by any of the kings for the religious instruction of the people." No wonder such consequences should have resulted (vv. 10, 11). Here is the secret for a revival, viz: the instruction of the people in the Bible by the best men in the church. This is worth tons of sermons on civic righteousness and reforms, and no end of so-called evangelistic campaigns," and religious "movements," which have so much of man in them and so little of God.

Verses 12-19 show that no monarch since Solomon equaled Jehoshaphat "in the extent of his revenue, the strength of his fortifications and the number of his troops." It pays to serve God.

Chapter 18 is the same as 1 Kings 22, which we considered in its place, commenting on the lapse it indicates. This lapse met its rebuke (19:2) and its punishment (c. 20). Note in the meantime 19:4, comparing again 17:7-11. And do not overlook 19:5-7. Judicial courts had been established earlier but here they are localized in the fenced cities. What a charge to the judges! It will be heard again when He comes who shall judge the people righteously! Verses 8-11 refer to a kind of supreme court established at Jerusalem.

Chapter 20 brings us face to face with a crisis in Judah (vv. 1, 2). How is it met by this pious king (vv. 3, 4)? Study the prayer, observing its argumentative character ending in an appeal (vv. 5-12). God loves to be thus argued with on the ground of His promises. Many such instances will be found later in the prophets. Compare Abraham (Gen. 18), and Moses (Exod. 32).

Questions.

1. How does chapter 10 illustrate the dogma referred to in the lesson?

2. Why did Rehoboam deal with his sons as recorded?

3. How may we account, humanly speaking, for Rehoboam's infidelity?

4. How does archaeological research corroborate the truth of any part of this lesson?

5. What, in general terms, was the character of Asa's reign?

6. How would you explain 16:12?

7. What religious instruction was adopted by Jehoshaphat, and what has it to teach us?

8. How does Jehoshaphat's reign show that it pays to serve God?

9. What lessons in prayer may be gathered from it?

JEHORAM TO HEZEKIAH

CHAPTERS 21-32

1. Jehoram, c. 21.

Jehoshaphat followed Rehoboam's example in arranging for his sons (v. 3), but without the hoped-for result (v. 4). Such a brother as Jehoram proved might be expected to act in his kingly capacity as verses five to seven testify. "Elijah" (v. 12) may be mistaken of the transcribers for "Elisha," as the former died earlier (2 Kings 2); unless we take the view in the margin that this was a "writing" he left behind him. For the fulfillment of this "writing" read the rest of the chapter. We had a much fuller account of this reign in 2 Kings.

2. Ahaziah, c. 22.

This king is called "Jehoahaz" in the preceding chapter (v. 17). The peculiarity in the figures (22:2) was noticed in 2 Kings 8:26, and the fact that his mother was the grand-daughter of Omri (v. 2). Note her influence (v. 3) like that of the mother of what other king recently considered?

In the story of verses five to nine, it is of interest to know that archaeological research has found the names of Hazael and Jehu on the Assyrian sculptures.

Athaliah's motive (v. 10) may have been inspired partly by anger at the destruction of her own house of Ahab, partly by the necessity of self-defense against Jehu, and partly by pride and ambition, since if any of the young princes became king his mother would supersede her in power and dignity.

Verse 12 means that the priests and their families, some of them at least, were privileged to dwell in the buildings in the outer wall of the temple.

3. Joash, cc. 23, 24.

"Chief of the fathers of Israel" (23:2), means Judah and Benjamin only, the name usually employed in this book for all that remained of Israel. 2 Chronicles 24:15-22 has no parallel in Kings. It mentions the honor shown Jehoiada. Burial in cities, except Jerusalem, was prohibited, and in that case only allowed to kings. What request did the princes make to the king after the death of the faithful priest (v. 17)? Does the next verse indicate its character? And was the king himself guilty (v. 21)? Compare Matt. 23:29-35. In this last passage Christ speaks of the slain prophet as the son of Barachias instead of Jehoiada, but possibly he was the latter's grandson. In his death the prophet said: "The LORD shall see and require" (v. 22), and for the fulfillment of the warning read the chapter to the end.

4. Amaziah, c. 25.

This history is divided into three parts: (1) the general account of the reign, and its spirit, especially at the beginning (vv. 1-4); (2) the conquest of the Edomites (vv. 5-13); (3) the idolatry of the king and its punishment at the hands of Israel (vv. 14-28). The second of these events is given with detail not found in the earlier record, and is valuable for the reply of God's servant to the king (v. 9), the lesson of which should not be disregarded. The third event also contains new matter (vv. 14-16), which explains why the calamity of the following verses was permitted.

5. Uzziah, c. 26.

Two periods suggest themselves in this case, early obedience and prosperity (vv. 1-15), and then pride and punishment (vv. 16-23). A comparison of the record of the first period with 2 Kings 14 and 15 shows new matter illustrating Uzziah's prosperity, who is there called "Azariah." This latter name is that of the Assyrian inscriptions also. Do not let verse five escape. "He sought God in the days of Zechariah, who had understanding in the visions of God." How valuable the prophets in the history of God's people, and especially those who understand the visions of God! There is a difference in prophets. Some understand what others do not. How necessary, therefore, that the Scripture interpreter should fear the Lord that he may possess his secrets.

Uzziah desired to exercise regal and sacerdotal functions at the same time, as in the case of pagan kings and emperors, but which was contrary to the divine law (Ex. 30, Num. 18). For the sin, compare 1 Samuel 13, and the punishment, Numbers 12, 2 Kings 5.

6. Jotham and Ahaz, cc. 27, 28.

Of Jotham's reign little need be said except to call attention to the lesson in verse six. The story of Ahaz is divided into four parts: (1) his general character and reign (vv. 1-5); (2) the invasions by Syria and Israel (vv. 6-15); (3) the alliance with Assyria (vv. 16-21); (4) the summary (vv. 22-27).

There is much that is new as compared with Kings, but the prophetic intercession for Judah with their brethren of Israel is particularly interesting (vv. 9-15). Was it their power, or God's judicial sentence that caused Israel to be victorious (v. 9)? How had they abused their opportunity? What should make them cautious and merciful (v. 10)? Verses 12-15 accord with the parable of the Good Samaritan (Luke 10), and Christ may have drawn upon this episode.

Ahaz's alliance with Assyria is attested by the Assyrian monuments. In the summary of the close of his reign, what language (v. 24) indicates the suspension of the worship of God in his time?

7. Hezekiah, cc. 29-32.

After the beginning of Hezekiah's history, we have, in chapter 29, the cleansing and consecration of the temple. In 30, the great passover. In 31, the religious reforms following. In 32, Sennacherib's expedition, and Hezekiah's sickness and the close of the reign. In Kings the military and political side of the reign is given more fully, but not the inner religious and theocratic side, as we see by comparing chapters 29-31 with the introductory verses of 2 Kings 18.

Noting a few outstanding points, "all the uncleanness" (29:16) means probably the sacrificial vessels formerly employed in idolatry, and possibly the remains of idolatrous offerings. "Ye have filled your hand unto the Lord" (v. 31 margin), means they had consecrated themselves to God (Ex. 28:41) after offering the expiatory sacrifices which preceded such consecration. Keep in mind that God accepts nothing from us as either gift or service until He accepts us. And we can be accepted only on the ground of the expiatory sacrifice of Christ. Note the last word of this chapter in the light of its context. That is the way a revival comes. O, that God would now surprise us with one!

Why could they not keep the passover in the appointed first month (30:2-4)? Was a change ever permissible (Num. 9:6-13)? Note the breadth of the invitation (vv. 5-9), and the reception it met from Israel (vv. 10, 11). See the difficulty in the case of Judah and the cause of it (v. 12.) "Healed the people" (v. 20) means forgave their guilt. "That they might be encouraged (steadfast) in the law of the Lord" (31:4), means that they might live carefree while performing their official duties.

Note that Hezekiah was a man of prayer and faith, who did not neglect means (32:1-8). To understand "he repaid not, etc.," (v. 25), compare 2 Kings 20:12, etc. How disappointing this is in so good a man, and what a lesson it teaches as to the need of prayer and watchfulness to the end of our lives (v. 31).

Questions.

1. Count the fulfillments of prophecy in this lesson.

2. What warning for mothers is found in it?

3. How is it corroborated by archaeology?

4. How may Athaliah's conduct be explained?

5. Recite the story of the reign of Joash.

6. Name the divisions of chapter 25.

7. What was Uzziah's sin?

8. Where is the parable of the Good Samaritan suggested here?

9. What comes first in the divine order, salvation or consecration?

10. What lession is taught by the latter part of Hezekiah's life?

MANASSEH TO THE CAPTIVITY

CHAPTERS 30-36

1. Manasseh and Amon, c. 33.

The history of the first-named is divided into three parts: (1) the outline of his character and reign down to the crisis of this punishment (vv. 1-10) (2) his affliction and repentance in Babylon (vv. 11-13); (3) his later career and death (vv. 14-20). The first part was considered in Kings. For the reference to "groves" and "the host of heaven," compare Deut. 16:21 and 17:3. It was in such groves, and on the high hills, and under the trees, that the heathen were guilty of their idolatrous practices. As a comment on verse six turn to Deut. 18:9, etc. Verse seven is a forerunner of what we read of the Antichrist in Daniel 7-9, Matt. 24, 2 Thess. 2, Rev. 13, etc.

God is merciful and long-suffering, but without avail (v. 10). The Assyrian king was Esarhaddon, son and successor to Sennacherib. "Among thorns" may mean that Manasseh was hiding in such a thicket, but some versions have another Hebrew expression translated "among the living," as intended to show only that he was taken alive. His condition was humiliating indeed, hands manacled and ankles fastened together with rings and a bar.

Observe the process of his repentance — affliction, supplication, humility, mercy, spiritual apprehension, restoration, reformation, zeal, prosperity, (vv. 12-16). Here is a good outline for an expository discourse. It was some political motive that induced the Assyrian to restore him to his kingdom, perhaps to use him as an ally against Egypt, "but God overruled the measure for higher purposes."

The story of Amon calls for no comment.

2. Josiah, cc. 34, 35.

The first ten years of this reign (vv. 1-7) are distinguished by a reformation and revival more thorough than that of Manasseh, and suggesting the one under Hezekiah. The exact chronological order is not followed by the great facts as the same as in Kings. That a king of Judah should have such influence among the tribes of Israel, is explained by the fact that the captivity of the latter had taken place, and the remnant remaining in the land kept in touch with Judah as their protector (v. 6). "Mattocks" has been translated "deserts" and may mean the deserted localities or suburbs of these tribes.

The remainder of this chapter has been alluded to sufficiently in Kings.

The first half of 35 is the account of the great passover, the origin of which was treated in Exodus 12, but a few features call for attention here. For example, "the holy place" in this case, (v. 5), means the court of the priests where the animals for sacrifice were slain, and the people were admitted according to their families, several households at a time. The Levites stood in rows from the slaughtering places to the altar, passing the blood and fat from one to another of the officiating priests. — *Bible Commentary*. The Levites, both here and at Hezekiah's passover, did more than the law, strictly interpreted, authorized them to do, but the peculiar conditions in each case justified the liberty. The singers (v. 15) were chanting Psalms 113-118, and doubtless repeating them over and over as each group entered the holy place. The comparison with Samuel's passover (v. 18) suggests that of Hezekiah's, and Solomon's (30:26), the distinction being found in the terms on which the comparisons are based. One perhaps on the grandeur of the ceremonies, and the other on the ardor of the people.

In the story of Josiah's death (vv. 20-27), we repeat what was said in Kings. Egypt and Assyria are rivals for world power, and Palestine is the buffer between them. Judah is Assyria's vassal, and it is Josiah's duty to oppose her enemy's advances. The "valley of Megiddo" is identical with the plain of Esdraelon of which we shall hear later. Necho's reference to God's command (v. 21) may not mean Jehovah, but some false god of Egypt, and yet verse 22 raises a doubt about it. For this reason, some think Jeremiah, who was a contemporaneous prophet in Judah, may have communicated such a revelation to the Egyptian king. If so, it adds a new cause for Josiah's death, for if the prophet revealed it to Necho, he would hardly have kept it a secret from Josiah.

Jeremiah's lamentation is not recorded (v. 25) except as it may be found unidentified in his book of Lamentations. The event is thought to be again referred to in Zechariah 12:11.

3. Jehoahaz, c. 36:1-4.

This was the popular choice to succeed Josiah, but being his younger son, there was a question of its legitimacy, which may explain, in part, his removal by the king of Egypt and the substitution of his older brother. His reign was short, and as we learn from 2 Kings 23:32, it was also wicked.

4. Jehoiakim, vv. 5-8.

His brother was no improvement (compare Jer. 22:13-19). At first the vassal of Egypt, he subsequently sustained the same relationship to Babylon, which had now become the head of the Assyrian empire, and had finally driven the Egyptians out of Asia. Rebelling against Babylon later on, the latter punished him (vv. 6, 7). Daniel was taken captive at this time (Dan. 1:1-6). Jehoiakim himself was not taken pris-

oner however, although that seems to have been Nebuchadnezzar's original intention. Compare with verse six, 2 Kings 24:2-7, Jeremiah as above, and also 36:30).

5. Jeholachin, vv. 9, 10.

This king is "Coniah" and "Jeconiah" in Jeremiah (cc. 22, 23), and according to 2 Kings 24:8, was eighteen years old instead of eight when he began to reign. This age seems corroborated by what our lesson says of him (v. 9). Compare also Ezekiel 19:1-9. "When the year was expired" (v. 10), means when the spring had come, and its opportunity for military campaigning.

6. Zedekiah, vv. 11-21.

As we know from Kings, Zedekiah was not the brother, but the uncle of his predecessor, but called the first-named in accordance with the Hebrew latitude in speaking of family relationships. Note the distinction given a prophet of God, implying both inspiration and authority (v. 12). Note carefully verse 21. We learnt in the Pentateuch that every seventh year in Israel was to be a sacred rest unto the Lord, the land itself was to lie fallow. But the greed of the people had disregarded this law, and now they were to pay the penalty as per Leviticus 26:33-35. Judah, providentially, was not colonized by other peoples, as was Israel, so that at the close of seventy years there might be a return (Jer. 25:12, 13).

This book concludes with an account of that return (vv. 22, 23), showing, in so far, that it was written after that event. The story of the return comes before us in detail in Ezra.

Questions.

1. Give in outline Manasseh's history.

2. How does he become a type of the Antichrist?

3. Who succeeded Sennacherib in Assyria?

4. How do you explain Josiah's influence in Israel as well as Judah?

5. What are the Passover psalms?

6. Name four great passovers of the people after entering Canaan.

7. What testifies to the people's love for Josiah?

8. Name Judah's kings, and give their relationship, from Manasseh to the captivity.

9. What hint is given in this book that it was written after that event?

EZRA

BACK TO THE HOMELAND

Chapters 1-6

1. Cyrus' Proclamation, c. 1.

Babylon has had its day, and with its downfall has come that of the Assyrian Empire. The Medes and Persians, with Cyrus at their head, are now in power, and in the providence of God, Daniel, the Jewish prophet and statesman, has influence at his court, as in that of Nebuchadnezzar. By a study of the earlier prophets, especially Jeremiah, he has become aware that the time is nigh for the captivity of Judah to end and his people to return to their land (Dan. 9:1, 2; Jer. 25:12-14). He knows, also, that two hundred years earlier, Isaiah had, by the Holy Spirit, mentioned Cyrus as the monarch by whose ukase this return would be brought about (Isa. cc. 44, 45).

Doubtless he told these things to Cyrus who issues this proclamation (v. 1) not from any intelligent desire to please Jehovah, but for political reasons. Nevertheless, thus is fulfilled again Romans 8:28.

The words of Cyrus (v. 2) are not merely oriental hyperbole, as we may judge by Jeremiah 27 and Daniel 2. It is anticipating too much to enter on these prophets now, further than to say that the dominion they speak of as divinely entrusted to Nebuchadnezzar and Babylon, was to be transferred to their successor down to the end of this age. Of these successors Cyrus and the Persians were the first.

"Sheshbazzar" (v. 8) is the Persian name for Zerubbabel (3:8; 5-16), who, though born in exile, was recognized as heir to the throne of Judah.

2. Zerubbabel's Company, c. 2.

"Province" (v. 1) refers to Judah, and indicates that it is no longer an independent kingdom, but a dependency of Persia. "Children" is not to be taken in the sense of little ones, but that of descendants or posterity. "Tirshatha" (v. 63) means "Governor."

Verse 64 says: "The whole congregation, together, was forty-two thousand three hundred and threescore." This amount is 12,000 more than the numbers when added together. Reckoning up the smaller numbers we find they amount to 29,818, in this chapter, and to 31,089 in the parallel chapter of Nehemiah. Ezra also mentions 494 persons omitted by Nehemiah, and Nehemiah mentions 1,765 not noticed by Ezra. If, therefore, Ezra's surplus be added to Nehemiah, and Nehemiah's to Ezra, they will both become 31,583. Subtracting this from 42,360, there will be a deficiency of 10,777. These are omitted because they did not belong to Judah and Benjamin or to the priests, but to the other tribes. The servants and singers are reckoned separately (v. 65), so that putting all these items together, the number of all who went with Zerubbabel amounted to 50,000 with 8,000 beasts of burden. [Davidson.]

3. The Altar and the Temple, c. 3.

The seventh month (v. 1) corresponds to our Sept. 15-Oct. 15, and was the time of the Feast of Tabernacles (Lev. 23). Jeshua (v. 2) was the hereditary high priest. "His (or its) bases" (v. 3) means the old foundations of the altar. After the altar which was necessary to be built first in order to sacrifice unto the Lord, the foundations of the temple begin to be laid (vv. 8-11). The sorrow of the older men (v. 12) was caused by the contrast between the prosperous circumstances under which Solomon's temple had been built, and those of the present. This second temple would be inferior in size and costliness, and destitute of the Ark, the Shekinah, the Urim and Thummim, and other features which contributed to the glory of the first temple. Read Haggai in this connection.

4. Adversaries, c. 4.

In verse one "Judah and Benjamin," and "the children of the captivity" are identical. "The adversaries," were the people settled in the land of Israel by the Assyrians after the captivity of the ten tribes. They intermarried with the Israelites who had been left behind, and their offspring went under the general name of Samaritans. Originally they were idolaters, but having received some instruction in the knowledge of the true God they claimed to be worshipping Him, though of course, in an ignorant and superstitious way. (Compare 2 Kings 17:24-41).

The refusal of their co-operation by the Jews was proper, but it brought serious and prolonged trouble to them (vv. 4, 5). (Compare John 4:9).

The nature of this trouble is shown in verse six, where "Ahasuerus" as commonly understood, is another name for the famous Xerxes king of Persia, although Anstey maintains that he is identical with Darius Hystaspes. The conspirators continued in the next reign also (vv. 7-16). "The great and noble Asnapper" (v. 10) is another name for Esar-Haddon, met with before, who transported these foreigners into the waste cities of Samaria after the captivity of Israel. The result of their efforts is shown in verses 23 and 24. "Darius" is sometimes known as "Darius Hystaspes," and was the second of that name since Cyrus. The work ceased for about fifteen years.

5. Renewal of the Work, cc. 5, 6.

Do not omit to read Zechariah at this point, and observe the effect of his words, heaven-endued, upon the leaders (vv. 1, 2). The men of verse three, like those of chapter four, verses seven and eight, were satraps or viceroys of Persia set over provinces in proximity to Judah, who felt it their duty thus to inquire and protest. Verse four

seems a mistranslation, and probably means that they inquired of the Jews instead of the reverse (see v. 10).

The Darius of chapter five acted differently from any of his predecessors. "Achmetha" (v. 2) is better known as "Ecbatana," the summer residence of the early kings of Persia. The work of the temple may proceed (v. 7), the Persian satraps are to assist (vv. 8-10), penalties are to follow interference (vv. 11, 12), and henceforth the turbulent Samaritans had better take care!

The work is ended (v. 15). Dr. Lightfoot says the foundation was laid April, 536 B. C., and the completion accomplished February 21, 515 B. C. The dedicatory feast is held with joy. Note the explanatory reason (v. 22). God receives the glory.

Questions.

1. What world-empire succeeded the Assyrian or Babylonian?

2. What prophet is used of God for the return of His people to Palestine?

3. Have you read Isaiah 44 and 45?

4. Are you familiar with Daniel 2?

5. What distinction belonged to Zerubbabel?

6. How many people of all classes returned in the first company?

7. What was the first religious work they set about?

8. What prophets, whose written works have come down to us, belong to this period?

9. Give the history of the Samaritans, so-called.

10. How many kings of Persia were named "Darius"?

EZRA AND HIS REFORMS

CHAPTERS 7-10

1. The Commission and Its Execution, cc. 7, 8.

The first of these chapters tells who Ezra was (vv. 1-6), the date and object of his journey to Jerusalem (vv. 7-10), the nature and extent of his commission from the king (vv. 11-26), and his feelings in the premises (vv. 27-28). The second, gives the number and genealogic record of the Jews who accompanied him (vv. 1-20), the spirit in which they entered upon the pilgrimage (vv. 21-23), the arrangements for guarding and delivering the treasurer in their keeping (vv. 24-30), their arrival and the fulfillment of their commission (vv. 31-36).

To consider chapter seven in detail, the Artaxerxes of verse one is considered as identical with the Ahasuerus of Esther's time, and Anstey regards him as identical also with the Darius Hystaspes named above. Ezra was a priest as well as a scribe (vv. 1-5). The "Seraiah" whose son (great grandson perhaps) he was, was the high priest slain by Nebuchadnezzar (2 Kings 25:18). Jeshua, with whom we got acquainted in the last lesson, was also his grandson, but probably in another branch of the family. "Scribe" is the same as doctor, teacher, or rabbi, one learned in the law of Moses and Jewish traditions and cutoms (v. 10).

How this Persian king came to be so interested is not known, unless, as some think, Esther had already become his queen, which would explain it. Others believe that after the death of the leaders of the earlier company, Zerubbabel and his associates, matters became so disordered in the province that leading Jews in Persia pleaded with the king to appoint this reform commission.

Observe the power granted Ezra to study conditions, as we now say (v. 14), to collect funds (vv. 15, 16), levy tribute (vv. 21, 22), appoint magistrates and judges (v. 25), and execute penalties (v. 26).

As to chapter 8, the number of male adults accompanying Ezra was but 1,754, but there should be added women, children and servants, making perhaps three or four times that number. Attention is called to verses 21 and 23. The danger of such caravans from the marauding Arabs was so great as to make a military escort necessary. But Ezra's sensitive regard for God's honor before the heathen would not permit his asking for one. It was a strong test of faith to which he and his companions were equal, and which God honored. May the principle of its lesson not be lost upon the reader.

2. Internal Conditions and How They Were Changed, cc. 9, 10.

This moral corruption (9:1, 2) is not inconceivable to those who know their own hearts and the nature of sin, but its effect on Ezra was what might have been expected under the circumstances (v. 3). His outward signs of grief were oriental. There is contagion in such grief which communicates itself to others animated by a like spirit (v. 4). It is thus revival spreads. One soul is awakened, and he awakens another. And if he be a pastor or leader of the Lord's hosts, like Ezra, the people gather round him, and results follow (9:4; 10:1-44).

Study the prayer carefully (vv. 5-15). The suppliant's attitude (v. 5), his sense of shame (v. 6), his unqualified confession (v. 7), his gratitude (vv. 8, 9), his deep conviction of sin (vv. 10-14), and his dependency only on divine mercy (v. 15).

Observe how God answered the prayer by graciously working on the people's hearts, the leaders first, and then the people generally. Shecanaiah (10:2), was a brave man in the attitude he took, for while his name does not appear in the subsequent list of offenders, yet those of his near relatives do (v. 26). Note the phrase (v. 2): "There is hope in Israel concerning this thing." Hope only, however, along the line of thorough repentance. Here is a text and subject-matter for a revival sermon.

Note the radical step taken by the leaders (v. 6-8), and its prompt result procedure as necessitated by the circumstances (vv. 10-17). This justifies the belief that provision was made for the unlawful wives and children that were put away.

Questions.

1. Have you familiarized yourself with the Persian kings of this period?
2. Who was Ezra?
3. What is a "scribe"?
4. How many were in Ezra's company of returning exiles?
5. How was their strong faith shown?
6. What illustration of the progress of a revival is found in this lesson?
7. What feature of Ezra's prayer most impresses you?

NEHEMIAH

BUILDING THE WALLS

Chapters 1-6

1. Prayer and Its Answer, cc. 1-2:8.

In this book it is to be kept in mind that the previous commissions to Zerubbabel and Ezra concerned only the repair of the temple at Jerusalem, and certain internal arrangements for the moral and material well-being of the people in their home towns. The walls and gates of the city, however, were still in the ruined condition in which they were left by Nebuchadnezzer after the siege. The consequences of this were detrimental to the people's peace, for such protection was practically their only defence against assaulting enemies.

Chislev was an early winter month. Shushan was the winter, as Ecbatana was the summer palace, of the Persian monarchs. Hanani may have been simply a relative, as we have seen how loosely these kinships are referred to (1:1, 2).

Nehemiah, though nothing more is stated of him, is likely to have been like Zerubbabel, of the royal family of David, and certainly he was a great patriot. Study his prayer carefully (vv. 4-11). Notice its deep earnestness (v. 4), unselfishness (v. 6), humility (vv. 6,7), faith (vv. 8, 9) and definiteness (v. 11). A cup-bearer to an oriental potentate (v. 12) held a confidental and influential office, affording him frequent access to his presence. At the meal he presented the cup of wine to the king, and since the likelihood of its being poisoned was ever present, he must be one in whom the greatest trust was reposed. Not infrequently, as a precautionary measure, the cup-bearer must first taste the wine in the king's presence before presenting it.

Four months elapsed between chapters one and two, though the cause is unknown. Nisan (2:1) was in the Spring. It awakened suspicion to appear before majesty with a sad countenance (v. 2), but in this case it gave Nehemiah his opportunity (vv. 3-8). The queen may have been Esther, though it is uncertain. God receives the glory (v. 8).

2. Progress of the Work, cc. 2:9-3:32.

"Beyond the river" means east of the Euphrates. "Governors" were in charge of the Persian dependencies in proximity to Judah (v. 9). "Horonite" seems to refer to a Moabitish town of that name. The Amonite "Tobiah the servant" may mean that he was a freed slave elevated to official dignity. Nehemiah enters on his task by a night survey of the ruins (vv. 12-16). Then he addresses the leaders, stirring them by his example and information about the king's commission (vv. 17, 18). The opponents (v. 19) were doubtless supporters or leaders of the Samaritans, met with in Ezra.

The priests take the lead in the work (3:1). The residents of Jericho have a section assigned them (v. 2), and other great families follow to the end of the chapter. Their names are recorded because the work was one not only of patriotism, but godly devotion, calling for faith, courage, and self-sacrifice.

3. Hindrances, cc. 4-6.

Ridicule was the first form the hindrances took (vv. 1-6), but Nehemiah made his appeal to God and continued the work until the wall was built "half the height" (R. V.). If his language in prayer seems harsh, recall what we have learned about Israel's position as God's witness and instrument in blessing the world. To frustrate her is to frustrate God, and work the sorest injury to human kind. These enemies are not personal to Nehemiah, but the enemies of God and of all the earth. Moreover, Nehemiah himself is not undertaking to visit punishment upon them, but committing them to God who doeth righteously.

Physical force was the next form of hindrance (vv. 7-23), but Nehemiah provided against it by day and night watches (v. 9), by arming the workmen (v. 13), and by detaining them all in Jerusalem (v. 22).

The hindrance of chapter five was not the same as the others, and did not arise from the outside, but it was a hindrance, nevertheless, that must have greatly weakened their hands (vv. 1-5). Nehemiah's action was bold and efficient. An assembly was called (v. 7), his own example cited (vv. 8-10), an appeal made (v. 11), a solemn agreement effected (vv. 12, 13). The verses following testify to the wealth of Nehemiah as well as his unselfish patriotism. Not only declining the emoluments of his office, he maintained an expensive establishment for the public good, and this for twelve years (v. 14). He appears self-righteous (v. 19), but he was not living in the Gospel dispensation.

In chapter six the external enemies once more come into view, whose policy has changed from ridicule and force to crafty diplomacy (vv. 1-4) with threats superadded (vv. 5-9). Nor are there wanting traitors within his own camp who seek Nehemiah's ruin, but in vain (vv. 10-15). Notice the intended disrespect in the "open" letter, which, in the case of so distinguished an official as Nehemiah (v. 5), should have been sealed, after the Persian custom. These were indeed "troublous times" (Dan. 9:25), but the man for the times had arrived.

Questions.

1. What material feature distinguishes the periods of the two books, Ezra and Nehemiah?

2. What is the meaning of "cupbearer"?

3. What outstanding features mark the character of Nehemiah?

4. What is the geographical designation of the enemies of Judah?

5. Name the three classes of hindrances emanating from them.

6. What were the hindrances of an internal character?

7. How long was the work in progress?

INTERNAL REGULATIONS

Chapters 7-13

1. A New Genealogical Record, c. 7.

The need for this assignment of duty to the two men named (v. 2), is not apparent unless Nehemiah contemplated a return to Persia. Later it will be seen that such return took place, but whether at this time or not, is not clear. To "fear God above many," as Hananiah did, is a great commendation. It was customary to open the gates of a city at sunrise, but to do so in this case before the inhabitants were well awake and stirring, might put them at a disadvantage before their enemies (v. 3). The new walls were built on the old foundations, but the city they enclosed did not as yet hold the old population, which explains verse four.

The genealogical record (v. 5) was doubtless that of Zerubbabel's day recorded in the book of Ezra, and if some differences are discovered between this and that, they may be accounted for by the different circumstances in the two cases. The first was prepared at Babylon and this in Judea, with almost a century intervening. Of course a particular object of this record was the purification of the priestly and Levitical line with reference to the temple service.

2. A Spiritual Revival, cc. 8-10.

It was in the seventh month (7:73), at the feast of tabernacles, that the stirring event of this chapter occurred. Ezra is in Jerusalem still, though during Nehemiah's governorship he has not been at the forefront. It may be that his time has been spent in preparing that edition of the Old Testament which has been associated with his name. His great usefulness is seen at this juncture

(vv. 1-8). Here is a great open-air meeting, and the Word of God has the place of honor. It is simply read and explained to the people, but as usual with mighty results. Behold the blessing which comes to a people when to a faithful ministry is added a godly ruler (vv. 8-15). Pastors will appreciate a good text for Thanksgiving Day in verse 10. There is nothing which brings such joy to people as a knowledge of God's Word, and nothing that makes them so practically mindful of others.

This feast proves a "protracted meeting", and is followed by a fast and other evidences of repentance (v. 9). Between the morning and evening sacrifices they devoted three hours to the Scriptures and three hours to prayer. Read the prayer carefully, which seems to have been uttered by the Levites on the "stairs," or pulpits, erected for the purpose, in the open. Perhaps we have here only the substance of the prayers, or it may be that Ezra prepared a general prayer for all to use. Notice the pathos of verses 36 and 37, and the covenant in which the proceeding ended (v. 38 and 10:1-39).

The points of this covenant are interesting. They bind themselves to abstain from heathen marriages (v. 30), to observe the Sabbath, to give the land its seventh year rest, and remit debts in that year (v. 31), maintain the temple service and support the priests (vv. 32-39).

3. A Patriotic Precaution, cc. 11, 12.

This measure (vv. 1, 2) was necessary to insure a proper guard for the capital. And as it involved danger and self-sacrifice on the part of the drafted ones they merited the public gratitude. Their names follow, and include the "Nethinim," a designation difficult to determine, but supposed to mean the descendants of the Gibeonites of Joshua's time, who were constrained to be hewers of wood and drawers of water. In any event they were men of humble rank in the service of the sanctuary. Various editorial comments occur in this chapter whose elucidation, in the lapse of time, is not easy. Some of these are the "second over the city" (v. 9), "ruler of the house of God" (v. 11), "the outward business" (v. 17), referring in general terms to assistants of the priests, collectors of provisions, leaders of the choirs, etc.

We may include in this division the dedication of the wall (12:27-47), in which the leaders, accompanied by the singers and people from all parts of the land marched around it, pausing at different points for praise and prayer, and the presentation of sacrifices. Some idea of the religious hilarity of the occasion may be gathered from verse 43. The explanation of verse 45 seems to be that the officials named saw that no persons ceremonially unclean entered the temple. This was the duty of the porters ordinarily (2 Chron. 23:19), but on special occasions singers were called on to assist.

4. A Moral House-Cleaning, c. 13.

Nehemiah has reported at the Persian court and again, after an unknown period, returned to Jerusalem (v. 6), and finding there great laxity in regard to the temple service, Sabbath observance, and heathen marriages, all of which he vigorously reforms. Eliashib's offense is the more reprehensible because of his sacred office (vv. 4, 5)—turning the house of God into a palace for the entertainment of his heathen relatives. It was to be expected that such conduct of the high priest would affect the people as shown in the verses following (10-14). When, however, the worship of God is neglected, his laws are generally dishonored (vv. 15-18). Note Nehemiah's decisive action in this case (vv. 19-22), and the pattern it affords for modern executives. There is this difference, however, that Nehemiah was an official over a people who had a fear of God in their hearts. Our executives serve a democracy where the people themselves are esteemed as the highest authority. "How far will the people sustain us?" is the question before their eyes in the performance of duty, and the execution of the laws. No wonder that their actions are often marked by timidity and insincerity. It will be only in the millennial age, which may God hasten, that conditions will produce and maintain governors of Nehemiah's type. Verse 25 shows that he was not influenced by the sentimentalism of these times to substitute reformatory measures in the place of punishment for wrong-doing.

Questions.

1. What was the commendation of Hananiah?

2. What explains the particularity as to genealogical records?

3. What may have been Ezra's great task at this period?

4. Tell the story of the revival of this period in your own words.

5. Who probably, were the Nethinim?

6. What three reforms are entered upon after Nehemiah's return from Persia?

7. What hinders executives such as he, today?

ESTHER

THE JEWS IMPERILLED

CHAPTERS 1-7

The events of this book belong chronologically after Zerubbabel's company have gone up to Jerusalem, and before the commissions of Ezra and Nehemiah. The scene is laid in Persia. Cyrus and Darius I have passed away, and Ahasuerus, son of the last named, and identified by some with Xerxes, and by others with Darius Hystaspes, is on the throne. He is a sensual, fickle, cruel despot. It was his great fleet that was defeated by the much smaller one of Greece at Salamis, about 480 B. C. He is mentioned in Ezra 4:6. He was succeeded by his son Artaxerxes, who figures in the later chapters of Ezra and Nehemiah.

The story of the book is well known, and may be divided as follows:

Queen Vashti's Fall, 1:1-22.
Esther's Exaltation, 2:1-23.
Haman's Conspiracy, 3:1-15.
Esther's Intervention, 4:1-7:10.
Haman's Judgment, 8:1-9:19.
The Commemorative Feast, 9:20-32.
The Epilog, 10:1-3.

1. Queen Vashti's Fall, c. 1:1-22.

Some think this feast (v. 3) was the occasion when the great campaign against Greece was determined upon. If a half-year seems long (v. 4), perhaps the time was extended to allow the different nobles and princes to "make their appearance at the court successively." The climax was the "garden party" of a week (vv. 5-7), although it should be understood that only men were present (v. 9). Verse eight seems to mean that in contrast with the customary excessive drinking, any were free to remain sober if they would. "Knew the times" (v. 13) is equivalent to "Skilled in the law."

2. Esther Exalted, c. 2:1-23.

When sober, the king ruled his action (v. 1), but had he changed his mind and restored Vashti, the consequences would have been serious to his advisers, hence their present counsel (vv. 2-4). "Things for purification" (v. 3) mean the oils for cleansing and anointing (v. 12). "She required nothing, etc." (v. 15), points to a desire of the virgins on similar occasions to bedeck themselves with ornaments, but Esther acted differently on the chamberlains advice, and with good results (v. 17). Note the expiration of four years between 1:3 and 2:7, which some think was occupied by the expedition against Greece, and for which secular history gives some justification. The incident of verses 21-23 is recorded here to explain that which follows later.

3. Haman's Conspiracy, c. 3:1-15.

The casting of the lot (Hebrew "Pur," v. 7), was for the purpose of selecting the most propitious day for the murderous undertaking Haman had in mind. While an idea as in verses six and nine would never occur to a revengeful man, it was different in the East. Massacres of a race, or a class, have at all times been among the incidents of history there. A great massacre of the Magi occurred only about fifty years before this, and a massacre of the Scythians fifty years before that again. The 10,000 talents (v. 9), or as some calculate it $12,500,000 of our money, was to be obtained by the confiscation of the Jews' property.

4. Esther's Intervention, c. 4:1-7:10.

It would appear by a comparison of verses 12 and 13 of the preceding chapter, that the Jews were for a whole year harassed because of their impending fate. This explains the opening verses of the present chapter (4: 1-3). Observe Mordecai's reliance on the promises of God concerning Israel (v. 14). They can not all be destroyed. God would not permit it, for it would defeat His purpose concerning the Messiah, the Redeemer of the world, and all else that was included in that purpose. Esther's request to fast is a call to repentance and a request for prayer (compare 1 Kings 21:27-29, Joel 1:14, and Jonah 3:5). Her boldness is seen in the following: She proposed to go to the king without being called; to make request for the change of a law which, according to Persian custom, could not be done; to reveal herself as a Jew; to place herself in opposition to the all-powerful favorite, Haman.

Rawlinson says the usual situation of the throne in the throneroom of an oriental palace, is one from which the monarch can see into the court through the doorway opposite to him (v. 1). Esther's tactful delay in making known her request (vv. 7, 8), was doubtless to further impress the king, or possibly to evolve her plan, which may not yet have been clear in her own mind.

God's hand is seen clearly in 6:1, which, compare with 2:23. The dramatic incidents of the chapter tell their own story as they swiftly pass before us. In 7:3, Esther's words are to be understood as offering her own life in the place of the people. The loss of the people would be a great damage to the king (v. 4). In the East at banquets they recline on couches (v. 8).

Questions.

1. What chronological place is occupied by this book?
2. Give some historical data of the king.
3. What great historical event may have intervened between the fall of the one queen and the exaltation of the other?
4. What does "Pur" mean?
5. Name some great massacres of this general period.
6. What shows Mordecai's faith?
7. What shows Esther's courage?
8. Give an illustration of the special providence of God in this lesson.

DELIVERANCE COMES

Chapters 8-10

1. The King's Decree, c. 8.

The "house" of Haman meant his possessions (8:1). His death, however, and Mordecai's distinction did not mean that the decree against the Jews had been annulled, which, indeed, could not be annulled, according to Persian law. This is the problem, now before Esther and Mordecai (vv. 3-6), and which the king solves by granting permission to the Jews to arm themselves against their executioners (vv. 8-11).

The effect of this measure on the Jews was what might have been expected (vv. 15-17). The meaning of the last sentence of the chapter is illuminated by Exodus 15:16 and Deuteronomy 11:25. The Persians felt that the God of the Jews was ruling over their destiny in a peculiar way.

2. The Heathen Massacre, c. 9:1-15.

The first part of this chapter records the successful stand made by the Jews against those who ventured to oppose them, and demonstrates that the God of their fathers was still their God. It reads like a chapter in Judges or Kings.

Rawlinson calls attention to the importance of verse three as bearing on verse 16. That the Jews should have been allowed to slay 75,000 Persians has been pronounced incredible, but it is not so when we see that the leaders of the nation took their side. The probability is, however that the slain were people of other, subject nations, for whom the Persians did not particularly care.

How does verse 10 show that the Jews' motive was not avarice but self-defense? The king's inquiry and Esther's reply (vv. 12, 13) indicate that danger still threatened the Jews in Shushan at least, unless further measures were taken. Haman's sons were to be hanged after death. "Hanged" here really means

"crucified," which was the Hebrew and Persian custom.

3. The Feast of Purim, vv. 16-32.

It seems that the Jews outside
of Shushan celebrated on the
fourteenth of Adar, but those
within could not do so for obvious reasons till the fifteenth. This
gave rise to different memorial
days until Mordecai settled the
matter as in verse 21. The whole
writing of Mordecai here spoken
of (vv. 20-25) may have included
the substance of the book we are
considering. Nevertheless a second document by Esther herself
seems to have been necessary to
finally determine the perpetuity of
the feast (vv. 28-32). The feast
is still kept by the Jews, proving the
authenticity of this book.

Mordecai's Greatness, c. 10.

The greatness of the Persian
king (v. 1) reflects on Mordecai
(v. 2), who is recognized even in
the kingly chronicles, and whose
exalted privilege becomes a benefit to all his race in Persia (v. 3).

Questions.

1. To what tribe and family
did Mordecai belong (2:5)?

2. What is Haman called
(3:5)?

3. What correspondence do
you see between the above and
what is recorded in 1 Samuel 15?

4. Have you compared the
passages of the Pentateuch
named in this lesson?

5. Why is the feast called
"Purim"?

6. Who may have been the author of this book?

7. How is its authenticity attested?

JOB

THEME AND OUTLINE OF THE BOOK

CHAPTERS 1-3

The theme of Job seems to be the meaning and object of evil and suffering under the government of a holy, wise and merciful God, and may be outlined thus:

1. The prologue, 1-2 (in prose).
2. The dialogue, 3-31 (in poetry).
3. The words of Elihu, 32-37 (in poetry).
4. The words of the Almighty, 38-41 (in poetry).
5. The response of Job, 42:1-6 (in poetry).
6. The epilogue, 42:7-17 (in prose).

The Key to the Book

The key to the book is found in the first chapter, which, after an introductory testimony to Job, translates the reader to heavenly scenes (verse 6).

The "sons of God" are angelic beings bringing in their reports to God, the mystery being that Satan is found "also among them." How the prince of darkness is granted access to God is a question these lessons cannot discuss; but we accept the fact and draw certain inferences therefrom.

He is seen here in his scriptural attitude of the accuser of the brethren; and when God taunts him, if one may so say, with the uprightness of Job whom he has been unable to corrupt, he at once charges him with a mercenary spirit, and declares that if God were to take his temporal blessings away from him he would be as bad as the rest.

God accepts the challenge and puts His servant into the hands of Satan for a period, and for the exercise of a terrible but limited power, that it may be seen if the charge be true.

In other words, it is not Job so much who is on trial as God. It is not a question of Job's loyalty so much as one of God's power. Is the grace of God able to keep one of His servants faithful to Him, though he be stripped of everything which men count dear?

The outcome was victory for God, and discomfiture for Satan, under circumstances calculated to prove a great comfort to God's people in every generation. This thought is suggested by the prologue, and which, kept in mind, lightens up the whole book.

The Discussion.

The dialogue proceeds on the question whether great suffering such as Job's be not an evidence of great sin, Eliphaz, Bildad and Zophar affirming and Job denying. The dispute is carried on in a series of three acts, each containing three arguments of the "friends" and as many defenses by Job, until the last, when Zophar is silenced, and Job apparently triumphs.

Job's defense is based on two grounds, (1) the admitted prosperity of the wicked, chapter 21, and (2) his own personal righteousness, chapters 29 and 31.

It would seem at first that his friends intended to comfort him, but were driven to accusation by the caustic character of his replies, caused no doubt, by his intense suffering. Whether his friends were sincere or insincere at the beginning must be determined by the view taken of chapter four. It can be so read as to suggest either view.

The words of Elihu also suggest a series of three acts, out of which we gather that he rebuked both parties to the debate, the friends for their accusations, which were unwarranted in great measure, and Job for his self-righteousness, equally unwarranted (32:1-3). His philosophy of the sufferings differs from the others in that he believes they were sent for the good of the sufferer, see chapter 33:28-30. The first part of his speech is addressed to Job, chapters 32 and

33; the second to the three friends, chapter 34; and the last to Job, again, chapters 35-37. As he closes a thunder storm is gathering, whose description forms a grand climax to his address, and out of which

The Voice of the Almighty
is heard.

The discussion thus far had been confined to the mystery of evil, and the balance is now restored by considering the mystery of good which the Almighty reveals. It is notable that He gives no explanation of Job's suffering, renders no decision on the subject in debate, and offers no hint of compensation to His servant for what he has endured.

The pervading idea of His revelation is that of power, absolute sovereignty, as though His design were to overwhelm Job and effect his unconditional surrender. The crisis in Job's life was like that of Moses as he stood in the cleft of the rock (Exod. 33, 34), or Elijah at Horeb (1 Kings 19), or Paul on his way to Damascus (Acts 9), and the result in Job's case is not unlike that in their cases.

Meditation on the book leads to the conclusion that such experiences as those of Job, and they come to every true child of God, may be for discipline and to teach submission so vital to be learned, but also to serve a purpose far exceeding human knowledge, in the superhuman world. Compare John 9:3; 1 Cor. 4:9; Eph. 3:10; 1 Pet. 1:12. What a dignity such a thought adds to the suffering for righteousness' sake!

Questions.

1. What is the theme of Job?
2. What is its outline?
3. What seems to be the key of the book?
4. How does Elihu's philosophy of suffering differ from that of the others?
5. For what three purposes may such affliction come on any saint of God?
6. Concerning the last purpose named, have you examined the Scripture passages indicated?

LITERARY STYLE OF THE BOOK

We have spoken of Job as in the poetic style, and something should be said about that style as applying not only to Job, but to the other poetical books of the Old Testament like Psalms, Proverbs, Song of Solomon and Lamentations.

While these books are poetical, to English readers neither the sound of the words nor the form in which they are printed in the King James Version, would suggest that idea.

As to the form, the Revised Version is an improvement, though it leaves much to be desired. As to the sound, the rhythm of Hebrew poetry is not found in it but in the recurrence of the thought. "Thought may be rhythmic as well as sound or language, and the full force of Scripture is not grasped by one who does not feel how thoughts can be emphasized by being differently re-stated."

Literary Parallelisms.

The grand peculiarity of Hebrew poetry, however, is the parallelism, a form of composition somewhat artificial, but which consists in the repetition of the main thought, usually with some modification of it.

These parallelisms are three classes—the synonymous, the antithetic and the synthetic.

In the synonymous parallelism the second clause is scarcely more than a repetition of the first, although there are many varieties of it so far as the length of the members is concerned. A good illustration of this parallelism is found in Job 6:5—

Doth the wild ass bray over his grass?

Doth the ox low over his fodder?

The antithetic parallelism is one in which the idea in the second clause is the converse of that in the first, a simple form of which is Proverbs 10:1—

A wise son rejoiceth his father;
But a foolish son is the heaviness of his mother.

In the synthetic parallelism the poet instead of echoing the former sentiment or placing it in contrast, enforces his thought by accessory ideas and modifications. For example, a general proposition is stated and the sentiment is then dwelt upon in detail. A specimen is found in Job 3:3-5:

O that the day might have
    perished in which I was
    born,
And the night which said, "A
    male child is conceived."
Let that day be darkness,
Let not God inquire after it from
    on high
Yea, let not the light shine upon
    it!
Let darkness and the shadow of
    death stain it;
Let a cloud dwell upon it,
Let whatever darkens the day ter-
    rify it!

Questions.

1. In what is the rhythm of Hebrew poetry?
2. What is meant by a literary parallelism?
3. Name and define the three leading classes of parallelisms.

FIRST SERIES OF THE DEBATE

Chapters 4-14

The first series of the debate may be outlined as follows:*
(1) With Eliphaz, 4-7.
  (a) Speech of Eliphaz, 4, 5.
  (b) Reply of Job, 6, 7.
(2) With Bildad, 8-10.
  (a) Speech of Bildad, 8.
  (b) Reply of Job, 9, 10.
(3) With Zophar, 11-14.
  (a) Speech of Zophar, 11.
  (b) Reply of Job, 12-14.
It is thought the debate may have occupied several days, by which supposition some of the difficulties of the book are re-

moved. In the first place, this leads to the opinion that the addresses were not impromptu, but that each speaker had time for the composition of his finished utterances in reply to the one who went before him.

In the second place, it throws light on the authorship of the book, because all the author had to do was to prepare the introductory and concluding historical statements, and then collect and arrange the speeches that had been actually made. These speeches would be preserved in the memory, and the work of the editor would be rather that of a compiler than an original author, although he may have been as inspired for the one work as for the other.

The debate is occasioned by the complaints of Job recorded in chapter 3, and up to which time his friends had been silent.

Eliphaz and Job.

Eliphaz commences with delicacy and candor, showing the inconsistency of a good man's repining under discipline, and advances the position that the truly righteous are never overthrown, while the wicked are always dealt with according to their sins. He establishes his position by a vision, and while he does not apply all he has said to Job, he yet leaves no doubt that it was intended for him, advising him to turn to God that he may find happiness and come to an honored old age.

Job replies justifying himself for complaining. He wishes he might die. His friends have disappointed him. They are a deceitful brook, but if they would use reasonable arguments he would listen to them. He describes his sufferings as one pursued of God, exhibiting much impatience.

Bildad and Job.

Bildad, who is provokingly severe, replies in chapter 8. Job is wicked and his children have been cut off for their wickedness. He exhorts him to repent and enforces his exhortations by the opinions of other men.

Job's reply covers chapters 9 and 10, and being calm at first he acknowledges God's supremacy and admits his own imperfection. The arguments of his friends, however, cannot be defended. He referes to his sorrows again and complains that God treats him as if he were a guilty man. His excitement grows until he again expresses the desire for death.

Zophar and Job.

Zophar, like Bildad, is somewhat violent. In his eyes Job has no sense, whom he rebukes for seeking to maintain innocence before God. Zophar's language is magnificent when he treats of the supremacy of God, but like the previous speakers, he exhorts Job to acknowledge his sins that he may find prosperity and peace.

The debate is closed by Job, who groups his opponents and answers them as a whole. He is sarcastic. He follows their example in quoting a number of proverbial sayings. He attacks their motives. Their arguments were unsound. They were mocking God by defending His government in such a way as they had done. They had cause for fear and trembling in consequence of this. He wishes that he might present his case directly before God rather than the tribunal of man. He would ask of God only two things, that He would withdraw His hand from him and not overawe him by His great power. His calamities are overwhelming, and he concludes with a pathetic description of the frailty and uncertainty of human life.

Note to Teachers.

To those using these lessons in classes, the author recommends that they employ each reference to any of the speeches as a basis for a question or questions on the text of the chapter as follows:

1. How does Eliphaz show delicacy of speech? How does he allude to the inconsistency of repining under discipline in the case of a good man? In which verses does he advance the position that the righteous are never overthrown? In which does he teach the opposite to this concerning the wicked? Can you give the details of his vision? Name the verses in chapter 5 in which he exhorts Job to turn to God. Name the verses in which he encourages him to do this.

2. How does Job express his desire for death in chapter 6? In what language does he express his feelings towards his friends? How is his impatience with God illustrated?

3. Give some illustrations of Bildad's severity. In what verses of chapter 8 does he draw comparisons from earlier authorities?

4. Give some illustrations of God's supremacy in chapter 9.

5. Give some illustrations of Job's sense of imperfection. Give some illustrations of his increased excitement towards the close of chapter 10.

6. Why should Zophar be described as violent? Give two or three illustrations of Zophar's magnificent description of God. In what language does he exhort Job to acknowledge his sins?

7. Indicate Job's sarcasm in chapter 12. How does he attack the motives of his opponents and the unsoundness of their arguments? In what language does he warn them? Give the verse in chapter 13 where he appeals directly to God. What language in chapter 14 justifies the last sentence in the text of our lesson?

*For this outline and the following credit is due to Dr. Albert Barnes.

SECOND SERIES OF THE DEBATE

CHAPTERS 15-21.

(1) With Eliphaz, 15-17.
     (a) Speech of Eliphaz, 15.
     (b) Reply of Job, 16, 17.
(2) With Bildad, 18, 19.
     (a) Speech of Bildad, 18.
     (b) Reply of Job, 19.
(3) With Zophar, 20, 21.
     (a) Speech of Zophar, 20.
     (b) Reply of Job, 21.

The second series of the debate is in the same order as the first, and with the same question in view.

Eliphaz and Job.

Eliphaz opens in chapter 15. Job is accused of vehemence and vanity; of casting off fear and restraining prayer; of arrogance and presumption.

God is vindicated by him, and the observations of the sages are quoted. A number of pithy and instructive sayings are used to show that wicked men are subject to sudden alarms and unhappy experiences.

Job replies, renewing his complaint of the way his friends have treated him, and of the intensity and injustice of his sufferings. His appeal is to God before whom his eyes pour out tears. In chapter 17 he prophecies that his trials will yet be a subject of amazement to good men.

Bildad and Job.

Bildad speaks in chapter 18 repeating the former accusation. In his estimation the laws of God's administration are fixed and it is an established principle that the wicked shall be punished in this life, which he illustrates by a number of maxims or proverbs. The student should enumerate these and distinguish between them.

There is nothing new in what Bildad says, but he is enforcing what he has previously advanced with greater emphasis.

In chapter 19 Job speaks more pathetically, exhibiting his character in a beautiful light. His language is sorrowful, his spirit tender and subdued. How long will his friends vex and crush him with their remarks? God has overthown him, fenced up his way, put away his friends. Even his wife and children are estranged from him.

Then, as Barnes says, there follows the most noble declaration in the book. "Conscious of the importance of what he is about to say, he asks that his words might be engraved on the eternal rock, and then professes his confidence in God and his assurance that he would yet appear and vindicate his character. Though now consumed by disease, and though this process should go on till all his flesh was wasted away, yet he had the conviction that God would appear on the earth to deliver him, and that with renovated flesh and in prosperity, he would be permitted to see God for himself."

Zophar and Job.

Zophar recapitulates the old arguments under a new form, and Job replies, closing the second series of the debate. All his strength is collected for this argument as though resolved to answer them once for all. He appeals to facts. The wicked alive, grow old, become mighty in power, etc. They openly cast off God and prosper in an irreligious life, although, as he admits, there are some exceptions. They are reserved, however, for the day of destruction and a future retribution they cannot escape.

Questions.

For questions, teachers are referred to what was said under "Note to Teachers" at the close of the preceding lesson. Examine the text of the chapters by the help of the various sentences and clauses of the lesson.

Ask yourself or your classes for example:

In what language does Eliphaz accuse Job of vehemence and vanity?

How many verses are taken up with these accusations?

To how many sages of ancient times does he refer, or how many of their observations does he quote?

Point out the literary beauty of some of these observations.

Discover the verse of verses in which Job prophesies the acquaintance of later generations with the story of his trial.

Count and distinguish between the maxims or proverbs of Bildad.

Memorize 19:25 to 27.

How many indisputable facts does Job refer to in chapter 21?

THIRD SERIES OF THE DEBATE

CHAPTERS 22-31

(1) With Eliphaz, 22-24.
    (a) Speech of Eliphaz, 22
    (b) Reply of Job, 23, 24.
(2) With Bildad, 25, 26.
    (a) Speech of Bildad, 25.
    (b) Reply of Job, 26.
(3) With Zophar, 27-31.
    (a) * * * * * *
    (b) Continuation of the reply of Job, 27-31.

The last speech Eliphaz makes, chapter 22, is a grand effort to refute Job based upon the latter's appeal to facts. There is more severity in it than he has shown before. He charges Job with cruelty, oppression and injustice as a magistrate. Therefore, no wonder such calamities had come upon him. Using the deluge as an illustration, he shows how God must deal with the wicked according to their deserts. Job is exhorted to acquaint himself with God and be at peace with Him, and all might yet be well.

Job replies pathetically. He has no human help, but turns to God. O, that he might come before Him! He cannot seem to find Him, yet he has confidence in Him. His own integrity is once more asserted. It was not true that God always dealt with men on earth in accordance with their character. The wicked often have long prosperity, though he admits they will ultimately be cut off.

Bildad attempts a reply in chapter 25, and yet he seems to realize that the controversy is decided, for he contents himself simply with a description of the power, wisdom and majesty of God, closing with the sentiment expressed before concerning the comparative impurity and insignificance of man. Bildad has, in fact, yielded the argument and retires from the field.

Job speaks in chapter 26 in a strain of irony. His friends have not enlightened him very much. His own views of the greatness of God are superior to those of Bildad. Notice the sublime description of the divine majesty which follows.

Zophar should have replied, but his lips are closed, and Job himself proceeds more calmly in chapters 27 to 31. Once more he refers to the government of God, giving, as Barnes expresses it, "a most beautiful description of the search for wisdom, detailing the discoveries of science in his time, and saying that none of them could disclose it, and concluding that true wisdom can only be found in the fear of the Lord. Once more he maintains his integrity, and concludes that if God would come forth and pronounce a just judgment on him, he would take the decision and bind it on his head as a diadem, and march forth with it in triumph."

Questions.

1. What illustrates the greater severity of Eliphaz?

2. How is Job's magisterial function referred to?

3. In what verses is the deluge spoken of?

4. Under what terms does Job affirm his integrity?

5. Quote some of the irony of Job.

6. Name some of the scientific discoveries of Job's day.

7. How beautifully is the search for wisdom described?

WORDS OF ELIHU AND THE ADDRESS OF THE ALMIGHTY

CHAPTERS 32-41

Elihu now comes forward with apparent modesty, and yet great pretensions. Young and inexperienced, he is nevertheless indignant at the manner in which the friends of Job have sought to reply to him. Professing that his views have been revealed from above, he undertakes to clear up all the difficulties in the case. Afflictions are for the good of the sufferer is his dictum, a thought which he exhibits in various lights.

He, too, reflects upon Job for his rashness and presumption, leaning rather to the side of his friends.

Chapter 32 is introductory, but in the following chapter he fully enters upon his argument. If Job had wished to bring his cause before God, let him now present it to *him*, i. e., Elihu, who assumed to take God's place. Job could not be correct in the claims he made for himself because God must be more righteous than man. God speaks to man in various ways to withdraw him from his purpose and save him from sin.

Job is not disposed to reply, although Elihu gives him an opportunity, and therefore the latter continues in chapter 34 to examine his case more particularly. Job had shown a spirit of irreverence which is rebuked. God's government is administered on principles of equity, and therefore Job must be a wicked man who is called upon to confess that his chastisement was just and to resolve to offend no more. In chapter 35, assuming that Job claimed to be more righteous than God, he examines the position, demonstrating its impossibility.

Having undertaken thus to vindicate the divine character, he proceeds to chapters 36 and 37 to state some of the principles of the divine government, illustrating, his views and showing the necessity of man's submission to God by a sublime description of the greatness of the latter, especially as manifested in the storm. To quote Barnes again, "There is in this description every indication that a storm is rising and a tempest gathering. In the midst of this tempest the address of Elihu is broken off and the Almighty appears and closes the debate."

The Address of the Almighty

The address of the Almighty covers chapters 38 to 41, and is represented as from the midst of the tempest. Its principle object appears to be to assert God's greatness and majesty and the duty of profound submission to the dispensations of his government. He appeals to His works, showing that man could explain little, and that, therefore, it was to be expected that in His moral government there would be much also above human capacity to understand.

Job is subdued and awed, and confesses his vileness in chapter 40:3-5. To produce, however, a more overpowering impression, and secure a deeper prostration before Him, the Almighty described two of the most remarkable animals He had made, with which description His sublime address concludes.

We agree with Barnes and others, that the general impression sought by this address is that of awe, reverence and submission. That God has a right to do, and that it is presumptuous in man to sit in judgment upon His doings. It is remarkable that God does not refer to the main point in the controversy at all. He does not seek to vindicate His government from the charges brought against it of inequality, nor does He refer to the future state as a place where all these apparent inequalities will be adjusted.

Job is humbled and penitent, chapter 42. His confession is accepted, and his general course approved. His three friends are reprimanded for the severity of their judgment upon him, while he is directed to intercede for them. His calamities are ended and he is restored to double his former prosperity.

Thus God shows Himself the friend of the righteous, and the object of the trial is secured by showing that there is true virtue which is not based on selfishness, and real piety that will bear any trial to which it may be subjected.

It shows that God is able to keep the feet of His saints, and that His grace is sufficient for them who put their trust in Him. We speak of Job as triumphant, but the more vital truth is that God is triumphant in the lives of His saints above the power of the evil one.

Questions.

1. Illustrate Elihu's modesty.
2. Do the same for his pretensions.
3. Show his indignation at the other friends.
4. What is his dictum?
5. How does he reflect on Job?
6. What principles of the divine government does he state?
7. How does he close his speech?
8. What is the chief object of the words of God?
9. How is Job affected by them?
10. For what omissions is God's address remarkable?
11. How is the matter concluded as to Job?
12. How about his friends?

THE PSALMS

INTRODUCTORY

1. Their Authors.

The Book of Psalms has sometimes been classified according to authors. For example, the titles indicate that seventy-three were written by David; fifty are anonymous; twelve have the name of Asaph, and ten that of Korah, or the sons of Korah; two are associated with Solomon and one each with Moses, Heman and Ethan.

A comparison of Acts 4:25 and Hebrews 4:7 shows that Psalms 2 and 95 respectively, were also written by David, though not ascribed to him in the book, and the question arises whether he may not have been the author of a still larger number of the anonymous Psalms. As some with the name of the sons of Korah were evidently written for them, may he have been their author as well? The same query arises about the 72nd Psalm, one of the two to which Solomon's name is attached. It might be added here that the titles of the Psalms are regarded by many as of equal authority with the text, and hence if we can ascertain what the title means, we may venture to build conclusions upon it.

2. Their Subjects.

The book again, has been classified according to subjects. Angus, in his Bible Handbook, has a convenient classification, giving the subject, and in each case the numbers of a few Psalms illustrating it. For example, there are Psalms of

Instruction, like 1, 19, 39.

Praise, 8, 29, 93, 100.

Thanksgiving, 30, 65, 103, 107, 116.

Penitence, 6, 32, 38, 51, 143.

Trust, 3, 27, 31, 46, 56, 62, 86.

Distress and Sorrow, 4, 13, 55, 64, 88.

Aspiration, 42, 63, 80, 84, 137.

History, 78, 105, 106.

Prophecy (Messianic), 2, 16, 22, 24, 40, 45, 68, 69, 72, 97, 110, 118.

3. Their Books.

It may seem strange to speak of the "Books" of the Psalms, but that expressed another kind of classification. The whole book has been divided into five books, each ending with a similar doxology, as follows:

Book I, Psalms 1-41.

Book II, Psalms 42-72.

Book III, Psalms 73-89.

Book IV, Psalms 90-106.

Book V, Psalms 107-150.

Notice the close of each of these books for the doxology.

There are those who question the value of this division, however, on the ground, first, that the title of the book itself in the Hebrew, (Sepher Tehillim), is singular rather than plural. It is not the "books" but the book of Psalms. Second, the numbers of the Psalms continue unbroken from the beginning to the end of the book. Third, there are other doxologies than those especially referred to, e. g., Psalms 117 and 134.

4. Their Unity.

The view of others, therefore, is that the Psalms comprise but one book with an order and unity throughout, the key to which is found in its final application to the millennial age and establishment of the kingdom of God on the earth. According to these, this explains what are known as the imprecatory or cursing Psalms. These have puzzled many, but when we consider them as terminating on that period when the era of mercy for the Gentile nations closes, and the time of their judgment begins, it lightens their problem very much.

In the same connection we should remember that the author is speaking in the prophetic spirit, and that the enemies are enemies of God whose permanent rejection of Him is implied. This view, moreover, explains those like the 91st Psalm which promise exemption from such things as pestilence and war. This Psalm was written doubtless on the occasion of Israel's deliverance from Egypt, but its language seems to indicate that it is a type of their greater and permanent deliverance in the time to come. This is strengthened if we conceive of the preceding Psalm as a picture of Israel to-day.

The opinion which sees the key to the Psalms in their millennial application also furnishes an explanation of the frequent references to Christ found in the Psalms.

Urquhart, who maintains the above view, regards the whole book as formed of a combination of twelve sections. Each of these contains a continuous recurring story of the establishment of God's kingdom on earth, in which Psalms of complaint and pleading on Israel's part are followed by those of jubilation for deliverance. In some of these jubilations the whole earth is seen to join. These twelve sections are indicated to him by the following jubilant Psalms: 10, 18, 24, 30, 48, 68, 76, 85, 100, 118, 136, 150. "In the first cycle of ten there is progress from the announcement of judgment (1), and manifestation of Christ (2), through His rejection (3-7), suffering and ascension (8), the waiting and persecution of His people (9), to the consummation of all things (10)." This analysis will not commend itself to all, but it is interesting and may lead to further thought.

5. The Messianic Psalms.

These are Psalms in which not only is the Messiah referred to, but in which He Himself in the Spirit is heard to speak. It is His feelings and experiences that are expressed rather than those of the human author. To know David it is necessary to study the Psalms as well as the historical books that refer to him, but this is even more necessary in the case of Jesus. In the Gospels we read what He said and did, and what was said and done to Him; in other words, we obtain a view of

the outside of His life, but in the Psalms we see the inner side, and learn how He felt and how He lived in the presence of His God and Father.

Questions.

1. How many Psalms, according to their titles, were written by David?

2. Classify the Psalms according to subjects.

3. Into how many books would some divide the Psalms? Give the Psalms in each.

4. What, in the judgment of others, is the key that unifies the Psalms?

5. What lightens the problem of the imprecatory Psalms?

6. How would you define a Messianic Psalm?

7. What is their value as applied to the Messiah Himself?

PSALMS 1-6

Psalm 1.

True happiness is the theme of this Psalm, whose author is unnamed. The negative side of true happiness is stated (v. 1), and then the positive (v. 2). Its reward follows (v. 3). Its nature and value are emphasized by a sharp contrast. Such a man is godly, his opposite ungodly (v. 4). The first is marked by stability, the second by instability (v. 4). The first has endless fruitfulness and blessing, the second has nothing and worse than nothing (v. 5), for he can not be acquitted at the judgment day. The secret of it all is found in Jehovah (v. 6). The Psalm is a summary of the whole book, and is appropriately placed at the beginning as a sort of preface.

Psalm 2.

Is prophetic and Messianic in one (see introductory lesson). It had a partial fulfilment at the first advent of Christ (Acts 4:25; 13:33), but a complete one is to follow at the second advent, as will be seen in the study of the prophets. The nations will rage and the kings of the earth again set themselves against Jehovah and His Christ under the lead of the Antichrist (vv. 1-3), but they will be regarded with contempt and terrified by divine judgments (vv. 4, 5). God's purpose will not be altered, which is to establish His Son upon His kingdom in the earth at Jerusalem (v. 6).

The Son Himself speaks at verse seven, the last clause of which refers to His inauguration as Mediatorial King, and does not in any way impugn His Deity. The Gentile nations are to be His in that day (v. 8), and although it will be the millennial day, yet its peace and righteousness will be secured through judgments and by the firmness of its Holy Ruler (v. 9). Kings and princes are warned to prepare themselves for its coming (vv. 10-12). "Kiss the Son" means submit to His authority, "lest He be angry and ye perish in the way, for His wrath will soon be kindled" (R. V.).

Psalm 3.

As its title indicates, should be read in connection with 2 Samuel 15. In his distress to whom does David appeal (v. 1)? Not only had men turned their backs upon him but it was charged that God had done so. Remember the possible reason for this suspicion in David's sin with Bathsheba, preceding this rebellion of Absalom. Does David still retain his faith in God's promises notwithstanding (v. 3)? What is the ground of his confidence (v. 4)? And its expression (vv. 5, 6)? What is the nature of his further appeal (v. 7)? "Cheek-bone" and "teeth" represent his enemies as wild beasts ready to devour him. By faith he already sees these enemies overcome, and praises God as his deliverer (v. 8).

The word "Selah" at the close of verse two is obscure, and may denote a pause or rest, in the singing, or an emphasis to be laid on the particular sentiment expressed.

Psalm 4.

A cry of distress is this, composed by David, it may have been, on the same occasion as the last. He is not trusting in his own righteousness, but God's righteousness (v. 1). The doctrine of imputed righteousness was apprehended by the spiritually enlightened in Old Testament, as well as in New Testament times. For a further illustration of this in David compare the opening verses of Psalm 32, with Paul's application of them in Romans 4.

David is encouraged to utter this cry by past mercies—"Thou hast enlarged me," and I trust Thee again. Verse 2 shows the source of his trouble. His "glory" may refer to his kingly dignity now dishonored by exile. But the schemes of his enemies were "vanity," and brought about by lying "leasing").

His confidence was in the divine purpose towards him (v. 3), and they who are against him are cautioned to repent and turn to the Lord (vv. 4, 5). In the midst of his afflictions he values the divine favor (v. 6), which brings more experimental joy to him than the husbandman knows at harvest time (vv. 7, 8).

"To the chief musician on Neginoth," indicates the purpose for which it was set apart as a musical composition. "Neginoth" were the stringed instruments used in the Levitical service, and the "chief musician" was the leader of that part of the choir.

Psalm 5.

Is a morning prayer (v. 3). The words "look up" are rendered "keep watch" in the Revised Version. The psalmist would keep watch on himself, that his life and conduct might be such as to insure the answer to his prayer (v. 4-7). The need of the player is indicated in verse eight. The enemies referred to are then described (v. 9), and their judgment committed into God's hands who defends the righteous (vv. 11, 12). "Nehiloth," means flutes or wind instruments.

Psalm 6.

Represents David in deeper distress of soul than we have found him hitherto. Conviction of sin is upon him. Those who have studied 2 Samuel will not need to be reminded of occasions for this experience, though the connection with Bathsheba will first suggest itself. He feels the justness of the divine rebuke (v. 1), but pleads for mercy (v. 2). The time of spiritual darkness has been long extended (vv. 3, 4). Will it end in death (v. 5)? He is heartbroken (vv. 6, 7). Enemies are rejoicing in his sorrow, but their glee is short-lived (vv. 7, 8). Light breaks, the morning dawn, tears are wiped away, for the Lord hath heard him! Begone, mine enemies, be ashamed and turn back (vv. 9, 10)!

Verse five need not be interpreted as expressing doubt of a future state, but may be simply a contrast between this scene of life and the unseen world of the dead symbolized by the "grave" (Heb. "sheol"). "Sheminith" means the "eighth," and perhaps this was a Psalm for the eighth key, or the bass of the stringed instruments.

Questions.
1. Memorize Psalm 1.
2. What is an appropriate theme for it?
3. State the two-fold application of Psalm 2.
4. Will the millennium represent only peace and cheerful obedience to God and His Son?
5. Did you re-read 2 Samuel 15?
6. On what ground might God have forsaken David according to Psalm 3?
7. What may "Selah" mean?
8. What great Gospel doctrine finds illustration in the Psalms of David?
9. Define "Neginoth" and "Nehiloth."
10. What is the Hebrew for "grave"?

PSALMS 7-10

The length of our lessons in this book are determined rather arbitrarily by the length of the different Psalms, or the special interest found in them. We have in mind weekly classes wishing to study the whole Bible in a connected way, and yet avoid tediousness in the process. The six Psalms included in the last lesson

might easily be read by the class in a week; and on the Lord's Day, the teacher with the assistance of the questions, would have little difficulty, in fastening the facts and their application on their minds in a way both interesting and profitable.

At the same time the average person, independent of any class preparation, reading a Psalm a day for private meditation, will probably find the brief comments and questions upon it as much as he will be able to assimilate.

Psalm 7.

We commence this new lesson with this Psalm because it offers a point of beginning in the title. This, however, is rather obscure since it is not clear who may be meant by "Cush." The margin of the King James Version identifies him with "Shimei" of 2 Samuel 16:5-14, which story it would be well to peruse again, although there are several incidents in Saul's persecution of David which would fit about as well. The word "Shiggaion" in the title means "a plaintive song or elegy."

David is persecuted (vv. 1, 2), and charged with wrong-doing to one at peace with him (vv. 3, 4). The charge is so false that he can safely offer the challenge in verse five. Jehovah is appealed to, and asked to sit in judgment on this matter: "Return, Thou on high" (v. 7). "My righteousness" (vv. 8-10) means his innocence of this particular charge. A warning is uttered against the wicked (vv. 11-13), whose folly is described in serious wit (vv. 14-16). David's experience illustrates these concluding verses more than once.

Psalm 8.

If the whole book of Psalms be considered a mountain range of poetic prophecy, then this is one of the highest peaks. Observe in the margin how frequently it is quoted in the New Testament, and applied to Jesus Christ. Read Hebrews 2:5-9 especially.

"O LORD, our Lord," gives better sense as "O Jehovah, our

Lord." His glory is in the Heavens as we see in verse three, and yet it is "above the heavens," both in kind and in degree. So great is His glory that He uses "the weak" things of the world to confound the things which are mighty." (Compare v. 2 with Matt. 11:25; 21:15 16, and 1 Cor. 1:27).

Verses 4-8 find a partial fulfilment in man as created in the first Adam, but their complete fulfilment is seen only in redeemed and regenerated man in the Second Adam. The passage in Hebrews shows this, and particularly alongside of 1 Corinthians 15:22-28.

"Upon Gittith" is "set to the Gittith" (R. V.) which, some think, means a tune of a joyous character.

Psalm 9.

Is one of the cursing or imprecatory Psalms which, as stated in the introductory lesson, find their key in the millennial age and the events introductory thereto.

It opens with rejoicing (vv. 1, 2). This rejoicing is for victory over enemies (v. 3) but they are God's enemies rather than the psalmist's. It is His coming (presence) that has overcome them. Moreover, they are nations rather than individuals. ("Heathen" in verse five, is "nations" in the R. V.) Their cities are destroyed (v. 6).

At the same time the Lord is seen sitting as King (v. 7, R. V.), judging the world in righteousness, comforting the oppressed, dwelling in Zion (vv. 9-12). All these are millennial figures. Israel is lifted from the gates of death (v. 13), and the great tribulation is over. She is praising God in Zion for the deliverance from the Gentile nations which are sunk in the pit they had digged for her (vv. 13-16). And so on to the end of the Psalm.

"Muth-labbed" may refer like "Gittith" to the name or character of the tune.

Psalm 10.

Seems allied in thought with that preceding, and the two may have been one, originally. The psalmist is not referring to personal experiences, but to those which are more general. It seems as though the poor and oppressed of the nation and the whole world were uttering their complaint through him.

Because God seems far away, the wicked are flourishing (vv. 1, 2). It would not be out of place to conceive of the wicked in this Psalm as personified in the Antichrist at the end of this age, when, as we shall learn later, he will be persecuting Israel as God's witness in the earth. This is not to say that, in no sense, the Psalm is applicable to an earlier period in the history of that people, but that in its fuller sense, it is for the time to come.

The wicked one is described as boastful, covetous, proud, atheistic, self-opinionated, bold, deceitful, oppressive, and cunning (vv. 3-11, R. V.). The "poor" means, as is customary in the Psalms, "the poor in spirit," described by Jesus in the Sermon on the Mount. They are sad and sorrowful sufferers for righteousness' sake, even though they may be rich in this world's goods. "Meek" would be a better word to describe them than "poor."

The description of the wicked oppressor is followed by the usual appeal to God (vv. 12-15), who is represented as reigning over the millennial earth, punishing the wicked, establishing the meek, and judging the oppressed against "the man of the earth" who, as has been said, may well be taken for the Antichrist.

Questions.

1. What is the title or inscription of Psalm 7?

2. What is the meaning of "Shiggaion" and "Gittith"?

3. Have you read 1 Corinthians 15:22-28 and Hebrews 2:5-9?

4. What is the key to the imprecatory Psalms?

5. To what period does Psalm 10 seem to apply?

6. Who are usually meant by the "poor" in these Psalms?

7. What title is given to the wicked one in Psalm 10?

PSALMS 11-17

Psalm 11.

A song of trust. The declaration of verse one. "In the Lord put I my trust," is buttressed by the reason in verse seven, while all between is descriptive of the condition in which David finds himself. Urged to flee from his enemies (v. 1), he shows the futility of the attempt (v. 2). The moral foundations are being undermined (v. 3), and only Jehovah is able to discriminate and judge (vv. 4-6).

Psalm 12.

The evil speaker. The close relation between this and the preceding Psalm is easily discovered. David's enemy is the deceitful flatterer (vv. 1, 2). But his judgment is of the Lord (vv. 3-5), the sincerity of whose utterances are in contrast with those of the enemy (vv. 6-8).

Psalm 13.

Sorrow. The Lord seems long in coming to His servant's relief from the slanderers in the Psalms preceding (vv. 1, 2). Will He never come (vv. 3, 4)? Yea, He cometh soon, and faith and hope rejoice (vv. 5, 6).

Psalm 14.

The whole world corrupt. All sinners are fools (v. 1) because they think and act contrary to right reason. First, they think wrong ("in his heart," Gen. 6:12), and then soon they act wrong (Prov. 23:7). This is true of the world generally (vv. 2-4). "Eat up My People" is a phrase denoting the "beastly fury" of the Gentile enemies of Israel. Verses 5 and 6 show their indifference rather than their ignorance of God. If the closing verse seems to refer to the period of the Babylonian captivity and therefore raises a question as to the Davidic authorship (see title), we should remember that the language is typical of any great evil, and that David may be speaking as in other instances, in the prophetic sense. In that case the

Psalm takes on a millennial aspect.

Psalm 15.

Holiness and its reward. Here a question is asked, verse one, which finds its answer in the verses following, the whole dialogue being summed up in the last sentence. To abide in God's tabernacle, etc., is to hold fellowship with God and enjoy the blessings incident thereto. These are for the man whose conduct is right, who is truthful, sincere, separate from the ungodly, and uninfluenced by covetousness and bribery.

Psalm 16.

Sometimes called "The Psalm of the Resurrection," is one of the great Messianic Psalms (see introductory lesson). While it is interesting to consider David as uttering the prayer, for it is a prayer, how much more so to think of Christ! On some mountain side, in the night's darkness, He may have poured out these petitions and praises. (For its Messianic application compare verses 8-11 with Acts 2:25-31, and 13:35). Observe the spirit of confidence (v. 1), loyalty to God (v. 2), love toward the saints (v. 3), separation from the world (v. 4), contentment (vv. 5, 6), obedience (vv. 7, 8), hope (vv. 9, 10), expectation (v. 11). The Revised Version throws light on the text. "Michtam" means "A Golden Psalm" (see margin) and such it is in its preciousness even above others.

Psalm 17.

Is a prayer in which vindication is desired. It makes such great claims that one thinks of it as Messianic also (vv. 1-4), and yet like Psalm 7, the writer may have some specific transaction in mind as to which his hands are clean. Note the testimony to the power of God's word (v. 4). What is asked is guidance (vv. 5, 6), and preservation (vv. 7, 8). The latter is desired from the wicked whose description follows as proud (vv. 9, 10), treacherous (vv. 11, 12), and yet prosperous in worldly things (v. 14). This prosperity is transient in comparison with his own expectation (v. 15). Have the Revised Version convenient in reading these Psalms, for the interpretation it casts on some obscure passages.

Questions.

1. What is the leading thought of Psalm 11?

2. Against what class of enemies are the psalmist's words frequently directed?

3. Why are sinners called "fools"?

4. Which of the Psalms of this lesson are millennial and messianic?

5. Have you compared the passages in Acts?

6. What does "Michtam" mean?

PSALMS 18-24

Psalm 18.

A song of victory. It opens with ejaculatory expressions of triumph for deliverance. All nature is described as convulsed when the Almighty presses to the rescue. The next division is meditation on the principles involved, the whole closing with a further outburst of triumph and confidence. 2 Samuel 22 is a copy of this ode saving a few variations, and the student is referred to our treatment of it at that place.

Psalm 19.

God's revelation in the world and in the Word. We have a contrast between these two in this Psalm. In verses one to six there is the general revelation of the heavens, "wordless but extending their sphere over the whole earth," which then specializes to the sun as the chief figure of it all. But in 7-14, the law is celebrated, whose function is to warn against sin, and by conformity to which only can our thought and conduct become acceptable to God.

Observe the literary beauty as well as the spiritual teaching in the description of the law—six names, six epithets and six effects. The clearer our apprehension of the law, so the Psalm teaches, the clearer is our view of sin, and the more evident that grace only can cleanse and keep us from it.

Psalms 20 and 21.

Are coupled in The Modern Reader's Bible, and called "An Antiphonal War Anthem." The first gives the prayers of the king and the people before the battle, and the second the thanksgiving after the victory.

As to the first, we hear the people (vv. 1-5), the king (v. 6), and then the people to the end. As to the second, the king is first (vv. 1-7), and then the people to the end. While this may be the historical setting of these Psalms, yet we are at liberty to apply their utterances in the spiritual scene to the experiences of believers in the Christian Church.

Psalm 22.

The Psalm of the Cross. Is this one of the great Messianic Psalms? Christ uttered the first verse on the cross (Matt. 27:46), and there is reason to think the words of the last were also heard. "He hath done it" (R. V.), in the Hebrew, corresponds closely to, "It is finished" (John 19:30). If this were so, may we suppose that the whole Psalm was the language of the divine sufferer as He bore our sins on the cross?

There are three strophes, or great poetical divisions, each associated with the phrase, "Far from me." The first covers verses 1 to 10, the second 11 to 18, the third 19 to 31. In the first, we have a cry of distress (vv. 1, 2), an expression of confidence (vv. 3-5), a description of the enemies (vv. 6-8), and a second expression of confidence (vv. 9-10). In the second, we have two descriptions, the surrounding enemies (vv. 11-13), and the sufferer's experiences (vv. 14-18). In the third the whole tone is changed to a note of victory (vv. 19-21), a testimony of praise (vv. 22-26), and a prophecy of resurrection glory (vv. 27-31).

The Psalm gives a graphic picture of death by crucifixion with circumstances precisely fulfilled at Calvary. As that form of death penalty was Roman rather than Jewish, we agree with the Scofield Reference Bible that the "proof of inspiration is irresistible." At verse 22 the Psalm breaks from crucifixion to resurrection (compare John 20:17).

Psalm 23.

The Shepherd Psalm is such a favorite with all as to make an attempted exposition almost an offence. Did David compose it as a youth tending his father's sheep? If not, it must have been when occupied in reminiscences of those early days.

Note the possessive, "*my* shepherd," and the future, "*shall* not want." Because the Lord is my Shepherd I am

Feeding on the Word—"pastures"

Fellowshipping the Spirit—"waters"

Being renewed—"restoreth"

Surrendered in will—"leadeth"

Trusting the promises—"fear no evil"

Enjoying security—"a table"

Doing service—"runneth over"

Possessing hope—"forever."

Psalm 24.

Is frequently defined as the Ascension Psalm. The Scofield Bible speaks of these last three Psalms, however, 22, 23 and 24, as a trilogy. In the first, the *good* Shepherd gives his life for the sheep (John 10:11), in the second, the *great* Shepherd "brought again from the dead through the blood of the everlasting covenant," tenderly cares for His sheep (Heb. 13:20), and in the last, the *chief* Shepherd appears as king of glory to own and reward the sheep (1 Pet 5:4).

From this point of view the order is: (a), the declaration of title, "The earth is the Lord's" (vv. 1, 2); (b), the challenge (vv. 3-6), it is a question of worthiness and no one is worthy but the Lamb (compare Dan. 7:13, 14; Rev. 5:3-10); (c), the king takes the throne (vv. 7-10), (compare Matt. 25:31).

Questions.

1. Where have we met earlier with the contents of Psalm 18?

2. What theme would you assign to Psalm 19?

3. Give the names, epithets and effects of the law.

4. What is the historical setting of Psalms 20 and 21?

5. How does John 19:30 suggest the last verse of Psalm 22?

6. Of what is this Psalm a picture?

7. What proof of inspiration does it contain?

8. By what name has Psalm 24 been called?

9. How may the last three Psalms be classified?

10. Amplify this last idea.

11. From this point of view, what is the order of Psalm 24?

12. What may have been the historical origin of the Psalm last named?

PSALMS 25-37

Psalm 25.

In the Hebrew this prayer is arranged as an acrostic, i.e., the first word of each verse begins with a letter in alphabetical order from A to Z.

Hereafter we shall not give as much attention to every Psalm as we have thus far, but trust the reader to do the analyzing after the examples given. The purpose of the Commentary is not so much textual explanation as a stimulus to Bible study in a broader sense, and it is assumed that the reader has been studying the Bible side by side with the Commentary from the beginning.

The more difficult Psalms, some of the more familiar and popular, and those distinctively Messianic and millennial may be treated more at length, but others must be passed over.

In the present instance the prayer is for defence (vv. 1-3), guidance (vv. 4, 5), forgiveness (vv. 6-11), etc., intermingled with testimony to the divine goodness (vv. 12-15).

Psalm 26.

Is another appeal to God on the basis of avowed integrity and innocence of the charges of enemies. Note the features of righteous character of which the psalmist speaks, as well as the description of his enemies. The Modern Reader's Bible names this Psalm, "Searchings of heart before worship."

Psalm 27.

Is called by the volume named above "An Anthem of Deliverance," and throughout it exhibits confidence, hope and joy, in God's worship, with prayer for help and guidance in danger. The secret of the psalmist's confidence is given in verse four as his delight in divine fellowship expressed in worshiping in God's tabernacle. God will protect and deliver him (vv. 5, 6). He will be more to him than earthly parents (v. 10). All he craves is guidance (v. 11). He concludes with counsel to others in a like case (vv. 13, 14).

Psalm 29.

"The Song of the Thunderstorm," encourages confidence in God by the celebration of His power in His dominion over the natural world. "Discovereth the forests" (v. 9) means "stripping them bare." In the midst of this sublimity God's worshipers cry, "Glory!" (R. V.)

Psalm 30.

States its occasion in the title, the reference being to David's own house or palace (compare Deut. 20:15; 2 Sam. 5:11; 7:2).

Psalm 31.

Is a cry of one in distress, which some have referred to as the period of David's persecution by Saul at Keilah. Read 1 Samuel 23:1-15, and then note in the Psalm, verses 4, 8, 10-15, 20-22.

Psalm 32.

Reads like "David's Spiritual Biography." It is thought to have been written after his sin with Bathsheba (2 Sam. 11, 12). He has been brought to repentance for that sin and forgiven (Psalm 51), and now is praising God for that forgiveness, and telling what

led up to it. It opens with a general declaration of his blessedness and why (vv. 1, 2). This is followed by his experience before forgiveness and when he was undergoing conviction of sin (vv. 3, 4). Confession brought forgiveness (v. 5). Let others act similarly in the same circumstances (v. 6). See what God is to him now (v. 7). The Psalm takes the form of a dialogue at this point, and God speaks at verses eight and nine, which should be read in the Revised Version. The whole concludes with a warning and exhortation (vv. 10, 11).

Psalm 33.

Is one of praise. It opens with a general chorus (vv. 1-3). This is followed by a semi-chorus (vv. 4-11), a second semi-chorus (vv. 12-19), and a final chorus (vv. 20-22). To follow this division suggested by the Modern Reader's Bible, is to obtain a good idea of the several subjects.

Psalm 34.

Has its occasion indicated in the title which refers to 1 Samuel 21:13. The name there is Achish, but some think Abimelech was the general name given the sovereigns of Gath at that time (Gen. 20:2). This is also an acrostic, and from a musical point of view consists of an introduction (vv. 1, 2), solos and choruses. For one solo, see verses 3-6, and for another 11-14.

Psalm 35.

May be read in connection with 1 Samuel 24, which some regard as its occasion. A comparison of that chapter will throw light on the meaning of several of its expressions.

Psalm 37.

Is one of the most popular of the Psalms of trust and confidence, whose contents are illustrated in David's personal history. It is an acrostic, which requires little in the way of explanation to any heart who really knows God through Jesus Christ. The theme is the prosperity of the wicked with counsel as to how the child of God should act in regard to it.

Questions.

1. What is an acrostic Psalm?
2. What earlier Psalm is suggested by the theme of Psalm 26?
3. Point out the poetic descriptions of a thunder-storm in Psalm 29.
4. What experience is Psalm 31 thought to describe?
5. Have you again read 1 Samuel 23:1-15?
6. Give a title of Psalm 32, and a reason for it.
7. What idea is conveyed by "semi-chorus"?
8. Memorize Psalm 37:1-9.

PSALMS 38-51

Psalm 38.

Is an appeal to God from chastisement because of iniquity (vv. 1-4). The mental anguish is described in figures of physical disease, and yet it is not impossible that such disease may have been part of the chastisement (vv. 5-8). The desertion of friends and the opposition of enemies also entered into it (vv. 10-17). There are verses susceptible of an application to Christ, but others would prevent its application as a whole to Him.

Psalm 40.

Is Messianic (cf. Hebrews 10:5 and the following verses). To quote the Scofield Bible: "It opens with the joy of Christ in resurrection (vv. 1, 2). Verses 3 to 5 give His resurrection testimony. The others are retrospective." "Mine iniquities" (v. 12) may mean "penal afflictions." This meaning is common (Psalm 31:11; 38:4); (cf. Gen. 4:13; Gen. 19:15; 1 Sam. 28:10; also 2 Sam. 16:12; Job 19:29; Isaiah 5:18; 53:11). It is also favoured by the clause "taken hold of me," which can be said appropriately of sufferings, but not of sins (cf. Job 27:20; Psalm 69:24). Thus, the difficulties, in referring this Psalm to Christ, are removed.

The language of verses 14 and 15 is not imprecatory, but a confident expectation (Psalm 5:11), though the former sense is not inconsistent with Christ's prayer for His murderers, as their confusion and shame might be to prepare them for seeking forgiveness (cf. Acts 2:37).

Psalm 41.

Closes "Book 1" of the Psalms (see introductory lesson). It celebrates the blessedness of compassionating the poor (vv. 1-3) which the psalmist contrasts with the treatment he received both from avowed enemies and professed friends.

Psalms 42 and 43.

Afford a good opportunity to speak of Hebrew poetry as illustrated in the Psalms. The rhythm of Hebrew poetry is not in the sound but in the recurrence of the thought. "Thought may be rhythmic as well as sound, and the full meaning of Scripture is not grasped by one who does not feel how thoughts can be emphasized by being differently re-stated." In this we see the wisdom of God as applied to the Scripture, for the poetry of the Bible can be translated into any tongue without serious loss to the thought, while of other poetry, depending as it does on the sound, this can not be said. The first of the two Psalms expresses the feelings of an exile from the altar of his God, and the spirit of the whole lyric is summed up in its refrain, a struggle between hope and despair:

Why art thou cast down, O my soul?
And why art thou disquieted within me?
    Hope thou in God:
For I shall yet praise Him,
Who is the health of my countenance
    And my God!

Quoting The Literary Study of the Bible: "This refrain is found to unify into a single poem Psalms 42 and 43; and the whole falls into "three strophies." Instead of "three strophies and a refrain," substitute "three verses and a chorus," and we have a more popular idea of the poetical form of the two Psalms.

Psalm 44.

The section of Psalms now entered upon introduces "The Sons of Korah," but whether they were written by them, or for them, as a class of the Levitical singers, is difficult to say. The present Psalm was penned with reference to a national calamity, just when, or what, is not known. But the psalmist recounts past deliverances in such crises as a ground of confidence and hope now.

Psalm 45.

Is Messianic, for the proof of which, see the marginal references to the New Testament. The divisions are: The beauty of the King (vv. 1, 2); His coming in glory (vv. 4, 5); His Deity and the character of His reign (vv. 6, 7); the Church as associated with Him in His earthly reign (vv. 9-13); Her virgin companions (The Jewish remnant?) (vv. 14, 15); the whole concluding with an illusion to His earthly fame (vv. 16, 17).

The Scofield Bible thinks this Psalm might be classed with the two following, as all three look "forward to the advent in glory." The same might be said of all down to and including Psalm 50, with the possible exception of 49.

To speak of Psalm 46 particularly: Israel is seen in great trouble but firmly trusting in God (vv. 1-5). The cause is the gathering of the nations against her. (v. 6). But God is with her and overcomes the nations, visiting them with judgment (vv. 7, 8). Following these judgments there is peace over all the earth (vv. 9-11). This is clearly millennial in its ultimate application.

Psalm 47.

Is of the same character. Psalm 52 also can hardly be read by anyone familiar with the later revelations of the Bible concerning the Antichrist without thinking of that arch-despot. He is overcome by the Lord (v. 5), and exalted over by the righteous (vv. 6, 7), whose trust in the mercy of God has not been in vain (vv. 8, 9).

Psalm 51.

Is historical again, and grounded on the sad event in David's life dwelt upon the Second Samuel. The Scofield Bible characterizes it in its successive steps as "The mould of the experience of a sinning saint, who comes back to full communion and service." (1) Sin is judged before God, verses 1-6; (2) forgiveness and cleansing are secured through the blood, verses 7-19; (3) the restored one is now filled with the Holy Spirit for joy, power, service and worship, verses 11-17; and is at last seen in fellowship with God, not about self, but Zion (vv. 18, 19). "Personally, while it was David's pathway to restored communion, dispensationally, it will be that of returning Israel at the end of this age (Deut. 30:1-10).

The other Psalms in this lesson give their historical setting in their titles, and the student of those preceding will interpret them with little difficulty.

Questions.

1. What verses of Psalm 38 would seem to prevent its Messianic application entire?

2. What Messianic Psalms are noted in this lesson?

3. In what does the rhythm of Hebrew poetry consist?

4. What advantage does this give the poetry of Scripture?

5. Repeat the "chorus" of Psalms 42 and 43.

6. Which Psalms of this lesson look forward to the millennial age?

7. On what historical event is Psalm 51 grounded?

8. What dispensational application is possible in its case?

PSALMS 67-78

The first half dozen of these Psalms form a group millennial and Messianic. The first is millennial. It is Israel who speaks, and the Psalm cannot be appreciated except as the word "us" in verse 1 is so applied. When God has mercy upon and blesses Israel in the latter days, His way will begin to be known upon earth, and His saving health unto all nations (v. 2). In other words, the present age is one of out-gathering, but the age to come (millennial) will be one of in-gathering. God is now calling out a people for His Name from all the nations to form the Church, the body of Christ; but then He will be gathering all the nations to Him through the witness and ministry of Israel. This is the age of the evangelism of the nations, that the age of their conversion.

Why will the people be praising God in that day? Let verse 4 answer. It will, however, not only be a day of righteous governing, but one of great material prosperity (v. 6). The cause of it all is again expressed (v. 7).

The Scofield Bible teaches that Psalm 68, which some think to have been composed at the bringing up of the ark, is from the prophetic view, entirely pervaded by the joy of Israel in the Kingdom, but a strict order of events begins with verse 18 which in Ephesians 4:7-16 is quoted of Christ's ascension ministry. Verses 21-23 refer to the regathering of Israel and the destruction of the Anti-christ and his armies, while verses 24-35 describe the universal Kingdom blessing.

Psalm 69.

Is Messianic as judged by the New Testament quotations indicated in the margin. It is the Psalm of Christ's humiliation and rejection (vv. 4, 7, 8, 10-12). Verses 14-20 point to Gethsemane, and verse 21 to the cross. The imprecatory verses 22-28, may refer to the present judicial blindness of Israel, verse 25 having special reference to Judas (Acts 1:20), who is typical of his generation which shared his guilt.

Psalm 72.

Is also Messianic. Whether composed by, or for, Solomon (see title), "a greater than Solomon is here." Millennial expressions prevail throughout, for it is a Psalm of the King when He comes in His kingdom. The difference in the imagery between

this and Psalm 2 will be observed, but both conditions as thus outlined will prevail in the millennial age. That of Psalm 2 precedes that of this Psalm and makes this possible. There is difficulty in applying verse 15 to Christ as it speaks of prayer being "made for him," unless we translate "for" by "to" as some have ventured to do, although without good authority.

Book 2 ends at this point, the opening of Book 3 being marked by a number of Psalms ascribed to Asaph of whose history nothing is known, except as 2 Chronicles 35:15 and Ezra 2:41 enlighten us.

The first of the Psalms of Asaph (73), is the most familiar, and suggests the language of Job and Jeremiah under similar circumstances (see Jer. 12:1-4). The psalmist is complaining of the prosperity of the wicked and the affliction of the righteous; but as his eye of faith is opened to the sudden and fearful ruin of the former his misgivings are removed; and in the reassurance of his heart he chides himself for his folly and praises God's love.

The opening verse is the conclusion at which he arrives at the close, although it is stated first. He had nearly fallen into infidelity (v. 2), the reasons for which are stated (vv. 3-12). It seemed as if there were no use in being good (vv. 13, 14). He wisely kept his complainings to himself however (v. 15); and when he came to know God better, which is the meaning of verse 16, he understood the enigma (vv. 18-20). His confession of the sin of unbelief follows (vv. 21, 22), and then the renewal of his faith and confidence to the end.

Some think Psalms 75 and 76 belong together, the one anticipating what the other commemorates, viz., the divine deliverance of Israel from their enemies on some signal occasion. Possibly 2 Kings 19:35 and Isaiah 37 throw light upon them.

Psalm 78.

Is applied by some, to the removal of the sanctuary from Shiloh in the tribe of Ephraim to Zion, of Judah; and consequently, the transfer of eminence from the former to the latter tribe. Though this transfer was God's purpose from the beginning, yet the psalmist shows it to have been a divine judgment on Ephraim under whose leadership the people had shown the sinful and rebellious character that had distinguished their ancestors in Egypt. Read in this light, the Psalm becomes doubly interesting and instructive.

Questions.

1. How would you characterize several of the Psalms of this lesson?

2. How is Psalm 67 to be interpreted?

3. On the question of salvation how may this age be compared with the one to follow?

4. When, presumably, was Psalm 68 composed?

5. What is its prophetic application?

6. Have you read Ephesians 4?

7. How is Psalm 69 characterized?

8. Which of the disciples is referred to prophetically in this Psalm?

9. Which is the great Messianic Psalm of the lesson?

10. What is the theme of Psalm 73?

PSALMS 79-108

The first Psalm in this lesson suggests Psalm 74 on which we did not dwell, but both of which depict the desolations of Judah by the Babylonians (cf. Jer. 52:12-24). On this supposition their date would be that of the captivity, and their author a later Asaph than the Asaph mentioned in David's time.

Psalm 80.

Has captivity features also, and some would say it relates to the ten tribes, as the preceding Psalm does to Judah. The next several Psalms are much alike in this respect and may easily be interpreted from that point of view.

Psalm 86.

Attributed to David, constitutes a break in the series, and is a prayer which we pause to analyze. Observe the touching picture in verse 1, a child with his arms around his father's neck. Observe the five requests for: preservation, joy, instruction, strength and encouragement, in verses 2, 4, 11, 16 and 17 respectively. Observe the grounds from the human side on which an answer is expected, his need, importunity (margin), trust, relationship to God (margin), verses 1, 3, 4 and 2. From the divine side he expected it because of God's goodness, greatness and grace, verses, 5, 10, 13.

Of the authors of Psalms 88 and 89 we know nothing save that their names are among David's singers (1 Chron. 6:18, 33; 15:17). There is little to show the occasion when they were written, but the last-named has been assigned to Absalom's rebellion. From that point of view it may be a contrast between the promised prosperity of David's throne (2 Sam. 7), and what now threatens its downfall; but in any event it is full of helpfulness in spiritual application.

Psalms 90 and 91 (especially the latter).

Rank with 37, 51 and 103 in popular favor, being quoted almost as frequently. The first is a contrast between man's frailty and God's eternity, and the second, an outburst of confidence in the presence of physical peril. Many a foreign missionary has found this last "a very present help in time of trouble"! The two Psalms are also capable of a dispensational application, the first referring to Israel's day of sorrow and repentance, and the second to her deliverance and protection from the tribulation to come. Satan's use of 91:11, 12, in the temptation of our Lord, will not be forgotten (Matt. 4:6).

Psalms 93-100.

Were applied by the Jews to the times of the Messiah, who

had in mind His first advent only; but we know in the light of subsequent events see their application to His second advent. In Psalm 93 He is entering on His reign; in 94 He is appealed to for judgment on the evil-doers; in 95 Israel is exhorted to praise Him, and warned against unbelief. The substance of the next four is found in 1 Chronicles 16, which was used by David's direction at the dedication of the tabernacle on Mt. Zion, which typified the dispensation of the Messiah.

A break appears at Psalm 101, where David is once more named, and is making a vow of consecration corresponding to Psalm 15. In Psalm 102 he is pouring out a deep complaint, prophetic of Israel's hour of tribulation and her deliverance therefrom (vv. 13-22). Observe that when the kingdoms of the earth are serving the Lord, men will be declaring His name in Zion and praising Him in Jerusalem. As we have seen earlier, that sacred city will be the centre of things in the millennial age.

Psalms 103-108.
Are all of praise. In the first, David rises from a thankful acknowledgment of personal blessings (vv. 1-5) to a celebration of God's attributes. In the next God is praised for His works of creation and providence. In the next Israel's special reasons for praise are enumerated, the thought being carried forward into the two succeeding Psalms, although the second of the two broadens out again into a celebration of God's mercy to all men in their various emergencies. It is one of the most beautiful of the Psalms and its structure affords another good opportunity to illustrate Hebrew poetry.

Questions.
1. To what period of Israel's history may Psalms 74 and 79 apply?
2. What other Psalms may here be included?
3. Have you studied Psalm 86 with the aid of the outline in the lesson?

4. Memorize Psalm 91.
5. To what period does the group 93-100 probably belong?
6. How would you designate the next group?
7. What is the refrain of Psalm 107?

PSALMS 109-119

The first psalm in this lesson is one of the imprecatory or cursing psalms, in the interpretation of which we should keep in mind the principles already stated, (1) that the writer speaks as a prophet; (2), that the enemies are not merely personal to him but enemies of God; (3), that they are not individuals so much as nations; and (4), that they are considered at a time when the incorrigible condition has been reached, and they have become permanently fixed in opposition to the Most High. The allusion to Judas (v. 8), suggests a symbolical character for the whole, and it would not be difficult to discover under the surface the lineaments of the Antichrist.

Psalm 110.
"The explicit application of this psalm to the Saviour, by Himself (Matt. 22:42-45), and by the apostles (Acts 2:34; 1 Cor. 15:25; Heb. 1:13), and their frequent reference to its language and purport (Eph. 1:20-22; Phil. 2:9-11; Heb. 10:12, 13), leaves no doubt of its prophetic character.

"Not only was there nothing in the position or character of David to justify a reference to either, but the utter severance from the royal office of all priestly functions (so clearly assigned the subject of this psalm) positively forbids such a reference.

"The psalm celebrates the exaltation of Christ to the throne of an eternal and increasing kingdom, and a perpetual priesthood (Zech. 6:13), involving the subjugation of His enemies and the multiplication of His subjects, and rendered infallibly certain by the word and oath of Almighty God." [Jamieson, Faussett and Brown.]

Psalms 111, 112.

Are frequently interpreted together, the first celebrating God's gracious dealings with His people, and the second carrying on the thought as an exposition of its last verse. Using that verse as a text, the whole of Psalm 112 becomes illuminative of it.

Psalms 113-118.

Of these psalms it may be said that the Jews used them on their great festivals, calling them the Greater Hallel, which means hymn. They contrast God's majesty with His condescension (113), they celebrate His former care of His people (114), they beseech Him to vindicate His glory over the vanity of idols (115), they praise Him for deliverance from peril (116), etc.

The last-named (116), is a particularly beautiful psalm, noting three distinct experiences of the Psalmist: love (vv. 1-6); rest (vv. 7-11) and gratitude (vv. 12-19). Love because God heard him, rest even when men are false to him, and gratitude expressed both with the lips and life.

Psalm 119.

Has several peculiarities. "It is divided into twenty-two parts, or stanzas, denoted by the twenty-two letters of the Hebrew alphabet. Each stanza contains eight verses, and the first letter of each verse gives name to the stanza.

Its contents are mainly praises of God's word, exhortation to its perusal, and reverence for it; prayers for its proper influence, and complaints of the wicked despising it. There are but two verses (vv. 122, 132) which do not contain some term or description of God's word. These terms are of various derivations, but used, for the most part, synonymously, though the variety seems designed to express better the several aspects in which our relations to the Word are presented.

The psalm does not appear to have relation to any special occasion of the Jewish nation, but was evidently "intended as a manual of pious thoughts, especially for instructing the young, and its artificial structure was probably to aid the memory." [Jamieson, Faussett and Brown.]

Questions.

1. On what principles are the imprecatory psalms to be interpreted?

2. What New Testament character is typically referred to in Psalm 109?

3. What proves the prophetic character of Psalm 110?

4. What does that psalm celebrate?

5. What designation has been given to Psalms 113 to 118, and when and by whom are they used?

6. Name six peculiarities of Psalm 119.

PSALMS 120-134

This group is differentiated by the title attached to each, "A Song of Degrees," or "A Song of Ascents." The title seems derived from the going up of the people to Jerusalem at the great festivals which came three times a year. (Compare Deut. 16:16; 1 Kings 12:27, 28, etc.); the thought being that they chanted the psalms at different stages in their journey.

The pertinency of this application of these psalms is more apparent in some than others. For example, Psalm 121 represents the pilgrim looking towards the goal of his journey, and inspired by its contemplation to apply the thought of the strength of its hills to the care of God for His people, and especially His care for them on their journey, by night or day (vv. 3-6). The spiritual application is easily suggestive. Psalms 124, 126, 129 and 130, suggest the Babylonian captivity. Psalm 134 represents the companies arriving at the sanctuary and calling on the priests to unite in praising God on their behalf, to which the priests reply in the language of the Mosaic blessing which they only could pronounce (v. 3).

Of the whole group Psalm 132 is the most important in some

respects. May Solomon have been its author? It opens with a declaration of his father David's zeal for the building of the temple (vv. 1-7). "Ephratah" (v. 6) is another name for Bethlehem (Gen. 48:7). "The fields of the wood" stands for "Jair" or "Kirjath-jearim" whence the ark was brought up by David to Jerusalem. The psalm next pleads with God for fulfilment of His promises to David concerning the temple (vv. 8-18). The Solomonic application is clear in verses 10-12, and yet, it has a typical reference to the Kingdom of our Lord Jesus Christ.

Questions.

1. How is this group of psalms designated?
2. What is the probable sense of that designation?
3. At what period may some of the group have been composed?
4. Show their pertinency, by the analysis of one or more of the group.
5. State the probable history of Psalm 132.
6. Interpret Psalm 134.

PSALMS 135-150

Psalm 135.
Praises God for choosing Jacob (vv. 1-4), extols His power in the natural world (vv. 5-7), and in the deliverance of His people from Egypt (vv. 8, 9) and bringing them into the promised land (vv. 10-12). All this is in contrast to the vanity of idols (vv. 13-18).

Psalm 136.
Is of the same character as the preceding, but is notable for the chorus attached to each verse—a chorus with which we have become familiar in other psalms (106:1; 118:1-4), and which may have been used by the people somewhat like the "Amen."

Psalm 137.
Is plainly identified as to its period and design.

Psalm 139.
Is perhaps the most sublime declaration of the omnipresence of God found in the Holy Scriptures. In the light of that attribute the Psalmist is willing to submit himself to the closest scrutinizing (v. 23), and for the reason indicated at the close. Who will follow in his train?

We have now reached another group of David's psalms (138-140) whose structure and style are like some of the earlier ones —complaint, prayer, hope, praise.

Psalm 142.
Is unique in the historical note attached to it. The "cave" spoken of may have been Adullam (1 Sam. 22:1), or Engedi (1 Sam. 24:3), but it is not necessary to believe that the psalm was composed while David was in the cave. It may have been written later when his experience in the cave furnished a good illustration of his present need and an argument for his relief.

Psalms 147-150.
Are thought to especially celebrate the rebuilding of Jerusalem, and correspond to the conditions in Nehemiah 6:16; 12:27 and other places, although their millennial application is not far to seek.

The last psalm is a fitting close to the book, "reciting the place, theme, mode and extent of Jehovah's exalted praise."

Questions.

1. What is a familiar chorus to the psalms?
2. What is the period and design of Psalm 137?
3. What divine attribute is the theme of Psalm 139?
4. What group of psalms is contained in this lesson?
5. What gives a historic touch to Psalm 142?
6. Of what period are the last four Psalms commonly interpreted?

PROVERBS

INTRODUCTION

That Solomon was the principle author of Proverbs is indicated by chapters 1:1, and 25:1, compared with 1 Kings 4:29-32. The last two chapters were the work of other authors to whom reference is made. See also chapters 25-29.

Their Character.

In Solomon's day there was a class of leaders in the eastern nations known as "teachers of wisdom," of which he was the most conspicuous; a supposition which gives countenance to the thought that the address, "My son," is not that of a father to a child, but a teacher to a pupil.

Most of the proverbs seem based merely on considerations of worldly prudence, which was quite like Solomon; but considering the Holy Spirit as the real author, we must believe that faith is the underlying motive productive of the conduct to which the reader is exhorted. Indeed, this is expressed in 1:17; 5:21; 15:11; 23:17-19; 26:10.

Luther called Proverbs "a book of good works"; Coleridge, "the best statesman's manual"; Dean Stanley, "the philosophy of practical life." Angus says, "It is for practical ethics what the psalms are for devotion;" Bridges says "that while other Scriptures show us the glory of our high calling this instructs us minutely how to walk in it;" Oetinger says, "The proverbs exhibit Jesus with unusual clearness." In the millennial kingdom doubtless it will constitute, with a portion of the Levitical ordinances and the Sermon on the Mount, the basis of the laws governing its citizens.

Their Literary Style.

Proverbs is classed with the poetical books of the Bible, but we must content ourselves with a single illustration of the poetic form taken from The Literary Study of the Bible.

In 4:10 we have a poem on The Two Paths. Its strophe and antistrophe consist of ten-line figures, varying between longer and shorter lines; the conclusion is a quatrain. This form is a reflex of the thought of the poem; the strophe describes the path of the just, the antistrophe the path of the wicked; the conclusion then blends the two ideas in a common image, as follows:

Hear, O my son, and receive my savings;
And the years of thy life shall be many.
I have taught thee in the way of wisdom;
I have led thee in paths of uprightness.
When thou goest, thy steps shall not be straitened;
And if thou runnest, thou shalt not stumble.
 Take fast hold of instruction;
 Let her not go:
 Keep her;
 For she is thy life
Enter not into the path of the wicked,
And walk not in the way of evil men.
 Avoid it,
 Pass not by it;
 Turn from it,
 And pass on.
For they sleep not, except they have done mischief;
And their sleep is taken away, unless they cause some to fall.
For they eat the bread of wickedness.
And drink the wine of violence.
But the path of the righteous is as the light of dawn,
That shineth more and more unto the perfect day.
The way of the wicked is as darkness;
They know not at what they stumble.

Questions.

1. What scriptures point to Sol-

omon as the principal author of
this book?

2. What scriptures indicate additional authors?

3. What may have been the origin of the book?

4. Is it, on the whole, a book of creed or conduct?

5. Compare it with the psalms.

6. Is it likely to have a future application? If so, when?

7. What is the literary form of the book?

8. Where is the poem on "The Two Paths" found?

CHAPTERS 1-3

The nature of this book makes divisions of its chapters rather arbitrary, and ours may not always be the best, but it is hoped it may prove useful in some degree. The opening of chapter four suggests a new beginning, for which reason we conclude this lesson at the close of chapter three.

It begins with an advertisement (1:1-6), in which mention is made of the author (v. 1), the object of the book (vv. 2, 3), and its great value (vv. 4-6).

Then follows its theme, "The fear of the Lord is the beginning of knowledge" (v. 7), of which the remainder of the lesson is a development or exposition. "Beginning" is rendered in the margin of the Revised Version "chief part." "The fear of the Lord" means a right state of heart towards God as opposed to the condition of an unconverted man. Put the two ideas together, and we learn that the chief part of all knowledge is to be right with God. In working out of the thought:

1. The teacher exhorts his "son" or pupil, to avoid vice (1:8-19).

2. He shows the ruinous conduct of the unwise, a warning placed on the lips of wisdom personified (1:20-33).

3. This warning is accentuated by contrasting the consequences of obedience and a striving after wisdom (2:1-3).

4. The Lord is shown as the protector of those who are wise in this sense (3:19-26).

5. The division concludes with an admonition to charity and justice (3:27-35).

Practical and Doctrinal Remarks.

In this part of the lesson we call attention to particular verses for explanation or application, acknowledging indebtedness to Arnot's "Laws From Heaven for Life on Earth."

1:23 is a text for a revival sermon, containing a command and a promise joined, like Philippians 2:12. It teaches in one sentence those two seemingly contradictory doctrines, the sovereignty of God, and the free agency of man. It is when we turn at God's reproof that He pours out His Spirit; though it be also true that unless His Spirit is poured out we can not turn.

1:24-32 offers an opportunity to preach on God's mercy to a rebellious people. He calls, stretches out His hands, counsels, and administers reproof. On the other hand men refuse, disregard, set at nought, reject. The natural consequence follows; sowing disobedience they reap judgment. That judgment consists in calling on God and getting no answer, seeking diligently and not finding Him. The passage closes with a promise to them that hearken—deliverance from death at last and freedom from fear now.

2:1-9 suggests Christ's words in Luke 11:9, "Seek, and ye shall find." The seeking is in verses 1-4, the finding in verses 5-9.

2:10-22 is an outline of "the way of evil" (v. 12, R. V.). The first step is "speaking froward things"; the second, leaving "the paths of uprightness," the feet soon follow the tongue (v. 13); the third, walking "in the ways of darkness" (v. 13); the fourth, rejoicing "to do evil" (v. 14); fifth, delighting "in the frowardness of the wicked," we can not take pleasure in doing wickedness without finding pleasure in seeing others do it; sixth, to complete the picture, the evil person here particularly in mind is seen to be a woman (vv. 16-22).

3:5, 6 presents one of the strongest promises of the Bible—

the first text from which the author of this commentary ever preached. Note how we are to trust, "with all thine heart." God complains as much of a divided allegiance as of none. Note the extent of our trust, "in all thy ways." "Few will refuse to acknowledge a superintending providence at certain times, and in certain operations that are counted great," but God wants us to confide in Him in the little, close, and kindly things.

3:11, 12 is quoted in Hebrews 12:5, 6. Note there how the inspired writer interprets the phrase, "My son." The speaker in Proverbs may have been addressing a pupil merely, but the Holy Spirit through him, "speaketh unto you as unto sons."

"Despise not," means do not make light of chastening or cast it aside as if it had no meaning for you; "faint not" touches the opposite extreme, do not be driven to despair by the experience. "The middle way is the path of safety."

3:13-20 is a description and appreciation of wisdom, which throughout this book means piety or godliness. In Ecclesiastes it is science. And yet piety or godliness hardly expresses it in the highest sense in which it is sometimes found, where as for example in these verses, it suggests Christ. He is the wisdom of God as we learn in the New Testament, who, by the Holy Spirit through the holy Scriptures is made unto us wisdom (1 Cor. 2). Such wisdom can not be planned, much less created by us, but must be "found" or "gotten" (v. 13).

Observe the figures describing it. It is precious merchandise (vv. 14, 15). It is a way of honor, pleasantness and peace (vv. 16, 17). It is a tree of life (v. 18).

Questions.

1. What is the chief part of all knowledge?

2. Give the five general divisions of this lesson.

3. Quote and give the doctrinal teaching of 1:23.

4. Quote and give the spiritual

significance of 1:33; 3:5, 6; 3:11, 12.

5. What does "wisdom" mean in this book?

CHAPTERS 4-7

These chapters begin with reminiscence. A father is reciting to a son the precepts taught him by his father in his youth, and which cover chapter four. Chapter five is a warning against the evil woman. Chapter six deals with suretyship, indolence, malice and violence, while chapter seven returns to the theme of chapter five.

In the first-named chapter occurs the beautiful illustration of Hebrew rhythm to which attention was called in Lesson 1; and following it we find in verses 18 and 23, two of as oft-quoted texts as are in the whole book.

The "just" man, as usual in the Bible, is he who is justified by faith and walks with God in a holy obedience. On him the Sun of Righteousness shines. His new life is at first like the morning light, a struggle between the darkness and the dawn. Ere long the doubt vanishes, and morning is unequivocally declared. The counterpart is fitted to overawe the boldest heart, "The way of the wicked is as darkness, they know not at what they stumble." The thought is that the darkness is in them and they carry it, an evil heart of unbelief, wherever they go.

As to the other text, notice the fountain—the heart (v. 23), and then the stream—the mouth, the eyes, the feet (vv. 24-27). The heart is kept by prayer and the Word of God, and then the life issuing from it is what it ought to be. The speech is pure, and true and potent. There are no secret longings and side glances after forbidden things, and the steps in matters of business, society, and the home are all ordered of the Lord. (Compare Christ's words, Matt. 15:18-20).

Family Joys.

We have spoken of chapter five as a warning against the evil woman, which is true of its first half; but the reader will observe how the warning is accentuated by the contrast of the pure and happy home life in the second half, beginning at verse 15. The former is a dark back ground to bring out the latter's beauty. The keynote of the first half is "remove far from her." She is deceitful (vv. 3, 4), unstable (v. 6) and cruel (v. 9). To associate with her means waste of property and health (vv. 8, 9), and at the last remorse (vv. 12-14).

The home in comparison is a pure and well-guarded well (v. 15). Read verses 16 and 17 in the Revised Version, and observe a husband's duty toward his wife (v. 18). Let him avoid biting words, neglect, unnecessary absences and the like. And as Paul says (Eph. 5:33), let "the wife see that she reverence her husband."

The suretyship against which we are warned (6:1-5) is of the inconsiderate kind. "That imprudent assumption of such obligations leaving out of account the moral unreliableness of the man involved." The advice is to get the quickest release possible (vv. 3-5). It does not mean that we should not kindly and prudently help a neighbor in financial need, if we can.

The "mother" of verses 20-24 must be one who knows God, for it is the instilling of His Word only in the heart of her child that can produce the results indicated. Observe it is a grown son here referred to as keeping his mother's law.

Questions.

1. What are the general subjects treated in these chapters?

2. Quote and explain 6:18.

3. What possible evidence is there in this lesson of our Lord's acquaintance with Proverbs?

4. What does this lesson teach about conjugal love? About parental authority? About suretyship?

CHAPTERS 8-9

In these chapters we have a public discourse of Wisdom (personified) (c. 8), and what Lange describes as an allegorical exhibition of the call of men to a choice of wisdom or folly, (c. 9).

It is really our Lord Jesus Christ putting forth this voice (8:1), and crying unto men at the gates of the city (vv. 4, 5). It is He who speaks the excellent things, (v. 6), and on whose lips wickedness is an abomination (v. 7). Of Him alone can it be predicted that there is nothing crooked (forward) in His mouth (v. 8), or to be desired in comparison with Him (vv. 10-18). It is He whose fruit is better than gold and who fills our treasuries (vv. 19-21). Were there any doubt of this identity would it not be removed by the remainder of the chapter? Who was set up from everlasting (v. 23)? Or, who was daily God's delight (v. 30)? And of whom can it be said that to find Him finds life (v. 35)?

The Redeemer Anticipating Redemption.

The heading of this paragraph expresses Arnot's conception of the latter part of the chapter, who says that, "if the terms are not applied to Christ they must be strained at every turn." Of course in a book writted by Solomon it could not be said that Jesus was born in Bethlehem and died upon the cross, but if the Holy Spirit wished to make known something of the personal history of Christ before His coming, how could He have done so in plainer terms than these?

Quoting the same in verses 30 and 31: "These three things are set in the order of the everlasting covenant: (1), the Father well pleased with His Beloved, 'I was daily His delight;' (2), the Son delighting in the Father's presence, 'rejoicing always before Him;' (3), the Son looking with prospective delight to the scene and subjects of His redemptive work, 'rejoicing in the habitable part of His earth; and my delights were with the sons of men.' "

The Marriage Supper in the Old Testament.

Arnot gives the foregoing title to the opening verses of chapter 9, where Wisdom, personifying the Son of God, has now come nigh unto men, having His habitation among them. Here we have the house, the prepared feast, the messengers, the invited guests, and the argument by which the invitation is supported. The positive side of that argument is: "Come, eat of my bread, and drink of the wine which I have mingled." The negative is: "Forsake the foolish, and live."

The closing of this chapter exhibits Christ's "great rival standing in the same wide thoroughfare of the world and bidding for the youth who thronged it." "All that is contrary to Christ and dangerous to souls, is gathered up and individualized in the person of an abandoned woman lying in wait for unwary passengers, baiting her hook with sin and dragging her victims down the incline to hell."

The reader will see how Proverbs may be fruitfully utilized in preaching the gospel.

Questions.

1. What have we in these chapters?
2. Who really is speaking here?
3. What proves it?
4. Analyze verses 30 and 31 from the New Testament point of view.
5. What parable of Christ is suggested in chapter 9?

Chapters 10-15

Some regard the division now entered upon as the original nucleus of the whole collection of proverbs (see the first sentence of verse one). The division extends really to the close of chapter 22, and contains "maxims, precepts and admonitions with respect to the most diverse relations of life." In so much of it as is covered by the present les-

son we have a contrast "between the godly and the ungodly, and their respective lots in life."

Following Zockler's outline in Langé we have this contrast set before us, first in general terms of the lesson, in detail, as follows:

(1) As to the just and unjust, and good and bad conduct towards one's neighbor, chapter 11.

(2) As to the domestic and public associations, chapter 12.

(3) As to the use of temporal good, and of the Word of God as the highest good, chapter 13.

(4) As to the relation between the wise and the foolish, the rich and the poor, masters and servants, chapter 14.

(5) As to the various other relations and callings in life, especially within the sphere of religion, chapter 15.

Memory Verses and Choice Texts.

This lesson is not suggestive of questions, but contains verses it would be well to memorize. For example, in chapter 10, verses 7, 9, 14, 22, 25; chapter 11, verses 1, 2, 13, 24, 25, 26, 30; chapter 13, verses 7, 15, 24; chapter 14, verses 10, 12, 25, 27, 32, 34; chapter 15, verses 1, 3, 8.

In Arnot's "Laws from Heaven for Life on Earth," there are helpful discourses on several of these texts, the titles of which will be appreciated by young preachers: "Posthumous Fame," 10:7; "The Center of Gravity," 10:9; "The Passing Whirlwind and the Sure Foundation," 10:25; "Assorted Pairs," 11:2; "Virtue Its Own Reward," 11:17; "Scattering to Keep, and Keeping to Scatter," 11:24; "Raising the Market," 11:26; "The Wisdom of Winning Souls," 11:30; "Man Responsible for His Belief," 14:12; "The Two Departures— The Hopeful and the Hopeless," 14:32.

Chapters 16-24

In these chapters we have a series of exhortations to a life of godliness expressed in general terms about as follows:

(1) Confidence in God as a wise ruler, chapter 16.

(2) A disposition of peacefulness and contentment, chapter 17.

(3) The virtues of affability, fidelity, and others of a social nature, chapter 18.

(4) Humility and meekness, chapter 19.

(5) Sobriety, diligence and kindness, chapter 21.

(6) Justice, patience, submission, chapter 21.

(7) The attainment and preservation of a good name, chapter 22.

(8) Warnings against avarice, licentiousness, and similar vices, chapter 23.

(9) Warnings against ungodly companionship, chapter 24.

CHAPTERS 25-29

This division of the book is introduced in the first verse of chapter 25, as the "proverbs of Solomon, which the men of Hezekiah, king of Judah, copied out." What these words mean it is difficult to say, except in the general sense that the teachers of Hezekiah's period selected and gathered together wise sayings that had been written, or handed down orally in previous generations. They may have been those of Solomon only, and yet his name may be attached to them simply because they were now made part of his general collection. They contain admonitions to the fear of God and righteousness, addressed partly to kings, and yet also to their subjects. They also contain warnings against evil conduct of various kinds, (c. 26); against conceit and arrogance (c. 27); against unlawful dealings, especially of the rich with the poor (c. 28); and against stubbornness and insubordination, (c. 29).

CHAPTERS 30-31

The last division consists of two supplements, one of the words of Agur (c. 30), and the other or Lemuel (c. 31).

Agur's words begin with an exaltation of the Word of God (vv. 1-6), followed by short and pithy maxims with reference to the rich and the poor, pride and greed, etc.

Lemuel's words open with a philosophical statement, applying chiefly to kings, followed by his well-known poem in praise of the virtuous woman.

ECCLESIASTES

INTRODUCTION

The ground for ascribing Ecclesiastes to Solomon is fourfold: (1) The indirect claim of the book as gathered from chapter 1, verses 1 and 12; (2) the general opinion of Jews and Christians from the earliest times; (3) the fitness of Solomon to write; (4) the lack of agreement among critics as to any other author or period.

There are different plans or theories of the book, but to the compiler of this commentary it is a kind of biography of Solomon's life, and yet one in which he not only records, but re-enacts his search for happiness, making of it a kind of dramatic biography.

In other words, Solomon rehearses the various phases of his former self, having fits of study, luxury, misanthropy, etc., all ending in disappointment. It is important to note that "wisdom" in Ecclesiastes means "science," while in Proverbs it means "piety." In the same connection, "vanity" here means not merely foolish pride, but "the emptiness of the final result of life apart from God" (Rom. 8:20-22).

They who hold this conception of the book are well represented by W. J. Erdman, in his concise work, entitled "Ecclesiastes," on which we have permission to draw for what follows. He calls it

"The Book of the Natural Man," by which he means man as he is "under the sun," compared with the man of Paul, whose "citizenship is in heaven."

The first proof is that the only divine name in the book is the "natural" name, God (Elohim), the significance of which all will recognize from our reference to it in Genesis. Jehovah, the name associated with the covenant of redemption, is not once employed; hence, man is seeking what is best "under the sun," but not seeking Him who is above the sun.

A second proof is the frequent use of "under the sun." "Man is looking up, not knowing what is beyond, except judgment."

A third proof is that all the experiences and observations of the book are bound together by the one question: "What is the chief good?" "Is life worth living?" While the answer is sought amidst general failure, contradictions, and half-truths, because man is out of Christ, and yet face to face with the mysteries of God and nature.

A fourth proof is what the book styles "the conclusion of the whole matter" (12:13, 14), which is that of the natural man only. "To fear God and keep His commandments," is right, but the author of Ecclesiastes confessedly has not done so, and yet he sees judgment in the distance and has no preparation to meet it.

"Where man ends therefore, God begins." The book of the natural man concludes where that of the spiritual man begins. The all-in-all of man under the sun convicts him of failure and guilt in order to lead him to the all-in-all of the man above the sun, the second Adam, who bare our guilt in His own body on the tree.

Is the Book Inspired?

This conception of the book explains why some of its conclusions are only partially true and others altogether false, such as 2:16; 3:19; 9:2; etc.

And if it be asked, How then can the book be inspired? the answer is that in the inspiration of the Bible we do not claim the inspiration of the men, but the writings; while in the latter case it is not meant that every word thus written is true, and in that sense God's Word, but that the record of it is true. That is, God caused it to be written that this or that man felt this or that way, and said thus and so, and hence the record of how he felt and what he said is God's record, and in that sense true and in that sense inspired.

CHAPTERS 1-2

1. The Prologue 1:1-11.

including (1) the general result of the whole search for good on earth, the record of which is to follow (vv. 1-3); (2) a symbolic illustration from nature of the monotony of human existence (vv. 4-7); (3) a plain statement of the facts in the case (vv. 8-11).

2. The Introduction vv. 12-18.

describing the seeker (v. 12); his method of search (v. 13), and the result in general (vv. 14, 15) and in particular (vv. 16-18).

3. Various Vanities.

and the conclusions drawn from them (2:2-26). The lust of the flesh (vv. 1-3); the lust of the eyes (vv. 4-6); pride of life (vv. 7, 8); conclusion (vv. 9-11). The vanity of wisdom (vv. 12-17); the vanity of work (vv. 18-23); conclusion (vv. 24-26).

CHAPTERS 3-4

1. Man's Times 3:1-11.

These are orderly and seasonable, but bring no permanent profit, because man is still ignorant of God's purpose in them all, He does not know how to fit his work into God's work. The conclusion follows (vv. 12-15).

2. God's Time vv. 16-22.

There is a suggestion in verse 17 that this is long. It will be a time, too, of judgment and manifestation (vv. 17, 18), and yet, and perhaps because of this, man's death is not different from the beast (vv. 19-21); conclusion (v. 22).

3. Sundry Wrongs and Vanities 4:1-16.

Oppression (vv. 1-3); envy (4:4-6); the lonely miser (vv. 7-12); political disappointment (vv. 13-16).

CHAPTERS 5-6

1. Varieties in Worship, 5:1-7.

On these verses the writer seems to muse on the relation of the unseen Being to the act of man in worship. "Mindful of man's jaunty liberalism and superstition, rash vows and wordy prayers, dreamy and unreal, because full of intruding vanities and worldly businesses, the preacher earnestly exhorts to few words and solemn steps." But even then it is the natural man only who is speaking in the exhortation, not the regenerate man, because he speaks "only of a God who is far away and looks upon sinful man on earth with cold, judicial eye, ready to destroy the work of man in wrath."

2. Vanities of Wealth, vv. 8-20.

Oppression of the poor by the rich (vv. 8, 9); dissatisfaction with mere abundance (vv. 10-12); hoarded riches an evil (vv. 13-17) conclusion (vv. 18-20).

3. Contradictions c. 6.

This chapter is a contradiction of the conclusion reached at the close of the preceding one. He thought it was "good and comely for one to eat, and drink and enjoy the good of all his labor," but now he is startled by discovering as a "common" experience that there are men of wealth and honor from whom God withheld this enjoyment (vv. 1, 2).

"Having begun his descent from the sunny slopes of a natural piety he sinks at last into the deepest melancholy." To be blessed with wealth, offspring, long life, and yet not have the "good" he once thought he had, were worse than never to have been. Before the mystery of it all he is dumb (vv. 11, 12).

CHAPTERS 7-9:12

The interval between this chapter and the preceding represents a pause in the writer's thought, and now he seems to "set out on a new quest for the chief good" in life. He will seek it in wise conduct. He will renounce feasting and trying the opposite (7:1-6); he will avoid extremes (7:15-18); no one is perfectly righteous (7:19-22); the worst thing he has found is woman (7:23-26); the conclusion is that man is indeed a fallen creature (7:27-29). "Inventions" in this last verse is to be taken in the sense of "tricks, evil artifices, and conceits."

The wise conduct which the preacher now proposes is to be exercised against temptations to disloyalty and rebellion in national and civic relations (8:1-8); and against the oppressions of tyrants and other injustices (8:9-13); and yet after considering it all, in his accustomed despair he reports to his favorite conclusion that there is "nothing in it," and he had better enjoy himself anyway (8:14-17).

This idea is carried over into chapter nine. The providence of God in human affairs is inscrutable (vv. 1-3), therefore the only thing to do is to enjoy this life cheerfully, and use it as profitably as possible (vv. 7-12).

Chapters 9:13-12:14

Erdman makes a new division here, and while others do not agree with him, yet there is that which suggests it, surely. To quote him, the preacher here seems to have returned to "the placid, philosophic mood again, in the cautious praise of wisdom (9:13-18). This praise is followed by a number of proverbs of natural wisdom and prudence (see chapter 10, especially verses 16-20).

In chapters 11 and 12 we have "the final sum and forecast," which is, that however pleasant at times life under the sun may be, everything that is to come, like everything that has been, will contain times of darkness. The whole period of life from childhood to old age is vanity (17:7, 8).

Therefore special exhortations to childhood and youth follow (11:9, 10). Rejoice if you will, but judgment follows.

These exhortations are accompanied by warnings against the evils and miseries of old age—the old age of a vainly spent life (12:1-8). And these lead to the epilogue of the book the mournful repetition of the monotonous refrain, "vanity of vanities, all is vanity." (12:8), and the great conclusion of man under the sun, "Fear God and keep His commandments" (12:13, 14). And why? Because judgment is coming, and yet no salvation is seen!

Summary.

"Thus in abrupt endings and sudden returns to the one great question of the book, the preacher keeps showing man to himself. Debating between the vanities of life and the gloom of the grave; the contentment of ignorance and the worth of wisdom; the vexations of riches and the miseries of poverty; the orderly 'times' of man and the 'eternity' of God; the wrongs which are not righted and the dead that can no longer be oppressed; a distant God and a becoming worship; the wonder why that women worth the name are so scarce, and the reason that things are as they are; the pride and fragrant joys of family life and the event of death that comes to all; the lifelong possession of all manner of earthly good and the final lack of imposing obsequies and an honorable grave; the problem of the proper conduct of life and the mystery of the divine purpose and plan; between such, and manifold more earthly things like these, and others too high for mortal men, the preacher keeps moving on to the discouraging conclusion."

That conclusion is the truth underlying all natural religions, the utterance of the universal conscience, namely, "Fear God; do right; thy judgment day is coming." It is some relief, amidst the wrongs and perplexities of the world, to look for a day of judgment to righten and clear up all, but, as has been said, there is no personal salvation in it.

Where man ends, however, God begins. The book of the natural man closes that the gospel of the Son of God may open.

An Alternative Outline

As some may find the preceding outline difficult to grasp, the following is added as suggested in part by the headings of the chapters in the Scofield Reference Bible:

1. The Theme (1:1-3).

2. The Theme Proved (1:4-3:22).

   (a) The transitoriness of all things (1:4-11).

   (b) The fruitlessness of power, wisdom or knowledge, to counteract evil (1:12-18).

   (c) The emptiness of pleasure, (2:1-3).

   (d) The emptiness of wealth and great works (2:4-11).

   (e) The limitations of wisdom (2:12-26).

   (f) The weariness of life (3:1-22).

3. The Theme Developed (4:1-10:20).

   (a) In the light of the oppressions and iniquities of life (4:1-16).

   (b) In the light of riches and poverty (5:1-26).

   (c) In the light of man's inevitable end (6:1-12).

   (d) In the light of incurable evil (7:1-29).

   (e) In the light of the mysteries of providence (8:1-17).

   (f) In the light of the world's wrong standards of values (9:1-18).

   (g) In the light of the anarchy of the world (10:1-20).

4. The best thing possible to man apart from God (11:1-12:12).

5. The best thing possible to man under the law (12:13, 14).

SONG OF SOLOMON

INTRODUCTORY

Internal evidence confirms the voice of antiquity that Solomon wrote this book (See 1 Kings 4:32). As it is called the Song of Songs, the title carries the idea that it is the best of all his songs. Moreover, although it is not quoted in the New Testament, yet it always formed part of the Old as far as we have record, and was in the canon of sacred Scripture which Jesus and His apostles recognized as such.

When it was written is not known, but its imagery seems drawn from the marriage of Solomon either with Pharoah's daughter, or some native of Palestine espoused some years later of noble birth, though inferior to her husband. For the first idea compare 1 Kings 3:1; 7:8; 9:24, with chapters 1:9, and 6:12 of the Song, and for the second, look at the Song, 2:1; 7:1; 1:6.

There are two characters who speak and act throughout, Shelomoh, a masculine name, meaning "peaceful," and Shulamith, a feminine form of the same name. See 1:6; 3:11; 6:13; 8:12. There is also a chorus of virgins, daughters of Jerusalem, 2:7; 3:5; 5:8, 9.

Towards the close two brothers of Shulamith appear (8:8, 9). See also 1:6). As in most Hebrew poetry, and indeed all ancient poems, there are no breaks to indicate change of scene or speakers, which is determined partly by the sense, but chiefly by the use of the original of the feminine and masculine pronouns.

The book is a description of wedded love; and yet, of course, it has a higher aim. It is noticeable that there is a sudden change from the singular to the plural in 1:4, which seems to indicate in the judgment of Angus, that Shulamith must be taken collectively; a fact which, put with others gives credence to the idea that the story should be applied to the history of God's chosen people and their relation to Him. Every reader of the Bible knows that the union of Jehovah with Israel, and that of Christ and His church are presented under the same figure of marriage. (See such passages as Psalm 45; Isaiah 54:5; 6; Jeremiah 2:2; Hosea 2:14-23; Matthew 9:15; John 3:29; Ephesians 5:23-27, etc.)

Outline of the Book.

The following is from Angus' Bible Hand-book:

1. Shulamith speaks, 1:2-6; then in dialogue with Shelomoh; Shul. 1:7; Shel. 1:8-11; Shul. 1:12-14; Shel. 1:15; Shul. 1:16-2:1; Shel. 2:2; Shul. 2:3.

2. Shulamith now rests, sleeps and dreams (Shelomoh addressing the daughters of Jerusalem and charging them not to wake her, 2:7; 3:5; 2:4-6; 8:3:4).

3. The daughters of Jerusalem see a nuptial procession approaching 3:6-11.

4. Dialogue between Shelomoh and Shulamith. Shelomah speaks 4:1-16; (as far as "flow out") Shul. 4:16; Shel. 5:1.

5. A night scene; Shulamith seeking for Shelomoh; meets and converses with the daughters of Jerusalem; Shul. 5:2-8; daughters of Jerusalem, 5-9; Shul. 5:10-16; daughters of Jerusalem, 6:1; Shul. 6:2, 3.

6. Morning scene; Shelomoh visits his garden early, and meets Shulamith; Shel. 6:4-10; Shul. 6:11, 12; the dialogue continuing to 8:8.

7. The brothers of Shulamith are introduced; the brothers speak 8:8, 9; Shulamith answers them, 8:10-12; Shelomoh speaks, 8:13; and Shulamith answers, closing the scene, 8:14.

CHAPTERS 1-2

For the following we are indebted to "An Exposition and Vindication of Solomon's Song" by James Strong, S. T. D., who combines the literal and allegorical modes of interpretation—the idea that the poem celebrates the royal marriage, and is also symbolic of the relation of Jehovah and His people in both dispensations. The details apply to the former, while the spiritual conceptions are foreshadowed in the latter.

Hebrew wedding festivities usually lasted a week, the marriage being consummated at the close of the first day, but here the nuptials seemed to have been postponed till the last day. The description, therefore, is not that of the honeymoon, but the wooing.

Strong distributes the drama into six acts corresponding to as many days—not extending into the Sabbath — and subdivides each into two scenes, morning and evening.

Act I. Scene 1.

This sub-section comprises verses 2-8 of chapter 1. The bride is an Egyptian princess, whose train of attendants has reached the royal portico at Jerusalem, and is met by the Israelitish maids of honor. Her thoughts are busy with anticipation of the greeting from her intended, and she expresses them, almost unconsciously, in the words, "Let him kiss me with the kisses of his mouth" (1-2). The ladies respond to the close of verse 3.

The bride orders the attendants to proceed. She being carried in a palanquin, a covered conveyance borne on the shoulders of men, and she exclaims, "Draw me," or "Bear me forward." The ladies respond, "We will run after thee!" Passing within the palace, she says, "The king hath brought me into his chambers" (his courts), and the ladies respond, to the close of verse 4.

The bride disparages her charms in verse 5, and a dialogue ensues between her and the ladies to the end of verse 8, where she is left awaiting the bridegroom in an ante-room.

If we seek the spiritual application of this, it is found in the expectant desire of true believers for the second coming of Christ.

Act I. Scene 2.

This scene runs from 1:9 to 2:6, and describes the introduction of the lovers to each other, in one of the interior reception chambers in presence of the attendants.

The bridegroom expresses his admiration of the bride (verses 9 and 10), and the attendants respond, verse 11. Probably the bride speaks (12-14), her observations inspired by a glimpse of the nosegay ("spikenard") at her bosom. Compliments are passed between her and the bridegroom (1:15-2:3), and probably the symbolic language is suggested by the garden and its fountains that lie before them.

The bridegroom and his attendants retire, but the bride continues addressing the ladies (4-6). Overpowered with emotion at her lover's favor toward her, she begs restoratives from them, although she sighs for his personal support to keep her from sinking.

The scene is emblematic of the church's rapturous contemplation of her glorified state with Christ. And there is that in it which suggests the declaration of John the Baptist: "He that hath the bride is the bridegroom; but the friend of the bridegroom which standeth and heareth, rejoiceth greatly because of the bridegroom's voice" (John 3:29).

Act II. Scene 1.

This scene (2:7-17) opens on the next morning, and represents the royal lover starting on a hunting trip. He serenades his sweetheart beneath her chamber window, urging her maidens not to awaken her (7). Her quick ear detects his voice, and she calls to her maidens concerning him (8-10), and repeats his song (10-14). A rougher voice, that of the gardener, is heard (15). Meanwhile the bride, having finished her toilet, is at the window acknowledging the song (16, 17).

CHAPTERS 3-5

Act II. Scene 2.

This scene embraces the first four verses of chapter 2, and is a soliloquy of the bride in the nature of a troubled dream—troubled because of anxiety for her lover's safety in the chase. It is emblematical of the temporary interruption experienced in the fellowship of Christ's people with their Lord.

Act III. Scene 1.

We are here dealing with the events of verses 5-11 of this same chapter, and which are supposed to have occurred on the third morning. The royal procession advances, bearing the spoils of the preceding day's excursion. Solomon again sends a caution to the bride's maids against breaking her slumber (5). She is alert, however, and exclaims to her attendants as in verse 6, who reply in verses 7 and 8. She recognizes the palanquin (9), and the maidens tell her of its construction (10). The latter are then permitted by her to make a closer inspection (11).

Act III. Scene 2.

We are now in the fourth chapter to which may be added the first verse of chapter five. Solomon has left the palanquin, and approaching the window of his bride, sings the praises of her person, which a partly drawn veil discloses (1-7). "His thoughts running upon his favorite rural haunts, he proposes future excursions to these spots, especially his garden, with which he compares his beloved in *her gorgeous* and perfumed attire" (8-16). She receives these ecomiums with modest silence, and then suggests that he do not wait for her to share his enchanting retreat. This observation he turns into another compliment that she herself, her presence, is his garden, whereupon, turning to his companions, he bids them share with him the luxury of the moment (v. 1).

There is a term occurring (1:2, 4; 4:10; 7:12) which Strong translates "loves" or "love tokens," and which, he says, can not mean kisses, or other found endearments as some have interpreted them; but as the contexts show, the cosmetic odors, perhaps from a lovecharm casket which the bride may have worn on the occasion. That no erotic sentiment is couched under the figures of this scene is shown by the closing invitation of the lover to his companions. From which we may conclude that no double meaning is intended by the similar metaphors in chapter 7, verses 7-9, following.

Compare corresponding passages of the Bible which express God's favor for His people and the love they should show towards Him (Isa. 62:5; Ezek. 16:10-13; Zeph. 3:14, 17; Eph. 5:25-27).

Act IV. Scene 1.

The morning scene of the fourth day (5:2-6:3) contains the recital of a nightmare illusion of the bride addressed to the ladies in her private apartment. In the opinion of Strong, verse 15 is to be interpreted of the snowy linen leggings, in contrast with the gilt sandals worn by Solomon. His knocking at the door for admission is borrowed in the Saviour's address to the church of Laodicea (Rev. 3:20). The description of the bridegroom's person is in keeping with the manifestations of the Redeemer in both Testaments (Ezek. 1:26, 27; Dan. 10:5,6; Rev. 1:13-15).

CHAPTERS 6-8

Act IV. Scene 2.

This sub-section corresponds to the afternoon of the fourth day, and carries us through chapter 6. The occasion looks like a formal visit of the bridegroom, with his courtiers, to the bride and her maids of honor. The place is a room in her future palace. Solomon begins his praises, 6:4-12, when the bride rises to retire, but the courtiers beg her to remain (13). The ladies inquire, "What will ye see in the Shulamite?" or, "Why do ye desire her to tarry longer?"

Act V. Scene 1.

On this, the morning of the fifth day, the bridesmaids are describing the nuptial wardrobe as they assist the bride in her toilet (7:1-6). Compare the wardrobe in Isaiah 3:16-24. See also a parallel in Psalm 45.

Act V. Scene 2.

The afternoon of the same day (7:7-8:3), is a representation of a more private interview between the two, when they avow their attachment for each other. As the week advances they are thus gradually brought into closer acquaintance with one another, and their affection increases. The bridegroom begins the conversation (7:7-9), and the bride responds in an undertone (10), but subsequently "reverts to the rural haunts of her maternal home," whither she would invite him (12, 13 and continuing into the next chapter).

The warmth of these expressions seem to many too amatory for spiritual interpretation, but following Strong, we keep two considerations before us (1), it is the bride who speaks in the most ardent terms, not the bridegroom, and it is only right to assume a pure and refined nature behind them appropriate to her sex and innocence; (2), it is no cold "platonic" love which the Bible employs as the emblem of Christ's feeling for His church, but something very different. See Ephesians 5:28-33.

Act VI. Scene 1.

This is the wedding day. Chapter 8, verses 4 to 7, may be taken as corresponding to the formal espousal in the presence of witnesses after the manner of the Hebrews.

Solomon arrives early (4), but the bride soon joins him, and then the guests are represented as asking the question in verse 5.

The bride is pointing out to the bridegroom the scene of their earliest acquaintance (5-7). (See the Revised Version for an improved rendering of this and other passages referred to.) Compare Jeremiah 2:2 for Jehovah's reference to the warmth of the early zeal of His people toward Him.

Act VI. Scene 2.

This synchronizes with the afternoon of the sixth day, and gives an account of the dower portion of the bride. "The matter is negotiated by her brothers, who, in their deliberations aside, speak depreciatingly of her as they had been accustomed to do ever since her tender age." It is they who speak in verse 8. When they say: "If she be a wall" (9), they refer to her external appearance suggesting to them the blank and unadorned structure facing the street in oriental houses.

The bride overhears, and interrupts indignantly in verse 10, reminding them that she has found favor in the eyes of her beloved. She then takes the negotiation into her own hands, settling "the income of her private estate upon the bridegroom" (11, 12).

The bridegroom now calls to her in verse 14 and she responds in the closing verse, which has been compared with the final invocation of the Apocalypse to the Lord Jesus, "Even so, come!"

Answers to Criticisms and Objections.

At the close of Strong's exposition there follows his vindication of the book in which he deals with criticisms and objections, some of the answers to which are here in a condensed form.

1. There are those who speak of the song as indecent, but this is explained by ignorance of the plot and its language. Even the bare outline of the former largely disproves this, to say nothing of the better translation which accompanies it and which our space

would not permit us to give except in a word here and there. There is a profound and hallowed instinct at the foundation of the marriage state, and where no sin is, it may be alluded to by lips of purity.

2. Some object that it is purely a love-song, nothing more, and therefore unworthy a place in holy writ; but Jews and Christians in all the ages have maintained its spiritual interpretation. They may have differed in the details of its application, but they have seen in it a foreshadowing of the relation of Jehovah to Israel, or Christ to His church.

Of course, a love-scene is the ground of the song, but its final import is of a higher significance. Figurative language has a twofold application, the literal and the symbolic, a present physical scene which is the type of a distant event or a spiritual principle. The physical is usually depicted with particularity, but it is not proper to pursue the parallel into all the minuteness of the application. To quote an authority on hermeneutics, "A parable does not run on all fours."

3. A third class have considered the book irreverent and deprecated addressing God in such familiar intimacy as its dialogues involve when considered symbolically. But the answer is first, that the language is not thought of as used by individuals in their personal capacity, but by the Jewish nation collectively, or the church considered as the bride of Christ. Charles Wesley, and other hymn-writers, employ the same sentiments in their lyrics intended for public worship. Secondly, the bridegroom typified here, is not God in His sovereign capacity, but the Redeemer in His revealed relation as partaker of our human nature. Moreover, the bride is not the church in her present weak and defective life and experience, but as presented unto Him, "not having spot, or wrinkle or any such thing" (Eph. 5:27).

4. A fourth class speak of the book as unedifying, which they think is justified by the fact that it is so little used. But there are other parts of the Bible of which the same might be said, and yet they are inspired, and "profitable for doctrine, for reproof, for correction, for instruction in righteousness" (2 Tim. 3:16), even though not as much so as other Scriptures. Strong maintains that the fault in this case lies largely in our poor version of the Song —poor not only in translation but arrangement. This is true not only of the King James' version but of more modern ones in English. The foregoing exposition furnishes a hint as to the possibilities in the book, did it have a better literary form.

ISAIAH

INTRODUCTION TO THE PROPHETIC SCRIPTURES

None of the prophets from the time of Solomon to the period when they began to write their prophecies, that is for two centuries, make any mention of the Messiah or His kingdom. The reason is that during that period the Messiah could not have been the object of hope to either kingdom taken as a whole, because the moral conditions were lacking. The promises respecting Him appealed to faith, and the prophets could not speak of future spiritual blessings to those who had no ear to hear. Their mission during that period was to convince the people of sin and seek to bring them to repentance, which was never expressed in any national sense. There were individuals who appreciated the Messianic hope, as our study of the Psalms showed, but this was not true of either Kingdom as such.

Why Prophecy Came to Be Written.

It was about the eighth or ninth century before Christ when the prophets began to record their prophecies. Before that time, God was present with His people in the theocratic sense, and communicated His will to them as need existed, by means of the Shekinah (Ex. 25:22) and the words spoken by the prophets (Deut. 18:18-22). These spoken words were for that time and generation in which the prophets lived, and were not necessary to be written down. When, however, this necessity arose, it spoke of the future withdrawal of God's presence and the consequent cessation of prophetic utterances. This meant in turn, a delay or postponement of the Messianic kingdom (Compare Amos 8:11, 12 and Lamentations 2:9). The prophets' words now were preserved for future generations because it became evident that both the kingdoms of Israel and Judah were to be scattered, in punishment for their sins.

The Mission of Written Prophecy.

Written prophecy, therefore, had a two-fold mission, one for the immediate present, and the other the remote future. The written messages revolve around three points: (1) The temporal and spiritual blessings which God would give Israel and Judah, if faithful; (2) the judgments that would fall upon them if unfaithful; (3) the renewed grace to them when they should become penitent.

There is variety in the detail with which the prophets write, but their points of agreement are as follows: (1) A day of retribution is coming on Judah and Israel, the end of which will bring repentence and prepare the way for the Messianic kingdom. While these judgments will affect Israel and Judah chiefly, yet they will fall also on the Gentile nations of the whole earth. (2) The tribes of Israel and Judah will be regathered to their own land, and a remnant purified by discipline will form the nucleus of the restored nation, where God will again dwell in temporal and spiritual blessing. (3) This restored nation will be the germ of the Messianic kingdom extending over the whole earth.

Why the Gentiles Are Addressed.

But written prophecy embraces God's words to Gentile peoples also. These words could not in the nature of the case always have been spoken to them, and even so, those peoples have long since ceased to exist as peoples.

Why, then, written and preserved? Not simply that we of these latter days may see their fulfillment, and thus have our faith confirmed, for this fulfillment cannot in many cases be proved because of our historical ignorance. They were written rather because the purpose of God in the Jews as a people, both as wanderers and when restored and dwelling in their own land, brings them into continued relations to other peoples, and especially to those dwelling immediately around them. And although the earlier peoples, as Edom and Moab, Syria and Egypt, may cease to exist, yet other peoples arise and the same relations in substance continue.

As His own chosen nation, through whom He will reveal Himself to the nations, the Jews hold through all time an official position and have a sacred character, and in the day of their restoration and of the judgment of the nations, the great question will be, how far have the other nations regarded them as His people, and so treated them?

For the substance of the above, indebtedness is acknowledged to Andrews' "God's Revelation of Himself to Man."

Questions.

1. Indicate the period marked by the absence of written prophecies in Judah and Israel.

2. Why was this true?

3. At about what period did written prophecy begin?

4. Prior to that time how had God communicated with His people?

5. Was the change from spoken to written prophecy a hopeful one, or otherwise?

6. State the two-fold mission of written prophecy.

7. Around what three points does written prophecy revolve?

8. On what three things do the prophets all agree?

9. Why were the prophecies concerning the Gentile nations recorded?

10. What kind of a position and character do the Jews hold through all time with reference to the Gentile nations?

11. What will be the great criterion of judgment upon the Gentile nations in the day of the restoration of Israel?

GENERAL DISCOURSES

CHAPTERS 1-5

The first five chapters of Isaiah form a natural division, to which, for want of a better title, we give that of *General Discourses*, or messages. The first is limited to chapter 1, the second covers chapter 5.

But first notice the introduction, verse 1. By what word is the whole book described? What genealogy of the prophet is given? To which kingdom was he commissioned, Israel or Judah? In whose reigns did he prophesy?

Examine 2 Kings, chapters 15-20, and the parallel passage in 2 Chronicles for the history of this period. It will be seen later that the prophet received his vision in the last year of Uzziah, so that few of his messages belong to that reign. In the days of Jotham and Ahaz Judah was menaced by Syria and Israel, and shortly after Ahaz came to the throne he made an alliance with Assyria against them. This was contrary to the divine will and gives occasion for much of Isaiah's prophecy, especially in the early part of the book. Assyria at first a friend, afterwards became the enemy of Judah, to the latter's serious loss. When Hezekiah came to the throne, however, he placed his trust in Jehovah and was able to resist the further inroads of Assyria. Familiarity with these facts is necessary to understand the allusions in Isaiah.

First Discourse. Chapter 1:2-31.

This discourse opens with an indictment against the people for their sin (2-4), ingratitude and sinful ignorance being emphasized. The name of Israel in these verses is to be taken in a generic sense as including Judah. Now follows a description of the present consequences of their sin (5-9). Notice the figure of speech —"a cottage in a vineyard." The cottage was the shelter of the keeper of the vineyard, but Judah's desolation at this time, represented a vineyard without fruit, the cottage alone indicating that it was a vineyard. In other words Jerusalem "the daughter of Zion" and the capital of the kingdom was about all that remained to her at this time. A remonstrance follows (10-15). "Sodom" and "Gomorrah" are used metaphorically. The people were hypocritical in their religious worship, and God was weary of it. He appeals to them (16-20). The appeal is recognized as fruitless, and judgments must follow, out of which purification and redemption shall come (21-27). This period of judgment runs throughout the history of Judah down to the end of this age, as indicated by verses 26 and 27, which speak of a time not yet realized in her experience. In other words Jerusalem on this earth shall some day be known as "the city of righteousness." This will be when Zion, or the kingdom of Judah, shall have been redeemed with judgment. The discourse closes with a further note of warning (28-31).

Second Discourse. Chapters 2-4.

This discourse opens where the previous one ends, viz. "in the last days" (2). Then the kingdom shall have been restored to Judah, and that nation shall have become the head of the Gentile nations on the earth, for such is the meaning of chapter 2:2-4. The millennial age is brought into view, when the other peoples of the earth are learning of God through the converted Jew, and when peace is reigning among them. This vision of future blessing for Judah is followed by a repetition of the indictment against the people for their present sin (6-9). They have been affiliated with the Gentile nations, luxuriating in their wealth, and worshiping their idols. The coming penalty on Judah is predicted (2:10-4:1). In the course of these verses note the rebuke to the pride of the men of Judah and the luxury of the women. The details of the attire of the women (3:16-26) has had light thrown upon it recently by oriental exploration. Seventeen of the twenty-one ornaments spoken of were those worn by the heathen goddess Ishtar. The Babylonian women copied the dress of their favorite goddess, and the Jerusalem women adopted their fashions. The discourse closes with a repetition of the future blessing promised (4:2-6).

The Third Discourse. Chapter 5.

The vineyard spoken of, and of which such care was taken is Judah (1-3). How Judah repaid God for this care is shown (4). The penalty is indicated figuratively (5-7). The remainder of the chapter gives in plain language the details of Judah's sin, and the penalty to be inflicted upon her.

Questions.

1. How many discourses are in the section?

2. Have you refreshed your memory by reading the chapters in Kings?

3. Give in your own words an outline of the first discourse.

4. How does the second discourse open and close?

5. Under what figure is the story of God's goodness and Judah's unrighteousness repeated in chapter 5?

PROPHET'S CALL

CHAPTER 6

This makes a short lesson but a distinctive one. The prophet is giving an account of himself, relating the circumstances under which he entered the prophetic office, and the authority by which he speaks.

The story divides itself thus: the vision (1-4); the effect of the vision in producing conviction and confession of sin (5); his cleansing from sin (6, 7); his call to service (8); the dedication of himself to that service (8); the divine commission given him (9, 10). This commission is of a discouraging character. The people will hear his messages but fail to be influenced by them. They will become more and more blind and deaf to the divine warnings, and neither will be converted nor spiritually healed.

This discouraging outlook brings the inquiry from the prophet (11), to which the Lord replies down to the end of the chapter. In other words, the people's blindness and sin will continue for a long while, but not forever. The oak tree retains its substance even after it is felled to the ground, and though Judah will be cast away, a remnant will be saved in the last day. This is the significance of the last clause of verse 13, which speaks of the holy seed as the substance, or the stock of the kingdom. By "the last day" is meant the end of the present age, which will be a period of great tribulation for the Jewish people, but, out of which a remnant will be delivered to become the nucleus of the millennial kingdom.

You have had attention called to the law of recurrence in earlier lessons, and will have noted its operation here. In each of the discourses in this book, and now in the story of the prophets' call, the same ground is being covered over and over again, only with added detail here and there. It is always, sin, penalty, repentence, blessing. What was said in the "Introduction to the Prophetic Scripture," is thus verified.

Questions.

1. What is the prophet doing in this chapter?

2. Can you give its outline from memory?

3. Have you been impressed with its value as a Bible reading or theme for exposition?

4. What is the significance of "the last day?"

5. Can you recall the definition of "the law of recurrence?"

JUDAH'S ALLIANCE WITH ASSYRIA

Chapters 7-9

Syria and Israel menaced Judah through Jotham's reign but the situation has become acute now that Ahaz is on the throne (7:1, 2).

The Promised Sign.

The Lord, through Isaiah, counsels and encourages the king at a crisis of affairs (3-16). Notice where the prophet is to meet Ahaz (3), where he and his military engineers may be conferring as to the water supply during the expected siege. Notice who accompanies the prophet, and his name which means "a remnant shall return" (margin). The name was doubtless known to the king and his party and was intended to inspire hope, as it pointed to God's purpose of ultimate blessing for Judah. Notice the design of Syria and Israel to overthrow the throne of Judah and set up their choice in the place of Ahaz (6). Ahaz' unwillingness to ask a sign (12), was not piety but the opposite, since he was intent on his own plan to invite the aid of Assyria and cared nothing for Jehovah.

The virgin is not identified, but within the period when she would become a wife and mother and her offspring old enough to discriminate between good and evil, a few years at the most, Ahaz' present enemies would be past the power to harm him.

Such is the immediate application, but the Holy Spirit had in mind a grander and fuller application, as we know from Matthew 1:23. This gives occasion to speak of another principle in the interpretation of prophecy known as the law of double reference. This is, when the precise time of particular events is not revealed, the prophets sometimes speak of them as continuous, and sometimes blend two events in one. The latter is the case here, and the birth of this child of the virgin, who became married in Ahaz' time, is a foreshadowing of the birth of Jesus Christ who was conceived by the Holy Ghost and born of the virgin Mary, who remained a Virgin until after the birth of her first-born Son.

Coming Judgments on Judah, 7: 17-8:8.

Ahaz' rejection of God, and his confidence in Assyria calls forth a prophecy of punishment

(17). Assyria will ultimately become Judah's enemy, (18-20), and the land be desolate of population and laid waste (21-25). After a parenthesis, in which similar catastrophes are spoken of in the case of Syria and Israel (8:1-7), Judah is again alluded to (8). When the king of Assyria is passing through Israel, and leading her people into captivity, he will sweep down into Judah also, and spare only Jerusalem, the capital of the nation. This prophecy was fulfilled in the story of Sennacherib and Hezekiah with which the book of Kings has familiarized us.

A Forecast of the End of the Age, vv. 9-22.

The law of double reference finds another illustration in the verses following. From the immediate judgments falling on Judah, the Holy Spirit leads out the prophet to speak of those to come at the end of the age.

Verse 9 is a picture of the Gentile nations federated under the man of sin, with whose character and work we have become partially acquainted. This federation will come to naught (10). The faithful remnant of Israel in that day are urged to make God their trust (11-18), while the nation as a whole will be walking in moral and spiritual darkness (19-22).

The Second Coming of Christ 9: 1-7.

This darkness and gloom will not continue forever (9:1-3, R. V.). The day is coming when the Gentile yoke will be removed from Israel under miraculous conditions foreshadowed by Gideon's victory over the Midianites (4). It is the coming of the Messiah to reign that will effect this (6, 7). Notice the law of double reference in these verses, where the first and second advents of Christ are referred to as continuous, or blended together in one. The last verse shows conclusively that the mind of the Holy Spirit is resting upon the millennial age.

Questions.

1. What nations are Judah's enemies at this time?
2. What was the design in Isaiah's being accompanied by his son?
3. Quote Matthew 1:23.
4. State the law of double reference.
5. What is the interpretation of 8:8?
6. To what period, presumably, does 8:9 apply?
7. Explain 9:4

JUDGMENT ON ASSYRIA

CHAPTERS 10-12

The verses intervening since the last lesson apply to Israel, and are comparatively unimportant; but at verse five of chapter ten begins a discourse concerning Assyria, running continuously to the close of chapter twelve. Assyria, which has been the ally of Judah, is to become her enemy, but the chastisement she is to inflict on Judah is in the divine purpose, up to a certain point (vv. 5, 6).

Assyria's motive is not the divine glory, however, but her own aggrandizement, which leads her to go further in afflicting Judah than God intends. She cares nothing for Jehovah, and esteems the God of Jerusalem no greater than the idols of the surrounding nations which she has overcome (vv. 7-11). Therefore, her day of retribution is coming (vv. 12-19).

But the day of her retribution is that of Israel's deliverance and triumph (vv. 20-34). "Israel" is used interchangeably with Judah when the history of that people at the end of the age is in mind. And that such is the case here is evident because Israel is found trusting no longer in any Gentile nation, but in Jehovah himself (v. 20). Also the saved remnant is spoken of (vv. 20, 21). Comforting language is used (vv. 24, 25). Israel's enemy shall be miraculously overcome, as were the Midianites under the Gideon (vv. 26, 27). Thus we have another illustration of the law of double reference, and two events wide apart in point of time are spoken of as though continuous.

As strengthening the thought that the end of the age is referred to, we find the second coming of Christ indicated and blended with His first coming (11:1-5. Compare v. 4 with 2 Thess. 2:8). A description of millennial conditions follows (vv. 6-9). The Gentiles are seen fellowshiping Israel (v. 10), while the latter are being gathered "from the four corners of the earth," the ten tribes and the two once more united in a single kingdom (vv. 11-13). The section closes with a song of rejoicing which will be heard in Jerusalem in that day, as recorded in chapter twelve.

Questions.

1. To which kingdom does the last part of chapter 9 seem to refer?

2. When is the name "Israel" used interchangeably with "Judah"?

3. Give four reasons for believing the end of the age is referred to in verses 20-24?

4. Quote 2 Thess. 2:8.

5. To what period did verses 6-9 refer?

6. When will the song of rejoicing (c. 12) be sung in Judah?

JUDGMENT OF THE GENTILE NATIONS

Chapters 13-27

This is a long lesson to read, but the study put upon it need not be proportioned to its length. There is a sameness in the chapters, and their contents are not unlike what we reviewed in the preceding lesson. Note the names of the nations and their continguity to God's chosen people. They have come in contact with their history again and again, for which reason they are singled out for special mention. It will be well here to review what was said about these Gentile nations in the "Introduction to the Prophetic Scriptures." Seven nations are named, a perfect number, indicating Gentilism as a whole, construed as the enemy of Israel. In their order we have Babylon (cc. 13-14); Moab (cc. 15-16); Syria (17); Ethiopia (18); Egypt (19, 20); Medo-Persia (21, 22); Tyre (23).

Then follows a picture of judgment in which all the nations seem to be included; but following the judgments on the Gentile nations, Judah is seen redeemed from her iniquity, delivered from her tribulations, and restored to her land (cc. 25-27). This whole section of the book, therefore, is on an enlarged scale, that which has been set before us several times.

For the purpose of the present study, therefore, and as a matter of convenience, these discourses might be grouped as one—climaxing, as in the other instances, in the ultimate triumph of the chosen people.

This idea, however, involves one of two things: Either these nations typify Gentile dominion in the earth at the end of this age, or else they themselves will be revived as nations with reference to the judgments of that day.

The evidence for their revival, however, is not apparent except in one case, that of Babylon (cc. 13, 14). The chapters referring to the overthrow of Babylon by the Medes and Persians, seem not to have been fulfilled in that event, except in part; from which the conclusion is gathered that a later and completer fulfillment is in store. There are corresponding passages in other prophets indicating this, and the book of Revelation (c. 18) seems almost to require it.

There are at least nine features of prophecy in these chapters not fulfilled in the earlier overthrow of Babylon referred to: The whole land was not then destroyed (13:5); the Day of the Lord did not then come (v. 6); the physical phenomena were not then seen (v. 10); the city itself was not then destroyed as Sodom, for the Persian victory was without blood, and the scepter passed gently into their hands. Moreover, the land still yields a princely income to its Turkish rulers, and a city and a village exist on the site of Babylon (vv. 19-22); the Lord did not then visit Jacob with rest, nor has He done so as yet (14:1-3); the king of Babylon therein minutely described, has not yet arisen, and seems to point to a greater and more august being than the world has ever seen (4:22); the Assyrian was not then trodden down in the land of Judah, nor was the yoke then removed from her (v. 25); finally, the divine purpose on the whole earth was not then fulfilled (v. 26).

Questions.

1. Have you examined the location of these seven Gentile nations on the map?

2. How is the law of recurrence illustrated in this lesson?

3. What two ideas about these nations are suggested in this lesson?

4. Have you read chapter 18 of Revelation?

5. What existing evidence is there that Babylon has not yet been destroyed as Sodom?

6. What great person seems to be referred to in chapter 14:4-22?

JUDAH AND EGYPT

Chapters 28-35

These chapters make a unit since, with the exception of the opening part of chapter 28, they chiefly deal with Judah's futile alliance with Egypt.

Chapter 28.

Israel, or the kingdom of the ten tribes, is addressed under the name of her leading tribe "Ephraim" (v. 1). Her great sin is strong drink. "The head of the fat valley" is Samaria the capital, which is soon to be overthrown by the Assyrians (vv. 2-4). Observe, however, the usual forcast of the end of the age and the coming deliverance and triumph of the faithful remnant (v. 5). This is a parallel to what we have seen in so many instances hitherto.

At verse 14, Jerusalem rather than Samaria, is addressed, Judah rather than Israel. The end of the age is in mind and the covenant with the Antichrist at that time (compare v. 15 with Dan. 9, especially v. 27). The Messiah is seen coming in judgment, and destroying the power of the Antichrist (compare 2 Thess. 2).

Chapter 29.

"Ariel," which means "the lion of God," is one of the names of Jerusalem (vv. 1-2). A siege is predicted (vv. 3-6), and while this may primarily refer either to that of the Assyrians under Sennacherib, or the Babylonians under Nebuchadnezzar, yet before the close of the chapter, the time of blessing portrayed for Judah shows a further fulfillment in the last siege of the united Gentile nations under the Antichrist. Again we find the parallel to earlier chapters, especially 10, and an illustration of the law of recurrence. Read also Daniel 11, Micah 4:11; 5:4-15, and Zechariah, chapters 12-14.

Chapter 30.

When Jerusalem was besieged by Sennacherib, and later by Nebuchadnezzar, she sought aid from Egypt, her natural ally, because of her proximity, but also because Egypt was Assyria's and Babylon's natural rival for world power. This was contrary to the divine will, for Judah should have trusted in God. Egypt's aid on both occasions was to no purpose as other Scriptures show, and the whole circumstance is typical of the end of the age. When, in that day, Jerusalem for the last time shall be besieged by the Gentile nations, again will her hope turn to the world which Egypt represents, and in vain. All this is set before us in what follows. We have (1) the alliance and its failure (vv. 1-7); (2) the nation warned but to no purpose (vv. 8-17); (3) the customary encouragement to the faithful remnant (vv. 18-21); (4) all of which is to be accomplished by the return of the Lord (vv. 22-23).

Chapter 31.

The alliance with Egypt is again condemned (vv. 1-3), and is quite unnecessary in view of Jehovah's purpose towards His faithful people in that day (vv. 4-9). It must be clear that these latter verses refer to the future since no such defence of Jerusalem by Jehovah has yet taken place.

Chapter 32.

The connection with the preceding is close. There Jehovah, the second person of the Trinity, is seen interposting on behalf of Judah, and here He is seen actually reigning over her in the millennial period following. Jesus Christ is the King (v. 1). Millennial blessings are portrayed (vv. 2-5). The Holy Spirit is poured out, and peace ensues (vv. 15-20). Read Joel 2.

Chapter 33.

Practically the same ground is covered here as in the preceding chapters. Judgment is pronounced on the enemy (v. 1); the prayer of the faithful remnant is heard (vv. 2-6); the judgment is seen in execution (vv. 7-12); the faithful are dwelling in safety and beholding the King in His beauty (vv. 13-24).

Chapter 34.

This is a parallel to chapter 24, and one of the darkest chapters in the Bible, describing a judgment world-wide. The indignation of God is upon all the nations and their armies, an enlargement of that spoken of upon the Assyrian, and of which that was a type (compare 2 Thess. 1:5-10).

Chapter 35.

After these judgments, blessing and glory are resting upon Judah. Evidently the millennium is once more pictured here.

Questions.

1. What central fact unifies these chapters?

2. To which kingdom does the opening prophecy of chapter 28 apply?

3. What specific sin is judged?

4. How was Samaria located topographically?

5. To what does 28:15 apply?

6. Are you familiar with 2 Thess. 2?

7. What does "Ariel" mean, and to what is the word applied?

8. Why, naturally speaking, should Judah have sought aid from Egypt?

9. What makes it clear that chapter 31 is future in its application?

10. Are you familiar with Joel 2?

11. Name two of the darkest chapters thus far met in the prophets.

12. What are some of the millennial features foretold in the last chapter of this lesson?

HISTORICAL PARENTHESIS

CHAPTERS 36-39

These chapters are a dividing line between what may be called Parts 1 and 2 of this book. They deal with Hezekiah's reign whose history has been considered in 2 Kings and 2 Chronicles.

The chapters are not arranged chronologically, as the event of chapter 38, Hezekiah's sickness and recovery, occurred prior to the siege of Sennacherib (cc. 36, 37).

The prophecies preceding these chapters predict the rise of the Assyrian power as the enemy of Judah and God's rod of punishment for them, which were fulfilled in Hezekiah's time; while those following look upon the nation as in captivity to Babylon, the successor to Assyria. It is in connection with Hezekiah's pride (c. 39) that this captivity is first definitely announced.

While the chapters following look upon the nation as already in Babylon, they do so chiefly for the purpose of assuring the faithful remnant of ultimate deliverance not only from the Babylonian captivity, but from all the nations whither the Lord has driven them, in the latter days.

In brief, chapter 36 reveals the Assyrian army before Jerusalem, and the effect upon the Jewish people. Chapter 37 shows the king in supplication to Jehovah with the effect on the invaders. 38 is the story of the king's sickness and healing, in which the prediction of the king's death alarms him because at this time he had no heir. Had he died thus, the messianic hope would have died with him.

In chapter 39 we have the circumstance of Hezekiah's boasting to the Babylonian ambassadors—exacting himself rather than Jehovah. It is in this connection that the prophecy of Babylonian supremacy is given. This is impressive, when we recall that Babylon had not yet risen into the place of power which was still held by Assyria. Only supernatural power could have revealed this to Isaiah. The reason why these Babylonians visited Jerusalem at this time may have been connected with their subsequent overthrow of that sacred city. Had the king glorified His God instead of himself might not the result have been different?

Questions.

1. To whose history does this parenthesis allude?

2. What is the relation of these chapters to those preceding and following?

3. Have you reviewed the chapters in Kings and Chronicles?

4. Where is Judah supposed to be historically, in the latter part of Isaiah?

5. Why do those later prophecies so regard Judah?

6. Give a brief outline of each chapter of the lesson.

7. What special cause of alarm was there is the announcement of the King's death?

8. What is the supernatural feature about the prophecy of Babylon's supremacy?

INTRODUCTORY TO PART II

The chapters of Part 2 (cc. 40-46), are chiefly millennial, and so different from the prevailing themes preceding, as to raise a query whether they were not written by some other author—a

second, or deutero-Isaiah, as some call him. We do not hold that opinion, the reasons for which are briefly stated in the author's Primers of the Faith.

In Synthetic Bible Studies, it was found convenient to treat this part as a single discourse—though doubtless, such is not the case in fact. As such its theme may be discovered in verses 1 and 2 of chapter 40—"Comfort." The prophet, though the Holy Spirit, sees the nation in the latter days, forgiven and at rest in Judea again. This is the "comfort" he is to minister to the faithful, and in the chapters following the elements of this comfort are explained. Or, to change the figure, on the assumption that the nation shall be forgiven and restored, these chapters reveal the factors or events leading up to that experience and that happy time.

These are in brief, seven:

1. God's providential care for the people of Judah during their scattered condition (see for example, the latter half of c. 40).

2. The work of the Messiah on their behalf, suffering for them first, and triumphing for them afterwards (see cc. 42, 50, but especially 53).

3. The outpouring of the Holy Spirit upon them (c. 44).

4. The overthrow of Babylon and all Gentile power as opposed to them (cc. 45-48).

5. Their recall to God's service (c. 49).

6. The divine oath concerning their redemption (cc. 54-59).

7. The predicted millennial glory (cc. 60-66).

Another way to treat this part of the book is to sub-divide it again into three sections to which consideration will be given in the lessons following.

Questions.

1. What chapters are included in Part 2?

2. What is the general character of the discourses of Part 2?

3. To what question has Part 2 given rise?

4. Is this opinion here entertained?

5. How may these chapters be treated homiletically?

6. What theme might be given them in such event?

7. How would you explain or justify this theme?

8. What other figure of speech might be applied to the interpretation of these chapters?

9. Can you name in their order the even elements of comfort?

10. How much of Isaiah 53 can you repeat from memory?

DELIVERANCE THROUGH CYRUS

Chapters 40-48

In this lesson Israel is seen prophetically in Babylon, but about to be delivered and restored. Primarily, the reference is to her restoration after the seventy years captivity, in which Cyrus, King Persia, is the instrument.

In chapter 40, the people are comforted (vv. 1-11), in the thought that God is so great they can not be forgotten (vv. 12-31). The first and second coming of Christ are blended in the first part of the chapter, and John the Baptist is the voice crying in the wilderness (Luke 3:1-6; John 1:23).

In chapter 41, Cyrus and his plans are predicted (vv. 1-7, but Israel is seen as God's chosen servant, and comforted in the midst of the coming turmoil (vv. 8-20). Jehovah challenges all false gods to foretell things to come, as He does (vv. 21-29).

Chapter 42 returns to the thought of the Servant of Jehovah, only now that Servant is the Lord Jesus Christ, rather than national Israel (vv. 1-4, compare with Matt. 12:14-21). Observe His work among the Gentile nations which is still future (vv. 5-16), and the appeal to deaf and blind Israel which must be awakened before that work shall begin.

Chapters 43-45 are connected, in which God is comforting Israel. See what he is and promises to be (43:1-7); How He will

chastise their enemies (vv. 8-17); the good things to come (vv. 18-20); especially the forgiveness of their sin (vv. 22-28); accompanied by an outpouring of the Holy Spirit, producing a great revival (44:1-5). Idolatry is again rebuked (vv. 21-23), and Cyrus is definitely named as their deliverer, between two and three hundred years before his birth (vv. 24-28). Josephus, the historian of the Jews, says, that when the attention of Cyrus was called to this fact, probably by Daniel, he was stirred to fulfill the prophecy. In chapter 45 Cyrus is first addressed (vv. 1-13), then Israel (vv. 14-17), and then the ends of the earth (vv. 18-25).

Chapters 46-47 belong together, describing the fall of Babylon under Cyrus, and yet carrying us forward to her final destruction at the end of the age (see chapter 14). Her idols are carried by beasts (46:1, 2), while Jehovah carries His people (vv. 3-7). Chapter 47 shows its application on its face.

Chapter 48 is a review of Jehovah's messages to Israel in the preceding chapters.

Questions.

1. What is the title of this lesson?

2. Under what condition is Judah seen?

3. What Gentile potentate is prominent?

4. What is the means of "comfort," Chapter 40?

5. What New Testament prophet is predicted?

6. What two servants of Jehovah are referred to?

7. Quote 44:3, 4.

THE MESSIAH REVEALED

Chapters 49-57

The thirty-two chapters deal particularly with the Person and work of the Messiah. Isaiah has sometimes been called "the evangelical prophet" because of the large space he gives to that subject—a circumstance the more notable because of the silence concerning it since Moses. The explanation of this silence is hinted at in the lesson on the introduction to the prophets.

In chapter 49, the Messiah speaks of Himself and the failure of His mission in His rejection by His nation (vv. 1-4). This rejection works blessing to the Gentiles (vv. 5, 6—compare Romans 11). Ultimately Israel shall be brought to Him and indeed the whole earth (see the remainder of the chapter). Zion, i. e., Israel, may doubt this (v. 14), but is made assured of it in what follows.

Chapter 50 is connected with the preceding verses 1-3 referring to Zion's restoration. But at verse 4 the Messiah bears witness to Himself again, His obedience, suffering and triumph down to the end of the chapter.

These verses furnish rich material for a Bible reading or expository discourse on "The Training of Jesus." (1), His Teacher: "The Lord God hath given me the tongue of the learned"; (2), the object of His teaching: "That I should know how to speak a word in season," &c.; (3), the method of its impartations: "He wakeneth morning by morning"; (4), the spirit of the pupil: "I was not rebellious." &c.; (5), the encouragement He receives; "The Lord God will help me"; (6), the counsel He offers to others: "Who is among you that feareth the Lord"? (7), the warning to the disobedient: "Behold all ye that kindle a fire."

In like manner 51 is linked to chapter 50, by the words of comfort to Zion which shall be brought to her through the Messiah's work on her behalf. Verses 9-11 are a prayer of faith of the faithful remnant which is answered in the remainder of that chapter and the following, down to and including verse 12.

Chapters 52:13-53:12 are a unit in their Messianic character. Christ's personal suffering and glorious triumph are depicted in the closing verses of chapter 52. His rejection by Israel in 53:1-6;

His submission, deliverance and reward (vv. 7-12).

Chapter 54 exhibits the result of this in Israel's conversion, restoration and earthly glory in the millennium. Observe the divine oath that this shall be brought to pass (v. 9).

Chapter 55 is the offer of this salvation to Israel, and requires no comment.

Chapter 56 shows that when this offer is at last accepted and the salvation experienced by Israel, it will mean similar blessing to the whole earth (vv. 1-8).

The rest of this chapter, and nearly the whole of the following one, describe the sad condition of Israel at present, but especially at the end period under the Antichrist 57:9). The section concludes with the customary promises to the faithful (57: 15-19).

Questions.

1. What is the chief topic of this lesson?

2. What name has Israel sometimes received, and why?

3. Explain the silence about the Messiah until this period.

4. Who speaks in chapter 49?

5. Have you read Romans 11?

6. Who speaks in chapter 50?

7. Memorize Isaiah 53.

8. State the connection between chapters 53 and 54.

MEETING OF THE AGES

CHAPTERS 58-66

We are drawing to the end of the present, and the opening of the Millennial age. The prophet's eye rests on the time when Israel is back in her land, the majority still unconverted to Christ and worshiping in a restored temple. There is a faithful remnant waiting for Him, though enduring the persecution of the false christ. This persecution may often be felt at the hands of their own brethren after the flesh. These facts must be assumed in the interpretation of these chapters, though they will not appear strange to any who have studied the preceding books in this commentary.

Chapter 58 opens with a renewal of the prophetic commission, suggesting that at the time of the end there will be a speical heralding of the Lord's coming as there was at His first coming (Mal. 4:5-6). Indeed the whole chapter suggests the preaching of John the Baptist. Their complaint in verse 3 is answered in the verses that follow (vv. 4-7). Their blessing depends on obedience (vv. 8-14).

Chapter 59 continues the thought, leading into a revelation of the divine purpose to interpose on their behalf in the person of the Redeemer. This interposition is for judgment (vv. 15-19), but to the penitent and believing it means forgiveness, sanctification and blessing forever (vv. 20-21).

Chapter 60 carries on the description of the blessing. It has actually come. The rest of the world may yet be in darkness, but not Israel (vv. 1, 2). Moreover, the latter has become light for all the rest. Millennial blessing pervades the whole earth (vv. 3-11). Israel is the arbiter of the Gentile nations (v. 12), and the latter are contributing to her greatness and benefit (vv. 14-16). Now the whole of Israel is converted and she has become great (vv. 21-22).

Chapter 61 shows the cause of the foregoing to be the work of the Messiah on Israel's behalf (vv. 1-3). The first part of this prediction was fulfilled at the first coming of Christ (see Luke 4:16-20). The first part ended at the proclamation of "the acceptable year of the Lord" (v. 3), but the second part begins "at the day of vengance of our God." This is the second coming. The rest of the chapter repeats what was said of the future blessings in the preceding one.

Chapter 62 carries on the thought of 61. Help will be found by reading the Revised Version side by side with the King James, and especially by observing the marginal readings.

Chapter 63 begins with the picture of judgment. The day of vengeance is ushered in by the coming of the Avenger, Christ, on behalf of His people against the oppressing Gentiles (vv. 1-6). The remainder of the chapter is identified with the following one, the two composing the intercessory prayer of penitent Israel in that day. Read and compare it with Nehemiah's prayer in the first chapter of his book and with that of Daniel 9. It also suggests many of the psalms. The closing two chapters are the answer to this prayer, and require no comment in the light of the principles of interpretation illustrated before.

Questions.

1. What period is in view here?

2. Whose later work is suggested in chapter 58?

3. How does chapter 60 show that the blessing on Israel is to precede that of the rest of the earth?

4. Have you read Luke 4:16-20?

5. What period is represented by the comma after the word "LORD," in Isa. 61:2?

6. Are you careful to note the marginal renderings in your Bible?

7. How would you designate the last part of chapter 63 and chapter 64?

JEREMIAH

THE PROPHET'S GENEALOGY AND CALL

CHAPTER 1

Introduction.

As we approach the second prophet it is timely to remind the student that this work is not designed to comment on every chapter and verse of the Bible. To do so would call for a number of volumes of this size defeating the purpose in view. Nor does the study of the Bible from the standpoint of the average Christian worker require this. Particularly is this true of the prophets, which, like the psalms, repeat themselves continually. Their principal contents were outlined in the lesson entitled, "Introduction to the Prophets," and more clearly defined in the lessons on Isaiah; and one who has thoughtfully pondered that "Introduction" and pursued those lessons, should be fairly competent to interpret Jeremiah on his own account.

There is this difference, however, between Isaiah and Jeremiah, in the latter, history is frequently blended with prophecy, particularly the history of the prophet himself. Moreover, the chapters are not arranged chronologically. For these reasons Jeremiah will be considered somewhat in detail, different lessons gathering round the leading events of his career.

It is assumed that before entering on the prophets at all, the reader has familiarized himself with the historical books of the Old Testament, which are as necessary to the understanding of the prophets as the foundation of a building is to its upper stories.

The first chapter of Jeremiah is full of interesting data, as for example—

(1) His Genealogy and Period vv. 1-3.

The "Hilkiah" named is another than he who found the lawbook (2 Kings 22:8), but since he was a priest, Jeremiah must have belonged to the tribe of Levi. Look up Anathoth on the map. Read 2 Kings 22-25 to refresh recollection of the period named in verses 2 and 3.

About fifty years had elapsed since the close of Isaiah's ministry, during which the kings were Manasseh and Amon, and the prophets Nahum, Zephaniah and Habakkuk.

(2) His Call vv. 4-10.

It is interesting that this was prenatal (v. 5). The prophet's diffidence growing out of his youth and inexperience is overruled (vv. 6, 7). He is assured of divine guardianship (v. 8) and entrusted with a divine message (v. 9). What a testimony to verbal inspiration is found in that verse! While distinctively a prophet to Judah, yet his ministry is wider (v. 10). It is mainly destructive in character or result, for while under four expressions judgment is set forth, only under two is a constructive task referred to.

(3) His Earliest Commission vv. 11-16.

Here two symbols are employed, and through the book the same form of teaching is used both for himself and the people. An "almond tree" blossoms early —God's purposes are maturing fast. A "seething pot" means trouble—the trouble is coming from the north.

(4) His Enduement for Service vv. 17-19.

Like Isaiah, the prophet's commission is discouraging, at least in the foreview. Enemies will oppose him—kings, princes, priests and people. And no wonder, because his speech will seem so unpatriotic, since he must proclaim the subjugation of Judah to Babylon, on account of her sins. But God will be with him. Note the figures of speech descriptive of his protection (v. 18), as well as the assured promise (v. 19). But the warning is equally significant (v. 17). The prophet's hope of success lies in his courage, and his courage depends on his faith.

Questions.

1. What peculiarity do we find in the books of the prophets?

2. How is the book of Jeremiah distinguished from Isaiah?

3. On what plan will this book be studied?

4. Name the four points in the outline of chapter 1.

5. Have you discovered Anathoth?

6. Have you read the historical chapters in 2 Kings?

7. Name the prophets between Isaiah and Jeremiah.

8. Quote verse nine of this lesson.

9. What form of teaching is frequently found in Jeremiah?

10. What is to be the burden of his message?

PERSECUTED IN HIS HOME TOWN

CHAPTERS 2-12

The length of this lesson may alarm, but preparation for it only requires the reading of the chapters two or three times. One who has gone through Isaiah will soon catch the drift of the Spirit's teaching and be able to break up the chapters into separate discourses and the discourses into their various themes. The main object of the lesson is to dwell on the prophet's personal experience in his home town which is reached in the closing chapters.

It is thought that the discourses in this section were delivered prior to the finding of the law-book in 2 Kings, which explains their more moderate tone as compared with the later ones, but this is a feature not relevant to this work.

Note in chapter 2 the divine expostulation (vv. 1-13); the reminder of the divine goodness (vv. 14-22); the vain excuses made by the nation (vv. 23-28); and the lamentation of the Lord over its condition (v. 29-3:5).

In chapter 3, beginning afresh at verse 6, we have God's complaint against Judah for learning nothing from "her treacherous sister," i.e., from Israel's experience (vv. 6-11); this is followed by a plea to that same Israel (now scattered through the north country by Assyria), to return if she would, and mercy would be shown her. In this connection the promise for the future is set before her (vv. 12-17); Judah and Israel will be re-united then, and so on to chapter 4:1-2.

Chapter 4 and the following, indicate that a mere outward reformation is not sufficient to bring divine blessing. Judgment is coming from the north! "A lion out of his thicket!" "A stormwind!" The prophet laments.

In chapter 7 there is a call to repentance and a spiritual religion. In chapters 8 and 9 coming judgment is again announced.

The Treachery of Friends.

Coming to chapter 11:18, we see the beginnings of the persecution that farther on became so bitter against the prophet as to make him a striking type of the suffering Saviour. It takes its rise among his neighbors and kinfolk in Anathoth. At first h is unsuspicious, but God reveals the plot to him. They would kill him, destroying the tree to be rid of the fruit. He appeals to God, whose answer is in the closing verses of the chapter. Anathoth was to suffer, but not immediately.

In chapter 12 the prophet expresses his surprise at this in the spirit of Job, and that of Psalms 37 and 73. The divine comfort he receives is to be told that worse things will follow. His friend Josiah is now on the throne, but wait till he is gone and Jehoiakim and Zedekiah reign! He is now like a man running a race with men, but then it will be like running a race with horses! He is dwelling in a land of comparative peace now, but then he will be in "the swellings of Jordan."

To understand this keep the politics of the period in mind. Judah is turning to Egypt for help against Babylon, the Gentile nation now in great power. But the divine purpose is that she shall submit herself to the yoke of Babylon. The prophet is proclaiming this against a strong party in the nation that will not have it so. They consider him a pessimist, a traitor to his country who must be silenced. And silenced he would have been if it were not for God.

Questions.

1. How should one prepare himself to get the results out of these lessons?

2. When, presumably, was this series of discourses delivered, and how is that fact supposed to be exhibited in them?

3. Name some of the leading features of these discourses.

4. Or whom is Jeremiah a type, and in what aspect?

5. Give the history of his earliest persecution.

6. Who is the human author of Psalm 73?

7. How does God "comfort" the prophet?

8. What is the outward cause of his persecution?

"IN THE SWELLING OF JORDAN"

CHAPTERS 13-20

God told the prophet worse was to come. "The Swelling of Jordan" would be experienced later, and in the present lesson, especially towards the close, we have an illustration of it.

There are things of interest to look at in the meantime, for example, an illustration of that symbolic teaching mentioned earlier.

1. In chapter 13 we have what two symbols? See verses 1-11 for the first and 12-14 for the second. The prophet acted these out before the people just as he was told. The significance of the first is apparent, the second means that the destruction of Jerusalem would be brought about by her own conduct. The evils in her would cause her to be filled with a rebellious spirit as with drunkenness. "Mutual self-seeking and distrust would produce a

condition where God could not pity."

2. Look at the prophet from the point of view of intercessor (cc. 14, 15), nothing more affecting in the same line being found anywhere in the Bible. Note the occasion (14:1-6); the first supplication (vv. 7-9); the divine reply (vv. 10-12); the renewal of the prayer and the excuse for Judah that is pleaded (v. 13); God's answer (vv. 14-18); the prophet's pleading and confession (vv. 19-22); his final rejection (15:1-9). See the personal lament and inquiry that follow (vv. 10-18), and God's comfort and instruction to him (vv. 19-20).

3. Chapter 16 has a peculiar interest as carrying out 1 Cor. 7:32, 33. The prophet's life must be an independent and separated one. He must be a celibate, and shun all social amusements (vv. 1-9). His attitude in these matters would be symbolic and give him further opportunity to instruct and warn the people (v. 17, and the following).

4. Another symbol in chapters 18 and 19, and a lesson about the divine sovereignty. Judah was a vessel marred in the making, not through want of skill on the potter's part, but because of resisting elements in the clay. It is to be broken that a better vessel may be made.

5. It is the use the prophet makes of this earthen vessel that brings on him the suffering recorded in the next chapter. Read chapters 19 and 20 together. He is in the swelling of Jordan now (20:1-2—compare Luke 20:2). See how he meets his enemy and God's in the next verses (vv. 3-6), remembering as he does, the divine warning not to be "dismayed at their faces" (c. 1). But when the crisis is past and he is in his own chamber, how discouraged he appears (vv. 7-10). He complains that God had coerced him into this ministry. He would turn his back upon it if he could, but God will not permit him. He is between two fires, persecution without and the Holy Ghost within, and the latter being the hotter

fire of the two he is compelled to the work again.

In other words God gains the victory in him (vv. 11-13), and he is at length able to sing praises to His holy name.

Questions.

1. From what chapter and verse is the title of this lesson quoted?

2. Name the two symbols in chapter 13.

3. What does the second mean?

4. What was the occasion of the prophet's intercession?

5. What two earlier servants does God name as having great power in prayer?

6. What is the general theme of 1 Corinthians 7?

7. What great doctrine is illustrated in the symbol of chapter 18?

8. Tell the story of the prophet's experience in chapter 20.

MESSAGES IN ZEDEKIAH'S REIGN

Chapters 21-24

These chapters furnish a convenient unit, as they are apparently a group of discourses delivered in Zedekiah's reign—the king of the captivity period.

The first, and one of the most interesting, is that concerning the seige (c. 21). Note the occasion (vv. 1, 2) and observe that "Pashur" was not he of the last lesson. The siege of Jerusalem by Nebuchadnezzar had begun and the king of Judah hoped the prophet would have some encouraging word from God for him and the nation. But the opposite was the case (vv. 3-7). The message to the people (vv. 8-10), was the theme Jeremiah had to proclaim for the greater part of his ministry down until the event occurred.

Chapter 22 is chiefly about the previous kings of Judah in Jeremiah's time. They need not weep for Josiah whom the Lord had taken to Himself (v. 10), but for Shallum (v. 11), another name for Jehoahaz (see margin), the son of Josiah who had been carried to Egypt as we saw in the book of Kings. They should not lament for Jehoiakim, now dead, for he qas unworthy of it (vv. 13-19). "Coniah," the fourth king (vv. 24-30), is another name for Jeconiah, the son of Jehoiakim, taken captive by the Babylonians, whose story we were made familiar with in 2 Kings and 2 Chronicles.

The twenty-third chapter contains one of those beautiful messages of the future redemption of Judah and Israel with which we have become acquainted in the Psalms and Isaiah (vv. 1-8). Observe the Messianic allusion in verses 5 and 6. And do not overlook God's testimony to His own Word that follows, coupled with the judgment pronounced on the false teachers who put their own word instead of it.

Chapter 24, the type of the good figs and the bad, explains itself. The Jews carried into captivity earlier than Zedekiah's time would have an opportunity to return from Babylon after a while, but those now in the land and to be carried away later would not have such opportunity.

Questions.

1. What is the title of this lesson and why is it given?

2. On what theme is the first discourse?

3. State the circumstances.

4. What four former kings of Judah are referred to?

5. What name is given our Lord Jesus Christ in chapter 23?

6. Can you tell the story of the good and bad figs?

MESSAGES IN JEHOIAKIM'S REIGN

Chapters 25, 26

Having just considered discourses in Zedekiah's reign, and now returning to that of Jehoiakim (25:1), it can be seen that the chapters are not arranged chronologically.

The first message is that of the seventy years captivity. We are familiar with that period as Judah's forced stay in Babylon, and it is interesting to see the place where it was definitely predicted (vv. 11, 12).

Note what leads up to the prediction, God's patience and faithfulness towards His people in their sin (vv. 3-7); and His choice of Babylon as the Gentile power, into whose hands He is pleased for the time being, in judgment on Judah, to commit the sovereignty of the earth (vv. 8, 9). Note what follows. Babylon's motive is selfish, and her time of punishment will surely come (vv. 12-14). Practically all the nations are now included in the coming judgment (vv. 15, to the end). The complete fulfilment is at the end of the age.

Some will be more interested in the next chapter, where the prophet because of his boldness (vv. 1-7) is arrested and threatened with death (vv. 8, 9). In this case the priests, the prophets and the people are against him, but not the princes (v. 10). This is the method God adopted in the execution of His original promise to Jeremiah (1:17-19). That is, He did not permit all of His enemies to be united against Him at the same time.

The prophet has a hearing (vv. 12-15). The princes express their opinion (v. 16). The elders give their judgment (vv. 17-19). A case is cited of a prophet who, unlike Micah, lost his life as the result of his fidelity (vv. 20-23). But happily that was not true of Jeremiah (v. 24).

Questions.

1. What period does this lesson cover?
2. Give the chapter of the seventy years captivity.
3. What distinction is divinely given Babylon?
4. How does God deliver Jeremiah from his enemies?
5. Give the history of the prophet's trial.

MESSAGES IN ZEDEKIAH'S REIGN—SECOND SERIES

Chapters 27-34

In some respects the most important chapter here is the first, which deals with Babylon's supremacy, and reveals the beginning of the "times of the Gentiles," or "the fullness of the Gentiles" (Romans 11:25). The term refers to the period when Israel, because of her disobedience to God, has forfeited her place of power in the earth and is scattered among the nations. It begins when God transfers this power to the Gentiles as represented by Babylon, and continues until Christ comes a second time for the deliverance of Israel from the Gentiles at the end of this age. The occasion of the transfer is set forth here.

Babylon is increasing in power, and threatening the smaller nations standing in the way of her mastery of the Mediterranean. These by their ambassadors are now in conclave in Jerusalem, presided over by Zedekiah, meditating the means of defense or opposition to the common enemy. God seizes the occasion to send the prophet to them with a revelation of His will in the premises (vv. 1-11).

Verse one speaks of it as in Jehoiakim's reign, but the context shows that it is an error.

With what symbolic action does the prophet introduce his message (vv. 2, 3)? What nations are represented in the conclave? What is the divine declaration he makes (vv. 6, 7)? What penalty is attached to the failure to comply with God's will (v. 8)? What promise to submission (v. 11)? What special message is vouchsafed to the king of Judah (vv. 12-15)? What other classes in Judah are addressed (vv. 16-18)?

When God calls Nebuchadnezzar His "servant" (v. 6), it does not mean that the king knows and consciously desires to please Him, but only that, like the king of Assyria before him, he is being used for the time being to execute

God's purposes of chastisement on His people.

Chapter 28 gives a fresh illustration of the persecution Jeremiah endured from the enemies of the truth. Read carefully it will explain itself. May its warnings and encouragements not be lost upon us.

Chapter 29 recalls the earlier one on the good and bad figs. To the "good figs" the prophet sends this letter (v. 1), that is to the earlier captives (v. 2), who are to return after seventy years as the others are not (vv. 10-14). To what evil teaching were they exposed in the land of their captivity (vv. 8, 9, 15-19)? What were the names of the false prophets (vv. 21-23)? What man tried to stir up evil against Jeremiah by a letter (vv. 24-29)? What punishment would befall him (vv. 30-32)?

Chapters 30 and 31 speak again of the future redemption of Israel. What command comes to the prophet touching this testimony, and why (30:1-3)? What language shows that the end of the age is in mind (vv. 7-9)? Have these words yet been fulfilled in Israel's history? Compare also verses 18-24, and indeed the whole of the next chapter.

Chapters 32 and 33 cover the same ground as the preceding chapters, except that they are more picturesque because of the real estate transaction they record. What was the period, and what was the prophet enduring at the time, and why (32:1-5)? What is he called upon to do (vv. 6-8)? What care is taken about this purchase (vv. 9-15)? What shows his surprise and ignorance of its meaning (vv. 16-25)? What question does God put to the prophet (vv. 26, 27)? Does this demand on the prophet to purchase the field indicate any change of God's mind concerning Judah and Babylon (28-35)? What does it indicate for the future, however (vv. 36-44)? Point out at least ten reasons to show that all of these last verses point to the future. The theme is continued into the next chapter, and the Messiah once more referred to as the cause of the restoration and blessing (vv. 15, 16). What name is given Him? And what corresponding name is to be given Judah in that day?

Chapter 34 is self-explanatory. A special offense on the part of the leaders brings a renewal of the prophecy of judgment.

Questions.

1. What chapter in this lesson is the most important, and why?

2. What is the meaning of, "the time of the Gentiles"?

3. Look up that phrase or its equivalent in your concordance.

4. Describe the occasion of chapter 27.

5. In whose reign did this take place?

6. Why is Nebuchadnezzar called God's "servant"?

7. Tell the story of chapter 28 in your own language.

8. Name the chapter containing the type of the good and bad figs.

MESSAGES IN JEHOIAKIM'S REIGN—SECOND SERIES

CHAPTERS 35-36

This lesson opens with the story of the Rechabites (c. 35). Verses 6, and 7 show the origin of their name and their "order," to quote a modern term. The principles of the latter were (1), abstinence from strong drink; (2), voluntary poverty; (3), a nomadic life. Verse 11 gives the explanation of their presence in Jerusalem. Verses 12-17 furnish the cause for Jeremiah's action in the premises, who is to use these followers of Rechab as a kind of object-lesson for Judah. Verses 18 and 19 are a benediction on them for fidelity to their vows. These vows were severely tested in one particular at least, as we see in verses 3-6. By comparing 2 Kings 10:15 it will be seen that the founder of the Rechabites was prominent in Jehu's time, and a maintainer of the true worship who assisted in the overthrow of Ahab's power.

Chapter 36 requires little explanation. Verses 1-4 are a witness to Jeremiah's authorship. Verse 5 shows him again a prisoner. At verse 9 a new section begins, in that Baruch who previously read the book in the court of the temple now has another opportunity to do so, the immediate outcome of which is stated in verses 11-15. From this incident grows another, viz., the interest of the princes both in the words of the book and the human author of them (vv. 16-19). At last their contents are set before the king (vv. 20-22), whose contemptuous treatment of them in the face of earnest protest is recorded (vv. 23-25). What divine judgment is pronounced against him (vv. 29-31)? And what is the further history of the words given to the prophet (vv. 27, 28, 32)? Note that in this new collection of writings we have more than a copy of the old, a much fuller record of Jehovah's revelations to the prophet. Note also the last clause of verse 26. How the Lord may have "hid them" is not revealed, but the fact recalls how Martin Luther was protected by God through the friendly and powerful Elector in the Wartburg.

Questions.

1. Give your recollection of the founder of the Rechabites as recorded in 2 Kings.

2. What were the principles of their "order"?

3. How did they happen to be in Jerusalem?

4. Tell the story of Jeremiah's testing of them.

5. What object had he in view?

6. What lessons may be gathered from the story?

7. Tell the story of chapter 36 in your own words.

8. What lessons may be gathered from it?

CLOSING EVENTS OF THE SEIGE

Chapters 37-39

We are again in Zedekiah's reign (v 1), and the same dis-

obedience as before marks the period (v. 2). We are astonished at the effrontery accompanying it, (v. 3). Note the occasion when this prayer is solicited (vv. 4, 5). Egypt has come up to help, and the Babylonians in consequence, have raised the siege in order to meet the approaching army. Is it not an indication that God has changed His mind about Judah after all? The answer is found in verses six to ten.

Verses 11-15 tell their own sad story. Notice the vacillation of the king (vv. 16, 17). Why does this man thus play hot and cold, and fast and loose with heaven? If God is the Lord, why not serve Him, and if not, why be interested to inquire of Him? Has this type of man yet vanished from the earth? How does he now lighten the prophet's suffering (vv. 18-21)? How does the last verse indicate the straitness of the siege?

In chapter 38, what illustration have we of the political weakness and the moral meanness of Zedekiah (vv. 1-6)? Whom does God now raise up to befriend His servant (vv. 7-13)? What further counsel of the king follows (vv. 14-23)? Is any change of the divine policy evident in this?

Although the king urges on the prophet a subterfuge (vv. 24, 35), there is no reason to feel that the prophet employed it. He probably did not tell the princes all that transpired, nor was there obligation on him to do so, but that he deliberately lied, even to save his life, is beyond belief (vv. 26-28).

In chapter 39 the end is reached. Compare verses 5, 6 with 32:4 and Ezekiel 12:13.

Note that a remnant is left in Jerusalem though the bulk of the people are deported (v. 10). Note the deference paid the prophet by the besieging army (vv. 11-14), and the manner in which God promised kindness to Ebed-Melech (vv. 15-18).

THE REMNANT AND THE PROPHET'S LAST MESSAGE

CHAPTERS 40-45

Chapter 40 opens with an account of Nebuchadnezzar's kindness to Jeremiah, inspired by what he had known of the latter's advice to his countrymen (vv. 1-4). Jeremiah had been the friend of Babylon, but not necessarily the enemy of his own nation. His patriotism was unquestioned, but the highest expression of his patriotism was his counsel to Judah to obey the will of God and submit to Babylon.

Jeremiah's choice of action is in verses five and six. The new governor is loyal and things promise well (vv. 7-12). But the Ammonites see an opportunity to get even with their old enemy and obtain control of their land through the treachery of an apostate Jew (vv. 13-16).

Chapter 41 narrates how the plot is carried out (vv. 1-10), and the resultant fear on the part of the people (vv. 11-18). This fear leads them to plan an exodus from Judah into Egypt.

Chapter 42 shows them consulting with the prophet before carrying out this plan, albeit they are determined to do it.

Chapter 43 is a prophecy of Egypt's conquest by Babylon (vv. 8-13) delivered after Jeremiah's arrival there (vv. 4-7). Today the place indicated in verse nine is marked by a ruined column.

Jeremiah's Last Message.

The contents of chapter 44 may be regarded as the continuation of the preceding, though how long after the entrance into Egypt the prophecy was uttered is impossible to say. Some have surmised twenty-five years. Certainly the Jews had spread themselves considerably (v. 1). The prophecy opens with a retrospect (vv. 2-6); but present conditions are no improvement over the past (vv. 7-10); only doom can await them (vv. 11-14). Opposition is aroused as of old (vv. 15-19), showing the former infatuation (v. 17). They had forgotten that God gave them these good things even when they were rebelling against Him (Hosea Chap. II). So men still trace misfortune to everything but the true cause, which is sin. Notice the prominence of women here, on whose regeneration that of society still depends. The prophecy concludes with the prediction of an awful judgment, the truth of which will be established by an appeal to history (vv. 20-30).

Baruch Counselled.

Chapter 45 is a word to Baruch, the prophet's amanuensis and friend, spoken doubtless at an earlier period than its position indicates, and some would say just after the events of chapter 36. Weighed down by responsibility and dismayed at the aspect of things, he is seeking better things for himself—an easier lot dare we say? At all events he is warned of his moral danger at the same time that he is promised physical deliverance at least, in the dire hour coming on the land (v. 5). He accompanied Jeremiah into Egypt, and to his labors doubtless, we trace the copies of these prophecies which have circulated in that country, and given rise to a Greek version of them (the Septuagint so-called).

Questions.

1. Explain Nebuchadnezzar's interest in Jeremiah.

2. Did this interest compromise the prophet's character of a patriot in any way?

3. What is Jeremiah's choice of a location, and with whom does he now take up his home?

4. Give the history of Gedaliah's brief authority in your own words.

5. Give the history of the people's dealings with Jeremiah at this crisis.

6. Analyze the prophet's last message.

7. Explain chapter 45.

LAMENTATIONS

"The touching significance of this book lies in the fact that it is the disclosure of the love and sorrow of Jehovah for the very people He is chastening—a sorrow wrought by the Spirit in the heart of Jeremiah. Compare Jeremiah 13:7; Matthew 23:36-38; Romans 9:1-5."—Scofield Reference Bible.

"As regards its external structure, the composition of the book, both as a whole and in its several parts, is so artistic, that anything like it can hardly be found in any other book of Holy Scriptures."—Lange's Commentary.

In the first place it contains just five songs, each limited to a single chapter. In the second place, there is a marked climax in the third song, with an ascent and a descent, a crescendo and decrescendo movement before and after it. About the middle of this song at verse eighteen, the prophet seems to have reached the deepest night of his misery, "but where the exigency is greatest, help is nearest. The night is succeeded by the morning (vv. 19-21), and with verse 22 breaks the full day."

Each of the songs contains 22 verses according to the number of letters in the Hebrew alphabet; in other words, it is an acrostic—a favorite form of Hebrew poetry. But in the third song each verse is divided into three members making in our English setting 66 verses. Other of its poetical features we can not dwell upon.

Analysis of the Chapters.

In chapter 1 the lament is over the ruin of Jerusalem and Judah, and is divided into two parts of equal length. The first is a description of the city, and the second the lamentation strictly considered. In both the speaker is the prophet himself (or an ideal person like the daughter of Zion, for example).

In chapter 2, the lament is over the destruction of the city, which is described and attributed to Jehovah. This also is in two nearly even sections. Verses 1-10 describe the judgment; verses 12-22 is the lamentation proper.

In chapter 3 is the climax where Israel's brighter day is contrasted with the gloomy night of sorrow experienced by the prophet himself. There are three parts in this chapter, divided as follows: Verses 1-18, 19-42, 43-66.

In chapter 4, Zion's guilt and punishment are described, the whole consisting of four parts which will be readily distinguished as verses 1-6; 7-11; 12-16; 17-22.

In chapter 5, the distress and hope of the prisoners and fugitives are expressed in the form of a prayer. Here the author lets the people speak, not as an ideal person but in the first person plural as a concrete multitude. There is an introduction (v. 1), two principal parts, verses 2-7 and 8-16, and a conclusion, verses 17-22.

For the above analysis of the chapter we are indebted to Lange.

Golden Texts.

There are some richly laden verses in this beautiful book, full of comfort and instruction for the saint and of homiletic value to the preacher. We indicate a few: 1:12; 1:16; 2:13; 2:14; 3:21-26; 3:31-33; 3:37; 3:39-41; 5:7; 5:16-17; 5:21.

Questions.

1. What fact gives this book peculiar significance?

2. Have you read Romans 11:1-5?

3. How does the literary structure of this book compare with other Scriptures?

4. Describe the third song.

5. What is an acrostic?

6. Have you memorized any of the Golden Texts?

EZEKIEL

THE PROPHET'S CALL AND PREPARATION

CHAPTERS 1-3

Ezekiel was carried to Babylon with King Jehoiachin, as we gather by comparing 1:1; 33:21; 40:1 with 2 Kings 24:11-16; and lived with the exiles on the river Chebar probably at Tel-abib (1:1, 3; 3:15). Unlike Jeremiah, he was married and had a stated residence (8:1;24:1, 18). His ministry began in the fifth year of Jehoiachin's captivity, and seven before the capture of Jerusalem (1:1, 2), when he himself was thirty years old (v. 1). His prophetic activity extended over a period of at least twenty-two years (1:2; 29:17), during which time he was often consulted by the leaders in exile (8:1; 14:1; 20:1), though his advice was not always followed. The time and manner of his death are unknown.—Davis' Bible Dictionary.

Like Daniel and the Apostle, John who, like himself, prophesied outside of Palestine, he follows the method of symbol and vision, or as we prefer to put it, God followed that method through him. And like them, his ministry was directed to "the whole house of Israel," the twelve tribes, rather than to either Judah or Israel distinctively, after the manner of the pre-exilic prophets. His purpose was twofold: (1) to keep before the exiles the national sins which had brought Israel so low; and (2) to sustain their faith by predictions of national restoration, the punishment of their enemies, and ultimate earthly glory.

Scofield divides the book into seven great prophetic strains indicated by the expression, "The hand of the Lord was upon me" (1:3; 3:14, 22; 8:1; 33:22; 37:1; 40:1), and seven minor divisions indicated by the formula, "And the word of the Lord came unto me." But although this is interesting and instructive, yet for our present purpose, we emphasize three main divisions only, as follows:

1. Prophecies delivered before the siege of Jerusalem, foretelling its overthrow (cc. 1-24). These correspond to the general character of Jeremiah's messages with whom for a while Ezekiel was contemporary.

2. Prophecies delivered during the period of the siege (cc. 25-32). These are chiefly about the Gentile nations.

3. Prophecies after the downfall of the city (cc. 33-48). These deal with the restoration entirely.

1. The Prophet Called.

Give the time, place and circumstances as indicated in verses one and two. Look at the map and identify the Chebar. Give the details of Ezekiel's biography in verse three.

Note the vision he beheld—the whirlwind, cloud, fire, brightness, color (v. 4); the four living creatures (vv. 5-14); the wheels (vv. 15-21); the firmament (vv. 22-23); the voice (vv. 24-25); the throne and the man above it (vv. 26-27); and finally, the definition of it all (v. 28). Note in the last verse that out of this glory the voice spake that directed the prophet. Freshen your recollection by comparing Exodus 3, 33 and 34; 1 Kings 19; Isaiah 6; Daniel 10; Acts 9; Revelation 1.

The "living creatures" are doubtless identical with the cherubim of the garden of Eden, to which further reference will be made in the next lesson.

2. Equipped and Commissioned.

Note the address "Son of Man" (v. 1). It is used by Jesus Christ seventy-nine times in referring to Himself, and by Jehovah ninety-one times in speaking to Ezekiel, which suggests that the prophet is considered in a priestly and mediatorial capacity. Or, we may take the thought of Scofield that in the case of our Lord it is His racial name as the representative man in the sense of 1 Corinthians 15:45-47. If so, applying the idea here, it means that Jehovah, while not forsaking Israel even in her disobedience and hour of punishment, would yet remind that people that they are but a small part of the race for which He also cares.

Note the relation in which the Holy Spirit comes to the prophet, and examine your concordance to see that "entering into him" is more of a New Testament than an Old Testament way of speaking of that relation.

Note finally, that like other recipients of God's revelation the prophet heard the voice that spake to him and recognized the speaker.

Now follow a description of the moral condition of the people to whom he is sent (vv. 3-5), and a warning to himself, corresponding to that in the case of Jeremiah (vv. 6-8). The demand for absolute obedience in the transmission of his message and his compliance therewith, are set forth symbolically in the figure of the book (2:9; 3:3), although the transaction itself is difficult to explain. Perhaps it took place in a vision. How does it show that only what God imparted to him was he to preach? How that he was to make it his own? How that in a spiritual sense he was to live on it? "Whatever its message, the Word of God is sweet to faith because it is the Word of God." (Compare Jer. 1:9; 15:16; Rev. 10:9, 10).

Questions.

1. When was Ezekiel made a captive?

2. What do we learn of his domestic history?

3. What method of teaching does he exemplify?

4. What was its purpose?

5. State the three main divisions of the book, with chapters.

6. What other men had corresponding visions of glory?

7. What, possibly, is the significance of the phrase "Son of Man?"

8. How is the inspiration of Ezekiel's message symbolized?

THE CHERUBIM

In our last lesson we had the first description of the cherubim met with in Scripture, although the beings themselves were brought before us in Eden (Gen. 3), and their images, or figures, in the tabernacle. In the latter case two were in the Holy of Holies over the Ark of the Covenant and others wrought in needlework upon the curtains of the sanctuary and the veil (Exodus 25-27).

Imperfect and erroneous conceptions of the cherubim have prevailed, as instanced in that they are almost always pictured as angels, which they are not, but rather the living embodiment of some important truth.

Familiar to Israel

That they were familiar Israel is seen in that Moses gives no description of them either in Genesis or Exodus. Is this accounted for by the circumstance that they continued to exist in Eden guarding the approach to the tree of life, and visible to man, say, down to the time of the flood? If so, Shem, who was contemporaneous with Abraham for 150 years, might easily have transmitted to him, and through him to his descendants, a knowledge of their appearance and of that which their presence was intended to teach.

But their appearance is not revealed to us until we reach Ezekiel, when they are presented as having in general, a human form, but each with four faces and four wings—one face of a man, another of a lion, a third of an ox, and a fourth of an eagle. Their motions were as swift as lightning, and the sound of their wings in flight as of great waters or a mighty host. A throne was in the firmament above them, and on the throne the divine glory in the likeness of a man. "This was the appearance of the likeness of the glory of the Lord," said the prophet, which shows the connection between it and our humanity in the person of Immanuel.

Subsequently, at chapter 10, the prophet speaks of seeing these beings again in the temple at Jerusalem, and identifies them as "the cherubim."

They are seen once more by John on Patmos (Rev. 4-5) where "they rest not day and night, saying, Holy, holy, holy, Lord God Almighty," and with the four and twenty elders they fall down before the Lamb and sing a new song—a song of praise for the redemption of man. This is very significant.

Type of Redeemed Humanity.

That they are beings designed to set forth some great truth of redemption is thus evident, since they are introduced at its opening scene in Genesis, and in its closing scene in Revelation, and associated with it throughout.

The symbolism of the faces of the cherubim considered together, gives us "the highest possible conception of life, with the noblest characteristics belonging to created intelligence."

The face of the man sets forth the highest ideal of wisdom and knowledge; that of the lion adds majesty and power; that of the ox, creative or productive industry; and the eagle, dominion and irresistible might, for "the range of his vision and the power of his flight, as well as his boldness and courage, are unequaled."

The other features, however, were equally striking. Eyes before and behind, show ceaseless vigilance and exalted capacities for knowledge; wings, denote a higher and wider sphere of service than simply the earth; going straight forward, never turning their bodies, as we must necessarily do, but with four faces always moving in the direct line of vision, points to a superior spiritual nature and undeviating integrity in God's service; their glorious appearance, also, like burning coals of fire, sparkling as burnished brass, has its significance.

If now, according to the ordinary principles of symbolic interpretation, we ask for the realization of all this, we may find it in our redeemed humanity when delivered from the curse, and restored, and glorified through Jesus Christ. The cherubim would seem to be the embodiment of that glory to which our humanity is destined in the resurrection state—that combination of powers and excellencies which shall be ours when our salvation is consummated in the life to come.

The Embodiment of the Glorified Life.

This is further corroborated by the fact that originally they stood within the prohibited bounds of paradise, and kept "the way of the tree of life;" i.e., they not only guarded it, but preserved the approach to it, as if until, in the fullness of time, redeemed humanity might have access to it again.

The divine presence since the entrance of sin, had withdrawn Himself from all familiar intercourse with men, no longer walking with them as in their innocence in paradise. But He had not withdrawn Himself from earth or from men altogether, since He might still be approached, and His favor secured at the gateway to the tree of life. Here the cherubim dwelt with the flaming sword of the divine presence between them. So also in the Holy of Holies in the tabernacle, their privileged place lies over the mercy seat, while here in Ezekiel's vision above their heads in the crystal firmament, the glory of the God of Israel in human form was seated on the throne.

Thomas Wicke, D.D., from whose "The Economy of the Ages" the above is an abridgment, regards the fact that the cherubim are always found in immediate connection with the surroundings of the divine presence, as declaring that those they represent have a right within the paradise of God—the blessed promise held out to our redeemed humanity. Compare Revelation 5:9, where the cherubim unite with the four and twenty elders in the song of redemption itself—the song of the Lamb.

SECOND VISION OF GLORY AND ITS RESULT

Remember that in the first part of this book, chapters 1-24, we are dealing with prophecies before the siege of Jerusalem and foretelling its overthrow.

The present lesson begins at verse 22 of chapter 3. (Compare verse 23 with 1:1, and verse 24 with 2:2 and Acts 2:4 and 4:31.) Verse 25 is to be taken figuratively. (Compare 2 Cor. 6:11, 12.) The same is true of verse 26, which means that as Israel had rejected the words of the prophets hitherto, the time had now come when God would deprive them of those words for the time being at least (1 Sam. 7:2; Amos 8:11, 12).

The Sign of the Tile. Chapter 4.

This sign (1-3) and those that follow immediately, were symbolic testimonies to the wickedness of the nation as well as prophetic of the coming siege. It is common to say that these things were performed in vision and not in external action, but we can hardly be sure of that. At all events the tile represents that God has set a wall of separation between Him and the nation, that can not be forced through. The second action, lying first on one side and then the other, (4-8) supplements the first. The third, eating the coarse and polluted bread, and by weight, is explained in the closing verses of the chapter (verses 16, 17). (Compare Jer. 52:6.) As to verse 12, the Arabs use beasts' dung for fuel, as wood is scarce, but to use that of man implies the most awful need. As to do so was in violation of the Mosaic law (Deut. 14:3; 23: 12-14), the command to the prophet, symbolized that now God's people were, as a judicial punishment, to be outwardly blended with the heathen (Deut. 28: 68; Hos. 9: 3).

The Sign of the Hair. Chapters 5-7.

This symbol (verses 1-4) is explained in the rest of the chapter.

The "knife" or "razor" was the sword of the enemy which God would use. The whole hair being shaven was a sign of humiliation (2 Sam. 10:4, 5). "Balances" expresses God's discrimination in the coming judgments. The "hairs" are the people in this case. One third was to be killed, another destroyed by famine and pestilence, and the remainder scattered among the Gentiles. The few to escape were symbolized by the hairs bound in Ezekiel's skirts, and even of these some were to pass a further ordeal (verses 3, 4). Compare these last-named verses with the story of the remnant in Jerusalem in Jeremiah 40-44.

Chapters 6 and 7 are a continuation of the subject of chapter 5, which our familiarity with the prophets preceding will simplify for us. The first of these may be divided into three parts. Verses 1-7 contain a message against Israel; verses 8-10, speak of that "remnant" which God always promised to spare because of their repentance, while the rest of the chapter, and the whole of chapter 7, is filled with the desolations God shall send upon the land for its iniquity.

Questions.

1. What characterizes the prophecies of the first 24 chapters of this book?

2. Have you read 1 Samuel 7:2 and Amos 8:11, 12?

3. To what do the symbols of chapter 5-7 witness?

4. What is symbolized by the coarse bread eaten by weight?

5. Give the interpretation of the symbol of the hair in your own words.

6. Have you refreshed your recollection by re-reading Jeremiah 40-44?

7. Analyze chapter 6.

VISIONS OF IDOLATRY

CHAPTERS 8-11

It is the general opinion that these chapters introduce a new stage of the prophecies, and that while those of the last lesson comprehended Judah and Israel, these refer more particularly to Jerusalem and the people of Judah under Zedekiah. The fuller story of this period was in Jeremiah.

The prophet is seen in his own house by the Chebar, and the elders of Judah are before him for instruction (8:1). "Elders" we understand to mean some who are in captivity with the prophet.

"The Visions of God to Jerusalem" (v. 3), concern the profanations of the temple and other wickedness of the people past and present, and because of which the partial captivity had befallen them which was speedily to be followed by a completer one.

As another puts it, the prophet was showing these things to the present generation of Jews in Babylon to justify to them the righteousness of God in their present chastening. There were some of the younger element who had been born in captivity and to whom these things presumably were unknown. The visions were so vivid to the prophet that it seems as if he were transferred back to Jerusalem at the time these things were occurring.

1. The Third Vision of Glory. 8:1-4.

Verse 1 compared with 1:2, raises the presumption that the "lying on his sides" (vv. 5, 6), had been completed. Verse 2, refers to a further manifestation of the Messiah as the Angel of the Covenant, in whose person alone God manifests Himself. (John 1:18). Verse 3, "the image of jealousy" was a heathen image worshiped with licentious rites and provoking God's jealousy (Exod. 20:5). Verse 4, refers to the Shekinah which still rested over the temple and upon the mercy-seat.

2. The Profanations of the Temple. 8:5-18.

The idolatries named (v.10) had been introduced from Egypt. "Chambers of his imagery," (v. 12) means his perverse imagination. "Tammuz" (v. 14) the

name of a heathen god, the Syrian form of Adonais. "The branch to the nose" (v. 17), refers to the sacred trees which were symbols in idol worship.

3. Sealing the Faithful. 9:1-11.

"Them that have charge over the city" (1) are doubtless angelic executioners of God's will as in Daniel 4:13, 17, 23, and elsewhere. The man with the ink horn (2) is thought to symbolize the Messiah, who is here marking His elect (v. 4, compare with Ex. 12:7, Rev. 7:3, and other places). The departure of the "glory of the God of Israel" (3) is significant, presaging His final departure from the nation which would be given over to its punishment. Quoting Scofield, "It is noteworthy that to Ezekiel, the priest, was given the vision of the glory departing from the cherubim to the threshold (9:3); then from the threshold (10:18); then from the temple and the city to the mountain on the east of Jerusalem (11:13), and finally returning again to the temple to abide permanently in the millennium (43:2-5).

4. The Judgments Spreading. 10-11:13.

"The wrath of God is now about to burn the city, as His sword in the hand of Babylon, had slain its inhabitants." This is the story of chapter 10, but in 11 we have a separate prophecy of the punishment of the corrupt princes. Their wicked counsel is indicated in verse 3, which agrees with what we saw in Jeremiah. They were ever contending against that prophet that his word was not true, and that destruction by the Babylonians was not coming. They, therefore, because of their unbelief, were responsible for the slain of the city (vv. 6, 7). Their judgment was certain (vv. 8-13).

5. Future Restoration Promised. 11:14-25.

Ezekiel wonders if there shall be no salvation (v. 13), and he is told that those who have been carried away, and whom the remainder in the land despised and sneered at for that reason, will be watched over wherever they are (v. 16). This leads to that prophecy of the future repentance and restoration of the nation with which we have become familiar in other prophets. Verses 17-21, is a picture of the millennial period.

Questions.

1. To what do the prophecies of this lesson more particularly refer?

2. What are the local circumstances under which they are delivered?

3. What specifically, do "the visions of God" concern?

4. Explain the difficult expressions in 8:1-4.

5. What is the definition of "Tammuz"?

6. How would you identify the man with the ink-horn?

7. What four journeys of "the Glory of the Lord" are recorded in Ezekiel?

8. To what period does 11:17-21 apply?

DISTRIBUTING THE RESPONSIBILITY

Chapters 12-15

While these visions and prophecies may be new as to the particular occasions for them, yet they are in substance the same as the preceding.

1. "The Prince in Jerusalem." 12:1-16.)

In chapter 10 we had a vision of the judgment upon the city of Jerusalem, in 11, upon the princes, and in this upon the king himself (10). The explanation of the action commanded the prophet in verses 1-7 is given in verses 8-16. It is thought that this was performed by him in vision only and not outwardly, but if so, its effect could hardly have been intended for those he was instructing but only for himself, which we doubt (v. 9). The whole thing typifies Zedekiah's flight by night. (Compare Jer. 39: 4.) He went out furtively as

digging through a wall, and covered his face so as not to be recognized.

2. The Nearness of the Event. Verses 17-28.

The infidels scoffingly said that because the threatened judgment was long in coming, it would never come (v. 22), but they are to be taught otherwise (vv. 23-25). As a matter of fact it was very near (vv. 26-28).

3. The Lying Prophets. 13:1-23.

The city, the princes, the king have each been singled out for judgment, and now come the prophets. Note where they obtained their false messages (v. 2), and the ill effect of them on the people (v. 6). Note the judgments to fall on them (v. 9), which probably means that their names would be erased from the registers like those who had died for their crimes (Jer. 17:13; Rev. 3:5; Luke 10:20). Moreover, they never would return from captivity. As teachers they were like men building up a wall with untempered mortar and their work would come to naught (vv. 10-16). There were false prophetesses as well as prophets (vv. 17-23). They "sew pillows to all armholes" might be rendered "to elbows and wrists," and the reference is thought to be the cushions which the prophetesses made to lean upon as typifying the tranquillity they foretold to them who consulted them. "Kerchiefs on the head of every stature" might be rendered on "men of every age," though its significance is doubtful. The prophetesses engaged in their wicked work for paltry fees (v. 19).

4. The Hypocritical People. 14:1-11.

The spirit in which some of the people sought the instruction of the prophet is shown in verses 1-5, and it is a judgment upon them that they shall listen to false prophets and be deceived. God will judicially darken the false prophet's mind to that end, or He will permit Satan to do it. The evil teaching of these false prophets, in other words, will serve the purposes of His just judgment. (Compare 1 Kings 22:23; 2 Thess. 2:11, 12).

5. Intercession Useless. Verses 12-23.

The inevitableness of the coming judgment on Jerusalem is shown in the discouragement of intercession on her behalf. Ezekiel had been pleading, but he might as well desist. Noah, Daniel and Job (vv. 14, 23) had prevailed with God on former occasions, but even their petitions would now be helpless. The reference to Daniel is interesting, for although his prophecies were mostly later than Ezekiel, yet his fame for piety and wisdom was already established, and the events recorded in the early chapters of his book had already occurred. But even he, though the Jews may have had their hopes turned towards his influence either in the court of Babylon or that of heaven, could not avert the approaching calamity.

6. The Burning Vine. 15.

The point of this vision seems to be that as the vine is worthless as wood so the people of Jerusalem have ceased to have any value in His eyes. They were once His vine, but now they shall pass from fire to fire until they come to naught.

Questions.

1. How does this lesson illustrate its theme?

2. What leads to the conviction that the prophets "removal" was acted outwardly?

3. What did it typify, and how?

4. What had become the proverb of the scoffers?

5. What judgment would fall on the false prophets?

6. Explain the figure of "untempered mortar."

7. Can you quote 2 Thessalonians 2:11, 12?

8. Who have divine testimony borne to them as men of power in prayer?

PARABLES AND RIDDLES

CHAPTERS 16-18

1. The Unfaithful Wife. Chapter 16.

The theme of chapter 16 is Jerusalem and her abominations (vv. 1, 2), but it is worked out in parabolic form, Jerusalem, or the nation of Israel, being personified as a female.

There are four stages in the story: (1) Jehovah adopts her as an infant (vv. 1-7); when attained to marriageable age she becomes his wife (vv. 8-14); as a wife she proves unfaithful (vv. 15-34); punishment follows (vv. 35-42); unexpected and unmerited restoration is promised (vv. 53-63).

Verse 7, first part, is corroborated by Exodus 12:37, 38. To spread a skirt (v. 8) was an oriental mode of espousal (Ruth 3:9). With verse 9 compare Exodus 19:12, and similar allusions. Verses 11-13 refer to the customary marriage gifts of one who was to become a queen. Verses 15-36 speak of her worship of idols after the manner of the surrounding nations, with which was accompanied gross sins of the flesh. Verses 35-52 refer figuratively to the shame, suffering, and loss, entailed by the Babylonian siege and overthrow—the enemy hurled stones at the siege and slew with the sword afterward (v. 40), and so on throughout.

The restoration was to be brought about at the end, not on the ground of Israel's repentance even, but of God's own promise to the fathers (v. 60). It would be His returning to them that would result in their returning to Him (v. 61).

2. The Eagles and the Vine. 17.

The "eagle" (v. 2) was the symbol of the Assyrian god Nisroch, and is here applied to the king of Babylon. "Lebanon" means Jerusalem, and "the highest branch" its King, Jeconiah, or Jehoiachin, whom the Babylonians carried away some time previously (2 Kings 24:8-16). The "city of merchants" is Babylon.

The "seed of the land planted" is Zedekiah placed on the throne of Judah by Babylon. Verse 6 means that at first Zedekiah was an obedient vassal to Babylon. The "eagle" of verse 7 is Egypt towards whom Judah turned in her heart, as a means of breaking the Babylonian yoke. But her scheme would not prosper (vv. 9, 10), as the remainder of the chapter shows.

3. Eating Sour Grapes. 18.

Verse 2 shows the people were charging injustice upon God, and claiming that they were suffering not for their own sins but their fathers, but He proves that this is not so. How does the last clause of verse 4 declare to the contrary? Note the following illustration of God's impartiality in a series of supposed cases: (a) a just man (vv. 5-9); (b) an unjust son of a just man (vv. 10-13); (c) a just son of an unjust man (vv. 14-18). "Righteousness," in verse 20 is not used as if any were absolutely righteous, which would contradict Scripture everywhere; but in the sense of seeking righteousness in God's way as far as that way had been revealed to them. In the light of the New Testament there is no ground of righteousness save that which is imputed for Christ's sake, and as the result of His atonement; but while this was not clearly understood by the Old Testament saints, yet it was the ground on which any righteousness of theirs could be accepted. This is brought out in verse 22, "in his righteousness that he hath done he shall live." Not "for," or "on account of" that righteousness, but "in" it. In the same manner, verse 31, shows not what man can do, but what he ought to do; and when he sees that he ought to make him a clean heart, and finds that he can not, he throws himself in his helplessness on God's mercy and receives it.

Questions.

1. Name the parables and riddles in this lesson.
2. Name the four stages in the story of the faithless wife.

3. On what final ground shall the future restoration of Israel be brought about?
4. What nations did the two eagles symbolize?
5. Tell this "riddle" and its interpretation in your own words.
6. In what sense only can "righteousness" be understood in this lesson?
7. What is the logic that causes man to cry out for mercy?

CLOSE OF PART ONE

Chapters 19-24

Lack of space makes it necessary to crowd the remainder of Part 1 into a single lesson, but nothing vital to its general understanding will be lost, as the chapters are, to a certain extent, repetitions of the foregoing.

1. Lamentations for the Princes. 19.

The theme of this chapter is found in the first and last verses. The "princes" are the kings of Judah—Jehoahaz, Jehoiachin and Zedekiah, whose histories were made familiar in the closing chapters of 2 Kings and 2 Chronicles. Judah is the lioness (2). Jehoahaz is the first of her young lions (3), and Jehoiachin the second (4-9). Zedekiah is probably in mind in verse 14.

2. Rejection of the Elders. 20.

Verse 1 gives the occasion for this message, which falls into two great parts. Verses 1-32 recite the peoples' rebellions against God during five distinct periods i. e., in Egypt (2-9), in the wilderness (10-17), on the borders of Canaan (18-26), when a new generation arose in Canaan (27-29), and finally in the prophet's own time (30-32). The explanation of verses 25 and 26 seems to be that God chastised them, as in Numbers 25, by permitting Baal's worshippers to tempt them to idolatry, ending in judgment upon them. The easy success of the temptor's arts showed how ready they were to be led astray (compare v. 39).

Verse 32 should not lightly be

passed over. It was in the heart of these Jews to live like the heathen round about them, and so escape the odium of having a peculiar God and law of their own. Moreover, they seemed to be getting nothing for it but threats and calamities, whereas the heathen seemed to be prospering. But God said it "shall not be at all," and how literally this has been fulfilled is seen in the later history of the Jews down to our day. As the Bible Commentary says: "Though the Jews seem so likely to have blended with the rest of mankind and laid aside their distinctive peculiarities, yet they have remained for centuries dispersed among all nations and without a home, but still distinct."

At verse 33, begins the second division of the prophecy. Lest the covenant people should abandon their distinctive hopes, and amalgamate with the surrounding heathen, God tells them that, as the wilderness journey from Egypt was made subservient to discipline, and also to the taking from among them the rebellious, so a severe discipline (such as the Jews for long have been actually undergoing) would be administered to them during the next exodus for the same purpose (v. 38), and to prepare them for the restored possession of their land (Hosea 2:14, 15). This was only partially fulfilled at the return from Babylon; its full accomplishment is future.

3. Three Messages of Judgment. 21.

The three messages in this chapter explain themselves to those who have followed the lessons thus far. The first might be designated the parable of the sighing prophet (1-7), the second, that of the sword of God (8-17), while the third is notable for the prophecy that thereafter there should be no true king of Israel till the Messiah came (26, 27; Acts 15:14-17).

4. Jerusalem's Present Sins. 22.

The repetition of Jerusalem's sins as given here suggests chapter 20; but there they were stated in a historical review, emphasis resting on the past, while here it is on the present.

5. Aholah and Aholibah. 23.

Here we have a parabolic portrayal similar to the adulterous wife in chapter 16; only that in this case it is not idolatries which are emphasized as violating the marriage covenant, but their worldly spirit, their alliances with the heathen for safety rather than confiding in God.

6. The Period of Silence Begins. 24.

"Ezekiel proves his divine mission by announcing, though three hundred miles away, the very day of the beginning of the siege of Jerusalem by Nebuchadnezzar" (1, 2). "The ninth year" means that of Jehoiachin's captivity, which was also that of Ezekiel.

There was a self-confident proverb among the people (11·3) expressed in the sentence: "This city is the caldron and we be the flesh." They meant that Jerusalem would prove "an iron caldron-like defense from the fire" of the Babylonian hosts around them in the siege; but God tells them that their proverb would fit the case in a different way (3-14). Jerusalem should be caldron set upon the fire, but the people, so many pieces of flesh subjected to boiling water within.

At verse 15 a period of silence begins for the prophet, covering the three years of the siege (compare verses 1 and 27 of this chapter, with verses 21 and 22 of chapter 33). The opening of the period is marked by a personal calamity—the death of the prophet's wife (16-18). Ezekiel is not forbidden sorrow, but only the loud expression of it after the oriental manner, that his countrymen might be moved to ask the question (19) whose answer constitutes the remainder of the chapter. When Jerusalem would be destroyed, the calamity would be so felt that the ordinary usages of mourning would be suspended, or perhaps it signified that they could not in their exile manifest their sorrow, but only "mourn one toward another." Thus the prophet was a sign unto them (24).

Questions.

1. What is the title of chapter 19, and to whom does it refer?

2. What gives occasion for the rejection of the elders (v. 20)?

3. Analyze the first part of this chapter.

4. Explain verses 25 and 26 and 32.

5. What Messianic promise is found in 21:27?

6. How would you explain chapter 33?

7. How does Ezekiel prove his inspiration in chapter 24?

8. How is the proverb about the caldron understood?

9. How long a period of silence is enjoined on the prophet?

JUDGMENT ON THE GENTILE NATIONS

Chapters 25-32

The prophet's "dumbness" enjoined in the last chapter, was only towards his own people, and the interval was employed in messages touching the Gentiles. These nations might have many charges laid against them, but that which concerned a prophet of Israel chiefly was their treatment of that nation—see this borne out by the text. Their ruin was to be utter to the end, while that of Israel was but temporary (Jer. 46:28).

Seven nations are denounced, "the perfect number, implying that God's judgments would visit not merely these, but the whole round of the Gentile world." Babylon is excepted here, because she is, for the present, viewed as the rod of God's justice against Israel.

Use the marginal notes of your Bible for light on, the historical references, and the maps for geographical data. A Bible dictionary also would be of much assistance.

"Men of the east" (24:4)

means the nomadic tribes beyond the Jordan.

The following from the Scofield Bible recalls earlier teachings of this commentary: "The prophecies upon Gentile powers (in these chapters), have had partial fulfilments of which history bears witness, but the mention of the 'Day of the Lord' (30:3), makes it evident that a fulfilment in the final sense is still future. These countries are once more to be the battle-ground of the nations."

Tyre. 26-28.

In the first of these chapters we have Tyre's sin (1, 2), her doom and the instruments of its execution (3-14), and the effect of her downfall on the other nations (15-21). In the second, we have a lamentation over the loss of such earthly splendor, and in the third, an elegy addressed to the king on the humiliation of his sacrilegious pride. This last is the most important chapter of the three.

As to the destruction of Tyre, secular history shows how accurately God's word has come to pass. "Though thou be sought for, yet shalt thou never be found again" (21). This is not to say that there should be no more a Tyre, but that there should be no more the Tyre that once was. As a matter of fact there were two Tyres in Ezekiel's time, old Tyre and new Tyre, the first on the main land and the other out in the sea; and as to the first not a vistage of it was left.

Passing over the "lamentation" attention is called to the description of the king of Tyre (28:1-19), which should be read in connection with that of the king of Babylon in Isaiah 14. The comment in that case fits this also, for although these verses are referring to the king of Tyre then reigning, Ithbaal II, yet they have evidently an ulterior and fuller accomplishment in Satan, or in his earthly embodiment, the beast, or the Antichrist, of Daniel 7:25, 11:36, 37; 2 Thessalonians 2:4, and Revelation 13:6. There are many expressions in the chapter which baffle our understanding at present.

Egypt. 29-32.

It should be remembered that "Pharaoh" was a common name of all the kings of Egypt, meaning, as some say, "the sun," others, "a crocodile," which was an object of worship by Egyptians. That nation was very prosperous and proud at this period, and no human sagacity could have foreseen its downfall as Ezekiel describes it, and as it came to pass, God's instrument was Babylon (29:19; 30:10), whose work is figuratively set forth in verses 4-12, of which 6 and 7 refer to the false confidence Israel reposed in Egypt during the siege, and which was recorded in Isaiah and Jeremiah. Note verses 13-15 in the light of the subsequent history of Egypt, and compare them with the promise to Israel (21). God's covenant with the latter holds good, notwithstanding for the present she is dealt with like the Gentiles. "In that day" means in the fullest sense, the coming Day of the Lord.

Reaching chapter 30 we find two messages, the first (1-19), a repetition, with details, of that in 29:1-16; and the second, a vision more particularly against Pharaoh himself.

"Heathen" (3) should be "nations," from which it will be seen that "the judgment on Egypt is the beginning of a world-wide judgment on all the Gentile people considered as God's enemies." "No more a prince of the land of Egypt" (13), means, no more an independent prince ruling the whole country.

Chapter 31 illustrates the overthrow of Egypt by that of Assyria, for although the former was not utterly to cease to be as in the case of the latter, yet it was to lose its prominence as an aspirant for world-dominion. Assyria was overthrown by the Chaldeans or Babylonians, and so Egypt would be.

Chapter 32 includes two lamentations rather than one, a fortnight apart in time, and divided at verse 17. Verse 7 may refer figuratively to the political sky, and yet the thought of supernatural darkness as formerly in Exodus 10:21-23 is not excluded. The second lamentation accompanies Egypt in imagination to the unseen world where she shares the fate of other nations (18 et seq.).

Questions.

1. What were the limitations on the prophet's dumbness?

2. Why were judgments pronounced against the Gentile nations?

3. How many nations are named, and what is the symbolism of that number?

4. Have these prophecies yet been entirely fulfilled?

5. Briefly analyze chapters 26-28.

6. What secondary, and yet complete application awaits the prophecy of 28: 11-19?

7. How would you explain 30:13?

BROKEN SILENCE

Chapters 33-37

Ezekiel's commission to his own countrymen is now renewed (21, 22), and evidences a new tone. "Heretofore his functions had been chiefly threatening, but now the evil having reached its worst in the overthrow of Jerusalem, the consolatory element preponderates." (See 22:11).

Verses 23-29 of the same chapter, have reference to the handful left in Jerusalem after the siege, the best commentary on which is Jeremiah 40-42. Verse 30 to the end describes conditions at Chebar. The last verse alludes to the news in verse 21. When they heard that report which took some time to reach them, they had reason to change their minds about the prophet and his work.

Many False Shepherds and the One True One. 34.

"The shepherds of Israel" (2), are not the prophets and priests so much (though they may be included), as the rulers—kings, princes, judges. The indictment against them extends to verse 10, at which point encouragement and comfort is given to the scattered sheep, the people of Israel. The language corresponds with that of all the prophets, and points to the regathering of the nation in the latter times, and their restoration and blessing in the land again (11-22). This will synchronize with the second coming of the Messiah, here called "my servant David" (24) and "a plant of renown" (29). That millennial conditions are in mind is evidenced by verses 25-28. "Though a number of the people returned after the seventy years' captivity, and though they had a larger posterity in the land, yet they were continually under the Gentile yoke, until in A. D. 70, they were finally driven away again in a dispersion which still continues."

Judgment on Mount Seir or Edom. 35.

This is placed here by way of contrast with Israel's promised blessing. The Edomites, descendants of Esau, Jacob's brother, had treated their kin shamefully in the past (5), therefore, unlike them their desolations should be perpetual (9). Remember that it is only in their national character of foes to Israel that they are to be destroyed. God is always merciful to individuals who repent. "When the whole earth rejoices" (14), means Judah and the nations that submit themselves to her God.

Moral Restoration. 36.

It is always understood that the national restoration of Israel implies their moral restoration. They will repent and turn to the Lord before the promised blessings shall be poured out upon them. It is this moral restoration which is foretold here.

We have first restoration of the land (1-15), and then the people (35:16, 37:28). Verses 19-22, like those that follow, are spoken anticipatively. Observe God's motive for restoring them (22, 23). Observe the symbolic allusion to their moral regeneration (25-27), and that afterwards comes the material blessing. Many will have been gathered back to their land before the moral cleansing takes place, but the blessing will be withheld till then (28-38).

Valley of Dry Bones. 37.

In this chapter we have in symbol what the preceding foretold in plain language—in other words what the prophet saw in vision. Verse 11 is the key to the chapter. The "bones" are the whole house of Israel on the earth at the time to which the prophecy refers, which is the beginning of the millennial age. The "graves" are the Gentile nations among which they shall be scattered. They shall be gathered out from among these nations back to their land (12). This will result in their conversion (13), after which they will be filled with the Holy Spirit (14). The two sticks (16) are Israel and Judah which shall again become one (17-27). Following this is a blessing on the whole earth (28). Compare Acts 15:16, 17.

Verse 8 indicates that the people will return to their land at first unconverted. "David my servant" (24) is generally understood of the Messiah. "The chapter, as a whole, presents a beautiful image of Christian faith, which believes in the coming general resurrection of the dead in the face of all appearances against it, because God has said it (John 5:21; Romans 4:17; 2 Corinthians 1:9)."

Questions.

1. Explain the title of this lesson.

2. Quote 33:11.

3. Who are the "shepherds" of chapter 34?

4. What title is twice given the Messiah in this lesson?

5. What explains the location of chapter 35?

6. What precedes the national restoration of Israel?

7. Explain Chapter 37.

8. Tell the story of that chapter in your own words.

9. What does verse 8 seem to show?

10. Of what is the chapter a beautiful image?

PROPHECY AGAINST GOG

Chapters 28-39

It is fitting that following the prediction of Israel's restoration and blessing, there should come another showing judgment upon her enemies. Only it is doubtful if these enemies are those spoken of hitherto. Those were contiguous to Israel, but his is a northeastern power which gathers its allies on the mountains of the Holy Land. There is reason to identify it with Russia. She and the northern powers allied with her have been the latest persecutors of dispersed Israel, "and it is congruous both with divine justice and God's covenants with Israel that destruction should fall at the climax of the last mad attempt to exterminate her in Jerusalem."

Let not the similarity of names with Revelation 20:7, 8 lead to the supposition that the same event is in mind, as that takes place at the close of the millennium, and this near its beginning.

Identification with Russia.

"Gog" is probably a common name of the kings of the land like "Pharaoh" in Egypt. "The chief prince" is more properly "Prince of Rosh" or "russ," which suggests Russia, to say nothing of "Meshec" and "Tubal," which are almost identical with Moscow and Tobolsk. It is more difficult to locate "Gomer" and "Togarmah," but the whole military combination never having been referred to prior to this time, strengthens the contention in favor of a Russian alliance of some sort.

The Period and the Plan.

Note the time and conditions in verse 8. "The latter years"— the end of this age. Israel is "brought back," restored, and is dwelling "safely" (also verse 11). Note the enemy's motive or plan (10-13), and compare that of Jehovah in permitting this to come to pass (14-16). The closing verses show the punishment superhuman in character, and final

in its result. No more fears for Israel until the muster of the nations at the close of the millennium.

Thoroughness of the Judgment. 39.

The prophecy is continued in this chapter, and verses 8-10 describe the going forth from the cities of Palestine to burn the arms of the foe. There is difficulty here, but "seven" is the sacred number (verse 9) indicating the completeness of the cleansing in Israel's zeal for purity. As Fairbairn says, "Nothing belonging to the enemy should be left to pollute the land. How different from the earlier times when Israel not only left the arms but the heathen themselves among them, to corrupt them."

A Public Burial Ground.

Where the enemy expected to take the land for a possession, he would find a grave. Verse 11 might be translated:

"I will give unto Gog a place for burial in Israel, the valley of the passengers on the east of the Sea; and it shall stop the passengers; and there shall they bury Gog and all his multitude."

The travelers shall not stop their noses because of the smell, but the great number of mounds in evidence shall stay their progress, and lead them to think upon the vengeance poured out. This is the sense of the passage.

In other words these graves shall be in no obscure spot, but in the direct pathway of travelers. Verse 15 is striking as compared with the foregoing. In verse 13, "all the people of the land" are burying the dead for seven months. In verse 14, at the end of that time, special men are employed to continue the task to a finish; while in verse 15, the passers-by are helping them by setting up a sign near any exposed bone to identify it until removed.

Verses 17-20 describe the fowls and the beasts feasting on the slain—by rams, lambs, goats, etc., (18) being meant men of different ranks and callings.

Questions.

1. With what Gentile nation is this chapter probably dealing?

2. State two or three reasons for your belief.

3. What period of time is in mind?

4. What shows the superhuman character of the punishment?

5. What illustrates its thoroughness?

THE MILLENNIAL TEMPLE

CHAPTERS 40-48

These chapters give a picture of the restored temple at Jerusalem during the Millennium, and of the worship of the Messiah when He shall exercise sway from that center to the ends of the earth.

Beginning with chapter 40:1-5, we have an introduction to the subject—the date as usual (1), the location and the opening vision. (The vision is of a city on the south); (2), a man with a measuring rod; (3), a building surrounded by a wall (5). In verses 6-16 the measurement of the east gate, the threshold, posts, porches, chambers, entry, pillars, etc. Following this (7-23), the outer court, the north gate and details corresponding to the preceding. Then the south gate with its appurtenances, and so on to verse 38. In 38-43 we have a description of the cells and entrances, the tables of stone for slaying the offerings, the inner cells for the singers (44-47), and finally the measuring of the porch (48, 49).

In chapter 41 the prophet views the house itself, and in 42 he sees the cells or chambers for the priests (1-12). This is followed by regulations as to eating, dressing of the priests (13, 14), the chapter closing with a general summary.

In chapter 43 a more august sight presents itself, the Shekinah, the visible glory of Jehovah is seen returning to dwell in the midst of His people (1-5).

Kelly says, "the force of this is clear enough. It is the sign of God's return to Israel which He had left since the time of their captivity in Babylon. When it left, Israel, or the Jews, ceased to be His recognized people, but when they are taken up again under the Messiah the glory comes back." (6-9.)

Following this we have the measurement of the altar, and statutes for the offering of burnt-offerings and the sprinkling of blood (13-17). But why is this, if we are dealing with millenial conditions? To this the author quoted above replies, that while Israel is to return to the land, and be converted and blessed, it will be still as Israel, not as Christians. In the present dispensation all believers, both Jews and Gentiles, belong to Christ in heaven, where such differences are unknown, but when this prophecy is fulfilled, and Christ's reign begins on earth, the distinction will be again resumed, though now for blessing, and not for cursing, as of old. He quotes verses 18-27 as decisive of this, since in these verses we hear of priests and Levites and the seed of Zadok entrusted with the duties of the altar.

Speaking of the offerings, they will be memorial, looking back to the cross, as under the old covenant they were anticipatory, looking forward to the cross. In neither case have animal sacrifices power to put away sin (Romans 3:25; Hebrews 10:4).—*Scofield.*

Five Views of Interpretation.

There are five interpretations of these chapters:

(1) Some think they describe the temple at Jerusalem prior to the Babylonian captivity, and are designed to preserve a memorial of it. But the objection is that such a memorial is unnecessary because of the records in Kings and Chronicles; while the description is untrue because in many particulars it does not agree with that in the books named.

(2) Some think these chapters describe the temple in Jerusalem after the return from the seventy

years in Babylon, but this can not be because there are more marks of contrast than likeness between the temple here described and that.

(3) Some think they describe the ideal temple which the Jews should have built after the seventy years' return, and which they never realized. But this lowers the character of the divine Word. Why should this prophecy in Ezekiel have been given if it was never to be fulfilled?

(4) Some think this temple in Ezekiel symbolizes the spiritual blessings of the church in the present age. But this appears unlikely, because even those who

meant, but a new dispensation with Israel on the earth while the church is in the air with Christ. This involves changes of immense magnitude.

An Architect's Testimony.

While lecturing in Edinburgh, the author received a communication from G. S. Aitkin, Esq., an architect of that city, who had studied this vision of the temple from a technical standpoint, and made a plan of it, finding a place for every measurement referred to.

The two points he settled were, first, as to the meaning of chapter

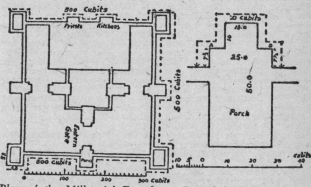

Plan of the Millennial Temple as Revealed to Ezekiel, and Enlarged Plan of Porch.

hold the theory can not explain the symbolism of which they speak. Moreover, even as symbolism it leaves out several important features of Christianity, such as the atonement and intercession of the high priest.

(5) The last view is that in the preceding comments, that we have here a prediction of the temple that shall be built in the millennial age. This appears a fitting and intelligent sequel to the preceding prophecies. A strong objection to its exists in that sacrifices and feasts are referred to, which seem contradictory to Christianity. But it should be remembered that Christianity is not

40:14, which he found referred to a girth measurement. This fixed the position of the outer gates in relation to the enclosing walls, and so determined the position of all the other parts following. The second point, that the five hundred cubit or "reed" dimension (chapter 42: 15, 16) was also girth and not linear dimensions, as hitherto maintained. The following is an extract of a paper prepared by him on the subject for the "Transactions" of the Royal Institute of British Architects."

"In the fourteenth verse of the fortieth chapter is mentioned the measurement that fixes the projections of the gate in relation to the enclosing walls; and as will be afterwards seen, the ultimate form and dimensions of the entire enclosure. Hitherto Ezekiel had been describing linear measurements, but now the expression 'Post of the court round about the gate' may be taken to imply that the prophet's companion made a girth measurement from the post of the court on one side right round the gate to the post of the court on the other side of 60 cubits. By deducting the girth of the porch, which is 45 cubits (see author's plan from A to B) from this 60 cubits 15 remain, or 7 cubits for each shoulder.

"The measurements of the buildings within the temple courts being completed, Ezekiel is brought through the eastern gate to the outside of the enclosing north, south, east and west wall, which are measured in his presence, and found to be 500 reeds, or, as corrected by the LXX, 500 cubits each.

"To meet this statement, Hastings' Bible Dictionary represents the temple area as enclosed with a straight lined wall, which, unbroken in outline, necessarily leads to so large an internal area as to require a greater number of courts than the inspired record allows.

"The author's plan, on the other hand, measuring around the broken outline which is obtained by adding the porches and the 'People's Sacrificial Kitchen,' 40 x 30 internally (chapter 46, verse 22), or (adding thickness of wall) 52 cubits by 42 cubits externally, secures the desired dimensions of 500 cubits for each side, the Priests' Kitchens (chapter 46, verses 19, 20) being substituted on the west side for the porches of the other three sides."

If this exegesis is correct, it is a further confirmation that the vision was the result of divine inspiration. Mr. Aitken did not understand what the intrinsic meaning of the whole passage might be, but it occurred to him, after listening to an exposition of the book by the present author, that it might refer to the future re-

building of the Jewish temple at Jerusalem.

Questions.

1. What picture is given in these chapters?
2. How is 43:1-5 to be explained?
3. Explain verses 13-17 of the same chapter.
4. Name the five views of the interpretation of the whole vision.
5. What is the position taken by the architect quoted?

CLOSE OF THE BOOK

CHAPTERS 44-48

1. The Gate of the Prince. 44:1-3.

As the glory of Jehovah had entered this gate (48:4, 5) it must hereafter be closed for all but His representative—the prince. This can not mean the Messiah, because the prince requires a sin-offering. (Remember that sin will be suppressed in that day, but not yet extirpated.) Doubtless this prince is a future prince of the house of David.

2. The Future Priests and Levites. 44:9-31.

Verses 9-14 show that the Levites who, in the earlier time had turned from God to idols, will be made to feel their shame since it is the days of the earthly kingdom that are here referred to, and righteousness (not grace) governs. The concluding verses of this chapter show conclusively, Kelly thinks, that they are dealing, not with Christian conditions, but with Israel again on the earth, and in covenant relations with God. 17-22, for example, is a repetition of the Levitical law for the priests, only with greater strictness. The priests' decisions are both for ceremonial and judicial matters (23, 24). Death may be rare and exceptional on the earth in that day, but it will still take place (25-27).

3. The Land and the Feasts. 45.

Jehovah's portion of the land must be set aside in acknowledgment of His claim to the whole, but He applies it for the sanctuary and they who minister there (1-5). The portion of the prince comes next, and then that of the people (6-8). Note the prophecy, "My princes shall no more oppress the people"—selfishness and greed must at last cease on the earth (9-12). Note, also, the religious dues to be paid (13-17). Also the fact of sin still existing (18-20), and the feasts (21-24), excepting, however, the feasts of weeks, or Pentecost. It might be thought that this would be the most prominent of the feasts during the Millennium, as that period is considered so peculiarly the era of the Holy Spirit which Pentecost represents, but the feast drops out of the list. Of course the Holy Spirit will be poured out on all flesh in that day, as the prophets foretell, but for a different object than now. Now he comes to baptize both Jew and Gentile into the body of Christ the exalted Head of the Church, this is the meaning of Pentecost, but then each Jew and Gentile will be blessed on their own ground, but there will be no union. There will be greater breadth of blessing then, but not the height and depth there is today.

The feast of tabernacle, however, is alluded to (25), because it most fully expresses their great ingathering when they rejoice before Jehovah, and look back on pilgrim days forever past (Kelly.)

4. Public Worship. 46.

The Sabbath is made much of, and the new moon (1). There is a distinction between the prince and the people, but neither goes within the temple to worship (2, 3). "There is no drawing near as we now do through the rent vail, for Israel is being blessed on earth, and not like the church in heavenly places." There is no longer an evening lamb, although the offering of the morning lamb continues (12-15). The jubilee year is re-established (16-18).

5. The Temple Waters. 47:1-12.

Compare with verses 1-5 of

this chapter Joel 3:18 and Zechariah 14:8, which show that the region of the Dead sea, which had been the embodiment of barrenness and desolation, is, in the coming day to be changed into a scene of life and fruitfulness. And the remarkable fact is that the waters increase continually, without the least hint, but rather to the exclusion of, accession from tributary streams. The whole thing is literal in fact, and yet supernatural in origin. For the healing effect of these waters read verses 6-12.

6. The Division of the Land. 47:13-48.

In accordance with Genesis 48:5 and 1 Chronicles 5:1 Joseph has two portions (13). The land will be rich enough not only for all Israel gathered there, but for the stranger and his children as well (22). And think of the largeness of vision of Israel in that day (23)! A comparison of chapter 48 shows the distribution of the tribes in the millennial kingdom will be different from that previously known, but we can not consider it in detail (1-29). The distribution is to be made by lot.

The last and chief glory is the presence of Jehovah in the city of His choice (30-35).

Questions.

1. What shows that the "prince" is not identical with the Messiah?

2. What consequence of sin will still be in evidence during the Millennium?

3. What notable feast of earlier Israel will be omitted in the Millennium, and why?

4. What ordinance of public worship shows the less desirable position of earthly Israel as compared with the heavenly church?

5. What other prophets corroborate Ezekiel concerning the temple waters?

6. Are these waters literal or only figurative?

7. What is the chief glory of the city of Jerusalem in the millennial age?

DANIEL

NEBUCHADNEZZAR'S DREAM

Chapters 1-2

Daniel, like Ezekiel, was an Israelite in Babylonian captivity, but of a little earlier date (1-4, compared with Ezekiel 1:1, 2). Of royal blood, fine physique, strong intellectuality and deep knowledge, he became trained in the language, traditions and astrological science of his captors that, with the other eunuchs, he might serve their king in responsible relations in the palace (4-7). For religious reasons, and out of reverence to the true God, he sought the privilege of abstention from a certain part of the physical preparation (8), with the happy result indicated in the chapter. God was preparing Daniel better than Nebuchadnezzar was and for a greater purpose than he knew.

The Testing Time. 2:1-30.

In process of time the testing came (1-13).

> "Each victory will aid you
> Another to win."

Daniel had won one, and his faith had been strengthened to essay another (14-16). We gather from these verses and the preceding that he had not been consulted with the heathen advisers above (2). Observe the character of his piety (17, 18), and note the first young men's prayer-meeting on record, and its results (19-23). "Belteshazzar" (26) is the Babylonian name bestowed on Daniel. Note his unfaltering witness to the true God (27-30).

The Dream and Interpretation. vv. 31-45.

At this point the book of Daniel differs from the preceding prophets in that they deal chiefly with Israel or Judah, and only secondarily with the Gentile nations; while he deals chiefly with the latter, and secondarily with the former. In other words, he is giving us the outline history of these nations during the time Israel is scattered among them in punishment, and up until the period of her restoration to her land and deliverance from their oppression.

Nebuchadnezzar's dream, which he interpreted, shows that this period of Gentile dominion in the earth, lasting from the time of that king, when Judah is taken from her land until the end of this age when she shall be restored there again, is divided among four world-powers (31-35).

The metal image equals Gentile dominion in all this period. The head of gold, the Babylonian power, the breast and arms of silver, the Medo-Persian power succeeding; the belly and thighs of brass, the Grecian; the legs and feet of iron and clay, the Roman. The stone "cut out of the mountain without hands" represents the Kingdom of the Messiah, which shall be set up on the earth at the end of this age, and whose establishment shall involve the demolition of all the earthly powers (36-45).

An interpretation of some of the difficulties follows: Note the two words of verse 31, "excellent," "terrible," as characterizing the history of the Gentile powers in all this period. They will have that to attract and that to repel to the very end. Note that the stone smites the image (34); in other words, the establishment of God's Kingdom on the earth will be with destructive judgments, as all the prophets have shown. Note that some day after the present kingdoms as such, are destroyed, but not before, God's Kingdom will be supreme in the earth (35). For the meaning of verses 37, 38, see Jeremiah 27.

Note that all the world-powers following Babylon will be inferior or to it in a descending scale (39, 40). Inferior not in territorial extent or military prowess, but in the character of their government. Babylon was an absolute monarchy, Nebuchadnezzar's word was law (12, 13). The Medo-Persian power represented a limited monarchy—Darius hearkened to his princes and his lords (6:4-16). The Grecian was weaker, in that after the death of Alexander the Great, the empire was divided into four parts. The Roman, the weakest of all, the clay mingled with iron, indicating the development of the democracy in the latter times; in other words, constitutional monarchies and republics.

Note particularly the fourth, or Roman, power (40-43). The two legs foreshadow the later division of that empire into the eastern and western halves. The ten toes speak of a time when five separate kingdoms shall represent each half. The iron and clay show the monarchical elements in more or less contention with the democratic, and vice versa. These governmental features are to characterize the end of this age (44), when God shall set up His Kingdom in the midst of heavy and destructive judgments.

Questions.

1. In whose reign was Daniel taken captive?

2. State in your own words his history down to the time of the dream.

3. How does his book differ from the other prophets?

4. State the beginning and the ending of Gentile dominion.

5. Name its four great historical divisions.

6. Shall this age end in peace or disorder?

7. Have you compared Jeremiah 27?

8. In what sense do the world-powers grow inferior to one another?

FROM NEBUCHADNEZZAR TO CYRUS

Chapters 3-6

The effect of the interpretation of his dream on Nebuchadnezzar is the inflation of his pride. To be sure, he was grateful to Daniel (2:46-49), to whom he offered worship, although the latter rejected it no doubt, as did Paul later (Acts 14:11-18). His apprehension of Daniel's God, however, is yet only as one amongst the national or tribal gods, although greater than they. This is clear from what follows in chapter 3:1-7, which is an attempt "to unify the religions of his empire by self-deification." The tower of Babel (Gen. 11) was an attempt of the same kind in the same place, and it will be again tried there by the "Beast," the last head of Gentile world-dominion (Dan. 7:8; Rev. 13:11-15; 19-20).

Speaking of the "Beast" brings to mind the tribulation Israel shall suffer at his hands; and the three faithful Jews of verses 8-18 are a type of the faithful remnant in that day which will not bow the knee to him (Isa. 1:9; Rom. 11:5; Rev. 7:14).

"The Son of God" (25) is translated in the R. V., "A son of the gods," and possibly refers to an angel which the king beheld (Psa. 34:7) though some apply it to the Second Person of the Trinity (Isa. 43:2). The result of Nebuchadnezzar's experience in this instance is a further confession of the true God, but still He is only the God of the Hebrews, ruler of angels and the rewarder of them who honor Him. At the conclusion of the next chapter his vision is cleared considerably.

The King's Confession. 4.

This next chapter is his confession in the nature of a general proclamation (1). The tree he saw in vision (10) symbolized himself grown great in the earth, as God, through Daniel, had foretold. Its hewing down (14) was the punishment coming on him for his pride. The stump left in the earth (15) was his return to power again after the lesson of his humiliation was learned. He became a lunatic, and lived like a beast for seven years (16). The reason for it all is in verse 17. Daniel is kind and sympathetic towards him though obliged to speak the awful truth (19). He is faithful also (27), and who can tell what the outcome may have been had the king heeded his warning? In a twelvemonth, however, the stroke fell (29-33). But at the end of the experience the king has a different testimony to bear of God (34, 35).

Passing of Babylon. 5.

Many years have elapsed since the events of the last chapter. Nebuchadnezzar is dead and his son-in-law, Nabonidus is reigning, with his son (and Nebuchadnezzar's grandson), Belshazzar, as co-regent (1). His name means "Bel protect the king," while "Belteshazzar," the name assigned to Daniel, means "Bel protect his life." In verse 2 Nebuchadnezzar is called "his father," but there is no discrepancy here, because the Semitic tongues have no equivalent for "grandfather" or "grandson." A corroboration of the position here assigned Belshazzar is found in verse 7, where the interpreter of the mysterious handwriting is promised the "third" place in the kingdom—Nabonidus being first and Belshazzar himself second.

The "queen" (10) is probably the aged widow of Nebuchadnezzar and grandmother of the present king, who has not forgotten Daniel, though her offspring and his court seem to have done so in their degeneracy. Like herself, the prophet is now old, perhaps eighty, but as the result shows, God has more service in store for him, and the honor that accompanies it. Note his words and the character of his indictment against the king (17-28). And yet the king acts like a king in verse 29. In that night the power was wrested from the Babylonians by the Medes and Persians, and the breast and arms of the image had become realized in history.

"Darius the Mede" (31) is unknown to history by that name outside of this book, and is not to be confounded with the later Darius of Ezra (5:15). When it is said he "took the kingdom," some think it means that it was taken in his name merely, but really by his general, who was also his relative, Cyrus, who afterward became king, and who is named at the close of chapters 1 and 6. There is obscurity surrounding this subject on which our space will not permit elaboration.

Daniel in the Lion's Den. 6.

Darius had heard of Daniel and his prophecies, and desired to honor him (1-3), but human jealousy is at work (4, 5). How does the first word of verse 7 prove that these rulers told a falsehood to the king? Is not this sin into which he fell practically the same as that committed by Nebuchadnezzar in chapter 3? Was ever faith more beautifully displayed than by God's aged servant in verse 10? Referring to our last lesson, how does verse 14 illustrate the inferiority in character of this kingdom over the preceding?

As another says, "Well may we think here of another law and another love." God's holy law condemned man, and justly so, yet He found a way to save him (2 Cor. 5:21). An absolute monarchy is what man wants, if only it be a holy monarchy. It was a terrific judgment that fell on Daniel's accusers, but remember the age in which it occurred, and also that it was not commanded by God, although permitted as a judicial retribution.

Notice in closing, the last verse of the chapter. Do we recall that Isaiah had prophesied of Cyrus between one and two hundred years before his birth (44-45)? He is the one under whom the Medo-Persian kingdom was consolidated, and who later gave liberty to the Jews to return to Jerusalem at the close of their seventy years' captivity, as we saw in Ezra (1:1-4). Doubtless Daniel's influence had much to do with this.

Questions.

1. How was Nebuchadnezzar affected by his dream?

2. Illustrate his development in the knowledge of the true God.

3. What was the motive or aim of his action in chapter 3?

4. To what event in the "end" period does this point?

5. Of what is the faithfulness of the three Jews a type?

6. Give the story of chapter 4 in your own words.

7. What was Belshazzar's relation to Nebuchadnezzar?

8. Who was the real conqueror of Babylon?

9. Quote from memory 2 Cor. 5:21.

10. Tell what you know of the story of Cyrus.

DANIEL'S VISION OF THE FOUR BEASTS

CHAPTER 7

This and the vision in chapter 8 are the prophet's "dream and visions," and not the king's, and they occurred apparently during his political retirement in the earlier years of Belshazzar (7:1, 8:1). They cover the same ground as Nebuchadnezzar's dream and give us in more detail, and from a different point of view, the same story of Gentile dominion from his period to the end of the present age. One difference is that Nebuchadnezzar's dream revealed the imposing outward splendor of the world powers, while Daniel's shows their moral character as indicated by ferocious and rapacious beasts. "It is remarkable that the heraldic insignia of the Gentile nations are all beasts or birds of prey."

The "sea," in Scripture, stands for the peoples of the earth (Isa. 17:5, Rev. 17:15). The "great sea" Daniel saw was the Mediterranean, the center of the prophetic earth. That is, where not otherwise indicated, the nations with which prophecy has to do chiefly, are those that border on that sea, or whose political affiliations are closely related to them.

The Four Beasts: 7:1-8.

The first of these two visions (chapter 7), when more closely viewed, resolves itself into four, with their interpretations, but we shall treat it singly.

The lion (v. 4) corresponds to the golden head of Nebuchadnezzar's image, and stands for Babylon. The bear (v. 5) corresponds to the breast and arms of silver, and stands for the Medo-Persian empire. Being "raised up on one side," means that one part of the empire was stronger than the other, which was Persia. The "three ribs in the mouth of it" are the three provinces conquered by it not long before, Susiana, Lydia and Asia Minor. The leopard (v. 6) is the Grecian empire, corresponding to the "belly and thighs of brass." The four wings denote the swiftness with which it carried its victories in every direction, and the four heads its ultimate partition into as many parts on the death of its great head, Alexander. The dreadful and terrible beast, too dreadful and terrible for a name (v. 7) corresponds to the legs of iron, and is equivalent to the Roman empire. Its ten horns, like the ten toes in the other case, speak of the ten kingdoms into which it shall be divided at the end of this age; while the little horn (v. 8) "who subdues three of the ten kings so completely that the identity of their kingdoms is lost," is the important additional feature of this vision over that of Nebuchadnezzar. We will again refer to this.

The Ancient of Days. vv. 9-14.

While these events are culminating on the earth others are transpiring in heaven—a great judgment scene is before us (compare Ps. 2; Matt. 25:31-46, and Rev. 19:19-21. "The Ancient of Days" is identified by some as the First, and by others as the Second Person of the Godhead (Rev. 1:12-14; John 5:22). The slaying of the "beast" (v. 11) means the destruction of the world powers as represented in their final form of the revived Roman Empire. As to the "rest of the beasts" whose dominion was taken away while their lives were prolonged for a season (v. 12), the meaning is that each of the preceding empires was, in turn, swallowed up by its successor, and lived in it, though it lost its place of independent power. "The Son of man" (v. 13) needs no identification as He comes forward to receive His earthly Kingdom—the stone cut out of the mountains without hands. (Compare the parable of the nobleman, Luke 19).

The Inspired Interpretation. vv. 15-27.

Note that while the Son of man receives the Kingdom (v. 13) "the saints of the Most High" take and possess it with him (v. 18). These may mean the faithful Israelites on earth, but the glorified church will be with the King as her Head in the air reigning over the earth.

The great interest for the prophet in this interpretation focuses on "the little horn" (v. 24), which is referred to under the title of the "Beast" in Revelations 13 and 17. He is a blasphemer of God and a persecutor of His saints (v. 25), who shall have great power for three and one-half years at the close of this age, and just before God interposes with judgments to set up His Kingdom. "Time" here stands for a year, "times" for two years, and "the dividing of time," half a year. (See Rev. 11:2, 3; 12:6.)

Questions.

1. To whom is this vision revealed, and at what period in his life?

2. How does it correspond with Nebuchadnezzar's dream?

3. How does it differ in its point of view?

4. What does the "sea" symbolize in the Bible?

5. What particular sea is now in mind, and what gives it its great importance prophetically?

6. Which was the stronger part of the second empire?

7. What is the interpretation of verse 12?

8. What is the meaning of "a time, and times, and the dividing of time?"

THE RAM AND THE HE-GOAT

Chapter 8

How much later was this vision than the preceding? Where was it revealed to Daniel (v. 2)? It is important to keep in mind that it covers the same ground as the preceding, except that the story begins, not with Babylon's supremacy, but that of the Medes and Persians represented by the ram (v. 3), though in the former vision by the bear. The higher horn of the ram is the Persian half of the empire. The united empire made conquests—west, north and south, but in its western campaigns it awakened the triumphing opposition of the Greeks represented by the "he-goat," whose "notable horn" was Alexander the Great (vv. 5-7). In the former vision this empire was represented by the leopard.

Verse 8 foreshadows the death of Alexander, and the division of the Grecian empire into four parts—Syria, Egypt, Macedonia, Asia Minor, under the rule respectively of four of Alexander's generals, Cassander, Lysimachus, Seleucus and Ptolemy.

Antiochus Epiphanes. vv. 9-14.

"A little horn," as in the preceding vision, comes out from these four (v. 9), whose power developed towards the south and east, and especially "the pleasant land," the land of Israel. The "little horn" is the eighth of the dynasty of Seleucus on the Syrian throne, whose name was Antiochus Epiphanes, although he was sometimes called "Epimanes," or the "madman," because of his life and deeds.

As an oppressor of the Jews he fulfilled the prophecy in verses 10-12, as will be seen by the book of Maccabees. "The host of heaven" and "the stars" are types of Israel, especially their leaders—the princes, priests, rabbis of the period, which was about 171 B. C.

"The prince of the host" (v. 11) is doubtless the Lord Himself, from whom the daily sacrifice was taken away, and whose sanctuary was polluted. Indeed, when Antiochus conquered Jerusalem he caused a sow to be sacrificed on the altar, and its broth sprinkled over the entire temple. He changed the feast of tabernacles into the feast of Bacchus, and greatly corrupted the Jewish youth who were spared from the sword, one hundred thousand of whom were massacred.

The time during which this continued is revealed by a conversation between two angels which Daniel in vision hears (vv. 13, 14). The 2,300 days is sometimes identified by going back from the time of Judas Maccabees' victory, or rather the date when he cleansed the sanctuary from its abomination, about December 25, 165 B. C., to 171 B. C., the date of the interference of Antiochus. This Antiochus is a forerunner, or an approximate fulfilment of that "little horn" spoken of in the preceding vision, and again in the closing part of the present one.

The Inspired Interpretation.
vv. 15-27.

The angel Gabriel here appears for the first time, and in the likeness of a man (vv. 15, 16), but it is evident that the interpretation he is to give has reference not so much to Antiochus and his deeds as to the greater than he who shall arise "at the time of the end" (5:17), the same one possibly, and the same period as are referred to in the preceding vision. "The time of the end" is identified in verse 19 as "the last end of the indignation," an expression frequently met with in the Old Testament, and meaning God's indignation against Israel on account of her disobedience and apostasy, an indignation which will be poured out upon her at the end of this age.

This being of whom Antiochus is the forerunner or approximate fulfilment, and who is possibly the same as in the preceding vision, is further described in verses 23-25. What language in verse 23 shows that he appears at the end of the age? How are his spirit and character described in the same verse? How does the next verse suggest superhuman agency in his case? And his animus towards Israel? Express the deceitfulness indicated in verse 25, in your own words. What language in this verse shows his opposition to the Messiah personally? How is his destruction expressed? (Compare 2 Thess. 2:8.) It may be objected that this being can not be the same as the "little horn" of the preceding vision, because that is seen to come up out of the ten horns; in other words, out of the Roman Empire or the last form of Gentile dominion on the earth, while this comes up out of the four, or the Grecian Empire, which is next to the last. But a simple answer is that he may come up out of the part of the Roman Empire which was originally the Grecian; in other words, that his rise may be expected in that quarter of the world and from such antecedents.

Nevertheless some think the "little horn" of this chapter, who shall arise at the end, is a different person from the one in chapter 7. They hold that he of chapter 7 will be the head of the revived Roman Empire, but that he of chapter 8 is another king of the north, who is to be the foe of Israel, and at the same time the enemy of the head of the revived Roman Empire. This may be true, and we would not dogmatize in a matter of such uncertainty, but we think the view suggested here of the identity of the two is the simpler and more practical one to hold awaiting light.

Questions.

1. How far is the scope of this vision identical with the preceding?

2. Name the geographic divisions of the Grecian Empire and their respective rulers.

3. Historically, who is meant by the "little horn"?

4. Give as much as you can of the history of Antiochus Epiphanes.

5. Of whom is he a type or forerunner?

6. What is meant by "the time of the end"?

7. What objection might be raised as to the identity of the "little horn" in chapter 7 with that of chapter 8?

8. How might it be met?

THE SEVENTY WEEKS

CHAPTER 9

Thus far in Daniel we have been dealing with the prophetic history of the times of the Gentiles, but now we return to that of his own people, the Jews.

Note the time and circumstances, verses 1, 2. The prophet is studying such books of the Old Testament as he possessed, especially Jeremiah, and knows the seventy years' captivity nears its end, therefore he is moved to offer one of the most notable prayers in the Bible. This prayer is divisible into confession, verses 3-15, and supplication, verses 16-19, and it is remarkable that in the former, holy man as Daniel was, he includes himself as partaker in the national sins. It is equally remarkable that his supplication is based on desire for God's glory, verses 17, 18. Israel has no merit to claim, but the Lord's honor is at stake. We have seen this before in the prayers of the patriarchs, the prophets and the psalmist, and we need to keep its lesson in mind.

Gabriel's Visit. vv. 20-23.
What mystery is shrouded in these verses! The nearness of heaven, the interest of God in the petition of His people, the nature and ministry of angels, the divine estimate of the saints, who can fathom these things?

Answer to the Prayer. vv. 24-27.
"Weeks," verse 24, might be translated "sevens," but whether is meant "seven" of days, or weeks, or months or years must be determined by the context. The context points to years, "Seventy sevens" of years, i.e., 490 years, are decreed upon Israel and the city of Jerusalem is the sense of the first phrase of

this verse. At the close of this period six things shall have been accomplished for that people. In other words, Gabriel's message is not merely an answer to Daniel's prayer about the return from the seventy years' captivity, but a revelation of the entire future of Israel from the end of that captivity to the end of the present age. This is evident from the nature of the six things mentioned:

1. To finish the transgression.

2. To make an end of sins.

3. To make reconciliation for iniquity.

4. To bring in everlasting righteousness.

5. To seal up the vision and prophecy.

6. To anoint the Most Holy.

The first three of the above refer to a time still future, for Israel's transgression is not yet finished, nor her sins ended, nor her iniquity covered. The time, therefore, is that spoken of by all the prophets, and especially named in Zechariah 13:1 and Romans 11:26-27. This is the time, moreover, when "everlasting righteousness" shall be brought in, otherwise the blessings of the millennial age. The vision and prophecy will be sealed then, in the sense that their final accomplishment in the history of God's earthly people shall have taken place. The most holy place will be anointed then in that new temple to be erected, as we saw in Ezekiel.

The Division of the Sevens.
"From the going forth of the commandment to restore and build Jerusalem unto Messiah, the Prince, shall be seven weeks," verse 25. This is the first of three divisions in this period of 490 years, and covers forty-nine years, seven weeks of years being equal to that number. This division begins to be counted "from the going forth of the commandment to build Jerusalem," which, it is commonly thought, means the twentieth year of Artaxerxes, King of Persia, who gave that authority to Nehemiah, in the month Nisan (see Neh. 2). It is proved historically that this was

454 B. C. During this period of forty-nine years the street and wall were built again "even in troublous times." (See S.P. Tregelles on Daniel.)

But to this period of seven weeks, or forty-nine years, is added another of three-score and two weeks, or 434 years, a total of 483 years, "unto the Messiah the Prince," i.e., until "Messiah be cut off," verse 26.

Observe that this period extends not merely to the birth but to the death of Christ, when He is "cut off, but not for Himself." It is now admitted that our Lord was crucified April A.D. 32, and those competent in such calculations show that this was precisely 483 years of 360 days each, allowing for leap years, changes in the Julian and Gregorian calendars and matters of that sort. That the Messiah was cut off, "but not for Himself," has been translated, "and there shall be nothing for Him," which probably means that He did not then receive the Messianic Kingdom.

[Anstey maintains that the point of departure for the 70 weeks is the first year of Cyrus. However the outcome is not different so far as the fulfilment of the prophecy is concerned, as the calculation in the other case is based, in his judgment, on an error of 82 years in the Ptolemaic chronology.]

"And the people of the prince that shall come shall destroy the city and the sanctuary," refers to the destruction of Jerusalem and the temple by the Romans under Titus, A.D. 70. They, i. e., the Romans, are "the people of the prince that shall come," but this "prince" himself is identical, not with the Messiah, but with the little horn of Daniel 7, the terrible despot who will be at the head of the restored empire at the end of this age.

The End Period

We now come to the last of the seventy sevens, or the closing seven years of this age. In other words, there is a long ellipsis between the close of the sixty-ninth and the beginning of the seven-

tieth week, indeed, the whole of the Christian age, of which more will be said later.

The events of the seventieth week begin with the words "and the end thereof shall be with a flood," which should be, as in the Revised Version, "his" end, not "the" end, for the allusion is still to the "prince that shall come," i.e., the Antichrist. The word "flood" also might be rendered "overflowing," which, to quote Tregelles, is doubtless the same overflowing as in Isaiah 10:22 and as that of the final crisis of Israel's history at the end of the age. The interval until this time will be characterized by war and desolation (compare Matt. 24:3-8).

"And he," i.e., "the prince that shall come," "shall confirm the covenant with many for one week." The "many" refers to the people of Israel then to be in their own land, but still in an unconverted state as far as the acceptance of Jesus as their Messiah is concerned. It will be to the mutual interest of the "little horn," i.e., the Antichrist, and Israel to enter into this covenant for seven years. There will be a faithful remnant, however who will not bow the knee to him— the covenant will be made with "many" but not all (compare Isa. 28:15-18).

He will break this covenant after three and one-half years and "cause the sacrifice and the oblation to cease," no longer permitting them to worship God in their newly-erected temple. Now begins their great tribulation,"a time and times and the division of time" named in chapter 8:25 (compare Rev. 13:5, 11-17).

The latter part of this verse has been translated thus: "And upon the wing (or pinnacle) of abominations (shall be) that which causeth desolation, even until the consummation and that determined shall be poured out upon the desolator."

The "abominations" are doubtless idols that shall be set up by this wicked prince to be worshipped in the temple, when the true God has been set aside,

Then the "consummation" comes and with it the judgment and desolation of the "desolator."

Questions.

1. With whose history are we dealing in this lesson?

2. What great feature marks the prayers of God's people in the Bible?

3. What are some of the suggestions growing out of Gabriel's visit?

4. What period of time is covered by the "seventy weeks"?

5. To what place and people does this period apply?

6. Name the six important things which will be accomplished in that people at its close.

7. When does this period begin and end?

8. Divide it into its three parts.

9. What event is identified with the first part?

10. With what event does part two close?

11. Explain the allusion to "the prince that shall come."

12. What age intervenes between the last two parts?

13. Tell what you know about the "covenant" of verse 27.

SUPPLEMENT ON BIBLE CHRONOLOGY

The last lesson referred to the lapse of time between the sixty-ninth and seventieth weeks, and as other lapses have been noted in the sacred chronology, it is desirable to devote a lesson to that subject.

The chronology of the Bible has a system of its own, whose center would seem to be the crucifixion of Jesus Christ. Forbes Clinton, an authority on such matters, has worked out the following dates without reference to any human system: Adam was created 4141 B. C., and Abram was called 2055 B. C., showing an intervening period of 2,086 years. But precisely the same period elapsed between the call of Abram and the crucifixion of Christ. The call of Abram, therefore, is the center date between creation and the cross, a supposition harmonizing perfectly with

the importance of that event in the history of redemption.

Cycles of Years.

To take another illustration, God's dealings with Israel are in cycles of 490 years. (1) The period from Abram to Exodus was 490 years, plus the fifteen years during which the bondwoman and her child (Hagar and Ishmael) dominated in Abram's tent, and which are not counted. (2) The period from Exodus to the dedication of Solomon's temple was 490 years, plus the 131 years of captivity in the time of the Judges, which are not counted. (3) From the dedication to the return from Babylon was 490 years, plus the seventy years of that capacity not counted. (4) From the return from Babylon to the beginning of the millennial age is 490 years, plus the dispensation in which Israel is dispersed, and which is not counted.

When God Does Not Count Time.

Prophetically speaking, God does not count time with reference to Israel while she is in captivity, or dispersion, or dominated by any other nation. In evidence of this, note that in 1 Kings 6:1 mention is made of the fourth year of Solomon as being 480 years after the Exodus. But we know from Numbers 14:33 that they were forty years in the wilderness; then, according to the Book of Joshua, they were thirty-seven years in conquering Canaan and up until the period of the Judges; Acts 13:20 shows that they were 450 years under the Judges; then they were forty years under Saul (Acts 13:21), and forty years under David (2 Sam. 5:4, 5): These periods total up 607 years, to which should be added the four years of Solomon referred to, making a total of 611 years.

How shall we explain this discrepancy, of which infidels and others have made so much? The answer has been stated above, that God does not count time prophetically while Israel is in captivity. For example, seven captivities are mentioned in the Book of Judges, one of eight years (3:8); eighteen years (3:14); twenty years (4:3); seven years (6:1); eighteen years (10:8); forty years (13:1), and twenty years (1 Sam. 7:2), making a total of precisely 131 years.

The above is a sufficient illustration of the principle.

We close this lesson with a rough diagram of the 490 years covered by Daniel 9:24-27, which may aid in fastening that important prediction in the memory:

Seventy-sevens—490 Years.

From the twentieth year of Artaxerxes to the end of this age.

Seven weeks, or forty-nine years. The street and wall of Jerusalem built.	Sixty-two weeks, or 434 years. At the close of this period the Messiah is cut off and has nothing. A. D. 32.	The Uncounted Period.	One week, seven years.
		1. Jerusalem destroyed, A.D. 70.	1. The Roman prince, or little horn in covenant with the Jews.
		2. Jews dispersed.	
		3. Jerusalem trodden down.	2. The covenant broken in the midst of the week.
		4. The church called out.	
		5. Apostasy of Christendom.	3. The great tribulation begins.
		6. Jews in part return to Jerusalem in unbelief.	4. Antichrist in power.
		7. Coming of Christ for the Church.	5. Christ appears to deliver Israel.

(See reference to Anstey in previous lesson.)

Questions.

1. What is peculiar to the chronology of the Bible?

2. What appears to be the central date between creation and the Cross?

3. How are God's dealings with Israel chronologically identified?

4. Name some of the cycles referred to.

5. When does God not reckon time prophetically in the case of Israel?

6. Can you illustrate this?

7. Name the chief events associated with the four periods of time in the preceding diagram.

"A GREAT WARFARE"

CHAPTERS 10-11:35

Note the late date of this prophecy (10:1), and the different rendering of a phrase in the Revised Version, where "even a great warfare" is substituted for "the time appointed was long." As the unveiling of the lesson will show, this phrase is an appropriate title for it.

Note the physical and spiritual preparation of the prophet for the revelation that follows (2-4), a condition into which he had doubtless brought himself by prayer. Had he been seeking of heaven an explanation of the previous mysteries—especially that of the ram and the he-goat? This seems probable, because what follows traverses so much of the ground of chapter 8.

Verses 5-9 bear so strong a resemblance to the description of the Son of Man in Revelation 1:12-17 as to suggest that it also is a Christophany, or manifestation of the Second Person of the Trinity. But this does not carry with it that it is He who touches and speaks to the prophet in the verses succeeding.

Mysteries of Satan's Kingdom.

Verses 10-14 are full of mystery, yet note first, the appreciation of Daniel in the heavenly courts (11); and then the testimony to the potency of prayer (12). But who is "the prince of the Kingdom of Persia (13)? Doubtless a spirit of eminence in the kingdom of darkness, to whose control Satan has committed the earthly affairs of Persia (compare Eph. 4:12). This interpretation seems confirmed by the reference to Michael, elsewhere known as the archangel, and who in the kingdom of light is the special guardian of Israel (10:21, 12:1; Jude 9; Rev. 12:7). What mighty power must Satan possess as judged by this verse, but what a relief to know that there is One stronger than he! Note in the conclusion of this section that the revelation now to be given chiefly concerns what we identify as the end period, the last seven years (14).

Intervening Events, 11:1–35.

Passing over the effect on the prophet, we come to the revelation of what shall take place between his time and that of Antiochus Epiphanes, with whom we were made acquainted in an earlier chapter.

The three kings of verse 2 were Cyrus, Ahasuerus (Cambyses) and Darius Hystaspes (see Anstey's, The Romance of Chronology, Vol. 1, p. 239). The fourth king was Xerxes (see Ezra 4:5-24). The "mighty king" (3) was Alexander the Great, while the next verse tells once more of the division of his kingdom at his death among his four generals.

Two of these kingdoms of the four now come into prominence, Egypt and Syria (5, 6), as those most closely related to Israel in their subsequent history. The "king's daughter" (6) was Bernice, offspring of Ptolemy II, who married Antiochus Theodus of Syria, but was subsequently poisoned by him. Her brother is referred to in verses 7-9—Ptolemy Energetes of Egypt.

Verse 9 is a mistranslation, and refers to the king of the north

(R.V.), whose sons (10) were nevertheless overcome by the Egyptian king, Ptolemy Philopater (11), who became weakened at length through licentious living (12).

We have now reached the period of about 200 B.C., when Syria, after many vicissitudes, turns the tide of battle in her favor under the leadership of one known as Antiochus the Great. He entered the Holy Land in the course of his campaign (13-16), treating it considerately, however, as the Jews had been his allies. The last part of verse 16 is an incorrect rendering and should be compared with the Revised Version. Later he made another effort to get possession of Egypt, the working out of his plan including a treaty engagement, and the espousal of his daughter, Cleopatra, to the Egyptian king, but the scheme did not succeed (17). Why the Cleopatra in this case is called "the daughter of the women" is not clear, but some suppose it to be because she was but a child and under the tutelage of both her mother and grandmother. Verses 18 and 19 speak of a contest with the Romans into which he unsuccessfully entered, and of his subsequent death.

Antiochus Epiphanes.

The brief reign of Seleucus Philopater B.C. 187-176 is depicted in verse 20, and then we come upon Antiochus Epiphanes, whose story continues through verse 35. "Vile" is "contemptible" in the Revised Version. This man was a younger son of Antiochus the Great, to whom the kingdom did not by right belong, but who stole the hearts of the people as Absalom did from David. He is the "little horn" of chapter 8, and as we have seen, forerunner of the greater "little horn" of the end period. Of his atrocities against Israel and the holy city and temple we read in the books of the Maccabees.

"The ships of Chittim" (30) are a Roman fleet whose power put an end to his victories in Egypt. Returning north, angry in his defeat, he committed those base things against Judea of which mention has been made and which are foretold again in verses 30-35. Apostate Jews sympathized with and aided him, as their successors will do in the case of his successor at the end period; but there were faithful ones under the lead of the Maccabees who valiantly resisted him (32). It was a period of testing for Israel, out of whose fires they came forth much purified.

Questions.

1. When was this prophecy revealed to Daniel?

2. How was he prepared for it?

3. What illustration of "the law of recurrence" is seen in this lesson?

4. Who presumably is the "man" referred to in verse 5?

5. Who is meant by "the prince of Persia"?

6. What relation does Michael bear to Israel?

7. Name the four kings of Persia referred to in verse 2.

8. What does this lesson reveal about Antiochus Epiphanes?

THE ANTICHRIST AND THE TRIBULATION

Chapters 11:36-12

In the introduction to this last vision of Daniel, it was stated (10:14) that it concerned his people "in the latter days," but thus far it has extended only to Antiochus Epiphanes and the Maccabees. The dividing line is at the close of verse 35 and the beginning of 36. In the former we read of the testing and purifying experiences of the wise ones in Israel "even to the time of the end," and in the latter of a certain "king" who "shall do according to his will." Most students agree, that the space between these two verses represents another lapse of time from the Maccabean period to the end of the age, and that the king now before us is the Antichrist of those coming days, who is referred to more particularly in Ze-

chariah 11:15-17, 2 Thessalonians 2:1, and Revelation 13:11-17. Some identify him with the "little horn" of chapter 7 and the "little horn" of chapter 8, whom Antiochus Epiphanes typifies. This, indeed, may be true, i. e., the restored head of the Roman Empire in that day, and the Antichrist, may be one and the same individual, but there are others who think that they may be two—of this we cannot now be certain.

The King Described, vv. 36-39.

He is self-willed, proud, blasphemous, successful, idolatrous, materialistic, and covetous. "The God of his fathers" (37) is a phrase indicative of his Jewish extraction; "the desire of women," is taken by some as signifying the true Messiah, to whom all pious Jewish women in pre-Messianic times desired to give birth. "The god of forces," or "a god of fortresses" (38, R. V.), is difficult to understand except in some materialistic sense. Shall we say it finds interpretation in Revelation 13: 11-17, by identifying the first beast as the restored head of the Roman Empire, and the second as this evil king, the Antichrist, who causes all men to worship the first? Is the first beast, this god, in other words?

The Last Campaign, vv. 40-45.

This king has enemies, the "king of the south" and the "king of the north" (40) of that period, but who they are cannot be conjectured. The last-named is more vigorous and successful, entering Jerusalem and overcoming countries (including the south country, Egypt, 41-43) until at length a menace in the east and north moves him to make quick work at Jerusalem (45), in which he meets his own inglorious end (compare Zech. 8 and 15, and Joel 2). It would appear from these passages that the coming of the Lord on behalf of Israel brings about his end, and we know that it is nothing less than this which also despatches the Antichrist (2 Thess. 2:8). There are deep things here for whose solution we can only wait, as Daniel was obliged to do (12:12).

Israel's Deliverance, 12:1-3.

The opening verses of this chapter, should be read in connection with Christ's words in Matthew 24, especially verse 21, and also Revelation 12, especially verses 7-12. Note the deliverance of the faithful remnant of the Jews in that day as shown in the latter part of verse 1, Zechariah 13:8, 9; Matthew 24:22. It is a question whether it is a physical or a moral resurrection that is spoken of in verse 2, but it would be harmonious with Ezekiel 37 to say the latter.

"They that be wise" (3), may be rendered "teachers," and refers doubtless to the faithful Jewish witnesses of the end period and the reward which comes to them; though, of course, it can be applied in a secondary sense to faithful witnesses anywhere and always, for "He that winneth souls is wise."

The Final Vision and Final Word to Daniel, vv. 4-13.

This book is still sealed to Daniel's people the Jews, but the time is coming when it will be unsealed (4). "The man clothed in linen" (5) is, it would seem, the same who appeared to the prophet at chapter 10:5, the blessed Lord Himself. Compare Daniel's question and its answer with Revelation 10:1-6. The answer once more identifies the last three and one-half years of the end period, "the time of Jacob's trouble," the 1260 days of Revelation 11 and 12. But verse 11 adds another 30 days, and what may be understood by this we do not know. In the meantime may the promise to Daniel be fulfilled to us in our place and measure, "thou shalt rest, and shalt stand in thy lot at the end of the days."

Questions.

1. What period of time is represented by the division between verses 35 and 36?

2. How might the "king" of verse 36 be identified?

3. How is he described?

4. Have you read Revelation 13?

5. Have you read Matthew 24?

6. Do you recall the subject of Ezekiel 37?

7. Where is found the verse "He that winneth souls is wise?"

8. Quote from memory the last verse of Daniel.

HOSEA

THE SWEEP OF THE BOOK

CHAPTERS 1-3

It will be seen by the opening verse of this lesson that we are back in the land of Israel before the Babylonian captivity. Examine 2 Kings 14-20 and the corresponding chapters in 2 Chronicles for the history of this period, and the more carefully you read those chapters the more interested you will be in Hosea, and the more you will get out of it. While four of the kings named in verse 1 reigned in Judah, and only the last-named, Jeroboam, in Israel, nevertheless it is to Israel rather than Judah that Hosea's prophecies apply.

The Prophet's Domestic History, 1:2-9.

God called upon him to do an unusual thing in taking an unchaste woman to wife (2), but it had a symbolical significance which the last part of the verse explains.

Other prophets, Isaiah, Jeremiah and Ezekiel, were called upon to do strange things with the same purpose, so we are not surprised. It was not wrong for Hosea to contract such a marriage because God commanded it, and because his motive was to exalt the woman to his own moral sphere. When he married her, and it became known in Israel, his opportunity came to show the loving-kindness of Jehovah to a nation that had no more to commend itself to Him than this woman had in Hosea's case. See the marginal references for the proof of this.

The children of his union are symbolical in their names (4-9). For historical reference to Jezreel and Jehu (4), see 2 Kings 10:11; but notice that there are two predictions in this verse, separated by the comma after "Jehu," which are at least forty years apart in their fulfilment. Judgment fell on the house of Jehu in Zachariah's reign (2 Kings 15:12), while the kingdom of Israel did not cease till the Assyrian captivity in King Hoshea's day (2 Kings 18).

It is with reference to this captivity that the names of the other two children are given (6,8,9). For the fulfilment of verse 7 see the marginal reference to 2 Kings 19:35 in the light of its context.

The Better Day Coming, vv. 10, 11.

Like all the prophets, Hosea speaks of Israel's happy future, which shall come to pass after the tribulation of which we learned in Daniel. How is her increase indicated? Her restoration to her own land? Her reunion with the two tribes? In explanation of the last clause it should be noted that the meaning of Jezreel is "the seed of God."

An Unfaithful Wife. 2:1-23.

This chapter begins at verse 2, and we see that Hosea's wife failing to appreciate her blessings, went after her former lovers, took up with her old life of sin again. In this the prophet's domestic history carries further the symbolical reference to Jehovah's relationship to Israel. That noation did in the spiritual realm what the wife did in the physical. It is difficult to determine just where the symbol ends and the history of Israel begins in the chapter, because the two are so closely blended, but there is little doubt that the nation is in view at verse 3 and the following. Students will recall earlier teachings about "the law of double reference" which finds illustration here.

Following through the chapter, note the punishment to fall on the adulterous nation (6-13); her political bewilderment (6); her disappointments in the expectation of help from the Gentiles (7); her deprivation of the divine blessing and the positive suffering entailed by it (9-13). All of these came to her in her captivity, and are her experiences still among the nations.

But again we see the future bright when, in repentance and faith, she returns to the Lord (14-16). "Ishi" means "My husband." "Baali," "My master, (see margin). Millennial conditions follow (17-23).

The Appeal to the Backslider.

"The law of recurrence," finds an illustration in chapter 3, where the story of the preceding chapter is repeated with additional data.

The prophet is commanded still to love his wandering and faithless wife as Jehovah still loves Israel in her disobedience (1). His love takes shape in material provision for her, though she is separated from him (2), as Jehovah is still caring for Israel that she should not perish from the earth. In the meantime the wife is not to take up with another husband, and the prophet will not marry again (3), the application of which is stated in the next two verses. The foregoing lessons in the prophets have made this plain.

Questions.

1 State the time of this book.

2. Have you re-read the history of the time?

3. To which of the kingdoms was Hosea particularly sent?

4. Relate the story of the prophet's domestic history in your own words.

5. What two prophecies are found in 1:4?

6. In the reign of what king of Judah was 1:7 fulfilled?

7. What is the definition of "Jezreel"?

8. What two laws of rhetoric find renewed illustration in this lesson?

JEHOVAH'S LOVE FOR ISRAEL

CHAPTERS 4-14

With Hosea begins the "Minor" prophets, extending to the close of the Old Testament, and so-called to distinguish them from the "Major," the first four already considered. The major are the more important not as to their contents but their size; and yet the minor prophets are, in principle, only repeating what the major prophets have recorded over and over again.

For this reason the minor prophets will be considered briefly. It may be repeated that we are not attempting to treat every chapter and verse in the Bible in detail. So far as the prophets are concerned, however, we have set forth the great subjects with which they alike deal, and in the laws of recurrence and double reference have indicated the path by which the student may with care find his own way through any of them. Of course, there always will be things calling for explanation which only the larger commentaries or Bible dictionaries can supply, but along the broader lines of study we trust these comments will be found helpful. In their use it is presupposed the reader is going through the Bible in regular order for the purpose of studying or teaching it in its completeness as a revelation of God.

The General Contents of the Chapters.

With the above understanding in view, it will be found that the following chapters in this book are simply giving in detail what the first three reveal in outline. They speak of Israel's unfaithfulness to Jehovah, and these enlarge on the expressions of that unfaithfulness.

For example, chapter 4 charges the nation with, "swearing and lying, and killing and stealing, and committing adultery" (2). People, priests and prophets are alike (45): Idolatry flourishes with all its licentious accompaniments (12-14): Judah is warned by Israel's declension (15-19) but the next chapter indicates that the warning will profit her little.

Chapter 6 opens with a prophetic expression of repentance on Israel's part—prophetic in the sense that as a nation she has not yet taken that attitude, although she will be led to do so in the latter days (1-3). Suddenly, at verse 4, Jehovah is introduced as pleading with her under the name of Ephriam her chief tribe, and pleading with her sister Judah as well. The plea is accompanied by explanation of their chastisement (4-11).

This thought is continued in the next chapters where Israel's folly in turning for help first to Egypt and then to Assyria, is pointed out (12). The marginal references direct the reader to Kings where these matters were spoken of in their historic setting.

The style of Hosea is abrupt and broken, but the ejaculations in which it abounds are frequently expressions of God's wonderful love for His people. Examine especially 11:1-4, 8, 9. Sometimes it is difficult to determine when the prophet is expressing only his own feelings toward his nation rather than Jehovah's, and yet even in those instances it is the Holy Spirit using the feelings of man to illustrate the tenderness of the heart of God.

The Appeal to the Backslider.

But the chapter expressing this tenderness the most is the last, and though the reader finds it necessary to hasten over those intervening, he should pause here.

Note God's appeal coupled with His condemnation (1). Consider His kindness in setting before His people the way to return (2, 3). They are to take words, not works—words of confession, faith, consecration, repentance. Look at the attitude in which He will meet them, and the promises He gives them (4-7). Here is growth, strength, expansion, loveliness and beneficence —all to be theirs in that day.

Verse 8 is a kind of divine soliloquy. Jehovah hears Israel's repentance, and her testimony to renewing grace, and assures her of Himself as its source.

The chapter closes with an exhortation as applicable to us as to her.

Questions.

1. To what division of the prophets does Hosea belong?

2. Why are the "Major Prophets" so called?

3. How would you describe the contents of the chapters of this lesson as distinguished from the preceding one?

4. What are some of the charges against the nation?

5. What characterizes Hosea's literary style?

6. How would you analyze chapter 14?

7. How would you descirbe verse 8?

8. Can you quote verse 9 from memory?

JOEL

The text of this lesson except the questions is taken from the author's "Synthetic Bible Studies."

Joel was probably the earliest of the prophets whose warnings have descended to us. His personal history is unknown further than the bare statement 1:1. His field of labor was presumably Judah rather that Israel, the southern rather than the northern kingdom, because of allusions to the center of public worship which was at Jerusalem, 1:9, 13, 14, 2:15, and because of non-allusions to Israel distinctively. Such places as 2:27, and 3:16 are thought to mean Israel as inclusive of Judah, i. e., the whole united nation. Although it is assumed, that Joel was the earliest of the prophets, yet the evidence is inferential rather than direct. He is presumably earlier than Amos who is known to have prophesied somewhere about the close of the eighth century B. C., because he seems to be quoted by Amos 5:16-18. He also refers to Amos 3:4-6, and to the same physical scourges as prevalent in the land, 1:4, 17, 20. (Compare the marginal references to Amos.)

General Outline of the Book. —As to the book itself we outline the contents of its chapters thus:

Chapter 3:

This chapter recures to the future blessing spoken of in the preceding chapter, for the purpose of amplifying some of its features, a peculiarity of all the prophets, as was indicated in one of our earlier lessons:

Questions.

1. What chronological relation does Joel bear to the other prophets?

2. To which kingdom were his messages sent?

3. What proof is there of this?

4. What future blessings are predicted for Israel?

5. When was the prophecy of 2:28-32 partially fulfilled?

AMOS

It will be seen from the opening verse that Amos, like Hosea, was a prophet sent to Israel, though his home, Tekoa, was in Judah. He was contemporary with Hosea for a while, though the latter prophesied longer than he.

After the introduction (1:1-3) there follows a series of messages concerning Gentile nations (1:4-2:3), each beginning with the words "For three transgressions . . . and for four, I will not turn away the punishment," an orientalism, meaning that it was not for three or four transgressions merely, but an innumerable number, that the judgments predicted were to fall.

These messages are succeeded by one to Judah (2:4, 5) while the remainder of the book is concerned with Israel.

The messages of Amos are more orderly than Hosea, and admit of homiletic divisions like the following: The first, beginning at chapter 2, verse 6, and concluding with the chapter, contains, (1), an indictment for sin (6-8), aggravated by the divine goodness toward them (9-12); and (2), a declaration of the judgment to follow (13-15). This sin is greed (6), lust (7) and oppression (8). The marginal references frequently give the meaning of expressions in the prophets. Compare Exodus 22:26 with verse 8 for example, and Jeremiah 11:21 with verse 12.

God will press them as a cart full of sheaves presseth the ground (2:13, R. V.). In other words none shall escape the Assyrian hosts when they come down against them (14-16).

The second discourse is limited to the third chapter, and contains, after the introduction, verses 1 and 2, (1), the prophet's justification of his message (3-8); (2) an indictment for sin (9, 10); (3), a declaration of punishment (11-15).

When God says, "You only have I known," etc., (2), He means what is expressed in Deuteronomy 7:6, Psalm 147:19, 20, and other places. Israel's punishment is proportioned to her privilege.

Amos prophesied because he could not do otherwise, is practically the interpretation of verses 3-8. As two do not walk together except they are agreed, or have made an appointment; as a lion does not roar when it has no prey, etc., so the fact that Amos prophecies is an evidence that Jehovah hath spoken to him (8).

Notice the suggestion of the preservation of a faithful remnant in the "two legs" or "piece of an ear" of a sheep taken out of the mouth of the lion (12).

Messages of this character continue till the seventh chapter when a series of visions begins.

In the first vision (1-3), Jehovah is withholding the coming judgment at the prophet's intercession, and the same is true of the second (4-6), but not of the rest (7-9; 8:1-3; 9:1-10).

And yet notice the conclusion of the last message growing out of the vision of the Lord beside the altar (9:8,9). He will not "utterly destroy." He will sift Israel "among all nations" as He has been doing all these centuries, but only the chaff will be destroyed.

This thought is amplified in the epilogue of the book (9:11-15), where the prophet definitely reveals the history of Israel in the latter days: (1) the kingdom is to be restored (11); (2) Israel is to be the head of the nations (12); (3) the land of Palestine is to be greatly increased in fruitfulness (13); (4) the cities are to be rebuilt (14); (5) the blessing is to be perpetual (15).

Questions.

1. To which kingdom was Amos sent?

2. What "orientalism" is employed by him and what is its meaning?

3. How do the messages of

Amos differ in form from those of Hosea?

4. Name some of the sins of Israel at this time.

5. Have you examined the marginal references?

6. How would you interpret 2:3-8?

7. What change in the character of Amos' messages take place at chapter 7?

8. What five promises are given Israel for the latter days?

OBADIAH

In all probability this prophet's period was just after the conquest of Judah by Babylon, and prior to that of Edom by the same people, which it is his mission to proclaim (1). Of all the nations afflicting the Jews the chief were the Assyrians, the Babylonians and Edomites; and although the last-named were their close relatives, they were the greatest enemies of all. The Edomites descended from Esau, the brother of Jacob, the ancestor of Israel. Examine the map to familiarize yourself with their territory, and by the aid of the concordance or Bible dictionary, refresh your recollection of their relations with Israel in the past. Compare also Jeremiah 49:7-22.

The Edomites were not thought of very highly by their neighbors (2), but were conceited in their own eyes. Why (3)? Would their supposedly impregnable situation save them (4)? What figures of speech are used to show, by contrast, the thoroughness of the destruction to fall upon them (5, 6)? Of what were they proud in addition to the physical features of their territory (8, 9)?

Why is this judgment to fall upon them (10)? Note what they did in the case of Judah in her day of need: (1) They stood aloof (verse 11); (2) they rejoiced in her calamity (verse 12);

(3) they boasted against her (same verse); (4) they shared in her spoiling (verse 13); (5) they prevented the escape of some of their people (verse 14); and (6) they actually delivered up some of them as prisoners (same verse). Is it to be wondered at that God should speak as He does (15, 16)?

And now mark the difference. Judah has been carried into captivity and her land was deserted, but was that condition in her case to continue (17)? On the contrary, what would be true of Edom (18)? In the day to come observe that while she will be swallowed up, Judah and Israel shall arise again, and possess not only their own land but that of Edom and Philistia as well (19, 20). It will be the day of the Messiah (21).

Questions.

1. What was Obadiah's period?
2. What is his mission?
3. What relation existed between the Edomites and Israelites?
4. Have you identified the territory of the first named on the map?
5. How did they show enmity toward Israel?
6. What contrast will be seen in Edom and Israel in the time to come?
7. When will that be?

JONAH

There is only one instance of Jonah's prophesying to his own people of Israel, 2 Kings 14:25. There he made a prediction concerning the restoration of the coasts of Israel, which was fulfilled in the reign of Jeroboam II about 800 B. C., showing that he lived earlier than that date. Of his personal history nothing further is known than what is found in this book.

Chapter 1.

Nineveh (2) was the capital of Assyria, and the reason Jonah sought to avoid the divine command against it (3) arose from his patriotism. As a student of the earlier prophets he knew what was to befall his nation at the hands of Assyria, and he shrank from an errand which might result favorably to that people, and spare them to become the scourge of Israel. The contents of the rest of the chapter requre no comment till the last verse, where it is interesting to note that it is not said that a whale swallowed Jonah, but "a great fish" which "the Lord had prepared."

Chapter 2.

Is self-explanatory, but it is interesting to observe Jonah's penitence under chastisement (2), the lively experiences he underwent (3-6), his hope and expectation even in the midst of them (4), his unshaken faith (5), the lessons he learned (8), and the effect of it all on his spiritual life (9). God could not afford to see him at liberty (10).

Is This Historic?

The question will not down, "Is this chapter historic?" The evidence for it is found: (1) In the way it is recorded, there being not the slightest intimation in the book itself, or anywhere in the Bible, that it is a parable. (2) In the evidence of tradition, the whole of the Jewish nation, practically accepting it as historic. (3) The reasonableness of it (see

the remarks under chapter 3. (4) The testimony of Christ in Matthew 12:38, and parallel places. There are those who read these words of the Saviour in the light of the argument of which they form a part, and say that they allude only to what He knew to be a parable, or an allegory, but I am not of their number. Jesus would not have used such an illustration in such a connection, in my judgment, if it were not a historic fact. (5) The symbolic or prophetic character of the transaction (see the remarks under chapter 4).

Worshiping the Fish God.
Chapter 3.

To grasp the significance of the events in this chapter it is necessary to know that the Ninevites worshiped the fish God, Dagon, part human and part fish. They believed he came up out of the sea and founded their nation, and also that messengers came to them from the sea from time to time. If, therefore, God should send a preacher to them, what more likely than that He should bring His plan down to their level and send a real messenger from the sea? Doubtless great numbers saw Jonah cast up by the fish, and accompanied him to Nineveh as his witnesses and credentials.

There are two side arguments that corroborate the historicity of this event. In the first place, "Oannes" is the name of one of the latest incarnations of Dagon, but this name with "J" before it is the spelling for Jonah in the New Testament. In the second place, there was for centuries an Assyrian mound named "Yunas," a corrupted Assyrian form for Jonas, and it was this mound's name that first gave the suggestion to archaeologists that the ancient city of Nineveh might be buried beneath it. Botta associated "Yunas" with Jonah, and the latter with Nineveh, and so pushed in his spade, and struck the walls of the city—*E. E. Helme, D.D.*

The Moral Miracle.

But before leaving this chapter observe that the moral miracle was greater than the physical. The sparing of a nation of confessed sinners, simply on their repentance and their giving heed to the message of the prophet, was more astounding than the prophet's preservation in the fish's belly (5-10)!

Chapter 4.

Especially the opening verse (1-3), corroborates the view that patriotism led Jonah to flee from his divinely-imposed duty. He could not bear to see his enemy spared.

From verse 5 we gather that he waited in the hope of seeing the destruction of the city; and yet how gracious God was to his narrow-minded and revengeful servant (6)!

Jonah a Type of Israel.

But we should not conclude this lesson without speaking of the dispensational significance of Jonah and his mission, which is a contribution to its historicity. To illustrate:

(1) Jonah was called to a world mission, and so was Israel.

(2) Jonah at first refused compliance with the divine purpose and plan, and so did Israel.

(3) Jonah was punished by being cast into the sea, and so was Israel by being dispersed among the nations.

(4) Jonah was not lost, but rather especially preserved during this part of his experience, and Israel is not being assimilated by the nations, but being kept for God.

(5) Jonah repentant and cast out by the fish, is restored to life and action again, and Israel repentant and cast out by the nations shall be restored to her former national position.

(6) Jonah, obedient, goes upon his mission to Nineveh, and Israel, obedient, shall ultimately engage in her original mission to the world.

(7) Jonah is successful in that his message is acted upon to the salvation of Nineveh, so Israel shall be blessed in that she shall be used to the conversion of the whole world.

Questions.

1. Have you read 2 Kings 14:25?

2. What was the motive for Jonah's disobedience?

3. Give five reasons for believing the historicity of this book.

4. Can you quote Matthew 12:38?

5. What explanation of this miracle is found in the worship of the Ninevites?

6. What two side arguments for the historicity of this event can you name?

7. What second miracle does this book contain?

8. Indicate the sense in which Jonah is a type of Israel.

MICAH

The little known of Micah is briefly stated. Calling himself a Morasthite indicates Moresheth, or Mareshah, as his birthplace in southwestern Judah, near Gath. The time of this prophesying is shown in the same verse by the reference to the kings of Judah, as between 758 to 700 B. C. He seems to have been the writer of his own book, if we may judge from the personal allusions in chapter 3:1, 8, and to have died in peace, judging by Jeremiah 26:18, 19. He is frequently referred to as a prophet, and his utterances quoted, not only in the instances above given, but in Isaiah 2:2-4 and 41:15; Ezekiel 22:27; Zephaniah 3:19; Matthew 2:5; and John 7:42. Jesus quotes him in Matthew 10:35, 36. For further references to his period, see our lessons on Isaiah.

1. A Description of Judgment.

Chapters 1-3 contain a description of the approaching judgment on both kingdoms—Israel and Judah. How do verses 1 and 5 of chapter 1 indicate that both kingdoms are under consideration?

Notice the order in which the three classes of hearers are addressed:

(1) The people at large, chapter 1:2.

(2) The princes, chapter 3.

(3) The false prophets, 3:5.

According to verse 11 what seems to have been the most crying sin of all? And yet notwithstanding their covetousness and greed, how did they show either gross hypocrisy or gross ignorance of God (same verse, last part)? It is at this point that the declaration of judgment is expressed, and in language which has been literally fulfilled, verse 12.

2. A Vision of Hope.

Chapters 4 and 5 unfold the future and happier, because holier, experience of the nation. The first four verses of chapter 4 are quoted almost verbatim in Isaiah 2, unless we reverse the order and say that Micah quoted Isaiah.

At what time are these better things to come to pass according to the beginning of this chapter? How are these things figuratively expressed in verse 1? It is not difficult to recognize in these figures of speech the exaltation of Jerusalem and Judah over all the nations in that day. But how does verse 2 show that the exaltation will not be exacting and tyrannous, but the opposite? What language shows that the millennial age is referred to, and no period which has yet appeared in the history of the world? How do verses 3 and 4 strengthen this conviction? What expression in verse 7 almost directly states this to be the case? In Joel we saw that prior to Israel's deliverance, and, as incident thereto, the Gentile nations will be besieging Jerusalem and desirous of seizing her, and that Jehovah will interpose on her behalf. How do the closing verses of this chapter parallel that prophecy?

Addressing ourselves to chapter 5, we discover what is the common teaching of the prophets that these good times coming for Israel and Judah are connected with the Person and work of the Messiah. How is that led up to in verse 2? To be sure, these words are quoted in Matthew 2, to apply to the first coming of Christ, but that does not exclude His second coming. Moreover, all the succeeding verses in this chapter point to events which did not occur at His first coming, but will be found to be uniformly predicated of His second coming.

3. A Contrast Drawn.

Chapters 6 and 7 present a "contrast between the reasonableness, purity and justice of the divine requirements, and the ingratitude, injustice and superstition of the people which caused their ruin."

The closing chapter is peculiarly affecting, a kind of soliloquy of repentance on Israel's part.

The better element among the people are confessing and lamenting their sinful condition in verses 1-6, but expressing confidence in God's returning favor (7, 8).

Putting all together, there are few verses in the Bible more expressive of quiet hope and trust than these. It is beautiful to see the spirit of confession and submission in verse 9, and the certainty of triumph over every foe, verse 10. Observe how Jehovah Himself speaks through the prophet in verses 11-13. (Revised Version). See the promise of interposition on Israel's behalf in that day, verse 15; and the confusion of the Gentile nations at their triumph, and their own discomfiture, 16, 17. Of course, the temporal blessings thus coming upon Israel are all predicated of their return to the Lord and His forgiveness of their sins (18, 19). Nevertheless these things will take place on the ground of the original promise to Abraham (20).

Questions.

1 What can you say of the history of Micah?

2. Name the three great divisions of the book.

3. Analyze chapters 1-3.

4. With what future event is the deliverance of Israel always associated?

5. What makes the closing chapter particularly affecting?

NAHUM

Isaiah concludes his work at about the end of Hezekiah's reign, which synchronizes with the captivity of the ten tribes of Israel by the Assyrians. At this period of perplexity, to quote Angus: "When the overthrow of Samaria (the capital of Israel), must have suggested to Judah fears for her own safety, when Jerusalem (the capital of Judah), had been drained of its treasure by Hezekiah in the vain hope of turning the fury of the Assyrians from her, and when rumors of the conquest of a part of Egypt by the same great power added still more to the general dismay, to reveal His tenderness and power (1:1-8), to foretell the subversion of the Assyrians (1:9-12), the death of Sennacherib the Assyrian king and the deliverance of Hezekiah from his toils (1:10-15)." The name of the prophet means consolation.

After the consolatory introduction which covers the whole of chapter 1, the prophet predicts in detail, the destruction of Nineveh, the capital of the Assyrian empire. Properly to grasp Nahum, one needs to compare it with Jonah, of which it is a continuation and supplement. "The two prophecies form parts of the same moral history; the remission of God's judgments being illustrated in Jonah, and the execution of them in Nahum. The city had one denunciation more given a few years later, by Zephaniah (2:13), and shortly afterwards (606 B.C.), the whole were fulfilled."

Questions.

1. Against what Gentile nation is this prophecy uttered according to verse 1?

2. Indicate the verses in chapter 1 that are particularly consolatory to Israel.

3. How is Nahum 2:2 rendered in the Revised Version.

4. How does chapter 3:7, 19 show the ultimate utter destruction of Nineveh?

5. How does 3:16 indicate the commercial greatness of that city?

HABAKKUK

Nothing is known of the personal history of Habakkuk, and but little as to the time when he prophesied. He is placed by some successor to Zephaniah, for he makes no mention of Assyria and yet refers to the approach of the Babylonian invasion. See 1:6; 2:3, 3:2, 16-19. The book seems to have been written by himself, as we judge from 1:2, and 2:1, 2.

His "burden" begins by lamenting the iniquity of his people 1:1-4. He then declares God's purpose of raising up the Chaldean nation as a scourge against them, 5-10. The probability is that the Chaldeans (or Babylonians) were still a friendly nation (see 2 Kings 20:12-19), but they were soon to march through the land as a ravaging enemy. There were three invasions by the Babylonians, as the second book of Kings showed us; in the reigns of Jehoiakim, Jehoiachin and Zedekiah, and it is thought Habakkuk alludes to all three. Verse 11 of chapter 1 might be taken as a prophecy of the disease that came over Nebuchadnezzar when, as a punishment for his pride, his reason was taken from him for a season. The chapter concludes with an expostulation to the Holy One for inflicting such judgment on Judah and for using a nation less righteous, as the prophet thinks, than themselves.

In chapter 2 he awaits God's answer to this expostulation (verse 1), and receives it (verses 2-4). This is encouraging. "The vision shall surely come and the just shall live by faith and wait for it." The continuation of the chapter is a prediction of the judgments that shall fall on the Babylonians for their cruelty and idolatry.

"The prophet, hearing these promises and threatenings, concludes his book with a song, of praise and prayer (chapter 3). He celebrates past displays of the power and grace of Jehovah, supplicates God for the speedy deliverance of His people and closes by expressing a confidence in God which no change can destroy."—Angus.

Attention is called to the words in chapter 2, verse 3, which the writer of Hebrews, according to the law of double reference, applies to the second coming of Christ (Hebrews 10:37, 38).

In the same manner notice verse 4 of the same chapter, "The just shall live by faith," and the application of it in Romans 1:17; 5:1 and Galatians 3:24.

Questions.

1. What are the terms of the indictment against Judah, 1:1-4?

2. What features of the military power of Babylon are noted 1:8?

3. How would you interpret 2:1?

4. Have you identified the New Testament reference in this lesson?

5. What are the terms of indictment against Babylon, 2:5-19?

6. Memorize 3:17, 18.

ZEPHANIAH

This lesson with the exception of the questions is taken from "Synthetic Bible Studies."

Little is known of the personal history of Zephaniah beyond the two facts in the first verse of this prophecy, the first bearing on his ancestry and the second on the period of his ministry. About fifty years have elapsed since Nahum, and Hezekiah has been succeeded by three of his descendants (see 2 Kings, chapters 20, 21). Manasseh and Amon were idolatrous and wicked, but Josiah now upon the throne, is righteous and God-fearing. The story of his reign is in the succeeding chapters of 2 Kings and should be read preparatory to Zephaniah, who prophesied in the earlier part of his reign and assisted him in his efforts to restore the worship of the true God. To quote Angus:

"The first chapter contains a denunciation of vengeance against Judah and those who practiced idolatrous rites; Baal, his black-robed priests (Chemarims), and Malcham (Moloch), being condemned (1-2:3). The second chapter predicts the judgments about to fall on the Philistines, those especially of the sea-coasts (Cherethites), the Moabites, Ammonites, and Ethiopians, and describes the desolation of Nineveh.

"In the third chapter, the prophet arraigns Jerusalem, but concludes with promises of her restoration in the latter day (3:1-7, 8-20).

"Coincidence of expression between Isaiah and Zephaniah are frequent, and still more between Zephaniah and Jeremiah. It may be added that the predictions of Jeremiah complete the view here given of the devastation to be ef-fected by Chaldea in Philistia and Judah."

In verse 8, observe the agreement with Joel concerning the gathering of the Gentile nations to judgment at the end of the present age. In verse 9, we see these nations, or the spared and sifted remnant of them, converted to God and serving Him with a ready will. In verse 10 they are bringing the sons of Israel back to their own land, the second gathering of them as explained in Isaiah. In verses 11 to 18, the cleansed, rejoicing, nation of Israel appears, dwelling in their own land. In verses 19, 20, we find the restored people a blessing in the whole earth as foretold in the original promise to Abraham, and in the millennial psalms. Verse 17 will repay careful meditation. The old marriage covenant between Jehovah and Israel is there depicted as gloriously restored (Is. 62:5; Hos. 2:19); the husband is rejoicing in His wife, resting in His love and joying over her with singing. "Rest" is translated in the margin "be silent," and this silence of Jehovah towards His people is no longer the silence arising from forbearance in order to punish at last (Psalm 50:21), but because He has nothing more to reprehend.

Questions.

1. Have you reviewed 2 Kings 20 and 21?

2. In whose reign did this prophet prophesy?

3. Name the nations denounced in Chapters 2 and 3.

4. How would you interpret 3:8-20 in detail?

5. How would you interpret 3:17 especially?

HAGGAI

This is the first of the post-Babylonian prophets—those who prophesied after the return from the seventy years' captivity. To be interested in this book therefore, one needs to read Ezra afresh, particularly chapters 4 and 5, for the mission of Haggai was to stir up the people of that time to rebuild the temple.

What excuse did the people make for not engaging in the work (2)? What showed their selfishness (4)? What showed their moral blindness (6)? What remedy for the material conditions indicated does God propose (7)? How is the divine judgment upon their neglect extended in verses (9-11)? What is the result of the prophet's indictment against them (12), and its effect in heaven (13)? How shall we explain this result from the spiritual point of view (14)? How much time is covered by the events of this chapter (compare first and last verses)?

Note the date of the second message beginning chapter 2, and compare Ezra 3:8-13. Some were discouraged because of their weakness and poverty, and felt that the temple could never be completed, and that in any event it would be outclassed by that of Solomon (3). How does God inspire them (4, 5)? Verses 6-10 are messianic, in which the first and second advents of our Lord are blended. The "shaking of the nations" seems future. "The desire of all nations" is taken as a personal designation of Christ, and yet the Revised Version renders it "the desirable things of all nations" which has a millennial flavor. Verse 9 is usually considered fulfilled by Christ's presence in this second temple.

Note the date of the third message (2:10). For the Levitical bearing of 11-13, compare the marginal references, Leviticus 10:10, 11; Deuteronomy 33:10; Numbers 19:11; Malachi 2:7, etc. Moral cleanness was not communicated by contact, but the same was not true of uncleanness. Israel was unclean in the spiritual sense, and all that they did in this way of divine service was correspondingly so (14), but in God was their help as the following verses prove.

God did not wait until the outcome of their labors testified to their change of heart, but from the day of that change His blessing began to be visited upon them (19). Previously, as the result of their disobedience, they reaped but ten measures of grain where they expected twenty, and twenty vessels of the fruit of the vine where they expected fifty; they had experienced blasting, and mildew and hail. But now all this would be changed, and the harvest plenteous. Let them take it by faith before the seed was in the barn, or the blossoms had come upon the trees (19).

Note the date of the fourth message (2:20). This is in the future, and recalls the forthcoming judgments on the Gentile nations of which the pre-exilic prophets have spoken. The period referred to is the end time. There are those who regard verse 23 as a prophecy of Christ of whom Zerubbabel is the type, though others take the words literally as foreshadowing the resurrection of the governor himself.

Questions.

1. To what period does Haggai belong?

2. With what historical book is this contemporaneous?

3. Have you re-read that book?

4. What was Haggai's mission?

5. How many of the questions on chapter 1 were you able to answer?

6. How would you explain the purpose of the second message?

7. To what period does the fourth message point?

ZECHARIAH

THE PROPHET'S OWN TIME

CHAPTERS 1-8

Zechariah, like Haggai, had a two-fold mission, to strengthen the hands of Israel for the rebuilding of the temple, and to quicken their hope as the earlier prophets had done, by painting in glowing colors the coming time of triumph over every foe.

This mission is set before us in a two-fold division of the book. Chapters 1-8 give us a series of prophetic visions bearing primarily, upon the prophet's own time, while chapters 9-14 deal chiefly with the events culminating at the end of the age and the opening of the millennium.

Part one, after the introduction, chapter 1: 7-6:8; might be outlined thus:

1. The prophetic visions, 1-6.
> The man among the myrtle trees.
> The four horns.
> The four smiths.
> The measuring line.
> The high priest in the temple.
> The golden candlestick.
> The flying roll.
> The woman in the ephah.
> The four chariots.

2. The symbolic crowning of the high priest, 6:8-15.

3. The instruction about fasting, 7-8.

The First Four Visions, 1-2.

To understand the first vision is the key to the rest. When was it received by the prophet? Chapter 1:7. Describe what he saw (8). Observe that two persons are referred to, the man upon the red horse, and the angel that talked with Zechariah, sometimes called "interpreting angel." The man on the horse seems afterward identified with "the angel of the Lord," verses 11, 12, one of the Old Testament names for Christ. It is presumable that the other horses had angelic riders also. Who are these described to be (10)? What report gave they of the earth

(11)? Prosperity and peace seem to have been characteristic, of all the peoples, while Jerusalem was distressed, the temple unfinished, and the remnant of the Jews there persecuted by enemies. Who now intercedes on behalf of Jerusalem and Judah (12)? Is the answer of Jehovah encouraging or the opposite (13)? What was His answer in detail (14-17)? Was the peace and prosperity of the Gentile nations an evidence of the devine blessing upon them (15)? Jehovah had used them to discipline His people, but what shows their selfish and wicked intent in the premises (same verse)? What does Jehovah promise shall be accomplished by the little remnant at this time (16)? What of the future (17)? This was fulfilled in the history of God's people at the time, in a measure at least. The temple was built, the cities restored, and Jerusalem and Judah comforted. And yet there is to be grander fulfilment in the days to come.

The two following visions, if we call them two—the four horns and four smiths (Revised Version), are closely connected with the one just considered. The four horns are the four world-powers (Babylonian, Persian, Greek and Roman) who scatter Israel, but the four smiths are four corresponding powers of some sort, not necessarily nations, which shall overcome them at the last and bring deliverance. We are almost necessarily shut up to the conclusion that this prophecy extends to the latter days by its reference to the whole of the four powers.

The next vision, that of the measuring line, presents no serious difficulty. Its significance explained (chapter 2:4, 5), is the same practically as that of the man among the myrtles. However it may have had an approximate fulfillment in the brother's own time, verses 10-13 indicate that it looks toward the future. What declaration in those verses seem to prove that?

The High Priest and Satan, 3.

To understand the meaning of the vision now reached, keep in mind that a cause of dejection of the Jews was their consciousness of past sin. They felt that God had forsaken them, and that their present calamities were the result. We see herein, a parallel to the spiritual condition of a true believer in our own day, whom Satan torments with the belief that he cannot be saved on account of his many sins. This is now set before us in symbol, only there is a nation in the case here, and not an individual, for Joshua the high priest represented Israel.

Where is the high priest seen to be (3:1)? It is thought that he was represented as in the holy place ministering at the altar. Who is seen with him, and for what malign purpose? We have here in symbol, Satan's temptation of the saint to doubt God's power to forgive and save. How is this goodness and power shown, in the next verse? On what ground is Jerusalem to be saved, on that of merit or of the divine choice? What does verse 3 teach as to the truth of Satan's insinuation against Israel as represented by the high priest? Does the imagery indicate the holiness or sinfulness of the people. Yet how is divine grace illustrated in the next command of Jehovah (4)? What did the removal of his filthy garments signify? What did the changed raiment signify? Compare Romans 3:22. What next was done (5)? By this act the clothing of the high priest was completed and he was fitted for his official service. Who is represented as "standing by" all this time as if interceding for Joshua (and through him for the nation), and to see that these commands were carried out and these benefits conferred? With whom have we identified "the Angel of the Lord"? What charge is now laid upon Joshua, and what privilege is connected with it (7)?

Questions.

1. Name the two-fold mission of this prophet.

2. Name the nine prophetic visions of Part I.

3. Give some reasons showing the application of these visions in the future.

4. What leads to that conclusion in the case of the four horns and the four smiths?

5. What is necessary to understand the vision of chapter 3?

THE PROPHET'S OWN TIME—

CONTINUED

CHAPTERS 4-8

The Golden Candlestick, 4.

The candlestick was a copy of that in the early tabernacle, but with what difference (verse 2)? From what source was its oil supplied (3)? What did this supply of oil from the trees symbolize (6)? The candlestick itself may represent the temple which the Jews were now essaying to build, or for that matter, the Jewish nation as a whole which was now sought to be re-established and become a light in the world. The difficulties in the way of accomplishing these things seemed insuperable, if the strength of man only should be considered, but God would interpose, and His Spirit do what human agencies could not do. How is this difficulty and its removal figuratively expressed (7)? How is the figure explained (8-10)? On what point did the prophet desire further light (12)? What reply was made to him (14)? By these "two anointed ones" is understood Zerubbabel and Joshua, the leaders of Israel at this time on whom, and through whom the Holy Spirit would be poured out for the successful termination of the work.

It is proper to use this symbol as applying to the church of the present day in its testimony and work; in which case the "two anointed ones" may represent any who "filled with the Spirit" are executing the Lord's will in power. At the same time the whole thing applies primarily to Israel, not only in the time of Zechariah, but in the last times when through the blessing of the Spirit, she shall be restored, and become a rejoicing in the earth. It is proper to add that the deeper meaning of verse 14 is probably Christ Himself, "The Priest upon His throne," who will supply Israel as He now supplies the church with His Holy Spirit!

The Flying Roll and the Ephah, 5.

The two visions in chapter 5 are mysterious and like the four chariots in chapter 6, seem to express the idea of judgment. That the "flying roll" has that significance would seem plain by a comparison with Ezekiel 2:9, 10, and Revelation, chapters 5 and 10, where similar figures have such meaning. We have seen that judgment is coming upon the Gentile nations, and that Israel also is to be purified before she is finally restored, and it may be that to both the present vision applies.

What is now seen (6)? An ephah or measure is an emblem of trade or commerce. What was seen sitting in the ephah? What is the woman said to symbolize (8)? The whole figure then represents wickedness in commerce. What is done with the ephah and whither is it carried? The land of Shinar suggests Babylon again, of whose revival in the latter days mention has been made. Every one knows that commercialism is prominent in Revelation 18 as the climax of ungodliness. Read that chapter in connection with Habakkuk 2:12, and James 5. Babylon is real, and the woman the commercial spirit that will reign there at the end. The spirit of self that prevailed in the Babylon of Genesis 11, will build up and prevail in the Babylon of Revelation 18. The description of the Babylon of Nebuchadnezzar's day will fit the one to come. It will be the city of "the prince of this world," the seat of the Anti-christ. It is noticeable that certain prophecies concerning

Babylon in Isaiah and Jeremiah have not yet been fulfilled, while these prophecies are closely identified with those in Revelation 17 and 18. The drift in our day is in the direction of a commercial center in the East.

The ninth and closing vision, chapter 6:1-8, furnishes another spectacle of judgments on the nations and the quieting of the divine Spirit with the result.

Crowning of the High Priest. 6.

The prophet is now called upon to do something in the nature of an object lesson to symbolize that great future event which will follow the judgments referred to, viz: the manifested reign of Christ over the millennial earth. Who have now come from Babylon on an embassage (10)? Whose guests are they (same verse)? What articles do they seem to have brought as gifts for the temple (11)? What is the prophet to do with some of this silver and gold? What is he to say in connection with this transaction (12-13)? What then shall be done with the crowns, and why (14-15)?

That this transaction is symbolic is plain from two or three points of view. In the first place, the royal crown did not belong to the high priest or any son of Levi, but to the tribe of Judah in the line of David. In the second place, there is the expression "Behold the Man whose name is the Branch!" To whom does that name belong? In the third place, we have the declaration, "He shall build the temple of the Lord." To whom in the fullest sense can this apply, save Christ? And then, "He shall bear the glory," and "He shall be a priest upon His throne." Of none other than Christ has this ever been predicted. He only is the priestly King. Compare Psalm 110, and Hebrews 7. What language in verse 15 bears a possible reference to the Gentiles in that day? On what condition is all this to be fulfilled (same verse)?

We pass over particular consideration of the two next chapters, which are in a sense parenthetical, although in accord with the whole book. Men of Babylon sent messengers to Jerusalem to inquire on the subject of ritual or ceremonial fasting. Had their fasting hitherto been acceptable to God and were they to continue it in the new regime? They are shown what a hypocritical thing that service had been hitherto; how it was such formalism and hypocrisy which had brought punishment upon their fathers: how that the fasting Jehovah desired was of a different nature, and finally, that in the blessed time coming feasting will take the place of fasting. These hints, will enable the reader to reach a fair understanding of the chapters in their present connection.

Questions.

1. What may the golden candlestick typify?

2. How might the reference to "the two anointed ones" be applied?

3. What about the flying roll and ephah?

4. What shows the crowning of the high priest to be symbolical?

5. Give briefly the substance of chapters 7 and 8.

END OF THE AGE AND THE OPENING OF THE MILLENNIUM

Chapters 9-14

It was stated that the first part of the book, chapters 1-8, referred chiefly, though not entirely, to the prophet's own time. The basis of all the prophecies in that part had a historical relation to the period then present. They were uttered, to encourage the people in rebuilding the temple. And yet there is not one of them that did not take cognizance of the far future. The discourses of this, the second part, deal almost entirely with the future.

It will aid in the understanding of these chapters if we recall a few historical facts. At the date of this book the Medo-Persian was the world-power to which the Jews were subject.

It was followed by the Greeks, and the Greeks by the Romans. During the Roman regime our Lord was crucified and Jerusalem destroyed. The present (i. e. our own time), is an interregnum so far as Jewish national history is concerned, which will continue till Israel is once more in Jerusalem, in covenant with Antichrist and about to pass through the tribulation prior to her final deliverance and blessing. Here are three periods in Jewish history which we may call, the Grecian, the Roman and the final periods. Zechariah, it is believed, treats of each of these in the chapters following.

1. The Grecian Period, 9-10.

You will recall from Daniel that this period begins with Alexander the Great, the notable horn between the eyes of the he-goat. When he crossed from Greece into Asia he swept down the Phoenecian and Palestinian coast of the Mediterranean, besieging and capturing Damascus, Sidon, Tyre, Gaza and other cities in the south Philistine country. But he passed by Jerusalem more than once without doing it harm. The Jewish historian Josephus explains this by a dream the great monarch had, and which was fulfilled by the appearance to him at Jerusalem of the high priest and his train. However this may be, the opening verses of chapter 9 give us the prophetic outline of his career at this time. Read verses 1-7. For the deliverance of Jerusalem which occurred, read verse 8.

But now we come to a further illustration of the law of double reference, for the verse which speaks of the deliverance of Jerusalem from Alexander, speaks evidently of another deliverance which can only find fulfillment in the latter times. What shows that this deliverance, thus foreshadowed, is connected with the coming of Christ (9)? When were these words fulfilled at least in part? (Matthew 21:5). What shows that their complete fulfillment is reserved for the latter times, or Christ's second coming (10-11)?

Verses 13-17 are obscure, but thought to refer to the period of the Maccabees who delivered their people for a while from the yoke of the tyrant Antiochus Epiphanes B. C. 170, or thereabouts, while the Grecians represented by him were still in power. However this may be, it is evident from what follows that, as in so many other instances, this deliverance foreshadowed a greater and final one to come.

The Roman Period, 11.

Greek supremacy is at an end, and we have reached the Roman period culminating in the rejection by the Jews of the Son of God. The eleventh chapter opens with a scene of judgment (verses 1-6). Then follows the cause of it (verses 7-14). In verse 4 the prophet is commanded to do a symbolic act, and in verse 7 he is in the performance of it. What was this act? There will be little doubt after reading the context, that in this act he is the type of the Good Shepherd, Jesus Christ. Compare Matthew 9:36, and John 10. What does the Shepherd carry with Him to guide and protect His flock? There is difficulty in the meaning of these staves unless we adopt that hinted at in verses 10 and 14, where "Beauty" seems to refer to the divine covenant, and "Bands" to the union between the ten tribes and the two.

Who are "cut off" in verse 8? It is supposed that these "three shepherds" stand for the three classes of rulers that governed Israel," priests, prophets and lawyers, Jeremiah 2:8, Matthew 16:21. Our Lord pronounced woes against them (Matthew 23), and when the city was destroyed their rule came to an end. What portion of the flock paid attention to and were fed by the shepherd (11)? Compare Matthew 5:3, 11:25; 1 Corinthians 1:26-29. How does verse 12 point to the rejection of the Shepherd by the flock? What is foreshadowed in the next verse? Who is

the prophet commanded to impersonate (15)? What person yet to come will answer the description in verses 16 and 17? Can this be any other ultimately than the Antichrist? Read John 5:43.

The Final Period, 12-14.

The prophecies in this section of the book are to be fulfilled at the end period frequently referred to. It is the time when Israel is once more in Jerusalem in the national sense, though at first in an uncovered condition.

We saw in Daniel that the Antichrist would at this time enter into covenant with Israel, and afterwards (in the middle of the last seven years), break that covenant. Then "the time of Jacob's trouble" begins, the nature of which will in part be the combination of the Gentile nations, i. e., the Roman world, against it. Antichrist will be at the head of this combination if we may judge from a comparison of Daniel with Revelations. It is at this point, when the nations are besieging the Holy City, that the "burden of the Word of the Lord begins (12:1, 2).

We can not outline these chapters in detail, nor is it necessary for those who have persued the earlier prophets in connection with these lessons. A hint here and there will suffice. For example, in this siege Jerusalem will for the first time be victorious (12:2, 3); the victory, however, will be of a supernatural character (48, R. V.); the conversion of the nation will accompany it (10), also 13:1, and it will take place coincident with the great tribulation (13:8), 9, 14:1-3); Christ shall appear to them (14:4); the earth will rejoice (9); and especially Judah and Jerusalem (10, 11); their enemies will be punished and the millennium will have begun (16, and the following verses).

Questions.

1. With what period chiefly, does this lesson deal?

2. Name the world powers of which these chapters treat.

3. Give the story of chapter 9:1-8.

4. What illustration of the law of double reference is here shown?

5. Who is suggested as a type of Christ in chapter 11?

6. For whom do the "three herds" stand?

7. To what time do chapters 12-14 refer?

8. Give an outline of their application.

[This lesson with the exception of the questions is from "Synthetic Bible Studies."]

MALACHI

This book is a continuous discourse, so that, properly speaking, there are no intervening events. The prophet is a contemporary of Nehemiah, following closely Zechariah and Haggai. The evidence of this is chiefly internal and gathered from two facts: (1) That the second temple was evidently in existence at the time, and (2) That the evils condemned by Nehemiah are those which he also condemns. This will appear as we proceed, but compare Malachi 1:7, 8; 2:11-16; 3:8-10 with the last chapter of Nehemiah, especially verses 10-14, 23-29.

Following an outline by Willis J. Beecher, we have:

The Introduction, 1:1-5.

What word in verse 1 indicates that the message, or messages, are in the nature of rebuke rather than comfort? With what declaration does verse 3 begin? While Jehovah thus declares Himself towards His Israel, how do they receive it? This skeptical insinuation in the interrogation, "Wherein hast thou loved us?" is a peculiarity of the book, and shows the people to have been in a bad spiritual frame, calculated to give birth to the practical sins enumerated later.

Be careful not to read a wrong meaning into that reference to Esau, as though God caused him to be born simple to have an object on which He might exercise His hate, or as if that hate condemned the individual Esau to misery in this life and eternal torment beyond. The hate of Esau as an individual is simply set over against the choice of Jacob as the heir to the promised seed of Abraham. Esau did not inherit that promise, the blessing to the world did not come down in his line, but that of his brother Jacob, and yet Esau himself had a prosperous life; nor are we driven to the conclusion by anything the Bible says that he was eternally lost. Moreover, the particular reference is not so much

to Esau as a man as to the national descendants of Esau, the Edomites, who had not only been carried into captivity as Israel had been, but whose efforts to rebuild their waste places would not be successful as in the case of Israel, because the divine purposes of grace lay in another direction.

The Second Division, 1:6-3:4,

consists of an address to the priests and Levites, more especially the former, in which they are charged with three kinds of offenses. The first is neglect of their temple duties, see chapter 1:6-2:9. The character of the offense is seen in verses 7 and 8, and 12 and 13 of chapter 1, while the punishment in the event of impenitence is in chapter 2:1-9. The second offense concerns unholy marriages, verses 10-16 of chapter 2. It was for this sin as well as the preceding one that Jehovah refused to accept their offerings (13, 14). Notice the strong argument against divorce found in verse 15. God made one wife for one man at the beginning though He had the power to make more, and He did this because of the godly seed He desired. The third offense is that of skepticism, and as Beecher calls it, a bad skepticism, for there is a species of doubt which deserves compassionate treatment and which cannot be called evil in its spirit and motive. That, however, is hardly the kind of doubt now under consideration (See chapter 2:17). This division closes, as does the division following, by a prediction "concerning a day in which the obedient and disobedient shall be differentiated and rewarded." This "day" we have often recognized as the "day of the Lord" still in the future both for Israel and the Gentile nations (3:1-4).

Notice the partial fulfillment of verse 1 in the career of John the Baptist, as indicated in the words and context of Matthew 11:10; Mark 1:2; Luke 1:76. But

the concluding verses of the prediction show that a complete fulfillment must be ahead. The offering of Judah and Jerusalem
has not yet been so purified by divine judgments as to be pleasant
unto the Lord as in the days of
old, but it shall yet come to pass.

The Third Division, 3:5-4:3,
consists of an address to the people as a whole, who like the
priests, are charged with three
kinds of offenses. The first is certain public wrongs in which are
grouped false swearing, adultery,
oppression and injustice (3:5-7).
The second is the failure to support the temple and its ministers
(3:8-12), in which case notice
the charge of divine robbery, and
the blessing promised to faithfulness in tithes. The third is the
same kind of skepticism as with
the priests (3:13-15). The prediction concluding this section covers verses 3:16-4:3, and is more
comforting in character than the
preceding one.

The Fourth Division, 4:4-6,
is a grand conclusion in which
the great day of the Lord is once
more referred to, and Elijah the
prophet named as His forerunner. We learn from Matt. 11:14,
Mark 9:11 and Luke 1:17 that
John the Baptist is to be considered the type of this forerunner, but that Elijah is to come
again to this earth is the opinion
of many. There are those who believe that he and Moses are the
two witnesses in Revelation 11
that shall do wonders in Jerusalem during the reign of the Antichrist.

Questions.

1. What is the peculiarity of
this book?

2. Give the proof that Malachi
is contemporary with Nehemiah.

3. How do you explain God's
"hatred" of Esau?

4. What argument against divorce is found here?

5. How do some interpret the
prediction about Elijah?

MATTHEW

INTRODUCTORY

About four hundred years have elapsed since Malachi, and no prophet has arisen in Israel. We left Israel under the dominion of the Persians, which was soon followed by the Grecians including the Syrian period in which Antiochus Epiphanes flourished, and the Maccabees, about one hundred and fifty to one hundred and seventy years before Christ. Then came the Roman period when the Messiah appeared.

At the outset, remember that the Old Testament promised an earthly Kingdom to Israel when the Messiah came, and for which the faithful were looking. Jesus was the Messiah though they knew Him not, and He had come to set up that Kingdom. Moreover, from the beginning of His ministry down to a certain point to be named later, He proceeds on the assumption that the Kingdom has come if the nation will receive Him. He is not received, but rejected, whereupon He changes the character of His teaching. He then begins to speak of the Church instead of the Kingdom, and to lay plans, humanly speaking, for the formation of a new body of people altogether. This body is composed of Gentiles as well as Jews, who sustain a peculiar relation to Him while the Kingdom is in abeyance, and indeed forevermore.

That phrase, "the Kingdom in abeyance," means that the Kingdom promised in the Old Testament is yet to be set up on this earth in Israel, with Jesus, the Messiah, at its head. This will be when Israel, punished and repentant, shall receive Him by faith as all the prophets have spoken. In the meantime the Church comes into view, with a unique origin, history and destiny, concerning which the New Testament treats almost exclusively.

The Transition Gospel.

How then shall we place Matthew's Gospel? Can we do better than to speak of it as covering the transition period, i. e., the period including the rejection of the Kingdom by Israel and the coming into view of the Church after the resurrection of our Lord?

Keep in mind that Matthew is writing for the Jewish people, and is seeking, under the inspiration of the Holy Spirit, to present Jesus to them as the One who fulfills the Old Testament features of the Messiah. For this reason the first Gospel is sometimes called the Gospel of the Kingdom, because more than any other, it dwells upon that aspect of the truth.

But this suggests that each of the Gospels has its own viewpoint of the history and work of the Saviour, to appreciate which is important in the study of that Gospel. In the Old Testament the Coming One is alluded to in different ways, but they have been reduced to four, as for example: He is the King of Israel, He is the Servant of Jehovah, He is the Son of Man, and He is the Son of God. This classification reappears in the Gospels, and as we shall see, Matthew reveals Him in the first particular, Mark in the second, Luke in the third and John in the fourth.

Questions.

1. How long an interim has taken place since Malachi?
2. Give an outline history of Israel during this period.
3. How does the Messiah change His teaching at a certain point, and why?
4. What is meant by "the Kingdom in abeyance"?
5. What period does Matthew's Gospel cover?
6. For what class of people is he writing?
7. What is this Gospel called, and why?
8. How may the other Gospels be classified?

THE ADVENT OF OUR LORD

CHAPTERS 1-2

In this lesson there are four divisions.

The Genealogical Table 1:1-17.

The Announcement to Joseph, 1:18-25.

The Flight into Egypt, 2:1-18.

The Return to Nazareth, 2:19-23.

I. We learned the value of genealogical tables to Israel in the Old Testament. This value applied to the separation into families and tribes with reference to the possession of Canaan; but it had a peculiar application to the Messiah also. He must come in the line of Abraham through David (v. 1), and no Israelite could be interested in one claiming to be He of whom this was not true. That Matthew should lay stress on this, and give the "generation" in detail is one evidence that his Gospel was addressed to Israel rather than the Gentiles. Neither Mark nor John gives a genealogy, and Luke's table (3:23-38), written for the Gentile, is a different one, and for a special reason does not pause at Abraham, but extends back to God, through Adam.

Reference will be made to Matthew's table again when we reach Luke's Gospel, but verse 16 is important, showing that "Joseph the husband of Mary" was legal heir to the throne of David, for the genealogical table following David's time is that of the kings. And also that although "the husband of Mary," he was not the begetter of Jesus as in the preceding cases. The changed expression is significant, "Mary, of whom was born Jesus." The latter did not come of natural generation, but in the manner indicated in the next chapter.

The "Mary" in this instance is always identified in the New Testament as the mother of Jesus, but there are five other Marys. "Mary Magdalene" (Luke 8:2); Mary, the mother of James the less and Joses, the wife of Alpheus and a sister of the Virgin (Matt. 27:56; Mark 15:40; John 19:25); Mary of Bethany, sister of Martha and Lazarus (Luke 10:39); Mary the mother of John Mark (Acts 12:12), and another Mary, associated with Paul in Rome (Rom. 16:6).

"Jesus" is the family name of our Lord. (Luke 1:31), the same as "Joshua" in the Old Testament, and means "Saviour" (v. 21); but "Christ" or "The Christ," in His official designation. "Christos" is the Greek form of the Hebrew "Messiah" (Dan. 9:25, 26), and means "The Anointed One." In the Old Testament, the prophet, the priest and the king were all anointed with oil, but Jesus their great antitype was anointed with the Holy Spirit (3:16).

II. Under "the announcement to Joseph," notice the testimony to the virgin birth (vv. 18, 20). Had Jesus been begotten after the flesh He would have been a sinner like us, and incapable of being our Saviour. And yet had He not been the legal descendant of Joseph, and heir to the throne, the Jews would have been justified in rejecting Him. Behold the wisdom and power of God! Compare the predictions of the virgin birth, Genesis 3:15; Isaiah 7:14; Jeremiah 31:22, and the corresponding account in Luke 1:28-35.

"His people" (v. 21) means in the first place the Jews, and then all who accept Him as their Saviour by faith.

Verses 22 and 23 are peculiar to Matthew, who, in writing distinctively for Israel, is careful to connect the events of Jesus' life with the Old Testament in which they believed and which contained His credentials.

III. "The flight into Egypt" is divisible into:

The visit of the wise men (vv. 1, 2).

The testimony of the priests and scribes (vv. 3-6).

The worship of the babe in the manger (vv. 7-12).

The warning to Joseph (vv. 13-15).

The slaughter of the little children (vv. 16-18).

1. This "Herod" is Herod the Great, an Edomite and appointee of Caesar. He was a cruel and despotic man, and his practical usurpation of the throne, and tyranny over the people, explain his apprehension (v. 3), on hearing that a true King of the Jews was born.

The "wise men" ("Magi" in Greek), were Gentile astrologers, occupied with occult things, foretelling events from the stars, etc. (Dan. 2:48), and earnest seekers after truth. Kepler, the astronomer, thought the "star" was a constellation of Jupiter and Saturn, but it is more likely to have been a miraculous sign from God. Nor is it necessary to suppose that it led them all the way from their eastern home, because verse nine indicates that when they started from Herod towards Bethlehem it reappeared to them. The way they came to expect a great King is suggested by their probable acquaintance with Balaam's prophecy in Numbers 23 and 24 and the predictions of Daniel.

2. The conduct of the priests and scribes illustrates a common phenomenon, viz, the truth held in the mind but having no power in the life. They knew where the Messiah should be born, but lacked the interest to inquire whether this were He. Their quotation (v. 6) from Micah 5:2, although its rendering suggests that it was taken not from the Hebrew, or Greek Septuagint, but probably a Chaldaic paraphrase.

3. Herod's interest (vv. 7, 8) was the grossest hypocrisy, but what a contrast is borne to it by these Gentiles worshiping, not the child's mother, but the child! Some find a significance in their gifts, "gold" representing royalty, "frankincense" purity, and "myrrh" suffering.

"We three kings of Orient are," is a line of a familiar hymn alluding to this visit, but is misleading, since there is nothing to indicate that they were kings, or that their number was limited to three. Another error is traceable to the picture representing them as worshiping a babe in a manger, whereas it is not unlikely that Jesus was a year old at this time. The reasons for thinking so are (1) that Luke 2:30 says, "when they had performed all things according to the law * * * they returned * * to Nazareth," while Matthew speaks of their going into Egypt after the departure of the wise men. (2), The shepherds in Luke 2, found "the babe wrapped in swaddling clothes lying in a manger;" but the wise men "saw the young child with Mary" in "the house." Possibly His parents returned to Nazareth after His birth, and then at the recurrence of the Passover the next year came down to Bethlehem again.

4. In the subsection designated as "The warning to Joseph," two prophecies find fulfillment. In verse 15, Hosea 11:1, and in verse 18, Jeremiah 31:15. The first found an approximate fulfillment in Israel, which in the Old Testament is sometimes called God's Son (Ex. 4:22; Jer. 31:9); but, according to the law of double reference, it has here an ultimate fulfillment in Christ who is often identified with Israel. The second causes Rachel, the beloved wife of Jacob, to personify Israel weeping for her children slain by Herod's sword. This weeping, in a sense, has continued ever since and will not end until Israel at last looks "upon Him whom they pierced" and mourns because of Him.

IV. "The return to Nazareth" demands attention because of the words "that it might be fulfilled which was spoken by the prophet He shall be called a Nazarene" (v. 23). The meaning is not clear because no one of the prophets calls Him by this name. However, all the prophets speak of Him in one way or another, as the despised or rejected One, and this in the eyes of a Jew is what it meant to be a dweller in Nazareth. The whole of Galilee was despised by them because it held so many Gentiles, but Nazareth was despised even by Galileans themselves. (Compare John 1:46.)

Questions.

1. Divide this lesson into four parts.

2. Name the two-fold value of genealogies to Israel.

3. What two facts give importance to 1:16?

4. Give the list of the "Marys" of the New Testament.

5. What are the distinctions between the two names of our Lord?

6. How are the wisdom and power of God shown in His birth?

7. What is peculiar to Matthew as writing for the Jews?

8. Analyze chapter 2 into its main divisions.

9. How may the Magi have known of the coming King?

10. What does the conduct of the priests and scribes teach?

11. Why may we think that chapter 2 refers to Jesus when a year old?

12. How may the last verse of that chapter be explained?

PREPARATION FOR HIS PUBLIC MINISTRY

Chapters 3-4:11

1. Baptized by John, 3.

For the earlier history of John the Baptist compare Luke 1. In verses 1-6 of the present lesson, however, we have the place and theme of his ministry, a statement of his official relationship to the Messiah, - his description, and an account of the interest awakened by his mission.

"The Kingdom of heaven," or "the heavens," (verse 2), means the earthly kingdom promised to Israel in the Old Testament, over which the Messiah was to reign. It is "the Kingdom of the heavens" in that it is the rule of the heavens over the earth (6:10). Compare Daniel 2:34-36, 44. It was the rejection of the Messiah that caused the postponement of this Kingdom until His coming again.

In 7-12 we have a reference to the religious leaders of the nation at this time, and a warning of judgment awaiting them. We met with "scribes" in the preceding chapter, and here we have "Pharisees and Sadducees." The "scribes" made copies of the sacred Scriptures, and classified and taught them (2 Sam. 8:17; Jer. 8:8), but by and by, they added to this other things not so necessary or lawful, and compelled the people to accept them or be charged with heterodoxy. This was the charge brought against our Lord Himself because He confined His teaching to the Scripture. Among the things they added were Hebrew legends (Gemara), and rabbinical rules on questions of ritual (Mishna), the two forming the Talmud of later times.

"Pharisee" comes from a Hebrew word meaning "separate," and identifies a sect whose origin dated from the return from Babylon. At first its object was to keep alive a reverence for the law of God, but later it degenerated into a traditionalism corresponding to the teaching of the scribes. Pharisees were zealous but self-righteous, and became the fiercest enemies of Jesus Christ. "Sadducees" some think were named after their founder Zadok. They were skeptics who denied the immortality of the soul. They also denied the oral tradition on which Pharisaic teaching was largely based. They were the rich and worldly people of Judea in our Lord's time. These definitions explain the hard names and the warnings applied to the Pharisees and Sadducees (v. 7). Their hypocrisy is seen in verse 8, their pride of race, verse 9, their speedy judgment, verse 10.

Baptism with water (v. 11) had been practiced among the Jews in connection with the proselytism of the Gentiles, and was the outward sign by which the latter signified the change of mind and purpose supposed to have taken place within, and which is really the meaning of "repentance." This baptism of John, however, is not identical with Christian baptism as will be seen later.

The last clause of verse 11 refers to Christ, who baptized His disciples with the Holy Ghost, after His ascension, on the day of Pentecost (Acts 2; 1 Cor. 12:13); and will baptize Israel with fire when He comes again in judgment (v. 12). This is an illustration of the law of double reference of which we learned in the Old Testament.

Verses 13-17 are the most important. The sinless one coming to a sinner to be baptized with sinners, how strange! No wonder John forbade Him. But it was not John's baptism He sought, although John baptized Him. John's baptism was the sign and seal of repentance to escape wrath, but Jesus had no need of repentance and no fear of wrath. His baptism was to "fulfill all righteousness" (15). In other words, the Father had made a covenant of redemption with the Son, in which the Son engaged to work out, as God Incarnate, through atoning sufferings and obedience, a perfect righteousness for sinful men. Of this covenant His baptism by John was the sign and seal. It was His own seal of consecration to His chosen work, and the Father's seal of faithfulness to the sufferer, the latter being proven by the open heavens, the descending dove and the paternal voice. Thus was He inaugurated into His great office. (Bishop W. R. Nicholson.)

2. Tempted by Satan. 4:1-11.

It is the Holy Spirit who is referred to in verse 1, and indeed, after His anointing by the Spirit, almost everything Jesus is said to have done, was accomplished, not in the power of His own natural spirit, but the Holy Spirit. It would have been wrong for Him to have entered into this temptation on His own account. The "Devil" of the same verse we became acquainted with as a personal being, in the Old Testament. But although he possesses personality, a word synonymous with self-consciousness, that is not to say that he appeared to Jesus in human form. The form he assumed is not revealed, although the temptation was objective in character, as was that of

the first Adam in Eden, with which it stands in contrast.

The temptation was three-fold, the appeal being directed to "the lust of the flesh, the lust of the eyes, and the pride of life" (1 John 2:16), which is all the devil has to offer. The Father had just testified to His Sonship, but He is tempted to doubt it because He is hungry (3). He has just declared His confidence in the Word of God (4), and He is tempted to presume upon it (5-7). He had been promised the Kingdom through the Cross, and He is tempted to obtain it in another way (8-10). As Scofield says, "Satan's one object was to induce Christ to act from Himself and independently of His Father," and Christ defeated him "by a means open to His humblest follower, the intelligent use of the Word of God."

This victory of Christ takes on great significance when we realize that as the second Adam He took the place of the first. What we lost in the first, we, who believe, have restored to us in the second. (Romans 5:12-21 and 1 Corinthians 15:20-22, 45-49.)

Questions.

1. Where do we learn the earlier history of John the Baptist?

2. Define "the Kingdom of heaven."

3. Define "scribes," "Pharisees," "Sadducees."

4. Give the history of the Jewish "Talmud."

5. What illustration of the law of double reference is found in this lesson?

6. What meaning is attached to Jesus' baptism?

7. What is the meaning of "personality"?

8. What was Satan's one object in the temptation of Christ?

9. What gives the temptation its great significance for us?

BEGINNING HIS MINISTRY

CHAPTERS 4:12-5:12

1. The Starting Point. 4:12-17.
For antecedent and parallel events, read John 1:15-51; Luke

3:1-20; 4:14-32, which explain why John the Baptist was imprisoned, and why Jesus left Nazareth. Identify Capernaum on the map, and read up its history in a Bible dictionary since it becomes important as the center of our Lord's ministry in Galilee. "Zabulun and Nephtalim" or Zebulun and Naphtali, we recognize as names of tribes of Israel and locations in Canaan called after them. Locate them on the map, and compare Isaiah 9:1, 2, R. V., which is to have a completer fulfilment at the second coming of Christ. The "Kingdom of heaven" He "began to preach" (17) was that which He came to set up in Israel had the nation received Him. Not a spiritual Kingdom only, but a manifested Kingdom like that of David, wherein righteousness should reign.

2. The First Followers. vv. 18-22.

He had met these men before (John 1), and called them to be His disciples. Having believed on Him, they are now called into His service.

3. The First Works. vv. 23-25.

The teaching was in the synagogues, and the preaching in the open air where the crowds gathered. Note the theme of His preaching, not the gospel of grace which now saves the sinner, but the "gospel of the Kingdom" the good news that the earthly Kingdom promised to Israel was ready to be set up if they would have it. By and by when His rejection by Israel is confirmed, this gospel ceases to be preached, and the gospel of grace takes its place. The gospel of grace is preached in the present dispensation of the church, but when the Church, the body of Christ, is complete, and caught up to meet Him in the air (1 Thess. 4:13-18), then the gospel of the Kingdom will be again preached because the Kingdom will be drawing near a second time. The miracles of healing are in connection with the gospel of the Kingdom. That is not to say that there are no such miracles at present, but only that they are peculiar to the set-

ting up the earthly Kingdom, and doubtless will be seen again in a marked manner as the day approaches. The Satanic counterfeits of these miracles now in many places would indicate that the time is at hand.

4. The First Discourse. 5:1.

Beginning here and extending to the close of chapter 7 we have what is called the "Sermon on the Mount" (5:1); but we are not to suppose that these words were all spoken at one time, or in their present connection. A comparison with the other Gospels suggest differently. For the purpose of the Holy Spirit in Matthew's Gospel however, it was desirable to group them as though they formed a single discourse. Addressing the Jew, he is showing that Jesus is the King who has come to set up His Kingdom, and in these words, chapters 5-7 sets forth at one glance the laws or code of that Kingdom. We must be clear about this. The "Sermon on the Mount" does not set forth the terms of salvation for sinners. Neither is it the experience which the Church will perfectly attain in this age, but is primarily Jewish and pertains to conditions on the earth when the manifested Kingdom of the Messiah is in vogue. It would be wrong to press this too far, and say that the "Sermon on the Mount" has no application whatever to the Christian Church or the times in which we live, for God is the same through all dispensations, and the underlying principles of His government never change. But just how to apply it must be determined in detail, and by the never failing light of the Holy Spirit who has been given to lead the Christian into all the truth (John 16:13).

The first twelve verses, or the "Beatitudes," constitute an exordium to the discourse, in which is set forth the characteristics of the heirs of the Kingdom. There are nine beatitudes, and dispensationally viewed, show us Israel, in the tribulation period awaiting the Kingdom. They will be poor in spirit, and shall get the Kingdom. They will mourn and shall be comforted. They will be meek and shall inherit the earth. They will hunger and thirst after righteousness, and shall be filled.

But in an accommodated sense the beatitudes apply to believers in the present age. There is a heavenly side and an earthly side to the Kingdom, and it is only those who are "poor in spirit," humbling themselves on account of sin and believing on the Lord Jesus Christ, who, through the new birth, receive the Kingdom. They who now mourn for their sins are comforted in forgiveness and cleansing through the blood. They who now hunger and thirst after righteousness are filled. As Weston says, we have here a picture of a redeemed and sanctified man, an ideal man whom the Saviour is to make actual by saving him from his sin.

For private study or classroom work, it would be desirable to include the whole of the Sermon on the Mount in one lesson, but for the purpose of this commentary, we pause here.

Questions.

1. Divide this lesson into four parts.

2. Did you read the scripture references for the antecedent or parallel events?

3. Have you looked up Capernaum?

4. Why does Matthew so often quote the Old Testament?

5. What is meant by the "Kingdom of heaven" in this case?

6. What is the distinction between "the gospel of the Kingdom" or "gospel of grace"?

7. What is set forth in the "Sermon on the Mount?"

8. What is set forth in the beatitudes?

9. What is their historical sense?

10. How do they apply to us in an accommodated sense?

THE CODE OF THE KINGDOM

CHAPTERS 5:13-7

The King has announced His kingdom at hand, and now de-clares the laws or code of that Kingdom. These which we began to speak of in the last lesson, have a two-fold application, ultimately to the Kingdom when it shall be set up, and approximately and in an accommodated sense to the Christian at present. Except that the first of these is kept in mind, confusion and uncertainty must attend the interpretation.

1. We have *two figurative descriptions of disciples,* (5:13-16), "Salt" and "Light." Salt is a preservative, and true Christian disciples counteract worldly corruption. They are the light of the world whose conduct is to reflect the Saviour. These two descriptions are a text for what follows, which shows how the disciple is to preserve the world and shine in it.

2. We have a statement of *Christ's relation to the law,* (17-20). His mission was not to set aside the Old Testament, but to fill it out, in that He obeyed the law perfectly, and fulfilled in Himself all the prophets had spoken of the Coming One. He also completely revealed the meaning of the Old Testament, which involves the warning of verse 19, made necessary by what He says in verse 20.

3. We have a comparison between *righteousness outward and inward* (21-48). The righteousness of the scribes and Pharisees was outward and ceremonial, that of the Kingdom of God on earth must go deeper. The spirit of murder is anger (21-22, compared with 1 John 3:15). "Raca" (a word of contempt) uttered against a brother will involve a condemnation by the Sanhedrin, and "thou fool" shall subject the guilty one to "hell fire" when the Kingdom is on earth. In the meantime these penalties show us God's estimate of sin now and always, and intensify our thanksgiving for the salvation we have in Christ.

As anger is the spirit of murder, so a lustful look is adultery (27-30). It were better to be blind than be guilty of it. The Greek word for hell is "Gehenna," the place in the valley of Hinnom where human sacrifices were formerly offered and which is used in Scripture as identical with "the lake of fire." Divorce is linked with adultery, and becomes adultery under the circumstances indicated (31, 32). The command against swearing (33-37) does not forbid legal oaths, but profanity, which includes expletives common in everyday speech. Retaliation (38-42) is personal, not judicial nor governmental. If the cause were that of another we have no right to do some of the things here commanded, or permit others to do them, but they are clearly within one's own rights. This is how men will act in the Kingdom, and how they ought to act now. And the absence of such a spirit shows how far we are from God, and what it is to be lost. What would become of us, without a Saviour! This leads to the law of love (43-47) which is as far from human hearts in their natural state as the foregoing. Our example is God (48), but who has attained to it? And if not, how can we see His face, except as He has in grace made provision for us in His Son?

4. Following these laws on our relation to others, we have *those touching the religious life*, i. e., our relations to God—almsgiving (6:1-4), worship (5-15), fasting (16-18), all of which must be done as in the presence of the Father. The "Lord's Prayer" will be dealt with in Luke.

5. Next are *laws relating more particularly to one's self*—trust (19-34), self-judgment (7:1-6), prayer (7:12), false teachers (13-20), future reward (21-23). Under the head of "trust," note (22-24), that the eye cannot look to earth and to heaven at the same time; and (34), that lack of trust is always pessimistic of the future. Under self-judgment, we are not denied privilege, or liberated from the duty, of passing upon the conduct of others and the evil that is in the world, which would be contradictory of Matthew 18:15-18, 1 Corinthians 5·12, 13 and other places; but to defer judgment as to motives, the sources from which such conduct or evil springs. (Rom. 14.) To abuse this spirit of restraint, however, and permit. evil to remain unjudged, would be to "cast that which is holy unto the dogs."

The reason for the "Golden Rule" (7:12) has been suggested thus: (1) We are to be careful about judging others; (2) we should seek divine wisdom in doing so; (3) which obtained, would lead us to act in love towards all. How many foolishly say that they live by the "Golden Rule"! But the Bible and experience·prove that no one has ever done so except Him who uttered it. And yet it is that by which the man out of Christ elects to be judged! What madness! Some tell us that Christ borrowed this word from the sacred books of the east, but this also is folly, for what is found there is merely a negative teaching, while this is positive. What you would not have others do to you, do not to them, is different from doing unto others what you would have them do unto you.

Under "false teachers," note that "fruits" (20) does not necessarily mean open immorality, but the counterfeit of the truth of God. False prophets and teachers are sometimes very attractive in their lives, but their words, rightly understood, are inconsonant with Holy Writ.

The conclusion of this discourse shows our Lord's mind to be resting on the end of the age, and the incoming of the Kingdom. Our study of the Old Testament taught us to interpret the phrase, "in that day" (22), in that way.

Questions.

1. What is meant by the "code of the Kingdom"?

2. What two figures of speech describe the relation of disciples to the world?

3. In what sense did Christ fulfill the law of the prophets?

4. What does "Gehenna" refer to, and how is it used in Scripture?

5. What kind of retaliation does our Lord refer to?

6. What is meant by "Judge not"?

7. Does any one really live by the "Golden Rule"?

8. What is meant by the "fruits" of false prophets?

CREDENTIALS OF THE KING

CHAPTERS 8-9

We have seen that the "Sermon on the Mount" was probably separate discourses grouped by the evangelist under the guidance of the Holy Spirit, for a particular purpose. That purpose was the presentation of Jesus to the Jews as the Messiah, the King promised them in the Old Testament. In like manner, the miracles now following were probably wrought at different times but grouped by the evangelist for the same purpose. Jesus had come proclaiming the Kingdom to be at hand; He had laid down the laws of the Kingdom, and now in these mighty works we have the credentials of the King.

There are ten in all, (nine being miracles of healing), to say nothing of the unclassified ones (8:16, 17; 9:35).

The Dispensational View.

Surely God only could do these things, and He through whom they were accomplished can be none other than the One He claimed to be. (Isa. 35:5, 6.) Their practical teachings have been made familiar in Sunday-school lessons, so that here attention may be given to their dispensational aspects. Gaebelein teaches that the cleansing of the leper stands for Jehovah in the person of Jesus among His people Israel; the healing of the centurion's servant, absent and healed by a word, represents this Gentile dispensation still running. When its course is completed, He will enter the house again in restored relations to Israel, as symbolized in raising the sick daughter of Zion, the mother of Peter's wife. Now come the millennial

blessings to all the earth—they brought Him those suffering from many diseases and He healed them all.

For the leprosy of Israel compare Isaiah 1:5, 6. Only God can heal that disease, and when Jesus spake the word, and sent the healed man to the priest, why did not the latter recognize Him? He, the priest, thus becomes the type of the unbelieving nation who ultimately rejected Him.

Grace now comes to the Gentiles typified by the centurion who manifests simple faith, drawing forth from our Lord the words prophetic of this dispensation, "Many shall come from the east and from the west, and shall sit down with Abraham, Isaac and Jacob."

The sick woman is typical of Israel whom the Lord has promised to heal at His second coming, and who will then become his minister (8-15). With the verses immediately following, compare Isaiah 53:4. The self-seeking scribe of verses 18-20 is a type of Israel filled with selfish expectations of earthly gain and glory, after the flesh and not after the Spirit.

Coming to the latter part of the chapter, we are reminded by the casting out of the demons, that Satan, the prince of the demons, will be cast into the bottomless pit when Christ comes a second time to deliver Israel (Rev. 20). From the dispensational point of view, the deliverance of these men foreshadows that of the faithful Jews in the tribulation, while the destruction of the swine indwelt by the demons, foreshadows the remainder of the nation rushing into the judgment awaiting them.

The healing of the paralytic (9:1-8) shows from another point of view what Christ will do for Israel when He comes again. He will pardon their iniquity (Isa. 43:25), and heal them of their sin in soul and body (Mal. 4:2).

The important feature in the call of Matthew (9-17) is the question of John's disciples and its answer. The explanation is that Christ is the bridegroom, and while He was with His disciples there could be no mourning; but by and by, He would be rejected, and then it would be different. Here follows a revelation of a new order of things. The old garment is Judaism with its legal righteousness, which cannot be patched up; i. e., law and grace cannot go together in the same system of faith. The new wine is Christianity, while the old bottles are the Mosaic institutions, a figure which teaches the same truth.

The miracles of verses 18-26 are typical. Christ is coming to bring life to Israel, the daughter of Zion; but while He is coming, the Gentiles, in parenthesis as it were, touch Him by faith, and salvation comes to them in that moment.

These hints are sufficient for our present purpose if they whet the appetite to turn to larger works and pursue the subjects further.

New and Important Words.
There are two or three words here which we meet for the first time. "Devils" is one, which in the Revised Version is rendered "demons." There is but one devil, Satan, but there are many demons. We know nothing of their origin save that they are not to be confounded with evil angels, as for instance in 2 Peter 2:4. Any Bible dictionary will furnish information concerning them.

"Lord". (Greek, *Kurios*), as applied to Christ, is met for the first time. It means "master" and may be used of merely human relationships, but in the New Testament is chiefly employed as the divine title of Jesus Christ.

"Son of Man" our Lord uses of Himself about eighty times. "Son of David" is His Jewish name, "Son of God" His divine name, and "Son of Man" his racial name. This latter conveys the thought that His mission transcends "in scope and result all merely Jewish limitations."

Questions.
1. What is signified by the title of this lesson?

2. How many miracles are in this group and of what nature chiefly?

3. Name the miracles in their order.

4. Give a general idea of their dispensational intent.

5. Explain Christ's references to the old garments and old wine bottles.

6. Distinguish between the devil and demons.

7. How is the word "Lord" commonly used of Christ?

8. What is the significance of the title, "Son of Man"?

EXPANSION AND OPPOSITION

CHAPTERS 10-12

The King has come, the code of His Kingdom is set forth, His credentials presented, and He now expands the testimony concerning Himself, with the result of increasing opposition. This expansion is connected with the commission of the twelve disciples (Chap. 10), and the opposition is revealed in various ways in the chapters following.

I. The Disciples Commissioned, 10.
Here we find "apostles" for the first time (v. 2), which means "those sent forth," an indispensable qualification for whose office was that of an eye-witness of the resurrection of Christ (Acts 1:22; 1 Cor. 9:1). The apostles were endued with miraculous powers as credentials of their ministry, and their work at this time was to announce to Israel only that the Kingdom was at hand (vv. 6, 7). The Kingdom is the one promised to Israel on this earth, and through Israel to the other nations. This explains things in the chapter, which if rightly understood, will keep us from reading into it that which does not belong there.

For example, the power granted in verses 1 and 8 was in connection with this preaching of the Kingdom, and withdrawn when the Kingdom was finally rejected by Israel; although it will be renewed when the faithful remnant of the Jews again go forth during the tribulation to preach the same Kingdom. In the meantime, the preaching of the gospel of grace, especially committed to Paul, who was not of the twelve, is accompanied by gifts of another kind (Eph. 4:10-12). Look at verses 11 to 15, where the "worthy" mean those looking for the Messiah promised by the Old Testament prophets. The gospel of grace is not offered to the "worthy," but to "whomsoever" will accept it. Or, take verses 16-23, which speak of the way the apostles' message would be received, and compare the prophecy they contain with the persecution in the Acts of the Apostles; or look at these verses in the light of the second coming of Christ, to which verse 23 refers. We learned in Daniel and elsewhere, that time is not counted in the history of Israel when she is not in her own land. Hence the testimony here begun by the apostles and continued up to Israel's rejection of the Kingdom, is an unfinished testimony, and will be taken up again when the Church is translated during the tribulation.

From this point to verse 33 we find encouragement. The disciples are identified with their Lord (vv. 24, 25); therefore, they need not fear (vv. 26-28), for He cares for them (vv. 29-33). Then follows a description of the age in which we live, a time of war rather than peace (34-36); of separation on the part of Christ's followers (vv. 37, 38), and yet with the prospect of a bright recompense (vv. 39-42).

Modern research throws light on a chapter like this. Take verses 9 and 10. Upon a monument at Kefr-Hanar in Syria, during this same period, one who calls himself "a slave" of the Syrian goddess tells of his begging journeys in her services, and uses the word for his collecting-bag here translated "scrip." He boasts that "each journey brought in seventy bags." The contrast with the followers of Christ is marked, who were neither to earn nor beg as they went forth with speed to herald His coming—Habershon.

II. Anxiety of John the Baptist, 11.

We are not surprised that as the testimony of Christ thus expanded (v. 1), John the Baptist in his prison should wonder. "Why, if this be the Christ, does He not take the Kingdom, or why does he not deliver me? Have I been mistaken in my witness to Him?" John is told to reflect upon the evidence and to wait (vv. 2-6).

How our Lord defends John, lest this act should reflect upon him (vv. 7-15)! Verse 11 has reference to John's relation to the Kingdom. The least in the Kingdom of heaven when it shall be set up upon earth, shall be greater than John could be before that time. The words do not speak of John in the moral sense, in which he was as great as any man born of woman, but in this dispensational sense. Verse 12 is capable of two interpretations, an external and an internal one. In the first, the enemies of Jesus and John are the "violent" who are rejecting the Kingdom by force; in the second, the "violent" are those who in face of the opposition are pressing into the Kingdom.

A description of that generation follows as a foolish one (vv. 16-19), but there were some who believed and are referred to in the words "wisdom is justified of her children."

As the judge of that generation our Lord now speaks (vv. 20-27). "Woe," is heard for the first time. In the coming day there will be different degrees of punishment (vv. 22, 24), responsibility being gauged by privilege. From the "wise and prudent" in their own eyes, i. e., the self-righteous Pharisees, these things were hidden, but were revealed unto "babes," the poor in spirit conscious of their need (v. 25). Our Lord now turns toward these in verses 28-30, in which he offers no longer the Kingdom, but rest and service to them that come to Him. Practically He has been rejected by the nation, and is approaching the turning point in His ministry, when the proclamation of the Kingdom shall cease.

III. Opposition Expressed, 12.

The enmity is coming to a head. In 1-8, the Lord of the Sabbath is unjustly accused of Sabbath-breaking, and answers His accusers by facts of Holy Writ. David, as the rejected king in his time, ate the shew-bread, and "Great David's greater Son" in His rejection is correspondingly guiltless. Next comes the temptation of 9-14, with the result that the opposition now becomes organized (v. 14), and the Lord withdraws Himself for His hour is not yet come. As He is departing, the incident of 22-30 takes place, when He is again charged as the representative of Satan (v. 24, compared with 9:34). The blasphemy against the Holy Ghost consists in attributing His work to Satan (vv. 31, 32). "A word against the Son of Man" might be forgiven, for the Holy Spirit still remained to convict one of that sin by testifying to Christ. But when the testimony of the Holy Spirit to Christ was rejected as in this case, there was no hope left.

The opposition increases by the demand for a sign (vv. 38-42). Had He not given sufficient signs? Jonah is a type of His own death and resurrection and He will give him as a sign. The Queen of Sheba is another sign. But Israel is like a man out of whom a demon had gone of his own accord, and comes back to find the place unoccupied and brings seven other worse spirits to fill the former abode. The nation, in other words, had been cured of idolatry by the Babylonian captivity, but now it was boasting of forms and ceremonies, traditions and self-righteousness. It was empty so far as the fear of Jehovah was concerned, and by and by the evil spirit would return, and the end of Israel, i. e., the period of the tribulation, would be worse than the first.

The Lord is rejected even by His family, as we judge by comparing the closing verses of this chapter with the reason in Mark 3:21. He declines to see them, and intimates the formation of a new family of faith.

Questions.

1. What is an essential qualification for an apostle?
2. What is the limitation of the apostles' commission at this time?
3. How does that limitation affect the teaching of chapter 10?
4. How may "violent" be interpreted in chapter 11?
5. On what principle will future retribution be rendered?
6. What is the blasphemy against the Holy Ghost?
7. How would you explain verses 43-45?
8. How would you explain Jesus' reference to His mother and His brethren?

THE TURNING POINT

CHAPTER 13

From the dispensational point of view, there is no chapter of the New Testament more needful to be understood than this. It contains seven parables, which now that the practical rejection of the Messiah by Israel has taken place, set forth the result of the gospel in the world down to the end of this age, when He shall come again. It is symbolic that our Lord now goes into a ship on the sea, the latter a type of the Gentile nations as compared with Israel; and also that He talks about sowing the seed in a field which is the world, as distinguished from laboring in a vineyard which is Israel (Isa. 5:1-7).

The parables are divided into two groups, the first four spoken before the multitude, and the last three in the presence of the disciples only. The first again may be divided in two—the sower, and the tares and wheat—referring more especially to the earlier history of Christendom; and the mustard seed and leaven describing its further progress and development.

I. The First Two of the First Group—The Sower and the Tares and the Wheat.

The Lord explains them, but prior thereto answers the question of the disciples (v. 10), in which He speaks of the "mysteries of the Kingdom of heaven." A "mystery" in Scripture is a previously hidden truth, now divinely revealed, but in which the supernatural element remains despite the revelation (Scofield). The "Kingdom of heaven," or, the "Kingdom of the heavens" as used here means that Kingdom which is to be set up on the earth, the truth concerning which is "left in the hands of men" while the King is absent, in other words, it stands for Christendom. It is given to true disciples to know the mystery of Christendom, but to others it is not given (vv. 11-17).

The parable of the sower needs no comment other than emphasis on the fact that all the seed sown does not bear fruit. The devil in the first case, the flesh in the second, and the world in the third, prevent it. In other words, all men will not be converted to Christ before the end of this age. This is brought out with more force in the second parable (vv. 24-30 and 36-43). The good seed here is not the gospel of the first parable, but that which the gospel produces, "the children of the Kingdom." These are sown among men, and Satan sows his seed with them. The children of Satan look as much like the children of God as tares look like wheat. Only the angels can separate them. Scofield says: "Mere unbelievers are never called the children of the devil, only religious unbelievers are called so," i. e., those who profess the name of Christ, and do not hold the truth of Christ (Matt. 13:38; 23:15; John 8:38-44, and other places).

II. The Second Two of the First Group—The Mustard Seed and the Leaven.

The mustard seed shows the rapid but abnormal development of Christendom to a great place in the earth. The fowls of the air mean unbelievers of various classes, who, for selfish reasons embrace Christianity and find shelter in its branches (Compare Dan. 4:20, 22 and Rev. 18:2). "Leaven" represents "a principle of corruption working subtly" and is used in Scripture invariably in a bad sense (Gen. 19:3; Matt. 16:11, 12; Mark 8:15; 1 Cor. 5:6-8, etc.). The teaching of the parable is that the gospel would be mingled with false doctrine, the latter increasing to the end of the age. (Compare here 1 Tim. 4:1-3; 2 Tim. 2:17, 18; 4:3, 4; 2 Pet. 2:1-3.)

III. The Third Group—The Hid Treasure, The Pearl, The Dragnet.

The multitude is dismissed, the Lord and His disciples have entered the house, and He is explaining the parable of the tares. After this He says, "the Kingdom of heaven is like unto a treasure hid in a field" (v. 44). The "field" was previously defined as the world. The hidden "treasure" is Israel (Exod. 19:5; Ps. 135:4). Christ is the "man who hath found" it. It is now hidden. Who knows where the "lost tribes" are? And even the Jew as we know him is in the world, and is in a sense lost there (Rom. 11:25). Christ has sold all that He had to buy the field. He gave His life for the world (1 Pet. 1:18), but He died in a special sense for that nation (John 11:51). What joy He will have when He takes His treasure to Himself (Deut. 30:9; Isa. 49:13; 62:4-7).

Christ is the "merchantman" of the next parable (v. 45), and "the pearl of great price" is the Church, for which He gave Himself (Eph. 5:25-33). "Ye are not your own but are bought with a price." There is beauty in the thought of the Church as a pearl whether we consider its origin, form, appearance or value. It comes into existence not mechanically but vitally, just as Christ forms His church by communicating His own life to it. The pearl comes from the sea as the Church comes from the nations symbolized by the sea. A grain of sand imbeds itself between the animal and the shell and creates a wound in the side of the animal in so doing. In the healing of the wound the animal deposits a thin crust of a bright aspect around this grain of sand, repeating the process till the pearl is formed, blending the colors of the rainbow. Eve was taken out of the side of Adam, and the side of Christ was opened that out of it He might build His Church, to which He addeth daily such as are being saved (Acts 2:41-47; Eph. 2:21; Col. 2:19, etc.).

The Dragnet

Is not the gospel net, but a picture of that which takes place in Christendom at the end of this age, i. e., after the Church is taken up into the air (1 Thess. 4:13-18).—Gaebelein.

The foregoing interpretation is unusual to those coming freshly upon it, but to others who have perused the lessons in the Old Testament prophets, it will appear perfectly consistent, and furnish a corroboration of the unity and divinity of the Bible.

Questions.

1. Name the parables in their order.

2. What is the scope of their interpretation?

3. What is meant by "the Kingdom of the heavens" as employed in this chapter?

4. What is a "mystery" in a scriptural sense?

5. What inference is clear from these parables?

6. Who are "the children of the devil," scripturally interpreted?

7. How is "leaven" invariably used in Scripture?

8. Give the interpretations of the "hid treasure" and the "pearl."

9. What four features give beauty to the pearl as a type of the Church?

THE FIRST MINISTRY TO THE GENTILES.

CHAPTERS 14-15

Jesus has come. He has proclaimed the nearness of the Kingdom, revealed its code or principles, presented His credentials, and sent forth His heralds. But He has been antagonized and practically rejected by the nation. Then comes the turning point, when He ceases to proclaim the nearness of the Kingdom, and discourses of it in mystery. In seven parables he outlines how it will fare among the nations in the absence of the King.

One might suppose that the teachings and the doings of our Lord to follow, would assume a different complexion from anything before. And, as a matter of fact such is the case in the judgment of those keen in dispensational discernment. But for the purpose before us it is undesirable to strain after such interpretations, and except where they are very clear, we shall content ourselves with the more practical line of comment as hitherto.

At the close of the thirteenth chapter (vv. 53-58), "they were offended in Him"; less and less is the nation disposed to receive Him as its Messiah, and because of the suspicions of Herod (c. 14:1, 2), He deems it prudent to withdraw Himself once more (vv. 13, 14). The events that follow in the chapter are the feeding of the five thousand, the walking upon the sea, the quieting of the storm, and the healing of the sick. All these are additional evidences of the grace and power of Jesus, leading to the conviction "Of a truth thou art the Son of God" (v. 33).

At chapter 15 the Pharisees once more seek occasion against Him (vv. 1, 2), but His disciples have broken no divine law, but only disregarded one of their traditions. The charge is not that their hands are soiled, but only ceremonially unclean (Mark 7:1-4). Christ takes the indirect method of reply by attacking the traditions (vv. 3-6). The fifth commandment is plain enough, but the Pharisees had supplemented it with interpretations, making it so burdensome, that devices had to be invented to neutralize them. But in neutralizing the traditions they had done away with the original law. A man to honor his parents must do so and so for them, they said, i. e., more than the commandment contemplated. But if "so and so" became irksome in any case, it was only necessary to affirm that the money it involved had been pledged as a gift to the altar, and then it need not be given to the parents. Thus the latter failed to be honored at all.

The boldness of Christ is marked in this instance (vv. 10, 11), giving further offence to His enemies (v. 12), His words calling for an explanation even to His disciples (vv. 15-20).

There is a dispensational color in the transaction following (vv. 21-28), which is the first recorded ministry of Christ to a Gentile and in a Gentile country. It comes close upon the aversion to Him of His own nation, and points prophetically to that "turning to the Gentiles" which marks the present age. The significance here is found in the woman's first appeal to Him as the "Son of David" (v. 22), to which as a Gentile, she has no right (v. 24); but when, dropping that, she throws herself upon His "uncovenanted mercies"— so to speak addressing Him only as "Lord," the plea is at once granted.

Questions.

1. What may be assumed as to the teachings of this Gospel following the turning point of chapter 13?

2. Name the leading facts of chapter 14.

3. To what conviction do they lead?

4. Explain in your own words chapter 15:1-6.

5. What gives a dispensational color to the story of the Syrophenician woman?

6. What is its prophetic application?

THE FIRST ANNOUNCEMENT OF HIS DEATH

CHAPTERS 16-17:23

In the first of these chapters there are several revelations, from one of which we take the title of the lesson.

We need not dwell on the first section (vv. 1-4), in which Jesus once more rebukes the Pharisees and Sadducees. Nor need we dwell on the second section which is self-explanatory (vv. 5-12). But at the third (v. 13-16) we reach something of much importance. Of course, Jesus knew what men said of Him, but the question of verse thirteen was to lead up to the confession of Peter, which in the outcome became His own formal claim to the Messiahship, the first He had made. The answer of verse 14 shows that the people knew Him not, as it is to-day, at the drawing to a close of the Christian age (compare 2 Peter 2 and 3). In the face of this, Peter's confession is wonderful, including "all upon which personal faith in the Son of God rests."

But it is wonderful also in that it is a supernatural revelation to Peter (vv. 17-20). The time is now ripe for Jesus to reveal that great fact, the mystery of His Church, which had been hid from former ages. There is in the Greek of verse 18, a play upon the words "Peter" and "rock." The first is "petros," which means "a little rock," a piece of a large rock. The second is "petra," which means "rock." Christ does not mean to build His Church on Peter, but on the confession of Himself as "the Christ, the Son of the Living God." Christ is the rock. Peter is careful to tell us this (1 Pet. 2:4-9). The word for Church, "ecclesia," is found here for the first time, and means an assembly of called-out ones. Israel was called out of Egypt and assembled in the wilderness (Acts 7:38), and the town-meeting at Ephesus was an assembly, an "ecclesia" (Acts 19:39). Observe the future tense, "I will build my Church." There was no

Church in existence before, nor did it subsequently come into existence till the day of Pentecost. Nor did Peter receive "the keys" of the Church, but of the "Kingdom of the heavens" (v. 19), which is "the sphere of Christian profession," or Christendom. A key is a badge of authority, and whatever it meant for Peter, it meant for all the apostles as is seen by comparing the whole verse with 18:18, where the thought is repeated and applied to all. Peter never assumed any special authority (see Acts 15:7-19; Gal. 2:11-15; 1 Pet. 1:1; 5:1). Just what is meant by the authority here conferred is not clear. Some think it was that exercised by Peter in opening the door of the gospel to the Jews on the day of Pentecost, and to the Gentiles in the house of Cornelius (Acts 2:38-42; 10:34-46). Others think it is a general authority constituted in the great commission (28-12). At all events, it was not what Rome thinks it is, for the eternal destiny of souls is held in the power of Christ alone (Rev. 1:18).

The first revelation of His death following is hardly second in importance to the preceding revelation of His Church, except that it has been anticipated; but the outcome of it in the case of the disciples is of the deepest instruction (vv. 21-27). The time had not come earlier for this revelation, and now that it had come how poorly prepared were the disciples to receive it (vv. 22, 23)! Peter's "rebuke" is explained by his expectation that the earthly Kingdom would be immediately set up, and his disappointment in losing the worldly advantages which would be his at that time. His temptation of Christ was not different in essence from that of Satan in the wilderness, who would have Christ take the Kingdom other than by the Cross (v. 23). This was the occasion for a discourse on the denial of self (vv. 24-27).

The closing verse of the section above indicates that the expectation of the disciples will be realized at the second coming of Christ, and to strengthen their faith as to this the transfiguration follows (16:28; 17:8). It is to the transfiguration that verse 28 refers, inasmuch as three of them standing there saw Him "coming in His Kingdom" in miniature, in that event. For an inspired corroboration of this, read 2 Peter 1:16-18. To quote the Scofield Bible: "The scene contains in miniature all the elements of the future Kingdom in manifestation: (1) the Lord, not in humiliation, but glory; (2) Moses, glorified, representing the redeemed who have passed through death into the Kingdom; (3) Elijah glorified, representing the redeemed who have entered by translation; (4) the three disciples not glorified, representing Israel in the flesh in the future Kingdom; (5) the multitude at the foot of the mountain (v. 14), representing the nations who are to be brought into the Kingdom after it is established over Israel. For the third point, read 1 Corinthians 15:50-53 and 1 Thessalonians 4:14-17; for the fourth Ezekiel 37, and for the fifth Isaiah 11:10-12 and many other places.

It remains to speak of the disciples' question about Elijah (vv. 9-13), suggested by His appearance on the mountain, and which carries us back to Malachi 3:1 and 4:5, 6. Here are two distinct prophecies, the first fulfilled in John the Baptist who had come "in the spirit and power of Elijah" (Luke 1:17); and the second yet to be fulfilled before the Lord returns a second time. This will be doubtless after the Church is translated.

Questions.

1. How many divisions have been found in this lesson?

2. To what was the confession of Peter equivalent so far as Christ was personally concerned?

3. Give in your own words the play on the words "Peter" and "rock."

4. Have you examined 1 Peter 2:4-9?

5. What is the Greek word for "Church," and its meaning?

6. When did the Church of Christ come into existence?

7. Have you examined the texts touching on Peter's supposed authority?

8. What are the views about the power of the keys?

9. What explains Peter's "rebuke" of Christ?

10. How is 16:28 explained?

11. How does the transfiguration show us Christ "coming in His kingdom"?

12. How would you explain Christ's words about Elijah?

THE SECOND ANNOUNCEMENT OF HIS DEATH

Chapters 17:24-20:16

The first announcement of His death and resurrection by our Lord in the last lesson, connected His suffering with the act of His own nation, while this predicts the part played in it by one of His own band (vv. 22, 23). It furnishes a starting point for a new lesson as in the other case.

The incident concluding chapter 17, is full of suggestive teaching. It is the temple tribute that is in mind, about sixty cents of our money, and Peter in saying "Yes," has already lost the significance of His confession of Christ. If He were "the Son of the living God," then was it not His glory that had appeared in the temple, and why should He pay tribute? But He surrenders His personal right, after He again makes it clear to His disciple. How His glory as Creator flashes forth in the miracle of the piece of money!

"At the same time" the disciples ask the question beginning the next chapter. Did our Lord's words about "the keys of the Kingdom of the heavens" in the preceding chapter awaken this inquiry? (Compare Luke 9:46.) How selfish and worldly was their ambition still! The Lord's answer (vv. 2-4), is what He gave to Nicodemus (John 3). It is a question whether in verse 5 the reference is to a "little child" in the literal or in the spiritual sense, but the words "believe in me" (v.

6), turn the scale in favor of the latter. Verses 7 and 9 are hard to apply in that connection, but they teach the necessity of removing all stumbling-blocks out of our way. Verse 10 brings us back to the little child in the literal sense. Some think the words mean that every such child has its guardian angel, some that every believer has such an angel. While others take the word "angel" in the sense of "spirit" (Acts 12:15), and interpret the passage to mean that if such little children, "who belong to the kingdom die, their disembodied spirits behold the Father's face in heaven,—in other words they are saved."

In the section now reached (vv. 15-20), we meet for the second and last time in this Gospel the word "Church," which has special interest because her executive power in the earth is spoken of. It is plain until we come to verse 18, which is to be understood not as limited to the apostles and their "successors" so-called, but as including the whole of the local church in any place gathered unto the name of the Lord Jesus. He sanctions in heaven what she thus binds or loosens on earth. What a promise that in verses 19 and 20! What mighty things has it accomplished, and it still holds good!

The law of forgiveness (vv. 21-35), is in answer to Peter's question, inspired by the preceding, probably. In that case, however, our Lord had been speaking about restoring a brother to the Church, while here it is a question of personal grievances, and the forgiveness must be unlimited (compare Luke 17:3, 4).

At chapter 19 we find Jesus in Judea again, His last visit there prior to His crucifixion. Had we this Gospel alone to consider it would appear as the first visit of Jesus after His baptism, but as a matter of fact there were at least two visits intervening, judging by John's record.

Once more His enemies are at His heels, this time on the divorce question (vv. 3-12). The Pharisees were divided about this, the school of Hillel holding that a man might put away his wife for almost any cause, and that of Shammai, only for adultery. Our Lord goes back of Moses to the beginning (vv. 4-6). Moses never commanded writings of divorcement, but allowed or suffered it (vv. 7, 8) in cases where there was suspicion of adultery (Num. 5). The actual sin was punishable by death. The Lord's command in the matter is plain and authoritative (v. 9). But the disciples think that under such circumstances it is better not to marry at all (v. 10), which leads Christ to say that some are unfitted for it by nature, some have been mutilated by wicked men, while some remain unmarried for the sake of the Kingdom (v. 12). All are not able wisely to remain unmarried, but where they are, it is not a man-enforced celibacy, but a divinely-bestowed gift. This seems to some to be the meaning of verse 11.

The incident of the little children (vv. 13-15) shows that the disciples had not caught the significance of the teaching of the previous chapter. But blessed be God, there is a place for children in the Kingdom. The parents in these cases must have been believers, setting an example to others to bring their offspring to Christ for His salvation and blessing.

The next incident brings before us a typical religious man of the world (vv. 16-26) through which we are taught that salvation is of God, and not dependent on the deeds of man. The Lord rebukes him for calling Him "good" (v. 17), because the young man was thinking of Him as a man merely, and "There is none righteous, no not one." He then meets him on his own ground. If he would do something to earn eternal life, there is but one thing to do; but this he is shown never to have done. If he really loves his neighbor as himself he would share what he had with his neighbor. The sequel shows how self-deceived he was (v. 22). "The eye of the needle" (v. 24) was a proverb among the Jews. After the gates of a city were closed at night, caravans could not enter.

There were narrow openings at the side large enough for the human traveler to pass through but not his beast of burden. This opening was called "the eye of a needle."

Out of this event grows the conclusion of this lesson down to 20:16. The self-seeking disciple again comes into view (v. 27), and also the condescension of our Lord Who does not rebuke but graciously instructs him (vv. 28, 29). The "regeneration" here means the renewal of the earth when the Kingdom is finally set up (Rom. 3:18-25).

"The Kingdom will be administered over Israel through the apostles according to the ancient theocratic judgeship (Judges 2:28)." But the promise holds something for all the faithful as well as the apostles (v. 29). The meaning of verse 30 is illuminated by the parable of the laborers in the next chapter which was uttered "to keep the disciples from a spirit of self-righteousness." God will give rewards in that day as may seem best to Him. They are not the legal outcome of our works even as saved sinners, but the expression of God's grace. We should be careful in the interpretation of parables not to seek a meaning or application of every detail, for in doing so we are as apt to teach error as truth.

Questions.

1. What distinction is made between the first and second announcements of Christ's death?

2. Paraphrase the story of the miracle of the tribute money.

3. How has the latter part of 18:10 been interpreted?

4. To whom do we understand the power of 18:18 to be granted?

5. Where is Jesus at the beginning of chapter 19, and thereafter?

6. What is the Lord's teaching about divorce?

7. What lesson may be learned from 19:13-15?

8. What is the main lesson

taught by the incident of the rich young ruler?

9. Explain the proverb "the eye of the needle."

10. What does "regeneration" mean, 19:28?

11. What is the main teaching of the laborers in the vineyard?

12. Of what are we to be careful in the interpretation of parables?

THE THIRD ANNOUNCEMENT OF HIS DEATH

CHAPTERS 20:17-22:14

With this third announcement our Lord has indicated the three classes of His foes, the leaders of His nation in the first announcement, one of the twelve in the second, and now the Roman Gentiles (vv. 17-19).

The ambitious request of James and John (vv. 20-28), is in keeping with the selfishness previously expressed by Peter. The immediate occasion for the request is found in our Lord's words which they had misunderstood (vv. 19-28). The gentleness of Jesus (v. 22) is as marked as in the other case. His "cup" stood for all the agony of the Cross, how could they drink it? Not the bodily agony merely, but that experienced in the withdrawal of His Father's face. They would indeed be partakers of His suffering in one sense (v. 23), not that from the side of God but from the side of man (Col. 1:24; Phil. 3:10; 1 Pet. 2:21), but their place in the Kingdom, when it should be set up, must be determined by the Father. Of course, the subjection He here expresses towards the Father, is not that of His divine nature, which was co-equal with the Father, but His human nature. It is as the glorified man at the head of the Kingdom He now speaks (1 Cor. 15:27, 28; Phil. 2:9-11). The indignation of the ten against the two was not because of the latter's presumption towards the Lord, but because of the advantage they were seeking over them. The ten, in other words, were as

selfish as the two; hence the rebuke and instruction following, for all.

The healing of the two blind men (vv. 29-34) recalls the instance of 9:27-31, but it is not the same. Mark 10:46 and Luke 18:35 mention but one man and the common explanation is that there were two miracles of the kind connected with this visit to Jericho, one as Christ entered and the other as He left the city. But some account for this seeming discrepancy in another way. For example, as son of David and heir to the throne, Christ was soon to be presented to Jerusalem, and ere this takes place He has the testimony of two witnesses that He is the Son of David, which was necessary according to the law. This they think, is the reason why two blind men are mentioned exclusively in Matthew's Gospel which is the Gospel of the Kingdom.

The entry into Jerusalem (21:1-11), which took place on the first day of the last week of our Lord's earthly life, is His formal offer of Himself to the nation as their King. This was necessary to His formal rejection by the nation, and is established by His fulfilment of Zechariah 9:9. This allusion to Zechariah's words would mark Him as an imposter or else their true Messiah. The leaders of the nation regard Him in the former light; and even the multitude, though they at first acclaimed Him as "the Son of David " (v. 9), in their cooler judgment settled on the simpler title of 5:11, and afterwards took up the cry "Crucify Him!"

This is the second time Jesus cleansed the temple (vv. 12-17), the first near the beginning of His ministry (John 2:13-16). It becomes a foreshadowing of His second coming to fulfill Malachi 3:3, the necessity for which appears in Daniel 9:27; Matthew 24:15, et seq.; 2 Thessalonians 3:4, 8. How different the scene in v. 14, type of that which shall follow also in that day when He comes again to Israel! The language of the chief priests and scribes (v. 15) accentuates the rejection of Him manifested all along. The 8th Psalm which Jesus quotes is Messianic, and His use of it is a further asseveration of His claim to be that Promised One. Bethany, the home of Martha, Mary and Lazarus, was His abiding place during this week (v. 17).

The barren fig-tree (vv. 18-22) stands for the nation of Israel. On seeing the leaves of profession, He had a right to expect fruit, but there was nothing on it for Him, though He hungered. Comparing Zech. 4:7, a mountain is used in Scripture to represent a large or difficult undertaking, in which sense probably it is here used (v. 21). If Israel at this time was a mountain in the way of the gospel, it could be removed, as it was removed, by faith, and cast into the sea of the nations (Gaebelein).

The climax is nearing. As the nation had rejected the Messiah, so now the Messiah rejects the nation in the parables following: The Two Sons (vv. 28-32); The Householder (vv. 33-46); The Marriage of the King's Son (22:1-14). The immediate occasion for them is in verses 23-27—another attack of the leaders. They were incensed at His action in the Temple on the previous day and the words He then spake against them. Behold the divine wisdom with which He now deals with them, silencing them utterly!

The first of these parables is interpreted by our Lord Himself. The second requires no extended comment. God is the householder, Israel the vineyard, the leaders of the nation the husbandmen, the servants the holy prophets, the son of Christ Himself. The chief priests and the Pharisees are condemned out of their own mouths (v. 41). The next verse is a quotation from Psalm 118, which is Messianic. Christ as the "Stone" is revealed in a threefold way. To Israel He was a stumbling-block and rock of offense, for He came to them not as a monarch but in the form of a servant (Isa. 8:14, 15; Rom. 9:32, 33; 1 Cor. 1:23; 1 Pet. 2:8). To the Church He is the foundation-stone and head of the corner (1 Cor. 3:11; Eph. 2:20-22; 1 Pet. 2:4, 5). To the Gentile world-powers, He is the smiting stone of destruction (Dan. 2:3, 4)—Scofield. The Kingdom would not be given to that generation which had rejected Christ, but to the faithful remnant in the latter days.

The third parable foreshadows more than the other two, as it brings in the Gentiles (vv. 8-10). Verse 3 applies to the offer of the Kingdom made to Israel up to the time of Christ's death and resurrection. Verse 4 perhaps applies to the renewed offer down to the time of its further rejection in the martyrdom of Stephen (Acts 7). Read especially Acts 3:19-21. Verse 7 applies to the destruction of Jerusalem by Titus A. D. 70. Verses 8 to 10 apply to the preaching of the gospel to the Gentiles beginning with Peter at Acts 10. The man without the wedding garment (vv. 11-12) may mean the mere professor in Christendom. "Many are called," and make this outward profession, but "few are chosen," in the sense that they really accept and put on Christ as their righteousness.

Questions.

1. How did Christ distinguish His foes in connection with the announcement of His death and resurrection?

2. What spirit was evinced by James and John?

3. What dispensational meaning is attachable to the healing of the two blind men?

4. To what was Christ's entry into Jerusalem equivalent?

5. What does His cleansing of the Temple foreshadow?

6. Of what is the barren fig-tree a type?

7. How would you interpret 21:21?

8. Name the three parables in which our Lord rejects the nation.

9. Name the three ways in which Christ is revealed as the "Stone."

10. Apply the parable of the marriage feast dispensationally.

WOE AND FAREWELL

CHAPTER 22:15-23

Another effort to "entangle
him in his talk," and a new
enemy, the Herodians. They were
the politicians of the time, a low
class of Jews who, for selfish reasons, favored the Roman rule represented by Herod. With flattery He is approached (v. 16),
but had He answered their question negatively (v. 17), the Herodians would have accused Him
before the Roman judges, while
affirmatively, the Pharisees could
have done so before the Sanhedrin. No true Messiah, they
would have said, would teach
subjection to the Gentiles. But as
before, He silences them, for had
they rendered unto God the
things that were God's, they
would not now be obliged to render anything unto Caesar (vv. 18-
22). The Sadducees were the ra-
tionalists who denied the future
life and all connected with it;
hence their question, although
founded on Deut. 25:5, et seq.,
was combined of ignorance and
sarcasm. There will be a resurrection but it does not imply marriage (v. 30). The proof of resurrection He employs (v. 32), is a
proof also of the inspiration of
the words of the original Scriptures. In the quotation from Exodus 3:14, the present tense of "to
be" is used, and on that He bases
His argument for the future life.
The Pharisees fare no better with
their inquiry than the other two
(vv. 32-40), and then our Lord
asks them a question which ends
attempts of this kind on their
part. He quotes Psalm 110 which
at once proves Him the Messiah
and the very God (vv. 41-46).

Now the declaration of the
judgments on His enemies. The
Scribes and Pharisees were the
national leaders of the Jews, in
which sense they sat in Moses'
seat, and it became necessary to
obey them. But to observe their
instruction was one thing, and to
follow their example was another
(v. 3). As to the first, compare
Rom. 13:1-7, and 1 Peter 2:13-
17. "Phylacteries," meaning

things to observe, get their name
from Exodus 13: 9-16, Deuteronomy 6:9 and the following
verses. A phylactery is a strip of
leather attached to a small box
containing a parchment copy of
Deuteronomy 6: 4-8. This strip
is used to fasten the box around
the head so that it rests in the
middle of the forehead. Another
is wound around the left arm.
This literal interpretation of the
Scriptures was for show (5-7).
And they not only loved show,
but to be addressed by high-
sounding names, which must not
be true of disciples of Christ (vv.
8-12).

The eight woes of the next
chapter all pronounced against
various forms of hypocrisy, and
with which our Lord closed His
public ministry, suggest the Beatitudes with which He opened that
ministry. We cannot do more
than touch upon a few of the distinctions He makes. The first,
that of hindering (v. 13), comes
home to preachers and teachers
of Christianity who are not regenerated and taught of the Spirit
in the Word. The second and
third, verses 14 and 15, need no
explanation. The fourth, verses
16-22, displays the ignorance of
the mere ritualist. The fifth and
sixth describe the formalist (vv.
23-26). The seventh is a figurative description of their religious
character (v. 28), and the eighth
no less so (vv. 29-31). They
made a show of zeal in adorning
the burial places of the prophets
their fathers had slain, and yet
they were exhibiting the same
spirit. Did our Lord ever utter a
severer word than verse 33? And
in that connection note the personal pronoun of authority—
"Behold, I send unto you prophets." All He there predicts was
soon fulfilled in the Acts.

Now the pathetic farewell (vv.
37-39). Their house is left unto
them desolate. It is Tuesday of
that last week, and as He leaves
the temple and the city it is not to
return until Thursday, the day of
the last passover and the betrayal. And yet His final word is one
of hope. Israel would see Him
again, i. e., at His second coming,

and the faithful remnant would exclaim "Blessed is He that cometh in the name of the Lord."

Questions.

1. Who were the Herodians?

2. What is the spiritual significance of the words, "Render unto Caesar," etc.?

3. How does the quotation from Psalm 110 prove the deity of Christ?

4. Explain the reference to the phylacteries.

5. How many "woes" are there, and against what feature of iniquity are they directed?

6. Quote our Lord's final word of hope.

THINGS TO COME

CHAPTERS 24-25

The present lesson connects itself with the last without a break. The disciples were mystified by what our Lord said about the "house," i. e., the temple, being left "desolate" (23:38), which explains why they called His attention to its grandeur and strength (24:1). His further observation (v. 2) deepened their wonder, hence their improvement of the opportunity on the Mount of Olives for the three questions of verse three.

The first was answered by the destruction of the temple under Titus, A. D. 70. But although Christ replies to this question as He does the other two, yet that reply is recorded only in Luke 21:20-24. The replies to the others follow.

Verses 4-14 are capable of a two-fold application. In the first place, they give in outline panoramic form the features of the present age during the absence of the King, and then in a more particular way describe the end of the age; for, as the Scofield Bible says, "all that has characterized the age throughout all these centuries gathers into awful intensity at the end."

What are these features? False Christs, wars, famines, pestilences, earthquakes, persecutions, apostasy, false teaching, abound-ing iniquity, and spiritual declension—just what Christendom in these twenty centuries records as fulfilling the words. Compare Daniel 9:24-27, and 2 Timothy 3.

To be specific as to verse 14, it refers to the proclamation of the good news that the Kingdom promised to Israel, and which both John the Baptist and Christ preached at the beginning, is again "at hand." This will be proclaimed at the end of the age, not by the Church, as we understand it, which shall have been caught up to meet the Lord in the air (1 Thess. 4:13-18), but by the Jewish remnant, the believing Israelites on the earth at that day (Isa. 1:9; Rom. 11:5; Rev. 14:6, 7).

Verse 15 points to the crisis at the end. "The abomination of desolation" (Dan. 9:27), which is the image of "the man of sin" (2 Thess. 2:3-8), and the "Beast" (Rev. 13:4-7) will then be set up in the temple of restored Jerusalem, and the hour of the Great Tribulation will have come. From this on (vv. 15-28), our Lord gives the details of this period. The believing Jews in Jerusalem at that time are warned to flee (vv. 16-20). A renewed warning is given as to false Christians (vv. 21-26). The sudden smiting of the Gentile world-powers is announced (vv. 27, 28 compared with Dan. 2:34). The glorious appearing of the Lord visible to the nations, together with the regathering of Israel as a nation are set before us next (vv. 29-31). The sign of the fig-tree is given (vv. 32, 33), and then "warnings applicable to this age over which these events are ever impending" (vv. 34-51); and yet, as stated above, especially applicable to the end period itself. The first verse of this last-named section (v. 34) requires special notice. The primary definition of the Greek word for "generation" is race, family, or stock, in which sense the word is evidently used by our Lord. The race of Jews (Israel) "shall not pass till all these things be fulfilled"—a promise to the truth of which the centuries bear witness.

Chapter 25 continues the discourse. The phrase "the Kingdom of heaven" or "the Kingdom of the heavens" recalls the parables of chapter 13, and applies to the same thing, viz. the sphere of professing Christianity, i. e., Christendom during the absence of the King. At the first, that is, after our Lord's ascension, the attitude of the disciples was that of going "forth to meet the bridegroom" (v. 1). In other words they were "waiting for the coming of our Lord" (1 Cor. 1:7). But "the bridegroom tarried," and "they all slumbered and slept" (v. 5). The "midnight" is coming however, when the cry is made "Behold the bridegroom!" The wise virgins are the true believers, "the oil in their vessels" (v. 4) symbolizing the indwelling of the Holy Spirit (Romans 8:9). The foolish virgins are the mere professors, as is evident from "I know you not" (v. 12). As this parable sets before us that testing of the Christian profession which the coming of the Lord will reveal, so the parable that follows sets before us the testing of service. The talents are the gifts God has bestowed on His servants to use for His glory (1 Cor. 12). Exercise of any gift will increase it through the Holy Spirit; and faithful service, though it be in the use of any one gift, will bring approval. The difficulty in the parable is the faithless servant, who must not be regarded as a true believer, but a mere professor as in the preceding case. A true believer would never call Christ a hard master.

The closing verses (vv. 31-46) do not contain a parable so far as the record goes, but for all we know a description of fact. It is a judgment scene, but not the last judgment (Rev. 20:11-15). The object of the judgment is the Gentile nations of the earth. The time is after the Church has been caught up to meet the Lord in the air, and when He has come for the gathering of the remnant of Israel at the end of this age. The place doubtless is Palestine. There is no resurrection here, no books opened, and nothing said

about the dead, all of which is in contrast to the last judgment. Moreover, three classes are present here, sheep, goats, and "My brethren," the test being not the possession of eternal life, but the treatment accorded by the nations to these "brethren." The latter are the "Jewish remnant who will have preached the gospel of the Kingdom to all nations during the tribulation." Examine Zechariah 14:1-5 and Joel 3 for light upon this judgment scene.

Questions.

1. How many, and what, were the questions asked by the disciples on the Mount of Olives?

2. What was the answer to the first question, and where is it recorded?

3. What two-fold application may be given to 24:1-14?

4. What features will mark this age increasing in intensity at the end?

5. How would you interpret verse 14 particularly?

6. What Old and New Testament passages are paralleled by verse 15?

7. What does "generation" mean, verse 34?

8. Who are meant by the wise and foolish virgins of chapter 25?

9. What is the distinction between the "testings" of the two parables in this chapter?

10. What is the difficulty in the second parable, and how would you explain it?

11. How would you distinguish between the judgment at the close of this chapter, and the last judgment in Revelation?

12. Who are meant by "My brethren"?

BETRAYAL AND ARREST

CHAPTER 26

This solemn chapter divides itself thus:

1. The counsel to kill Jesus, vv. 1-5,

2. The anointing of Jesus, vv. 6-13,

3. The bargain of betrayal, vv. 14-16,

4. The last Passover, vv. 17-25,

5. The institution of the Lord's Supper, vv. 26-29,

6. The prediction of Peter's denial, vv. 30-35,

7. The agony in the garden, vv. 36-46,

8. The betrayal and arrest, vv. 45-56,

9. The hearing before Caiaphas, vv. 57-68,

10. The denial of Peter, vv. 69-75.

As to the first point (vv. 1-5), note that Christ predicts His death for the fourth time, adding the manner of it, and the time it would take place. What a calm walking up into death it was! But see how Satan, through the human conspirators, would hinder, if he could, the offering of the sacrifice at the appointed time! (v. 5).

As to the second point (vv. 6-13), we learn from John 12:1-8, that the woman was Mary, the sister of Lazarus, leading to the presumption that Simon the leper was her father, and possibly one whom Jesus had healed. The circumstance that one Gospel speaks of her as anointing Jesus' head and the other His feet, shows that the "ordinary anointing of hospitality and honor" included both. Matthew mentions the first as in harmony with the general purpose of his Gospel to reveal Jesus as the king. John reveals Him as the Son of God, in which the attitude of Mary at His feet is in harmony. Verse 12 is significant, indicating that Mary understood more of Christ's death than the disciples; in which connection note that she is "not among the women who went to the sepulchre to embalm His body." The cost of the ointment (John 12:5), equals about $50, which as values are to-day compared with those times would mean six times as much, or $300. A laborer's daily wage at that time being a penny, one understands the "indignation" of the disciples (v. 8). But how blessed to obtain our Lord's interpretation of the act (v. 10)! Let us bring our best to Him no matter what men say. To Him let it be brought. There is much charity and philanthropy in our day in which the glory of the Lord Jesus Christ is not considered.

As to the third point (vv. 14-16), compare Psalm 41:9; 69:25; 109:8; Zechariah 11:12, and observe from Luke 22:3, that Satan entered into Judas, and that the price for which he sold our Lord was that of a slave (Exodus 21:32).

Coming to the Passover (vv. 17-25), let it not be supposed that because of the different accounts in the four Gospels there is any conflict among them, even though we may not be perfectly able to harmonize them. For the Passover itself, and what it commemorated, we refer to Exodus 12.

The institution of the Lord's Supper which followed (vv. 26-29), marked the end of the Mosaic dispensation. The Passover had fulfilled its purpose as the paschal lamb to which it pointed, was to be slain the next day. Hence the inauguration of a new feast embodying the fundamental truth of Christianity as that had embodied the fundamental truth of Judaism (Weston). And the fundamental truth of Christianity is "remission of sins." "Remission" means to send off, or away, i. e., to separate the sin from the sinner. In this respect there is a difference between human and divine forgiveness. The first remits the penalty, which is all that it can do, while the second remits the sin. And the latter can do this, because with God, forgiveness always follows the execution of the penalty (see Lev. 4:35; Heb. 9:22). We are forgiven for Christ's sake, in the sense that Christ has borne the sins of the believer in His own body on the tree. What meaning must be wrapped up in verse 29, "new with you in my Father's kingdom!" Who can fathom its depths?

Concerning the agony in the garden (vv. 36-46), we must not suppose the "cup" was the fear of mere physical pain or death, in which event Christ would have been lacking in the courage and faith of many an ordinary martyr. Moreover, He need not have died at all had He desired otherwise (John 10:17, 18). The "cup" must have been the making of His soul an offering for sin (Isa. 53:10), including the withdrawal of His Father's face on account of that sin (Psalm 22:1)—not His own sin of course, but that of the whole world (1 John 2:2). The value of His petition is seen in the testimony it bears to the necessity of the atonement, showing that without the shedding of His blood there could have been no remission.

Other events in this chapter we pass over to speak of them in the next lesson, pausing a moment to allude to the seeming discrepancy in the account of the denial of Peter (vv. 69-75). Comparing the story here with the corresponding places Mark 14, Luke 22, and John 18, it is to be kept in mind, that an excited crowd had gathered and that Peter was questioned in two places; with the servants (Matthew 26:58), where the first charge was made (v. 69); and in the porch where a great number of people would be gathered, and where the second and third charges were made by another damsel and by the crowd.

Questions.

1. Name the ten great facts of this lesson.

2. How would you harmonize the two accounts of the anointing of Jesus by Mary?

3. Name the events on the night of the Passover.

4. What is the origin of the Passover and what did it commemorate?

5. How does "remission" differ from "forgiveness," and why?

6. How should we interpret the "cup" spoken of in Gethsemane?

TRIAL AND CRUCIFIXION

Chapter 27

This chapter opens with the delivery of Jesus to Pontius Pilate, the Roman governor (vv. 1, 2); then follows the account of

Judas' remorse (vv. 3-10); Jesus is now questioned by Pilate (vv. 11-14); Barabbas is released and Jesus is condemned (vv. 15-26); He is crowned with thorns and crucified (vv. 27-44); He dies (vv. 45, 46), and is buried (vv. 57-66).

The account of Judas' remorse (vv. 3-10) seems to contain two discrepancies. For example, verse 5 compared with Acts 1:18, the explanation of which is that he fell after the hanging. Verses 9 and 10 may allude to Jeremiah 18:1-4 and 19:1-3, but if so, the application is remote, since Zechariah 11:12, 13 fits the case more exactly. Perhaps this is a copyist's mistake, although there is another explanation. In the Jewish canon the books of the prophets began with Jeremiah, and sometimes his name was given to the whole section of the prophets just as we use David's name for any of the Psalms, or Solomon's for the Proverbs, though there were other authors in each case.

Note that Jesus' reply to Pilate, "Thou sayest" (v. 11) is equivalent to a declaration that He was what Pilate said, "The King of the Jews."

Note Pilate's testimony to the innocense of Jesus, and that according to Roman law He was condemned unjustly (v. 24.)

Note Jesus' consciousness to the end, as illustrated in his refusal to sip the stupefying drink (v. 34).

The inscription on the Cross is recorded differently by the evangelists, but this does not imply a contradiction or weaken the argument for the inspiration of their records. The inscription was in three different languages involving a different arrangement of the words in each case. Secondly, no one of the writers quotes the entire inscription. Thirdly, they all agree in emphasizing the one great fact that He was "the King of the Jews." Fourth, their narratives combined give the full inscription, as follows:

"This is Jesus, The King of the Jews"

"The King of the Jews"

"This the King of the Jews"

"Jesus of Nazareth, the King of the Jews."

It is consistent with the strictest view of the inspiration of the original autographs that the Holy Spirit may have had a purpose in causing the four different records to be written, and that the purpose was to bring out in relief the charge made against Jesus, as that charge was in itself the strongest testimony to His Messiahship and the fulfilment of the Word of God.

The words "yielded up the ghost" (v. 50) should not be passed over. They mean "dismissed His spirit," and imply an act of His will. Christ did not die like other men who cannot help themselves, but because His work was done His life was laid down of His own volition. (Compare Mark 15:37; Luke 23:46; John 10:18; 19:30). This is an inferential testimony to the sacrificial character of His death.

The "veil of the temple" (v. 51) separated between the Holy Place and the Most Holy the latter that into which the High Priest alone entered once a year with the blood of atonement (Exod. 26:31; Lev. 16). It was a type of the human body of Christ, and its rending signified that "a new and living way" was opened for believers into God's presence (Compare 9:18; 10:19-22).

The resurrection referred to (vv. 52, 53) was one of the most remarkable testimonies to the deity of Christ and the divinity of His work on the Cross. Did the bodies of these saints return to their graves? It is usual to imagine so, but they may have ascended to heaven with Jesus when He "led captivity captive" (Eph. 4:8-10). See "Progress in the Life to Come," by the author.

Questions.

1. Name the seven chief events of this chapter.

2. Name the parallel Scriptures.

3. How would you harmonize verse 5 with Acts 1:18?

4. How would you explain the different reports of the writing on the Cross?

5. What evidence have we here to the voluntariness of Christ's death?

6. What was the significance of the rending of the veil?

7. Have you read Ephesians 4:8-10?

RESURRECTION

Chapter 28

Perhaps the most important comment we can make on this chapter will be the order of the ten events on the day of which it speaks. (1) The three women, Mary Magdalene; Mary, the mother of James; and Salome, start for the sepulcher, followed by other women bearing spices. (2) These find the stone rolled away and Mary Magdalene goes to tell the disciples (Luke 23:55-24:9; John 20:1, 2). (3) Mary, the mother of James, draws near the tomb and discovers the angel (Matthew 28:2). (4) She returns to meet the other women bearing the spices. (5) Peter and John arrive, look in and go away. (6) Mary Magdalene returns, sees the two angels and Jesus (John 20:11-18). (7) She goes to tell the disciples. (8) Mary, the mother of James, returns with the other women, all of whom see the two angels (Luke 24:4, 5; Mark 15:15). (9) They receive the angel's message. (10) While seeking the disciples are met by Jesus (Matthew 28:8;10).

Another comment of interest is the order of the appearances of Jesus on this day. (1) To Mary Magdalene (John 20:14-18); (2) To the women returning from the tomb with the angel's message (Matthew 28:8-10); (3) To Peter (Luke 24:34; 1 Cor. 15:5); (4) To the two on the way to Emmaus (Luke 24:13-31); (5) To the apostles in the absence of Thomas (Luke 24:36-43; John 20:19-24).

In dividing the chapter we have (1) The narrative of the resurrection with the appearance of

Jesus to the women (vv. 1-10); (2) The false invention of the Jews (v. 11-15); (3) The gathering in Galilee (vv. 16-20).

We can only touch upon the most important things, one of which is Christ's reference to His disciples as His "brethren" (v. 10). For the first time does he use that word in such connection, showing that until His death and resurrection on their behalf the relationship had not become possible. (Compare Ps. 22:22 and Heb. 2:11, 12).

Another important thing is verse 13, "Say ye, His disciples came by night, and stole Him away while we slept." We give excerpts from Gaebelein on this verse: "The watch recover from their fright, and some hasten to the city. Surely something happened or why should they leave their post to make a report? Then it is strange they went to the priests first and not the Roman governor. This was an irregular proceeding, from which we conclude that what they had to report was of greater importance for the priests than Pilate. Who knows but these priests had instructed the guard that if He should come forth they were to come to them first of all? Their report was a witness of the resurrection and that the tomb was empty.

"The Sanhedrin was hastily summoned to receive the report in an official way. The straightforward statement, as men of military training are apt to report, made doubt about veracity impossible. To impeach them would have been insane. But what would happen if this truth got out among the people?

"The resurrection must be denied which could only be by inventing a lie. The only possible lie was that His disciples stole the body. The story is incredible. It is easier to believe He arose from the dead than to believe what the Jews invented about His resurrection. The disciples had forgotten about the resurrection promised and they were a scattered, poor, timid lot of people. But even if they had been anxious to

steal the body, how could they have done it? Here was the company of armed men. Then there was the sealed, heavy stone.

"But the ridiculous side of the lie came out with the report the soldiers were to circulate. The disciples came and stole the body, while they were sleeping! It is incredible that all these men had fallen asleep at the same time, and so fast asleep that the commotion of rolling away the stone and the carrying away of the dead did not disturb them. Furthermore, sleeping at a post meant death for the Roman soldier. One might have nodded and risked his life, but that all slept is an impossibility. But the report is foolish; they were asleep, and while asleep witnessed how the disciples stole the body of Jesus! It was a miserable lie, and is continued to the present day."

We might mention here the testimony of Josephus, who says in his antiquities: "He appeared to them alive on the third day, as the divine prophets had foretold these and ten thousand other wonderful things concerning Him."

A third matter of importance is the "Great Commission" as it is called (vv. 19, 20). Note the word "Name" as indicative of the Trinity. It is not names but "Name." "Father, Son and Holy Spirit is the final name of the one true God. * * *The conjunction in one name of the three affirms equality and oneness of substance." Note the peculiarity of the terms. This is the Kingdom commission, as another expresses it, not the Christian commission. The latter is in Luke, distinctively the Gentile Gospel, but not here, which is distinctively the Jewish Gospel. And this is all the more remarkable because in Luke, the disciples are commanded to go to the Jews (24:47), while here they are commanded to go to "all nations." It points to the close of the age when the commission will be carried out by the faithful remnant of the Jews so often spoken about. It has not yet been carried out. The story of the Acts is not its fulfilment. Its accomplishment has been interrupted, but will be taken up before the Lord comes to deliver Israel at the last.

Questions.

1. Repeat the order of the events on the day of resurrection.

2. Do the same with reference to the appearances of Jesus.

3. Divide the chapter into three parts.

4. How would you answer the argument that the disciples stole the body of Jesus?

5. What is the significance of the word "Name" in the "Great Commission"?

6. How do you distinguish the "Commission" in Matthew from that in Luke?

MARK

INTRODUCTORY

As Matthew wrote for the Jew, so Mark wrote for the Gentile. In illustration of this we find that with a single exception at the beginning of his Gospel, Mark practically omits all reference to the Old Testament prophets. This shows that he is addressing a people to whom such references were not necessary as in the other case, even if they would have been intelligible. In other words, the Gentiles knew nothing of the sacred Scriptures, and were not expecting the Messiah of whom they spake. As carrying the thought further, Mark omits the genealogical table of Matthew, since it is not necessary for him to prove to Gentiles that Jesus descended from Abraham through David. More careful examination shows that all the omissions in Mark's Gospel are of an especially Jewish character. It will be seen too, that Mark explains Jewish words and customs which would be left unnoticed if he were addressing Jews (5:41; 7:1-4, etc.).

There were two great Gentile peoples of that day, the Romans and the Greeks, and Mark is addressing the first-named. The Romans represented the idea of active power in the world, and their ideal was military glory. They were the people who did things. Their highest conception of power and authority was themselves, i. e., the Roman state, which they worshipped in the person of its emperor. Their spiritual need as a people grew out of this fact, for they were failing to attain their ideal in the state. With all their power and authority, injustice, cruelty and suffering still prevailed, and would continue to do so.

Mark's Gospel fits into this condition of things. It sets forth Jesus as the active Servant of Jehovah. It is marked by energy, power, movement, particularly attractive to the Romans. It is the briefest Gospel, containing but sixteen chapters in comparison with the twenty-eight in Matthew, showing it to be intended for a people of action rather than meditation. The discourses of Jesus are omitted, rather than His deeds, as for example, the Sermon on the Mount, the charge to the disciples, the message on His second coming. And then, too, the things which Mark records as distinguished from Matthew, are those calculated to arouse the attention of men of affairs and action. In this connection note the frequent employment of the words "straightway" and "immediately," which are the same word in the original, and occur not less than forty times.

Speaking of Jesus as the Servant of Jehovah, it is to be remembered that he was so announced by the Old Testament prophets. (See Isa. 42:1; 43:10; 49:6, and elsewhere. Also Zech. 3:8, Mark 10:45; Phil. 2:7, etc.). It is not our idea to follow this thought closely in commenting on the Gospel, but it may be interesting to give the following outline of it from that point of view, in Gaebelein's Analysis of Mark:

Part 1. The Servant; Who He is and How He came. 1:1-13.

Part 2. The Servant's Work; not to be Ministered unto, but to Minister. 1:14-10:52.

Part 3. The Servant in Jerusalem. Presented as King and Rejected. Chapters 11-13.

Part 4. The Servant giving His life as Ransom for Many. Chapters 14-15:47.

Part 5. The Servant Highly Exalted. Risen and Ascended; His Commission to His Servants. Chapter 16.

Questions.

1. Give four reasons for believing that Mark wrote for the Gentiles.

2. Describe the Romans and their spiritual need.

3. Give three reasons for believing that Mark wrote for the Romans.

4. From what point of view does Mark present Jesus?

5. Give Gaebelein's outline of Mark.

BEGINNING OF CHRIST'S MINISTRY

CHAPTERS 1:1-2:12

Study this lesson in comparison with Matthew to discover what Mark omits and what, if anything, he adds; and then consider the same in its bearing on the object or purpose of the gospel as described in the "Introductory" lesson.

The following analysis will aid:

Introduction, 1:1.

Testimony of John the Baptist, 1:2-8.

Testimony of God the Father, 1:9-11.

Victory in the Wilderness, 1:12, 13.

Call of the Disciples, 1:14-20.

Works of Power, 1:21-2:12.

The introduction is without a parallel in the other Gospels. Its abruptness is almost startling, but the chief feature of it is its testimony to Christ's deity. The Servant of Jehovah is at the same time "the mighty God" (See Isa. 9:6).

John's testimony is paralleled in Matthew 3:1-11, but here it is much briefer (See the last lesson). Compare the intervening chapters of Matthew and observe in detail what Mark has omitted —the genealogy, the Virgin birth, the visit of the wise men, the sojourn in Egypt, the settlement in Nazareth. None of these important events evidently falls in with the purpose of this Gospel. The Romans will be attracted by activity and strength, and hence the writer begins at once at the ministry of Christ.

God's testimony to His Son is paralleled in Matthew 3:13-17. Note here the first use of "straightway," as referred to in "Introductory," and that Mark says —Jesus "saw the heavens opened." Among minor points Mark's Gospel is notable for descriptive details of this kind.

The wilderness victory is found in Matthew 4:1-11, and the student will be impressed with its succinctness here. Compare "driveth" with "led" in Matthew, and note the bearing on the supposed objective of this Gospel. The different temptations are omitted, but reference is made to "wild beasts," which is also characteristic.

For what is placed here under the call of the disciples, see Matthew 4:12-22 and the comments there.

The works of power are paralleled in part in Matthew 8 and 9. Note another descriptive touch in Mark's reference to the healing of Peter's wife's mother, "He took her by the hand and lifted her up" (1:31). Also his reference to Christ's early rising to pray (v. 35), and His being "moved with compassion" in the case of the leper (v. 41). He alone speaks of the "four" men who bore the one sick of the palsy (2:3).

Questions.

1. Did you read again the chapters in Matthew leading up to the events of this lesson in Mark?

2. What strikes you as peculiar in verse 1?

3. Among minor points for what is Mark's Gospel noted?

4. What four illustrations of this are found in the last division of this lesson?

5. Have you examined a map in connection with this lesson?

FROM THE CALL OF LEVI TO THE TEACHING BY THE SEASIDE

CHAPTERS 2:13-3:35

The events are:

The call of Levi, 2:13-20.

Parables of the cloth and the bottles, 2:21-22.

In the cornfields on the Sabbath, 2:23-28.

Healing the withered hand, 3:1-5.

Healing the multitudes, 3:6-12.

Choosing the twelve, 3:13-21.

The unpardonable sin, 3:22-30.

New relationship, 3:31-35.

We will not in every case name the parallel passage in Matthew, which can be learned by the marginal references in one's Bible. It is assumed that every reader or student has a Bible of this character which he consults. He will look for the comment desired under our treatment of Matthew in that place, while in Mark we will limit ourselves to what is peculiar to that writer.

The "Levi" of 2:13 is identical with Matthew. He took toll, or collected the taxes for the Roman government, which made him an object of hatred to his own people and one who was despised as an apostate. Mark mentions the fact omitted by Matthew, that the feast of verse 15 was in Levi's house.

In the incident of the withered hand also, there is an addition not found elsewhere, indicating that Mark was a close observer of his Master's actions and interpreter of His feelings (3:5).

The choosing of the twelve (3:13-21) has quite a different context in Mark from Matthew. Christ is on the mountain, but the Sermon on the Mount is not given. Notice, too, that the surnames of James and John are found here only (v. 17). And do not pass over verse 21, which is peculiar to Mark. "Friends" there means "kinsmen."

A very important addition is that under the head of the unpardonable sin (v. 29). "Danger of eternal damnation" is rendered in the Revised Version "guilty of an eternal sin," which teaches us the awful nature of ascribing the work of the Holy Spirit to Satan, and also the certainty of eternal punishment. If there is such a thing as eternal sin, there must be eternal punishment to accompany it.

Questions.

1. What are the leading incidents of this lesson?

2. Who was Levi?

3. What is characteristic of Mark as a reporter?

4. Name the things peculiar to Mark's record.

5. What two great doctrinal truths are here emphasized?

PARABLES AND MIRACLES

Chapters 4, 5

This lesson contains the parables of the sower, the candle, the seed growing secretly and the mustard seed (4:1-34); and the miracles of the stilling of the storm, the healing of the Gadarene and the woman with the issue of blood, and the raising of Jairus' daughter (4:35-5; 43).

The parables of the sower (4:1-20) and the mustard seed (30-34) are the only two out of the seven in Matthew 13 which Mark records. The whole of the seven taught the mystery of the Kingdom in its present form which explains their presence in Matthew, the Gospel of the Kingdom; but why two of them are given in Mark, and only two, is not easy to determine. Keeping in mind, however, that Mark presents Jesus as the Servant of Jehovah, it may be because these two miracles relate to His work of ministry. Mark adds an interesting sentence to the parable of the sower (4:13) which indicates that it is fundamental in its character and teaching, and that until it is understood, the others cannot be.

While the parable of the candle (4:21-25) is in Matthew yet it is found there in another setting. In the present instance, taken with that of the sower, it seems to teach that the word of truth sown in the heart is not only to give life and yield fruit, but to shine forth in testimony. The "bushel" stands for the cares and material things of life, and the "bed" for ease and comfort. We should be careful that our testimony be not hindered either in the one way or the other.

The parable of the seed growing secretly (Chaps. 26-29) is peculiar to Mark, and teaches that the spiritual processes of the Word of God are mysterious in human life, and will only be known by the matured fruit at the harvest day.

In the story of the stilling of the storm (4:35-41) we have another characteristic touch of Mark (v. 36).

He also describes the condition of the Gadarene with the greatest fulness (5:1-20), and alone gives verse 26 in the story of the woman with the issue of blood.

Questions.

1. Name the events in this lesson in their order.

2. Why, presumably, are but two out of the seven parables of Matthew 13 found in Mark?

3. Can you quote and explain the sentence added by Mark to the parable of the sower?

4. What does the parable of the candle teach?

5. Explain the figures of speech in that parable.

6. What is taught by the parable of the seed growing secretly?

7. What are the characteristic touches of Mark in 4:36 and 5:36?

8. What descriptions of the demoniac are peculiar to Mark?

EXPANSION AND OPPOSITION

CHAPTERS 6, 7

These chapters deal with Jesus' visit to Nazareth (6:1-6); the commission of the twelve (7-13); the martyrdom of John the Baptist (14-29); the report of the twelve (30, 31); the feeding of the five thousand (32-44); Jesus walking on the sea (45-52); healing at Gennesaret (53-56); opposition of the Pharisees (7:1-23); dealing with the Syrophoenician woman (24-30) and recovering the deaf and dumb man (31-37).

Read Matthew 13:53-58 in comparison with Mark's story of Jesus' visit to Nazareth, and discover what is peculiar to the latter in verses 3-6. In the same way compare Matthew 15:13, with verse 31 of this lesson for a statement only given by Mark. Another calls attention to the fact that our Lord does not say anything about the success of the disciples when they make their report to Him in this instance; in which silence on His part we find a necessary warning against all self-exaltation. It is of His power and grace that we are able to do anything with success or acceptance in His sight.

What notable feature of the walking upon the sea does Mark omit as compared with Matthew?

We considered the opposition of the Pharisees (7:1-23) in our comments on Matthew, but note here in detail the circumstantial evidence that Mark was writing for a Gentile people who were in consequence unfamiliar with Jewish customs 1-4).

In the case of the Syrophoenician woman note the comment of Mark (24), and the fuller description (25, 26, 30). What he omits is also significant, the appeal to Jesus as "Son of David," See the comment on Matthew 15:21-28.

The story of the healing of the deaf and dumb man is peculiar to Mark.

Questions.

1. Name the different events of these chapters.

2. What is peculiar to Mark in the story of Jesus' visit to Nazareth?

3. What statement is peculiar to Mark with reference to the report of the twelve?

4. What does the silence of Christ teach us in this instance?

5. Have you reviewed our comments in Matthew on the story of the Syrophoenician woman?

REACHING A CRISIS

CHAPTERS 8, 9

The four thousand fed (8:1-9); the leaven of the Pharisees

(10-21); the blind man of Bethesda (22-26); Peter's confession (27-38); the crisis of the transfiguration (Chapter 9, 1-13); the lunatic healed (14-29); Christ's prediction of His death (30-32; ambition rebuked (33-37); sectarianism rebuked (38-41); future retribution (42-50)—these are the topics or events of the present lesson.

In the second of these events, observe a further illustration of Mark's power of observation and the minuteness of his record in particular cases—Jesus "sighed deeply in His spirit" (8:12).

The third is recorded only by Mark, and has an illuminating note attached to it in the Scofield Bible. It will be observed that the man was "led out of the town" (Bethsaida). This town, as appears from Matthew 9:21-24 had been abandoned to judgment, and Christ would neither heal nor permit further testimony to be borne there (v. 26 of the lesson). But while Bethsaida's probation as a community was ended, yet He would still show mercy to individuals. It suggests Rev. 3:20.

Mark, as usual, gives the briefest account of Peter's confession, and does not mention the Church. The mention of the latter is dispensational and is found in the dispensational Gospel of Matthew. Notice verse 33, "when He had turned about and looked on His disciples"—characteristic of Mark.

The warning about future retribution (9:42-50) peculiar to Mark, is one of the most solemn in the Bible. "Where their worm dieth not, and the fire is not quenched," can hardly yield other meaning than the eternal conscious punishment of those who die in their sins. How awful the thought! What a motive for earnestness in soul-winning!

"Every sacrifice shall be salted with salt," is an allusion to Leviticus 2:13. The salt represents the power of the Holy Spirit to keep us from all that tends to corruption. "Have salt in yourselves" really means to be filled with the Holy Spirit. God grant it to us.

Questions.

1. Name the topics or events of this lesson.

2. Name some illustrations of Mark's peculiar characteristics as a writer, found in this lesson.

3. What peculiarities do you find in the miracle at Bethsaida?

4. What is the doctrinal teaching in 9:44, 46, 48?

5. How would you interpret 9:49, 50?

NEARING THE END

CHAPTERS 10, 11

In these chapters we have (1) teaching about divorce (10:1-12); (2) blessing little children (vv. 13-16); (3) the story of the rich young man and its lessons (vv. 17-31); (4) Christ's second prediction of His death (vv. 32-34); (5) the ambitious request of James and John (vv. 35-45); (6) the healing of Bartimeus; (7) the formal entry into Jerusalem (11:1-11); (8) the cursing of the fig tree (vv. 12-14); (9) the cleansing of the temple (vv. 15-21); (10) teaching about prayer (vv. 22-26); (11) discussion with the rulers (vv. 27-33).

It will be worth while to compare the teaching about divorce with Matthew 19:1-9, for the points of difference between them. Both the evangelists record the same incident, but reading of the two together throws light upon it. This does not mean that one contradicts the other, but that under the guidance of the Holy Spirit one describes the event as he saw it, and the other does the same. Again, one lays emphasis on this feature of the dialog between Christ and the Pharisees, and the other on that.

But note Mark's particularities about the next event as compared with Matthew. Jesus "was much displeased," he says, "moved with indignation" (margin). Verse 15 is original with Mark, and so is the record that Jesus took the little children "up in His arms" and "blessed them." In the same way observe the details in the story of the rich young man. His running and kneeling. "Jesus beholding him, loved him." "Jesus looked round about." Also the astonishment of the disciples and Jesus' explanation (v. 24).

The second prediction of Christ's death has similar features. Mark says "they were amazed," doubtless at His calmness in walking into the face of death, when even "they were afraid." "He took again the twelve." "And shall spit upon Him." Mark alone mentions this in Christ's prophecy.

There is no contradiction between Mark 10:35 and Matthew 20:20, for if their mother spake for them it were really James and John who were speaking. All the disciples recognized this, for it was the sons they rebuked and not the mother.

The healing of Bartimeus as we noted in Matthew, stands at the beginning of the end of Christ's earthly life, and is the prelude to the great events following in Jerusalem. It holds the same place in the three Gospels. The apparent contradiction as to whether one or two men were healed, is referred to in our notes on Matthew. But note the details in Mark (vv. 49, 50, 52).

The entry into Jerusalem is equally graphic. "A colt tied, whereon never man sat." Note the details also in 11:5, 6 and 11.

We can not pursue these comparisons, but trust interest has been awakened to lead the reader to do so for himself.

Questions.

1. Give the details of these two chapters.

2. What is the most important difficulty you note in Christ's teaching on divorce as between Mark and Matthew?

3. Have you reviewed our notes on Matthew with reference to Bartimeus?

4. What are the details peculiar to Mark in 11:5, 6 and 11?

5. Have you pursued the comparisons throughout this chapter?

QUESTIONS AND ANSWERS

Chapters 12, 13

The parable of the householder (vv. 1-12); the question of tribute (vv. 13-17); the question about the resurrection (vv. 18-27); the question about the first commandment (vv. 28-34); the question about the son of David (35-40); and the incident of the widow's mite constitute the contents of chapter 12. Chapter 13 is the discourse of Christ about His second coming delivered to the disciples on the Mount of Olives, also in response to questions.

It will be recalled from our study of Matthew that the parable of the householder found in that Gospel (21:33-46), was one of the three in which Christ formally rejected His nation, after the latter, by its rulers had definitely rejected Him. It will be seen by comparison that Mark, as is His wont, passes on with celerity, omitting those features of the story which were not necessary for his purpose as in the other Gospel.

With the question of tribute, begins that series of special temptations of Jesus devised by His enemies toward the last to entrap Him in His speech. The Pharisees and Herodians come first (see Matt. 22:15-22.) The Sadducees next (Matt. 22:23-33). The scribe, representing the lawyers next (Matt. 22:34-40), and finally Christ silences them all by His question concerning Himself (22:41-46). We have included in this last section the few verses in which Mark refers to the discourse against the scribes and Pharisees, which in Matthew occupies the whole of chapter 23 (the "Woes"). And yet brief as Mark is, his abridgment contains "the chief characteristics of the corrupt leaders of the nation," which are religious vanity, hypocrisy and greed.

The incident of the widow's mite is not found in Matthew, but is in Luke (21:1-4). How appropriately it follows Christ's denunciation of the Pharisees who "devour widow's houses" (v. 40). Note the detailed description here. Where had Jesus located Himself? What was Jesus doing? Whom and what did He see? What is the value of "two mites"? What does Jesus now do? What does He say? What is the estimate of, or enconium on, the widow? Which gave the more, she, or the rich, and why?

In the occasion for the Olivet discourse, what interesting fact is given by Mark not mentioned by Matthew (13:3)? In treating of this discourse in Mark, Gaebelein says:

"Mark's report is the briefest, Matthew's the longest. Omitted in Mark are the parables, which have special reference to the Christian profession (Matt. 25) and the judgment of living nations (c. 25:31-46). These belong in Matthew, but would be out of keeping with the purpose of Mark. The service of our Lord, as we have seen, is in the foreground. The three characteristic discourses in Matthew nowhere else reported in full are: 1. The Sermon on the Mount, which is the proclamation of the King. 2. The parable discourse in Matthew 13, the mysteries of the Kingdom. 3. The Olivet discourse, Matthew 24-25, the future of the Kingdom. But why should there be anything at all in the Gospel of Mark about the future things, such as the end of the age, and His return in glory, if only the Servant is described? It will be seen that the predictions are in part at least in view of this *service*. He forewarned them as His servants of what was to come after His departure."

Questions.

1. Name the leading incidents of this lesson.

2. To what group of parables does that of the householder belong?

3. To what series of questions does that of the tribute belong?

4. What chapter of Matthew contains the woes against the Scribes and Pharisees.

5. What does Mark omit from the Olivet discourse?

THE BETRAYAL AND ARREST

CHAPTER 14

This chapter corresponds with the 26th of Matthew, and contains the plots of Jesus' enemies (vv. 1, 2); His anointing at Bethany (vv. 3-9); the bargain of Judas (vv. 10, 11); the last Passover and the Lord's Supper (vv. 12-25); Peter's denial predicted (vv. 26-31); the agony in the garden (vv. 32-42); the betrayal and arrest (vv. 43-52); the hearing before the high-priest (vv. 53-65); Peter's denial (vv. 66-72).

Mark's talent for details is seen in his giving a specific money value to the ointment which Mary used, 300 pence, while we shall never cease to be grateful to him under God, for quoting Christ's laconic commendation of her, "She hath done what she could" (vv. 3-9). How many sermons have these words preached, and what comfort have they brought to those whose limited ability has permitted only little ministries!

It is Mark who tells us that the Sanhedrin was "glad" at the chance to bargain with Judas for the life of Jesus (vv. 10, 11).

It is he who mentions the "two" disciples sent forth to make ready the Passover, and who indicates how the man was identified at whose house it was to be eaten. He also gives details of the conversation held with him (vv. 12-25).

Christ's prediction of Peter's denial (vv. 26-31) is made more graphic by the statement concerning the cock crowing "twice," which is referred to again at the time of its fulfillment.

In the Gethsemane crisis, according to Mark, Christ prays that "the hour" might pass from him (vv. 32-42).

And an interesting detail is that of the young man who at the betrayal fled away naked, and whom tradition identifies as Mark himself (vv. 43-52).

In the hearing before the high-priest, note that significant touch, Peter "warmed himself"; and that other about the witnesses agreeing not together (vv. 53-65).

Questions.

1. Give the facts of this chapter.

2. Indicate some of the interesting details it contains, peculiar to Mark.

3. How was the host of the Passover feast identified?

4. What item of Mark's personal history is supposed to be found in this chapter?

5. How does he indicate the injustice of Jesus' trial?

CRUCIFIED AND RISEN

CHAPTERS 15, 16

Jesus before Pilate (15:1-15); mocked by the soldiers (16:23); nailed to the cross (24-41); buried in the tomb (42-47); risen from the dead (16:1-18); ascended into heaven (19-20)— are the closing events in Mark's Gospel.

As in other instances, Mark's account of the trial before Pilate is the briefest while that of Matthew is the longest in the Gospels. The former, however, especially emphasizes the religious hatred of the people. He also describes more particularly the charge laid against Barabbas (15:7) who was released, though guilty and condemned; and this because the Lord Jesus took his place. "Christ was his substitute," says another, "and Barabbas when released might have looked up at Him on the Cross, and have said, 'He died for me, he paid my penalty',—a blessed illustration of the atonement."

Mark says, "they clothed him with purple" (17), while Matthew describes it as a "scarlet robe" (27-28) but as Lange explains, the scarlet military robe was meant to represent the imperial robe, and hence called in the symbolic sense purple.

Note how Mark dwells on the personality of Simon the Cyrenian (21). The reason he was drafted to bear the Cross was that Jesus' strength was exhaust-

ed and He could not Himself bear it. This seems implied in the word "bring" (22). They had to bring, in the sense that they had to bear, or carry, Jesus to Golgotha, they had to hold Him up on the road. As one says, what an appearance He must have presented after all the scourging and other indignities He received! How His face must have been marred by the blows, and how His sacred head must have bled from the cruel crown of thorns! It is Mark only who mentions that the wine (or vinegar) they gave Him was "mingled with myrrh," which was considered an anodyne to deaden pain. It was for this reason Jesus refused it. Mark says it was "the third hour" when they crucified Him, while John says the sixth (c. 19, 14); there is a difficulty here, but the latter alludes to the Roman method of computing time and the former the Hebrew.

Mark mentions the "boldness" of Joseph of Arimathea in begging the body from Pilate (43). "Boldness" in the face of the Sanhedrin to which he belonged, and at whose insistence it was that Jesus had been crucified. One must be a converted Jew in these days and experience his persecution and torture at the hands of his own people, to understand something of what this may have meant to Joseph (Compare Isa. 53:9).

Coming to the resurrection chapter, we again observe the brevity of Mark compared with Matthew. For the order of events on the resurrection day compare the comments on Matthew 28. Mark especially mentions Peter (7), which is the more noticeable because he also describes Peter's denial in the fullest way. The passage from verse 9 to the end of this chapter is not in the two most ancient manuscripts, the Sinaitic and Vatican, and others have it with partial omissions and variations, but it is quoted by some of the fathers of the second and third centuries. The whole church, practically, has accepted it as genuine from that period.

The "Great Commission" in

Mark (15:18) differs from Matthew. In the former the Kingdom is not in view, but "the Servant having given His life as a ransom, the good news is to go forth." Signs were to follow them that believe. These signs did not follow all even in the apostles' time, but they did follow some. And if they do not follow now, it is because there are other evidences more suitable for the later periods of Christianity. As a matter of fact, however, such signs do still follow the preaching of the gospel on foreign mission fields, and doubtless will be practically universal again as the end of the age draws near and the coming of the King.

Mark records the ascension as Matthew does not, and even penetrates the clouds and sees Christ in heaven at the right hand of God. But He sees Him working with His disciples even though He is in heaven (20), and refers to it in a word found nowhere else in the Gospels. How fitting thus the close of that Gospel intended for the active energetic Roman!

Questions.

1. Name the closing events in this Gospel.

2. What illustration of the atonement is found here?

3. Why was Simon drafted to bear Christ's Cross?

4. How do you harmonize the two accounts as to the hour of the crucifixion?

5. Can you quote Isa. 53:9?

6. What do you know about the closing verses of the Gospel?

7. What comment may be made on 16:17, 18?

8. What new thought about the life of our ascended Lord does Mark express?

LUKE

INTRODUCTORY

Luke, like Mark, wrote for the Gentiles, but for a different class than he. While Mark had the Romans in mind, the writers of the first three centuries testify that Luke wrote for the Greeks, and this is corroborated by the internal evidence of the book itself.

Characteristics of the Greeks.

We have seen that the Romans represented the idea of activity or power, but the Greeks that of reason and culture. While the Roman ideal was military glory, that of the Greek was wisdom and beauty. The Roman felt his mission to be that of government, but the Greek that of education. The Greek was seeking the perfect, the ideal man, and as illustrating this fact they made their gods in the likeness of men.

How Luke's Gospel Meets this Need.

The Gospel of Luke meets this need of the Greeks by presenting Jesus as the perfect, the ideal, or universal man. Dr. D. S. Gregory in his excellent book, "Why Four Gospels?" sums up the reasons for this opinion in the following way:

(1) Luke himself was a Greek, though a proselyte to the Jewish religion. He was moreover, a cultivated man as is indicated in the general style of his writing. And he was a travelling companion of Paul, the great apostle to the Gentiles, especially the Greeks.

(2) His gospel is the most orderly history of the sayings and doings of Jesus, and evidently prepared for a thoughtful and philosophic people.

(3) Speaking further of its style, it is remarkable for its poetry, song, eloquence and for the depth and sublimity of its thought. Differing from Mark it abounds in the discourses of Jesus, as though the people for whom it was intended were accustomed to think and meditate.

(4) This Gospel also omits the distinctively Jewish portions of the record found in the other Gospels, and also the distinctively Roman features such as the vivid pictures and the activity associated with Mark.

(5) Furthermore, it gives those incidents in the life of our Lord which more especially demonstrate his interest in the whole race. For example, the genealogy of Jesus is traced through Adam to God, and the sending out of the seventy is mentioned as well as the twelve, for the former were not limited in their work to Israel. Also a good deal of space is given to the ministry of Jesus among the Gentiles beyond the Jordan (9:51-18:30). The parable of the good Samaritan, and the healing of the ten lepers are also recorded, both of which are peculiar to Luke, and especially cheering to the Gentiles.

(6) This Gospel again, contains peculiar marks of the humanity of Jesus (10:21; 22:43, 44; 23:46; 24:39), although Luke emphasizes His Deity as do all the evangelists.

Questions.

1. For what class of Gentiles did Luke write?

2. How does he present Jesus as distinguished from Matthew and Mark?

3. Describe the Greeks as distinguished from the Romans.

4. How is Luke personally distinguished from other evangelists?

5. How does the plan of his Gospel compare with theirs?

6. Describe the style of his Gospel.

7. How do the omissions and additions of Luke's gospel bear on the thought that he was writing for the Greeks?

THE EARLY YEARS OF JESUS

CHAPTERS 1-2

There is a preface to Luke's Gospel (vv. 1-4). "While Matthew and Mark tell us of *whom* they write (Matt. 1:1; Mark 1:1), Luke and John tell us *why* they write" (Compare John 20:31). Luke wrote for the instruction of Theophilus (Cf. Acts 1, 2), whose name indicates that he was a Greek, while "most excellent," suggests that he may have been of high rank.

There were many records of our Lord (v. 1), received from eye-witnesses (v. 2), but Luke "had perfect understanding of all things from the very first" (v. 3). The Greek reads "from above," as if his information was confirmed by revelation. (Compare 1 Cor. 11:23).

Luke contains much found in no other Gospel, practically the whole of this lesson for example.

(1) Visit of the Angel to Zacharias vv. 5-25.

(Note the historic date (v. 5); the character of the husband and wife (v. 6); their domestic disappointment (v. 7); the angel's visit (vv. 8-12); the prayer, which was more than answered (vv. 13-17); the acts of unbelief and its punishment (vv. 18-22); the consummation of God's promise (vv. 23-25). With verses 8 to 12 compare Mal. 3:1; 4:2, 5, 6. Not since that prophet's time, 400 years before, had there been communication from Jehovah to His people, but He was now visiting them again (Cf. Dan'l 9:25, 26).

(2) Visit of the Angel to Mary vv. 26-38,

Two sons were to be born, both named by the angel. Both would be great, but of John it is added, "in the sight of the Lord" (v. 15). Its omission in the case of Jesus is an incidental reference to His deity. The former "would be filled with the Holy Ghost," the latter conceived of the Holy Ghost. In this He stands alone. He became man in a way peculiar to Himself, since as God, He was from all eternity. (See verse 35). Genesis 3:15 "the seed of the woman," now received elucidation and fulfilment. Also

Isaiah 7:14. Note particularly verses 32 and 33 and their relation to prophecies like Isaiah 9:6, 7. These verses (in Luke) are yet to be fulfilled, for although Christ is now seated at the right hand of the Throne of God, this is not the throne of David.

(3) Visit of Mary to Elizabeth vv. 36-56,

is told in a way requiring no comment.

(4) Zacharias' Prophecy vv. 57-80,

is remarkable as the first through a human channel since Malachi; and also as a partial fulfilment of Malachi.

(5) Birth of Jesus 1-20.

Note the time and occasion (vv. 1-5). "All the world" means, "The inhabited earth," or as usual in the New Testament, the sphere of Roman rule at its greatest extent. Compare Daniel 2 and 7, which reveal the nature and extent of the Gentile world empires. Cyrenius was twice governor of Syria, and this enrollment was ordered during his first term (see Revised Version). Note the fulfillment of prophecy in verse 4 by comparing 1 Sam. 17:12; Micah 5:2.

(6) Presentation in the Temple vv. 21-38.

With the first four verses compare Exodus 13:12, 13; Lev. 12:8; Num. 18:16. Observe that Mary was necessitated to offer a sacrifice (v. 24) because sinful as other women. Her child was holy, being conceived of the Holy Ghost, but not she. The story of Simeon is beautiful (vv. 25-35), a Spirit-led man all through, and in nothing more than this, that in blessing Joseph and Mary, he did not bless the child. "The less is blessed of the greater" (Heb. 7:7). Anna's story is beautiful, but the thought we dwell on is that "she spake of *Him* to all *them that looked for redemption* in Jerusalem" (v. 38). Alas! none others would give heed, even as to-day.

(7) Jesus at the Passover vv. 39-52.

Eleven years of our Lord's earthly life are comprehended in verses 39 and 40. He grew in stature, and increased in strength (the words "in Spirit," are not in the Revised Version). He was filled with wisdom and God's grace was upon Him. And yet He was like other boys but without sin. His wisdom and grace are illustrated in the incident following (vv. 42-51), in which three things are noticeable." (1) As a child He kept His place, asking and answering questions, but not teaching; (2) as the Son of His Divine Father He was conscious of being about His Father's business; (3) as the child of His human mother, He was subject unto her." We read of Him not again for eighteen years!

Questions.

1. How do the first two evangelists differ from the last two in what they tell about their messages?

2. Have you read Acts 2:1, 2?

3. What leads us to think that Luke's record was confirmed by revelation?

4. Name the seven leading facts of this lesson.

5. In what does Jesus stand alone among human beings?

6. How many Old Testament passages are referred to in this lesson?

7. How many have you verified?

8. What does "All the world" mean?

9. What shows Mary to have been a sinner?

10. How many years, in round numbers, were spent by our Lord in Nazareth?

PREPARATION FOR PUBLIC MINISTRY

CHAPTER 3

(1) Ministry of John the Baptist is the first event here (vv. 1-22), in which we note another mark of history characteristic of Luke (vv. 1, 2). Also he quotes more

fully from Isaiah 40 than the preceding evangelists, and for the purpose of giving the words, "all flesh shall see the salvation of God." The quotation is from the septuagint, and is in harmony with Luke's objective towards the Gentiles, as He distinctively shows that the grace of God in Christ is for all people who will accept it, and not for Israel only. We have met with John's preaching in the other evangelists, but not with the allusion to the different classes (vv. 10-14). The baptism of Jesus by John and its significance, have been spoken of in Matt. 3, but Luke alone tells us that the Lord was "praying" as heaven was opened unto Him (v. 21). Was He supplicating His Father with reference to Isaiah 61, now about to be fulfilled?

(2) Genealogy of Mary is the next division (vv. 23-38). We say "Mary" because that is the generally accepted view of the differences between this list of names and that in Matthew. The latter gives us the genealogy of Joseph saying, "Jacob begat" him (1:16). In what sense, therefore, can Luke call him "the son of Heli" (v. 23)? The answer of some is, that inasmuch as the latter does not say Heli begat Joseph the inference is that he was as husband of Mary the son-in-law of Heli, who was, like himself, a descendant of David. That he should in such a case be called "of Heli" is in accordance with Jewish usage (1 Sam. 24:16).

(3) The temptation of Christ (4:1-13), is dealt with in Matthew as the supreme testing through which He, as man, must pass in preparation for His great work. The moral order of the temptations as Luke presents them is observable, "corresponding to those by which Eve was seduced" (Gen. 3:6), and which, according to 1 John 2:16, is a kind of general principle with Satan in dealing with humanity. Christ resisted the temptations in obedience to the Word of God. Our first parents knew the Word of God and quoted it, but did not obey it. What a contrast! "Had they kept the Word it would have kept them" (Ps. 17:4).

Stuart referring to the *moral* order of the temptations as Luke gives them, calls attention to the fact that it was not the actual order in which Satan presented them and which is given by Matthew, who says the temptation on the pinnacle was the second and not the third. Of course there was a Divine reason for these differing records, and we have here an evidence of the guidance of the Holy Spirit in the writing of the four Gospels. The same author suggests how the temptation illustrates that much may go on in the world without man's knowledge. Who saw our Lord on the pinnacle of the temple, and Satan with Him, and yet how momentous to the world was the event!

(4) Return to Galilee vv. 14, 15.
is notable from the fact that He did so "in the power of the Spirit." The reference is to the Holy Spirit of which He was "full," and by Whom, as we see in the next lesson, He was now anointed. It is instructive that all Jesus is said to have done after this anointing, was done not in the power of His natural spirit, but the Holy Spirit. What a lesson for His disciples! If He were anointed, may not we, and if He required it for service, how much more we?

Questions.
1. What are the leading events in this lesson?
2. What is the significance of Luke's quotation from Isaiah?
3. What special feature is mentioned by Luke in connection with the baptism of Jesus?
4. How is the genealogy in Luke explained in comparison with Matthew?
5. What distinction is mentioned as to the order of the temptations in Matthew and Luke?
6. Can you quote Psalm 17:4 from memory?
7. What practical truth is taught in the closing verses of this lesson?

THE MINISTRY BEGUN

Chapters 4:16-5:16

(1) At Nazareth vv. 16-30.
It was the custom for visitors to be granted the privilege of reading the Scriptures on such occasions (vv. 16, 17), and Jesus read from Isaiah 61. Perhaps it was not the appointed portion for that day, which may explain the last sentence of verse 20. However, when He began to apply the prophecy to Himself (v. 21), there was astonishment indeed, for nothing like that had ever been heard. Verse 23 indicates the state of mind and heart of His hearers. He knew the rejection before Him was such as had been meted out to Elijah and Elisha, and as God had worked by them among the Gentiles so would He do again. This aroused enmity, with the result of verses 29 and 30. · A comparison of Isaiah 61:2, affords an instance of "the exquisite accuracy of Scripture," since Jesus stopped midway in the verse. The first half is connected with His first Advent and the present dispensation of grace, and the second, with His second Advent and the judgments to follow.

(2) At Capernaum vv. 31-44.
The leading events here are the casting out of the demon (vv. 33-35), and the healing of Peter's wife's mother (vv. 38, 39), both of which are referred to in Mark 1, the second also in Matt. 8. Matthew 4 tells us that Christ made His home at this time at Capernaum, while Luke (4:23) tells us *why* He did so. Note in the case of the demon: (1) that demons know their ultimate fate; (2) that Jesus will not receive their testimony to Himself though it be true; (3) that there is a distinction between them and the persons they inhabit and control. But why were the people amazed (v. 36)? To cast out demons was not new (Matt. 12:27), but the way and the power by which Jesus cast them out was altogether new. Compare the testimony of Nicodemus

(John 3:2, last clause). Notice verse 40, "He laid His hands *on every one* of them, and healed them," and also verse 43. What labor it represents!

(3) At Gennesaret 5:1-11.

The great draught of fishes is original with Luke, but calls for little comment. But note Peter's confession of sin in verse 8. *Sin*, not *sins*. It is his *state* of which he speaks, and not particular transgressions. What he *is*, not what he has *done*, utterly unfits him for the Divine presence, and he can find no comfort in that presence until his old nature has been taken away and a new put in its place. Nor is verse 11 less remarkable. "They forsook all and followed Him," because one who could do what they had just seendone, was able to meet all their needs henceforth including those of their families.

(4) In a Certain City vv. 12, 13.

With the exception of Miriam (Num. 12), this is the first illustration of the healing of leprosy in Israel, where the law of Leviticus xiv could have been acted upon. No wonder the fame of Jesus spread abroad (v. 15)! Who could work this miracle by His own power save the God of Israel?

Questions.

1. Name the geographical divisions of this lesson.

2. Have you examined a map in its study?

3. Can you quote Isaiah 61:1-3?

4. Give in your own words the Old Testament incidents referred to in 4:26, 27?

5. What is noticeable about Jesus' quotation of Isaiah 61:2?

6. Why did Jesus change His residence from Nazareth to Capernaum?

7. What three things do we learn about demons?

8. Quote John 3:2.

9. What is most noticeable in the story of the great draught of fishes?

10. How does the cleansing of the leper prove the deity of Christ?

TEACHING

Chapters 5:17-6:49

1. Forgiveness of Sin vv. 17-26.

Comparing this with Mark 2:1, we find it took place in Capernaum, and possibly in the house in which our Lord dwelt (Matt. 9:1). What a proof it contains of the deity of Christ.

2. Jesus' Earthly Mission vv. 27-32.

"Levi" as we saw in Mark 2, is Matthew whose faith in following Jesus is more remarkable than that of Peter, for he had more to relinquish. He soon showed his faith further by his works (v. 29). But though he made "a great feast" for his Lord, yet the latter made a greater one for him and for others like him in verse 32.

3. Fasting vv. 33-39.

To impose fasting on disciples who were enjoying His presence, would be like patching an old garment with a piece out of a new, and so both would be spoiled. A new era had begun and everything must be in harmony with it. The joy of the disciples could not accommodate itself to old forms and practices. Nevertheless, till others had proved what that joy was, they would naturally be satisfied with practices to which they had been accustomed (v. 39).

4. The Sabbath Day 6-1:11.

The events of these verses are recorded by Matthew and Mark also, and we need dwell on them but briefly. The Pharisees were not zealous of God's law but of their traditions super-added to the law, which practically made it of no effect. There was no law of God against doing what Jesus' disciples did, nor would God command His people to starve because it was the sabbath. Works of necessity might be done on that day as the Pharisees themselves taught. The disciples were hungry and in want because they were suffering rejection with their Lord. This is the significance of His reference to David, who also was suffering rejection as God's anointed when he partook of the shewbread and was sinless in so doing.

5. Happiness and Woe (vv. 12-26).

We do not dwell again on the choice of the twelve (vv. 12-16), having spoken of it in Matthew only to observe that Luke records that the night previously our Lord spent in prayer. But at verse 20 He begins to speak of the heavenly calling of those who are rejected on earth. This is not that the earthly kingdom will never be set up or Israel blessed in it, but only that for the time being the called out ones for heaven are addressed (Hebrew 3:1). Four beatitudes are named, poverty, hunger, sorrow, excommunication might be their lot on earth, but great their reward in heaven (vv. 20, 21). As another puts it, "the antidote is given before the trial comes."

6. Treatment of Enemies vv. 27-36.

It is natural to think that Luke is here giving a synopsis of the "Sermon on the Mount" recorded more fully in Matt. (cc. 5-8), but we face the difficulty that these words were spoken "in the plain" (v. 17). Shall we say that the same instruction was given more than once? There is nothing in the verses different from Matthew, and we only note that the whole teaching is not that of righteousness under the law but of grace, which was entirely new to the hearers. Verse 30 is not to be taken unqualifiedly but in connection with our treatment of enemies—if any of them should even ask aught of us it is to be given.

7. Treatment of Fellow-disciples (vv. 37-45).

8. Summing up vv. 46-49.

Questions.

1. Name the seven subjects of teaching in this lesson.

2. How does the incident first-named prove Christ's deity?

3. Explain "the new wine in old bottles" in your own language.

4. Where is the parallel between Christ's disciples and David in the incident of 6:1-11?

5. What experience of our Lord preceded the choice of the Twelve?

6. What is the comparative character of this whole teaching of Christ?

7. Can you quote 6:46?

HIS FAME SPREADING

CHAPTERS 7, 8

1. The Centurion's Servant 7:1-10.

Matthew describes the centurion as personally entreating our Lord (8:5-13), but Luke tells how he first approached Him through the Jewish elders and then through other friends.

2. The Widow of Nain vv. 11-17.

is a story original with Luke. Note that no appeal was made to our Lord in this case, but that His compassions was awakened by the sight itself. This was probably the first occasion when He raised the dead, which accounts for the effect and testimony in verses 16 and 17.

3. Christ's Witness to John the Baptist vv. 18-35.

As the fame of the wonder-worker spread it reached John the Baptist in prison (cf. 3:19). For John's doubts, and our Lord's discourse concerning him see Matt. 11.

4. The Woman That Was a Sinner vv. 36-50.

The Pharisee was willing to show Jesus the outward honor of an invitation for selfish reasons, but had no love for Him, as his treatment showed. Houses in the east were easy of access, and on occasions when distinguished rabbis were entertained, outsiders were admitted to listen to the conversation. Reclining at the table with the feet extended outward, made possible the action of this woman. It was grace in her that drew her to Jesus as her Saviour, hence she had already been forgiven ere she washed His feet. In other words, as the latter part of verse 47 shows, she was not forgiven because she loved, but she loved because she was forgiven. It is solemnly suggestive that she was the only one in that company to whom such an announcement of forgiveness was made. They all heard it, including the host, but none seemed to desire it for himself.

5. The Parable of the Sower 8: 4-15.

Before reaching this parable it is pleasant to read of the women ministering of their substance not to Jesus only, but to "them," i. e., He and His disciples (vv. 2, 3, R. V.). Compare this with the earlier suffering and need in the cornfield. We pass over the parable because of our comment in Matthew, but add a remark of Stuart, that "in Matthew the fruitful ones hear and understand; in Mark they hear and receive; in Luke they hear and keep." These words are alike in that to understand, receive, and keep the Word are all requisite to fruit-bearing.

6. In the Gerasene Country vv. 26-39.

The remaining incidents of the chapter have been touched upon in the other Gospels, but we pause at the visit to the Gerasene country. A practical thought has been suggested to us here. viz: that if men can be the mouthpiece of demons, "why should it be difficult to believe that a man may be the mouthpiece of the Spirit of God?" Matthew speaks of two men though Mark and Luke call attention to only one. Was it because of this one's subsequent request (v. 38)? What a contrast in this he presents to the other people of that country! They wished Jesus to depart, but he wished to go with Him. Salvation makes all the difference as to whether one desires the Lord's presence or not. But the Lord

wanted a witness in Gerasene and could not spare this man to come with Him (v. 39). Does the man's work afterward explain what Mark says of this country at a later time (Mk. 7:31-37)?

Questions.

1. How does Luke's account of the centurion's action differ from Matthew?

2. How is the raising of the son of the widow of Nain distinguished?

3. How was it possible for the incident of v. 11, 36-50 to occur in Simon's house?

4. What three things are necessary in a Christian to fruit-bearing?

5. What desire does salvation awaken in the human heart?

THE TWELVE AND THE SEVENTY

CHAPTERS 9, 10

The events of chapter 9 with a single exception, were dealt with in either Matthew or Mark. Luke, however, adds items of fresh interest to some of them which the student can easily discover by comparison.

Chapter 10 has three subjects original with Luke: (1) the sending forth of the seventy (vv. 1-24); (2) the lawyer's question and its answer (vv. 25-37); and (3) the story of Martha and Mary (vv. 38-42).

The sending forth of the seventy fits into the purpose of his gospel to reach the Gentiles. The twelve apostles were sent only to the lost sheep of the house of Israel, but these went "into every city and place whither He himself would come." In most other respects the charge to the seventy was like that to the twelve. When they returned and reported the subjection of demons unto them (v. 17) our Lord's reply was an "earnest of complete victory over all the power of the enemy." They had spoken of demons but He speaks of Satan (v. 18), and the downfall of the one presaged that of the other. It is instructive that our Lord defines demons as being in nature spirits (v. 20). Nor let the story pass without noting His prayer in verse 21, which occurs in Matthew in another place (chapter 11:25-27). Stuart believes Luke has correctly located it because of the words "In that hour," for otherwise we would not have understood the full significance of the passage.

The lawyer's question (vv. 25-37) suggests Matthew 22:34-40 and Mark 12:28-34, and yet it is a different occasion. Certainly our Lord's reply including the story of the good Samaritan is original with Luke and peculiarly suited to the Gentiles for whom he wrote. The Jewish priest and Levite passed by the wounded man, but the Gentile Samaritan befriended him. The lesson taught is that anyone in need is our neighbor, without reference to his nationality, religion or character.

We linger a moment at the story of Martha and Mary (vv. 38-42), to speak of a unique reason for its position here, suggested by Stuart. The lawyer in the preceding incident had not gotten eternal life, and the question is how could any man obtain it? The answer is given in the attitude and occupation of Mary as distinguished from Martha. To sit at Jesus' feet, and hear His word is the way of blessing.

Questions.

1. What is the title of this lesson, and why?

2. What three utterances about the transfiguration are original with Luke?

3. Name the three events of chapter 10.

4. How does the record of the sending forth of the seventy fit into the purpose of this Gospel?

5. What are demons?

6. Have you compared Matthew 11:25-27?

7. How is the story of the good Samaritan fitted to this Gospel?

8. What is the great lesson of that story?

9. What is the way to find eternal life?

DOCTRINE OF PRAYER

CHAPTER 11

We name this lesson after its chief topic, for as the Scofield Bible says, we have here "the central New Testament passage on prayer." The disciples' request (v. 1) is answered first by a model prayer (2-4), then by a story or parable about prayer (vv. 5-10), and finally by setting before them the chief object of prayer (vv. 11-13). The "model" contains fundamental principles of prayer, (a) the right relationship, that of a son to a father; (b) the right attitude, worship, "Hallowed be Thy Name, Thy Kingdom come, Thy will be done"; (c) the right spirit, love, trust, holiness (vv. 3-4). "Used as a *form*, the Lord's prayer as it is called, is, dispensationally, upon legal ground, rather than that of grace. It is not in the name of Christ for example, and makes human forgiveness the condition of Divine forgiveness"—*Scofield*. Christians have always used it however, and will continue to use it, but they must think into it the conditions of their standing in Christ. The parable following teaches importunity and intercession for others, and shows in its application that the reason for prayer from the Divine side is God's desire for the fellowship of His creatures. That is why He waits to give till we ask and seek, or to open unto us until we knock. The chief object in prayer is the Holy Spirit. Here it should be remembered, we are on Old Testament ground, and "to go back to this promise is to forget Pentecost, and to ignore the truth that now every believer has the Holy Spirit dwelling in Him (Romans 8:9-15; 1 Corinthians 6:19; Galatians 4:6; 1 John 2:20-27)." It is right for us to seek to "be filled with the Spirit" (Ephesians 5:18) but not to seek the Spirit Himself, Who is already ours if we are Christ's.

The subsequent events are (1) the false charge against Jesus and His reply (vv. 14-28); (2) the challenge for a sign (vv. 29-32;

(3) the parable of the lighted candle (vv. 33-36), and (4) the denunciation of the Pharisees (vv. 37-54). The first three were found in Matthew, but the last, while suggesting Matthew 23:13-35, is the record of a different occasion, verses 37-41 make this clear, but in reading them we must not misinterpret verse 38 to mean that our Lord was physically unclean, but only ceremonially so (cf. Mark 7:3). His reply to His host is difficult to understand at verse 41, but the Revised Version throws light upon it. "Lawyers" (v. 45) is really the same as "Scribes," and so throughout the Gospels. We have seen that the scribes made copies of the Scriptures, and classified and taught the precepts of the oral law as well. Verse 51 is very solemn. For Zechariah's death see 2 Chronicles 24:21.

Questions.

1. What gives distinction to this chapter?

2. Analyze the "Lord's Prayer."

3. What is its place dispensationally?

4. What three things are taught or suggested in the parable about prayer?

5. What is the place of verse 13 dispensationally?

6. What are the other events of this chapter?

7. Have you reviewed Mark 7:1-4?

8. What was the work of a "lawyer"?

WARNINGS

Chapter 12

This chapter, almost entirely original with Luke, consists of four warnings against hypocrisy (1-12), covetousness (vv. 13-24), carelessness (vv. 25-48, ignorance (vv. 49-59).

1. Hypocrisy (vv. 1-12).

Note the fearlessness of Christ (v. 1), and in the same verse the typical use of "leaven" in the sense of evil, which is never used otherwise in the Bible. Hypocrisy will not avail in the day of judgment (vv. 2-3), and one of its causes, the fear of man (v. 4), is supremely foolish in the light of responsibility to God (v. 5), and in the light of His abounding care for us (vv. 6-7). The lesson is that of open acknowledgment of Jesus Christ in order to receive His acknowledgment of us, (vv. 8-10), even though it means trial and suffering (vv. 11-12). The explanation of verse 10 seems to be that one might speak against the Son of Man and do it ignorantly. But it is the office of the Holy Ghost to testify to Christ and make Him known, and thus he who rejects that testimony puts himself outside of the pale of salvation and hence, forgiveness.

2. Covetousness vv. 13-24.

There is a closer connection in thought between this and the foregoing than appears at first. The disciple might be called a fool who would act according to the foregoing, but the *real* fool is now brought into view. He is a covetous man (cf. Ezek. 33:31) for that was the animus of him who made this request of Jesus (vv. 13-15). The latter was setting forth the heavenly calling, but his questioner thought only of his possessions in the present life. This explains the parable that follows (vv. 16-21), and in the light of it all the verses are to be interpreted down to 48, but especially to 34. "Take no thought" (v. 22) means no anxious, worrying thought indicative of a lack of faith and knowledge of God in Christ. The birds of the air and the grass of the field might teach us lessons (vv. 24-28). Such a spirit belongs to the world, but not to the family of God (vv. 29-34).

3. Carelessness vv. 35-48.

is connected with covetousness, for he who is absorbed in the things of earth is not getting prepared for those of heaven, which will be his when the Lord comes again. It is to be noted that He comes before daybreak (v. 38) hence, the need of always watching, and working too (vv. 42-48, cf. with 1 Cor. 15:58). The unfaithful disciple, the merely professing Christian will have his portion with the unbelievers.

4. Ignorance vv. 49-59.

is the cause of carelessness. In other words we are not to expect peace and worldly co-operation in the present age but unpopularity and divisions. Happy are we, if warned by our surroundings we take the right course (v. 57) for judgment cometh (vv. 58-59). In the "Sermon on the Mount," our Lord used similar language, but then as another says, He was pressing on His *disciples* the importance of reconciliation with an adversary. Here He is teaching the multitudes a similar lesson in view of the judgment, but in both instances we are reminded that there is no mercy for the guilty at the bar of God. "Now is the accepted time, to-day is the day of salvation."

Questions.

1. Name the four warnings of this chapter.

2. Analyze verse 1-12.

3. Why is blasphemy against the Holy Ghost unpardonable?

4. Who is a fool?

5. Periodically considered, when may the Lord be expected?

6. Why should men accept Christ now?

JUDGMENT AND PENALTY

CHAPTER 13

There is such a close connection between the opening of this chapter and the close of the preceding, that it were better not to have separated them. Jesus had been speaking of judgment and penalty, and now came those to Him who put a case or two which seemed to illustrate what he said (vv. 1-15). But they are mistaken, as He teaches them. "Those events had a voice for the living, and concerned not only the dead."

The parable of the barren fig-tree is intended to impress this still further (vv. 6-9). The Jewish nation was the fig-tree, and for the three years of Christ's ministry there had been no fruit from it. A little longer delay would be granted, and then it would be cut down, but not *rooted up*, observe. This agrees with all the prophets, that a goodly remnant will in the future spring up and bear fruit.

All that follows down to and including verse 21, is related to this same teaching. For example, the spirit of the ruler of the synagogue (vv. 10-17), showed the unlikelihood of any change in the nation; while the parables of the mustard-seed and the leaven foreshadowed what we were taught in Matthew 13 from another point of view. In other words, the Jews were to lose their place as God's witnessing people on the earth for the time being, and His Kingdom would come to embrace the Gentiles. Both of these parables treat of Christian profession, the first (vv. 18-19) showing its spread from a small beginning, and the second (vv. 20-21) "its permeation by a generally accepted creed, as leaven permeated the dough." There is no thought in either of the parables however, that the Gospel would spread over the whole earth in this age, nor have we found this taught anywhere in the New Testament.

The remainder of the chapter consists of Christ's teachings on His way toward Jerusalem (22), and they too, bear on the general subject of judgment and penalty. The question in verse 23 is answered only indirectly. Each one is to make sure of his *own* salvation. It is no ideal picture that is set before us in the verses following (vv. 25-30), for it is the Judge of that solemn day Himself Who speaks. The Pharisees, troubled at His words, but hypocritically professing interest in His safety, warn Him in verse 31, but they might spare themselves their pains, for He was walking deliberately towards death, which, for Him, could take place only in Jerusalem.

Questions.

1. Tell the story of verses 1-5 in your own words.

2. Give an interpretation of the barren fig-tree.

3. Do the same for the two parables of the lesson.

4. Memorize verse 24.

PARABLES OF GRACE

Chapters 14-15

1. The Selfish Guest c. 14:1-14.

We pass over vv. 1-6 which set forth the occasion for the first parable. The lesson from this first parable is, that if in natural things such selfishness was unbecoming, how much more on the spiritual plane? (cf. 1 Peter 5, 5-6; Isa. 57:15).

2. The Great Supper vv. 15-24.

This was spoken on the same occasion as the other and in response to the remark of verse 15. Christ had spoken of reward at "the resurrection of the just" (v. 14), for those who, in the spiritual sense, acted on the principle He had laid down. But the resurrection of the just will take place at His second coming, although that of the unjust, or unbelieving, will not occur for at least 1,000 years thereafter (John 5:28-29) (Acts 24:14; 1 Cor. 15:23; Rev. 20:5-6). Those who will share in that first resurrection are described in verses 21-23. The leaders of Israel are represented by those first invited to the supper (vv. 17-20). The common people were the next class (cf. v. 21, with the first five chapters of the Acts). The Gentiles were the last (cf. v. 23 with Acts 13:46, 28:23-28, etc.).

3. The Tower and the Field of War vv. 25-35.

The Saviour is again on the road, and admonishes the multitudes as to the spirit of true discipleship in the two parables that follow, closing with the simile of salt. True disciples were the salt of the earth (Matt. 5:13), but mere profession in that direction was as useless as salt which had lost its saltness.

4. The Lost Sheep, the Lost Coin, and the Lost Son c. 15:1-32.

The foregoing chapter deals with grace in a subjective way, acquainting us with the subjects of it and the danger of rejecting it, and adding exhortations for those who have received it. But in this we have the objective side, and behold the joy of God in bestowing it. It is fitting that these parables should have been spoken in the presence of the "publicans and sinners," and to understand their teaching we should remember that they, being Israelites, were on the same ground of privilege as the Scribes and Pharisees who objected to them. Hence the form of the parables— a sheep wandering from the *flock*, a piece of money out of a number of pieces in the *house*, a prodigal son gone from the *parental roof*. If the shepherd and the woman could be so concerned under the circumstances, was it surprising that God should care for His immortal creatures, and especially His chosen people? Separating these first two parables, the first shows the activity of the Lord under the similitude of the shepherd, and the second, that of the Holy Spirit under the similitude of the woman. In other words, men are not only guilty (Rom. 3:19) as indicated by the wandering sheep, but they are by nature dead (Ephesians 2:1) as seen in the lifeless coin. The Son of God removes the guilt by His death and Sacrifice, and the Holy Spirit quickens the sinner. The third parable divides itself in two at verse 24. The meaning of the first part is plain, that God welcomes the penitent sinner and rejoices over him. And that of the second part also, that the murmuring Scribes and Pharisees are depicted by the elder brother. We thus learn that self-righteous people, like the latter, who is not seen to enter the father's house, are in danger of excluding themselves from heaven through failure to understand and delight in salvation by grace.

Questions.

1. How many parables are here treated?

2. Divide them into those subjective and objective.

3. Give the dictionary meaning of these terms.

4. Can you quote 1 Peter 5:5-6?

5. What period intervenes between the two resurrections?

6. How many passages of Scripture are referred to in this lesson, and how many have you verified?

7. Distinguish the work of the two Persons of the Godhead in the parables of the lost sheep and the lost coin.

8. What do we learn from the case of the elder brother in the parable of the prodigal?

USE OF OPPORTUNITY

CHAPTERS 16-17:19

In the last lesson thought was turned towards the heavenly calling of the disciple, of which earthly wealth is not necessarily a part. To the Jews, this was "a great change, which we who, unlike them, never had a country on earth allocated to us, cannot well understand." For this reason our Lord now changes the character of His instruction, and shows in the parable of the unjust steward the results of the right use of opportunity, and in the story of the rich man and Lazarus, the perilous consequences of the opposite.

"The lord" of verse 8 is not Jesus Christ, but the steward's earthly master who commended him for his foresight. The world which the sinner serves commends him in the same way for similar chicanery. On the other hand, verse 9 is to be understood as in the Revised Version. It is not "when ye fail," but when "it shall fail," the mammon of unrighteousness the worldly possessions leased to you for a little while, that the eternal friends you have made by the righteous use of it will "receive you into the eternal tabernacles." We thus see that our future possession "so apt to be viewed as airy and intangi-

ble, comes out as a solid and substantial reality."

Of course the covetous Pharisees deride Him for teaching like this (vv. 13-15), therefore, after He rebukes them for their fleshly desires (v. 18), He enforces what He has said by the story that follows (vv. 19-31). It is not said that this is a parable, and for aught we know there may have been two such men on earth "whose history in the other world answers to that set forth in language suited to the day." "The vail is here lifted by Him who was competent to do it, and the condition of the lost in the unclothed state laid bare before us." Of what use then is earthly wealth so dearly prized by the covetous, if it be expended only in gratifying the selfish desires of its possessor?

This lesson will not be too long if we include the next chapter down to verse 20, where we reach a natural division of the book. The chief feature of that chapter is the healing of the ten lepers (vv. 11-19), but the transition to it is our Lord's discourse to His disciples on the duty of forgiveness (vv. 1-10). The occasions for the forgiveness would be many and unavoidable in a life of sin (vv. 1-2), but it should never be omitted (vv. 3-4). In the presence of such an obligation the disciples might well say "Lord increase our faith!" (v. 5). And yet as He teaches them, it is not faith they require so much as obedience. This obedience should be displayed without self-glorying (vv. 6-10).

Following Stuart, the story of the ten lepers illustrates four principles of the gospel: (1) the Lord visited the scenes of their wretchedness unasked; (2) they owned that among themselves, Jews and Samaritans there was no difference; (3) they supplicated divine mercy as those who felt their need of it; and (4) manifesting the obedience of faith they got the desired blessing. It is not till after all this that any difference is seen, and that in the case of the Samaritan. "He who was the most signal example of grace of them all, most valued it." But what a gainer he was by turning back to glorify God! (v. 19).

Questions.

1. In what sense does Christ now change the character of His instruction?

2. Who is meant by "lord" in verse 8?

3. How does this lesson show that the future hope of the saint is solid and substantial?

4. Have we any positive ground for calling the story of the rich man and Lazarus a parable?

5. How does the incident of the ten lepers illustrate the principles of the gospel?

COMING OF THE KINGDOM

CHAPTERS 17:20-18:30

A transition of thought and teaching is marked by the demand of the Pharisees, "when the Kingdom of God should come" (c. 17:20)—the Kingdom of which He had said so much, and which they had been led to expect by the Old Testament prophets. In our Lord's answer, "within you" (v. 21) is to be taken in the sense of "in the midst of you" (see R. V. margin), the meaning of which is seen in the context. The note in the Scofield Bible is informing here: "The Kingdom in its outward form as promised to David and described by the prophets had been rejected by the Jews, so that during this present age it would not 'come with observation' i. e., with outward show, but in the hearts of men. Meantime however, it was among them in the Person of the King and His disciples."

The Kingdom would come some day *with* observation, but prior thereto persecution and suffering would be the lot of Christ's disciples, so that they would long for its speedy appearing (v. 22). They should be careful lest they be deceived (v. 23), for when it came it would be as open as it would be unexpected

(v. 24). Its unexpectedness to the world is illustrated (vv. 26-30), and its discriminating judgments (vv. 31-37). Of course, the coming of Christ here referred to is not His coming for His Church which will be caught up to meet Him in the air (1 Thess. 4-16), but His manifestation to the world and to Israel after that has taken place.

In view of the persecution and suffering to be experienced prior to that day, the resource of the disciples must be prayer (c. 18:1-8). The "widow" is doubtless the godly remnant of the Jews, to which the disciples in their day belonged, and which will be found on the earth between the translation of the church and the appearing of Christ referred to above. Verse 8 confirms this application, since the word "faith" there means not "personal faith, but faith in the whole body of revealed truth." In other words, it will be a time of such apostasy that the truth of God will have departed almost entirely from the earth.

But other traits should characterize the saints of God at that trying time, of which He speaks first in parabolic form (vv. 9-14), and afterwards plainly (vv. 15-30). The traits emphasized in the parable are lowliness of spirit based on a right apprehension of sin and faith in sacrificial atonement. The Greek for "Be merciful" is used in the Septuagint and in the New Testament in connection with the Mercy seat (Exod. 25:17, 18, 21; Heb. 9:5), and the publican was "thinking not of mere mercy, but of the blood-sprinkled Mercy-seat." His prayer has been paraphrased thus: "Be toward me as Thou art when Thou lookest upon the atoning blood."

The thought is carried out in connection with the blessing of the little children (vv. 15-17), see especially the last-named verse. And also in the story of the young ruler (vv. 18-30) found as well in Matthew and Mark. This last shows the hindrance against which all are to be warned who would enter into the Kingdom.

Questions.

1. Whence is obtained the title of this lesson?

2. What is the meaning of "the Kingdom of God is within you?"

3. How would you explain verse 22, chapter 17?

4. What aspect of the "Coming of Christ" is referred to in the closing part of this chapter?

5. How would you interpret the parable of the widow and the unjust judge?

6. What is the meaning of "faith," 18:8?

7. How do you understand the publican's prayer, "Be merciful?"

REJECTION

Chapters 18:31-19

At this point we enter the period of Christ's formal rejection by His nation with which we have been made acquainted in the other synoptics, and hence we pass on to that which is peculiar to Luke, the conversion of Zaccheus (c. 19:10).

Jesus never declined an invitation to hospitality, but this is the first instance in which He ever invited Himself (5). Murmured at for lodging with a "sinner," He justified the act (vv. 9-10) and then spake the parable of the pounds (vv. 11-17) to "dispel the mistaken supposition that the Kingdom of God would immediately appear."

In this parable Christ is the nobleman. The pound represents the opportunity for service given each of His disciples, and on that disciple's use of it will be determined his place in the Kingdom, when the nobleman returns to set it up. This parable differs from that of the talents (Matt. 25:14-30), though the two resemble each other. This speaks of opportunity, that of ability; and yet they agree in this, that the character of the service in the age to come will be that of ruling. But notice the reference to the "citizens" as distinguished from the servants. When Christ went away these two classes were left on the earth, and when He comes back the same two classes will meet Him, friends and enemies. Hence there can be no millenium before He comes. Notice also where this parable was spoken—Jericho. There was still to be seen there a palace of Archelaus, who had gone to Rome to get Kingly power confirmed upon him. His citizens did send after him to frustrate his object, but he returned to reign in spite of all their efforts to influence Caesar against Him. As their attempt failed in the one case, so will it in the other. (Stuart.)

The triumphal entry into Jerusalem (vv. 28-48) we pass over as sufficiently treated in Matthew 21, dwelling a moment however, on verses 41-44 which are original with Luke. Compare here chapter 13:34-35. Christ's was the only sad heart in that rejoicing multitude, and sad not for Himself but the city that was soon to finally reject Him.

Questions.

1. What three things in this lesson are original with Luke?

2. Why was the parable of the pounds spoken?

3. How does this parable differ from the "talents"?

4. Wherein do they agree?

5. What rendered the speaking of this parable in Jericho specially appropriate?

THE LAST TEACHING IN JERUSALEM

Chapters 20-21

The facts of this lesson are: (1) the challenge of the chief priests and scribes as to the authority of Jesus which, as we saw in Matthew 21, was equivalent to their formal rejection of Him who had just entered their city as the Messiah in fulfillment of Zechariah's prophecy; (2) the parable of the vineyard which, as we saw in the same place, was equivalent to His formal rejection of the nation; (3) the questionings of the Pharisees, the Sadducees and the scribes, "that they might take hold of His words, that so they might deliver Him unto the power and authority of the governor," (19-47); (4) the incident of the widow's mite (c. 21:1-4), dealt with in Mark 12; (5) the Olivet discourse on His second coming, being a shorter record of that in Matthew 24, and covering in this chapter verses 5-34.

In the questioning of the Sadducees (c. 20:27-40) Luke gives particulars unnoticed by the other evangelists. He adds the words of Jesus, (v. 36) explaining why they who are counted "worthy to attain that world and the resurrection from the dead, neither marry nor are given in marriage," because they never "die any more" but, in that sense, "are equal unto the angels." In other words the ordinance of marriage is not needed to perpetuate the race. A further particular is at verse 38, "For all live unto Him." Death does not terminate man's existence — either that of the righteous or the wicked, the believing or the unbelieving. As unclothed spirits they live before God, and of course this will be true in the further sense on the resurrection of their bodies from the dead.

Another particular peculiar to Luke is in the Olivet discourse. Verses 20 and 24 are not given by Matthew or Mark. The whole of that section in Luke refers to the siege of Jerusalem by Titus A. D. 70, when the city was taken; but that siege foreshadows the greater one at the end of this age of which we learned in the Old Testament. In the siege at the end of the age the city will not be taken, but be delivered by the appearing of Christ (Rev. 19:11-21). The references in Matthew and Mark unlike this in Luke, are to this last siege and not to the earlier one. In Luke, the sign is the compassing of Jerusalem by armies (v. 20), but in the other gospels it is the abomination in the holy place (2 Thess. 2:4)—(Scofield Bible). There is no contradiction among the evangelists as to this, as a comparison shows that questions touching both the commencement and the end of Jerusalem's trouble were put to Christ by His disciples. But the different narrators give those which relate to our Lord's reply as each was guided of the Spirit to record them. The trouble of Jerusalem caused by the rejection of Christ, began with the siege under Titus, but will not end till the times of the Gentiles have run their course. (Luke 21:24).

Questions.

1. Name the great facts of this lesson.

2. Why is there no marrying in the resurrection life?

3. What words of Jesus prove life after death?

4. What essential difference is there between the siege of Jerusalem, A. D. 70, and that at the end of the age?

5. To which does Luke refer?

6. How would you harmonize the different statements of the evangelists on this point?

LAST DAY UPON EARTH

Chapters 22-23

Here we meet the momentous events recorded in Matthew 26 and 27 and Mark 14 and 15, and there treated as fully as space permitted.

The incidents peculiar to Luke are first, the explanation of Judas' conduct that Satan entered into him (c. 22:3). Satan can enter into no man without his own consent, but the only safeguard against that is the new birth, (John 3); second, the information that Peter and John were the two disciples sent to make ready the passover (v. 8); third, the report of the strife among the disciples at that feast (vv. 24-30); fourth, the prediction of Peter's fall as the direct result of the work of Satan upon him—(vv. 31-34). Satan's desire here should be understood as comprehending *all* the twelve, although it is Peter only for whom the Lord would pray as the one in danger. We cannot fail to contrast the sin of Peter with that of Judas, the former being forgiven while the latter was not. Peter a child of God was *ensnared* by Satan, Judas, a child of the devil was his *tool*. That is the great difference which faith produces; fifth, the story of Gethsemane is enriched by Luke in the mention of the angel from heaven strengthening Jesus, the drops of blood He sweat, and the circumstance that it was "for sorrow" the disciples slept (vv. 39-46); sixth, in the arrest, Luke alone reports the words of Jesus to the betrayer, "Betrayest thou the Son of Man with a kiss"? the request of the disciples whether they should "smite with the sword?" and the healing of Malchus' ear (vv. 47-53). Last, but not least, so far as Chapter 22 is in mind, it is Luke who tells us that "Peter remembered the words of the Lord" about his denial of Him, after the latter had "turned and looked upon Peter" (vv. 61-62).

Coming to the next chapter, Luke tells us the nature of the indictment against Jesus before Pilate, and perhaps the very form of it (v. 2); and he alone gives us the hearing before Herod (vv. 6-12). On the way to Golgotha, he describes with detail the procession. Simon the Cyrenian is bearing the cross "after Jesus" (v. 26); that is, as some think, Jesus Himself is bearing the cross, but the other is carrying "the lighter end of it behind Him." A great multitude are following, and lamenting women among them (v. 27). To these Jesus addresses the warning of verses 28-31 not recorded elsewhere. Luke also gives the correct meaning of Golgotha (Aramaic) and Calvary (Latin) as "the Skull" (v. 33).

Luke's account of the crucifixion is different from the others. Matthew and Mark bring out men's hatred of Christ in the fullest way, John presents Him as a Divine Person in Whom is the calmness of One who knew whence He was, but Luke shows us "the Man Christ Jesus, suffering, but showing grace even on the cross." Of the seven sayings on the cross three are found only in Luke, one when interceding for His murderers, one when about to breathe out His life, and the third when His reply to the penitent thief.

The story of the thief is original with Luke, who presents Him as a witness to Christ little expected at that moment and in that place. But what a miracle of grace is he—a malefactor saved, blessed, and received into Paradise!

Questions.

1. In what chapters of Matthew and Mark are the events of this lesson paralleled?

2. Name the incidents in Chapter 22 peculiar to Luke.

3. Do the same with Chapter 23.

4. Contrast the sin of Peter with that of Judas.

5. Give the Aramaic sayings of Jesus on the cross as recorded only by Luke.

6. Give the Aramaic and Latin words for "the place of a skull."

FIRST DAY OF THE WEEK

Chapter 24

The order of our Lord's appearances on this day was given in the comment on Matthew 28, and need not be repeated. Indeed all of the events in the chapter were dealt with there, except the walk to Emmaus (vv. 13-35). Three score furlongs represent nearly eight miles (v. 13). Cleopas, one of the two on this journey is not met with elsewhere, and is to be distinguished from the "Clopas" of John 19:25. Luke has sometimes been identified as the other, but this is conjecture. The story runs on smoothly and requires little explanation; but, following Stuart, we remark on the wisdom Christ displayed in dealing with the men. He brought them to the written word, and He left them there (vv. 25-27), furnishing no fresh revelation, but expecting them to rest on the old one. What He expected of them, He still expects of His disciples, and the sooner we realize and act on it, the sooner will we have peace.

Another interesting item is the reference to Simon Peter (v. 34) which no other evangelist mentions, but which Paul records later (1 Corinthians 15:5). The reason for silence concerning it was the question of communion with His Lord that had to be settled for Peter. Could he again enjoy it after what he had done? "That visit settled it," says Stuart: "We say *visit* because evidently it was the Lord who sought him out." He "hath appeared unto Simon." The effect of this interview on Peter is seen in John 21:7.

Luke is very definite concerning the evidences of Christ's resurrection. "A spirit hath not flesh and bones, as ye see me have" (39). There is no mention of blood, for that is the life of the flesh (Lev. 17:14), and was poured out when He died for guilty men.

Luke's version of the commission to the disciples is new, in that "repentance and remission of sins" were to "be preached in His Name among all nations, beginning at Jerusalem" (v. 47). This is "the gospel of the grace of God" (Acts 20:24), and is to be distinguished from the gospel of the Kingdom which our Lord Himself and His disciples preached throughout His earthly life. That gospel will be preached again as we have seen (Matt. 24:14), but not until after the translation of the church, and Israel takes up her mission once more among the Gentiles.

Power was needed for the preaching of this gospel, and it is promised (v. 49), but our Lord must first ascend ere it can be "shed forth," hence the record following (vv. 50-51). This reference to the ascension in Luke makes his Gospel the most complete outline of the four, for it begins with the announcement of the birth of John the Baptist as none of the others do, and closes with this event which Mark alone alludes to but in the briefest manner. Speaking of verse 51, the Scofield Bible says very beautifully, "the attitude of our Lord here characterizes this age as one of grace, an ascended Lord is blessing a believing people with spiritual blessings. The Jewish, or Mosaic age was marked by temporal blessings as the reward of an obedient people (Deut. 28:1-15). In the Kingdom or Millennial age, spiritual and temporal blessings unite."

Questions.

1. Have you reviewed the order of our Lord's appearances?

2. How was Christ's wisdom displayed on the walk to Emmaus?

3. What reason for silence is suggested in regard to our Lord's appearance to Simon?

4. Why is the mention of "blood" omitted in the testimony to Christ's bodily resurrection?

5. What is the distinction between the two "gospels" mentioned?

6. In what sense is the third Gospel the completest?

7. Distinguish among the three ages, the Jewish, Christian and Millennial.

GOSPEL OF JOHN

INTRODUCTORY

The first three gospels are called the Synoptics, from two Greek words which means "a view together," the idea being that they set forth the same general view of the story of Jesus Christ, and contain much the same material although differently arranged. They were the earliest gospels, in circulation within twenty-five or thirty years of the Ascension, and did the work of an evangelist in carrying the knowledge of Jesus to peoples theretofore ignorant of Him. From among these peoples thus converted to Jesus, Jews, Romans and Greeks, the Christian church was founded, and to this latter body, composed of all three classes, the Gospel of John was addressed.

The Reason for John's Gospel.

Thirty years, more or less, had elapsed since the Synoptics, and with the growth and development of the church had come up questions for settlement that the fourth gospel was designed to meet. These touched on the Person and work of Jesus as the Messiah, his nature and the significance of His death, so that in answering them John reveals the profoundest truth found in the gospels. For the same reason John's Gospel is nearly altogether new as compared with the Synoptics. This is not to say that John invented what he wrote, or that the substance of his Gospel was unknown to the other writers, but only that, in the wisdom of God, the relation of such things as he records was held back until the period when it was particularly needed and could best be understood and appreciated. John was the last survivor of the twelve, dying near the close of the first century, kept on the earth by divine Providence, until, like his Master, he, too, had finished the work given him to do.

Proof of Later Date.

The proof of the later date of John's Gospel is in such references as 1:32, and 3:24, which assume a previous knowledge of the facts on the part of his readers. It is found also in the omissions of all the material of the Synoptics down to the passion. There is only one exception to this, the feeding of the 5,000 which was retained in John probably in order to introduce the discourse on the Bread of Life (chapter 6).

There is a further evidence of the later date of John in that which, at the same time, affords an illustration of its profounder character, viz., the prevailing use of words belonging to the later rather than the earlier experiences of Christianity such as: Sinner, Repent or Repentance, Righteous, Justify, Believe, Love, God as Father, World as Renewed, Humanity, Truth, True, Light, Life and Eternal Life.

Depth of Its Teaching.

Further illustration of its profundity is found in the miracles it records, which show a higher degree of power than those in the Synoptics, and testify the more emphatically to the divine origin of Jesus' message, and by inference to the Deity of the Messenger. Witness the turning of the water into wine (chapter 2), the healing of the nobleman's son in the same chapter and that of the impotent man in chapter 5. Also the man born blind (9), and the raising of Lazarus (11).

The nature of the discourses in John's Gospel illustrates the same thing. They are on the profoundest themes which fell from the lips of our Lord. For example: The New Birth, The Living Water, The Honor of the Son, The Living Bread, The Good Shepherd, The Farewell Discourse.

Consider also the doctrines emphasized in John's record. Take those related to the Godhead alone. Observe how he speaks of God in the abstract, 1:18, 4:24, 5:37. No such teaching about God is found anywhere in the Bible outside of the epistles of this same evangelist and those of Paul. Observe how he speaks of God as Father, 3:16, 5:36, 6:37, 8:18, 10:30, 17:11. Of the person of Jesus Christ as related to the Father, 1:1, 14, 18, 5:17, 18, 26, 14:9, 10; and as related to man, 1:4, 6:46, 8:40-46, etc. Of the Holy Spirit, 3:5, 4:14, 7:38, 14:12, 16, 26, 15:26, 16:7. Of course, in these instances it is frequently Christ Himself who is speaking and John simply reporting or quoting Him, but the point is, it was left for John to do this, to report Him in these deeper and profounder utterances which are so important for the church to know.

Questions.

1. Why are the other gospels called the Synoptics?

2. What was their accomplishment?

3. How much later than they was this gospel written?

4. What was the particular object of this Gospel?

5. How does it compare in character and contents with the others?

6. What was the date of John's death?

7. Have you examined the proof texts as to the date of this Gospel?

8. What further evidence of a late date can you indicate?

9. Give one or two illustrations of the profundity of this Gospel.

10. Name some of its great discourses.

DEITY OF JESUS CHRIST

Chapters 1-2:12

This portion of the Gospel is chosen as a lesson because it gives an opportunity at one view to consider the Deity of Jesus Christ as *declared* in the preface 1.1-14, as witnessed to by the testimony of the Baptist, 1:15-34, and demonstrated in the first visit to Judea after the baptism, 1:35-2:12.

1. Preface. 1:1-14.

Observe the earliest illustration of John's presentation of Jesus as the Son of God. Nothing corresponding is found in the Synoptics. John asserts the Deity of Jesus, showing Him to be the Creator of all things and the source of all life (verses 1-5). He emphasizes the point by comparing Him with John the Baptist (6-9). He is careful, too, to proclaim Jesus as the source of the renewed spiritual life of man, the eternal life which is coincident with salvation (10-13). And yet side by side with these testimonies he demonstrates His perfect humanity (14).

"Word" is the Greek *Logos* which means (1) a thought or concept, and (2) the expression or utterance of that thought. And thus as a designation of Christ it is peculiarly applicable because in Him are embodied all the treasures of the Divine Wisdom or the collective thought of God (1 Cor. 1:24; Eph. 3:2; Col. 2:2, 3), and also because from all eternity, but especially in His incarnation, is He the utterance or expression of the person or "thought" of God (John 1, 3-5, 9, 14-18; 14:9-11; Col. 2:9)—Scofield Bible.

2. The Testimony of John the Baptist. 1:15-34.

Every student will be impressed with the originality of this Gospel concerning the testimony of John the Baptist. Nothing corresponding is found in the Synoptics. Observe his testimony to the pre-existence and deity of Jesus Christ (15-18), and to the sacrificial nature of His death (29). It was questions of this character which arose for settlement in the early church and which John the evangelist was retained on the earth to answer. Was Jesus God as well as man? Was His death a sacrifice for human guilt? How clearly the Baptist's witness bears upon these points.

3. The First Visit to Judea. 1: 35-2:12.

It is a peculiarity of the fourth

Gospel that it dwells upon the ministry of Jesus in Judea while the others mention more especially His ministry in Galilee. In Matthew, after the narrative of the baptism, there is scarcely any allusion to Jesus visiting Judea until the nineteenth chapter, which was His last visit. A convenient division of the present Gospel will be along the line of these different visits.

This first includes the baptism, overlapping what we described as the testimony of John, and might be said to begin at verse 29 instead of 35. Besides the baptism it includes the call of the first four disciples (35-51), a call preliminary to the more formal call in the other gospels. In connection with the call of Nathaniel, Christ's reference to the prophetic symbolism in Jacob's dream of the ladder points to the Millennial age, when visible communication may be carried on between earth and Heaven.

This first visit to Judea ended with His return to Capernaum in Galilee, on which journey was wrought the creation of wine out of water at the wedding feast. The nature of this miracle and the bearing of its record upon the peculiar position of John's Gospel has been alluded to in "Introductory."

Questions.

1. Why have these chapters been chosen as a lesson?

2. How is the Deity of Christ brought out in the "preface"?

3. What does "Word" mean, and how does it show the Deity of Christ?

4. Have you examined the texts in Corinthians, Ephesians and Colossians?

5. How does John the Baptist witness to the Deity of Christ?

6. On what feature of Christ's ministry does this Gospel dwell?

7. What events are included in the first visit to Judea?

8. What kind of a work was the turning of water into wine?

SECOND VISIT TO JUDEA

CHAPTERS 2:13-4

With reference to what occasion, and hence at what period of the year, did this visit take place (2:13)? With what display of Jesus' authority and power is it associated (14-17)? Comparing this with Matthew 21:12, 13, it would seem that this transaction was repeated at the last Passover. In what manner did He refer at this time to His death and resurrection (18-22)? What great discourse of Jesus is associated with this second visit to Judea (3:1-21)? Where did this discourse occur presumably (2:23)? How does the theme of this discourse demonstrate the profundity of this gospel, and bear out the theory that it was written for the church? How further does John the Baptist bear testimony to Jesus on this visit (3:25-36)? An analysis of this testimony like that in the first chapter, would make an excellent sermon, or Bible reading. He testifies (1) to Jesus, relationship to His people (verse 29); (2) His growing influence and authority (30); (3) His exaltation (31); (4) His truth (32, 34); (5) His supreme power and grace (35, 36).

What reason is assigned for Jesus' departure from Judea at this time (4:1-3)? Whence did He journey, and what route did He take (3, 4)? What exhibition of grace was associated with this journey (5-42)? Select some passages in this part of the chapter which harmonize with the design of John's Gospel. What about verses 10, 14, 24? How long did Jesus remain in Samaria, and where did He next go (43)? What miracle is connected with this return journey to Galilee, and how does it bear on the purpose of John's Gospel (46-54)? An allusion to this miracle was made in the introduction to our study of John.

We must not pass the teaching in 3:3-8 about regeneration. We see how essential it is because the natural man can not "see," apprehend, the Kingdom of God without it. Read here Jer. 17:9; 1 Cor. 2:14; Rom. 8:7, 8; Ps. 51:5; Eph. 2:3. As to its nature or source it is a supernatural, creative act of the Holy Spirit, not reforming our old nature, but giving us a new one alongside of the old (John 1:12, 13; 2 Cor. 5:17; Eph. 2:10; 4:24). There is but one condition for our receiving it, viz.: faith in the crucified and risen Lord (John 3:14, 15, 16; Gal. 3-24). This gospel is richly set before us in the familiar 16th verse referred to above. Salvation may be said to be its theme, and we find in it: (1) its source, the love of God; (2) its ground, the gift of Christ; (3) its means, faith; (4) its need, "should not perish;" (5) its result, eternal life; (6) its extent, "whosoever." That word "perish" must not be misunderstood. It is translated "marred" in Mark 2:22 and "lost" in Matt. 10:6 and other places, but nowhere does it signify cessation of existence.

The great teaching in chapter 4 is suggested in verses 6-14 about the Holy Spirit, whose indwelling in the believer is set before us in the Symbol of the living water. Other truths are the nature of God (24), the revelation of the Messiahship (26), the governing motive of Jesus (34), and the miracles of verses 46-53.

Questions.

So many questions are asked in the text of the lesson that but few are required here.

1. What is the doctrine in chapter 3:3-8?

2. Tell what you have learned about it in this lesson.

3. How many of the corroborative scriptures have you examined?

4. Analyze John 3:16.

5. What do we learn about the Holy Spirit in chapter 4?

THIRD VISIT TO JUDEA

CHAPTERS 5-6

1. This visit like the second was occasioned by the Passover, and a year later (6). What miracle was wrought on this occasion (5:2-9)? With what effect on the unbelieving Jews (10-16)? How does Jesus justify such labor on the Sabbath day (17)? On what two-fold ground did His enemies seek to kill Him (18)? The latter of these grounds, because He said "God was His Father," is deeply important. The Revised Version translates it because "He also called God His OWN Father." The Jews understood Him to declare God to be His Father in a sense in which He was not the Father of other men. This is why they said He made "Himself equal with God." The importance of this is seen in that it contains a direct claim on Jesus' part to be equal with God, i. e., a claim of absolute Deity.

The Jews so regarded His words, and Jesus took no pains to correct that impression, on the contrary, His words that follow are an argument to prove that He was God. Almost all the verses down to 31 prove this, but especially verse 23. This discourse concludes with a supplementary one on the Four Witnesses (32-47). We have here cited by Jesus Himself, the witness of John the Baptist (32-35), the witness of His own marvelous works (36), the witness of the Father (37, 38), and the witness of the Holy Scriptures (39), but how vain so far as moving the wills of His unbelieving countrymen was concerned (40)!

2. Leaving Judea again, where do we next find Jesus (6:1-3)? What miracle is associated therewith (5-13)? This is one of the few miracles found in the other gospels which is also recorded by John, and for the reason doubtless of leading up to the discourse on the Living Bread. What effect had this miracle on those who saw it (14)? What did they propose to do with Jesus in consequence of their opinion (15)? What did the knowledge of their purpose lead Jesus to do? What bearing has His action on the incident in chapter 18:10, 11, and His words before Pilate in the same chapter, verse 36? To what

place did Jesus depart? What miracle took place during the night (16-21)? Where next do we find Jesus (22-24)? It is at this point the discourse is given to which reference has been made, and which is one of those which give the gospel its distinctively spiritual character. At what place was this discourse given (59)? How does it seem to have been received by the people generally (41, 52)? How by the disciples (60, 66)? What foreshadowing of His death does He reveal (66-71)? Why did He confine His ministry to Galilee just now (7:1)?

3. The importance of these two chapters grow on one as establishing the Deity of Christ, and the vital character of the work for man which He came into the world to do. As illustrating the latter, consider especially verses 37-40 in the discourse on the Living Bread: (1), the Father gives His chosen ones to the Son; (2), the Son receives all such; (3), the reason for His so doing is His devotion to His Father's will; (4), His will is that He lose none of those the Father gives Him; (5), the means by which this choice of the Father becomes operative in individual cases is faith, "believing on" the Son.

Another way to treat this chapter is to divide it into four parts designated by the attitude of the multitude towards our Lord; (1), Discussion (four dialogs) (25-40); (2), Dissatisfaction, (41-51); (3), Dissension (52-59); (4), Defection; (60-66). The foregoing is quoted from an unknown source.

Questions.

1. What occasioned this visit to Judea?

2. State the circumstance under which Jesus claimed equality with God.

3. What four witnesses does He produce to substantiate His claim?

4. What distinction is accorded the miracle of the loaves and fishes?

5. Analyze chapter 6:37-40.

6. Analyze the chapter as a whole.

FEAST OF TABERNACLES

CHAPTERS 7-10:21

The story of the fourth and last visit to Judea is too long and important to gather into one lesson, and will be broken up into three or four, the first of which bears the above title.

1. How did the brethren of Jesus regard Him at this time (7:2-5)? What hesitancy did He exhibit in going up to this feast (6-9)? This feast took place in the fall, corresponding to our October. This chapter and the next are identified as those of the Controversies in the Temple. They represent periods of sustained contention with enemies such as are described nowhere else in the gospels. The crisis indicated in the Synoptics is now rapidly approaching. Examine in this connection verses 12, 13; 20, 26, 27, 30, 32, 43, of chapter 7. What effect had Jesus' answers to His opponents upon the officials (45, 46)? What authoritative person speaks on His behalf at this critical moment (50-52)?

2. Where did Jesus pass the night after this exhausting day (8:1)? Where is He found the next morning (2)? With what work of courage and grace does the day begin (3-11)? Who came off victor in that contest of light and darkness, Jesus or His adversaries (6)? The controversy begins again by Jesus' bold declaration of Himself as "the Light of the World," a declaration which, if unsupported by the truth, makes Him an imposter, but otherwise establishes His right to be all that this gospel claims for Him—that He is God. Observe the features of the controversy all through this chapter, but especially at verses 13, 19, 25, 37, 48, 52, 59. Observe, too, the repeated declarations of Jesus bearing upon the dignity of His person, as in verses 16, 18, 19, 23, 28, 36, 42, 46, 51, 56, 58. It is comforting that His testimony was not

fruitless in discipleship (30).

3. As Jesus passed from this murderous crowd, what miracle is wrought (chapter 9)? What explanation does Jesus afford as to why this man was born blind (3)? How does this work of power and mercy effect the enemies of Jesus, does it soften or harden their opposition (16, 28, 29)? What did they finally do to the man (34)? What does "cast him out" probably mean? Compare verse 22, last clause. How does Jesus make a further claim of Deity in addressing this man (35-37)? It is to be observed in this connection that the discourse on the Good Shepherd, in chapter 10, grew out of the casting out of this man from the synagogue because of his confession of Jesus. The Scribes and Pharisees are the "hirelings" Jesus has in mind, who showed themselves to be such in their treatment of this man. Notice how this discourse also falls into harmony with the purpose of John's Gospel to present the highest aspect of Christ's Person and work, for example, compare His utterances in verses 10, 11, 15, 17, 18. His work is clearly that of a substitute Saviour, and yet none other than God could speak of Himself thus. What opposite results were produced by this discourse (19-21)?

4. Reference was made above to chapters 7 and 8 as those of the controversies in the Temple. The first controversy has been described as touching the character of Christ's teaching and the condition for testing it (15-30); the second, as touching the character of the Sabbath day (21-24); the third, on the divine character of Christ Himself (25-31); the fourth, on His approaching disappearance, its nature and object (32-36). Another outline is the following: controversy one, on the source of His knowledge (14-24); controversy two, on the origin of His being (25-31); three, on the mysteriousness of His sayings (32-36). In the same way chapter 8 might be regarded as a controversial discourse on (1), the nature of His mission

(12-20); (2), its need (21-30); (3), its result (31-36); (4) possibly, its motive (37-58).

Speaking specifically of chapter 10 and the discourse on the Good Shepherd it may be stated that the Shepherd work of our Lord has three aspects: (1), as the Good Shepherd He gives His life for the sheep; (2), as the Great Shepherd He intercedes for them as one alive from the dead, and hence is caring for and perfecting them (Heb. 13:20); (3), as the Chief Shepherd He is coming again in glory to reward the faithful under shepherds (1 Pet. 5:4).

Questions.

1. When do the feasts of the Passover and the Tabernacles relatively occur?

2. How would you characterize chapters 7 and 8?

3. How is Jesus proven to be God in this chapter?

4. Analyze chapter 8.

5. Name the three aspects of Christ's work as Shepherd.

FEAST OF THE DEDICATION AND THE HOME IN BETHANY

CHAPTERS 10:22-11

1. The Feast of the Dedication took place midway between that of the Tabernacles and the Passover, or some time corresponding to our December or January. It is mentioned no where else in the Bible, and it is not positively known just what it commemorated.

Where Jesus had been in the meantime is not revealed except that it is not stated that He returned to Galilee. We dwell on this period to call attention to the same features as in the previous one, viz: the putting forth of the boldest claims on Jesus' part, followed by conflict with His opponents. For the claims consult verses 28 and 30, and the conflict, 31 and 39. What was the sequel of this appearance so far as Jesus was concerned (40, 41)? Notice that in the face of all the criticism and opposition, the disciples continually increased (42).

We should not leave this without a further word on verse 30, which literally translated is, "I and My Father are one thing." (Bishop Ryle.) Christ does not say "One" in the masculine, but in the neuter gender. That is, He and His Father are not one in Person, but one in nature, power, will. It silences those who say there is but one Person in the Godhead, and those also who say that the Son is inferior to the Father.

Our Lord's defence of this language against the charge of blasphemy (33-36), is an argument from a lesser to a greater. In Psalm 82, the inspired writer is speaking of the position and duties of princes and rulers, whose elevation above other men and consequent responsibility was so great, that compared with them, they might be called "gods". If then no fault is found with them, who receive this honor by grace, how can He deserve blame Who possesses this honor by nature? "Sanctified" (34) means "set apart," and the verse teaches the eternal generation of Christ. The Jews did not understand Christ to claim to be "god" in the sense of the 82nd Psalm or they would not have threatened to stone Him; but God in the sense of Deity, and hence Christ's acceptance of that claim, as in chapter 5, is an assertion of that fact on His part.

2. We now come to chapter 11, where we find Jesus in Bethany. Here occurs the raising of Lazarus. In the Synoptics we read of the raising of Jairus' daughter and the son of the widow of Nain. In the first case death had just ensued, and in the second but a single day had intervened. Here, however, Lazarus had been four days dead. Of course, with God it is no harder to restore life in the one case than in either of the others, and yet all must be impressed with the gradation of difficulty illustrated in the three, and that the most difficult, humanly speaking, should be recorded only in John's Gospel. This, like so many other features,

shows the purpose of this gospel to set forth Jesus in the highest aspect of all, that of the Son of God—the Son of God giving life to the world. What a wonderful declaration that in verse 25!

Speaking of this miracle in general terms, Bishop Ryle makes three good points: (a), it was intended to supply the Jews with one more incontrovertible proof that Jesus was the Messiah (cf. again their question in 10:24), (b), it was meant to prepare their minds for our Lord's own resurrection. They could not say when the tomb of Jesus was found empty, that His resurrection was an impossibility; (c), it is the most credible of all our Lord's miracles, and supported by the most incontrovertible proof.

Questions.

1. When did the Feast of Dedication take place?

2. Explain 10:30.

3. Explain 10:33-36.

4. With what circumstances are we impressed in comparing the raising of Lazarus with the other two restorations to life?

5. Quote from memory 11:25, 26.

6. What three good points on this miracle are made by Bishop Ryle?

APPROACH TO THE HOLY OF HOLIES

Chapters 12-13

1. A footnote of the Scofield Bible which suggests the title of this lesson is well worth quoting: "chapters 12-17 are a progression according to the order of approach to God in the Tabernacle types. Chapter 12 in which Christ speaks of His death answers to the brazen altar of burnt offering, type of the cross. Passing from the altar toward the holy of holies, the laver is next reached answering to chapter 13. With his associate priests now purified, the High Priest enters the holy place in the communion of chapters 14-16. Entering alone the holy of holies, the High Priest intercedes

17. It is not for the salvation of His own for which he intercedes, but their keeping and blessing. His death has saved them, and this is assumed as accomplished (17:4)."

2. The facts of chapter 12 are the supper at Bethany (1-11), the triumphal entry (12-19) and the visit of the Greeks concluding the chapter. The first two having been touched upon in the synoptics, let us consider the last which some regard as the second great temptation in Jesus' life. The considerations justifying such a view are found in the effect which the request of the Greeks to see Him made upon Jesus: "Now is my soul troubled," "Except a corn of wheat fall into the ground and die," "Father, save me from this hour." Also in the heavenly testimony to His Sonship which was again afforded Him. The thought is that the Greeks, whether heathens or proselytes to the Jewish religion, had come to invite Jesus to return with them to their own land. We have seen what the Greek race stood for, what their ideals were, and how likely they would have been to make a god of Jesus had He consented. It was a temptation not unlike that of Peter, when in Matthew 16, he sought to dissuade Jesus from going to the Cross, or, like that of Satan in the wilderness, when showing Jesus "all the kingdoms of the world and the glory of them." He said: "All these will I give Thee if Thou wilt fall down and worship me." This view assumes deeper significance if we recall that the time these Greeks approached Jesus was when He had most come to realize that "He had come to His own and His own received Him not." It was when He was rejected by His own nation that this sister nation, great in much that the world called greatness, came to Him thus and said, "Come with us and we will receive, honor, and deify Thee!" Ah! if He had, what would have become of this poor lost world (20-36)?

3. We should not pass to the next chapter without observing in passing the additionally strong testimony John bears as his manner is, to the Deity of Jesus. See for example, the argument to be drawn from verses 37-41, especially the last-named. Look up the quotation in Isaiah 6 and ask yourself whether John's testimony must not be utterly dishonored unless Jesus is God incarnate. How corroborative of this are Jesus' own words in verses 44, 45. What is the leading event in chapter 13? What is the lesson taught in this transaction (12-16)? And yet is there not more than a lesson in humility here? What of the mysterious teaching in verses 8, 9? We have here a symbolic representation of Christ's intercessory work for His people. They are already "clean" so far as their salvation is concerned because of faith in Him, and on the ground of His finished work on the Cross; but passing through the world brings daily defilement which requires daily cleansing, for which provision is made by His intercession as our High-priest. Compare 1 John 1, 9. Peter's words in verse 8, illustrate the mistake of the sinner with reference to Christ's atonement; while those in verse 9, illustrate the mistake of the saint with reference to His intercession.

What omission is found in this gospel with reference to the events of this last Passover night as compared with the Synoptics? What additional details of the betrayal are given here (18-30)?

Questions.

1. What justifies the title to this lesson?

2. What are the three great facts of chapter 12?

3. What significance is attached by some to the visit of the Greeks, and why?

4. With what other temptation of Jesus is this classed?

5. How do verses 37-41 compared with Isaiah 6:1-4 prove the Deity of Jesus Christ?

6. What verses in chapter 12 teach the sacrificial character of Christ's death?

7. What symbolic representation is afforded in chapter 13?

8. Explain the spiritual distinction between "bathed" (R. V.) and "wash his feet" in verse 10.

9. What two mistakes are illustrated in Peter's words?

10. Can you quote from memory 1 John 1:9?

CENTRAL TEACHING OF JESUS CHRIST

CHAPTER 14

1. The title of this lesson is borrowed from Bernard's volume on chapters 13-17 inclusive. Others call the chapters the heart of the heart of the Gospel. Commonly chapters 14-16 are known as the farewell discourse to the disciples, which occurred in the same place and on the same occasion as the washing of the disciples' feet. Indeed there seems to have been two discourses on the occasion, the one limited to chapter 14, and the other to 15 and 16.

2. Chapter 14 as to subjects might be thus classified: the preparation for Christ's Second coming (1-3); the identity of the Father and the Son (4-15); the office of the Holy Spirit in the Church (16-26); and the bequest of peace (27-31). We have seen that the Second Coming of Christ is to be conceived of under two aspects, a coming for His saints (1 Thess. 4:14-17), and a Coming to judge the nations (Matt. 24:29, 30), and it is the first of these aspects that is here referred to. The "Father's house" not God's dominion is in the foreground. It has " 'mansions' which suggests settled continuance and secure possession," "many" mansions, not in the sense of ampleness only, but variety. Jesus' going is necessary to prepare them, for they were not open to the sons of men till the Son of Man was glorified (see the Author's "Progress in the Life to Come") and yet their preparation was not enough, but there is the added grace of the Coming again to receive His disciples unto Himself.

This is not a continuous coming again but a final and collective one (Rev. 22:20). It is a re-union too, "Where I am, there ye may be also" (cf. 12:26; 17:24; 2 Cor. 5:8; Phil. 1:23).

3. The next subject (4-15) is introduced by the suggestion that disciples sometimes know more than they suppose or use (4). "Cometh unto the Father" (6), is to be construed not only as coming to Him in glory at the last, but coming to Him in a reconciled relation now through faith in Christ. Verses 7-11 contain truths too deep for human understanding, and we can only say in the face of them that the more we know of the Son, the more we know of the Father. The first half of verse 12 refers to the miraculous gifts the apostolic church exercised, and the last to the moral and spiritual effects of the preaching of the gospel from that day to this. The reason for these gifts and these effects is twofold, "because I go to my Father" and because "Whatsoever ye shall ask in My name, that will I do." The only qualification to this asking and receiving is "that the Father may be glorified in the Son" (13).

4. The subject following (16-26), is in harmony with the foregoing, because as the result of His going to His Father the Holy Spirit was given to the Church, through whose power the mighty works are done and prayer made efficacious (Zech. 4:6; Rom. 8:26, etc.). This is the first time the Holy Spirit is named as Christ's special gift to His people. Of course He was the regenerator, guide and aid of the Old Testament saints, but His relation to New Testament saints is peculiar as we shall see later. Several things are here taught about Him. He is a person for the words do not fit an influence or an inward feeling. His special office is to apply the truth to the heart. He is the eternal possession of the believer. His coming to dwell in him fulfills the deep mysterious sayings of verses 17-23: "I will come to you"; "because I live you shall live also";

"Ye in me and I in you"; "make our abode with Him."

5. In the conclusion of this chapter there is a difficulty at verse 28, where our Lord says, "My Father is greater than I," but where He means as touching His manhood simply (cf. Phil. 2:7). And yet why does He say that the disciples ought to rejoice at His going to the Father because the Father is greater? Perhaps because then He would resume the glory He had with Him before the world was, or perhaps then He would receive the kingdom which in the eternal counsels the Father had prepared for the Son as mediator. "If I had not placed Myself in a position of inferiority to the Father by becoming man for man's sake, you would have no hope for your souls. But now the work is finished, and I return to My Father and ye ought to be glad." The last words of verse 31 indicate some kind of a break in the discourse, and make it a suitable place to bring the lesson to a close.

Questions.

1. Why is this title given to our present lesson?

2. In what terms do others designate these chapters?

3. Name the different subjects of chapter 14.

4. Expound verses 1-3.

5. Explain verse 12.

6. What do we learn about the Holy Spirit here?

7. Explain verse 28.

CENTRAL TEACHING—
CONTINUED

CHAPTERS 15-16

Bernard speaks of the fundamental subject of what follows in this discourse as "that of the relation of believers to Jesus Christ in respect to practical life under the coming dispensation."

1. The relation of members who share in His life and thereby bring forth fruit unto God (15:1-8).

2. The relation of friends who share in His love and maintain its continuance and manifest its effect by love to each other (9-17).

3. The relation of followers who share in His work toward the world, and therefore in its enmity (18:16, 3).

4. The relation of adherents on whom He bestows a share in His own Spirit, the comforter, advocate and teacher (16:4-15).

Then follow answers to thoughts raised in the minds of His hearers, renewed warnings, promises and assurances, closing with a sad intimation of desertion, which passes again into a note of peace and victory.

Under the first of the above relationships (1-8), we learn that the union between Christ and His true disciples is a living one—the branch lives in the vine and the vine in the branch. All the meaning that can be gathered out of that simile belongs to the Christian's faith. We learn also, that there are false Christians as well as true ones, branches which appear to be joined to the vine and yet bear no fruit. Further, we are taught that the only satisfactory evidence of being a true Christian is fruit. Again, that fruitfulness is increased in such by God's providential dealing with them. Verse 7 is a distinct promise of power and success in prayer as a result of fruit bearing.

Under the second relationship (9-17) think of the measureless compass in the words, "Even as the Father hath loved Me, so have I loved you" (9); think how simple it is to continue in that love, just to keep His commandments; and the two-fold motive for so doing, that He may have joy in us, and that our own joy may be filled full. Note the high privilege of a believer in verse 15 and compare it with Gen. 18:17.

As to the enmity of the world, how kind that our Lord should relieve His disciples of fault or blame in the promises (18-21)! Verse 22 does not teach that they would not have been sinners at all had not Christ come, but that they would have had a less degree of guilt (cf. John 9:41).

In the teaching about the Holy

Spirit there is a mysterious saying at verse 7 of chapter 16. It is hard to understand why it could be good for Christ to go away from His disciples, but the fact remains that when He went away and the Comforter came at Pentecost the faith of the disciples became a new thing altogether. The Acts of the Apostle will -teach us this. If Christ had remained bodily with them He could not have been in more places than one at the same time, and there would have been far less room for the exercise of their faith, and hope and trust. And what about His exalted life in heaven as our High Priestly intercessor? How could His people have continued without that? Verse 8 is also mysterious. As commonly understood, it describes the ordinary operation of the Holy Spirit in saving sinners, but there is more in it. Bishop Ryle thinks it means that when the Spirit came at Pentecost He would stop the mouths of enemies, and oblige them however unwillingly, to think of Christ and what He taught very differently from what they were thinking now. The Acts illustrates this for there was a peculiar irresistible power accompanying the work of the Apostles which neither the heathen nor the unbelieving Jews were able to resist or gainsay. Witness the stoning of Stephen, Acts 7, and Pliny's famous letter to Trojan about the Christians. Verses 12 and 13 of this chapter are "Christ's preauthentications of the New Testament." He would leave many things to be revealed for example, and this revelation would be completed after the Spirit came (cf. 1 Cor. 14:37 and Rev. 22:19).

But there is nothing in this sublime discourse of more practical value than what it teaches about prayer. See 14:13, 14, 15:16, 16:23-27. To ask the Father in Christ's name is in advance of asking for His sake. To ask in His name is as though He asked Himself with all the assurance of answer which such a fact implies. This is the privilege of the true believer who is thus a member of Christ's body, and of Him only, and it is a revelation of truth which Christ at no time had made known to His followers until now, doubtless because they were not prepared to receive it.

Questions.

1. Name the four different relations of believers to Christ treated of in this discourse.

2. What are the subjects concluding chapter 16?

3. What do we learn from the parable of the vine and the branches?

4. What is the high privilege of a believer as stated in 15:15?

5. Explain 15:22.

6. Explain 16:7 and 8.

7. How would you characterize verses 12 and 13, and why?

8. What does it mean to pray in Christ's Name?

THE INTERCESSORY PRAYER

CHAPTER 17

1. This chapter because of its subject, and its great preciousness is worthy to stand out by itself. Bernard divides the prayer into three great parts and a sequel: (1) for His work and glory, 1-5; (2) for the disciples, 6-19; (3) for all believers, 20-24; (4) the sequel, 25, 26. The first and second part he subdivides again into two sections, 1-3, and 4, 5, and 6-10 and 11-19 respectively. The third into three, 29-32, 23, 24.

2. The Scofield Bible divides it into seven petitions: (1) that Jesus may be glorified as the Son who has glorified the Father, (2) for restoration to the eternal glory, 5; (3), for the safety of believers from the world, verse 11, and from the evil one, verse 15; (4), for the sanctification of believers, 17; (5) for the spiritual unity of believers, 21; (6) that the world may believe, 21; (7) that believers may be with Him in heaven to behold and share His glory, 24. The same source notes the five gifts which Christ bes-

towes on them whom the Father gives Him; Eternal life, 2; the Father's Name, 6:26; the Father's words, 8:14; His own joy, 13; His own glory, 22.

3. We have here the only long prayer of our Lord which the Holy Spirit has thought good to record for our learning. And how wonderful it is when we think of the One Who prayed it! One Person of the adorable Trinity praying to another Person of the Trinity! Or when we think of the occasion on which it was prayed, the night in which He was betrayed! Or those for whom it was prayed, disciples soon to forsake Him and flee, and other believers like ourselves, so unworthy of it all, or finally, when we think of its terms, the character of its petitions. Wonderful indeed! Perhaps it was prayed in the room where the Lord's supper was instituted, but from the closing words of chapter 14 it seems likely to have been uttered in some quiet place outside the walls, and before the crossing of the brook Cedron (18:1).

4. Among the utterances, we note especially the last clause of verse 1, which proves, inferentially, the equality of Christ with God. Then verse 3 as a description of saved souls. Of course, head knowledge is not here meant, but that to which we have been renewed by the Holy Spirit through faith in Christ (Col. 3:10). God known out of Christ is a consuming fire. A question of grave importance arises at verse 12. The "but" in this case is not exceptive but adversative as Bishop Ryle thinks. It does not mean that Judas was once a true believer who became lost, but should be read: "Those to whom Thou gavest Me I have kept, and out of them not one is lost. But there is one soul that is lost, even Judas, the son of perdition." This view is confirmed in John 18:9, where no hint is given of any exception having been made by our Lord in the previous instance, when John of course, heard Him speak. Verse 17 seems to us next in importance. Sanctification there is in the experimental sense. Saints are sanctified the moment they accept Christ in that they are then set apart for God, but after that they are expected to become sanctified in that their life and conduct are to measure up to their position. In this verse we see such sanctification to be an obligation; and also that it is the work of God in us, He must do the sanctifying; and yet there is an instrument or means to be used to that end, even His Word of truth. Without a knowledge of God's Word in us the Holy Spirit has nothing on which He can work so to speak, hence the primary importance of Bible reading and study.

Verse 19, in this connection must not be misunderstood. Christ Himself required no sanctification in the sense of experience or growth. He was always perfect and without sin. The word in His case is the same as "consecrate" or "set apart." He offered Himself to God as a sacrifice in other words, that His people might be both justified and sanctified. To pause next at verses 21-23, the unity of believers there sought is not that of any visible church or denomination, but that of the church considered as the body of which He is the Head, and which was effected potentially on the day of Pentecost (Acts 2:1-4; 1 Cor. 12: 13; Eph. 4:1-6). We express this unity not in forms of worship, discipline or government, but in oneness of will, heart, doctrine and conduct.

Questions.

1. How does Bernard divide this prayer?

2. How does Scofield divide it?

3. What are the gifts Christ bestows on His disciples?

4. What makes this prayer wonderful?

5. Where, presumably, was it uttered?

6. What question arises at verse 12 and how is it answered?

7. What are we taught about sanctification?

8. What are we taught about Christian unity?

AT MAN'S JUDGMENT SEAT

Chapters 18-19

1. A way to study this lesson is to compare the text with the corresponding places in the synoptics and observe what is original to John. Any "Harmony" of the Gospels would furnish valuable aid. For example, it is John who named "the brook Cedron" or "Kidron," and identifies the "garden" (18:1). The others speak of "a place called Gethsemane," etc. but nothing more. He alone tells us that Judas "knew the place," and why (2), 18:4-8 is new, and one sees its fulness as the design of that Gospel is to emphasize the power and Godhead of Christ. Here we learn the name of the high priests' servant Malchus (10). Again from 13 to 17 is original, and from 17 to 23, also verses 29, 32 and 34-38. These give details of Peter's denial of His Master, and Jesus' hearing before the Sanhedrin and before Pilate.

2. John gives no record of the agony in Gethsemane, which otherwise would have appeared between verses 1 and 2 of chapter 18. Verse 2 affords one of the many illustrations in this chapter of the voluntariness of Christ's death. He did not hide Himself, but went where He could easily be found. Verse 4 is to the same purport. With verse 6 compare Ps. 28:2. Let not verse 8 be passed without noting the illustration of Christ's constant watchcare and protecting power over all His believing people. Verse 9 shows that one way He keeps His people faithful is by keeping them from being tempted above what they are able to bear. The circumstance in verse 13 is mentioned only by John, and is explained by some in saying that Annas, having served his time as high priest, was living in the same place with his son-in-law. Certainly their relations were intimate judging by Luke 3:2. There was disorder in the office of the high priest at this period, which must be kept in mind in considering the difficulties of this chapter, verse 24 for example. Then too, for wise reasons, the Holy Spirit may have led one writer to dwell more on one set of facts than another. If each had told the story in the same words, the whole would have been less satisfactory.

3. The larger part of chapter 19 is new with John. The events are the crowning with thorns (1-3); the appearance before the multitude (4-13); the final rejection (14, 15); the crucifixion (16-37); the entombment (38-42).

The outstanding figure from the point of view of human iniquity is Pilate, the double-minded, cruel deceitful Pilate. Note the scourging of Jesus, verse 1, and remember that "by His stripes we are healed" (Isa. 53:5). Matt. 27:29 tells us that this took place in the "Common hall," the soldier's guard room, the character of which may be imagined by what we know of similar places in modern days. The Roman legionaries were expert in torturing prisoners. Verse 7 refers to Lev. 24:16. Verse 14 means that it was the day before the great Sabbath of the Passover Week (Mk. 15:42). There is a difficulty in that John speaks of the 6th hour and Mark the 3rd, a common solution being that the latter reckoned by Jewish and the former Roman time. Note how the close of verse 15 stamps the Jews at this time as an apostate nation. With the word "delivered" (16), compare Rom. 4:25; 8:30, and with "led," Isa. 53:7; Acts 8:32. With "went forth" (17). Compare Lev. 16:27; Heb. 13:12.

At verse 24, Bishop Ryle calls attention to the importance of interpreting prophecy literally, of which importance there are several illustrations in the chapter, for example 36, 37. At verses 28-30, observe another proof of the voluntary character of Christ's death, as the final separation between body and soul could not take place until He willed it. The author just quoted, thinks the "Blood and water" (34), was a symbolic fulfilment of Zech.

13:1, which the student will look up. Verse 38 was predicted in Isa. 53:9, which should be translated, "His grave was appointed with the wicked; but with the rich man was His tomb."

Questions.

1. Do you possess a "Harmony of the Gospels?

2. Name some of the events original to John in these chapters.

3. Name some of the proofs of the voluntariness of Christ's death.

4. What is one of the means by which Christ keeps His people faithful?

5. How often is Isaiah 53 quoted in this lesson?

6. How would you harmonize the difficulty in verse 14?

7. Name some of the illustrations of the importance of interpreting Old Testament literally when it can be done.

AFTER THE RESURRECTION

Chapters 20-21

1. The Fact of the Resurrection, 20:10.

The original features are Mary Magdalene's message to Peter and John and the visit of the last two to the tomb. Perhaps the most notable verse is the 7th which shows the deliberate manner in which the resurrection took place. Everything contradicted the idea that the body had been stolen. Why thus, should the linen clothes have been left? The quantity of linen must have been large when 100 pounds of aromatic powder had been used wrapping the body.

2. The Appearance to Mary Magdalene, vv. 11-18.

The critical verse is the 17th. In view of Matt. 28:9, why should Christ say "touch Me not"? Was it because several women were present then, and here but one? Was it because she evinced extravagant joy in some way? Or was it because Christ would now teach her of the new relationship to His disciples He

was about to assume? (cf. 2 Cor. 5:15-17). And then the words, "I am not yet ascended," what is their significance in this case? We must confess inability to answer these questions satisfactorily.

3. Appears to the Ten, vv. 19-23.

With what body did Christ arise? It was of a more spiritual kind than He had before, because He appeared in the room without unfastening the doors, and yet it was a real human body and not a mere shadow or spirit. "Peace be unto you" was not merely a formal salutation, but a re-assurance that all had been forgiven them. The breathing on them is a strong intimation that the Holy Ghost proceeded from Him, and hence another indirect proof of His Godhead (John 1 :33; Acts 2:33). It is difficult to interpret the sense in which they now received the Holy Ghost, since they had received Him at their regeneration and conversion (1 Cor. 12:3); and receive Him again on the day of Pentecost (Acts 2). May it be that this was a special enduement of power for the intervening period before Pentecost? Of course the authority to remit sins is not absolute but declarative, just as the high priest in the old economy pronounced who were clean and who were unclean as to leprosy. It was God who cleansed in the one instance or forgave in the other, but the evidences of either might be made known through His representatives.

4. The Appearance When Thomas Was Present, vv. 24-29.

Here is strong indirect evidence of the truth of the scriptures, as an impostor would not have told us of the unbelief of an apostle! Christ's words to Thomas are a warning to all who demand an excessive amount of evidence before they believe. And yet when Thomas did express his faith, "My Lord, and My God" became an unanswerable testimony to Christ's Deity. It was said in the presence of ten witnesses and our Lord accepted it as a fact.

5. Summing up the Testimony, vv. 30, 31.

These verses are parenthetic and break the thread of the narrative. If the Gospel ended here they might apply to the whole of what the evangelist had written; but as another chapter follows he is probably referring only to the proofs of the resurrection.

6. The Sea of Tiberias, 21.

There is little requiring explanation in these verses, but the Scofield Bible offers a good interpretation of them. The whole chapter it entitles, "The Risen Christ is Master of our Service." Verses 3 and 4 show us service in self-will under human leadership, and verse 5, the barren results. Verses 6 to 11 on the other hand, show us Christ-directed service and its result while 12-14 indicate that the Master is enough for the need of His servants. Then in 15-17 we have the only acceptable motive in service. 18 and 19, the Master appoints the time and manner of the servant's death. 20-25, if the Master returns the servants will not die.

"Naked," verse 7, means the absence of a loose outer garment, the same which he "girt" about him afterwards. That the number 153 has some symbolic significance seems probable, but up to the present it is only speculation to inquire. The "third time" (14) means doubtless, the third time Christ appeared to any number of the disciples gathered together. "Lambs" in contradistinction to "sheep" means probably the young and weak in spiritual experience, whatever their years. Verses 18 and 19 shows that the future history of every saint is known to Christ, and it is commonly supposed that in fulfillment of them Peter was crucified as a martyr. The latter is interested to know of John's future and is gently rebuked for it (20-22). Verse 22 is mysterious, and has never been fully explained and is distinguished as having given rise to the first tradition in the church (23). This tradition though early and common, was nevertheless false. It is always better to say, "I do not know," than to build up a conclusion on a false premise. In verse 24, John alludes to himself and his authorship of this Gospel, while in 25, according to Calvin, he employs a figure of speech for commending the greatness of Christ's works.

Questions.

1. What are the features original to verses 1-10?

2. Which is the most notable verse, and why?

3. What explanations have been offered of verse 17?

4. How might the breathing upon them of the Holy Ghost be explained?

5. What two-fold evidential value is attached to 20:24-29?

6. What spiritual interpretation of chapter 21 has been suggested?

7. What gave rise to the first tradition in the Church?

ACTS OF THE APOSTLES

FROM THE RESURRECTION TO PENTECOST

CHAPTER 1

Following our plan in the preceding books, we waive the consideration of the human authorship of the Acts and other questions of Biblical introduction and enter at once on the text. It is assumed from verses one and two compared with the opening verses of the third gospel, that "Luke, the beloved physician" (Col. 4:14), was the author chosen by the Holy Spirit. It is also assumed from verse two, that it is not so much the acts of the apostles he here records, as the acts of Jesus Christ through the apostles in the power of the Holy Spirit.

These two verses constitute the first division of our lesson. The second includes verses 3 to 11, being an outline of the events from the resurrection to the ascension. The features to note are (a), the evidence of Christ's bodily resurrection in verse 3, accentuated by His mingling with the disciples for six weeks; (b), the teachings "pertaining to the kingdom of God" which are outlined in the verses immediately following (vv. 4-8); (c), the Ascension (v. 9); (d), the promise of His return (vv. 10, 11). Under (b), our Lord taught three things: first, the distinction between receiving the Holy Spirit and the baptism of the Holy Spirit (vv. 4, 5); secondly, the distinction between the church of Christ and the kingdom of Israel (vv. 6, 7); and thirdly, the distinction between the evangelization and the conversion of the world (8).

As to the first of these three things, these disciples had previously received the Holy Spirit in regeneration or else they had not been His disciples at all (to say nothing of the specific experience in John 20:22), yet they were to be "baptized with the Holy Spirit not many days hence." As to the second of the things, the kingdom of Israel promised in the Old Testament, and of which so much has been said in previous lessons, was not immediately to be set up, the church of Christ was to take its place for the time being, but that did not mean that the promise concerning it had failed. It was coming on the earth, but "the times" and the "seasons" were in the Father's keeping. Witnessing unto Christ was left for the disciples in the meantime, but nothing was said about waiting for the conversion of the world before that witness could have accomplished its purpose. As to the Ascension, the probability is that the "cloud" was not the vaporous material of which we are cognizant, but the Shekinah Glory which overshadowed Christ on the Mount of Transfiguration. The testimony of the angels to His return shows that it will be a personal one in the sense of a visible appearing.

The remainder of the chapter requires but little explanation. The "upper room" (v. 13) may have been the same as that in John 20:19. Observe the presence of Mary and the brethren of Jesus (v. 14) with the others, and in no position of superiority whatever. The "scripture" Peter refers to (v. 20) is Psalms 69:25 and 109:8. That he should have been so intelligent and positive in his position is probably explained by such post-resurrection teaching of Jesus as Luke 24:27, 46, and verse 3 of this same chapter. There is no contradiction between verse 18 and Matt. 27:5, as doubtless the rope broke by which the traitor hanged himself. Notice the qualifications for an apostle (v. 21). The "lot" was legitimate at that time, as the disciples were still on Old Testament ground (Prov. 16:33), but for us to use it would not be equally so, as we have the complete Word of God and the Holy Spirit to lead us into the meaning of it.

Questions.

1. Who was the human author of this book?

2. How does the text lead to that conclusion?

3. What four things are included in the second division of this lesson?

4. What three things did Jesus teach pertaining to the Kingdom of God?

5. What "cloud" may that have been in which our Lord ascended?

6. What is the testimony of the angels as to the character of His Second Coming?

7. What explains Peter's intelligent leadership in the choice of Matthias?

THE FORMATION OF THE CHURCH

CHAPTER 2

1. The Descent of the Holy Spirit, vv. 1-4.

"The Day of Pentecost" alludes to the Levitical feast, with which we became acquainted in the Old Testament. The word is Greek, meaning "fifty," the feast occurring 50 days after the offering of the barley sheaf in the Passover feast. It commemorated the wheat harvest and was sometimes called "the Feast of Harvest" (Ex. 33:16), or "the Feast of Weeks," (Ex. 34:22), or the "Day of the First Fruits" (Num. 28-26). After the Babylonian captivity it came to commemorate the giving of the law on Mt. Sinai. There is reason to believe that on this occasion it occurred on the Lord's Day, which explains the declaration in verse one. The "wind," the "tongues" and the "fire" were not the Holy Spirit but the signs of His advent. Their being "filled with the Holy Ghost" was the fulfillment of Matt. 3:2, Luke 11:13, John 1:33; 7:37-39; 14:16, 17, Acts 1:5, etc. This was the gift of the Spirit, the promised Comforter, the baptism of the Holy Ghost. He came to dwell in the believers individually, and yet that individual indwelling by the Spirit, naturally resulted in a corporate work, uniting them all in one body which is the church of Christ (1 Cor. 12:13). Since that day, whenever a sinner believes on the Lord Jesus Christ, he shares in that baptism and becomes a member of that one body, of which Christ is the head, (1 Cor. 6:19; Eph. 1:23; 4:3-6). From a scriptural point of view, it is therefore improper for a believer to pray for the gift of the Spirit, or for a greater baptism of the Spirit, because these blessings are already his; but it is different with reference to being filled with the Spirit, if one may judge by Acts 4:8, 31; 6:5; 7:55; Eph. 5:18.

2. Immediate Effects vv. 5-13.

The first of these was given in verse four, the speaking "with other tongues as the Spirit gave them utterance;" the second was the coming together of the multitude in consequence of this, and the third, the conclusion the latter reached. As to the first, the thought is that the disciples, not of their own volition, but as instruments of the Holy Spirit, proclaimed not the gospel as such, but the praises of God in various languages theretofore unknown to them. Their act had been symbolized in the cloven tongue of fire that had sat upon each, and it prophesied that the Holy Spirit had come to make known through them the gospel to all nations under heaven. It is not likely that they continued thus to speak in different tongues. In Acts 10:46 it is referred to again as an evidence that the Gentiles had received the gift of the Holy Ghost the same as the Jews had on the Day of Pentecost, and in Acts 19:6 it shows that the Jewish disciples of John had received it, but beyond this it is not named further and these were all special and initial cases. The passage in 1 Cor. 14 will be considered when it is reached. In the meantime a caution is necessary because phenomena of this character can so easily be counterfeited by evil spirits.

3. Peter's Discourse vv. 14-36.

This may be divided at each of the verses where he directly addresses his hearers: "Ye men of Judea" (v. 14); "Ye men of Israel" (v. 22); "Men and Brethren," or simply "Brethren," as the R. V. puts it, (v. 29). In the first division he disposes of the charge of drunkenness, and shows the relation of that which had occurred to the prophecy of Joel 2:28, 29. He does not say that Pentecost was a complete fulfilment of that prophecy, which will not take place until the end of the age, but it was a foretaste of it. In the second division, he describes the death of Christ and charges that sin upon them; and in the third, he affirms His resurrection as proven by the scriptures, by the testimony of the disciples who were its eye-witnesses (Ps. 16), and by the event that was just transpiring.

4. The First Converts vv. 37-47.

Questions.

1. What does "Pentecost" mean and to what does the feast allude?

2. Have you re-examined the New Testament scriptures which predicted this event?

3. How does 1 Cor. 12:13 explain this event?

4. What is the thought of verse four?

5. Of what was their act at once a symbol and a prophecy?

6. Why is a caution necessary about "speaking with tongues"?

7. Analyze Peter's discourse.

THE OFFER OF THE KINGDOM RENEWED

Chapters 3-4:30

The disciples are still in Jerusalem, and the preaching is still limited to Jewish hearers, and in a sense we are still on Old Testament ground. An illustration of this is found in the previous lesson, for example: where in 2:38 to "repent and be baptized" was essential "for the remission of sins" and to "receive the gift of the Holy Ghost." But this is no longer so when the Gentiles are being approached (10:44-48). The Jews who had openly rejected Jesus of Nazareth must openly accept Him in order to receive the blessing, but with the others grace deals in a different way. That is not to say that repentance and baptism are no longer necessary; indeed repentance is always involved in saving faith; but baptism now follows the gift of the Spirit as a sign of it, rather than precedes it as a condition.

As a further illustration of Old Testament conditions the disciples are still worshipping in the Temple (v. 1), at one of whose gates this miracle occurs in the Name of the rejected and now risen One (vv. 2-11). It is Peter's discourse in this case that justifies the title of this lesson, especially verses 19-26. This work had not been wrought in the names of the apostles but in Christ's Name, Whom they had crucified (vv. 12-16). This fulfilled prophecy (vv. 17-18). Let them now repent that the Lord may "send the Messiah who hath been appointed for you" (v. 20 R. V.). The inference from all this to the end of chapter is that had they as a nation repented, the Messiah would have returned at that time to set up His kingdom in Israel.

But the opposite took place as indicated in the next chapter, the facts of which are (a), the arrest of Peter and John (vv. 1-3); (b), their defense (vv. 5-12); (c), their threatening and their deliverance (vv. 13-22); (d), their return "to their own company" with the spiritual quickening that followed (vv. 23-30).

Questions.

1. What is to be remembered in the study of this part of the Acts?

2. Give an illustration of this from the preceding chapter.

3. Also from this lesson.

4. What justifies the title of this lesson?

5. What inference is deducible from this?

VARIED EXPERIENCES

CHAPTERS 4:21-5

1. Unity of Love 4:31-37.

The quickening in the last lesson was associated with another outpouring of the Holy Spirit but not another "baptism," and some who had been filled before were refilled, with results following: (a), courage in preaching (v. 31); (b), unity of soul (v. 32); (c), power in testimony (v. 33); (d), love in practical conduct (vv. 34-37). This last result has sometimes been quoted as favoring Christian communism, but it is to be remembered that it was voluntary in origin, temporary in duration, and limited in its application. Where such communism is the result of the work of the Holy Spirit on regenerated hearts, and accompanied by such fruit as it here revealed, no one need have any apprehension in regard to it.

2. Pride and Hypocrisy vv. 1-11.

But there is mildew in every garden, and the opening of the next chapter shows its presence here. Notice in verse three the testimony to the personality and power of Satan, and the personality and Deity of the Holy Spirit. One can not "lie" to an "influence" or a mere "principal of good." Moreover, in verse five the Holy Spirit is identified as God. The penalty on Ananias and Sapphira does not necessarily involve eternal retribution, inasmuch as, notwithstanding their sin, they may have been in vital relationship to God through faith in Christ (1 John 1:8). But it is an illustration of God's chastening His people on earth, paralleled by the cases of Nadab and Abihu and Achan in the Old Testament (Lev. 10; Josh. 7), and the Corinthians in the New Testament (1 Cor. 11:30-32). (Compare here 1 John 5:16).

3. Power and Persecution vv. 12-42.

Note in passing, the continued growth of the Church (v. 14); the unusual nature of the signs wrought by Peter (v. 15); the continued enmity of the Sadducees because the apostles preached the resurrection (vv. 17-18); the supernatural deliverance (vv. 19-24); the defence before the Sanhedrin (vv. 25-32); the unexpected advocate (vv. 33-39); the penalty (v. 40); the effect on the apostles and the church (vv. 41-42).

Questions.

1. What were the results of the filling with the Holy Ghost?

2. What are the distinctions between the charity of the early church and the modern communism?

3. What sin in the heart led to the open hypocrisy of Ananias and Sapphira?

4. How is the Deity of the Holy Spirit proven in this lesson?

5. Is there a distinction between the Divine retribution of the unbelieving and the Divine chastening of the followers of Christ?

6. Give some Old and New Testament illustrations of the latter.

7. Give in your own words the story told above under the head of "Power and Persecution."

FIRST CHRISTIAN MARTYR

CHAPTERS 6-7

The Church was being blessed and multiplied but the conditions were not perfect. The flesh was asserting itself. Verse 1 carries us back to the close of chapter 4, and we see that the charity which led to hypocrisy there, led to "murmuring" here. "Grecians" should be translated "Grecian Jews" to distinguish them from the native born. The apostles who had been distributing the alms could do so no longer, and hence the institution of the office of "deacon" (v. 5), after the Greek of "serve tables" (v. 2). (It is an interesting fact that their names are all Greek.) Note in passing, the exalted nature of the Christian ministry (v. 4), the high qualifications of those who even should carry on the secondary work of that ministry (v. 3), the democratic nature of the church assembly, and yet the respect for order and authority (v. 6). The whole multitude selected the deacons, but the Apostles ordained them. Note also the direction in which the truth of the gospel was now advancing (v. 7).

The above leads up to the personal history of Stephen, whose ministry was not limited to that of an almoner, and who was endued with miraculous power (v. 8). Verse 9 is explained by the fact that in addition to the Temple in Jerusalem there were many synagogues, where the Jews from different countries assembled according to local preferences. (The "Libertines" were Jews from Rome). "The servant is not greater than his Master," and if false witnesses caused the death of the One, the other need not expect different treatment (vv. 11-14), but the Master has not forsaken His servant (v. 15).

The defense of Stephen before the Sanhedrin (c. 7) is a historical address carrying his hearers through the glory of God's dealings with Israel from the call of Abraham to the building of Solomon's Temple, special emphasis being laid on Joseph and Moses who were remarkable types of Christ (vv. 2-50). One instinctively feels that he was proceeding to a climax in his witness to Christ and the resurrection, when he was diverted by the gathering opposition of his hearers, and broke off in the language of rebuke at verses 51-53. Their fury vented itself upon him at this time (vv. 54, 57, 58); but he was marvellously sustained, and had a marvellous testimony to bear of what he saw, which enabled him, as his Saviour before him, to pray for the forgiveness of his murderers with his last breath.

A comparison of Stephen's words with the Old Testament records shows certain variations, but the Holy Spirit through him may have been adding details to that record. On the other hand, Stephen was a Grecian Jew, using doubtless the Septuagint or Greek translation of the Old Testament, which would explain some things.

Note in verse 55 the first manifestation of the glorified Christ on record. Note in verse 58 the illegality of Stephen's judges when compared with John 18:31. And in the same verse the presence of Saul, who, in a sense, owed his conversion to this scene, and of whom we are soon to learn more. (Cf. 22:20).

The second offer of the kingdom to Israel is brought to an end here, and in our next lesson we enter on the transition period through which the story of the Church passes out of the Jewish into its Gentile stage.

Note in closing, that the name "Jesus" (v. 45), should be rendered as in the R. V. "Joshua," the two in the original being the same.

Questions.

1. To what earlier event in the history of the Church is the opening of this lesson related?

2. What is the significance of "Grecians" in 6:1?

3. Whence does the word "deacon" originate?

4. What distinguished men of Israel were now uniting with the Church?

5. What is the interpretation to be put upon the synagogues of the Cyrenians, etc.?

6. What was the character of Stephen's defense before the Sanhedrin?

7. What important epoch is thought to have come to an end at this time?

TRANSITION PERIOD

CHAPTERS 8-9:30

We explained in the last lesson the meaning of the "transition period", which continues to chapter 13. The first sentence in chapter 8 is more properly the concluding one of chapter 7, although it introduces the account of the persecution following in which Saul was the leader (8:1-3). With the account of this persecution cf. Heb. 10:32-34, and for Saul's part in it, Acts 22:4, 19, 20; 24:10, 11 and parallel places.

"The blood of the martyrs is the seed of the church," as the results in verses 4-8 bear witness. Notice in this case that every one was a preacher, somewhat as in the later instances of the Waldenses and Huguenots. John 4:42 shows how the soil had been prepared in Samaria. Miracles were in order here because the New Testament had not come into existence, but in our day faith in the Word of God is substituted for them.

Simon, or "Simon Magus," was one of Satan's instruments to anticipate the coming of the gospel and counterfeit God's power (vv. 9-11). Cf. 2 Thess. 2:9 for the multiplication of such persons towards the end of the age. His pretended faith deceives even Philip (v. 13).

Verses 14-17 have led to error in two directions. Some teach therefrom that one may believe in Christ and yet not possess the Holy Spirit, and whose reception it is claimed is distinct from conversion. While others affirm that the laying on of hands as in the rites of confirmation and ordination, are needful to His reception. The correction of these things is found in the dispensational character of this part of the book. The Samaritans who had a controversy with the Jews (John 4:19-24), had to be identified with those in Jerusalem, after their conversion, hence the gift of the Holy Spirit was withheld in their case till Jerusalem sent the apostles to them.

To quote Gaebelein, Peter uses the "keys" here as with the Jews on the day of Pentecost and the Gentiles later in the case of Cornelius (Acts 10). Nowhere in the New Testament is it taught that the believer on Christ should seek the gift of the Holy Spirit afterward, nor that He is to be received only by the laying on of hands. The believer may be "filled with the Spirit" many times, but the Spirit comes to dwell in him once and forever.

"Simony" is the name given to the offence of the imposter recorded in 18-24, and it stands for any attempt to make merchandise of the gifts of God. In so far as Christian Science, claiming to be a divine religion, seeks pay for its healing benefits, it is guilty of this sin.

The remainder of the chapter is quite plain. As a soul-winner all must be impressed with Philip's obedience (vv. 26, 27), tact and intelligence (vv. 30-35) and success (v. 38), but the explanation is that he was "full of the Holy Ghost," Acts 6:3. Verse 37 is omitted in the Revised Version given Paul as not belonging to the text. It states a great and important truth, but it anticipates the later teaching of Christianity which was given Paul to reveal (Acts 9:20; Gal. 1:12). The catching away of Philip (v. 39), suggests 1 Thess. 4:17, and is a kind of type of that which will occur when the Church as a whole has finished her labors here, and will be translated to "meet the Lord in the air."

We include the conversion of Saul in this lesson, as the opening of chapter 9 leads us back to that of chapter 8, showing the intervening narrative as a parenthesis. With the exception of the descent of the Holy Spirit, the conversion of Saul is the most important event in the book. For something of his early history see Acts 22:3, 28; 23:6; Gal. 1:13, 14; Phil. 3:5, 6. What happened on the way to Damascus was unique (vv. 3-7), and will not be repeated till Zech. 12:10 is fulfilled at the end of this age. It is related twice again, and with more detail, in chapters 22:5-16, 24:12-18. The "light out of heaven" (9:3) was doubtless the Glory of the Lord, but later on it is the Lord Himself Who appears unto Saul. For proof of this cf. verse 5 with verses 17 and 27 of the same chapter, also 26:16, 1 Cor. 9:1 and 15:8, 9.

Note the identification of the Lord and His people, the Head and the members of the body in the words, "Why persecutest thou Me?" Note the correspondence in the two visions to Saul and to Ananias (vv. 6, 10-16), which establishes the actuality of the occurrence. Note the particularities of God's knowledge of man,—the name of Ananias, the city, the street, the house in which he dwelt, the name of Saul, his birthplace, his present occupation! How real and startling it all is! And Ananias is an ordinary disciple, not an apostle, to whom the great commission is accorded (Gal. 1:1). Note the first indication of what Paul's mission is to be (v. 15). Note that he was first filled with the Spirit and afterward baptized (vv. 17, 18), which was different from Acts 2:38; 8:16 and 10:44. "Evidently had there been uniformity in all these cases it would have resulted in the belief that to receive the Spirit, the same method always must be followed, which has to be avoided. It is to be remembered that these cases were all unique as taking place in the Jewish and the transition stages, while the present method of receiving the Spirit is revealed in Eph. 1:13."—*Gaebelein.*

We pass over the remainder of this story except to notice verse 23. The many days doubtless included the journey to Arabia and back spoken of in Gal 1:17, and which will be treated when that epistle is reached.

Questions.

1. What is meant by the transition period?

2. Have you carefully examined the other scriptures referred to in this lesson?

3. What is now substituted for miracles?

4. In what two directions has the translation in 8:14-17 led to error?

5. In what is the correction found?

6. What is "simony"?

7. What marks Philip as a soul-winner?

8. What is suggested by his being caught away?

9. What comparison is made between the conversion of Saul and other events in this book?

10. How is God's knowledge of

our intimate life shown in this lesson?

11. What did we note about receiving the Holy Spirit?

12. What is included in the "Many days" of 9:23?

DOOR OPENED TO THE GENTILES

CHAPTERS 9:31-11:18

The closing of the 9th chapter shows Peter on a tour of visitation, and the instrument of two great miracles, it being significant that the greater of the two was in answer to prayer (v. 40). Almost all the commentators regard these miracles as having a bearing on the crisis of the Chruch recorded in the next chapter. In that chapter Peter is again to use the "keys," this time in opening the door of the gospel to the Gentiles. Indeed, since the occupation of a tanner was unclean in the eyes of a Jew because of the handling of the skins of dead animals, it is seen that Peter in Joppa is already breaking with the customs of his nation.

As an introduction to chapter 10, carefully read Paul's words in Eph. 2:11-18. Note, in passing, that the Caesarea in this case was not that of Matt. 16, but another city of the same name located near Joppa, which the Emperor Augustus gave to Herod, and which the latter greatly beautified.

The description of Cornelius (vv. 1-8), shows this Gentile Roman soldier very near the kingdom of God, and an example of how God will reveal more light to any man who lives up to the light he has. But the need of this "more light" in the sense of the knowledge and acceptance of Jesus Christ as a Saviour, is also revealed with equal clearness.

Passing to the vision of Peter (vv. 9-3), the "vessel" represents the Christian church; the "four corners," the four corners of the earth; the clean animals, the Jews; the unclean, the Gentiles. In the Church however, all are cleansed (read here 2 Cor.

6:11 and Eph. 3:6). The Lord providentially interprets the vision in verses 17-20. Note the proof of the personality of the Holy Spirit found in verses 19 and 20—"the Spirit said * * *I have sent them."

We are now in the centurion's house and listening to Peter's sermon (vv. 24-43). He has had his eyes opened to the great truth expressed in v. 34. This does not mean that any man merits God's acceptance by his natural morality, for the true fear of God and the working of righteousness are always the result of His grace. It means that God vouchsafes this grace to men of every nation, whether Gentile or Jew. Verse 43 emphasizes this, being the first echo of John 3:16 in the history of the Church.

That the household of Cornelius acted on this promise by faith is seen in the result (vv. 44-48), which demonstrates that the Holy Spirit is given to men without either water baptism or the laying on of hands, but simply by believing (Gal. 2:2). Water baptism followed, but not as an act of Peter himself as is worth noticing (v. 48).

The next chapter indicates that party spirit showed itself early in the Church. "They that were of the circumcision" (11:2), means the Palestinian Jews as distinguished from the Grecian Jews or "Hellenists" as they were sometimes called, and who were born in Greece. The priests and the Pharisees belonged to the former who were more zealous for the letter of the Mosaic law than the others (Acts 21:20). As we shall see later (c. 15), they thought it necessary for a Gentile to become a Jew before he could be saved i. e., he must submit to be circumcised at least. But Peter rehearses all the circumstances in the case of Cornelius, and at this junction they appear to be more than satisfied (v. 18).

Questions.

1. Name the two miracles of Peter at the close of chapter 9.

2. What is Peter about to do in chapter 10?

3. Have you read Eph. 2:11-18?

4. Give a brief history of Caesarea.

5. What does the history of Cornelius teach?

6. Explain the housetop vision.

7. What proof of the personality of the Holy Spirit is here found?

8. How is 10:34 to be interpreted?

9. How is the gift of the Holy Spirit received?

10. What distinguished the Palestinian Jews from the Hellenists?

THE CHURCH AT ANTIOCH

CHAPTERS 11:19-13:3

By connecting the first verse of this lesson with 8:4, it will be seen that all intervening is a parenthesis, an important one indeed, but making it necessary now to return to the martyrdom of Stephen for a new start. Be sure to consult a map for the localities in verses 19 and 20. Antioch now coming into prominence as the headquarters of the Gentile church, was a beautiful and influential city, but luxurious and immoral. It was founded about 300 B. C. Saul's great life work really begins here (v. 25), and here also the name of Christianity takes its rise (v. 26). Antioch is said to have been famous for its witty epigrams, and it is thought that such was the origin of the name "Christian." The Church there was richer in this world's goods than at Jerusalem, which enabled the Christians to show the beautiful spirit of verse 29.

Another parenthesis meets us at chapter 12, the closing verse of which brings us back to Antioch. Chapter 12 is of events in Jerusalem, the martyrdom of James by Herod, the imprisonment and deliverance of Peter, and the fate of the wicked king.

To begin with the last-named. Four Herods are mentioned in the New Testament, Herod the Great who killed the innocents in

Bethlehem, Herod who killed John the Baptist, this Herod, and him before whom Paul stood later on.

The story of this, the second persecution of the Church is told in verses 1 to 5. The James here mentioned was the one honored by our Lord on the Mount of Transfiguration, and in Gethsemane. See also the memorable circumstance in Matt. 20:23. Peter was now the only apostle remaining in Jerusalem. The four quaternions, 16 soldiers, "to keep him," suggest that the enemies of the Church in Jerusalem had not forgotten his earlier deliverance (c. 4).

The story of the present deliverance is told in verses 6-17, and is so plain we need not dwell upon it.

The judgment on Herod (vv. 18-23), suggests to some "the presumption and fate of the Anti-christ," who also will persecute the Jewish saints, claim divine honors and assume the place of God (2 Thess. 2:3-8).

In verses 24, 25 Barnabas and Saul have returned from their mission of bearing the alms of Antioch to Jerusalem and have brought John Mark with them.

It is now that Antioch comes to the front as the second great center of Christianity, and with it Paul, no longer called Saul, the great apostle to the Gentiles. The time is supposed to be toward the spring of A. D. 46. Verses 1-3 tell the story. Five names are given, one of them very prominent in social circles—Manaen, a foster-brother of Herod. Note the phrase "they ministered to the Lord." How? Just by quiet worship. And, Oh! who can measure the results to the Church and to the world that came of it! What a contrast with the present-day "Movements" of one kind and another, the banquets, conventions, newspaper advertisings, photos, and "whoop-'em up" song services, to say nothing of meetings for the so-called deepening of the spiritual life. The simplicity of ministering to the Lord strikes us here, and the circumstance that He Himself is present to guide into large things through the voice of His Spirit. Who can be recognized by all who are holy enough and quiet enough to hear.

The laying on of hands in this case is hardly identical with modern "ordination," but simply the testimony of the church to the genuineness of the call that had been received, and their outwardly expressed "fellowship and identification with the two" who had thus been set apart by the Holy Spirit. This is the way all true missionary work should begin, and the only way to insure a blessing.

Questions.

1. With what earlier event is this lesson connected?

2. Have you located the cities on the map?

3. What do you know about Antioch?

4. To what locality do the events of chapter 12 belong?

5. Name these events.

6. Identify the different Herods.

7. Identify James, the first of the apostles to suffer martyrdom.

8. Of whom may this Herod be taken as a type, and in what particular?

9. At what date did the great work of missions to the Gentiles begin?

10. What is here meant by ministering to the Lord?

PAUL'S FIRST MISSIONARY JOURNEY

Chapters 13:4-14

Note who was the real inspirer and director of this missionary journey "sent forth by the Holy Ghost" (v. 4). This does not contradict the last phrase of the preceding verse which, properly rendered, is "they let them go." Study the localities of Seleucia and Cyprus on the map. What was the first port of Cyprus at which they preached (v. 5)? Note that they began their work in the synagogues because it was the Divine order to preach to the Jew first (Rom. 1:16), and because this assured them a waiting audience. The kind of ministry John Mark rendered is not stated, and some think it may have been of a domestic or personal kind. The emphasis in this part of the journey is on the events in Paphos, which place the student should identify. Those versed in dispensational matters speak of Elymas as a type of apostate Judaism which has turned away from the truth and perverts the right ways of the Lord. As he tried to keep the Word of God from the Roman governor, so the Jews tried to keep it from the Gentiles as a class; while on the other hand the judgment falling on him is also significant. Blindness has been put upon the Jews judicially, and they are groping in the darkness without a leader. Cf. the story (13:6-1) with such a passage as Isa. 6:9, 10, for example.

Leaving the island for the continent of Asia Minor at verse 13, we find that verse to contain two interesting things. Paul is now first called by that name and begins to take the first place in the narrative as compared with Barnabas or any other fellow-worker. Also John Mark is pointed out as a deserter for some cause, just what is not known. Cf. here Acts 15:38 and 2 Tim. 4:11, the first of which shows that Mark was to be blamed, and the second that he was subsequently restored to Paul's fellowship. The word Paul means "little," but why it was now assumed by him is not known, except it be as expressing his estimate of himself spiritually.

"Antioch in Pisidia" (v. 14) was a region sometimes known as "Galatia" and as one of Paul's most important epistles was sent there it gives special interest to this part of the story. Furthermore we have here a sample of Paul's preaching as in the case of Peter at Pentecost, and also an intimation of how he found access to the people in the synagogues. The order of exercises there is given in verse 15. From 16 to 41 is the sermon, which differs from Peter's in an important way. Peter addressed the Jews

distinctively, and before the final offer of the kingdom was withdrawn from them for the time being, and hence he offered forgiveness on the ground of repentance and baptism. But Paul speaking to Gentiles as well as Jews, and proclaiming the gospel of grace as distinguished from that of the kingdom, "utters a truth for the first time which Peter did not declare" (v. 39). See comments on chapter 3.

The sermon breaks itself up into three parts: a historical retrospect (vv. 16-25), an unveiling of the gospel (vv. 26-39), and a warning (vv. 40, 41). "Ye that fear God" in contrast with "Men of Israel" (v. 16), means the devout Gentiles who sometimes worshipped in the synagogues. Observe that while Paul addresses himself chiefly to the Jews (v. 23), yet true to his commission these others are not forgotten— "Whosoever among you feareth God" (v. 26). The gospel part of the sermon is a model for all time, a statement of facts (vv. 27-31), a glorious declaration based upon them and buttressed by holy writ (vv. 32-37), and the whole pressed home in a personal application (vv. 38, 39). The warning seems to have been drawn forth as was that of Stephen, by a spirit of opposition rising among his hearers.

The effects of the sermon are pointed out in verses 42-44, both Jews and Gentiles having been impressed, some of whom were saved. The next week shows a change in the situation explained in verses 44-48. "Ordained" in the last-named verse is not to be interpreted as an arbitrary act on God's part, although it remains true that their acceptance of eternal life by faith shows that He had chosen them to that end. There was a wide work of evangelization in this place (v. 49), but at length the gospel messengers were forced out into other regions (v. 50). "Devout and honorable women," means doubtless Jewish worshippers who were wives of the rulers of the city.

We need not dwell on the story

of Iconium (14:1-5) except that the missionaries abode there a long time before persecution drove them forth, and that a great multitude of both Jews and Gentiles believed.

The events at Lystra are full of dramatic movement (vv. 6-20). The supernatural deliverance of Paul suggests Job 2:6. But is it not amazing that they should have returned, without fear, through the cities in which they had so recently suffered persecution (v. 21). Some have calculated that the whole of this journey covered about a year and a half.

Questions.

1. Who originated this missionary journey?

2. What geographical relation does Cyprus bear to Syria and Asia Minor?

3. In what sense may Elymas be spoken of as a type?

4. What is the meaning of the word "Paul"?

5. Describe the simple service of the synagogue.

6. Analyze Paul's sermon at Antioch.

7. Give the story of Lystra in your own words.

FIRST GENERAL CHURCH COUNCIL

CHAPTER 15:1-35

This lesson is one of the most important in the whole historical part of the New Testament. It is the record of the first general council of the Church, called to settle the fundamental question as to how a man may be just with God. We have become acquainted with "they of the circumcision" who, at chapter 11, objected to Peter's fellowship with the Gentiles in the case of Cornelius. The party was strong and growing stronger. As Jews of the stricter sort they could not understand how Gentiles could become Christians without in a sense first becoming Jews. Their theory is expressed in verse 1. Some of them, who have come to be styled "Judaizing teachers," had followed Paul and Barnabas to An-

tioch and sought to undermine their work there. The immediate result is given in verses 3 and 4. The second of these two verses should be read in connection with Paul's account of this gathering in Gal. 2. The appearance of Peter (vv. 7-11) is his last in this book, and it is remarkable that as an apostle of the circumcision so called (Gal. 2:8), he should have been used by the Holy Spirit to reprove the error of the Judaizing teachers. He does so by a plain relation of facts, an interrogative argument and a statement of belief. The preciousness of that statement is enhanced by a recurrence to the later dark ages of the Church when its momentous truth was obscured by the sacramentalism of the papacy.

But the settlement of this great doctrine is not the only feature marking the value of this Council, since we have in the inspired words of James following (vv. 13-18), the Divine program for the whole of this age and the following. Here we have the great truth of the dispensations so necessary to the understanding of the Bible, and so little appreciated by many Christian teachers to-day. As another puts it, "How different would be the work of our large denominational gatherings if the facts here alluded to were taken into consideration?" Here is the order of events: First, God is now in this Christian age visiting the Gentiles "to take out of them a people for His Name." This, in other words, is a time of outgathering of an elect number from the nations to form the Church or the body of Christ (cf. Eph. 3:6 in the light of its context). Secondly, "After this" Christ "will return" (v. 16). The feature of the return of Christ here spoken of is not that for the translation of the Church which is His body (1 Thess. 4:16-18), but His visible return in power and glory of which the Old Testament prophets speak. This is that second feature of His second coming to which reference has been made before in these pages. It follows the rapture of the

Church synchronizing with the threatened judgments on the living Gentile nations and the deliverance of Israel from her great tribulation. Thirdly, following this event will transpire the building again of "the tabernacle of David" (v. 16), in other words the restoration of the kingdom to Israel (cf. Luke 1:32, 33). Finally, i.e., during the Millennial Age "the residue of men" will "seek after the Lord." (Cf. Isa. 2:2, 11:10, 60:5, etc.)

The divine program enunciated by James is followed by his "sentence" (v. 19), which is, in effect, the judgment of the whole assembly now reduced to writing, and to be transmitted to the churches by a committee of the brethren named in verse 22. All that the Gentiles are asked to abstain from are those things more or less associated with idolatry (v. 20), and which were not distinguished as Mosaic prohibitions, but based on the earlier covenant of Noah (Gen. 9:4), binding equally on Gentile and Jew. Nevertheless, verse 21, indicates that in the abstinence therefrom they were to show a suitable respect for their Jewish neighbors who were instructed in these things in the Old Testament scriptures, of which the Gentiles until that time were ignorant.

The remainder of the lesson requires no comment.

Questions.

1. With what event does this lesson deal?

2. What question, or doctrine, was now settled?

3. What was the contention of the "Judaizing" teachers?

4. In what epistle does Paul refer to their false teaching?

5. What is the nature of Peter's address on this occasion?

6. What other feature gives an outstanding character to this chapter?

7. What is the divine order of the ages as indicated here?

8. What was the final "Sentence" of this Council?

SECOND JOURNEY

CHAPTERS 15:36-18:22

Though the text of this lesson is long, it will be interesting to read it through at a single sitting, and get the whole journey at one view. The events are clear cut, easily remembered and apparent in their spiritual teaching.

Starting Forth.

It begins with the "contention" between Paul and Barnabas— men "of like passions" with ourselves, which was providentially overruled so that two missionary journeys grew out of it instead of one (15:36-41). Note that there were churches in "Syria and Cilicia" though no account is given of their origin beyond that of Antioch. It is a hint of the activity of the preachers of the Word, and the extent to which the gospel may have spread in that early time far beyond the record.

The story of the second visit to Lystra (16:1-3), gains interest from the subsequent prominence of Timothy, of whom further data are found in the epistles Paul afterward addressed to him. His circumcision is no evidence of inconsistency on Paul's part, since no question of principle was involved, but only expediency (v. 3). As Timothy's father was a Greek, it would be known that he was uncircumcised which would prevent this ministry among the Jews (cf. here 1 Cor. 9:20).

The outstanding feature of this journey is in verses 6-10 of this chapter. "Asia" (v. 6) was a name given to a large part of the coast of Asia Minor especially on the southeast. Why the Holy Spirit forbade the missionaries to preach there at this time, or the manner in which the prohibition was communicated, is not stated; but we know that later a great work was wrot there especially in Ephesus. The story is repeated with reference to the North (Bithynia), and as the only point of the compass left is the West, they make for the seaport of Troas. The student is urged to identify these localities on the map. At Troas special direction is required, for the sea is to be crossed, and God meets the need in the vision vouchsafed to Paul. At this point interest is added by the pronoun "we" in verse 10, indicating that the author, Luke, has now joined the party.

Experiences in Philippi.

Their stay at Philippi is full of movement (vv. 12-40). It was an important city founded by Philip of Macedon, inhabited chiefly by Roman citizens, but lacking in a Jewish population as is shown in the fact that it contained no synagogue (v. 13). It is unusual to read of a woman (Lydia) as engaged in commercial pursuits on her own account in that early time, but she seems to have been an exporter of Thyatira, noted for its purple dyes (vv. 14, 15).

The case following is that of demon possession, with phenomena not very different from modern clairvoyance or the spiritualistic seance (vv. 16-18). Of course the resultant proceedings were all illegal (vv. 19-24), but how greatly was God glorified thereby (vv. 25-34)! Verses 35-38 are an illustration that a Christian may with dignity insist upon his legal rights. Immunity from corporal punishment was one of the most valued privileges of Roman citizenship, and to impose it was a crime in the eye of the law. No wonder the magistrates were afraid. But learn the lesson of these verses concerning the way of Satan with the gospel. He first applauds and seems to help it along by flattery and with advertisement (v. 17), but when his testimony is rejected, he shows his true character (v. 19). Paul's preaching aimed at the idol worship of Rome which gave the excuse of verses 20, 21. Let us also be impressed with the simplicity of the gospel in verse 31. To believe on the Lord Jesus Christ is simply to commit one's self to Him to be saved. Nothing else is to be done, for God has put away our guilt in His atonement, and offers reconciliation for our acceptance. Note the reference to the jailer's "house." No one can be saved except by the exercise of a personal faith in the Saviour, but there is great encouragement here for the Christian parent to bring his offspring to the Lord in full assurance.

Thessalonica to Athens.

Thessalonica now claims our attention (17:1-9), a most influential city then and now, located on the Agean Sea, and on the direct route to Rome. Paul's method with the Jews is further presented here in verses 2 and 3. He employed the Old Testament scriptures. He *reasoned* with them, doubtless in the form of questions and answers. They were expecting the Messiah, the Christ, and he showed them that when He came it was necessary according to their own scriptures that He should suffer, die and rise again from the dead. Establishing these points he was then ready to show that "this Jesus Whom I preach unto you is the Christ," because He has fulfilled these things. The customary results follow, faith in some, envy and opposition in others, persecution, and removal to another place. The experience is repeated in Berea (vv. 10-14), and then we find Paul at Athens (vv. 16-34), still at this time "the intellectual and artistic capital of the world." It was also a religious capital, the strongest in Greek mythology, as illustrated in the text. The "Areopagus" (v. 19) was a court somewhat like the Roman Senate; and here Paul addressed the philosophers and leading citizens in terms familiar to them. Their "unknown God" he introduces to them as the Creator of all things and the "Lord of heaven and earth," and the future judge of men through His Son Jesus Christ, Whom He hath "raised from the dead" (vv. 23-31). The poets he quotes (v. 28) were Cleanthus and Aratus, whom he tactfully employs against their countrymen, whose boasted philosophy was "ignorance" (v. 30). The times of this ignorance God had "winked at" hitherto, overlooked in other words. Not in the sense that they would not be held to account or judged for it, but that He had sent them no special revelation of Himself until now. There is no distinctive application of the gospel here, and possibly because Paul's hearers were not prepared for it, but still his testimony was not in vain (v. 34).

Corinth and Ephesus

Corinth was the capital of Achaia, the lower peninsula of Greece; and in comparison with Athens, a great commercial center, cosmopolitan in its population, and as immoral as could well be conceived. The record of Paul's experiences here is varied by several details, for example his association with Aquila and Priscilla; the reference to his trade, for all Jewish lads, no matter what their circumstances, were taught trades; the encouraging vision he received; the length of time he remained in the city; the turning of the tables on his enemies; the Jewish vow he assumed, etc. (18:1-18). To speak of the vision, judging by verse 5, and also by certain allusions in Paul's two epistles to this Church, there was special need of it at this time. He seems to have been much depressed, and the Lord graciously desired him to be without anxiety. This explains why he remained there so long. The event before Gallio brings to mind one of the incidental evidences of the historical accuracy of this narrative. He is called the "deputy" of Achaia, and as a matter of fact that is what he was only, and not a proconsul, for at this time Achaia was united to Macedonia. Somewhat later it was constituted a province on its own account, and then came to have its own proconsul. The "vow" which Paul took may have been one of those concessions to the Jews he thought needful for expediency's sake.

Ephesus next reached (vv. 19-21), was just across the Aegean Sea from Corinth, and was the capital of the Roman province of Asia, noted for its commerce, but particularly for its temple of Diana (Artemis). There was a large Jewish population there, and they were accorded special privileges by the local government. We shall learn more of Paul's work there in our next lesson.

Questions.

1. What hint does this lesson give of the development of Christianity at this time?

2. Have you read 1 Cor. 9:20?

3. Have you traced this journey on the map?

4. Name the four missionaries in the journey.

5. How were the rights of Paul and Silas infringed upon in Philippi?

6. What is it to believe on the Lord Jesus Christ?

7. What encouragement for Christian parents is found here?

8. What is the meaning of 17:30?

9. Tell the story of Paul's stay in Corinth in your own words.

10. What was the geographical relation of Corinth and Ephesus?

THIRD JOURNEY

CHAPTERS 18:23-21:17

As in the last lesson, it is recommended that the text of the present one be read through at a single sitting, and two or three times if possible, before considering the comments, which then will be more valuable.

Some time had been spent again in Antioch, after which the whole territory of Phrygia and Galatia, in Asia Minor, was once more traversed for the purpose indicated in 18:23. Ephesus was duly reached (19:1), where Paul found a condition of things explained by the closing verses of chapter 18. Apollos does not seem to have been a Christian till Aquila and Priscilla met him, but he had been awakened by the ministry of John the Baptist, and was learned in the Old Testament Scriptures. The "disciples" Paul met (19:2), were possibly those of Apollos' ministry, whom he (Paul) brought out into the full fellowship of the gospel (vv. 2-

7). "Since ye believed" of verse 2, should be rendered *"when* ye believed." There was something lacking in these disciples which Paul observed, and which led him to put this question, because the reception of the Holy Spirit is the test of true discipleship (Rom. 8:9). (See comment on 2:5-13.)

Verses 8-20 show an unusual work of grace in and around Ephesus at this time. "The school of Tyrannus" (v. 9) was the convenient meeting place. The special miracles by Paul (v. 11) were an offset to the unusual power of the evil one there. This power showed itself in the "vagabond Jews" of verse 13 who suffered justly for their wickedness (v. 16), and whose defeat wrought gloriously for the Gospel (v. 17). There was much of this occultism in Ephesus, the overthrow of which is portrayed in the bonfire of the books of the black art, the cost of which was about $10,000.

But the spread of the Gospel exhibited itself also in the undermining of the controlling trade of the city, with the consequences following (vv. 23-41).

Chapter 20 is a diary of an extended journey from Ephesus to Macedonia (vv. 1, 2), when again Paul must have visited Philippi, Thessalonica, Berea, etc. Then he came down into Greece, possibly Athens, certainly Corinth saw his labors again. Here his purpose to cross by sea to Syria was interfered with by plots against his life, so that he retraced his steps into Macedonia, and crossed again to Troas (vv. 3-6). A week in Troas was made memorable by his discourse till midnight, and the miraculous recovery of the young man Eutychus (vv. 7-21). Note that this gathering of the saints to "break bread," i. e., observe the Lord's supper, was on the first day of the week, strengthening the conviction that the Lord's day had taken the place of the Jewish Sabbath as the time for Christian assemblies. Twenty miles on foot, and apparently alone, brought Paul to Assos, and thence by ship to Mitylene, and finally Miletus (vv. 13-16).

A tender episode meets us here in his farewell discourse to the beloved elders (bishops or presbyters) of the church at Ephesus (vv. 17-38). Three of his discourses have been reported hitherto somewhat at length, but this is especially interesting as the first spoken to the church. The others were missionary discourses. He first testifies to his own integrity as a minister (vv. 18-21); he then alludes to the bonds and afflictions that await him (vv. 22-27); a charge to the elders follows (vv. 28-31); a further testimony to his faithfulness (vv. 32-35); the prayer of farewell (vv. 36-38). Space will not permit elaboration, but verse 28 should not be passed over in its clear testimony to the oneness of God in Christ. "The Church of God which He purchased with His own Blood." The Deity of our Lord is here asserted, and the priceless cost of our redemption. There is no suggestion of an "apostolic succession" in verse 29, but just the opposite; a prophecy by-the-way, finding fulfillment in all the centuries, and never more positively than now. The beatitude of verse 37 was evidently current in the early church in addition to those recorded in the gospels, and this reference to it gives it inspired authority.

The journey continues until Jerusalem is reached (21:1-17), the most important features of which are the warnings of the apostle not to go to Jerusalem at all (4:10-14). The second says that these warnings were not merely from man but from the Holy Spirit. How then can we explain his neglect of them? Shall we say that they were not in the nature of a command, but a testing? Verses 11-13 suggest this. There is one other difficulty in this chapter, where the prophesying of women is referred to (v. 9), and which seems to contradict Paul later on in 1 Cor. 14 and 1 Tim. 2. We can not explain it, except to suggest that possibly this prophesying was in private rather than the public assembly.

Questions.

1. Have you read the text of this lesson as requested?

2. Why did Paul take this journey through Asia Minor?

3. What is suggested in this lesson as the test of true discipleship?

4. State in your own words the story of Paul's ministry in Ephesus at this time.

5. What makes memorable his stay at Troas on this journey?

6. Analyze his discourse to the elders of Ephesus.

7. What two great doctrinal truths are emphasized in 20:28?

8. Quote the new beatitude of verse 37.

9. What do verses 11-13 suggest concerning Paul's warnings?

TUMULT IN JERUSALEM

Chapters 21:18-23

The stirring events in this lesson are: 1st, Paul's ceremonial vow (21:18-26); 2d, his apprehension by the Jewish Mob (vv. 27-30); 3rd, his speech to them on the castle stairs (v. 31-22:21); 4th, his colloquy with the Roman soldiers (vv. 22-29); 5th, his defense before the Sanhedrin (v. 30-23:11); 6th, the plot to murder him (vv. 12-22); 7th, the escape to Caesarea (vv. 23-35).

As to Paul's vow, it is to be kept in mind that the Judaizing element in the church increased as its numbers increased, and while they had accepted the Lord Jesus Christ as Saviour, yet they were also zealous for the law of Moses. They can be sympathized with in this, considering their past history as Jews; but not when they attached a saving value to the law, or attempted to force its observance upon the Gentiles. To propitiate them and promote peace, Paul was tempted to compromise in the matter of this vow whatever it may have been, and he fell into a snare. It might be said in extenuation that the pressure was exceedingly strong upon him.

Of course it was not these Judaizing Christians who set upon him in the temple, but out and out Jews who hated Christianity altogether, and to whom the opportunity had been given by the action of Paul in yielding to the prejudices of the others.

His speech on the castle stairs constitutes: 1st, an account of himself as a Jew (vv. 1-5); 2nd, the story of his conversion (vv. 6-16); and third a declaration of his divine commission (vv. 17-21). In the story of his conversion some have found a difficulty in that Paul says his companions saw the light but heard no voice, while in chapter 9, Luke reports that they heard the voice. The explanation probably is that they heard the sound of the voice but were unable to understand the words. What he says of his divine commission here is not given in chapter 9, and is especially interesting and important on that account. It is a chapter of his inner life which otherwise never would have been known.

In Paul's defense before the Sanhedrin some think he was acting in the flesh, and after his own will rather than in the Holy Spirit. This is a serious charge to make and great caution is necessary, but the circumstances supposed to justify it are the abruptness of his beginning without waiting to be questioned, and his apparently self-righteous spirit (23:1), his offensive epithet to the high priest (v. 3), and his cleverness in dividing the council (v. 6). If there be anything in such a supposition, we are all the happier for the evidence in verse 11, that it was all right once more between the Lord and himself before the next day arose.

We need not continue our comments further in this case.

Questions.

1. Give the outline of this lesson.

2. How would you explain the occasion for Paul's vow?

3. Do you see clearly the distinction between Jews, and those here called Judaizers?

4. Analyze Paul's speech on the castle stairs.

5. What serious reflection is

sometimes cast upon Paul at this crisis, and on what grounds?

6. What Divine comfort or justification of Paul does the record contain?

PAUL A PRISONER AT CAESAREA

Chapters 24-26

There are three dignitaries of the Roman Empire before whom Paul now has a hearing—Felix, Festus and Agrippa.

The circumstances in the first instance show the great importance the Jewish leaders attached to the matter, since the high priest himself journeyed to Caesarea as an accuser of Paul, bringing with him not only a number of the elders but a Roman lawyer (34:1). The latter's indictment of Paul contains three counts, that of a political plotter, a religious heretic, and a violater of the temple (vv. 5, 6). Paul denies the first, admits the second, and challenges evidence of the third (vv. 12-20). "More perfect knowledge of that way" (v. 22), means that Felix knew much about Christ and Christianity though himself not a follower of the Nazarene.

"Drusilla" was a sister of Agrippa of whom the next chapter speaks, and a daughter of the Herod who martyred James (c. 12). She was not a lawful wife of Felix, having deserted her own husband to live with him. Of course the plot to kill Paul when he should return to Jerusalem (25:3), was not known to Festus, which makes it the more remarkable that he decided to keep him in Caesarea, and shows the hand of God in the premises.

Agrippa was king of Chalcis, holding the title by the grace of the Roman Emperor, and Bernice was his sister. The hearing before them was made a great state occasion (v. 23). Paul's opening words are courteous and tactful (26:2, 3). He reviews his past life as a Pharisee (vv. 4-11). He recounts once more his heavenly vision, his conversion and commission (vv. 12-18). The last verse is a remarkably condensed statement of the Gospel, referring to (a), Man's condition by nature, blinded, darkened and under the power of Satan; (b), the power of divine grace to give liberty and light to him including forgiveness, and an inheritance among the saints; (c), the instrument of it all—faith in Christ. Next, Paul speaks of his unjust treatment at the hands of the Jews, and the protection of God accorded him. The verdict follows in verses 30-32.

Questions.

1. Name the Roman dignitaries of this lesson.

2. Give the specifications against Paul.

3. What biographical data can you give about Drusilla?

4. How is the hand of God seen in the action of Festus?

5. Give an exegesis of 25:18.

6. What was the verdict of Festus and Agrippa?

A PRISONER AT ROME

Chapters 27-28

The reader is urged to add to the interest of this lesson by the further use of the map. The sea journey is marked by different stages—from Adramyttium to Myra (vv. 1-5), from Myra to the Fair Havens (vv. 6-8), from Fair Havens to Melita or Malta (v. 6-28:1), from Melita to Syracuse (vv. 2-12), from Syracuse to Rhegium, Puteoli and Rome (vv. 13-15).

The most interesting stage is the third which covers the shipwreck, and of which it is said that "in all classic literature there is nothing which gives so much information of the working of an ancient ship." Moreover, "historical research has confirmed the facts of the chapter and identified the scene of the wreck." The narrative has often been used in an allegorical sense to portray the history of the church, and also the history of the salvation of a single soul, but into this we have not time to enter. Gaebelein has a striking observation on Paul's warning to the centurion and the shipmaster (27:19, 11) saying, "we can think of other warnings given through the great apostle, warnings concerning the spiritual dangers, the apostasy of the last days, the perilous times of seducing spirits and doctrines of demons. The professing church has forgotten these, for which she is drifting, cast about by every wind of doctrine and rapidly nearing the long-predicted ship-wreck." Alas! how true this is!

The phrase "barbarous people" (28:2), is not to be understood as meaning savages, but simply foreigners to the Greeks. All who did not speak their language were called "barbarians." What a striking fulfillment of Mark 16:18 is found in verses 2-6! Read verses 15 and 16 in comparison with Rom 1:11-13, written years before, and be impressed with the different way in which Paul entered Rome from that which he expected. Note in verse 17 how consistent is his method of preaching the Gospel with the principle he laid down in Romans 1:16, "to the Jew first." Note too, his quotation of Isaiah 6 in verses 25-27, when the Jews turned their back upon his message, and how sadly those words of the prophet have been fulfilled in the history of their nation from that day to this. But the latter part of Romans 11 should be read in the same connection, to learn what God's gracious purpose is for that same people in the time to come. Verse 28 marks a larger beginning of the world-wide proclamation of the "salvation of God" among the nations. This proclamation however will one day close as that same chapter of Romans (11) foretells, when it will have come to pass that they too have judged themselves "unworthy of eternal life."

Paul is now a prisoner in Rome where he remains for two years actively engaged not only in preaching the gospel by word of mouth, but expounding its deeper truths through the epistles he wrote from his prison house to the churches of Ephesus, Colosse and Philippi. There is reason to believe from his later pastoral epistles that he was liberated after his hearing before the Emperor, and once more took up his itinerary among the churches and in unevangelized parts. He was arrested a second time however, as we may gather from the same sources, when, according to tradition, he was beheaded in Rome for his testimony to the Gospel and the Saviour he loved.

Questions.

1. Name the stages of Paul's sea journey.

2. How is the word "barbarous" explained?

3. Have you read the latter part of Romans 11?

4. What church epistles were written from Rome by Paul?

5. What have history and tradition to say concerning the subsequent life of this great apostle?

EPISTLE TO ROMANS

INTRODUCTION AND THEME

Chapter 1:1-17

It is not known how, or when, the church at Rome was founded, but probably by Jews who received the Gospel in Jerusalem on the day of Pentecost (Acts 2). We shall see later that neither Paul nor any other apostle had as yet visited that metropolis, although Paul had a great desire to do so; and as another says, it was natural that "he should wish to announce before his coming the distinctive truths which had been revealed to and through him. He would desire the Christians in Rome to have his own statement of the great doctrines of grace so assailed everywhere by legalistic (Judaizing) teachers."

He was now in Corinth doubtless on his third missionary journey (15:22-29), and Phoebe, a deaconess of the church at Cenchrea, the seaport of Corinth, was about to visit Rome (Rom. 16:1); a circumstance of which he avails himself to send this letter.

1. It opens, as is usual in Paul's epistles, with a greeting or salutation (vv. 1-7), in which is given the author's name and spiritual relation to Jesus Christ, his official designation and the object of it, and an announcement of the church or persons addressed. It is Paul who writes, and he is a bond-servant of Jesus Christ. As such he has been made a messenger of the Gospel of God (v. 1). This Gospel, which means "Good news" or "glad-tidings," was not altogether new because it had been promised through the Old Testament prophets (vv. 2 cf. Gal. 3:8). It concerned the Son of God, Jesus Christ our Lord, an account of Whose Gracious Person and work follows (vv. 3-5). The testimony of this Gospel committed to Paul, was worldwide including them at Rome (vv. 5-7).

2. The salutation is followed by a thanksgiving (vv. 8-12) for the "faith" or standing in grace of the church at Rome (v. 8), which leads to an expression of the apostle's longing to visit them (v. 10); not merely for social reasons, but spiritual benefit (vv. 11, 12). It is here we learn that he had not visited them before, and that no other apostle had done so, for if so, the "spiritual gift" (v. 11) would doubtless have been imparted; while on the other hand it was a Pauline principle not to build on another man's foundation (Rom. 15:20, 21; 2 Cor. 10:14-16).

3. The thanksgiving is followed by a statement of the theme of the epistle, for it is more than a personal letter, a treatise, in short, on the great subject that had been committed to Paul (vv. 13-17). "Let" (v. 13), is obsolete English, meaning "hindered." "Barbarian" (v. 14), signifies "foreigner," the Latins (Rome) were foreigners to the Greeks. "Unwise" is to be taken only in a comparative sense. The Greeks regarded themselves as the "wise" people of the world, cultivated in human philosophy, while all others were unwise by contrast. That which Paul is ready to preach at Rome is the "Gospel" (v. 16), called as we saw in verse 1, "the Gospel of God." The words "of Christ," (v. 16), are omitted in the Revised Version. It is the "Gospel of God," i.e., "the widest possible designation of the whole body of redemptive truth." This might be called the theme of the epistle, unless we prefer to take that which is the essence of the Gospel as inferred from a later verse, "The Gift of God's Righteousness."

This Gospel "is the power of God unto salvation to every one that believeth." The dynamic He uses to lift men out of the death of sin into the life of righteousness, for "salvation" means just that, including, as another puts it, "the ideas of deliverance, safety, preservation, healing and soundness." And the essence of its power lies in this, that "therein is revealed a righteousness of God by faith unto faith" (v. 17 R. V.). It is very necessary to understand that phrase "a righteousness of God," which is the key to the epistle, and does not mean the righteousness which God *is* in His own nature, but a righteousness which He *gives* to men freely, on the exercise of their faith in Christ. To quote Lange's Commentary, it is the rightness which proceeds from God, i. e., the right relation in which man is placed by a judicial act of God." Or to quote the Scofield Bible, the righteousness is "Christ Himself, Who fully met in our stead and behalf every demand of the law, and Who is by the act of God, 'made unto us * * * righteousness' (1 Cor. 1:30)." "As it is written 'He that is righteous by faith shall live' " (Hab. 2:4, Lange).

Questions.

1. By whom presumably, was the church at Rome founded?

2. Why may Paul have wished to write this letter?

3. What gave him the opportunity to send it?

4. Divide this lesson into three parts.

5. What leads us to think Paul had never visited Rome?

6. What is the theme of the epistle?

7. What other theme is preferred by some?

8. What ideas does the word "salvation" include?

9. Does "righteousness of God" mean what God is, or what God gives?

10. Give the definitions of that phrase in Lange and the Scofield Bible.

MAN'S LOST CONDITION BY NATURE

CHAPTERS 1:18-3:20

We saw in the last lesson that man if he would be saved must become righteous before God, and the righteousness which alone satisfies Him is that which He Himself supplies. We now learn what man's condition is which makes this a necessity. In other words this lesson, constituting the second general division of the epistle, gives us (1), a Divine declaration about sin (1:18-21); (2), shows it to be punitive and degenerative in its effects (vv. 22-23); and (3), teaches the universality of its extent (2:1-3:20).

1. As to the Divine declaration about sin, we perceive that not only is there a righteousness from God revealed from heaven, but "a wrath of God" as well. The first gives the remedy, the second the penalty if the remedy is not applied. "Who hold the truth." might be rendered "who hold *down* the truth." That is, the truth of God, whose saving power might be known to men, is held down, does not get a chance to be known, because of man's unrighteousness (v. 18). This truth might be known by the facts of creation. Not that the Gospel of redemption is revealed in nature, but sufficient of God is thus revealed, i. e., His eternal power and Godhead, "to have kept men true to Him essentially," so that they are without excuse (v. 20). This is seen in what follows: Man once knew God, the story of Eden shows this: but he is now fallen from God, through his own ingratitude and conceited reasonings. The fall is moral, rather than intellectual, for his "foolish (senseless) *heart*" is "darkened" (vv. 18-21).

2. Sin at once becomes punitive and degenerative. Observe the down-grade: failure to glorify God; ingratitude; vain reasonings; darkened moral nature; turned into fools; worshipping natural objects, men, birds, beasts, reptiles, given over to uncleanness in the dishonoring of their bodies among themselves (vv. 22-25 and practically to the end of the chapter). In passing, it should be said that the horrible details of this indictment against the Gentile world is established by the "classics" of Greek and Latin literature, showing that these things were true not merely

of the low and ignorant, but the high and cultured of Paul's day. (See Testimonium Animae, or Greek and Roman before Jesus Christ, by E. G. Sihler, Ph.D.)

3. This thought is now elaborated, which shows the philosophers and moralizers of Greece and Rome to be no better than the others (2:1-3). They were incapable of judging others; only God could do that, Who is no respecter of persons (vv. 6-11). His judgment would be just both as against the Gentiles and Jews. The former had not the revealed law as did the latter, i. e., they did not have the Old Testament scriptures, but would be judged by the law written in their hearts (vv. 12-16).

Special attention is now given the Jews because they had the Old Testament scriptures, and while equally sinful with the pagan Gentiles, were yet trusting in their knowledge of the letter of the law as making them better than they (vv. 17-20). The answer assumed in the case of each question in verses 21-23 is affirmative, as is proven by the concluding verses of the chapter.

4. Did this mean then, that the Jew had no advantage whatever over the pagan Gentile? No, for the reason in c. 3:1, 2. It was an advantage for the Jew to have the Scriptures even though some did not believe them (vv. 3, 4). Verses 5-8 are parenthetical, and the main question is taken up again at 9. The Jews are morally no better as a class than the pagans, as proven by the facts of history just alluded to (vv. 21-24), and by their own Scriptures (vv, 10-18 cf. with Ps. 14:1-3, 53:1, 5:9, 10:7, 36:1). These were the things which their own "law" said, and said to them as Jews, because the Gentiles did not know that law, did not have the Old Testament scriptures. Therefore the "mouth," i. e., the boasting of the Jew was stopped as well as that of the Gentiles, and "all the world." Jew and Gentile, were "guilty before God" (v. 19). This proved that as the result of the works of the law no man could be accounted right-

eous before God, for as a matter of fact, the clearer one apprehended the law the more condemned as a sinner he became (v. 20).

Questions.

1. What did the previous lesson teach us?

2. What are we to learn from this lesson?

3. Divide this lesson into three general parts.

4. What two great things are revealed from heaven?

5. Why are men without excuse for their ignorance of God?

6. Name some of the steps in the downgrade of sin.

7. What is the bearing of contemporaneous literature on Paul's indictment of the pagan world?

8. By what two lines of proof are the Jews proven as guilty as the Gentiles?

9. How would you interpret 3:20?

NATURE AND EFFECT OF THE GIFT OF RIGHTEOUSNESS

CHAPTERS 3:21-5:11

1. If a righteousness were not obtainable by the works of the law as we saw in our last lesson, then a Jew especially, might well ask in surprise how it *were* obtainable? To which the apostle replies, that "now apart from the law a righteousness of God is manifested," (3:21 R. V.), i.e. a righteousness which may become man's without the keeping of the law. This righteousness he describes as (a), "witnessed by the law and the prophets," in other words, taught in the Old Testament as well as the New Testament; (b), obtained through faith in Jesus Christ (v. 22); (c), without respect of persons, Jew or Gentile (vv. 22, 23); (d), the free gift of God's grace (v. 24); (e), based upon the death of Jesus Christ (v. 25); (f), and its bestowment declarative of God's righteous character (vv. 25, 26). "His righteousness" in these last two verses does not refer as in the earlier instances, to the right-

eousness He gives, but the righteousness He *is*. It means that He is perfectly consistent with His own law and holiness in freely justifying a sinner who believes on Christ, because Christ has fully met every demand of the law on his behalf (10:4). In this connection "propitiation" should be understood clearly. It does not convey the idea of placating an angry God, but of "doing right by His holy law and so making it possible for Him righteously to show mercy"—Scofield Bible. Christ so honored the law by enduring its righteous sentence that God who ever foresaw the cross, is vindicated in having "passed over" sins from Adam to Moses (5:13), and the sins of Jewish believers under the old covenant, and in justifying sinners under the new covenant.

2. To appreciate chapter 4 go back to the phrase, "witnessed by the law and the prophets" (3:22). "The Law of the Prophets" was one of the names given by the Jews to the Old Testament. The "Law" meant the Pentateuch or the first five books of Moses and the "Prophets" the remainder of the Old Testament. Paul was showing that the salvation or justification by faith he preached was Old Testament truth, and in the present chapter he confirms the fact by the instances of David and Abraham. The illustration from Abraham is found in the "Law" and that from David in the "Prophets." Abraham's case is first treated (vv. 1-4), and then David's (vv. 5-8). To Abraham he returns at verse 9, showing in what follows how justification is entirely distinct from ordinances. Verses 18-25 should be pondered because of their simple and picturesque presentation of the theme. Abraham believed God's testimony about Isaac in the face of nature to the contrary, and this faith "was counted to him for righteousness" (v. 22). We have only to believe God's testimony about Jesus Christ, Whom Isaac typified, to receive the same blessing in the same way. Verse 2 of this chapter must not be thought to contradict James 2:24, because these two scriptures are but two aspects of the same truth. Paul here is laying down the principle which James is applying; or to put it better, Paul is speaking of that which justifies man before God, and James of that which justifies him before man. The former alludes to what God sees —faith, and the latter to that which man sees—works. The one has in mind Gen. 15:6, and the other Gen. 22:1-19—Scofield Bible.

3. There are three great results of justifying faith as indicated in chapter 5:1-11—peace with God, access unto God, and rejoicing before God (vv. 1, 2). The rejoicing is in three things, (1), hope of the glory of God (2), tribulations (3), God Himself (v. 11). The rejoicing in tribulations is a theme full of interest. We rejoice because the tribulations of a justified man work "patience," the patience "experience," and the experience "hope," that "maketh not ashamed" (vv. 3-5). The "experience" in this case is experience of the love of God Who comforts us in our tribulation, sanctifies it to us and delivers us from it. This experience assures us of His love for us, the Holy Ghost thus 'sheds it abroad in our hearts,' and in consequence of that assurance our hope of beholding and partaking of His glory grows the brighter. We know that we shall not be ashamed of, or confounded in regard to the fulfilment of that hope. Verses 6-10, important as they are and full of the riches of Christ, are in a sense parenthetical to the main line of teaching in this section. Bishop Moule suggests a rendering of verse 10 of great beauty—"We shall be *kept* in His life."

Questions.

1. What is meant by righteousness "apart from the law"?

2. What is meant by "witnessed by the law and the prophets"?

3. How do you distinguish the "righteousness of God" (vv. 25, 26), from the same phrase as used earlier?

4. How do you understand "propitiation?"

5. What part of chapter 3 is illustrated by chapter 4?

6. What is the meaning of "The Law and the Prophets"?

7. Why is the phrase used in this case?

8. What is the substance of chapter 4?

9. How does Abraham's justification illustrate ours?

10. Harmonize 4:2 with James 2:24.

11. Name the three results of justifying faith.

12. Name the three causes of rejoicing.

MAN IN RELATION TO THE FIRST ADAM AND THE SECOND ADAM

Chapters 5:12–7:6

1. "Wherefore" leads back to chapter 3, where the apostle is referring to the sinful condition of all men. It was by one man that sin entered the world bringing physical death as a penalty, and that all have sinned is proven by the fact that all have paid that penalty (v. 12). To be sure the law was not given to Moses till Sinai, but as "death reigned from Adam to Moses," it is evident that there was a transgression of another law than that written on stone, for "sin is not imputed when there is no law" (v. 13). For the nature of this other law compare again 2:15.

2. But as sin came through the first Adam, so the gift of righteousness came through the second Adam. It was just one offence that brought the condemnation, but the gift of righteousness covers "many offences" (vv. 16, 19). It was the giving of the law at Sinai that revealed how many these offences were (v. 20) for "by the law is the knowledge of sin" (3:20). Nevertheless, though sin was thus seen to abound, yet "grace did much more abound" (v. 20). "Sin" as used here is different from "sins," the former referring to our fallen nature, and the latter to manifestations of that nature.

3. What Paul had said about grace abounding where sin abounded, might lead an uninstructed mind to infer that it put a premium on sin. Or in other words, if man were justified by faith only, what provision was made for a change of character? How did salvation by grace affect one's experience as well as his standing before God? Chapters 6 to 8 work out this thought as follows:

(a) The believer is identified with Christ in His death and resurrection (6:1-10). The baptism into Jesus Christ (verse 3), is the pentecostal experience which becomes the birthright of every believer the moment he believes. He is then baptized by the Holy Spirit into the body of which Christ is the Head (1 Cor. 12:13); and being so baptized he is considered as one with Christ as any member of a human body is one with the head of that body. This means of course, that he is regarded in God's sight as having died when Christ died—he was "baptized into His death." The sequel however, must be equally true, and he is regarded as having risen from the dead when Christ rose. Hence he is now in a legal or judicial sense walking before God "in newness of life." Being dead he "is freed from sin" (v. 7), i. e., having legally died in Christ when Christ died just as every member of a body dies when its head dies, he has paid the penalty of his sin in Christ, and having now arisen in Christ after the payment of that penalty, "death hath no more dominion over him" (v. 9), he has not again to pay the penalty of sin.

(b) It is now his duty to reckon this to be true, and no longer to allow sin to reign in his "mortal body" (v. 11). The way to accomplish this is not by efforts and resolutions on his part, but by yielding his new life unto God. He yields his new life by yielding the members of his body unto God—his eyes, ears, tongue, hands, feet, brain, etc. (v. 13).

(c) The result will be his deliverance from the dominion of sin —God will see to it (v. 14). The old relation of the man to the law of sin, and his new relation to Christ are illustrated by the effect of death upon servitude (vv. 16-23). The old servitude was rendered to sin the end of which was death. But death in another form, i. e., crucifixion with Christ, has now intervened to free the servant from sin, and enable him to become the servant of God with "fruit unto holiness and the end everlasting life" (v. 22). The relationship is next illustrated by marriage (7:1-6). Death dissolves the marriage relationship, and as natural death frees a wife from the law of her husband, so crucifixion with Christ sets the believer free from the law, or rather its penalty resting upon him on account of his sin.

"Newness of spirit" and "oldness of the letter" (v. 6) are expressions requiring a word of comment as we meet with them again in another epistle. By the "letter" is meant the Mosaic law, and by the "spirit" the powers and relationships of the new life in Christ Jesus (cf. 2 Cor. 3:6).

Questions.

1. What is the significance of "wherefore" at the beginning of this lesson?

2. How is it proven that all men have sinned?

3. Did you cf. 2:17?

4. What is the distinction between "sin" and "sins"?

5. What thought is it that chapters 6-8 are working out?

6. What is the meaning of "baptized into Jesus Christ?"

7. How may the dethronement of sin be accomplished in a believer?

8. What two illustrations of this truth are employed in this lesson?

9. Describe "oldness of letter" and "newness of spirit."

VICTORY AND SECURITY

Chapters 7:7-8

That part of chapter 7 on which we now enter is biographical, giving Paul's experience at a period when, though, regenerated, he was still living under the law and in ignorance of the deliverance to be had in Christ. It is a revelation that the believer possesses two natures—that of the first Adam received at his physical birth, and that of the second Adam received in regeneration by the Holy Spirit through faith. The man here described has been baptized into Jesus Christ, is judicially free from the law, and is walking in newness of life, and yet sin reigns more or less in his mortal body. How is he to be delivered from it? In chapter 6 Paul taught that it was by yielding oneself to God, as the result of which sin would not have dominion over him. In chapter 7 he shows in his own person the need of doing this, while in chapter 8 he describes the Divine process by which the change from defeat to victory is thus produced.

1. He makes clear that the Christian believer is not made holy by the law (7:7-14). There was a time when, as a Jew, he thought he had kept the law (Phil. 3:6), but now as a regenerated Christian he had come to see the law in a new light, i.e., as spiritual, and that which was not sin theretofore now became so. Then he had thought himself "alive" in a spiritual sense, but now he perceived that he was really dead.

2. He shows the conflict of the two natures under the law (vv. 15-25). He spoke of himself as "carnal" (v. 14), by which he meant that, as a believer, he was still more or less under the power of his fallen nature, i. e., he did things that were wrong and yet it was not the new Paul that was doing them but the old Paul, "sin that dwelleth in me" (vv. 17, 20). This "sin," this "old man" was like a dead body lashed to his back, was there no deliverance from it? He thanked God that there was such deliverance through Jesus Christ.

3. This deliverance he now reveals (8:1-27. (a) It is the Holy Spirit dwelling in the believer who sets him "free from the law of sin and death" (vv. 2-4). In

his fallen state he was subject to a bias or tendency towards sin, the outcome of which was death. But now as a regenerated man that bias or tendency is broken. (b) The Holy Spirit also gives him a spiritual mind to desire this new freedom (vv. 5-10). (c) And the spiritual power to exercise the desire (vv. 11-13). (d) And the spiritual motive to lay hold of the power (vv. 14-25). (e) And the spiritual wisdom to appreciate the motive (vv. 26, 27). The spiritual motive to lay hold of the power of the Holy Spirit for a life of victory, is that of our relationship to God as His children, which implies joint heirship with Christ. This heirship is so glorious in its full manifestation that the whole creation is groaning for it, because it means its deliverance from bondage.

4. The practical conclusion to be drawn from all this on the part of the believer is stated in verse 28,—a conclusion which reaches into the glorified state (vv. 29, 30). The man Whom God has called in Christ to be his, is already considered "glorified," so certain is that event to follow in his experience. No wonder that the challenges of verses 31-35 should follow. Read them in the Revised Version.

Questions.

1. How is the latter half of chapter 7 described?

2. Of what is it a revelation?

3. What does chapter 8 describe?

4. What does 7:7-14 make clear, and how?

5. What is shown in chapter 7:15-25, and how?

6. By whom is deliverance from the power of sin wrought in the believer?

7. Name the five-fold process by which this is done.

8. What is the spiritual motive for a life of victory?

9. Quote the practical conclusion of 8:28.

10. How far does this extend in its application??

PARENTHESIS CONCERNING ISRAEL

CHAPTERS 9-11

These chapters carry us back to the third where Paul proved the lost condition of the Jew as well as the Gentile. But if this were so it might be charged that the Old Testament promises to Israel had failed, which he now shows is not the case. His line of argument is threefold: first, some of Israel were already saved (c. 9); secondly, all of Israel might be saved but for unbelief (c. 10); thirdly, all of Israel would be saved ultimately (c. 11).

1. Chapter 9 might be divided thus: (a) The apostle's solicitude for Israel (vv. 1-5), whose sevenfold privilege he names. There is a difficulty of interpretation in verse 3, which might be helped by a slight variation in the translation, which some have rendered: "I have great heaviness * * * for my brethren (for I myself were wishing to be accursed from Christ)." The thought may be that he is expressing sympathy with them in their spiritual darkness, because he was once in a like case. (b) The fact that some of Israel were saved (vv. 6-13). The Word of God had taken some effect for there were Israelites who had believed, and were now counted not only as Abraham's natural posterity but his spiritual children. This principle of selection was illustrated in the choice of Jacob over Esau. "Hated" (v. 13), must not be understood of arbitrary wrath, but only as expressing choice. (c) The sovereignty of God in such a choice is defended (vv. 14-24), for His mercy is under His sovereign will. The reference to Pharaoh must not be understood of arbitrary action on God's part, but as involving the free choice of the wicked monarch. God did not put forth effort to change that choice, so that the hardening of his heart was the penal consequence of his folly. (d) The Old Testament predicted the rejection of Israel and the calling of the Gentiles

(vv. 25-33). (Cf. Hos. 1:10, 2:23; Isa. 10:22, 23, etc.)

2. The whole of chapter 10 shows that the rejection of Judah is due to their unbelief, i. e., to their desire to work out under the law a character or righteousness which would satisfy God, instead of accepting a righteousness from Him by faith (vv. 3, 4 cf. with v. 10).

3. Chapter 11 shows that the setting aside of the nation has not been perpetual. In the *first* place, there was a remnant of the faithful even at the present time, of whom the apostle was one (vv. 1-6). Indeed, there always had been such a remnant. There was one in Elijah's day (cf. vv. 2-7 with 1 Kings 19:18). There was one in Isaiah's day (Isa. 1:9). During the captivity there was such a remnant, and at the end of the 70 years a remnant returned to the land. Look at Luke 2:38 for one at the period of the first advent of Christ. There are believing Jews in our day who constitute such a class, and we have seen in our Old Testament studies that the prophecies focus on the deliverance of the remnant during the tribulation (Rev. 7:3-8). It is of the hopes and fears of this last-named that the Millennial psalms treat.

In the *second* place this chapter indicates that the national blindness of the Jews had been foretold (vv. 7-10). But in the providence of God it gave an opportunity to the Gentiles (vv. 11, 12), which the latter are warned to profit by (vv. 13-22). Throughout this warning there are several intimations of the restoration of Israel as a nation (vv. 12, 15, 16). This is what is meant by "their fulness," "the receiving of them," etc. The "first-fruit" and the "root" are Abraham, and the "lump" and the "branches" the offspring that came from him.

Finally, it is definitely stated that the nation shall be restored (vv. 23-36), by which is meant the faithful remnant at the end of the age. The "fulness of the Gentiles" (v. 25) means the completion of God's purpose in them at that time, i. e., the whole body of Christ, the Church, will have been called out from among them, and caught up to meet Him in the air (1 Thess. 4:13-18). Observe the reference to Christ's second coming in verse 26, and to the fulfillment of God's original promise to Abraham in verse 29. "Without repentance" means without a change of mind on His part.

Questions.

1. To what past of the epistle does this lesson carry us back?

2. What possible charge is it intended to refute?

3. Give the refutation in outline.

4. Name the seven great privileges of Israel.

5. How is 9:3 sometimes rendered?

6. How is the hardening of Pharaoh's heart to be explained?

7. What explains the rejection of Israel as a nation?

8. Trace the history of the remnant of Israel in the Bible.

9. What is the meaning of the "fullness of the Gentiles"?

PRACTICAL APPLICATION

CHAPTERS 12-16

1. In the 6th chapter Paul revealed the secret of experimental sanctification as the yielding of one's self unto God, in which case sin would not have dominion over one, while in the 8th he showed the Divine process of that sanctification as the work of the Holy Spirit in the believer. Having now finished the doctrinal part of his epistle, he returns to what he then said (c. 6) and *exhorts* to that yielding on the ground of the "mercies of God" of which he had been speaking throughout (12:1, 2). The presenting of our bodies is the same as the yielding of our members in chapter 6. This exhortation is followed by a promise that we shall not be "conformed to this world," but be "transformed by the renewing of your mind." In other words the Holy Spirit will do His work in us as the result of which we shall experience, i. e.,

do, the "good, acceptable and perfect will of God."

2. The verses, and indeed the chapters that follow to the end of the epistle, indicate the ways in which this will should be done: (1) In the exercise of spiritual gifts as members of the body of Christ (vv. 3-8); in our social duties as Christian brethren (vv. 9-16); (3) in our general conduct towards the world (vv. 17-21); (4) in our subjection to human governments (13:1-14); and (5) in our ecclesiastical relations concerning doubtful things (14:1-15:13).

3. This last will repay further exposition. "Him that is weak in the faith," is the Christian brother with scruples on matters of Christian practice, such as the eating of meats and the observance of fast days (14:1-9). He is not to be denied fellowship on that ground, since he is thus walking out of regard to God's honor. On the other hand, he is not to judge the brother who does not see the particular matter just as he does. The whole question of judging or criticising one another then comes under review (vv. 10-11), after which the apostle turns to the consideration of the "strong" brother who does not possess these scruples. He has a right to his Christian liberty in the premises, but he should not press it to the point of "stumbling" his weaker brother (vv. 13-18), but seek peace (vv. 19-21). If he has the "faith" to believe that he is at liberty as a Christian to do thus and so, let that be a matter between him and God, but let him be careful lest in openly exercising that faith or Christian privilege he does not bring himself under self-judgment (v. 22). If he has a doubt about his liberty in the premises, he had better not "eat" as that will thus condemn him. To insist on his liberty when he is in doubt about it is "sin." The better plan is to follow Christ's example (15:1-4), which is the apostle's prayer for them (vv. 5-7). [The difficulty as to the strong and the weak had probably arisen between the Jews and Gentiles,

which may explain the remaining verses of this section (vv. 8-13)].

4. The epistle concludes as follows: (a) A reference to the apostle's special ministry to the Gentiles (15:14-21); (b) another expression of his desire and purpose to visit Rome (vv. 23-33); (c) individual remembrances, in which it is interesting to observe the references to Paul's personal acquaintances and relatives (16:1-16); (d) a warning and exhortation (vv. 17-20); (e) friendly greetings, a benediction and an ascription of praise to God (vv. 21-27).

In this last, Paul incidentally mentions "my Gospel," and also "the mystery which was kept secret since the world began, but now is made manifest" (vv. 25, 26). Just what this "mystery" is as distinguished from the "Gospel," will appear more particularly in the epistles to the churches at Ephesus and Colosse, although chapter 6 of this epistle gave us an introduction to it in the believers' identification with Christ. The full truth of the mystery is found in a right conception of the church of Christ as distinguished from the kingdom of Israel, and the union of Jew and Gentile believers in this age in that mystical body of which Christ is the Head.

Questions.

1. To what chapter, and what thought in that chapter, are we carried back by the beginning of this lesson?

2. What is the promise attached to the yielding of our bodies to God?

3. What will be the result of the renewing of our minds?

4. In what ways is our doing of the will of God to be shown?

5. Who is meant by "Him that is weak in the faith"?

6. Why should he not be denied Christian fellowship?

7. What is the Christian obligation of the "weak" brother?

8. What is the caution given to the strong brother?

9. Give an outline of the conclusion of this epistle.

FIRST CORINTHIANS

10. What is the explanation of the "mystery" here named?

THE CAUSE AND CURE OF FACTIONAL DISPUTES

CHAPTERS 1-4

This epistle was written by Paul probably during the latter part of his long visit to Ephesus, and it will add interest to its study to re-read Acts, chapters 18-20, which speak of his visit to both cities, Ephesus and Corinth. The occasion for its writing as given in chapters 1:11 and 7:1, was a visit to Paul of members "of the house of Chloe," who brought a written communication to him as well as verbal reports of conditions in the Church. These conditions were not good, as indicated in their party divisions (cc. 1-4), their tolerance of gross immorality (cc. 5-6), their erroneous views in regard to marriage (c. 7), their abuse of Christian liberty (cc. 8-10), their disorderly conduct in the assemblies of worship (cc. 11-14) and their false teaching touching the resurrection of the dead.

Indeed, as one carefully reads the epistle he wonders how such people could be Christians at all, until he recalls the distinction, made clear in the New Testament, between the believer's legal standing before God in Christ, and his actual walk or experience in it. As we saw in Romans, the moment one believes on Christ, he becomes justified from all sin, i. e., the condemnatory guilt of it is removed, he receives a righteousness from God which perfectly satisfies God, and he is adopted into the Divine family. But now the work of grace begins in Him by the Holy Spirit, in distinction from the work of grace wrought *for* him by Christ on the cross, and in the measure in which he comes to know the will of God through His Word, and yields himself thereto, he becomes more and more conformed to the image of Christ.

These Corinthians may have been in Christ, but they were walking inconsistently, and the purpose of this epistle is to set them right, and to set us right through them.

1. After the salutation (1:1-3) and the thanksgiving on their behalf (vv. 4-9), the apostle enters into the difficulty of their party divisions. Some were "Paulinians," some "Apollonians," some "Cephasites," and some, perhaps the most contentious of all, "Christites." Paul was innocent of fomenting these discords (vv. 14-17), and so doubtless had been Apollos and Cephas, but the root of the matter lay in the false intellectualism of the Corinthians. They were Greeks for the most part, and the Greeks gloried in human philosophy and worldly wisdom, the application of whose principles to the teaching of Christianity had made all the trouble.

2. In meeting the situation, Paul shows in three ways that the Gospel is not human wisdom (1:18-3:4): (a) by the mystery of the cross, which "is to them that perish foolishness, but unto us which are saved, the power of God." "The wisdom of the wise" had been unable to save men in the past, but the preaching of the cross had effectually accomplished it (vv. 18-25); (b) by the elements composing the Church, which were not for the most part the worldly-wise and great, but the opposite. God had made Christ to be unto them wisdom however, in the sense that He had become their righteousness, and sanctification and redemption (vv. 26-31); (c) by the apostle's own example, who had not appealed to their intellectualism, but had simply preached Christ crucified (2:1-5). This last point must be guarded though, as there was danger of men esteeming the gospel to be destitute of wisdom of any kind; (d) it is therefore shown to be the wisdom of God (v. 7); which only the Spirit of God could reveal to men (vv. 8-11), but which had been revealed

to Paul, and was being revealed through him to others (vv. 12, 13). Only the spiritually-enlightened however, were capable of receiving it (2:13-3:4).

In the verses last indicated, Paul speaks of three classes of men, the "natural," the "spiritual" and the "carnal." The first is man considered as fallen and unsaved; the second, as he who is saved and, being filled with the Spirit, is walking in fellowship with God; the third is saved, but still walking "after the flesh," a "babe" in Christ.

3. But the Corinthians had not only a false view of the Gospel, confounding it with human wisdom, but also a false view of their Christian teachers which had contributed to their divisions. Paul deals with this beginning at 3:5-4:2: (a) Christian teachers are simply ministers (3:5-11), whose reward depends on their faithfulness (vv. 12-15); (b) the Church should not glory in them, for out of Christ their wisdom is foolishness, and in Christ, they are all alike the possession of the whole Church (3:16-4:2). In connection with the reference to rewards (3:14, 15), remember that the subject applies only to those who are already saved by grace, and it is grace to which any saved soul is indebted for reward.

4. These divisions somehow involved a question of Paul's apostolic authority, and to its defence he applies himself to the end of the lesson: (a) all human estimates of men are inadequate, and for a just judgment we must await the Lord's second coming (4:3-5). Another calls attention here to the interesting point that four standards of judgment are referred to, those of our friends, the world, ourselves, and the Lord. Our own judgment is not to be depended upon absolutely, any more than that of other people; (b) the question of his authority had arisen out of the vanity of their hearts (vv. 6-8). They were "puffed-up" and vainglorious now that he was absent from them, and having begun to apply their worldly wisdom to the Gospel, they felt that they could get along without him, and boasted of it. They felt themselves to be "full" and "rich," and reigning "as kings" without him. There is irony, and yet an earnest longing in the words, "I would to God ye did reign, that we also might reign with you," his allusion being to the second coming of Christ; (c) the apostles, himself doubtless being chiefly in mind, were objects of contempt and suffering to the world both of angels and of men (vv. 9-13) —a testimony that other intelligences than ourselves, both good and evil doubtless, are interesting in the working out of God's purpose of redemption through His church; (d) His motive in thus writing was to warn them as his children in Christ, for which reason he was soon to send Timothy to them, and would ultimately visit them himself again. Upon their reception of this admonition would depend whether he would come to them "with a rod, or in love and the spirit of meekness."

Questions.

1. What is the theme of this lesson?

2. When and where was this epistle written by Paul?

3. What was its occasion?

4. Describe conditions in this church.

5. Harmonize these conditions with the Christian profession.

6. In what did the root of their party divisions lie?

7. In what three ways does the apostle meet the situation?

8. How is the third point guarded?

9. Discriminate among the three classes of men.

10. What further had contributed to these party divisions?

11. In what two ways is this met?

12. How does Paul defend his apostolic authority?

THE SANCTITY OF THE HUMAN BODY

CHAPTERS 5-6

1. One of the demoralizing things reported to Paul was the incest dealt with in chapter 5, and aggravated by the fact that the Church instead of excommunicating the offender had become "puffed up" over it! This was an illustration of what their worldly wisdom in the Gospel had resulted in (vv. 1, 2). Paul had already "judged" this person and directed the Church to come together and solemnly deliver him "to Satan for the destruction of the flesh that the spirit may be saved in the day of the Lord Jesus." This means (a) that Satan is an executioner of Divine punishment upon the saints in the present time, the saints who live in disobedience; (b) that the Church, considered as the body of Christ, has the authority to deliver such an one into his hands for that purpose; (c) that the punishment is limited to the flesh, the human body, and can not touch the soul; (d) that the object is to affect the soul indirectly, by bringing the disobedient to repentance, confession, and the experience of that spiritual cleansing which will be the means of keeping him saved "in the day of the Lord Jesus Christ" (cf. Luke 13:16; 2 Cor. 12:7; 1 Tim. 1:20). In other words, the punishment is the means of grace necessary to retain such a saint in the fellowship of God (vv. 3-5). Note "destruction" in verse 5, which is the Greek word used in 1 Thess. 5:3, 2 Thess. 1:9, 1 Tim. 6:9, etc., and does *not* mean annihilation. The bearing of this is important on the subject of the future retribution of the wicked.

But before leaving the case of incest note the warning (vv. 6, 7), the exhortation (v. 8) and the added instruction (vv. 9-13). To permit sin to remain in the Church unrebuked would mean the spread of it. The Church was "unleavened" in that all who truly belonged to it had their guilt purged away by the sacrifice

of Christ, therefore let them see to it that what was true of their legal standing before God, become true in actual experience. Paul had written them an earlier epistle of which we have no further record, but in which he had warned them not to keep "company with fornicators." This did not mean that they could shun such in the necessary business of the world, but that they must do so in the fellowship of the Church. They were not expected to act as judge in regard to the people of the world, but it was their duty to do so in the Church, hence the excommunication of this "wicked person" was demanded.

2. The allusion to "judging" brings up the question of lawsuits in chapter 6. Saints should not bring their disputes before the world's courts because of the incongruity of it (vv. 2-4). The language gives a most exalted conception to the dignity of the Church when she shall be reigning with Christ in the ages to come. During the time being however, could they not find men among them competent to judge between their brethren? And if not, were it not better to suffer wrong?

There is ground for thinking that the law-suit eliciting this rebuke, was linked in some way with the incest under consideration, as Paul now returns to the subject of the sanctity of the human body. The body is holy, (a) because in the sight of God it is washed, sanctified and justified. Therefore, while certain liberty in the use of it might be allowable to a Christian, it were inexpedient to press that liberty for the reason (as in Romans 14), that it would bring him under the power of carnality (vv. 9-12). But the body is holy, (b) because it is the Lord's. The worldly-minded Greeks considered the law of adjustment as settling the matter. Meats were for the belly, and so the belly must have been made for meats, on which principle they would justify the gratification of any bodily passion. But meats and the physical organ to receive and assimilate them were temporary and would be destroyed, while the body in its essentiality would be raised from the dead. This was true because our bodies are the members of Christ who was raised from the dead. How could we employ the body in fornication under such circumstances? (vv. 13-18). Finally, the body is holy, (c) because it is the temple of the Holy Ghost, for which reason, and because we "are bought with a price" we are to glorify God in our body (vv. 19, 20). It is not the 7th commandment which the apostle invokes in this case, but the sacredness of the believer's new relationship to Jesus Christ.

Questions.

1. What is the sin dealt with in this lesson?

2. What is the teaching of chapter 5:4, 5?

3. What may be learned from the use of "destruction" in 5:5?

4. What is the meaning of "unleavened"?

5. What allusion shows the great dignity of the Church?

6. On what three grounds is the body holy?

7. What is the meaning of chapter 6:13?

THE CHRISTIAN AND MARRIAGE

Chapter 7

1. It seems a strange inconsistency that a church "puffed up" over an incestuous person in their midst, should have scruples about the lawful marriage of a Christian, but such seems to have been the case. Paul yields the point on which some insisted, that it was desirable for a Christian man to remain single (v. 1), at least at that period and in those circumstances, provided he could do so without sin. But as the temptation in that case would be strong, he advised marriage (v. 2), and also that married persons should live together as becometh the conjugal relationship (vv. 3, 4). Exceptions to this for religious reasons, should be but temporary, lest the same temptation should overtake them as the unmarried (v. 5). By this however, he meant not to command them to marry, but to assure them as Christians of permission to do so (v. 6). He himself was unmarried, but all men did not have the same gift of control in that particular as he (v. 7), hence the advice following (vv. 8, 9).

Separation or Divorce.

2. From the general subject of marriage, he proceeds to that of separation or divorce as between two parties who are believers, which he forbids (vv. 10, 11). As he quotes our Lord in this instance he doubtless has in mind Matt. 5:32, which makes the one exception of adultery. He next touches the question where one is a believer and the other an unbeliever (vv. 12-16). Here he is himself speaking because the particular aspect of the subject is one on which our Lord had not expressed Himself while in the flesh. This shows that he places his own words on the same level of authority as those of our Lord, thus making the strongest claim of inspiration for them. Two such persons, he teaches, were not to separate simply for religious reasons. If a pagan wife wished to remain with her husband who had become converted to Christianity, he was not to divorce her. And if a pagan husband wished to remain with his wife after she had become converted she was not to leave him. The unbelieving partner in either case would be "sanctified" by the other in the sense that the other might continue in the relationship without impairing his or her sanctification (cf. 1 Tim. 4:5). The clause, "else were your children unclean," etc., is difficult, but may mean that such children were by the faith of the Christian parent brought into a nearer relationship to God than otherwise. It is to be remembered that this is where marriage was contracted before either husband or wife was converted. Christians are forbidden to contract such marriages. (Cf. v. 39 with 2 Cor.

6:14). Continuing the theme, the apostle says, if the unbelieving partner departs let him or her depart: "a brother or sister is not under bondage in such cases." His meaning is again doubtful. Not under bondage to renounce the Christian faith, or not under bondage to remain unmarried, which? Both views have advocates, but the latter is to be accepted with caution and with the understanding that human courts have rights in the case which Christians are bound to respect (cf. Rom. 14). The interpretation of verse 16 depends somewhat on the accent in reading it. If emphasis be laid on *"save,"* it is a plea to hold on to the unbelieving partner as long as possible in the hope that he or she may be saved. If it be laid on *"knowest,"* it is to relieve the mind of the Christian partner from an undue anxiety in the premises.

3. From the separation of married couples on religious grounds, the apostle digresses to speak of separation in other relationships for the same reason, applying it to Jews and Gentiles (vv. 18, 19), and to bondmen and freemen (vv. 20-24). The idea is that Christianity interferes only indirectly with existing institutions. It makes men free *in* but not *from* the responsibilities of their present positions, where those positions are not in themselves sinful. It teaches us to be indifferent in a sense to our external relations.

Celibacy.

4. Celibacy is the theme of verses 25-35, which the apostle opens by saying he is giving his own "judgment" or "opinion," having received "no commandment from the Lord." This means that the Holy Spirit has granted him no revelation or instruction on this particular point, which, while it qualifies the *authority* by which he speaks on it, does not qualify his inspiration. In other words, he is as truly inspired to say that he is simply giving his own opinion as he is inspired to say anything else. This has an important bearing on the whole question of inspiration, and is an assurance that where the apostle does not state to the contrary, he is always giving us the mind of the Holy Spirit. On general terms he would recommend celibacy because of the "present distress," i.e., the persecution and affliction being experienced by the church (vv. 15-27). While to marry was not sin for either sex, yet he would spare them in the trouble just ahead, and which would bear harder upon the married than the unmarried (v. 28). In this light the verses following are to be interpreted (vv. 29-35).

5. But at verse 36 he is referring to a Christian father's responsibility as to the marriage of his virgin daughter. It was humiliation in a Greek household for such to "pass the flower of her age" unmarried, and if a father felt the need of doing so he might give her in marriage without incurring sin in so doing. Nevertheless, if he acts in the opposite way he is also doing well, or better (vv. 37, 38).

6. The second marriage of widows is the last subject (vv. 39, 40), where the important clause is added that they are to marry "only in the Lord"—Christians are at liberty only to marry Christians. Paul's opponents in Corinth who held a different view of this matter, claimed to be acting by the Spirit of God, hence the irony of the closing remark, which is an irrefutable testimony to the authority with which he spake, "I think that I also have the Spirit of God," (R. V.).

To avoid misunderstanding, it should be said that we have not here the whole of the apostle's views on marriage, much less the whole of the New Testament teaching about it, but only so much as connects itself with the questions put to him at this time.

Questions.

1. What is here taught about marriage and the conjugal relation?

2. What strong claim of inspiration is here made?

3. What explanation of verse 14 is suggested?

4. What of verse 15?

5. How would you read verse 16?

6. What is here taught concerning the relations of Christianity to existing institutions?

7. Why does the apostle advise celibacy?

8. How would you explain verse 36?

CHRISTIAN LIBERTY AND ITS ABUSE

Chapters 8–10

The Christian Church was composed largely of Gentiles, who, when they were pagans, worshipped idols, with animal sacrifices and feasts in the idols' temples. Having become Christians, their practices were discontinued, though pagan neighbors might occasionally invite them, in a social way, to join in such feasts. The question had arisen as to their Christian liberty to accept such invitations. A "liberal" party in the church not only favored it, but indeed regarded the acceptance of such invitations as necessary to testify their freedom in Christ. There is no such thing as an idol, said they, and hence Christians are as much at liberty to eat meat offered in sacrifice to idols as any other meat, and in an idols' temple as well as any other place.

1. In reply, Paul admits the fact and the inference arising from it (8:4-6). They were at liberty to eat this meat and in an idol's temple, *provided* they had only themselves to consider. But there was their weak Christian brother, the man not gifted with as much spiritual knowledge as they, and who, though trusting Christ for salvation, still had a lingering idea that "an idol was something in the world." If the "strong" brother, he who was spiritually enlightened, ate this meat in the idol's temple, the weak brother might do likewise, but what the one might do with impunity the other could not do without sin. Hence the liberty of the one became the stumbling-block of the other (vv. 7-10). This made it serious for the strong brother to press his "knowledge," or his "liberty" to that point (vv. 11, 12). Personally, Paul's example was different from this (v. 13).

2. Continuing the reference to his own example in chapter 9:1-23, the apostle reminds them of the grounds on which he might claim all the liberty they had, or more. He was an apostle, he had seen Jesus Christ (Acts 9), they, the Corinthians, were the fruit of his ministry (vv. 1, 2). He was at liberty to eat and drink as he pleased, to marry, and have a wife accompany him on his itineraries as others did (vv. 3-6). He had a right to claim pecuniary support from the churches in his labors on their behalf (vv. 7-14). But he had foregone all these privileges for the gospel's sake (vv. 15-18). For the same reason had he accommodated himself to Jewish prejudices (vv. 19-20), and to Gentile peculiarities (vv. 21-23).

The Christian Race.

3. He shows that there is a practical motive for Christians acting on this principle (9:24-10:15), by employing an illustration from the Olympian games. Christian believers were like men running a race, but it was one thing to run and another thing to win the prize. Here again comes in the distinction between salvation and the rewards of faithfulness (see c. 3). The athlete knew the need of curtailing his liberty in certain directions in order to gain the race, and Paul appreciated the principle in spiritual things. Did he not deny himself lest he would be unfit for service, and lack of service meant, in the end, loss of reward (vv. 24-27). "Castaway" here does not mean loss of salvation, but loss of the opportunity to serve as one who is saved. The thought is continued in chapter 10, where a leaf is taken from the history of Israel. All the Hebrews originally were partakers of the same privileges—the guiding cloud, the passage through the Red Sea, the manna, the smitten rock, type of our salvation through the smitten

Christ (vv. 1-4). But many of them failed of the ultimate goal and never entered Canaan, because of their after conduct in the wilderness (vv. 5-11). A warning follows (v. 12) with accompanying encouragement (v. 13), and then an exhortation (vv. 14, 15).

4. The practical motive however, is more than the thought of reward for fidelity, it is that of positive danger in the face of the opposite (vv. 16-23). This is suggested already in the story of Israel, but more than suggested in what follows. The idolatrous feasts are in contrast with the Lord's supper, the one the worship of demons, the other the true God, between which there can be no fellowship. One or the other must be renounced. To tamper with demons is to challenge Divine wrath, with which we are unable successfully to contend. While the exercise of the fullest Christian liberty in these matters may be lawful for me, says the apostle, nevertheless it is not expedient, it will not be found to edify or build me up in Christ, for which reason it will not be acted upon.

5. The conclusion of the matter is: (a) do not be seeking your own advantage but another's (v. 24); (b) if the sacrificial meat is offered for sale in the public market, you may buy and eat it without compunction (vv. 25, 26); (c) if a pagan neighbor ask you for a meal at his private house you are at liberty to partake of it (v. 27); but (d) if in the course of the meal it is referred to as of a religious character, desist from eating, not for your own sake so much as that of the other (vv. 28-30). In other words, (e) act on the principle of verses 31, 32, and (f) follow my (Paul) example (10:33, 11:1).

Questions.

1. State in your own words the occasion Paul had for writing these chapters.

2. What is the main argument Paul presses against the abuse of Christian liberty?

3. In what respects did his example agree with his precept?

4. What motive governed him?

5. What is the significance of "castaway" in this case?

6. What further motive does Paul refer to?

7. How does he conclude, or sum up, the case?

CHURCH DISORDERS

CHAPTER 11

1. This chapter begins properly at verse 2, and treats of disorderly conduct of the women in the church assemblies, and of the misuse of the Lord's supper. "Head" is used in the sense of source of dominion because it is that which directs the body, and the man is the "head of the woman" because she is under authority to him, the reference being to married women and their husbands. "The head of Christ is God," when Christ is considered in the mediatorial sense, and from the point of view of the Godman. Of course both men and women are equal in God's sight when salvation and all the spiritual blessings in Christ are under consideration (Gal. 3:18), but human society could not exist without certain distinctions. It is evident that from this standpoint, the Christian women at Corinth went too far, and misinterpreting their newfound liberty in Christ, were overstepping bounds in an unbecoming way. As F. W. Robertson expressed it, "large principles when taken up by ardent and enthusiastic minds, without the modifications of experience, are almost sure to run into extravagance, and hence the spirit of law is by degree reduced to rules, and guarded by customs."

2. The offence of these women was praying and prophesying with uncovered heads, or rather unveiled faces, contrary to the custom of the times for both Jews and Gentiles, the headcovering being a symbol of the woman's subordination to the man. It is difficult to say what is meant by the man dishonoring

his head, since it is uncertain whether by his "head" is meant the Lord Jesus Christ. And in the same way we do not know whether the "head" which the woman "dishonoreth" is her own head, or her husband regarded as her head. We only know that it is the true glory of every creature to fulfill the law of its being (vv. 3-6).

3. The argument against this conduct on the women's part follows in verses 4-7: (a) the woman has present a visible superior in man created in God's image. He as the highest earthly being represents God's glory. Woman, as such, is not the representation of God's glory on earth, but to all inferior beings represents man's glory sharing his superiority over them (v. 7); (b) woman was created second to man as to substance (v. 8), and service (v. 9); (c) woman should consider the presence of the angels who are invisible spectators of Christian assemblies. This last is a mysterious subject, not merely that angels are present, but that women should exhibit modesty or the sign of subordination in their presence. Dean Stanley in his comment on this passage, thinks it may refer to evil angels and their unlawful intercourse with human flesh as spoken of in Genesis 6. Immodesty on the women's part might give them unholy opportunity, for as Robertson again says, "It is impossible to decide how much of our public morality and private purity is owing to the spirit which refuses to overstep the smallest bound of ordinary decorum."

4. The apostle balances the whole subject as between man and woman in verses 11 and 12, and sums up so far as the latter is concerned by a couple of questions, the bearing of which is that the absence of a veil is uncomely (vv. 13-15). If however, they continue to be contentious in the matter notwithstanding his rebuke, he would have them know that their conduct is without precedent (v. 16).

The Lord's Supper.

5. It is not a far cry from this to the disorder associated with the Lord's supper, and which the apostle approached by a general statement (vv. 17-19). It should be said that the divisions here are not doctrinal so much as social cliques. They came together for a general meal prior to the Lord's supper, and made it a sort of indoor picnic. The rich brought plenty to eat and drink while the poor had nothing. If this was what they desired to do it should be done in their own houses and not in the general assembly. The original institution of the rite is now referred to and its significance enlarged upon (vv. 23-26). A warning follows (vv. 27-37), in which "unworthy" is not to be understood as discouraging penitent sinners from partaking of this blessed feast, but to be taken in the sense of "an unworthy manner." To be "guilty of the body and blood of the Lord" means to commit an offence against Him, while "damnation," (v. 29), is to be taken in the sense of judgment as illustrated in verses 30-32. "Not discerning the Lord's body" means not appreciating the significance of His atonement, or the mystical relationship in which they as believers stand toward Him their Head, and which the Lord's supper so peculiarly makes manifest. Their erroneous practice in this particular had brought chastisement of a physical kind upon them; from which if they had "judged" themselves by putting away the sin, they would have escaped. Nevertheless, it was a mercy of God that they were thus chastened, which showed that they were His children, and not the people of the world, for there is a great distinction between chastisement and condemnation.

Questions.

1. Where does this lesson begin, and of what two things does it treat?

2. What does "head" mean, and what is the significance in each case of the "head of the

woman," and the "head of Christ"?

3. Can you quote Robertson as to the application of large principles?

4. What was the particular offence of these women?

5. Give the three-fold argument against their conduct.

6. Define and describe the "divisions" referred to in the second case.

7. What does each of the following expressions mean: "unworthy", guilty of the body and blood"; "damnation"; "not discerning," etc.?

8. What two things does Paul discriminate in this lesson?

SPIRITUAL GIFTS

CHAPTERS 12-14

The theme of this lesson is closely related to the preceding, for the church disorders included not only unbecoming conduct of the women in the public assembly, and an unworthy observance of the Lord's supper, but an unholy emulation in the matter of spiritual gifts.

1. After a brief introduction (vv. 1-3), the apostle discusses the origin of these gifts as not natural to the believer, but the special bestowment of God. God the Father is the worker of them, God the Spirit their distributor, and God the Son the One on Whose behalf they are administered (12:4-6).

2. As to their nature, there are nine—wisdom, knowledge, faith, healing, miracles, prophecy, discerning of spirits, tongues and interpretation of tongues (vv. 7-11). Of course, the above means "wisdom" and "knowledge" in the things of God; "faith," not merely for the acceptance of Christ, which is assumed, but for special purposes or objects, "prophecy," not in the sense of foretelling, but *forth*-telling, speaking "to edification, exhortation and comfort" (14:3).

3. The object and use of the gifts is for the profit of the whole body of Christ, into which believers have been baptized by the Holy Spirit (vv. 12, 13). They are in Christ what the foot, the hand, the ear, the eyes are in the human body (vv. 14-21). Hence honor, unity, sympathy, and mutual joyfulness should pervade and prevail (vv. 22-26). There are differences among these gifts, and the best are to be coveted, but all depend on the spirit in which they are exercised (vv. 27-31).

4. This leads the apostle to speak of the abuse of the gifts of which the Corinthians had been guilty, and which consumes the whole of chapter 13. Of what value is any of these gifts to their possessors without "*love*," which is the meaning of "charity" in this chapter (vv. 1-3). Love is now defined (vv. 4-7) and its supremacy and permanency affirmed (vv. 8-13). A time is coming when prophesying and speaking with tongues will be no longer required, and the knowledge we now have will appear childish in comparison with what we shall have, but not so with love, which, like faith and hope, is eternal. Therefore follow after *love* (14:1).

Speaking With Tongues.

5. Returning to the choice among the gifts the preference is given to prophesying (14:1-25), especially as compared with "tongues," because the latter had been the chief cause of the unholy emulation referred to, and also of gross disorder in the public assembly. The value of prophesying is stated in verse 3. "Tongues" should not be exercised unless an interpreter is present (v. 5), and for reasons indicated (vv. 6-14). Paul's own custom or example is now stated (vv. 15-19), an exhortation follows (v. 20), and a declaration of the purpose of "tongues" concludes this part of the subject (vv. 21-25).

"Tongues" are a sign not for believers but unbelievers, and not for their conversion evidently, but simply as a demonstration of Divine power. It is far different with prophesying which practically is identical with preaching and testimony, for this serves both for believers and unbelievers.

6. The order in which the gifts are to be publicly exercised is now given (vv. 26-35). The form of worship was very democratic, the people generally participating, reciting psalms, giving instruction, speaking with tongues, interpreting tongues, uttering a "revelation." As to this last, it would appear that until the New Testament was written, new revelations suited to the new dispensation were given to certain of the prophets. Care was to be taken that not more than two or three should speak in an unknown tongue, and not all at once, but one by one. Moreover, in the absence of an interpreter they should not speak at all. The same method should be followed by the prophets. Nor let any say when he felt a desire to speak, that he could not wait until another had concluded (vv. 32, 33).

In such meetings when the whole church came together in one place, women were to keep silence. This is the interpretation the Scofield Bible puts on verses 34 and 35, but there is a difficulty here in the light of 1 Cor. 11, where women are not forbidden to pray and prophesy in public.

7. The contentious spirit of the church is rebuked as in chapter 11. They were evidently seeking to establish a precedent of their own in these matters (v. 36), but that which Paul is writing to them is the commandment of the Lord (v. 37). Whatsoever they did was to be done "decently and in order," (v. 40).

Questions.

1. Name the seven divisions in the text of this lesson.

2. Name the nine spiritual gifts.

3. What is meant by "prophesy"?

4. How should "charity" be rendered in chapter 13?

5. Which of all the gifts is to be preferred, and why?

6. What restriction is placed on "tongues" and why?

7. What is the meaning of "revelation" in this case (v. 26)?

8. What principle is to be maintained in the public gatherings?

RESURRECTION OF THE DEAD

CHAPTERS 15-16

They were not only questions of casuistry that disturbed this church, but deeper ones—especially that of the resurrection of the dead. We may gather the real nature of this difficulty by the manner of Paul's treatment of it.

1. He dwells on the fact of Christ's resurrection (vv. 1-11), in which he furnishes incidentally a definition of the "Gospel" he preached. This consists of just three counts, Christ died for our sins, was buried, and rose again. The proof that he rose again is two-fold, the Old Testament scriptures (v. 4), and human witnesses. Just where or how the former testified to His resurrection is not apparent to the casual reader, but a student like Paul found it in both type and prophecy. Compare also Christ's words to the two disciples en route to Emmaus (Lk. 24). The proof from the human witnesses (514 in all) is given in detail (vv. 5-8). "Born out of due time," some would translate "before the due time," as though Paul were thinking of the national new birth of Israel which is to be. His conversion by the appearance of the Lord at Damascus (Acts 9), was an illustration before the time of what will take place when the Lord reveals Himself to that people at the end of this age (Ezek. 20:35-38; Zech. 12:10-13:6; Rom. 11:25-27).

2. Passing from the fact of Christ's resurrection he proceeds to the inference from and the importance of it (vv. 12-19). Christ having arisen, the fact of a resurrection can no longer be disputed (vv. 12, 13, 16). To dispute it would render nugatory the whole scheme of the Gospel on which depended their salvation

and the future life (vv. 14, 17, 18, 19). Strange that Christians should find it possible to question the resurrection of Christ, but still are there some inconsistent and ignorant enough to do so.

3. The order of the resurrection follows (vv. 20-34). The resurrection of Christ insures that of all men (vv. 20-22), for both the wicked and the good, the unbelieving and the believing shall be raised, "some to everlasting life, and some to everlasting shame and contempt" (1 Jno. 5:28, 29; 1 Tim. 4:10). But they will not be raised all at once. Christ is the first-fruits Whose resurrection has already taken place. The second installment of the resurrection will consist of true believers, and come forth at His second advent (1 Thess. 4:13-18). The third and last will consist of the rest of the dead which will come forth after the millennium and at the end of the world (v. 24 cf. with Rev. c. 20). The "kingdom" spoken of is that promised to David and his seed (2 Sam. 7:8-17; Zech. 12:8; Lk. 1:31-33). It is that which was announced as "at hand" when Jesus Christ came (Mt. 4:17), but which was rejected by the Jews when they rejected Christ and crucified Him (Mt. 11:20; 21:42, 43). At His second coming, and after the Church has been caught up to meet Him in the air, the King will restore the Davidic monarchy in His own Person, regather Israel, establish His power in the earth and reign with His church 1,000 years (Mt. 24:27-30; Acts 15:14-17; Rev. 20:1-10). This is the kingdom which at the end of the millennium, will be delivered up to the Father, that God (i. e. the Triune God) "may be all in all" (v. 28). The subjection of the Son spoken of in this verse is not that of the Son as the Second Person of the Trinity, but as the Mediatorial King of the earthly kingdom. The language in verse 29 is difficult, but is evidently a challenge of some kind to their reason, like that which follows. Why should Christians expose themselves to the peril of their Christian testimony, as Paul himself was doing daily, if the resurrection of the dead were not a fact? Why not live to please the flesh? Alas! some seemed to be doing so whom he would warn (vv. 30-34).

The Nature of the Risen Body.

4. Now comes the teaching as to the nature of the resurrection, i. e. the resurrection body (vv. 35-50), which, in a word, will be related to the mortal body as the harvest is related to the grain that is sown (vv. 35-38). That is to say, the body that is raised will be the same as to identity with that which was buried, but not the same in other respects—it will be incorruptible, glorious, powerful, spiritual, "the image of the heavenly." Verses 45-49 are deeply interesting. "The first man Adam was *made* a living soul." i. e. he *derived* his life from another, even God. "The last Adam was made a quickening Spirit," gives a truer meaning by omitting the italicized words "was made," so as to read, "the last Adam a quickening (i.e., a life-giving) Spirit." He did not derive His life, but is Himself the fountain of life, and gives that life to others (Jno. 1:4; 5:21; 10:10; 12:24; 1 Jno. 5:12). Because He lives we shall live also.

5. But all believers will not die (vv. 50-57). These verses should be read in connection with 1 Thess. 4:13-18, as they similarly teach that the bodies of living believers will be instantaneously changed from corruptibility and mortality to the opposite, at the coming of the Lord.

6. The theme is concluded by a reference to the practical effects of the doctrine, which carries us into the 16th chapter as far as verse 4. It should confirm our steadfastness in the Christian faith, at the same time that it quickens our service (v. 58). A good outlet for this service in the case of the Corinthians is that named at the opening of chapter 16, the means of whose execution are detailed in verses 2-4.

7. The concluding instructions and greetings in the epistle (16 5-22) hardly furnish material for

another lesson, and may be included in this. Paul will not visit them at present though he is just across the Aegean Sea, but will pass through Macedonia first and come to them later, probably wintering there (vv. 5-9). He commends Timothy to them whose arrival en route to Ephesus they may expect (vv. 10, 11). Apollos is also referred to in brotherly terms (v. 12), though he had spoken plainly about him in the body of the letter. Those who had specially ministered to him are named (vv. 17, 18). The token of validity in his letter is important (v. 21). "Marantha" means "Our Lord Cometh." With that hope before him he had begun his letter, and with that hope he laid down his pen.—Synthetic Bible Studies.

Questions.

1. Divide chapter 16 into 6 parts.

2. What is Paul's definition of the Gospel?

3. How many eye-witnesses of Christ's resurrection does Paul indicate?

4. What may "born out of due time," mean?

5. When will the second and third installments of the resurrection army come forth, and of whom will they be composed?

6. What is meant by "kingdom" (v. 24)?

7. How will the resurrection body compare with the mortal body?

8. Give the meaning of verses 51-53.

9. What is the two-fold practical effect of the doctrine of the resurrection?

SECOND CORINTHIANS

THE APOSTLE'S EXPLANATION

CHAPTERS 1-2:13

Paul had left Ephesus where his first epistle had been written to this Church, had crossed into Macedonia, and was now in Philippi. (Cf. Acts 19:23-20:1-3 with chapters 8:1-9:2 of this epistle.) The reception given his first letter had been generally favorable, but all had not submitted to his rebuke, and the adversaries who opposed his teachings before were more virulent than ever, now seeking to undermine his authority as an apostle. It was therefore with a two-fold purpose he wrote this second letter, to comfort some whom he had "made sorry" by his previous one, and to defend his character and authority against those who impugned both. For this reason, as Alford says, "we find consolation and rebuke, gentleness and severity, earnestness and irony succeeding one another at short intervals and without notice." To quote the Scofield Bible, his spiritual burdens were of two kinds, solicitude for the maintenance of the churches in grace as against the law-teachers, and anguish over the distrust felt towards him by Jews and Jewish Christians. The latter rejected the revelation through Paul of the doctrines of grace, grounding themselves, probably, on the kingdom teachings of our Lord (Rom. 15:8), seemingly oblivious that a new dispensation had been introduced by Christ's death. It was this that made necessary a defense of the origin and extent of his apostolic authority.

The first seven chapters are taken up with an account of his principles of action; chapters 8 and 9 are an appeal for the collection for the poor saints at Jerusalem; and the remaining chapters are a straight out defense of his apostolic authority.

The particular part assigned for this lesson is the writer's explanation of his conduct with respect to his promised visit (see the close of the first epistle), and with respect to the case of incest (see c. 5 of the same).

The customary salutation or greeting, (1:1, 2), is followed by the usual thanksgiving (vv. 3-7), in which the apostle mentions his sufferings for Christ's sake, and the relation they bear to this church as an example of patient endurance and Divine consolation. He enlarges on his sufferings, going into detail as to one particular, to magnify the power of God in his deliverance as from the dead (vv. 8-10). Tactfully he mentions his confidence in their interest in him (v. 11), arising, as it must, out of his faithful service on their behalf (vv. 12, 13), which they for the most part were ready to acknowledge (v. 14). Note the exception in this last verse, and its indirect allusion to his enemies, ("in part").

At this point he begins his explanation of his change of mind about visiting them, of which his enemies had taken advantage. His first thought had been to go to Corinth direct from Ephesus, then north into Macedonia where he now was, and returning to Corinth proceed thence into Judea (v. 16). Passing by Corinth and going into Macedonia instead, was not a mere whim of his carnal nature, not an indication of trifling indecision or fear, but to spare them the further rebuke which must have fallen on them (1:17-2:4).

He next refers to his previous directions about the incestuous person, whom he now recommends to be forgiven and restored (vv. 5-11).

Perhaps the last two verses (vv. 12, 13) suggests a further reason for his going into Macedonia before visiting Corinth.

Questions.

1. Have you examined the scripture passages referred to in this lesson?

2. For what two-fold purpose was this epistle written?

3. What is peculiar as to its literary style?

4. What was the nature of Paul's spiritual burden?

5. Give the general outline of the whole epistle.

6. What is the particular theme of this lesson?

7. Analyze the lesson by verses.

THE TRIUMPHS OF PAUL'S MINISTRY

CHAPTERS 2:14-4:7

1. Pursuing the consideration of his principles of action, Paul now shows his ministry to have been a triumphant one, notwithstanding the opposition of his enemies (vv. 14-17). The triumph however, was of God's power and grace, and not in himself. Note the comparison between himself and the false teachers (v. 17).

2. It was not only a triumphant ministry but one fully accredited by themselves (3:1-5).

3. It was a spiritual ministry as distinguished from one of legalism (vv. 6-18). This is the meaning of "the letter killeth, but the spirit giveth life" (v. 6), the first referring to Judaism and the latter to the Gospel of grace. Not that Paul would disparage the former which was glorious in its revelation (v. 7), but the latter more so (vv. 8-15). Prof. Robertson in, "The Glory of the Ministry" gives a beautiful exposition of the last-named verses. The glory of Moses was (1), a *real* glory—"the ministration of death written and engraven in stones, *was glorious*"; (2), a *hidden* glory—"Moses put a veil over his face"; (3) a *temporary* glory— "Israel could not steadfastly look to the end of that which is abolished"; (4), an *overshadowed* glory—"if the ministration of condemnation be glory, much more doth the ministration of righteousness exceed in glory"; (5), a *defective* glory—"Who hath made us able ministers of the New Testament; not of the letter but of the spirit"; (6), an *ineffective* glory—"their minds were blinded." Verses 13 and 14 referring to Exodus 34:33-35, are rather obscure because of a wrong rendering of the Old Testament passage. The Revised Version indicates that the Israelites saw the glory on Moses' face as he spake; but when he had ceased, the veil was put on that they might not look on the end, i.e., the fading of that transitory glory. To quote Alford, they were permitted to see it as long as it was necessary to be seen as a credential of his ministry but then it was, withdrawn. Thus the declaration of God's will to them was not in openness of speech, but interrupted and broken by intervals of concealment. This was not the case in the Christian dispensation of which Paul was a minister.— Synthetic Bible Studies.

4. It was an honest ministry (4:1-7), for the reason that the apostle's life harmonized with the truth he preached (vv. 1, 2); because it was Jesus Christ he preached and not himself (vv. 3-6); and because the power in which he preached was of God (v. 7).

Questions.

1. What four points concerning Paul's ministry are here named?

2. How do you understand the distinction between the "letter" and the "spirit"?

3. Give an analysis of 3:8-15.

4. How does the Revised Version throw light on Ex. 34:35?

5. On what grounds was Paul's ministry honest?

TRIAL OF PAUL'S MINISTRY

CHAPTERS 4:8-5:21

1. His Sufferings 4:8-15.

"Troubled," "perplexed," "persecuted," "cast down"—what a story! "Pressed on every side, yet not straitened," not so hemmed in but that he could still proceed with his work; "perplexed, yet not in despair," bewildered like a man going in a circle, put to it, yet not utterly put out; "pursued, yet not forsaken," hunted like a wild animal, yet not abandoned to the foe; "smitten down, yet not destroyed," thrown to the ground but able to rise again—"The Glory of the Ministry." But not merely resigned, he has come to rejoice in his sufferings because of his relationship to Jesus Christ (10, 11). For the meaning of these last-named verses, compare Col. 1:24; 1 Cor. 15:31; and Rom. 8:36. Indeed verse 11 is a sufficient comment on verse 10. Death (12) was working in Paul, physical death, but it was "working out for the good of the saints who were benefited by his ministry." He speaks this by the same faith which stirred the Psalmist (verse 13 cf. with Ps. 116:10), and it is this faith that gives him the bright outlook for himself and his faithful hearers as expressed in verse 14, and which he amplifies in the next division.

2. His Comfort 4:16-5:8.

(a) Inward spiritual renewing day by day (16); (b) the relation between his earthly suffering and heavenly glory (17, 18); (c) which includes the resurrection of his body (5:1-4); (d) his confidence rests on the eternal purpose of God in his redemption, and the indwelling of the Holy Spirit in his soul (5); (e) so that he is always of good courage whether in his physical body or out of it (6-8).

3. His Ambition 9-13.

"Wherefore we labor," might be rendered "wherefore we are ambitious." "Present or absent" has reference to the Lord's second coming. Paul might be "present," i. e., in his physical body on the earth when He came, for like all true and intelligent disciples, he was expecting Him in his own generation; and yet he might be "absent," in the sense that he had passed out of the body in death. But in either event he must appear before his "judgment seat" when He came (10). This "judgment seat of Christ" is not that in Rev. 20, which is the last judgment and takes place at the

end of the world, but it is one before which disciples, and they only, shall stand at the Second Coming of Christ. Notice that they are to "receive the things done" in the body. In other words, it is not for them a judgment unto condemnation because they are already by faith "in Christ Jesus" (Romans 8:1). It is not to determine the question whether they are saved or lost, which was settled the moment of their accepting Christ, but rather that of their reward or loss of the reward in the Kingdom of Heaven then to be manifested (1 Cor. 3:11-15). "Terror" (verse 11) should be rendered "fear," and refers to the godly fear Paul had with reference to that judgment, his reverent desire to enter upon his reward, and which explained his earnestness as a soul-winner. God was his witness to this, and he trusted the church at Corinth also was. If so they might properly speak of it before his enemies (12) who were reflecting on him as one who was out of his mind (13).

4. His Motive 14-21.

"The love of Christ" here means primarily His love for us as indicated in what follows. "Then were all dead," should be, "Then all died," i. e., all true believers have died to the guilt and penalty of sin because they are members of Christ (Rom. 6). But they are now alive in Him in a new sense (v. 15), and being thus alive they are not to live for "themselves," their own satisfaction and glory, but for Him. As a matter of fact this was Paul's governing principle, he says (16). "Henceforth know we no man after the flesh," means that his relationship to his fellow men is no longer that of his former unregenerated state. Indeed this includes that knowledge of Christ he then had concerning Whom he says. "Know we Him so no more." He knows Christ differently now from the way he knew Him before his conversion (Acts 9). This explains verse 17. Now all these new "things" come from God and are the consequence of our reconciliation to Him by Jesus Christ (18). This reconciliation is enlarged upon (19-21). God Himself was reconciled, God as manifested in Christ. And His method of reconciling men to Him was not to impute (or charge) their trespasses unto them. This act of grace He was able to express because He had imputed those trespasses unto His Son, mankind's substitute, Who had no sin. The ministry of this reconciliation had been committed unto Paul who, with his fellow-preachers, was an ambassador for Christ, the mouth-piece of God, beseeching men to accept the reconciliation thus wrought out for them, by accepting the Reconciler, Jesus Christ.

Questions.

1. Name the four principal subdivisions of this lesson.

2. What five considerations ministered to Paul's comfort in the midst of his trials?

3. To what event does "present or absent" have reference?

4. Explain 5:10, and 16.

5. Analyze verses 19-21.

HIS APPEAL TO THE CHURCH

Chapters 6-7

1. Not to Receive the Grace of God in Vain, 6:1-10.

These Corinthians as believers on Jesus Christ, had received the grace of God in their justification and all which it implied; but they would have received it "in vain" did it not bring forth the proper fruit in their lives. That such is the meaning is evident by verse 3: "Giving no occasion of stumbling that our ministration be not blamed," which is the negative side. And by verse 4: "In everything commending ourselves as ministers of God," which is the positive side. Now follows a flight of eloquence in praise of Christian ministration (vv. 4-10). We use "ministration" rather than "ministry" because while Paul has himself in the foreground, he is not limiting what he

says to "ordained ministers," but includes all Christians. Notice the rhetorical device in the grouping of the experiences by the use of the words "in," "by," "as," (Greek, *En, Dia, Hos*). The first touches environment (vv. 4, 5). The second, conduct (vv. 6, 8). It was in the midst of such untoward environment to quote "The Glory of the Ministry," that Paul found the graces of the heart to grow "like orchids on the wild rocks." In this second group of experiences there is progress over the first. "By" suggests aggressive conflict in the spiritual sense— "The atmosphere of conflict, the swing of victory." The third group is one of paradoxes (vv. 9 10). Light and shadow interplay, and as the work quoted above says, "One can get a double report on almost any man's life unless he has been a nonentity." This is particularly true of a Christian, and in a good sense, since he must almost of necessity appear as one thing to the world and another to the household of God able to appreciate spiritual things.

2. Not to be Unequally Yoked Together 6:7-11:1.

This division is a continuation of the foregoing about receiving the grace of God in vain, and the great New Testament classic on Christian separation. To quote the Scofield Bible: Separation in Scripture is twofold; "from" whatever is contrary to the mind of God; and "unto" God Himself. The unequal yoke is anything which unites a child of God and an unbeliever in a common purpose (Deut. 22:10). Separation from evil implies (a) separation in desire, motive and act, from the world, in the ethically bad sense of this present world-system (see Rev. 13:8); and (b) separation from believers, especially false teachers, who are "vessels unto dishonour" (2 Tim. 2:20, 21; 2 John 9-10). Separation is not from *contact* with evil in the world or the church, but from complicity with and conformity to it (John 17:15; 2 Cor. 6:14-18; Gal. 6:1). The reward of separation is the full manifestation of the divine fatherhood (2 Cor. 6:17, 18); unhindered communion and worship (see Heb. 13:13-15), and fruitful service (2 Tim. 2:21), as world-conformity involves the loss of these, though not of salvation.

3. Not to Reject the Apostle Himself and His Teachings 7:2-16.

Note the seven reasons for this: For the 1st see verse 2; for the 2d verse 3; for the 3d verses 4, 14, 16; for the 4th verse 5; for the 5th verses 6, 7, 13; for the 6th verses 8 to 11; for the 7th verse 15.

A brief word on verses 8-11: Paul regretted his previous letter because it had made them sorry; but now he did not regret it because it had made them sorry in the right way, "after a godly manner." They had sorrowed with a sorrow never to be regretted. Verse 11 shows in what manner this was true.

Questions.

1. For what three things did Paul appeal?
2. What is meant by receiving "the grace of God in vain"?
3. Why do we use the word "ministration"?
4. What rhetorical device is here used?
5. What does separation from evil imply?
6. Name the seven reasons for Paul's personal appeal.

CONTRIBUTION FOR THE SAINTS

Chapters 8-9

The mother church at Jerusalem was passing through stormy days, and its common chest was replenished by all the daughter churches. Macedonia, in its poverty, had contributed liberally but the wealthy and flourishing Corinthians had been backward, and the apostle devotes nearly one-sixth of his present letter to arguments and pleadings for greater generosity on their part. He enjoins the duty of giving:

1. By the example of the churches in Macedonia (8:1-4). They were poor, yet lavish. The effect of divine grace on their hearts.
2. By the sense of congruity in the Christian life (8:7). They already abounded in other gifts such as faith, utterance and knowledge; liberality therefore was expected. Its absence would be a defect in the symmetry of their spiritual experience.
3. As a proof of their love and gratitude to Jesus Christ (8:8, 9), who, though rich, yet for their sakes had become poor.
4. In consideration of what they professed to be willing to do. Regard for their promises (8:10, 11).
5. The offering would be appreciated not according to its size, but the spirit in which it was given (8:12).
6. The care of the poor saints should not fall on a few but all should be equally burdened (8:13-15).
7. The apostle's honor was at stake (8:24, also 9:3, 4). He had boasted of their willingness.
8. As they sowed they would reap (9:6).
9. God was able to reward them (9:8-11).
10. They would thus glorify God (9:13).
11. They would thus secure the prayers and love of the saints (9:14).

The foregoing is abbreviated from "Synthetic Bible Studies," but there is further homiletic value in the following division of the chapters in the Scofield Bible: The example of Macedonia (8:1-6); the exhortation, (vv. 7-15); the messengers, (8:9-16:5); the encouragement (vv. 6-15). From the same source we get a summing up of the Christian doctrine of giving, as follows:

(1) It is a "grace," i.e. a disposition created by the Spirit (8, 7). (2) In contrast with the law, which imposed giving as a divine requirement, it is voluntary, and a test of sincerity and love (8:8-12; 9:1, 2, 5, 7). (3) The privilege is universal, belonging, ac-

cording to ability, to rich and poor (8:1-3, 12-15. Cf. 1 Cor. 16:1, 2). (4) It is to be proportioned to income (8:12-14. Cf. 1 Cor. 16:2). The O. T, proportion was the tithe, a proportion which antedates the law (Gen. 14:20). (5) Its rewards are (a) joy (8:2); (b) increased ability to give in proportion to that which has been already given (9:7-11); (c) increased thankfulness to God (9:12); (d) God and the gospel glorified (9:13, 14).

Questions.

1. Have you carefully examined the eleven arguments for Christian giving?

2. Divide the eleven arguments among the four homiletic divisions of the chapter.

3. Summarize the doctrine of Christian giving.

DEFENCE OF HIS APOSTLESHIP

CHAPTERS 10-13

At this point Paul begins his personal defence which concludes the epistle. And here we perceive more particularly that interchange of gravity and irony to which reference has been made, and which causes these chapters to be so difficult of explanation.

The apostle's critics had reflected on his personal appearance (10:1, 7, 10); on what they were pleased to consider his carnality (v. 3); his lack of eloquence (11:5) and his lack of dignity (11:7-10). We shall find it inconvenient to deal with these subjects otherwise than as they come before us in the chapters.

Chapter 10. They said that in their presence he was "base" or "lowly," but that absent he was bold as indicated in his letters (v. 1). He besought them therefore, to heed his words that he might not have occasion to be "bold" against them when he was present (v. 2). He had particular reference to some who regarded him as walking "according to the flesh." They would see that any

spiritual weakness in his conduct did not show itself in the weapons or results of his spiritual conflicts with the enemies of the truth (vv. 3-6).

They were looking on the outward appearance, despising him and conceitedly claiming some special relationship to Christ for themselves. He meets this by a presentation of his *true* claims, as to which he might go further without idle boasting and justify any expressions of apostolic power in his letters (vv. 7-11). In proof of this he appeals to facts including his work among them in Corinth (vv. 12-14); and delicately intimates that when the present trouble was at an end, they would assist him to extend his ministry further (vv. 15-18). (Cf. Romans 1:10; 15:28.)

Chapter 11. His pleadings continue because of his love for them and his fear of their beguilement. They were tolerating those who were preaching another gospel to them, and surely they might bear with him, since he was in no respect inferior to those "overmuch" apostles (vv. 1-6). Verse 2 is very interesting. For an explanation of "a godly jealousy" see Exodus 20:5, and Joshua 24: 19. For "one husband" and "chaste virgin" see 1 Corinthians 1:12. The espousal in this case took place when they were converted to Christ, the presentation will take place when He comes again. Verse 3 is interesting from another point of view, since it shows that Paul regards the fall (Genesis 3) as historical. Note also that the tempter did not propose to take Eve's allegiance away from God entirely, but only to corrupt her faith, which was enough. At this point he refers to their assumed contempt because he had not demanded pay from them, explaining the reasons for his conduct (vv. 7-12), plainly characterizing the "false apostles" (vv. 13-15). They have compelled him to boast (vv. 16-33) for which he apologizes. Verses 23-27 reveal a life of hardship far beyond anything told of Paul in the Acts. Verse 19 is ironical.

Chapter 12. Here we come to "visions and revelations" vouchsafed to him. In these there could be no self-commendation, but only that of a man in Christ lifted out of his own individuality, and thought worthy of such grace on account of being in Christ. His only object in boasting of such an one was to bear witness to the supernatural life he was living and that such glorious things had been granted him. In behalf of himself he would boast only in his infirmities (vv. 1-6). —Lange. Verses 7-10 are self-explanatory except as to the nature of the "thorn in the flesh." It has been spoken of as "chronic ophthalmia, inducing bodily weakness and a repulsive appearance" (Galatians 4:15), but no one knows what it was. The Corinthians should not have made it necessary for him thus to speak of himself; they should have spoken on his behalf (v. 11), for the signs of an apostle were wrought by him among them (vv. 12, 13). The insinuation about his having ministered to them without monetary gain is once more referred to, in order to say that he will continue to do so. He is their parent, and parents lay up for the children (vv. 14, 15). Those he had sent to them had followed his example in this respect (vv. 16-18). The church, however, must not suppose that in what he was saying he was excusing himself to them. On the contrary he was doing all things for their edifying (v. 19), and in the hope that when he visited them the third time, it might not be with a rebuke and with sorrow because of their sin (vv. 20, 21).

Chapter 13. He emphasizes the rebuke and chastening that await some on his third coming if they do not repent (vv. 1-10), closing with an exhortation (v. 11), salutation (vv. 12, 13) and benediction (v. 14).

Questions.

1. What is the general theme of this lesson?

2. In what four ways had Paul's critics reflected on him?

3. Why had Paul declined material support from the church at Corinth?

4. What kind of apostles were these who were comparing themselves with Paul?

5. What kind of life was Paul really living?

6. Why should the Corinthians have commended Paul?

7. With what does he threaten the church on his next visit?

EPISTLE TO THE GALATIANS

INTRODUCTORY

The Acts of the Apostles records that Paul visited the province of Galatia in Asia Minor twice, on his second and third journeys, but no mention was made of any particular city or town at which he stopped on either occasion. Acts 16:6, 18:23. It was on the third journey, and probably during his long stay at Ephesus, though some would say at Corinth, that this epistle was written. The occasion for writing it carries us back to the fifteenth chapter of Acts and the story of the first Church council held at that time. The Judaizing teachers there referred to tracked Paul's footsteps everywhere, seeking to circumvent the preaching of a free Gospel and teaching the need of circumcision and other observances of the Mosaic law in order to salvation. They had good soil to work on in Galatia, for the people seem to have been of a demonstrative and fickle mind. (1:6, 4:9, 4:15, 16, 5:15.) That this was the condition of things in the church, and that many had already fallen into the snare of seeking to supplement faith by works is further evident from 1:6-9, 3:3, 4:9-11, 5:3, etc. The object of the epistle, therefore, is to restore these people to the faith, and in the working out of that object the epistle becomes an inspired classic on that fundamental doctrine of Christianity, Justification by Faith.

It would seem that the false teachers in order to undermine the confidence of the people in the Gospel itself, must first accomplish the same purpose with reference to the apostolic authority of Paul. They must first destroy his authority as an inspired apostle before they could weaken the foundations of the Gospel he preached. This they sought to do using Peter as a sort of comparison and contrast. The last-named preached no different Gospel from Paul, but being the apostle to the circumcision, i.e., the Jews, (Galatians 2:6-9), presented it from the Jewish standpoint, while Paul as the apostle to the uncircumcision did the same from the Gentile standpoint. We can see how there may have been some differences in the mode of presentation which gave opportunity to these unsanctified Jewish Christians to denounce Paul as unorthodox. They had an advantage also in that Paul was not one of the original twelve.

The plan of the Epistle lends itself to a three-fold division. Chapters 1 and 2 are of a personal character in which Paul defends his apostolic authority; chapters 3 and 4 are doctrinal, in which he defends the Gospel or the doctrine of justification by faith; while chapters 5 and 6 are practical and contain the application of the doctrine to the daily life of the individual Christian.

Questions.

1. How often did Paul visit Galatia?
2. What two cities have been named as the abode of Paul at the time of writing this epistle?
3. Tell the story of Acts 15.
4. Describe the Galatian people.
5. What was the object of this epistle?
6. What was the method of the false teachers?
7. Name the three divisions of this epistle.

PAUL'S DEFENCE OF HIS AUTHORITY

CHAPTERS 1-2

Paul defends his authority in five ways. On the ground of
1. His Divine call, 1:1.
2. His Divine revelation of the Gospel, 1:11, 12.
3. His independence of the other apostles, 1:15-24.
4. His endorsement by the church, 2:1-10.
5. His rebuke of Peter, 2:11-14.

Speaking of his Divine call,

some would say that his reference to man-made apostles has an application to the choice of Matthias in Acts 1, though there may be a question about this. In like manner, his reference to the way in which he received the revelation of the Gospel recalls the circumstances of his conversion in Acts 9, as well as the experience referred to in verses 17 and 18 of this chapter. In the section treating of his endorsement by the church there is an allusion (chapter 2:1, 2), to the journey and its results spoken of in Acts 15 at the time of the first general council of the church to settle the question of justifiication. Particular attention should be called to his bold and consistent attitude with reference to the circumcision of Titus (3-5), an allusion to which was made in our study of the Acts. It is noticeable, too, that Paul makes as much of his final endorsement by the church as of his independence of the leaders of the church prior thereto. He would give his adversaries no advantage over him, as if they should say he were too independent and could not be acknowledged by them until he had received the acknowledgment of the accepted authorities. His rebuke of Peter shows him to have been naturally the stronger character of the two, and in consideration of the fact that Peter was doubtless being quoted by his opponents, proves a convincing argument for his own authority.

In verse 17 of chapter 2, the Scofield Bible has this illuminating footnote: "If we Jews, in seeking to be justified by faith in Christ, take our places as mere sinners like the Gentiles, is it therefore Christ who makes us sinners? By no means. It is by putting ourselves again under law after seeking justification through Christ, that we act as if we were still unjustified sinners, seeking to become righteous through law-works."

Questions.

1. Give the five arguments of Paul in defence of his apostolic authority.

2. Recall the circumstances of His call to the Apostleship.

3. Recall the circumstance of his endorsement by the church.

4. What shows his tact in offsetting any advantage against him?

5. Explain 2:17.

JUSTIFICATION BY FAITH

CHAPTERS 3-4

1. Having established his authority as an apostle, and his right to expound the Gospel he had received; Paul now enters upon the elucidation of the latter, or rather proceeds to the defense of its cardinal teaching. This is the doctrine that man is justified only by faith in Jesus Christ without the works of the law. The same doctrine was enlarged upon in Romans, only there he was expressing the Divine side of its truth while here he is showing the human side. There he taught that God justified man by giving him a rightness or righteousness that satisfied His justice, here he teaches that man receives this blessing simply by believing on Jesus Christ. The false teachers had denied this and had led some of the Galatians back to the law of Moses both as (in part at least), the ground of their justification and the means of their perfection in holiness. Paul shows the untruthfulness and futility of this in the following way:

1. By their own experience of the effects of faith in the Gospel, 3:1-5.

2. By the history of Abraham the founder of the Jewish Nation, 6-9.

3. By the teachings of Old Testament Scriptures, 10-12.

4. By the nature of the work of Christ, 13, 14.

2. The first might be called the *"argumentum ad hominem."* It was evident to these Galatian christians that they had received the Holy Spirit. But how had they come to receive Him, through observing the Mosaic law or the preaching of the Gospel? The answer, of course, was foreseen. It was as the result of Paul's

preaching and not the observance of circumcision or anything else. Why then did they need to supplement the work of the Spirit by that of the flesh?

The second argument is well adapted to refute the Judaizing teachers, since Abraham was the founder of their faith. And yet Abraham clearly was justified by believing on God and before he was circumcised.

The argument from the teachings of Scripture requires no explanation, since the passages quoted plainly state that if one elects to be saved by the law and not by grace, he can only be saved by keeping the whole of it. Circumcision nor ceremonialism of any kind were not enough.

The work of Christ did away with all these things which only foreshadowed Him. He hath redeemed us from the curse of the law, why then dishonor His work and put ourselves voluntarily under that curse a second time? The whole argument is clear and convincing.

3. But at this point the apostle supplements his argument by a brief disquisition on the

Relation of the Law to the Promise.

He anticipates a possible objection to his argument. It were as though some one should say: Granted that God saved Abraham or accounted him righteous on the ground of his belief in His promise; iis it not true that 430 years after that promise to Abraham He gave the law to Moses? And was not this law to take the place of that promise as a ground of human righteousness? Paul answers, No. (verses 15-18). His imaginary interlocutor then inquires, Why was the law given? What purpose does it serve? Paul's reply discloses two points: —(1), the law was given because of transgressions, etc., verse 19. As the transgressions of men multiplied and became aggravated, God was obliged to come to His people in an entirely new way, in a more distant revelation than existed in the time of the patriarchs. "The law was given, not

so much in order to prevent transgressions, as to bring men under a more strict accountability for them, and a more plainly expressed curse." This brings us to (2), the law was our schoolmaster to bring us to Christ, verse 24. The Greek word for schoolmaster here means a faithful slave entrusted with the care of a boy from his tender years till puberty to keep him from physical and moral evil, and accompany him to his studies and amusements. He approached his charge with commands and prohibitions, and in a sense with limitations of his freedom. All this as a means to an end, viz: that the boy might be trained for mature age, and the assumption of that higher grade of life for which he was destined. (Lange). Thus the law leads men to Christ. It restrains and rebukes us, it shows us our sin and danger, it condemns us, and thus makes us feel the need of a Redeemer and prepares us to receive Him when presented to our faith. Compare Romans 10:4.

4. Paul continues this general subject throughout chapter four, climaxing the whole in the allegory of Sarah and Hagar, (21-31). This is not to say that the story of Sarah and Hagar was not historical in Genesis, but only that the apostle uses the fact in an accommodated or allegorical sense for illustration. The design seems to be to show the effect of being under bondage of the Jewish law as compared with the liberty of the Gospel. Hagar and her son were treated with severity, cast out and persecuted, and became a fit representation of Jerusalem as it was in the time of Paul. Sarah and Isaac enjoyed freedom and sonship, and became correspondingly a fit representation of the New Jerusalem or the true kingdom of God. Which would these Galatian Christians choose, to remain under the freedom of the Gospel, or voluntarily put themselves into the bondage and under the yoke of Judaism?

"The allegory is addressed to justified but immature believers, who, under the influence of legalistic teachers, "desire to be under the law," and has therefore no application to a sinner seeking justification. It raises and answers for the fifth time in this epistle, the question; Is the believer under the law?"—*Scofield Bible.*

Questions.

1. What has the writer entered upon in this part of the epistle?

2. What is the difference between Galatians and Romans as to the teaching about justification?

3. Name the four direct arguments for justification by faith in Chapter 3?

4. Amplify the first argument.

5. What is the title of the supplemental argument?

6. For what two-fold purpose was the law given after the promise?

7. How would you state the teaching of the allegory?

PRACTICAL APPLICATION

Chapters 5-6

In applying the doctrine Paul urges his readers to stand fast in the liberty of Christ, (5:1-12), but in doing so not to abuse that liberty, (5:13-6:10). He mentions four ways in which it may be abused:

Uncharitableness, 13-15.

Uncleanness, 16-25.

Pride, 26-6:5.

Selfishness, 6-10.

The first-mentioned warning or exhortation speaks for itself. They were to give over contending on this matter and everything else, and live in peace.

The second is important as showing that sins of the mind (20), as well as of the body (19, 21), are classified as of the flesh; that the practice of such sins eternally disinherits (21), and that the Holy Spirit is given to believers for the purpose of overcoming them (17). Read this last verse in the Revised Version and see the different construction put upon the word "may" instead of "can" in the last phrase.

The "pride" referred to in the third instance is spiritual pride;

in which connection note the contrast between verses 2 and 5 of chapter 5. The Greek word for "burden" is not the same in both cases and the statements are not contradictory. In the first instance Paul tells them to bear with others' "burdens" of infirmity in sympathy; and in the second, that self-examination will make them feel they have enough to do with their own "load" of sin without comparing themselves boastfully with their neighbors.

What in the fourth place is called selfishness, might be equally described as parsimony. Verse 6 seems to refer to the care they should evince for their spiritual teachers in their temporal concerns; and the reference to "sowing and reaping" in the following verses primarily alludes to the same thing.

In closing the lesson note verse 11 for its bearing on 2 Thessalonians 3:17.

"How large a letter," really means "with how large letters." The apostle, as was stated in the treatment of 2 Corinthians, had a serious affliction of the eyes, a common disease in the East, which caused him to usually dictate his letters. He seems to have had no amanuensis at hand just now, but the urgency of the situation at Galatia made it necessary to write to them with his "own hand," even though with pain and difficulty.

Questions.

1. From the positive side, what application does Paul make of this whole epistle?

2. From the negative side, what obligations does he lay upon his readers?

3. What three great facts about sin are taught in Chapter 5:16-25?

4. Explain the two-fold use of "burden" in Chapter 6?

5. To what particular sin does Chapter 6:7, 8 refer?

6. How would you explain 6:11?

*The body of the teachings on this epistle is taken from the author's "Synthetic Bible Studies."

EPISTLE TO THE EPHESIANS

THE BELIEVER'S BLESSINGS IN CHRIST

CHAPTER 1

This is the first of what are called the "prison" epistles, because written by Paul while a prisoner at Rome, (Cf. 3:1, 4:1, with Acts 28).) The others are Colossians, Philippians, and Philemon. The apostle wrote these with the chain upon his wrist.

This also, (with Colossians), contains the profoundest truth God has been pleased to reveal to His People, even that of the Church considered as the body of Christ, "the mystery which was kept secret since the world began, but now is made manifest" (Romans 16:25, 26). To quote "Synthetic Bible Studies": "The Church is a body distinct from the Jews on the one hand or the Gentiles on the other. Neither is it identical with the kingdom, but separate from it. It is something unique, not heard of in the Old Testament, and especially given to Paul to reveal. It had its earthly beginning after Christ's ascension into glory. It will have its earthly ending when He comes again, and it is caught up to meet Him in the air (1 Thessalonians 4:13-18). Thenceforward the Church will reign with Him over the earthly kingdom to be set up. The Church is composed of both Jews and Gentiles, and is called The Body of Christ (Cf. 1 Cor. 12:12-27; Col. 1:18, 24; 2:10, etc.)"

1. The apostolic salutation, 1:1, 2, contains the first allusion to this "mystery" in the phrase "to the faithful *in* Christ Jesus." "In" Him, just as the members of our body are in us, i.e., vitally one with us.

2. The thanksgiving in the next verse carries the thought further —"hath blessed us with all spiritual blessings in heavenly places *in* Christ." Note the past tense, "hath blessed," indicating that it is not something God is doing, or is about to do, but something He has done in the case of every believer, once and forever. Note the comprehensiveness of the work, "*all* spiritual blessings." There is no blessing God has purposed for the saint that is not already his potentially, in Christ. In the physical realm, the new-born infant is potentially the man, and all his earthly life is simply the working out, the developing of that which was his in the beginning; so in the spiritual sense of the saint in Christ. The phrase "in heavenly places" does not qualify this at all, since it does not mean that these blessings will not be ours, or not be realized in any sense, till we get to heaven. They are "in heavenly places" in the sense that their source, the One in Whom they are located, and from Whom they flow, Jesus Christ, the Head of the body, is in heaven.

The Four Great Blessings.

3. The verses following, 4-14, describe these blessings, of which there are four all-inclusive ones. First, the believer is "chosen" in Him (vv. 4-6). The *period* of choice was "before the foundation of the world"; the *purpose*, that "we should be holy and without blame before Him"; the *ground*, "the good pleasure of His will"; the *object*, or motive, "the praise of the glory of His grace." "Holy and without blame" does not mean merely that this will be true of us in the life to come, but that it is true now, not experimentally indeed, but positionally, or legally, as we stand before God uncondemned in Christ. Secondly, the believer is redeemed in Him (vv. 7-10). The redemption was necessary that thus by the removal of sin, the choice of God might become operative in our case. This redemption includes the forgiveness of our sins, and more. It means the revelation to us of the mystery of the Divine will (v. 9). Being now sons of God through His grace, we are given the mind of God. The Father reveals His

purposes to His children. These are stated in verse 10. "The dispensation of the fulness of the times," is by some understood as the Millennial age which follows the present one; but there are others who think it refers to an age succeeding that and prior to Eternity. "That word 'fulness of the times,' seems to imply not only the fulfilment of the broken purposes and plans of past dispensations, (broken by man's sin), but also a duration of time in comparison with which all past ages shall be but as fragments, while this will be complete." Thirdly, the believer is inherited in Him (vv. 11, 12). Verse 11 should be read in the Revised Version. It is not only true that "we have obtained an inheritance" in God through Christ, but that God has obtained an inheritance in us. We are His purchased possession, and hence we may be persuaded that He is able to keep that which we have committed against that day (2 Timothy 1:12). Fourthly, the believer is "sealed" in Him (vv. 13, 14), the Holy Spirit Himself, Who dwells in the believer, being that seal. "In the symbolism of Scripture, a seal signifies a finished transaction (Jer. 32:9, 10); ownership (Jer. 32:11, 12; 2 Tim. 2:19); and security, (Esther 8:8; Dan. 6:17; Eph. 4:30)"— *Scofield Bible.*

Prayer for Enlightenment.

4. The apostle concludes the revelation of these blessings with a prayer for spiritual enlightenment on the part of his readers, that they may understand and appreciate their meaning (vv. 15-23). It is not enough that the Holy Spirit reveal a great truth like this to Paul, or inspire Him to record it, but the same Spirit must accompany it to the minds and hearts of his readers or hearers if it is to be effective in their faith and experience. They require "the spirit of wisdom and revelation" (v. 17), in order to know "the hope of His calling," "the riches of the glory of His inheritance in the saints," and "the exceeding greatness of His power

to usward who believe" (vv. 18, 19). Their calling, these riches and this power have just been revealed in the preceding verses, but who can know them without the aid of the Holy Spirit? Consider the "power" for example. It is that which in Christ raised Him from the dead and set Him at the right hand of God, and put all things under His feet (vv. 20-22). This power will do the same for us who are in Christ. It will do so because He is the "Head over all things to the Church" (v. 22). Speaking in the physical sense merely, if one's head is raised from the dead and exalted to a place of power and dignity, every member of the body united to that head, living in it, and in which it lives, must necessarily be raised and exalted also. The head, in a physical sense, finds its completeness, its "fulness" in the body it governs and to which it gives life, and so in the spiritual sense, the Church of Christ, which is His body, is His "fulness" in the sense that He fills it all in all things (v. 23). How much we need the aid of the Holy Spirit to apprehend these things, and make them our glorious possession!

Questions.

1. What is the title of this lesson?

2. Name the "prison" epistles, and state why they are so called.

3. What is the great truth revealed in this epistle, and how does it compare with other features of inspiration?

4. What is the Church, and its earthly history?

5. Have you re-read 1 Corinthians 12:12-27?

6. How would you illustrate the phrase "*in* Christ"?

7. What is the sum of the believers' blessings in Christ?

8. Name these blessings in their order.

9. What may be understood by "the fulness of the times"?

10. What does a "seal" signify in the symbolism of Scripture?

11. Explain the necessity for Paul's prayer in this case.

12. Have you offered the same prayer for yourself?

ADDRESS TO THE GENTILES

CHAPTER 2

This Church, like all the others, was composed of both Jews and Gentiles, but chiefly the latter. Paul is the apostle to the Gentiles and he never loses sight of this calling in his speaking or writing. It is especially necessary that he now address himself to them, because of the nature of the truth he is here revealing, which is the union of Gentile and Jew in the mystical body of christ. The chapter shows us three things: (a), our condition by nature (vv. 1-3); (b), our change from nature to grace (vv. 4-10); (c), our condition by grace (vv. 11-22).

1. Our Condition by Nature vv. 1-3.

"Dead in (or through) trespasses and sins." Spiritual death is meant, consisting in alienation from the life of God, being destitute of His Spirit (Eph. 4:18, 19). It continues after the physical dissolution of the body, and consists in external separation from God in conscious suffering (2 Thess. 1:9; Luke 16:23). The Scripture speaks of this latter as the second death (Rev. 2:11; 20:6, 14; 21:8). But in this life to be "dead in trespasses and sins" is equivalent to be walking "according to the course of this world" (vs. 2); to be doing this is one with holding allegiance to Satan, "the prince of the power of the air, the spirit that now worketh in the children of disobedience." And there is no exception to the rule, for all mankind before they come to Christ have this manner of life. In other words, they are following after the desires of the flesh, their fallen nature, for which reason they are exposed to the wrath of God against sin (v. 3).

2. Our Change from Nature to Grace vv. 4-10.

God, and not ourselves, is the cause of this change. God in the going out of His mercy and love toward us (v. 4). The great instrumental means is Christ, and the method employed is to quicken, raise us up, and make us "sit together in heavenly places" in Him (vv. 5, 6). Observe the past tenses here. He "*hath* quickened us." Believers are already spiritually alive in Christ. He "*hath* raised us up." In the mind and purpose of God, believers are already physically raised from the dead. "Together" with Christ are they raised, the philosophy of which is seen as we retain in mind the illuminating figure of the human body. If, in the physical sense, one's head is raised from the dead, must not the same be true of all the members of His body? And so, in the spiritual sense, if Christ is the Head of the body His Church, and if He is risen from the dead, must not His whole body be risen? It is nothing to say that so far as believers are concerned this is not yet true in an experimental sense. The point is that in God's mind and purpose it is true, and with Him time is not counted. He hath "made us sit together in heavenly places in Christ Jesus." In other words, we who believe, are already exalted with Him. "Heavenly places," literally translated, is "the heavenlies," and means "that which is heavenly in contradistinction to that which is earthly." We are already in the "heavenlies" in Christ in the sense that (1), we are partakers of His heavenly nature (2 Pet. 1:4), and life (Col. 3:4; 1 Jno. 5:12); (2), we enjoy the same heavenly fellowship (Jno. 20:17; Col. 1:24; Phil. 3:10; Heb. 2:11; 1 Jno. 1:3); and (3), we have a heavenly inheritance (Rom. 8:18-21; 1 Pet. 2:9; Rev. 1:5, etc.). The object of God in thus changing us from nature to grace is expressed in verse 7, and corresponds to chapter 1, verses 6, 12 and 14, "the praise of His glory," especially the glory of His grace. From the human side, all this comes to pass through faith— "not of works" (vv. 8,9). And indeed, on our part there can be no good works acceptable to God, until this change occurs. It is then we are created anew in order to bring forth such works (v. 10). This last is the present and earthly effect of our changed condition.

3. Our Condition by Grace vv. 11-22.

Verse 11 shows that Gentiles rather than Israelites are particularly in mind. Before becoming Christians they were "separate from Christ" (v. 12 R. V.), in that they did not belong to the commonwealth, or nation, of Israel. Not belonging to Israel they were "strangers from the covenants of the promise" (R. V.). The "promise" was that of the coming of the Messiah, the Christ, in connection with which, and for the carrying out of which, God entered into many covenants, or agreements with Israel, as the Old Testament has shown us. To none of these covenants did the Gentiles bear any relation. Hence the latter were without hope in the world such as Israel had, and being without such hope, they were practically "without God." They were thus "afar off" from Israel in point of privilege and blessing, but now, being in Christ Jesus, they had been "made nigh" (v. 13). Christ had become their "peace," He had brought the Gentile and Jew together, by breaking down that which had separated them (v. 14), "even the law of commandments in ordinances" (v. 15). This He did by His death on the cross, having fulfilled the law in the ceremonial sense and kept it in the moral sense, on their behalf. He had thus made in Himself of the two men, Jew and Gentile, One New Man, by which is meant not an individual believer, but that mystical conception, CHRIST, spoken of in 1 Corinthians 12:12. The CHRIST there, as we saw, meant not the Personal Christ, but the Personal Christ plus the Church considered as His body, the members of which are baptized into Him by the Holy Spirit. This is THE GREAT MYSTERY of which Paul speaks here, and which he had been especially commissioned to reveal. How wonderful it is! Both these two classes, Jews and Gentiles, have been reconciled to God "in one body by the cross" (v. 16), in the sense that Christ's work on the cross took away the enmity between them both and God. He thus preached peace with God to both, to the Gentiles "afar off" from God, and to the Jews "that were nigh" in comparison with them as indicated in verse 12. These both, Jew and Gentile now alike through Christ, had access by the Holy Spirit "unto the Father" (v. 18). The Gentiles, in comparison with the Jews, had been "strangers and foreigners," but were now "fellow-citizens with the saints." In verse 30 the figure is changed to a building to which Christ is the Chief Corner Stone. In Him "each several building" (R. V.), "groweth into a holy temple in the Lord" (v. 21). This holy temple is "a habitation of God through the Spirit." Because the Holy Spirit dwells in every believer, He dwells in the whole company of believers, and this means that He dwells in the Church, which is His habitation (cf. Rev. 21:2, 3).

Questions.

1. Why is it specially necessary for the apostle to now address himself to the Gentiles?

2. What three things are shown in this chapter?

3. How do verses 2 and 3 explain being "dead in trespasses and sins"?

4. What is God's method in changing men from nature to grace?

5. What is the significance of the past tense in the working out of this method?

6. What is meant by "heavenly places"?

7. What object has God before Him in all this?

8. Analyze verse 12.

9. What is meant by "one new man"?

10. Explain verse 18.

AN EXPLANATORY PARENTHESIS

CHAPTER 3

At the beginning of this chapter, Paul is about to exhort the Church in a practical application of the doctrine he had expounded. Indeed, he has gotten as far as—"For this cause I Paul, the prisoner of Jesus Christ for you Gentiles," when the divine impulse leads him to digress. This digression, covering the remainder of the chapter, is an explanation of the special ministry given him for the Gentiles (vv. 2-4). This ministry was a "mystery" unrevealed in the Old Testament, for the reference to the "prophets" in verse 5 means the New Testament prophets particularly Paul himself. That the apostle is not referring merely to the gospel of salvation is clear because that was no "mystery" (Rom. 9:24-33; 10:19-21). What he *is* referring to is (v. 6), "that the Gentiles should be fellow-heirs, and fellow-members of the body," i.e., the body of Christ, the Church, of which he has been speaking. This unique "body" was a mystery "hid in God" from the beginning of the world (v. 9), whose revelation at this time was for the purpose stated in verse 10. That verse shows the Church to be "the lesson-book for the angels." They had seen God's ways in creation, and at the deluge, and in Israel, but here is something that not even the Scriptures had hinted at, that was never promised in the Old Testament, something kept entirely secret between the Father and the Son.

Prayer for Strength.

Some conception of the nature and greatness of this truth thus revealed, may be gathered from the prayer that follows. As that in chapter 1 was for spiritual enlightenment, this is for spiritual strength. "We have this treasure in earthen vessels," the apostle says in another place, and earthen vessels break easily, and are unable to stand too great a strain. To contain such a truth, we need the aid of the Holy Spirit, hence the language of verses 16 to 19. As Kelly puts it, "the prayer in chapter 1 was for a deep and real apprehension of their standing before God; here, it is rather for practical, inward power, by the Holy Ghost. In a word, it is here a question of actual state, of the affections having Christ within, of being rooted and grounded in love, that they might be thoroughly able (for so it means), to lay hold of that which is indeed measureless. The apostle does not say what it is of which they are to lay hold, for verse 18 has no ending. It brings you into infinity. It can be nothing else, indeed, than the grandeur of that 'mystery' of the believer's oneness with Jesus Christ. All things are for the glory of the Son, and the saints in Him are to have the very highest place with Him over all."

Hence the ascription (vv. 20, 21). In this, He does not say above all that we *can* ask or think, but all that we *do* ask or think. We *can* ask more than we *do* ask, because of "the power that worketh in us," i. e., power of God. In chapter 1, we saw the power of God working for us; here, we see it working in us. There, it raised us from the dead; here, it gives us entrance into His love and fulness. No wonder the apostle exclaims, "Unto Him be Glory!"

Questions.

1. What is the literary character of chapter 3?

2. What is the nature of this digression?

3. What is meant by the "mystery"?

4. What is the subject of this prayer in comparison with that in chapter 1?

5. What added thought have we here concerning the Divine power in relation to the believer?

THE CHRISTIAN'S WALK

CHAPTERS 4:1-5:21

At 4:1 the apostle returns to the exhortation and practical application on which he had started at 3:1. The Ephesian Christians had been called with a holy calling (vocation) and now they were to "walk worthy" of it. "Walk" occurs five times in our lesson, giving completeness to it.

1. Walk in Unity 4:1-16.

The unity referred to, is that which has been made among Christians by the baptism of the Holy Spirit into Christ (vv. 3-6). It is not anything they are to make for themselves, or which they can make, but something they are to endeavor to "keep." The way to keep it is expressed in verse 2. The occasion for the exhortation is suggested in verses 7 and the following, which recall the strife in the Corinthian Church about spiritual gifts, only there the stress was laid on the gifts, while here it bears on the persons who receive the gifts, or rather who themselves are gifts to the Church (vv. 8-11). These apostles, prophets, evangelists, pastors and teachers are given for "the perfecting of the saints," their increase in the knowledge of Christ, and the latter in turn are to engage in ministering for the building up of the whole body (see the Revised Version). This is to continue till the body of Christ is complete, i.e., "till we all come . . . a perfect (full grown) man" (v. 13). This "man" does not mean any individual man, but the "MAN" referred to in chapter 2:15, the "MAN" composed of the Personal Christ as the Head, and the members of the Church as His body. We Christians are all to "grow up into Him in all things, which is the Head, even Christ" (v. 15). Each member of the body has a part to perform in its development (v. 16).

2. Walk in Purity 4:17-5:2.

"Not as other Gentiles walk," in vanity, ignorance of God, lasciviousness (vv. 17-19), falsehood, anger, theft, idleness, corrupt speech, etc. (vv. 25-31). These things are to be "put off," or in other words, "the old man," i.e., our old fallen and corrupt nature is to be put off at the same time that "the new man," i.e., the new nature in Christ Jesus is to be "put on." This means as we have seen in Galatians 5:16-25, that there should be an actual, experimental living of Christ in us, and by us, every day. But this is only to be obtained through the renewing of the spirit of our mind (v. 23). That is, the Holy Spirit must renew us day by day with strength to accomplish it (3:16-19).

3. Walk in Love 5:2.

This section really begins at 4:31, 32. Walking in love is being kind and tender-hearted to one another in Christ, which graces show themselves in the absence of bitterness and wrath, anger, clamor and evil-speaking. Christ Himself is an example, and His work for us the motive of this love.

4. Walk in Light v. 8.

This section probably begins at verse 3 and runs to 14. The darkness which is the absence of light is shown in the sins of fornication, uncleanness, covetousness, filthiness, foolish talking, and the like, with which we are to have no fellowship, but rather to reprove (v. 11). This very reproof is light (v. 13).

5. Walk in Wisdom vv. 15-21.

"Not as fools, but as wise, redeeming the time," or "buying up the opportunities" as it might be rendered. The wisdom spoken of is "understanding what the will of the Lord is" (v. 17), which can only be ours as we are "filled with the Spirit" (v. 18). When we are thus filled with the Spirit, our fellowship with one another in Christ, is one of joy, gratitude, loving submission (vv. 19-21).

Questions.

1. What is the title of this lesson?

2. What suggests it in the text?

3. In what five ways is the Christian's walk outlined?

4. What is the nature of the unity in which they are to walk?

5. How may this unity be kept?

6. What gifts are here referred to?

7. For what purpose are they bestowed?

8. How long is this work to proceed?

9. What is meant by "man" in verse 13?

10. What is meant by the "old man," and the "new man" in verses 22 and 24?

11. How can we put on the new man?

12. What is the result of being "filled with the Spirit"?

APPLICATION TO THE THREE CLASSES OF THE SOCIAL ORDER

CHAPTERS 5:22-6:24

In the last lesson Paul spoke of the Christian's "walk" in general terms, but now applies the thought particularly to (a), wives and husbands (5:22-33); (b), children and parents (6:1-4); (c), servants and masters (vv. 5-9), summing up the whole in verses 10-18. The epistle concludes with a brief reference to his personal affairs (vv. 19-22), and a benediction (vv. 23-24).

Speaking of the application to the three classes of the social order, it is noticeable that the apostle begins with the duties of the inferior or subjected party in each case, an arrangement not accidental, as may be judged by comparing Colossians 3:18-4:1, as well as 1 Peter 2:18, and the subsequent verses. As another suggests, "one reason for this may be that the duties of submission and obedience are so incomparably important to all the interests of human life." Furthermore all these duties are here seen in special connection with the believer's standing in Christ.

In the instance of wives and husbands, we are not to suppose that there is anything derogatory to the former in their submission, "since subordination and order are the great characteristics of God's workmanship." Christ is equal to God and yet as the Son

He is submissive to the Father. Is that derogatory to Him? Of course, the reference here is to the *saved* woman, and one who so appreciates her stand-in Christ as to feel the fitness of things resulting therefrom.—Bishop W. R. Nicholson. Moreover, as the same spiritual teacher says, husbands are not directed to *command* but to love their wives. The right to command is implied but not enforced. The husband's love, on the other hand, includes every attention to his wife, the reposing of his confidence in her, and the enjoyment with her of their oneness in Christ. Under these reciprocal conditions submission is likely to be a delight. Verses 30 and 31 of this section are quoted from Genesis 2:23, 24, which suggests a beautiful type of the Church as the bride as well as the body of Christ (2 Corinthians 11:2, 3).

In the instance of children and parents, observe that the former are addressed as though they were present in the church assemblies where this letter was read, and expected to give their personal attention to it, to understand it, and obey its teachings the same as their adult associates. Observe too, that they were *saved* children, and able to appreciate their obligation to obey their parents because with them they were "in the Lord." One such inspired declaration as this is an all-sufficient answer to much of that newer pedagogy in our Sunday schools which leaves the supernatural almost out of account.

Children need the Word of God as much as their parents do, and if it be given to them clear and simple, the Holy Ghost is able to illuminate it to their understandings and apply it to their hearts. They who are substituting something else in its place in our Sunday schools are assuming a responsibility from which the wise may well shrink. Observe finally, in this connection, that fathers are not to be unduly severe with their children, but to temper and qualify their government as becometh them that are in the Lord.

In the instance of servants and masters, the former are to be understood as slaves, but not necessarily of an inferior race. They may have been captives taken in war, and in many respects the equal of their masters, and yet they were to be obedient, "as unto Christ." They were in Him just as their masters were, but this would not alter the relation they bore to them, for Galatians 3:28 has reference to salvation in Christ, and does not contravene the established relations of life. But there are obligations for the Christian masters also (v. 9).

In the previous lesson we dwelt on the Christian's *walk*, but now we come, in the summing up of the article, to the Christian's *warfare* (5:10-18). The Scofield Bible divides these verses thus: the warrior's power (v. 10); the warrior's armor (v. 11); the warrior's foes (vv. 12-17), and the warrior's resource (v. 18).

Questions.

1. What three classes of the social order are named?

2. Why presumably, does the apostle begin with the duty of the subjected party first?

3. Show that there is nothing derogatory in the subjection of a wife to her husband.

4. Under what conditions is such submission likely to be a delight?

5. What inferences are to be drawn from the address to "children" chapter 6:1?

6. What caution does this suggest to Sunday school teachers?

7. Have you looked up the reference to Galatians 3:28?

8. To what does that reference refer?

9. What new idea about the Christian is suggested in the summing up of the epistle?

10. Analyze verses 10-18.

EPISTLE TO THE PHILIPPIANS

INTRODUCTORY

As we saw earlier this is one of the "prison" epistles of Paul, written at Rome where he was awaiting a hearing before Nero because of his witness for Christ (Acts 28). Its occasion is stated in chapter 4:10-18. Epaphroditus had brought him the gifts of the church at Philippi, and now that he was returning to Macedonia he is commissioned with this letter of appreciation and loving instruction. It has sometimes been called the epistle of Christian experience, as it deals with conduct rather than doctrine, and yet there is doctrine in it too, precious and important.

For the history of the Church, read again Acts 16. It is probably nine years since the events of that chapter, and Paul has visited the Church twice since that time. But how it has grown! Now it has "bishops and deacons," it is full of love and good works; it is affectionately mindful of Paul—and yet it has some trouble too, a tendency to separate into cliques, as we shall see. And there were also emissaries of error there, false professors and pharisaic disciples—all this comes out in the text.

The Scofield Bible indicates the divisions by chapters thus: Taking as the key-verse 1:21, "For me to live is Christ and to die is gain," Chapter 1 reveals "Christ as the believer's life, rejoicing in suffering"; Chapter 2, "Christ the believer's pattern, rejoicing in lowly service"; Chapter 3, "Christ the believer's object, rejoicing despite imperfections"; Chapter 4, "Christ the believer's strength, rejoicing over anxiety."

Questions.

1. Where, and under what circumstances was this epistle written?
2. What was its occasion?
3. How has it sometimes been designated?
4. Where do we find the history of the church at Philippi?
5. What is called the key-verse of this epistle?
6. Classify its chapters according to this key-verse.

JOY IN SUFFERING

CHAPTER 1

1. The epistle opens with the customary salutation or greeting (vv. 1-2). Timothy is named with Paul, not that he is a co-writer, but a co-worker in Philippi, and hence known to the Church. He is however, Paul's companion in Rome at this time. Note the important expression *"in* Christ Jesus," which was explained in Ephesians. Note the advanced development of the Church— "bishops and deacons" or "overseers and working-helpers."

2. Then comes the thanksgiving (3-8). Note the Christian fellowship expressed in verse 5, the Philippian church being particularly active in co-operating with Paul. The thought is carried forward into verse 7, verse 6 being a parenthesis. Their long consistency in Christian service leads Paul to feel convinced that they were planted on the rock which could not be shaken. They would certainly see the glory of Christ (v. 6).

3. Returning to the thought of his love for them, note his fourfold prayer on their behalf: (a), that their love (for one another) might abound; (b), that they might approve the excellent things, or rather "try the things that differ" (R. V.); (c), that they might be sincere and not stumbling-blocks to others; (d), that they might be filled with the fruit of righteousness.

4. A further division begins at verse 12, where the apostle speaks of his position and circumstances in Rome in language justifying the title of the lesson. His sufferings as a prisoner have proven beneficial to the Gospel, in that it is known "in all the palace" and outside, that he has committed no crime but is there

because of the Messiah of Israel, the Saviour of the world (v. 13). This knowledge is spreading in two ways (vv. 14-17). The contentious preachers are troubling him personally, but nevertheless the Gospel is spreading through their contention (v. 18) and he rejoices. These will be a blessing to him in the end, through the fulness of the Holy Spirit in answer to their prayers. Of this he will not be disappointed, he feels sure (v. 20).

5. A fifth division suggests itself at verse 21, where passing from his present experiences to his future hope, he glides naturally into a vein of exhortation. His "consciousness and experiences of living are so full of Christ," and hence so full of blessing, that the act of dying to be with Christ would be only to increase his blessing (vv. 21, 23). If he lives however, being acquitted at his trial, he will have more fruit in earthly labor for Christ (v. 22). It is difficult which to choose, but he is confident that the Lord's will is for him to remain with them longer (vv. 24-27). However, whether he returned to them or not let their conduct be ordered right. Let them be steadfast, united and courageous (vv. 27, 28). To their enemies this will be an evidence of the perdition that awaits them, but to themselves an evidence of their salvation. This is a great boon that has been granted them to suffer for Christ, as he, Paul, had suffered and was now suffering.

Questions.

1. Why is Timothy named with Paul in the salutation?

2. Analyze Paul's prayer.

3. How would you explain verse 21?

4. How would you explain verse 28, last clause?

JOY IN SERVICE

CHAPTER 2

1. Expressed in Unity.

We here touch the weak point in the spiritual life of this church —a tendency toward dissension and separation. It is sad, as another says, that this tendency "is not least likely to be operative where there is a generally diffused life and vigor" in a church, just as a state of lukewarmness may favor an outward tranquility. Paul plies his arguments against it, saying in effect, if there is any such thing as comfort drawn from our common union in Christ, any such thing as fellowship in the Holy Spirit, or human tenderness and compassion, show it toward me, by giving up your pride and self-will and becoming of one mind.

2. Expressed in Humility vv. 5-11.

This leads to a deeper note. Unity presupposes humility, and here the great example of Jesus Christ is used. "Being in the form of God." (v. 6) is translated by Bishop Moule, "in God's manifested Being subsisting," (cf. John 17:5). "Thought it not robbery," he translates, "reckoned it no plunderer's prize," i.e. "He viewed His possession of the fulness of the Eternal Nature as securely and inalienably His own." And so "made Himself of no reputation," or so made Himself void by His own account (v. 7). The idea is, that so sure was His claim of Deity, that with a sublime unanxiety He could empty Himself of the manifestation and exercise thereof to take "upon Him the form of a servant." We should be careful to note however, that, as the Scofield Bible says, "nothing in this passage teaches that the Eternal Word (John 1:1) emptied Himself of either His divine nature or His attributes, but only of the outward and visible manifestation of the Godhead." "He stripped Himself of the insignia of His majesty"— Lightfoot. Taking "the form of a servant" means assuming our human nature; and then He stooped even lower, i. e., unto death, in obedience to His father. And lower yet, "even the death of the cross" (v. 8), unimaginable as to its pain, and so humiliating that to the Jews it was the symbol of the Divine curse, and to the Romans so degrading, that Cicero said it was far from their bodies not only, but their imaginations. But think of the reward of such humility (vv. 9-11). The "Name Which is Above Every Name" is His "not only as He is from all eternity, but as He became also in time, the suffering and risen Saviour of sinners." Of this whole passage Bishop Moule well says, "Nothing but the orthodox creed, with its harmonious truths of the proper Godhead and proper Sonship of the Lord Christ, can possibly satisfy the apostolic language about His infinite glory on the one hand, and His relation to the Father on the other."

3. Expressed in Watchfulness vv. 12-16.

"Work out your own salvation" means "develop" it. It had been given to them in Christ, and now they were to set themselves to the "business of the spiritual life." But to guard against the thought of personal ability or merit in the premises, they are reminded of the Divine indwelling (v. 13), by Whose power it is that progressive as well as immediate sanctification is secured. The "fear and trembling" does not indicate a suspicion lest the salvation will be taken from them, but the solemn watchfulness to be exercised lest they grieve the Spirit of God (Ephesians 4:30).

Three Great Human Examples.

The chapter closes with great human examples following the Divine one—Paul himself (vv. 17, 18), Timothy (vv. 19-23), Epaphroditus (vv. 24-30).

Paul fears his reference to having "run in vain" (v. 16) may be misunderstood, and he assures them that if his life were poured out on their behalf, it would be well worth while because of their service of faith. He views them in their consecration as a burnt-offering to God, upon which his own life-blood might be poured out as a drink-offering (cf. Numbers 15:5). How sad the thought in verses 20, 21! The

other Christians who were by him and whom he might send, were pleading excuses of one kind and another, but they knew Timothy of old, and could trust him (vv. 22, 23). It was necessary however, for him to return Epaphroditus to them, who had brought their gifts of love to his prison-house (v. 25), and who had been very sick (v. 27), occasioned in some way by his fidelity to them in his service for Paul. Such men as he were to be held "in reputation."

Questions.

1. What was the weak point in this church?

2. How would you interpret verses 1 and 2?

3. Who is the great Example of humility?

4. What caution is necessary in the interpretation of verses 6-7?

5. In what sense is verse 9 to be applied to Christ?

6. How are we to understand verse 12?

7. Name the three great human examples of unselfish devotion to Jesus Christ.

JOY IN PRAYERS

CHAPTER 3

1. This chapter opens with a warning against the Judaizing teachers whom we have met before (vv. 1-3), and who followed Paul everywhere teaching that the keeping of the ceremonial law of Moses was necessary to salvation. The "dogs," the "evil workers" and the "concision" of verse 2 all refer to them, the last word being a parody of what circumcision meant in the Old Testament. These false teachers were not the true circumcision, or the true Israelites, who are described in verse 3.

2. This reference to the true circumcision leads Paul to speak of himself (vv. 4-14). If any spiritual value lay in pedigree or outward zeal, he might well claim it (vv. 5, 6); but his estimate of these things since his conversion to Christ is expressed in what fol-

lows. He counts them not merely worthless but ruinous, being a "loss," "a robbery of the true blessing." "That I may win Christ" (v. 8) might be rendered "that I *might* win." "He thinks the past over again," says Bishop Moule. "The righteousness which is of God by faith" (v. 9) is expounded in our treatment of Romans 1:17. "That I may know Him" (v. 10), means with an inward spiritual intuition, as the One Whose resurrection assures me of justification and coming glory, for Whom I daily take up the cross of suffering, being thus brought more and more into harmony ("conformity") with that surrender He made in achieving my salvation. The outcome of this knowledge is an attainment "unto the resurrection out from the dead" (v. 11, R. V.). The reference is to the first resurrection, that of the saints which takes place at Christ's second coming (1 Cor. 15:23; 1 Thes. 4:16; Rev. 20:4-6. This is that for which Christ had laid hold of Paul at his salvation, and toward which he was ever pressing (vv. 12-14).

3. The reference to himself and his purpose eventuates in an exhortation (vv. 15-21). "Perfect" (v. 15), means not sinlessness which Paul himself had not reached (v. 12) and which no saint reaches in this life, but rather "Christian maturity and entirety of experience," which those in Christ as long as these Philippians were should have known. "Thus-minded," means of the same mind as Paul, who rested immovably on Christ for His acceptance with God, and pressed forward without rest in the path of obedience. Did they not see eye to eye with him on all these matters it would yet be revealed to them (v. 15), but in the meantime let them fully live up to the light they had (v. 16). From the above it will be seen that Paul has in mind another class of false teachers besides the legalists (Judaizers). These were those with false notions of holiness, who so presumed on the atoning merits of Christ as to disclaim any need

of seeking conformity to His life. They walked as enemies of Christ, though professing His name, and indulged in gross sins (vv. 18, 19) on the ground that it made no difference if their spirits soared in a higher region. This was the teaching of a false philosophy known as "Gnosticism" of which we shall learn more in Colossians. Some of the "Gnostics" were ascetics while others were libertines, both practices springing from the same root of error, viz: a wrong conception of the human body in the scheme of redemption (cf. 1 Corinthians 6:12-20). To both schools, spirit was good and matter evil; but one sought to wear out the body by beating and abusing it, while the other let it have its own way as that which was soon to perish. These all minded "earthly things," but the true Christian the heavenly things (v. 20). The latter is a citizen of the heavenly city, where he will be forever with the Lord (1 Thessalonians 4:17), and is therefore 'obliged by his nobility' to live as one who belongs to and represents it. When our Lord comes out of that city for us, He will not destroy or annihilate our present bodies, but wonderfully change them like unto His own "glorious body" (v. 21).

Questions.

1. With what does this chapter open, and why?

2. What does the apostle count "loss"?

3. What does "perfect" mean in verse 15?

4. Define "Gnosticism."

5. Give an interpretation of verse 21.

JOY IN ANXIETY

Chapter 4

1. The chapter opens with another exhortation to unity, but this time in a specific case (vv. 1-3). Two Christian women, probably deaconesses, like Phoebe (Romans 16:1), were at variance. The spirit of self had got in and Paul pleads with them

to come together again, and pleads with his "true yokefellow," whoever he may have been, to help them do it.

2. This leads to a statement of a great truth about self-will (vv. 4-9). In the first place, to "rejoice in the Lord" is an antidote to self-will (v. 4). In the second place, the absence of mere self-will in a Christian should "be known to all men," i. e. it should be a reality in his life, and for the reason that the Lord is always "at hand" to help and to calm his spirit. In the third place, since the occasion of the Christians' self-will is likely to be some cause for anxiety about himself, he is to remove this by telling it to the Lord (v. 6). Thus God's peace will garrison his heart, keeping it as with a sentinel from being invaded by disquiet, giving rise to self-will. The Christian who thus draws his strength from God is able to act on the advice of verse 8, and to follow the example of Paul in verse 9. How wonderful the grace of God in Paul, when he might dare to remind them of himself in these respects, not in egotism, but in sober and blessed fact!

3. The remainder of the letter is taken up with personal matters. The church at Philippi had contributed to the apostle's physical needs through the ministration of Epaphroditus. They had aided him in his necessity before; but some time had elapsed since they had done so, because they "lacked opportunity" (vv. 10). The apostle was not complaining. He had not wanted anything, not because he had much, but because he had learned to do with little (vv. 11, 12). This was not a natural gift of his, but a supernatural enduement (v. 13). Nevertheless the kindnesses of the Philippians were appreciated,

and especially because they were the fruit of Paul's ministry among them, which ultimately would bring reward to them— "abound to your account" (vv. 14-17). This would be true because they did it for him in the Name of the Lord, Who would supply all their need (vv. 18, 19).

Note in the closing salutation, "They that are of Caesar's household" (v. 22), which means Christian believers "gathered from the retainers of the palace." Quoting Lightfoot, "the household of Caesar embraced a vast number of persons in Rome and in the provinces, all of whom were either actual or former slaves of the Empire, filling every description of office more or less domestic." It should be added that they were not necessarily of inferior races, but captives taken in war, just as the Hebrews were made to serve at the court of Babylon. "Their associations and functions," adds Lightfoot, "give a noble view of the power of grace to triumph over circumstances, and to transfigure life where it seems most impossible."

Questions.

1. Explain verses 1 to 3.
2. State in your own words the inspired teaching about "self-will."
3. State in your own words Paul's feeling about the ministrations of this church to him.
4. Who are meant by "Caesar's household"?
5. How is the "power of grace" illustrated in them?

Colosse was an important city of Phrygia in Asia Minor, east of Ephesus. It is not definitely known that Paul visited it, and yet it is assumed he did so on his third journey. The epistle was written while he was a prisoner at Rome (4:8) and sent by Tychicus, (4:7, 8).

EPISTLE TO THE COLOSSIANS

INTRODUCTION

Colossians bears a somewhat similar relationship to Ephesians as that of Romans to Galatians. That is, it makes a pair with that epistle, the two being written almost simultaneously. It was sent by the same messenger also (compare Ephesians 6:21, 22) and contains some of the same expressions (compare 1:4 with Ephesians 1:15, and 1:14 with Ephesians 1:7). See also the prayers in the two epistles and the references to the Body of Christ.

The central theme of Colossians is Christ, while that of Ephesians is the church. In the first-named we have the Head of the Church, and in the last-named the body of the church, and both are seen exalted on high. (Colossians 1:18, Ephesians 2:6). Perhaps it would be well to designate the theme of the epistle as, "The Headship of Christ," or "The Believers' Union or Identification with Christ."

Definition of Gnosticism.

It was occasioned by the fact that the spiritual life of the church was threatened by false doctrine, a mixture of Judaism (2:16) and Oriental mystic speculation (2:18). That there were Jews in large numbers in that region is certain, says Bishop Nicholson*, and that there was a Jewish sect precisely answering to the false doctrine condemned in this epistle is certain. The sect was the Essenes, who, unlike the Pharisees and Sadducees, do not appear in the Gospel narratives, because their principles withdrew them from the daily life of the Jewish people and immured them in convents. They were essentially a Gnostic sect, and Gnosticism, under whatever variety, was characterized by three features: (1) An exclusive spirit. The word means one who claims pre-eminent knowledge. It was an intellectual caste, with a process and

oaths of initiation. (2) Speculative tenets on creation, evil, emanations, angels. Creation was not by the Supreme God, according to them, since He could have nothing to do with matter which is inherently evil, but must have been by one or more of angelic emanations from Him. Those emanations or angels are to be worshipped. (3) Ethical practice. Either a rigid asceticism, because of matter being the abode of evil, or unrestrained licentiousness, on the principle of not condescending to care at all about a thing so inherently evil as matter.

Paul assails the exclusive spirit of intellectual caste (1:28), and as in his other epistles, insists upon the free offer of the Gospel to all men, but now from a different point of view. Here it is as opposing *intellectual* exclusiveness, and not, as in Galatians, *national* exclusiveness. "Perfection" was a great Gnostic word, and that word the apostle here appropriates to the position in Christ of every believer. He also attacks the speculative tenets of angelology and the idolatrous practice of angelolatry (1:15-19; 2:18), opposing to them both the true ideas of Christ in His Person and His mediation. And he utters his condemnation of a very peculiar ethical practice (Col. 2:16, 23), protesting not alone against "holy days, new moons, and Sabbaths" (strictly Jewish observances), but against the asceticism with regard to "drinks," and the "neglecting of the body" (which was wholly of Gnostic origin): and opposing to both of these Jewish and Gnostic practices the believers' life in Christ.

It has been well said that "the Colossian heresy was no vulgar falsehood. At the bottom of it there was an earnest, unsatisfied desire of the soul; a sense of need unrequited; an aching void the world had never filled. In its doctrine of the mediation of angels and the consequent removal of God from contact with the inherent evil of matter, it claimed to honor the supreme majesty of the Deity, and at the same time to show forth its own humility, as shrinking amid the evils of human nature, from any direct converse with God; while yet in its asceticism it honored itself and ministered to the pride and vanity of self-righteousness. It was human nature as essentially displayed everywhere and in all ages; the circumstances and the particular tenets ever changing, but the affectation of humility and the proud, self-righteous spirit ever remaining the same. And thus it is that the Colossian heresy was an anticipation of the errors of today, and that the apostles' confutation of it supplies the needed instruction for ourselves."

*Oneness with Christ, a practical commentary on the Epistle of the Colossians.

Questions.

1. Have you examined the map for Colosse?

2. Define the relationship of this epistle to Ephesians?

3. How does its theme differ from Ephesians?

4. What two forms of false doctrine is here touched upon?

5. Describe the Essenes.

6. What three features characterized "Gnosticism"?

7. What makes this epistle of practical value to-day?

THE DOCTRINAL PART

CHAPTER 1

The chapter divides itself into a salutation (vv. 1, 2); a thanksgiving (vv. 3-8); a prayer (vv. 9-14), and a three-fold declaration concerning Jesus Christ (vv. 15-29). This declaration sets forth His Godhead (vv. 15-17); His reconciling work (vv. 18-23), and the mystery of His indwelling in the believer, and hence in the church which is His body.

1. The salutation is scarcely distinguishable from those considered in the preceding epistles.

2. The thanksgiving is for the faith of the church, their love to the saints, and the hope laid up

for them in heaven (vv. 4-5). "In all the world," (v. 6), does not mean literally in every place, but is used simply as expressing the proper area of the preached Gospel, in which sense it was the whole world. The reference to Epaphras (v. 7) leads some to think that he, rather than Paul, had planted this church, but if so, he was doubtless a fruit of Paul's labors at Ephesus.

3. The prayer is a single petition, but it has a great scope, "that ye might be filled with the knowledge of His will in all spiritual wisdom and understanding" (v. 9). This knowledge of God's will as revealed in His Word, applied to them by the wisdom of the Holy Spirit, would enable them to "walk worthy of the Lord unto all pleasing" (v. 10). And this walk would show itself in four ways: fruitfulness, growth, patience and thankfulness (vv. 10-12). The thankfulness would be expressed for their share of "the inheritance of the saints in light." They were sufficiently assured of it to give thanks for it, because they had been delivered "from the power of darkness, and translated into the kingdom of His dear Son" (v. 13). This was something that they knew, and they were not walking well-pleasing unto the Lord, if they did *not* know it, and were not continually praising Him for it.

The Godhead of Christ.

4. This reference to the Kingdom of Jesus Christ, leads to the thought of His Person and Glory. "The *image* of the invisible God" (v. 15) means more than a likeness. Two men are alike but one is not the image of the other. On the other hand, the head on a coin is not only a likeness of the sovereign but his image—a *copy* of him derived from and representing him. So Christ is the representation of His Father because derived from Him (Philippians 2:6; Hebrews 1:3). There are then three teachings in this phrase, "Christ is the Son of God, He is the Eternal Son of God, He is God," (Nicholson).

His *eternal* Sonship is seen in that He is not called the Son merely by reason of His incarnation, but as the image of God "prior to all creation," as the next phrase may be rendered. It was not the incarnation which made Him the image of God, but being His image, the incarnation brought Him, so to speak, within our grasp. Moreover, a corroboration that He was "before all creation," is set before us in the next two verses.

5. This declaration concerning His Godhead is followed by one concerning His reconciling work (vv. 18-23). He is not only the Head of the universe as God, but the Head of the church as the God-man. And He is the Head of the church, because He is the beginning of the church. And He is the beginning of the church because He is the first-born from among the dead (v. 18), for the church is made up of raised ones like Himself. Now are they raised in a spiritual sense by faith, but when He comes again they will be raised in the bodily sense and glorified with Him. Being thus Head of the universe and Head of the church, the first in creation and the first in grace, in all things He has the pre-eminence, "for it pleased the Father that in Him should all fulness dwell" (v. 19), i. e. the whole fulness of the Godhead (see 2:9).

The Gnostics taught that a fragment of the Deity was given to the various Divine emanations or angels, who, according to their false philosophy, were generated from the Supreme Deity. The fragment became less and less, in proportion as any one of these emanations was removed from the Deity, but still each had a fragment. A smaller fragment was found in man also. The Greek word for "fulness" was "*pleroma*." Paul takes this word, and wresting it from their perversion of it, "appropriates it to Christ in the utmost extent of its significance." Inasmuch as in Him all the fulness of the Godhead dwelt, therefore it was possible "by Him to reconcile all things unto Himself" (v. 20), to bring them out of the deranged condition in which they were on account of sin into harmony with Himself.

Reconciliation Through Christ.

" 'Reconciliation' is that effect of the death of Christ on the believer, which, through Divine power, works in Him a thorough change toward God from enmity and aversion to love and trust. It is never said that God is reconciled. God is propitiated (Romans 3:25) but the sinner is reconciled (2 Corinthians 5:18-21)."—Scofield. This reconciliation is true not of all things absolutely, but of "all THE things," or to give the exact order in the Greek, "THE all things," which it pleased God thus to reconcile. These things are those of earth and heaven, we perceive, but not hell (cf. Matthew 25:46; Revelation 20:10). Among these especially, are men who believe on the Lord Jesus Christ (Mark 16:16). They were once alienated from God and enemies to Him, but now are they reconciled by Him (v. 21), through the sacrifice of Christ, and presented "unblameable and unreprovable to His sight" (v. 22). This means that such is the position of the believer now, on the earth, the moment he believes on Christ (see our comment on Ephesians 1:4). The proof of it is that he is continuing in the faith (v. 23), "Preached to every creature under heaven," means among all mankind, in all countries, in contrast to Judaism, for example, which was limited to one nation.

Christ Dwelling in Us.

6. We now come to the still deeper mystery of Christ's indwelling in the believer (vv. 24-29). Paul had spoken of his ministry (v. 23), which caused him suffering (v. 24). This suffering had been endured on their account, but he rejoiced in it nevertheless. "The afflictions of Christ in my flesh," means probably his own afflictions, and yet also Christ's, on the principle that the Head suffers in the sufferings of His members (Acts 9:4, 5;

Matthew 25:40, 45; 1 Corinthians 12:12; 2 Corinthians 1:5). "He was going on to endure whatever remained of the afflictions which God had appointed for him to endure," in the exercise of his ministry for them. His was a special ministry, a dispensation of God had been given him "to fully preach the Word of God." This included the revelation of the mystery expressed in the words, "Christ in you, the hope of glory" (v. 27). This mystery is something more than the gospel of our salvation, for that had not been "hid" in the Old Testament. It is an altogether unique blessing, belonging only to the church of this dispensation, and is the indwelling of Christ. And note that this indwelling itself is not the "glory" spoken of but the *hope* of the glory. The glory includes our resurrection bodies; our new hearts in "unhindered development of Christly life"; our coming back with Christ again to earth, and sharing in the triumphs of His reappearing; our sitting with Him on His throne as He has sat down with His Father on His throne; and finally the glory which shall endure "to all the generations of the age of the ages" (Ephesians 3:4), for when at length the millennial church shall have been transferred to her place among the glorified, then shall there be "a new heaven and a new earth." Oh, the glory of being a Christian!

Questions.

1. What title do we give to this chapter?

2. Divide the chapter into three main parts.

3. What three-fold declaration about Christ does it contain?

4. What is the meaning of the phrase "in all the world"?

5. What is the single petition of Paul's prayer?

6. In what way are Christians to "walk worthy of the Lord"?

7. For what should the thankfulness of Christians be ever expressed?

8. What is the difference between a likeness and an image?

9. Why may we speak of Christ as the Eternal Son of God?

10. How did Christ come to be the Head of the church as well as the universe?

11. What was the teaching of the Gnostics about the nature of the Deity?

12. Define reconciliation.

13. To what is this Divine reconciliation limited?

14. What is meant by the "afflictions of Christ in my flesh"?

15. Describe in a phrase the ministry Paul was commissioned to reveal.

16. What are some of the things which the promised glory includes?

THE POLEMIC PART

Chapter 2

The Apostle spoke (1:24, 28, 29) about the suffering entailed by his ministry, and the labor endured to present "every man perfect in Christ Jesus." Of course, he means every Christian man, and by "perfect in Christ Jesus," so far as the present life is concerned, he means, not perfect in the sense of faultless or sinless, but perfectly justified, and sanctified, and perfectly made meet for glory in Him. The word "perfect" is here borrowed from the heathen mysteries and appropriated to the Gospel in condemnation of them. Perfection such as that of which he speaks is not found in them, but in Christ.

The word "every" used three times in 1:28, is important— warning, teaching, presenting *every* man. It harmonizes with the word "all" before "wisdom" in the same verse, and strikes at the Gnostic exclusiveness to which reference has been made. In the wisdom of God in Christ there are no restrictions as to persons or subjects, the whole Christ is preached to every man, and every man has the same opportunity to possess "the riches of the glory."

The subject of the apostle's suffering and toil is carried over into chapter 2, the first three verses of which really belong to chapter 1. The latter part of verse 2 reads in the Revised Version: "That they may know the mystery of God, even Christ, in whom are" etc. In other words, Christ Himself is the mystery of God, "as incarnating the fulness of the Godhead and all the divine wisdom and knowledge for the redemption and reconciliation of man." Now the reason of Paul's conflict on behalf of these Colossian christians is that they may not be enticed away from this precious truth by the false (Gnostic) teachers (4-7), nor enslaved by their empty philosophy (8-15), nor judged in their Christian liberty (16, 17), nor robbed of their reward (18-23).

1. "Lest Any Man Should Beguile You With Enticing Words,"

or beguile you by false reasoning in persuasive discourse. The only safeguard against this is stated in verse 6. They had "received Christ Jesus," and now they are to "walk" in Him, to put forth all their energies as consciously in Him. And to encourage them to do this the apostle calls attention to the good that is among them for their comfort (5).

2. "Beware Lest Any Man Spoil You Through Philosophy and Vain Deceit,"

i.e., enslave, lead you away as his prey. Paul does not characterize *all* philosophy in these terms but only *the* philosophy which is empty deceit, i.e., the philosophy of these Gnostics, somewhat like that of modern times standing under the names of Spinoza, Herbert Spencer and others. It is according to the tradition of men and has no support from revelation. Such teaching is after the world and not "after Christ." In Christ we are "complete," and need nothing more since Christ is God (9, 10). We are "complete" or "filled full" in Him in the sense that His merits, His righteousness, His preciousness, His life, His Sonship, His heirship, His glory, have all been made over to us by Divine grace

through faith (Rom. 8:10-18; 28-39).—*Nicholson.* In detail, we are circumcised in Him (11) i.e., in a spiritual sense, and need not the ritual circumcision as the false teachers claimed. We Christians possess all that was symbolized by that rite, i.e., the putting off of our fallen and corrupt nature. This took place when we died in Christ and were "buried with Him in *the* baptism" (12), i.e., the baptism of the Holy Spirit (1 Cor. 12:13; Rom. 6:4). And having thus died and been buried with Him, we are risen again in Him, and are walking before God "in newness of life" (Rom. 6:4). What then do we require of man-made philosophies? Think what God does, in and through Christ, for the soul He saves! (a) He quickens, i.e., makes us alive in a spiritual sense; (b) He forgives all our transgressions; (c) He blots out "the handwriting of ordinances that was against us." These "ordinances" are His decrees written on the tables of stone in the ceremonial law of Moses, and in our moral nature. In them we find our own handwriting that is "against us," for we assent to the fact that the law is good, and that it is our obligation to obey it. Nevertheless, God blots this out, cancels the bond, erases the signature, pays the debt.—Nicholson. (d) He gets such a victory for us over all our spiritual enemies as is expressed in verse 15. The principalities and powers of darkness seized upon the human nature of Christ our substitute, as if to prevent Him from going to the cross and dying for our redemption. But He overcame them, "made a show of them openly," by rising from the dead, and in His triumph we triumph.

3. Let No Man Therefore Judge You.

"The apostle is here striking at the practical error of the false teachers as expressed in their excessive ritualism and vigorous asceticism." Eating and drinking were referred to in the Mosaic law, but the Gnostic went far beyond that as we may judge further from Rom. 14:2 and 1 Tim. 4:2, 3. "The Sabbath" (16) is referred to from the Jewish point of view. "The rest of one day in seven as expressive of the law of creation, and as supplying the principle which underlies the fourth commandment, he does not here include." He does not merely forbid the observance of these things but going further, forbids Christians to let any one "judge" them, or take them to task concerning them. These things are not a basis of judgment concerning our standing in Christ, but on the contrary, so far as they are part of the Levitical system, they are only the shadow cast in advance of the work of Christ. "The body" the substance, "is of Christ" (Heb. 10:1). The ancient Jew took the shadow as foretelling the body, but the modern ritualist takes the shadow instead of the body."

4. "Let No Man Beguile (rob) You of Your Reward."

In verses 18-23 we have "a description of one whose views of the truth are diametrically opposed to those taught by the apostle in verses 9, 10." (a) He takes delight in "humility and worshipping of angels." This is the mock humility such as we see in the Roman Catholic Church, as though Christ were too high for these false teachers and they must have lower beings for mediators. (b) He "dwells" or takes his stand upon "those things which he hath seen" (18, R. V.). In other words, he does not walk by faith but judges by his natural experiences. For instance, an uninfluential man cannot enter the presence of a human king except as some one introduces him, so Christ, although a Godman, is in the judgment of this false teacher, too high for human fellowship except through lower mediation. And yet there is a slightly different interpretation suggested by Sir William Ramsey. He thinks the force of "intruding into" is gotten only when regarded as a quoted word, and a sarcastic reference to an act by which, once on a time, the false teacher had

symbolically expressed his choice of a so-called "New Life" in the heathen "Mysteries."

These were the things he had "seen," and he was now taking his stand upon them, urging them as needful in the Christian life. If the Christians at Colosse aspired to be "perfect" they must enter upon a higher course of asceticism, self-denial and humiliation after these heathen mysteries. (c) This false teacher is "vainly puffed up by his fleshy mind," by the mind of his fallen and corrupt nature. (d) He does not hold the "Head," i.e., he has no clear and definite views concerning Christ as the Head of the Church which is His body. In other words, he may be a professing Christian, but he is not a member of the true church of Christ.

The practical inference or conclusion follows in verses 20-23, which it will be more convenient to deal with in the succeeding lesson.

Questions.

1. Why is this lesson called the "Polemic" part of the epistle?
2. What is the meaning of "perfect in Christ Jesus"?
3. In what sense is Christ "the mystery of God"?
4. What four-fold reason is given for Paul's conflict?
5. How are we "complete" in Christ?
6. What was symbolized by circumcision?
7. If we are true Christians when was our fallen and corrupt nature put off?
8. Explain "blotting out the handwriting."
9. Explain verse 15.
10. What is meant by "judge you," verse 18?
11. How would you explain "intruding," verse 19?
12. What is the practical conclusion in verses 20-23?

THE HORTATORY PART

Chapters 2:20-4

1. The Christian being "dead with Christ," is dead "from the

rudiments of the world"; in other words, worldly methods of obtaining "perfection" are something with which he has nothing to do. Why then should he act to the contrary, "after the commandments and doctrines of men"? (20, 22). Why should he ascribe salvation or any part of it, to things which "perish with the using"? Why should he come under a law which says "touch not, taste not, handle not," as though it possessed sanctifying grace? As one who is saved, there are many things he will not touch, nor taste, nor handle, as the next chapter indicates, but this is different from attaching a meritorious value to such things, as these false teachers did. Such things have "a show of wisdom" in men's eyes perhaps, but are of the nature of "will worship," self-imposed ordinances, and nothing more. No neglect of the body, no asceticism of this kind can extirpate evil appetites or get rid of sin (23).

2. On the other hand, the Christian having "risen with Christ" as we have seen, let him seek, i.e., set his mind on things above (3:1,2). For these things, compare Matthew 6:33, Phil. 3:20. To seek them means to inquire about and ask for them, as they are revealed in Holy Scripture. The encouragement to do this is found in verses 3 and 4 (cf. 1 John 3:1-3).

3. The Christian who does this will soon be exhibiting the fruit of it in a life of *real* holiness as distinguished from the counterfeit recommended by the Gnostics. This holiness will show itself in two ways, by a putting off (5-11) and a putting on (12-17). The true Christian realizing his risen life with Christ will "mortify" put to death the members of his body, in the sense that he will eschew the things named in verses 5-9. He will do this through the power of the Holy Spirit who dwells within him, and by whom he is "renewed in knowledge after the image of Him that created Him." Verse 11 means that this "new man" is not depending on the distinctions

therein indicated, all of which are obliterated in Christ. But the true believer will not only put to death the things named, but clothe himself with a heart of compassion, kindness, humility, meekness, long-suffering, forbearance, forgiveness, love, peace and thankfulness.

4. We have said that this would be done through the power of the Holy Spirit dwelling in the believer, but the instrument He uses is the "Word of Christ" (16), i.e., the Holy Scriptures. The believer in whose heart that dwells richly, will ever be acting on the principle of verse 17.

5. The apostle now applies all this to the three classes of the social order (3:18—4:1), as he did in Ephesians, to which lesson the student will turn.

6. The conclusion of the epistle is an appeal for prayer (4:2-4); counsel as to conduct toward the world (5, 6); personal matters including commendations of and salutations from fellow workers (7-15); directions concerning the epistle (16); a charge to one of the elders (17), and the benediction (18). Note how aptly the subject of prayer is introduced, following as it does the opening up of the whole subject of practical holiness. How shall we obtain the power to practice such holiness without prayer for the Holy Spirit's aid? Note that while the brotherhood of Christ is a world in itself, yet the Christian has responsibilities toward others (5). To "walk in wisdom" with reference to the unconverted means Gospel knowledge applied in common sense. It means the "conscious blessedness of the life of the Christian as a visible fact," but no "stage effects" no self-conceit and no more oddities. The Christian should evince a true sympathy with all genuine human interests while yet in earnest for the salvation of souls. He should "redeem the time," or "buy up the opportunity," in the sense of knowing just when and how to act in such cases with reference to the world around him. Speech "alway with grace, seasoned with salt" (6) means the

right adaptation and point in our remarks in addressing the unsaved, as indicated in the last clause of the verse. The allusion to Laodicea (13, 15, 16) brings to mind that of 2:1, and gives occasion to say that it, and Hierapolis and Colosse lay very near each other. It is interesting to note that an epistle had been sent there as well as to Colosse, though we have no further record of it. Moreover, the circumstance that the epistles were to be interchanged is a hint as to the way in which the church of the first century determined the Canon of the New Testament. There was in other words, a circulation of the inspired teachings, and a searching into them by all the Christians in every place.

Questions.

1. Interpret in your own words verses 20-23.

2. In what two ways is true holiness exhibited?

3. What does verse 11 mean?

4. What connection in thought is there between verses 16 and 17?

5. What does "walk in wisdom" mean?

6. What is meant by speech "seasoned with salt"?

7. What hint have we here as to the determination of the Canon of the New Testament?

FIRST THESSALONIANS

REMINISCENT

CHAPTERS 1-2:16

For the story of the founding of this Church by Paul, examine Acts 17. We call the first section of the epistle the reminiscent part, because the apostle is referring to what had taken place in Thessalonica at that time.

1. It opens with the usual salutation 1:1, in which Silas and Timothy are named with Paul, not as co-writers, but co-workers with him when in that city, and so known to the church.

2. The thanksgiving follows, 2-4, in which is mentioned a triad of graces (3) that had been produced in these young Christians, testifying assuredly to their election of God (4).

3. Next comes a testimony to the church of the deepest interest (5-10). Through receiving the Word of God in the Holy Ghost, they had become imitators of Paul and of the Lord (6) to such an extent that all the saints throughout Greece were reaping a blessing from their lives (7). Travelers passing from them to other parts, were carrying the news of what God had done for them, so that Paul's own witness was made unnecessary (8). It was an evidence of his ministry among them as the result of which they had "turned to God from idols" (a "work of faith"); "to serve the living and true God" (a "labor of love"); and "to wait for His Son from heaven ("patience of hope"). The explanation of it all is found in verse 5.

4. The testimony to the church leads to a testimony concerning himself (2:1-16), not for his own praise, but the magnifying of the grace of God in Him. In verse 5 of the previous chapter, he had shown that the wonderful result of the gospel among them was explained by the power of the Holy Ghost, with which it had been preached; and this power, in turn, was explained by the "man-ner of men we were among you for your sake." Again, in verse 9, he referred to the "manner of entering in we had unto you," while in chapter 2, he expatiates upon it. In other words, "the manner of man" he had been was expressed (a) *by courage and devotion* (cf. verses 1 and 2 with the story in Acts 16). (b) *by faithfulness and impartiality.* His preaching had not been of deceit (error), uncleanness, guile, flattery, covetousness, or vain-glory. The gospel had been committed to him by God, as a sacred trust; and since to God he must give account of his stewardship, he ministered it not to please men but God, "which trieth our hearts" (3-6). (c) *by kindness and affection.* His gentleness was like that of a mother nursing her children (see R. V.) His affection was shown in the self-denying labor of tent-making in which he engaged to earn his living, that he might "not be chargeable" to them for his support (7-9). (d) *in holiness and consistency* of life (10-12). No wonder therefore that they received his message as the "Word of God" and not the word of men (13); nor that it should have affectually wrought in them as it did "in the churches of God in Judea" (14-16).

Questions.

1. Have you read Acts 16 and 17 in connection with this lesson?

2. Why is this lesson called "Reminiscent"?

3. Why are Silas and Timothy named?

4. What triad of graces was seen in these young Christians?

5. How do you explain 1:7?

6. What is the theme of chapter 2?

7. How had Paul's Christian character been exhibited among the Thessalonians?

8. What was the result?

PERSONAL AND
CONGRATULATORY

CHAPTERS 2:17-3

1. Paul's Desire to Revisit the Church (2:17-19).

Satan hindered in the execution of this desire in ways indicated in Acts 17, viz, by stirring up opposition on the part of the Jews. Observe the teaching here as to the personality of Satan, his hatred of the true church, and the power he has to use agents in opposition to it. Paul's desire to visit the church is explained by his interest in the saints (19). Observe here the reference to the Second Coming of Christ, and the teaching of Paul that he would then meet his converts, and know and rejoice over them in the Lord's presence. What an answer to the question so often raised, Shall we recognize each other in the future life?

2. Timothy's Mission to the Church 3:1-5.

Refer to Acts 17 and observe the circumstances under which Paul was left at Athens. Driven out of Thessalonica and Berea, by persecution, the brethren had sent him there. Observe the reason why Timothy was returned to Thessalonica; to establish and comfort the young saints (2). Their affliction arising out of their faith was great, and though they had been warned of it (4), yet they might have succumbed under it, and Paul's labor on their behalf would in that sense have been "in vain" (5).

3. Timothy's Report of the Church 6-10.

Their faith was firm, their love warm, their remembrance of Paul keen, and he was comforted. This was life for him, to know that his children in the faith stood "fast in the Lord." (8).

4. Paul's Prayer for the Church 11-13.

That he might see them again and that their love might increase toward one another, and toward all. But all this would be fulfilled in permanent perfection only at the Coming of Christ (13).

Questions.

1. What are the four main points of the lesson?

2. How did Satan hinder Paul?

3. What light does this lesson throw on the question of future recognition of believers?

4. Why did Timothy return to Thessalonica?

5. What was the nature of his report to Paul leading to the writing of this letter?

HORTATORY AND
INSTRUCTIVE

CHAPTERS 4:1-5:12

Timothy reported some things that called for exhortation and instruction. In the first place, fornication was indulged in by some who had no proper understanding of its sinfulness (4:1-8). This inconsistency is probably explained by the circumstance that the church was composed of Gentiles chiefly, rather than Jews. (See Acts 17 and compare such passages in the epistle as 1:9.) Paganism, out of which they came, knew not the meaning of "sin," and as for "fornication" it may be said to have been part of their religion, just as the grossest licentiousness is now connected with certain forms of heathen worship. Under these circumstances these young Christians may have been slow to apprehend their duty in the premises and the real meaning of "sanctification." This exhortation had its effect, however, for in Paul's second epistle to the church he does not mention the offence.

In the second place, the imminency of our Lord's return which had taken hold of this church, had reacted in some cases in the direction of idleness (9-12). If He were coming so soon, why such carefulness as to physical necessities? The answer is practically that of John Wesley, that if one knew He would come to-morrow, the duties of to-day should be performed just the same. "Study (or be ambitious) to be quiet," attend to your business, work for two reasons: (a) that you may be able to pay your honest debts, especially to the world's people with whom you deal, and (b) that you yourselves may have your physical necessities supplied (12).

The Dead and the Living Saints at Christ's Coming.

But the chief difficulty in the church was doctrinal, arising also out of a misapprehension about the Lord's Second Coming. The difficulty concerned the relation of the dead to the living saints at His coming (13-18). There was a fear that the departed would be at some disadvantage in the matter of time when that event took place. But Paul teaches (a) that the dead saints will return with Christ (14); (b) that their bodies shall be raised first (15, 16); (c) that the translation of the living saints shall then follow (17, 18). In other words, something like that which took place in the lives of Enoch and Elijah in earlier dispensations, will take place in the life of the whole church, i.e., the true body of Christ in the present dispensation. Paul taught this "by the word of the Lord" (15), which means not any word which our Lord spake on the subject while on earth, but a special revelation vouchsafed to Paul after He had arisen from the dead.

The subject is continued into the 5th chapter where the first three verses treat of the condition of the world when Christ comes, and the next eight are an exhortation to the church. The world will be taken unawares, but the church should not be so taken (4, 5). To guard against this the church should be wide awake concerning this doctrine and the hope of His coming (6-8). The reason for this is that while "wrath" awaits the world in that day, "salvation" in the fullest sense awaits the church (9). Whether we are "awake," i.e., alive on the earth when He comes, or "asleep" and come with Him, we shall "live together

with Him" as the close of the preceding chapter indicated.

Questions.

1. What three subjects called for exhortation and instruction?
2. How do we explain the presence of "fornication" in this church?
3. What reason is there to believe that Paul's words were heeded?
4. What probably led to idleness?
5. How does Paul meet the situation?
6. What was the doctrinal difficulty in this church?
7. What three things does Paul teach about the second coming of Christ for the church?
8. What shows that the world will be unprepared for His coming?

CONCLUSION

CHAPTERS 5:12-28

This is a brief lesson, but the text is sufficiently distinct from the foregoing to warrant separate treatment. It is hortatory and instructive as that was, but exhortation prevails.

"Them which labor among you" (12) are doubtless the elders of the church Paul had set over them. "To know them" is the same as "to esteem them" (13). But this esteem is associated with a joint responsibility with them for the proper discipline of the church (14, 15). "The feeble-minded," has reference not to intellectual but spiritual defectiveness—not strong in the qualities of faith and hope and courage.

Joy should be perpetual (16) because it does not depend on outward circumstances, but an inward condition. Prayer should be "without ceasing" (17), not in the sense that nothing else was to be done, but that this should be the habit. The true believer talks with God more continually and intimately than with any human being however near and dear. "Thanksgiving" always accompanies prayer (18) "This is the will of God * * * concerning you," may mean the thanksgiving itself, or it may mean the experience which calls for it. Note that we are not commanded to be thankful *for* everything, but *in* everything. Of course, only the true believer is here in mind, as indicated by the expression "in Christ Jesus." (See our lessons in Ephesians and Colossians.)

The next four verses have a close relationship. "Prophesying" (20), as we judge from 1 Cor. 14, was apt to be despised in comparison with other spiritual gifts; but to despise it in the sense that its proper exercise was restricted would be to "quench the Spirit" (19) and thus "limit the Holy One of Israel." To be sure,

there was a danger of false teaching coming in by that channel, but the remedy is in verse 21, especially in view of the general caution in verse 22, which should read "avoid every form of error."

The prayer of verse 23 is beautiful and convincingly determining that man is a trinity. Some think that Paul is here again expressing his conviction or hope of an imminent return of our Lord, and praying for their "spirit and soul and body" to be kept entire, intact, i.e., without death until then, though the next verse rather raises a question as to that.

Note the authority and importance attaching to an inspired letter of this kind (27).

SECOND THESSALONIANS

THE THANKSGIVING

CHAPTER 1

This epistle was written by Paul soon after the previous one, and for a reason not very different. Acts 17 shows that Paul emphasized the second coming of Christ at Thessalonica, which is corroborated by 1 Thess. 1:10. It grew out of this that the anxiety was felt touching the relation of the dead to the living saints at His coming, which was dealt with in 1 Thess. 4:13-5; 12. But another error arose from the same source which was fostered by false teachers. These had even forged a letter in Paul's name, claiming that "The Day of the Lord" had already come, alarming many and leading them astray (2 Thess. 2:1, 2). To meet this Paul writes this second letter, the chief interest in which begins at the "Thanksgiving" for their growing faith and abounding love (1:3). All this was in the midst of persecutions and afflictions endured because of that faith (4), and was a token to them that God had counted them worthy of the kingdom of God which was to be set up when Christ came (5). The church would be at rest with Christ in that "Day" when those who afflicted her would themselves be afflicted (6, 7). But the "Day" Paul now has in mind does not synchronize precisely with the coming of the Lord for His church as taught in 1 Thess. 4:13-18. In other words, to rehearse what has been taught in other parts of this Commentary, the second coming of Christ is an act of two scenes. There is a "coming" for His church when the latter shall be caught up to meet Him in the air, and then, after an interval, how long or short it is impossible to say, there is a "coming" or a "revelation" in judgment on the unbelieving and wicked nations of Christendom that are left behind. It is this latter aspect of the Second Com-

ing, that associated with judgment, which the Old Testament prophets are ever speaking of as "The Day of the Lord." They say nothing about His coming for His church, as indeed they say nothing about the church, but focus their attention upon the end of the age, when only Israel and the Gentile nations will be on the earth and the church shall have been taken away.

That Paul is speaking of this here is indicated in verses 7-10. The Lord Jesus will be "revealed from heaven with the angels of His power" (R. V.), "rendering vengeance." This shall take the form of "everlasting destruction from the face of the Lord and from the glory of His power." This is not annihilation, it is well to observe, but conscious separation from Him. And the time it will take place is "When He *shall have come* to be glorified in His saints" (10). The Greek second Aorist is used here, indicating that the event spoken of, the glorifying of Christ in His saints shall have taken place. In other words, it is after the translation of the church, as we understand it, that "the Day of the Lord" is ushered in with its attendant judgments.

The apostle closes his allusion to these matters with the prayer of verses 11, 12.

Questions.

1. What can you recite as to the occasion for this epistle?

2. What shows the boldness of the false teachers in this case?

3. For what does Paul thank God on behalf of these Thessalonian Christians?

4. Of what were their afflictions a token?

5. What can you recite about the second coming of Christ?

6. What do you understand by "The Day of the Lord"?

7. When will it be ushered in?

THE REVELATION OF THE MAN OF SIN

CHAPTER 2

At this chapter we have the reference to the false teachers and their teaching. The first two verses should be read in the Revised Version which brings out the meaning clearer, for what the false teachers said was, that "The Day of the Lord *is now present."* Therefore what the Apostle announces to take place before that "Day" comes, does not apply to the coming of Christ for His church, (an event which, so far as we know, may be very near), but to the judgments that are to fall on the ungodly after the church has been taken away. Such is the significance of verses 3 and 4.

That which is to take place is (a) "a falling away," an apostasy in Christendom, and (b), the revelation of "the man of sin" (or lawlessness). This "man of sin," who was foretold by Daniel, by Zechariah, and by Christ Himself as we have seen, is described as opposing and exalting himself against "all that is called God," in the sense that he gives out that he himself is God, and men are ready to believe him. "The temple of God" (4) as we have seen (Daniel 9; Matt. 24), is the Jewish temple re-erected in Jerusalem, for the Jews are to return there, at first in an unconverted state so far as the acceptance of Jesus as their Messiah is concerned.

The apostle had informed the Thessalonians of these things when he was with them (5), and furthermore that a restraining power was holding back the full development of this "man of sin" until his time came (6). Just what this power is we are left to conjecture, but doubtless it is the Holy Spirit who dwells in the church. Imagine the church translated out of the earth, and the ascent of the Holy Spirit in consequence, and what restraining power would be left to hold back the hordes of wickedness in the earth, and prevent Satan

from having his way in the full development of "the man of sin"? The doom of the latter is given in verse 8, and an added description follows in verses 9 and 10. Satan gives him his power, but he is able to deceive only those who "received not the love of the truth" (10). The truth was revealed to them and rejected, for which reason that moral and spiritual weakness which made them a prey to the delusion, fell upon them as a Divine judgment (11, 12). There is a solemn warning here for those who are being tempted by Spiritualism, The New Thought, Christian Science and kindred teaching.

It is a relief to turn to the apostle's address to the true believer in verses 13-15, and as we close the lesson let us for ourselves offer the prayer of verses 16 and 17.

Questions.

1. Have you read verses 1 and 2 in the Revised Version?

2. What did these false teachers teach?

3. To what event do verses 3 and 4 apply, in general terms?

4. What two things must transpire prior to The Day of the Lord?

5. What is intended here by "the temple of God"?

6. Who presumably is holding back the full development of this apostasy?

7. What is the doom of "the man of sin"?

8. What class of people only will he be able to deceive?

9. What warning have we here?

10. Have you offered the prayer of verses 16 and 17?

CONCLUSION

CHAPTER 3

The concluding chapter consists of an exhortation to pray for its author (vv. 1, 2); an expression of his confidence in the faithfulness of those he is addressing (vv. 3-5); a command to them concerning their separation from the unfaithful (vv. 6-11); a command to the unfaithful themselves (12-15), a benediction and a superscription (vv. 16-18).

There is but one thing for which Paul would have them pray on his behalf viz. that he may be "delivered from unreasonable and evil men." These men were in the church in the visible sense, not the invisible, for they did not have "the faith" (R. V.) It was these more than the people outside who were hindering the Word from running and being glorified.

What a sweet thought that is in verse 5, "the patient waiting for Christ." It is only the scoffer, walking after his own lusts who says, "Where is the promise of His Coming"? (2 Pet. 3:3, 4). Let us not through any undue impatience be classed with them. He "will come and will not tarry" (Heb. 10:3, 7).

The unfaithful ones are the same as he addressed in 1 Thessalonians 4:10-12, and who evidently did not heed that exhortation. And yet, they might be saved men notwithstanding (see verse 15).

The token of validity (v. 17) is interesting in the light of 2:2. Hereafter the forger will have to be doubly bold.

No questions are required for this lesson.

FIRST EPISTLE TO TIMOTHY

INTRODUCTORY

We now reach the Pastoral Epistles* of which there are three, 1 and 2 Timothy and Titus. They are so called because their contents are chiefly directions regarding the pastoral work of ministers. It is evident that they deal with persons and things belonging to a late period in the Apostolic Age. The heretics mentioned in them indicate this. These are of a Jewish character, for they profess to be teachers of the law (1 Timothy 1:7), and are described as of the circumcision (Tit. 1:10), and as causing men to attend to Jewish fables (3:9). And yet they are not the same Judaizing teachers with which we became acquainted in Acts (15), and Galatians, or even Colossians. They have progressed further on the "down grade," and "are involved in a total apostasy from God and from good." They had lost all true understanding of the law (1 Tim. 1:7); had repudiated a good conscience (19); had become hypocrites and liars (4:2); were branded with immorality (4:2); of corrupt minds, using religion to better themselves in the world (1 Tim. 6:5; Tit. 1:11); subverters of the faith (2 Tim. 2:17); victimizing foolish persons to their ruin (2 Tim. 3:6); confessing God with their mouths, but denying Him in their works, abominable and disobedient, and for every good work reprobate (Tit. 1:16). A dark catalogue this, corroborating the teaching of 2 Thessalonians as to the working already of the apostasy in the church. The false doctrines attacked by Paul in his earlier epistles were now bearing fruit in laxity of life and morals.

Date of the Epistles.

It is clear from the foregoing that the date of these epistles must have been later than the period of Paul's history covered by the Acts, and that they were probably written after his liberation from imprisonment. There is reason to believe that he was imprisoned a second time, and in the interval between the first epistle to Timothy and that to Titus were written, while the second to Timothy followed during the second imprisonment, as it is thought.

Following Alford, Paul, after the imprisonment mentioned in the Acts, journeyed eastward as he anticipated in his letters to Philemon (22), and the church at Philippi, 1:26; 2:24. He visited Ephesus again, and doubtless took further journeys West occupying three or four years. At Ephesus he left Timothy and passed into Macedonia (1 Tim. 1:3), from which he wrote him the first epistle. Not far from this time he must have visited Crete in company with Titus and have left him there to complete the organization of the churches. This will appear when we come to the study of the epistle to Titus, which it is thought was written somewhere in Asia Minor, and when Paul was on his way to winter at Nicopolis in Greece. It was at this place he was arrested again probably, "as implicated in the charges made against the Christians after the fire in 64 A.D., and sent to Rome." Once more in that city, he is treated no longer with the courtesy of his former residence there but as an ordinary criminal (2 Tim. 2:9). All his Asiatic friends avoided him except Onesiphorus (2 Tim. 1:16). Only Luke was with him. Timothy is entreated to come to him before winter (2 Tim. 4:21). He is expecting execution (2 Tim. 4:6), and in view of it he writes his second epistle to Timothy, about A.D. 67 or 68.

History of Timothy.

For the beginnings of Timothy's history you will need to recur to the sixteenth chapter of the Acts. He was converted perhaps on the occasion of Paul's first visit to Lystra, since it was on his second visit he was chosen to be his traveling companion.

He accompanies Paul throughout that second missionary journey, wintering with him at Corinth, and seems to have been with him pretty steadily, except for the commissions on which he was occasionally sent (Acts 19:22; 1 Cor. 4:17, 16:10), not only throughout the second, but the third journey as well. About A.D. 62 or 63 he was with the Apostle while the latter was a prisoner at Rome (Col. 1:1; Philemon 1; Philippians 1:1). In 66 or 67, after that imprisonment, he was left by Paul in charge of the church at Ephesus. It was while he was here that he received the first epistle or letter from Paul. A year later it may be, the second was written, when Paul was again a prisoner, and Timothy repairs to Rome to visit him, after which nothing further is heard of him.

In his character he was a very earnest and consecrated man, and yet timid and diffident, and hesitating to deal with certain difficulties of his work. Compare here 1 Corinthians 16:10; 1 Tim. 4:12; 5:23; 2 Tim. 1:5, 7; 3:10.

Questions.

1. Name the Pastoral Epistles and state why they are so called.

2. To what period do they belong, and why is it so believed?

3. Describe the heresies therein referred to.

4. Give Paul's history between the close of the Acts and the writing of 2 Timothy.

5. Give an outline of Timothy's history.

*The lessons on the Pastoral Epistles, except the questions, are taken from the Author's Synthetic Bible Studies.

CHIEFLY PERSONAL

CHAPTER 1

1. The Salutation, 1:1, 2. In this notice the beautiful designation of our Lord Jesus Christ as "Our Hope." He Himself is our Hope. And when we remember that these words were written by Paul in his later years, they are all the more affecting. And notice the designation given Timothy in verse 2. What bearing has this upon the proposition that he probably owed his conversion to Paul's labors?

2. A reference to Timothy's mission at Ephesus, 3, 4. We have referred to the circumstance of his being left there by Paul, in our introduction. It seems to have necessitated urging on Paul's part. What language indicates as much? What charge was he to lay upon the teachers at Ephesus? In what two directions (especially Jewish) were they inclined to digress from the Gospel? What would be likely to be the outcome of such digression?

3. A description of the false teachers, 5-7. In this description it will be noted that the root of the offense, was in swerving from love, for such is the correct translation of the word "charity" in verse 5.

4. A description of the true use of the law, 8-11. These false teachers pretended to discourse of the law, by which is meant the law of Moses, without really knowing the subject on which they spoke. The law did not apply to those who were saved under the Gospel, but it had the same bearing as ever to the unbeliever.

5. A digression to the circumstances of his own conversion, 12-17. This springs from his allusion to the Gospel in verse 11, a Gospel committed to his trust as a steward to proclaim. He does not spare himself in extolling the grace of God toward him (13-15), and he used his own history as an example and encouragement to the worst of sinners (16).

6. A personal charge to Timothy, 18-20. This charge is the single one to fight the good fight of faith, to which he is stimulated by two considerations. The first is the "prophecies which went before" on him, the supernatural predictions of his future; and the second, the failure of some who had started in the fight with him and fallen back. The good fight of faith in his case is that which was personal to himself, and that

which concerned his ministry. It is not the conflict of the Christian life in general which Paul refers to so much, as that of a leader in the church against the opponents of a pure Gospel.

Questions.

1. What title is given Jesus Christ in this lesson?

2. What led to the defection of these false teachers?

3. How does Paul consider his ministration of the Gospel?

4. What is meant by the fight of faith in Timothy's case?

5. How many questions are in the body of this lesson, and how many have you answered satisfactorily?

CONCERNING PUBLIC PRAYER

CHAPTERS 2–3

Chapter 2 is taken up with regulations concerning public prayer. First, he directs that intercessory prayer be made for all men (verses 1-7). What class of men is especially singled out (2)? What selfish motive on the part of the church should induce such intercessory prayer? And yet what higher motive is suggested (4)? What does this verse suggest as to the object of such intercession so far as those in authority are concerned? On what ground may such intercession be made (5, 6)? It seems evident that intercession was not being made in this church at Ephesus. Perhaps persecution at the hands of the authorities had caused it to be less earnestly conducted, or perhaps a party spirit had something to do with it; at all events the church needed to be stirred up to it, and Timothy to get them doing it. This was part of the good warfare he was to wage.

Second, he refers to the way men should pray (8). "Everywhere" may refer to every place the worshippers were in the habit of assembling in Ephesus. There may have been several bodies of believers there meeting in different places. The fact that men without distinction of ministerial functions were to pray is significant. Not only were the deacons, or elders, or presbyters, or bishops, to pray, but the "men" were to pray. There is no priesthood in the church except the common priesthood of believers. But how were they to pray? "Lifting up" the hands was a Jewish custom in prayer and seems to have been adopted in the church.

But what kind of hands were the men to hold up? "Holy hands" are those not stained with sin (Psalm 25:4; 26:6; James 4:8). If we regard iniquity in our hearts God will not hear us. "Without wrath and doubting" might read without wrath and disputing or contention. No religious disputes, no outbreaks in daily life could be permitted where prayer was to be engaged in.

All expositors are agreed that "I will" of verse 8 should be carried over to verse 9. The latter then would read, "In like manner, I will that the women adorn themselves,", etc. What, in this case, would be the force of the expression "in like manner"? Is it meant, as A. J. Gordon asks, that he would have the men pray in every place, and the women "in like manner" be silent? Or would he have the men lifting up holy hands, and the women "in like manner" adorning themselves? So unlikely is either of these that many expositors supply the word "pray" in verse 9 to complete the sense. The two verses would then harmonize like this: "I will therefore that men pray everywhere lifting up holy hands, and in like manner, I will that women pray in modest apparel," etc., to the end of verse 10. Compare 1 Corinthians 11:5.

At verse 11 there is a translation, and the Apostle passes on to something new. What is that new thing about woman he now takes up? Not her relation to public prayer, but her relation to her husband, especially in the matter of public teaching in the church. The command to silence here suggests 1 Corinthians 14:34, 35, where the context shows that there were various forms of disorder and confusion in the church assemblies, especially the making remarks and asking questions about the words of others, from which women, who seem to have been the chief offenders, were enjoined.

But what about teaching? "I suffer not a woman to teach." To teach and to govern are the special functions of the presbyter or elder. The teacher and pastor, named in the divine gifts to the church (Ephesians 4:11), are considered by some to be the same; and the pastor is generally regarded as identical with the bishop. Now there is no instance in the New Testament of a woman's being set over a church as bishop, or teacher or ruler. What then if we say it is to this, to which Paul here refers?

The reason why woman is placed in subjection to man as stated by Paul in verses 13 and 14 is sufficiently plain, but there is a mystery about verse 15. Certainly it does not mean that the mere act of child-bearing saves a woman, which would contradict the primary truth of the Gospel that we are saved by faith and not works. As a matter of fact, moreover, the word for child-bearing here includes more than the act of giving birth, and means the proper nurture and training of children. Conybeare & Howson's note of this reads: "The apostle's meaning is, that women are to be kept in the path of safety, not by taking to themselves the office of the man (taking part in the assemblies of the church), but by the performance of the peculiar functions which God has assigned to their sex."

Chapter 3 is a charge to Timothy concerning the selection and the duties of church officials. First, he treats of bishops or overseers (1-7). It is to be remembered that the word "bishop" here is the same as "presbyter" or "elder" elsewhere, and does not mean a higher and distinct order of the ministry. See Titus 1:5, compared with verse 7 of the same chapter. Secondly, he treats of deacons (8-13). Then, to quote Alford, he brings these

directions to a close by a solemn statement of their object and glorious import (14-16).

Questions.

1. What probably explains the occasion for these instructions about prayer for rulers?

2. What illustrates the common priesthood of believers?

3. How might the difficulties in verses 9-15 be explained?

4. What about verse 15 especially?

5. Does the proposed definition satisfy you?

6. What is the particular theme of chapter 3?

7. How many orders of the ministry are here taught?

CONCERNING FALSE TEACHERS

CHAPTER 4

In verses 1-6 these false teachers are foretold and described. At what period are they to appear? Notice that this agrees with Paul's teachings to the Thessalonians about the apostasy. It also has a bearing upon the current question as to whether the world is growing better or worse. That question is too vast for mortal to answer, and we can only fall back upon what God says about it. In this and in other places, He has told us what to expect as the end of the age draws near, and it is for us to square our understanding and conduct accordingly.

Notice the detail of the Holy Spirit in describing these false teachers. They shall be under what kind of influence (verse 1)? What two leading tenets of their system are mentioned in verse 3? How does the Apostle contradict these teachings in verses 4 and 5? Here we need to guard against the disposition to limit the application of this false teaching to Roman Catholicism. Celibacy and abstinence from meat suggest that phase of Christianity, but the teachings of the occult sciences, Christian Science included, enlarge our horizon considerably in estimating what the Holy Spirit meant in this case.

Verses 7-16, or perhaps beginning at verse 6, may be regarded as an exhortation to Timothy himself to that steadfastness and growth in his Christian life and calling so imperative in view of the false teaching he was called upon to combat, the germ of which had already sprung up. How does verse 7 indicate that, in Paul's estimation, these heresies were mere "abstract speculations without any connection with the historical realities and practical tendencies of Christianity"? The reference to "bodily exercise" in verse 8 is interesting. According to many it had reference to the physical abstinence from certain food, from marriage, etc., referred to above, which the heretics commended, but which Paul condemned. According to others, he means the gymnastic exercises so much in vogue with the Greeks, especially the Olympic games. He would have the youth Timothy appreciate that the exercise begins with the inner man.

Questions.

1. What bearing has this chapter on the question whether the world is growing better or worse?

2. To what current heresies besides Roman Catholicism may verses 1-6 apply?

3. How does Paul feel about these heresies in his day?

4. In what way may the reference to bodily exercise be explained?

MATTERS ECCLESIASTICAL AND SOCIAL

CHAPTERS 5-6

Chapter 5 gives directions concerning Timothy's management of Church affairs, first, as to his behavior towards the older and younger members of the flock, of both sexes (1, 2). Secondly, as touching widows (3-16). By "widows indeed," verse 3, Paul means those who had no near relatives to support them (see verses 4 and 5), and who were trusting in God (verse 6). At this point the Apostle turns from the widows themselves to the persons whose duty it was to support them (8), returning to the widows again, for the purpose of treating the subject from a different point of view, viz: that of the church deaconess, as many expositors believe (9, 10). The younger widows were not to be inducted into this office from the likelihood that, desiring to marry again, they should thus become unfaithful to their covenant (11, 12), and also for the reason named in verse 13. Of course, Paul does not mean that it was sinful for young widows to marry a second time, or he would not have recommended it in verse 14, but that it was a breach of their faith to Christ after having betrothed themselves to Him, so to speak, for this service. Verse 16 recurs to verse 4, about the pecuniary support of widows by their relatives that the Church may be relieved of the burden.

Third, he speaks of Timothy's relation to the elders, i. e., the presbyters of the Church (17-22). The Greek word for elders here is the same as in verse 1, but while in that case elder men merely were intended, here the context shows an official distinction. The directions concern the pecuniary provision for these Church ministers (17, 18), the esteem in which they should be held (19), and yet the impartiality with which they should be treated in the event of wrongdoing (20, 21). In the same connection, Timothy receives a caution about the selection of men for that office (22). The chapter draws to an end with advice to Timothy in regard to his health. It seems quite irrelevant to the main subject and yet was suggested doubtless by the command at the end of the preceding verse. Speaking of the irrelevancy, it is worth while quoting Dr. Paley that it affords a strong incidental proof of the genuineness of the epistle. It is incredible that an imposter forging the name of Paul should give a direction like this, so remote from everything else discussed. "Nothing but reality," he says, "the real valetudinary situation of a real person, could have suggested it."

Two other verses follow, perhaps intended to restrain Timothy from hasty judgments, referred to in verse 22, in the selection of men for the ministerial office. There are some men whose faults are very apparent, but others who can be known only by an after judgment. With reference to the latter great circumspection on the part of Timothy is urged. The same facts, however, apply to good works as well as evil, so that Timothy might be consoled in the thought that if he had unwittingly overlooked some of the latter class, they would sooner or later come to the light.

In the final chapter ecclesiastical matters give place to those of a different character. The "servants" in verses 1 and 2, are bond-servants. After laying down the law in relation to them, Paul digresses into a criticism of those who teach otherwise concerning them (3-5). It surprises us to learn of the hyprocrisy of these false teachers even in those early days, since the Apostle speaks of them as using godliness for a way of gain. A show of Christian life for them was a lucrative business, (compare\ Titus 1:11). This digression leads to another, for the reference to godliness and gain brings up the whole question of earthly riches in the life of the

disciple (6-10). There is a sense in which true godliness does bring gain, if it be mingled with contentment, but contentment takes wings in the case of those whose condition is outlined in the verses following. The warning against this sin associated with the love of money leads to an earnest exhortation to Timothy personally, and a doxology springing out of it, when the theme is returned to again for a charge concerning the rich (17-19). The epistle concludes with another personal address to Timothy to keep the trust committed to him, avoiding the errors before enumerated.

There is much in this epistle of deep practical value to-day, and especially applicable to ministers, Sunday-school teachers, Christian workers and Church leaders of every kind. May the Holy Spirit Himself apply it to us!

Questions.

1. What three classes of directions are given Timothy in Chapter 5?

2. Who are meant by "widows indeed"?

3. What is the instruction about elders?

4. What incidental proof of genuineness does Chapter 5 afford?

5. To what depth did the hypocrisy of the false teachers go?

6. How is the question of earthly riches treated?

7. To whom is this epistle of practical value?

SECOND EPISTLE TO TIMOTHY

PERSONAL TO TIMOTHY

CHAPTER 1

When Paul addressed his earlier letter to Timothy, the latter was in Ephesus, and there are reasons to believe he was still there.

Paul was now a prisoner in Rome for a second time, awaiting a hearing before the Emperor, and he was not being treated with the consideration shown him on the earlier occasion (Acts 28), but like a common prisoner. The immediate occasion for this letter grew out of this, for he is anxious to have Timothy and Mark as his companions (1:4, 4:9, etc.). He is conscious that his death by martyrdom could not long be delayed, for these were the days of wicked Nero, and not knowing whether he should see Timothy again, or not, he was desirous of adding still further to the instructions he had given him.

There is reason to believe that Timothy required these encouragements in a marked degree. His character was not of the stuff that Paul's was made of. He suggests the diffidence of Jeremiah in the Old Testament, without some of the redeeming qualities he possessed. For references to the lack of courage of Timothy, see 1:5, 7; 3:10.

1. Salutation, 1:1, 2.

2. Thanksgiving, vv. 3-5.

In this thanksgiving on Timothy's behalf, there is a reference to his spiritual history which seems to have come down in his mother's line.

3. Exhortation, vv. 6-14.

The exhortation which follows, and which has grown out of the remembrance of Timothy's past life and the piety of his ancestors, contains three or four natural divisions.

(a) An exhortation to firmness in the faith (6-8). This can be cultivated, stirred up. It is inherent in the spiritual gift he received from God at the time he was set apart to the ministry, and is not consonant with fearfulness, the moral cowardice to which he seems to have been addicted, but is evinced rather in the exercise of suitable discipline in the spirit of love (Revised Version), and in boldness of testimony even to the point of suffering.

(b) This exhortation enforced by the character of the Gospel and the mercy of God (9-11).

(c) Finally, the Apostle cites his own example (12-14). He suffers for his testimony, and is not ashamed of it; he is willing to suffer, he counts it worth while, in the light of his faith. Let Timothy profit in word and deed by what he sees in him.

4. Description of False Brethren, vv. 15-18.

This exhortation to Timothy gathers force from the circumstance that some who professed fealty to Christ have been guilty of defection, if one may judge by their desertion of Christ's servant in his trial (15). Their action, however, serves to bring out the stronger the love of another brother for whom he prays (16-18).

Questions.

1. Locate both Paul and Timothy at this time.

2. State the possible reason for this epistle.

3. Analyze Timothy's character and temperament.

4. Divide the chapter into 4 parts.

5. Analyze the exhortation in the chapter.

INSTRUCTING A TEACHER OF TEACHERS

CHAPTERS 2-4:8

The instruction may be divided into three or four parts.

(a) He is instructed concerning his duty as a teacher of teachers (2:2), but in that connection is again exhorted to firmness, or rather to strength and "hardness," which are practically the same (verses 1 and 3). What figure of speech does Paul use to illuminate his theme? What particular lesson would be drawn from it (verse 4)? What second figure does he use at verse 5? Here is a reference to the Olympian games. How must a man have contended in order to win the crown? What third figure is used at verse 6? What reward does the faithful husbandman receive? It is easy to see from these illustrations the direction in which this young minister required encouragement and warning. He must separate himself from the world, strive faithfully and obediently, and work diligently to receive the blessing. In this connection, what fact was he to keep in mind (8)? Note how Paul once more digresses to his own example. He was not laying upon Timothy any burden he did not himself bear. Indeed, on behalf of the Gospel just spoken of, he suffered "hardship," (for so the word "trouble" should be translated in verse 9), and he also endured (10). For whose sake was it done? And why? Speaking of the "eternal glory" the elect were going to obtain, was it an assured experience for them (11-13)?

(b) Again, in this instruction to Timothy as a teacher of teachers, he is directed to caution them about idle and foolish words (14). But no sooner is this dictum laid down than he is once more exhorted as in the other case, to be the kind of teacher he would have others be. To what is he exhorted in verse 15? What do you suppose that expression means, "Rightly dividing the word of truth?" In reply, note the three classes of peoples into which Paul divides mankind in 1 Corinthians 10:32. Do you not think that "rightly dividing the word of truth" must mean giving to each of these their "portion of meat in due season"? But how can this be done where one is ignorant of the dispensational teaching of the Bible, which we

are trying to emphasize in this Commentary? What is to be avoided in this teaching (verse 19)? To what physical disease is that kind of foolish teaching likened in the next verse? How careful we need to be not to allow our study of dispensational truth to become fanatical gangrene! How much we need the wisdom from above, the balance of mind and heart which the Holy Spirit alone can supply!

But we need not pursue our inquiries into this chapter further. The same mingled exhortation, instruction and warning continue throughout, and can be brought out by the student through questioning and patient waiting for the answer to suggest itself as above.

(e) Proceeding to chapter three, Timothy receives instruction concerning the last times, i. e., the times at the end of the present age. What kind of times does the Spirit of God, say they will be (1)? The word "perilous" is in the Revised Version "grievous." What shall constitute their grievous character (2-5)? What class of persons are designated as influenced by these things, and why (6,7)? How does the Apostle seek to strengthen Timothy against these things by his own example (10-13)? And what exhortation does he now receive (14-16)? What tribute to the Holy Scriptures is in verse 15? And how is their authority and infallibility affirmed in the following verse? The Revised Version renders this verse a little differently, but this is one of the places where the King James translation is to be preferred not only as the stronger, but also the more scholarly of the two. To what "charge" to Timothy does this allusion to the Holy Scriptures lead (4:1, 2)? What consideration adds solemnity to that charge (1)? What consideration makes that charge to be necessary (3, 4)? What office is Timothy to exercise in addition to that of an overseer and teacher in order to "make full proof" or fulfil his ministry (5)? What consideration personal to Paul, adds solemnity to this exhortation (6-8)?

Questions.

1. How many of the questions in the text of the lesson have you answered?

2. How often does Paul allude to his own example?

3. Can you quote 1 Corinthians 10:32?

4. Can you quote 2 Timothy 3:16?

5. What was Timothy to be besides an evangelist?

PERSONAL TO PAUL

CHAPTER 4:9-22

We have now passed beyond the portion of the epistle devoted to instruction and reached that in which the writer deals with personal matters (4:9-22). An aged prisoner in Rome, awaiting trial, and almost certain execution, he is, alas! forsaken by many who should have stood by him. Demas has left him, Crescens, and even Titus. He wishes Timothy to hasten to his side, and to bring Mark with him. It has all been made up with Mark since the sad affair in Acts 13. He needs his cloak too, and parchments. He can not at this moment forget that man Alexander. Is he the Alexander named in Acts 19? Doubtless. Timothy is warned against him, for he is still in Ephesus.

Paul has had one hearing before Caesar and another is coming. At the hearing, however, he was sadly deserted by his friends. O! the grief of defection! Nevertheless the Lord stood by him, and He will continue to do so. Friends are saluted at Ephesus. Hasten Timothy, I want you.

No questions are called for as following this lesson.

EPISTLE TO TITUS

HIS COMMISSION

CHAPTER 1

The epistle to Titus was written prior to the second to Timothy. Alford, and others, suppose that after Paul's liberation from prison (see Acts 28), he journeyed eastward as anticipated in Philemon 22 and Philippians 1:26, 2:24, and visited Ephesus again. Other journeys to the West followed, occupying three or four years, during which time, he visited Crete in company with Titus, leaving him there to complete the organization of the Church in that neighborhood. This Church had probably been founded prior to this time, and now the same heresy is beginning to show itself as in the church at Ephesus over which Timothy had been set.

The epistle to Titus was probably written from some point in Asia Minor where Paul was stopping on his way to winter at Nicopolis in Greece (3:12), Crete is a small island to the west of Cyprus and where the waters of the Mediterranean and Aegean Seas meet. No account is found in the Acts as to the circumstances under which the Church originated there, but it is probable the Gospel was borne to the island by the Jewish converts at Jerusalem on the Day of Pentecost.

Of Titus himself little is known. The earliest references to him are in Galatians, where we learn that he was a Gentile, probably one of Paul's converts, who accompanied him and Barnabas to Jerusalem at the first council (Acts 15). See Galatians 11:1-4. He is mentioned again in 2 Corinthians, where he seems to have been sent by Paul on a mission to Corinth from Ephesus (2 Corinthians 8:6, 12:18). See other references to him in that epistle, in chapters 2 and 7. For a number of years he is lost sight of after this, until we now find him at Crete. His later career does not seem to have been all that it might have been so far as his loyalty to the Apostle is concerned, if we may judge from 2 Timothy 4:10. During Paul's second imprisonment at Rome he seems not to have remained with him.

The epistle may be outlined thus:

1. The Salutation, 1:1-4.

2. The Commission to Titus, vv. 5-9.

In these verses it will be seen that the duties of Titus at Crete were substantially those of Timothy at Ephesus. Reference to that will throw light on this.

3. The Description of False Teachers, vv. 10-16.

The need of elders and overseers such as Paul had indicated, was seen in the heresies that were in the Church, and which were of the same character as those mentioned in the epistle to Timothy. The errorists were chiefly Jews (10). The language in verses 12 and 13 is striking, since Paul there quotes from one of their own poets against them (Epimenides), whose witness is borne out by Livy, Plutarch, Polybius and Strabo, who speak of the Cretan's love of gain, natural ferocity, fraud, falsehood, and general depravity. Titus did not have an easy place to fill, and his work ought to bring comfort to Christian workers under not very different surroundings to-day.

There is a statement in verse 15 that calls for particular attention. "To the pure all things are pure" is an aphorism greatly abused. To understand it, turn back to 1 Timothy 4:4. The reference here in Titus is the same as there, (and in Romans 14:20), to the eating of meats which the Jewish law forbade on ceremonial grounds. The Jewish professing Christians referred to previously as false teachers, were seeking to impose these customs upon the converts from Gentilism, and Paul was withstanding them by saying, as he had contended all along, and as God had taught Peter in Acts 10, that there was nothing of this kind unclean in itself. That is, it was not sinful for a Christian to eat such things. The "pure" means those who are sanctified by faith, true believers on the Lord Jesus Christ. Such are not bound by the Jewish commandments in eating and drinking, but are at liberty to eat all the creatures of God set apart for their use, without sin. How monstrous in the light of the true meaning of the words, for people to employ them as a permission to look at obscene pictures in art galleries, and listen to lewd stories, and read impure books, and witness impure plays. These actions on their part testify that they are not the "pure" Paul has in mind, but the defiled and the unbelieving, referred to later in the same verse. "They profess that they know God, but by their works they deny Him."

Questions.

1. Locate Crete.

2. Give the history of Titus.

3. Describe the Cretans.

4. Explain the phrase, "To the pure all things are pure."

5. How are these words frequently misapplied?

CONCERNING CHURCH MEMBERS

Chapters 2-3

Paul now enters upon instructions to Titus as in the case of Timothy concerning different classes in the Church. Aged men are first spoken of, verses 1, 2. It is sound doctrine that these be of the character described. Aged women are next referred to (3), and under cover of that exhortation comes an allusion to the younger women (4, 5). Titus does not exhort the young women directly on the themes indicated, but indirectly through the older women. A hint for Christian workers in our own time, and especially in slum districts, where discretion is to be observed between the sexes. The young men come in for treatment next (6), to whom Titus, himself a young man, was to set the right example (7, 8). Then follows an exhortation for servants, where bond-servants or slaves are meant (9, 10). "The duties of these last, and indeed of all classes, are grounded on the moral purpose of God in the Gospel concerning us" (11, 14). These last-named verses are full of strong meat, and will bear close analysis. See what the Christian's hope is, in verse 13. Observe the two-fold object which Christ had in view in the work of the Cross, verse 14, and the obligation it lays upon believers, verse 12.

Pastors will find a fine outline here for an expository discourse on "Four Great Things": (a) A great revelation (11); (b) A great obligation (12); (c) A great inspiration (13); (d) A great salvation (14).

All these classes are now put in mind of their obligations with reference to the civil powers, and to outsiders and unbelievers generally (3:1-3); an exhortation affording another opportunity of contrasting the present state and condition of believers with that in which they were prior to their salvation. Here we find a precious declaration of Gospel truth which should be learned by heart (4, 7). The theme is salvation. How not was it effected? How was it effected? What period of time? What is the result? The eighth verse might be included as showing the obligation of the saved growing out of their salvation.

Another sermon is suggested here on "Salvation from Start to Finish." (a) Our condition by nature (3); (b) Our change from nature to grace (4-6); (e) Our condition by grace (7, 8).

Titus was to constantly affirm these things, avoiding other things and subjects that might come up (9). What a lesson for the ministers of our own time! Finally, he is directed how to deal with these false teachers and their followers (10, 11).

The remainder of this chapter

is taken up with personal directions and commissions.

Questions.

1. What hint for Christian workers is found in this lesson?
2. Analyze 2:11-14.
3. Analyze 3:3-8.

EPISTLE TO PHILEMON

Philemon, like some other of the epistles, is not located in the canon chronologically. It will be seen to have been written by the Apostle while a prisoner at Rome, and the supposition might be that the second imprisonment was meant, because it follows 2 Timothy. But it was addressed to Philemon, beyond doubt, on the earlier occasion. See verse 22 as a hint of this. In verse 23 Epaphras is named as one known to Philemon, who according to Colossians 1:7, and 4:12, was a minister at Colosse, and perhaps Philemon and his household were members of his flock. As Philemon owed his salvation to Paul, (verse 19), we may believe that the latter had made his acquaintance during his stay in Ephesus and its vicinity, (Acts 19, 20), for Colosse was in that neighborhood.

Philemon had a slave named Onesimus who seemed to have run away from his master, perhaps having stolen from him besides (18), and had found his way to Rome, and was thrown into the way of Paul. We would rather say God led him into the way of Paul. Perhaps he had known Paul when he lived with Philemon at Colosse. At all events, the circumstances are changed now, and under the power of a burdened conscience, and perhaps the condition in which he finds his old friend as a prisoner, he is moved to give more earnest heed to the message, is converted and is rejoicing in the Lord.

But one of the first duties of the converted man, is confession and restitution of wrong. Onesimus knows this and is ready to return, but shrinks from doing so unless he shall have some document to show the genuineness of the change wrought in him, and some plea from the friend of both his master and himself that may intercede for him; and what a loving letter Paul writes.

Outline of the Epistle.

The epistle begins with the salutation, verses 1-3. "The church in thy house," is mentioned, showing that in the primitive times the gathering of Christians were in private homes.

Now comes the Thanksgiving, 4-7. Paul had good reason to remember Philemon in thanksgiving and prayer, for see what kind of man he was!

Following the thanksgiving is revealed the reason for the letter, the plea for Onesimus, 8-21. He pleads though he might command (8, 9). Onesimus has been converted by him while a prisoner in Rome (10).

Onesimus means "profitable," but he had not been profitable to his master therefore, he had belied his name. He had now, however, become profitable to both Philemon and Paul (11). Paul would like to have kept him, he was so profitable to him, only he had not the mind of Philemon on the subject, and did not feel at liberty to do so (12-14). He was returning now to Philemon in a new relationship (15, 16). It were worth while to have lost him for a while to get him back forever! What a striking testimony that saints shall know each other in the life to come! But he was now coming back not merely as a slave, but a beloved brother! This does not mean that the old relationship as master and slave should be dissolved (see 1 Corinthians 7:17-24), but only that it should now be continued under these more blessed circumstances. Observe how delicately Paul pleads for him on the ground that he is now his (Paul's) brother (16, 17). Paul is willing to assume whatever pecuniary responsibility might be attached to his running away, but tactfully insists that if Philemon considers, he will regard himself as still in the Apostle's debt (18, 19).

Following the plea, the letter concludes with personal allusions, and the benediction (22,

25), Who of the brethren named in verse 24 were with Paul in his second imprisonment? Which one did he ask to come unto him? See 2 Timothy.

Its Place in the Canon.

If some ask why such a personal letter should find a place among the inspired books of Holy Scripture, it would seem sufficient to refer to the glimpses it affords of the social intercourse of Christians in the primitive days.

But there is something else here, viz: Christianity does not rashly interfere with existing institutions, even when they are inimical to its principles. Philemon was not bidden to give Onesimus his freedom. Does Christianity, then, countenance human slavery? Nay, wherever Christianity has made headway, slavery has fallen. The truth makes free. The union of believers in Jesus Christ promotes love to one another, and love ministers to freedom.

There is still another lesson to be drawn. As Paul found Onesimus wandering from his master's house, so the Lord Jesus Christ found us wandering from God. As Paul pleaded for the restoration of Onesimus, asking that what he owed might be placed to his account, so Jesus Christ acts as our Advocate with the Father, having borne our sins. As Philemon received Onesimus on Paul's account, so God has received us, and made us what we never were before, "profitable" unto Him—"created in Christ Jesus unto good works which he hath before prepared for us to walk in them."

Questions.

1. State what you know of the acquaintance of Paul and Philemon.

2. State what you know of the history of Onesimus.

3. State the four divisions of this epistle.

4. What reason is suggested for its appearance in the canon?

5. What moral lesson is found in it?

6. What spiritual analogies does it suggest?

EPISTLE TO THE HEBREWS

INTRODUCTORY

In the case of Hebrews there is uncertainty as to the authorship. It may have been written by Paul, or Apollos, or some one else, we can not tell absolutely. There is also uncertainty as to the Church. While Jewish Christians are in mind, yet there is no positive knowledge as to where they were located, whether at Jerusalem, Alexandria, or Rome.

But while uncertainty exists as to these particulars, there can be none as to the reason for writing the epistle. No one can read it carefully without perceiving a two-fold object, viz: to comfort the Christians under persecution, and to restrain them from apostasy on account of it. And the persecution must have been very severe, judging by the nature of the temptation to which it gave rise. For the apostasy contemplated was not like that of the Galatians, the supplementing of faith by the words of the law, but the renunciation of that faith altogether and the return to Judaism. It is the assumption that the temple was still standing with its glorious history and magnificent priesthood, and that the followers of Moses were allowed to pursue their religion in peace. All this was different from the outward meanness and poverty, and tribulation of those seeking to follow the Nazarene.

Theme.

There were many lines of argument open to the Apostle (for convenience, we assume the writer to be Paul), by which to counteract this tendency towards apostasy, but he chooses only one, viz: *Christianity is superior to Judaism as seen in its Founder, Christ.* The tempter is represented as urging that Judaism was introduced by "the goodly fellowship of the prophets." "Christ is superior to the prophets!" Judaism was ministered to Israel through angels. "Christ is superior to the angels!" Judaism owes its position to Moses. "But Christ is superior to Moses!" Judaism is associated with the divinely-instituted priesthood of Aaron. "Christ is superior to Aaron!" These are the main points, but the whole revolves around the single argument already indicated.

And yet the Apostle does not go straight on with his argument. He makes a digression, sometimes at the close of a division of his theme, and sometimes in the middle of it, warning his hearers, comforting or exhorting them to steadfastness in the faith. This we shall see as we proceed.

General Outline.

The general outline of the epistle is something like this: (1), Christ is shown to be superior to the prophets 1:1-3; (2), Superior to the angels, 1:4,2:18; (3), Superior to Moses, 3:1-19; (4), Superior to Joshua, 4:1-16; (5), Superior to Aaron, 5:1, 10:18. These divisions with the parenthetic warnings and exhortations make up the book.

Questions.

1. What two uncertainties exist as to this epistle?
2. What was the two-fold occasion for its writing?
3. What was the nature of the temptations in this case?
4. What is the single theme of the epistle?
5. Of what does it consist beside argument?
6. Give the general outline.

CHRIST AND THE ANGELS

CHAPTERS 1-2

While in these chapters, the comparison is chiefly between Christ and the angels, yet they open with an important contrast between Him and the prophets (1:1-3), in which His superiority is seen in seven particulars:

He is God's Son;
He is Heir of all things;
He made the worlds;

He is the Express Image of God;

He Himself purged our sins;

He upholds all things;

He is sat down at the right hand of God.

The "Express Image" of God is equivalent to "God." Our comment on Col. 1:15 will aid here, or compare this same epistle with 10:1, where "image" is used for the very substance of that which is referred to, though in the Greek it is not so strong a word as that in the lesson.

Christ however is superior to the angels in five particulars: (a), they have the name of angels, He the Name of Son (1:4, 5); (b), they are worshippers, He is the Worshipped (v. 6, R. V.); (c), they are creatures, He the Creator (7-12); (d), they are the ministers of salvation, He is its Author (13, 14); (e), they are subjects in the age to come, He is its Ruler (2:5-9). The amplification of the last thought is majestic, bringing out the four steps in the work of the Redeemer from His incarnation until His ultimate triumph over every foe. For a little while was He lower than the angels, i.e., during His earthly humiliation; now He is crowned with glory and honor; during the millenium will He be set over the works of God's hands, and finally in the age that follows will all things be put under His feet (6-9). For all this His suffering was necessary, not for His own sake but our sake (v. 10). We have become sons of God through faith in Him, in which sense He that sanctifieth and we who are sanctified "are all of one." i. e., our origin is from God. This explains the verses that follow to the end of the chapter.

In this lesson we meet with the digressions spoken of, one occurring in the middle of the argument, chapter 2:1-4, and another at its close, 2:9-18. The first is warning, the second comfort. If the earlier dispensation, that of Judaism, punished every transgression and disobedience, how shall we escape if we neglect this greater light, the heavenly origin of which was demonstrated by witnesses confirming and being themselves confirmed? And then on the other hand, think of your privileges! your exaltation to the position of "brethren," and your claims upon the Lord of glory as your true High Priest, faithful, merciful, capable and sympathetic.

Questions.

1. Name the seven particulars in which Christ is superior to the prophets.

2. What is the equivalent of the words, "Express Image of God"?

3. Name the five particulars in which Christ is superior to the angels.

4. Bring out the four steps in the work of the Redeemer.

5. What is the meaning of the phrase "All of one"?

6. What two "digressions" are found in this lesson?

COMPARED WITH MOSES AND JOSHUA

CHAPTERS 3-4

The superiority of Christ to Moses is shown in chapter 3, the comparison in which case runs in two parallel lines of two members each:

(1) Moses a servant over God's house, 3:5.

(2) Christ a Son over His own house, 3:6.

That is an interesting phrase, "Whose house are we," (verse 6), suggesting a plan for a sermon. In what sense are believers Christ's house?

He built them—"without Him was not anything made that was made."

He bought them—"Ye are not for your own, for ye are bought with a price."

He occupies them—"Ye in me and I in you."

As in the preceding instances we have a digression at this point in the nature of warning (7-19). In the first reading omit the parenthesis after "wherefore" (3:7) down to the close of verse 11, which will simplify the thought. The idea is that because of the greater importance of the New Testament revelation over that of the Old Testament as evidenced in the superiority of the Messenger, we should take heed lest through unbelief we fall away from God, as did Israel in the wilderness. They tempted God, and as a result, the males over twenty years of age were not permitted to enter into the rest of Canaan (16-18). The Holy Ghost used that sad episode in their early history as a warning to them at a later time, i. e., in David's day (vs. 7, etc., cf. with Ps. 95:8-11), and it was just as applicable now to these Hebrew Christians. Therefore, they should exhort one another against "the deceitfulness of sin" and to steadfastness in the faith.

The allusion to the rest of Canaan naturally leads to a comparison of Christ with Joshua in chapter 4, which may be outlined thus: (a), Israel failed of God's rest through unbelief (3:16-19); (b), We Christians may fail of God's rest through unbelief (4:1, 2); (c), This rest is not Canaan however (3-9); (d), but the rest of faith in God through Christ (v. 10); (e), which is to be diligently sought (11-13). The proof that this rest is not Canaan is two-fold: (a), it was spoken of long before Canaan was revealed, even at the creation of the world (3-5); and (b), it was spoken of long after Israel had entered Canaan as something still to be had. This last thought is brought out clearer in the R. V. where "Jesus" of verse 8 is translated "Joshua," which has the same meaning.

It is important to understand what this rest is. In the first place, it is God's rest and not our rest. And God's rest does not mean cessation from work on His part, but rather his joy and delight in that work as good and perfect. In this sense He rested from creation on the seventh day, a rest which was marred by sin, but now the new rest of which He speaks is that of redemption, typified by Israel's deliverance from Egypt and entrance into Canaan. As a matter of fact God rests in Christ as the Redeemer and Restorer of fallen man, and where He rests there only can we rest. It is not death that can be rest to us, but only Christ, and this because the secret of our unrest is sin and He only can take away sin in every aspect of it. Of course, the *perfect* enjoyment of this rest is still future. "There *remaineth* a rest for the people of God." It is not a rest of inactivity, but of peace and harmony with all that is within and around us. Glory to God for this expectation! The sense in which we are diligently to seek it (11), is not that of self-righteous works on our part, but a carefulness not to fall into unbelief. The relation of the words that follow in this chapter (12-16) with those preceding, seems in general terms to be this: The Christian is to rest in faith, and labor to enter into the rest that remaineth, but this means that he must be guided and instructed by the Word of God, and upheld and encouraged by the sympathy and intercession of His Great High Priest.

Questions

1. State the two parallel lines of comparison between Christ and Moses.

2. In what senses may it be said that we are Christ's "house"?

3. Explain the warnings in verses 7-19.

4. Give an outline of Chapter 4.

5. What two facts prove that "rest" other than Canaan is intended?

6. How would you explain the "rest"?

7. When will this "rest" be perfectly entered upon by the Christian?

8. In what sense are we to seek it?

9. What relation do the concluding verses of the chapter bear to the preceding?

CHRIST AND MELCHISEDEC

CHAPTERS 5-7

It has already become evident to the careful reader that the author of this epistle is particularly desirous to bring out the comparison between the priesthood of Christ and that of Aaron. He approached it at the close of chapter 2, (17, 18), and was on the point of making the comparison (3:1) when he was led into the digression about Moses (2-6), and then Joshua (4:4-11). But he returns to it again at the close of chapter 4 (see 14-16), and at the beginning of chapter 5 clears the way for its discussion by the dictum that *Christ was a priest.* This is necessary to be proven before he can advance, and he proves it in two ways. Christ was a priest (a), in that He possessed our human nature with its capacity for sympathy (1-3), and (b), in that He received the Divine appointment to that office as Aaron did (4-10). His appointment however, was after another order than Aaron—that of Melchisedec (6, 10), of whom he will speak later after another digression of warning and encouragement.

Teaching About Apostasy.

This digression covers 5:12-6:29, and consists (a), of an explanation as to why they should be so seriously tempted to apostatize (vv. 11-14). They had become "dull of hearing," spiritually deaf to the appeals of the Gospel. They had been in the faith long enough to become teachers of others, and yet they themselves needed teaching again, even in the A B C of the Scripture. They were still babes in Christ, as indicated by their lack of experience in the word. (b), The offset to this, or the remedy for their situation, was to grow in grace and Divine knowledge (6:1-3). To leave "the principles of the doctrine of Christ" does not mean to discard the foundation of the Gospel but rather to build upon it. "Perfection" refers not to sinlessness but to full growth in the knowledge of Christ. "Repentance for dead works" means those not wrought for God's glory. "Faith towards God," was so primary that once experienced it was inconsistent to think of its

being "laid" again. "The doctrine of baptisms" may mean "washings," "ablutions," after the purifying of the Jews. "Laying on of hands" was a symbolic act among the Jews connected with prayer and invoking the divine benedictions. Note that "the resurrection of the dead" with "eternal judgment," which some professing Christians in these days affect to doubt, was considered a primary doctrine of the New Testament Church. The six particulars here named were fundamental, and yet as Dr. Saphir says, they did not set before these Hebrew Christians with sufficient fullness the truth of which they stood in need to keep them from apostasy, and to strengthen them in their sore temptation. (c), The peril of their situation is set forth in verses 4-8. Some think these "present the case of a Jewish professed believer who turns back from Christ after advancing to the very threshold of salvation," but who never experienced real faith. But we differ, and hold the opinion that a true believer is meant. It is not said however, that such a one will be lost (indeed the opposite is shown to be the case (v. 9), but this warning is given to keep him from being lost. (d), Their encouragement in the premises follows (9-20). They were bringing forth the fruit of the Spirit, let them thus continue in well-doing (10-12). Their salvation was secured by the divine promise confirmed by the divine oath (12-18). Nay more, they had laid hold upon the hope, which as an anchor of the soul had entered into that which is within the veil. Jesus Himself was their hope, and He had entered there "an high-priest forever after the order of Melchisedec."

Melchisedec a Type.

We are now brought back again to Melchisedec, who is described and compared with Christ (7:1-3). For his historical record see Gen. 14:17-20. He is a type of Christ in his office as a king-priest (cf. Zech. 6:12, 13); in his name, "king of righteousness" (Isa. 11:5); and his location, "king of Salem," i.e., peace (Isa. 11:6-9). Also in the fact that he had "neither beginning of days nor end of life." This last does not mean that it was literally so in his case, but that so far as the record went it appeared so. Compare here John 1:1; Rom. 6:9; Heb. 7:23-25. After this description and comparison the inspired writer shows the superiority of his order to that of *Aaron* in seven particulars (4-24): Abraham gave him tithes (4-6); he blessed Abraham (6-7); he was an undying priest, i.e., so far as the record goes he did not see death (8); the unborn Levi (or Levitical priesthood) paid him tithes in the person of Abraham (9-10); the permanence of his priesthood, continued by Christ, implied the abrogation of the whole Levitical law (11-19); his priesthood was founded on an oath (20-22); it was intransmissible, not being vacated by death (23, 24). The whole argument is summed up in verses 25-28.

Questions.

1. What seems to be the chief purpose of the author?

2. Indicate his approaches to it.

3. In what two ways is Christ shown to be a priest?

4. Name four main divisions of the digression in this case.

5. What is the meaning of these words or phrases: "Perfection," "Repentance for dead works," "the doctrine of baptisms"?

6. What is the object of the warning in 6:4-6?

7. In what ways is Melchisedec a type of Christ?

8. Name the seven particulars in which his order shows superiority to that of Aaron.

THE PRIESTHOOD OF CHRIST AND THAT OF AARON

CHAPTERS 8-10:18

1. Christ is a priest of a better covenant than Aaron. Chap. 8.

Better not morally, but efficaciously, i.e., established on better promises (6), in the sense (a), that they are written on the heart rather than tables of stone (10); (b), that they are universal in their application and not limited to a single people, Israel (11); (c), that they bring with them eternal forgiveness.

2. Christ is a priest of a better tabernacle. Chap. 9:1-14.

(a), It is not a material but a spiritual structure (11);

(b), It is not hallowed by the blood of beasts but by His own blood (12);

(c), It stands not for temporary but eternal redemption (12-14).

3. Christ is a priest of a better sacrifice. Chap. 9:15-10:18.

(a), Not a sacrifice of calves and goats (19) but the sacrifice of Himself (9:23);

(b), Not a sacrifice to be repeated every year (25) but offered only once (9:26);

(c), A sacrifice which does away with the covenant of the Old Testament and establishes that of the New (10:5-9). The reference to the sacrifice offered but once is worked out richly: first, the fact is stated (9:24-26); secondly, an inference is drawn from it (10:1-3); third, the fact is emphasized anew (4-13), and finally its precious truth is applied (14-18).

Questions.

1. In what sense is the covenant of Christ's priesthood better than that of Aaron?

2. In what sense is it established on better promises?

3. In what sense is Christ a priest of a better tabernacle?

4. In what sense is He a priest of a better sacrifice?

5. Have you tried to work out in detail the exposition of Chapters 9:24-10:18?

TRIUMPHS OF FAITH

CHAPTERS 10:19-12:29

This lesson covers one of the many digressions alluded to and is first, an exhortation (10:19-25); secondly, a warning (26-31), and thirdly, an expression of comfort (32-39). This last touches on the principle of faith and gives occasion for an exhibition of its triumph in the lives of the Old Testament saints that makes the 11th chapter rank with the most notable in the Bible.

1. The exhortation (10:19-25) keeps in mind that these Hebrew Christians were sorely tried by persecution and seriously tempted not merely to backslide, but to apostatize, i.e., give up Christianity altogether and return to Judaism again. The inspired writer is seeking to restrain them from so doing by the argument that Christianity is superior to Judaism as seen in its Founder, Christ. All that was symbolized in Aaronic priesthood is realized in Christ's priesthood. The Aaronic priest passed through the veil of the temple into the Holy Place, while Christ through His suffering humanity passed for believers into glory. The Aaronic priests were purified from ceremonial defilement by being sprinkled with blood (Ex. 29:21, Lev. 8:30), and washed in the laver of pure water, but the Christian believer's sins are so surely put away that as priests unto God they may draw near in fulness of assurance. Therefore they should hold fast the confession of their faith and provoke, urge, one another to love and to good works, the means of doing which was best found in the sacred assemblies which they were not to forsake.

2. The warning (26-31) does not call particularly for explanation.

3. The comfort (32-39) is notable for its reference to the reward to be realized by the believer at the second coming of Christ. Verse 37 might be rendered "for yet but a very very little while," showing that the Christians of that generation were expecting Him in their own day, which should be true of every generation. Speaking of "faith" in verse 38, Farrar says it is "introduced with the writer's usual skill to prepare for the next great section of the epistle."

What Faith Does.

Entering on that section the same author remarks that it would have been fatal to the peace of mind of Jewish converts, such as here addressed, to feel that there was a chasm between their Christian faith and the faith of their past life. Hence the inspired writer shows that there is no discontinuity of that kind. Their faith was identical with, though transcendently more blessed than that which had sustained the patriarchs, prophets and martyrs of their nation. Verse 1 of chapter 11 defines faith rather in its effects than its essence; i.e., it tells what it does, bringing the assurance of things hoped and the proof of things not seen. In verses 2 to 40 we have the fruit of faith, or its effect, in detail. In 12:1-4 we have the testimony of faith, in 5-11 its comfort, in 12-17, its duty, in 18-24 its encouragement, and in 25-29 its warning.

It is noticeable that passing from particular to general illustrations of faith, we have in 11:32-34 those of active, and in 35-38, those of passive faith, most of which are gathered from the books of Joshua, Samuel, Kings and Chronicles, though doubtless the time of the Maccabees is also in mind. Verses 39 and 40 may be paraphrased thus: these had all good witness borne to them through their faith, but still they did not see the fulfillment of the one great promise, which awaited the dispensation to follow.

The "witnesses" of 12:1 are not "spectators" of us on earth, but "testifiers" to us of what faith can do. In other words they are those of the preceding chapter from whose lives we are to learn. The remainder of the verse is athletic in its figures of speech. The athlete lays aside every heavy or dragging article of dress, and so we should throw off "the clinging robe of familiar sin," "looking unto Jesus" not only as a higher example of faith than any previously named, but as "the author and finisher of our faith." From Him our faith comes, and by Him it is sustained to the end.

The reference to Esau 16, 17 is ambiguous, and may mean that so far as his father Isaac was concerned, there was "no place of repentance," in the sense that Isaac had no power to change his mind and alter his promise. Or it may mean that Esau could not avert the earthly consequences of his folly, or regain what he had once flung away. And another says, "the text gives no ground for pronouncing on Esau's future fate, to which the inspired writer makes no allusion whatever."

Notice six particulars, some try to discover seven, in which Mt. Sinai and Mt. Zion are contrasted in verses 18-24.

Questions.

1. Divide the chapters of this lesson into four main parts.

2. Give in your own words the substance of the exhortation.

3. How does 11:1 define "faith"?

4. Give an outline analysis of chapters 11 and 12.

5. What books of the Bible furnish most of these examples of faith?

6. How would you explain 12:1?

7. How would you explain the reference to Esau?

8. Do you find six or seven particulars of comparison in verses 18-24?

CONCLUDING EXHORTATIONS

Chapter 13

Farrar thinks that the exhortations of this chapter being mostly of a general character, probably formed a characteristic feature in all the Christian correspondence of this epoch—interesting if true.

1. Brotherly Love, Verses 1-3.

A virtue undreamed of until the time of Christianity, but peculiarly necessary among members of a persecuted sect like these Hebrew Christians. (Cf. Rom. 12:10; 1 Thess. 4:9; 1 Peter 1:22; 1 John 3:14-18). Here it was expected to take a very practical turn, made necessary by the absence of places of public entertainment like our hotels and boarding-houses (Rom. 12:13; Tit. 1:8; 1 Tim. 3:2; 1 Peter 4:9). For illustrations of the latter part of verse 2 see Gen. 28:2-22; Judges 13:2-14; also Matt. 25:35-40. If Paul was the writer of this epistle, how particularly touching is the reference in verse 3? "Being yourselves also in the body," may be related to what he says to the Colossians (1:24; see comment).

2. Chastity, Verse 4.

Light is thrown on the meaning here by the R. V. (Cf. Acts 15:20; 1 Thess. 4:6). The Gospel of Christ introduced a wholly new conception of the sin of fornication which among the heathen was not regarded as a sin.

3. Contentment, Verses 5 and 6.

"Conversation" here means "your turn of mind," let it be "free from the love of money." The rest of the section gives a good reason for such trustfulness.

4. Steadfastness and Heavenly-mindedness, Verses 7-16.

Verse 7 is rendered in the past tense in the R. V. "them that had the rule over you," which is more consistent with the words "whose faith follow." "The end of their conversation" means "the outcome of their life and testimony." Their "faith" is expressed in the terms of verse 8, to which the readers are further exhorted in verse 9. The close of verse 9 points back again to the Jewish ceremonials they had left and to which some of them were being tempted to return again. Such sacrificial altars they did not require as they had a better one (10). Christ Himself is the Christian's "altar" as well as that which is upon it. On Him the Christian feeds in a heavenly and spiritual sense. Verse 13 is another of the many exhortations for these Jewish Christians to separate themselves from their past at whatever cost for Jesus' sake, while verse 14 offers the encouragement for them to do it (Cf. Phil. 3:20). The sacrifices we have to offer through Christ are not the bodies of beasts, but thanksgiving and good works (15:16).

5. Spiritual Obedience, Verse 17.

6. Prayer for the Writer, Verses 18, 19.

7. Benediction, Verses 20, 21.

8. Conclusion, Verses 22, 25.

Questions.

1. What is Farrar's idea about these exhortations?

2. What two practical applications of brotherly love are indicated in the lesson?

3. How are we to understand verse 4?

4. Why may true Christians be content?

5. What summing up of the Christian's faith is found in verse 8?

6. How would you explain verses 9 and 10?

7. What sacrifice has the Christian to offer?

8. Memorize the benediction of verses 20, 21.

EPISTLE OF JAMES

INTRODUCTORY

We have now reached that part of the New Testament containing the General or Catholic epistles. They are so called because addressed not to any particular individual or Church, but to the Church at large. And yet this is not true of all of them, not true of this one, which is addressed to a particular class of Christians named in the first verse.

There are three persons named James in the New Testament. One was the brother of John, another the son of Alpheus, and a third the brother of our Lord, who is commonly supposed to be the author in this instance.

A peculiar interest attaches to the fact that, as the brother of our Lord, he did not believe on Him as the Messiah up until the resurrection perhaps. Compare John 7:5 with Acts 1:13, and 1 Corinthians 15:7. His conversion may have taken place at the time mentioned in the last named Scripture, which, if so, accounts for his presence with the Church as shown in the reference in the Acts.

As to his religious character, he was a very strict Jew, a faithful observer of the law, both moral and ceremonial, without, of course, relying upon it as a ground of salvation. He gave Paul and Barnabas the right hand of fellowship in their work among the Gentiles, but personally he remained attached to the Jewish form of Christianity. His place in the Christian scheme was to win over the Jewish people, and no one probably was better fitted for this than he.

Persons Addressed

The epistle is addressed "to the twelve tribes scattered abroad," which proves its Jewish designation; but that they were Christian Jews is shown in the salutation, where James styles himself "a servant of Jesus Christ."

As to their social condition they seem to have been composed of rich and poor, the tendency of some of the former being to oppress and despise the latter, as we shall see. Like all the other classes of Christians, they were passing through trial, and like them, too, more or less under the influence of false teachers. The doctrine of justification only by faith was being perverted among them, and from various points of view, their condition was unsatisfactory. The writer comforts them in their trial, but rebukes them for their sins, and seeks to give them instruction concerning the matters in which they were in error.

The style of the epistle is vivid, sententious and yet rich in graphic figure. There is not the logical connection found in Paul's writings, the thoughts rather arranging themselves in groups strongly marked off from one another; but yet the writer goes immediately into his subject, and with the first sentence beginning a section says at once what is in his heart. The first words of each section might almost serve as a title for it, while that which follows is the development, ending usually in a kind of recapitulation. (How to Study the New Testament, second section, pp. 163, 164).

*The Comments on this epistle are taken from Synthetic Bible Studies.

Questions.

1. What is the meaning of "Catholic" epistles?
2. Describe the three persons named "James."
3. Give a sketch of the supposed author of this epistle.
4. Describe the persons addressed.
5. Describe the style of the epistle.

INSTRUCTIONS
CONCERNING TRIAL

CHAPTER 1

"Temptations," in verse 2, is in the sense of trials (see Revised Version margin). Why should they be received with joy (verse 3)? In what spiritual condition will such a reception and use of trial result (4)? What will effectually aid in that direction (5, 8)? Along what lines of trial were they being exercised (9, 11)? Notice that the poor man is to find comfort in his truly high estate in Christ, while the rich man is to find comfort in a truly humble spirit before God in view of the facts referred to.

But there are two kinds of testings which come upon believers, those already spoken of as "trials," whose source is divine, and whose purpose is strengthening and purifying, and those now brought into view as out and out "temptations," not from God, but from themselves. What reward comes to the disciple who successfully encounters these (12)? What is their immediate source and outcome (13, 15)? What three arguments are presented in verses 13, 17 and 18, to show that God is not the author of these temptations? On the ground, then, that we have our good from God, and our evil from ourselves, what lesson is drawn (19, 20)? Speaking of our being "swift to hear," whose words has the writer in mind (21)? What shows, however, that the "hearing" he has in mind is a very practical experience (22, 25)? Speaking of our being "slow to speak," how does he emphasize its importance (26)? In what does "pure religion" consist other than in mere talk (27)? Remember that James is talking to believers in Christ, to those who supposedly have "religion," and he is merely instructing them how it should be manifested. Men are not saved by benevolence and kindness to the widowed and the orphaned, or even by strenuous efforts after a pure life, but by Christ, who bore their sins in His own body on the tree; yet they show that they are saved by such works as these spoken of in the text.

Questions.

1. In what sense is "temptation" (v. 2) to be understood?

2. How are the rich and the poor comforted?

3. How many kinds of testings come on believers?

4. How would you explain verse 27?

RESPECT OF PERSONS AND
FAITH AND WORKS

CHAPTER 2

We next have some instruction or admonition concerning respect of persons, or the relation of the rich and the poor, 2:1, 13. This would seem to be connected with the trials of the poor mentioned in chapter 1. It not infrequently happens that the people who complain of the abundance of the rich, are the most obsequious in their conduct, as if they expected something from them as a result. Perhaps it was so here. Or it may be, that this instruction laps on more closely to what had been said about "pure religion," and visiting the fatherless and widows, and keeping one's self unspotted from the world, 1:27.

Respect of persons was incompatible with these things. Note that the Revised Version translates "have" of verse 1 by "hold." These two things could not be held at one and the same time. What instance is given of holding it (2, 3)? Of what wrong would they be guilty in such a case (4)? What kind of judges would such partiality show them to be (same verse)? What would demonstrate the unwisdom as well as unkindness of such partiality (5)? What would show their meanness of spirit (6)? Their disloyalty to their Saviour (7)? On what principle should they exercise themselves toward rich and poor alike (8)? How were they in danger of violating this principle (9)? What fundamental truth about sin is enunciated in this connection (10, 11)?

3. Some instruction on the relationship of faith and works, 2:14-26. If the subject of respect of persons grew out of the declaration about "pure religion" at the close of chapter 1, there is reason to believe the same of the present subject.

Before considering the verses, it may be well to remark on a criticism sometimes made that James is here contradicting Paul. The latter insists upon faith without works, while the former insists upon works with faith. But there is no contradiction, because Paul is laying down the principle of salvation, while James is showing the working of that principle in the life. Paul as well as James insists upon a faith that brings forth fruit, and was himself a fine example of it. The epistle of James was written at an early period, before Paul's epistles were generally known and before the council at Jerusalem (Acts 15), which may account for this treatment of the subject of faith from a different standpoint to that made necessary by the admission of Gentiles into the church.

Observe the change the Revised Version makes in the last clause of verse 14. "Can THAT faith save him?" Faith saves, James declared, but it is not the kind of faith which produces no fruit. It is not dead faith, but living faith. What illustrations of a fruitless faith are in verse 16? And verse 19? What illustrations of a fruitful faith are given in verses 21-25. Read carefully verse 22, which teaches that Abraham's faith was simply shown to be faith, a perfected thing by his obedience to God. So our faith in Christ can hardly be called a saving faith if it works no change in our lives and produces no results.

Questions.

1. What two things are discoursed of in this lesson?

2. What presumably, led the writer to speak of the first?

3. Which seems more likely from the context, that "Assembly" (v. 2) means a plan or worship or a lawcourt?

4. What indicates that James is not contradicting Paul in regard to justification by faith?

5. What is the test of saving faith?

CONTROL OF THE TONGUE

CHAPTER 3

The third chapter contains instruction or admonition concerning the control of the tongue, 3:1-18. Just as the instruction in the other instances grew out of something written in the first chapter, so also here. He had exhorted them to be "swift to hear and slow to speak"; following that he had showed them how to hear in the sense that they must be doers of what they hear; and now he would show them how to be slow of speech in the sense that they should "set a watch before their mouths and keep the door of their lips."

"Masters" in verse 1, is really "teachers." This shows the direction of their temptation to talk too much. They affected teaching, after the manner of those rebuked by Paul in his letters to Timothy and Titus. There was danger in their doing this, as verse 1 indicates. A heavier responsibility rested upon teachers than upon the taught, and there was the likelihood of stumbling in that capacity (v. 2).

Note how he speaks first, of the power of the tongue (3-5). What three illustrations does he employ? Secondly, he speaks of the evil of the tongue (6). How is it described? What does it do? Whence the source of its iniquity? Thirdly, he speaks of its uncontrollableness (7, 8). With how many wild, and subtle, and strong things, does he compare it in this regard?

After speaking of the tongue in general terms, how does he apply the subject to the present condition of things (9, 10)? By the use of what similes does he seek to better it (11, 12)? What is the relation between wisdom and speech (13)? What does the strife of tongues indicate as to the condition of the heart (14)? What is the source of such strife (15)? Its product (16)? How does true wisdom compare with it as to its source, character, and effects (17, 18)?

The questions in the text of this lesson render unnecessary any at the end.

WORLDLY MINDEDNESS

CHAPTERS 4-5

Like other divisions of this epistle this is so connected with the last, and grows out of it so naturally, that it is difficult to say where the division occurs. The writer had been speaking of envying and strife in expression through the tongue, and now puts in his plow deeper to show their source in the antecedent condition of the heart. "Lust" is not to be taken in the limited sense of sensuality, but in the broader, sense of worldly pleasure or gratification of any kind.

Verse 2 presents difficulty. Consistency makes it necessary to suppose that James is here addressing Christians as throughout the epistle, and yet how incongruous to think of Christians committing murder to gratify their desires! Luther translated "kill" by "hate," and doubtless expressed the real meaning by so doing, although, to quote Neander, "James used the stronger expression in order to designate the epistle with the utmost precision the nature of that evil which, whatever may be the outward form of manifestation, is still the same."

Nor let it be thought strange that such persons should be referred to as engaging in prayer (v. 3), for nothing is more common than for worldly-minded Christians to supplicate heaven for the gratification of desires entirely selfish, giving no consideration either to God's pleasure, or the well-being of their neighbors. How plainly James reveals the cause for the non-results of such prayers!

What names does he bestow upon these worldly-minded Christians (4)? How does the language of this verse indicate that he has in mind adulterers in the moral and spiritual sense—professing loyalty to God and yet consorting with the world? What shows the incompatibility of such things? Verse 5 should be read in the Revised Version, showing that the Holy Spirit who dwells in the believer is not a spirit of envy. What was their hope under such circumstances of sin, and in what direction should they look for deliverance (6)? What prerequisite was necessary to obtain this grace (6-10)? How did the want of humility show itself in their prayers (11, 12)?

But this worldly-mindedness took to itself various forms, and James addresses himself to another in the verses following. What false reliance is spoken of in verse 13? How is it rebuked (14)? What advice and admonition is given (15, 16)? It was not enough for them to know this truth, how does he teach them the need of acting upon it (17)?

What further application of worldly-mindedness follows in chapter 5? Who are addressed now? What warning is given them? "Ye have laid up your treasure in the last days," is the way verse 3, last sentence, should be rendered. How vividly it applies to-day!

Are we not nearing the last days, and are not treasures heaping up as never before? What three charges are laid against the rich here (4, 6)? Fraud, voluptuousness, injustice! How awful to think of these things under the cloak of Christianity! Or shall we say that James is here referring to the rich outside the Christian church altogether? It is difficult to say. Notice carefully, however, the judgments coming upon these rich people. What miseries indeed!

The epistle closes as it began, with comfort for the tried and oppressed, verses 7-20. What hope is set before the oppressed laboring men (7, 8)? How different from the strike and the boycott? If the rich of our day be at fault, are not the poor equally so, the Word of God being the standard? What examples of long-suffering patience are set before them in verses 10 and 11?

What closing recommendations and exhortations are set before all concerning oaths (12)? Concerning heavenly-mindedness in the opposite experiences of life (13)? What specific directions concerning the sick (14-16)? What testimony to the efficacy of prayer? How is it illustrated (17, 18)? With what statement of the believer's privilege and obligation does the epistle close (19, 29)?

Questions.

1. How would you connect this lesson with the last?

2. What does "lust" mean?

3. What difficulty is presented in this lesson?

4. What hinders prayer?

5. Who are meant by spiritual adulterers?

FIRST EPISTLE OF PETER

THE LIVING HOPE

Chapter 1:1-12

The opening of this epistle reminds us of Paul in its salutation, verses 1 and 2. Here we have the author's name—Peter, his official designation—an apostle of Jesus Christ, and a characterization and location of the people addressed—"strangers scattered throughout" the provinces of Asia Minor named. This last phrase is rendered in the Revised Version, "sojourners of the dispersion," which indicates that they were chiefly Jewish Christians not at home in their own land. But nevertheless, they were at home with God, for they are spoken of as "elect," or chosen ones, and it is interesting to note the operation of the Three Persons of the Godhead in their election—the Father, the Son and the Holy Spirit. The First, called them, the Second redeemed them, the Third satisfied or set them apart for God forever.

The salutation is followed, as also in Paul's epistles, by the thanksgiving (3-12), which contains as well a statement of the theme of the epistle which is, "The Living Hope." Seven things are told us of this Living Hope: (1) Its source, "the abundant mercy of God"; (2) its ground, the new birth, "begotten again"; (3) its means, "the resurrection of Jesus Christ," involving His death, of course; (4) its nature, "an inheritance," etc.; (5) its security, "reserved" for us, "who are kept" for it; (6) its consummation "in the last time," which as is shown later, means not the end of the world, but of the present age which synchronizes with the Second Coming of Christ; (7) its effect, joy, "wherein ye greatly rejoice." This rejoicing is experienced even in the midst of trial (v. 6), because that trial will redound to our "praise, and honor and glory" at Christ's Second Coming. "The end of your faith" (v. 9), means that at which

faith aims or in which it results, which the apostle says the believer is now *"receiving,"* now bearing off as a prize in the present earnest of the Spirit he enjoys, in the present peace of reconciliation, in his growing sanctification and eager anticipation of eternal joy.

The closing part of this section (9-12) is a strong declaration of the supernatural character of the Holy Scriptures. The "Salvation" just referred to had been prophesied of in the Old Testament, concerning which its writers had sought and searched diligently. That for which they searched was the time of the sufferings and subsequent glory of Christ. The Holy Spirit had led them to write of that time, and now the same Spirit revealed unto them the meaning of what they had written. He instructed them that they had written not for their own age but this age, when that which they had written was being preached in the demonstration of the same Holy Spirit (v. 12). We thus see that the Holy Spirit inspired the Scriptures, reveals their meaning, and accompanies their preaching and teaching, or else that preaching or teaching is in vain.

Questions.

1. Give the details of the "Salutation."
2. Who are meant by "strangers" here?
3. What is the theme of the epistle?
4. Name the seven things spoken of it.
5. Explain verse 9.
6. What three-fold relation does the Holy Spirit bear to the Holy Scriptures?

OBLIGATIONS OF THE HOPE—UPWARD

Chapters 1:12-2:10

"Wherefore" at the beginning of this lesson shows that as the result of what has gone before something is expected. They who have been begotten again to this Living Hope have obligations arising from it.

1. The first is *Hope* (13-16). The difference between "hope" in verse 13 and that in verse 3 is, that there it represented the believer's standing or position before God in Christ, and here his experience and exhibition of it. Having been begotten again unto a Living Hope, he is now to hope for it with all sobriety and concentration of mind. As he does so hope it will affect his character and conduct (14), for no longer will his daily life be run in the mould of his former desires in sin, but will be holy as God is holy (15, 16).

2. The second is *Fear* (17-21), godly fear, of course, not the fear of a criminal before a judge, but that of an obedient child in the presence of a loving father. Two motives are given for it, one, the thought of judgment, (17), and the other, the cost of our redemption (18, 19). The judgment is not to determine the question of salvation, which is settled for believers as soon as they accept Christ, but to determine their fidelity as disciples and the place of reward awaiting them in glory.

3. The third is *Love* (22-2:3). Believers have "purified their souls," not in an absolute experimental sense, but in the judicial sense that they now have a right standing before God. This they did "in obeying the truth" of the Gospel, which they were enabled to obey "through the Spirit"; in other words, by the aid of the Holy Spirit. Being in this position they are able to "love one another," and being able to do it imposes the obligation to do it. (22). The thought is extended in the next verse which reveals that believers are "brethren" in that they have all been "born again" by the one "seed," which is the incorruptible Word of God. The "love" they are to exercise toward one another is defined in the opening verses of chapter 3, and in order to obtain the strength to exercise it they are to draw on the Word of God. That which instrumentally brought them into life will sustain them in it continually (2, 3).

4. The fourth is *Praise* (4-10). The Lord Jesus Christ referred to in verse 3, is "a Living Stone," Whose life has been communicated to believers, making them "living stones" (5). They thus form a spiritual temple, and, abruptly changing the figure, they are the "priesthood" in the temple. As such they have spiritual sacrifices to offer (5), the chief of which is to "show forth the praises of Him Who" redeemed them (9, 10).

These four obligations of "The Living Hope" are referred to as the "upward" ones in the sense that, with one exception, they are due to God directly. The exception is that of *"Love"* which is due to God indeed, but exercised indirectly through the brethren. The obligations following in the epistle are for the most part outward toward the world, and inward toward one another as fellow-believers, fellow-members of the family of God or of the Body of Christ.

Questions.

1. What is the significance of "Wherefore"?

2. Name the four "obligations" in this lesson.

3. Why are they called "upward"?

4. What is the difference between "hope" in verse 3 and in verse 13?

5. What are the two motives for godly fear?

6. Expound in your own words 1:22-2:3.

7. Do the same with 2:4-10.

OBLIGATIONS OF THE HOPE—OUTWARD

CHAPTERS 2:11-4:6

The writer had dropped his pen, but takes it up again at verse 11. To "abstain from fleshly lusts that war against the soul," is limited and defined in the next verse. The pagans round about were speaking against the Christians as evil-doers. Their increasing numbers were emptying the Pagan temples, and threatening in so doing, not only the Pagan religion but the state itself, for the Romans worshipped the state in the person of the emperor, and at this time Rome controlled the world. The duty of the Christians, therefore, was to have their conduct so seemly and consistent in the eyes of their watchful and jealous neighbors that by their "good works," those neighbors might in the day of their visitation by Divine grace glorify God for them.

There were two ways in which this seemliness was to show itself, or rather two obligations to be borne by the Christians toward the pagans: one was submission (2:13-3:7), and the other testimony (3:8-4:6).

The submission was comprehensive in scope, covering the three classes of the social order: governmental (13-17), industrial (18-25), conjugal (3:1-7).

The testimony was to be marked by four things: readiness, intelligence, meekness and consistency of life (3:15, 16).

The last point calls for amplification because of some obscurity in the text that follows. It is the writer's desire all through the epistle to use the example of Christ to enforce his exhortations. For example, in chapter 2 (18-25), household servants are urged to patience under even unjust treatment by their Pagan masters on the ground that when Christ "was reviled," He "reviled not again." "But committed Himself to Him that judgeth righteously." And so here it is said that it is better to "suffer for well-doing than for evil doing" (17). Why? Because Christ so suffered even unto death (18), but was quickened and raised from the dead; and even more, has "gone into heaven and is on the right hand of God, angels and authorities and powers being made subject unto Him" (22). We Christians should arm ourselves with the same "mind" that He had (4:1). We, too, should be willing to suffer in the flesh. He who has this purpose in his heart

"hath ceased from sin" in the sense indicated in verses 2-4; i.e., he will separate himself from all evil-doers even if he suffer for it so far as his life in the flesh is concerned. There were some indeed, who had suffered even unto death (6); but it was to this end that the Gospel had been preached to them while they were alive, that they might know that, though they were thus judged, thus treated according to the will of men as regards the flesh, yet they would live by the will of God as regards the spirit. And, of course, as Christ triumphed over His enemies and entered into glory, the same would be true of them.

A further difficulty appears at 3:19, where Christ in triumphing over His enemies is represented as preaching "unto the spirits in prison." "Preaching" here is not the word commonly used for preaching the gospel, but means "to herald" or "to proclaim." That which Christ heralded or proclaimed was His triumph over His enemies through the Cross (Col. 2:13-15). "Spirits" presumably, does not refer to men but angels, the evil angels who "kept not their first estate, but left their own habitation," "in the days of Noah." (See our comments on Gen. 6:8, and compare also 2 Peter 2:4, 5, and Jude 6, 7.)

Questions.

1. Explain 2:11, 12.
2. Name the two "outward" obligations of "The Living Hope."
3. Name the three kinds of submission enjoined.
4. In what four ways was the testimony to be marked?
5. Explain 4:1-6.
6. Explain 3:19, 20.

OBLIGATIONS OF THE HOPE—INWARD

CHAPTERS 4:7-5:14

1. Hospitality, 4:7-11.
by which we understand spiritual rather than physical hospitality, though the latter need not be excluded from the thought. Verses 10 and 11 for example, suggest 1

Cor. 12; Rom. 12:3-8; Ephesians 4:7-16, etc., in which Paul is teaching the duty of the members of the Body of Christ to minister to one another of their spiritual gifts without judging.

2. Patience, vv. 12-19.

Verse 12 shows that the opposition to the Christians at this time was exhibited in more than a "speaking against" them as earlier passages record. "The fiery trial among you" is the rendering of the Revised Version—it was already there. Verse 13 is characteristic of Peter, who always throws forward the fact of the present suffering of Christians unto the light of their future glory, for which reason he is called the apostle of hope (cf. 1:3, 7, 11; 5:1, 4, 10). If Christians were unwilling to suffer for righteousness' sake it was an evidence of a low spiritual state. Let them remember therefore, that time of judgment he had referred to in 1:17.

3. Fidelity, 5:1-4.

In this instance "elders," in the sense of pastors are particularly addressed, when once more the heavenly glory is brought forward as a motive for their conduct.

4. Service, vv. 5-11.

"Elder" in this instance has reference, not to office, but age.

The younger members of the flock, and indeed all of them, are to gird themselves with humility "to serve one another" (R. V.). Fear should move them to do this, "for God resisteth the proud." The hope of reward should move them, for He "giveth grace to the humble," hence the exhortation of verse 6. It costs something to humble one's self. It makes us anxious about our possessions or our position in life, but let us cast that anxiety upon God, for it is His business to care for us (7). "It matters to Him about you," is a literal and beautiful rendering of that verse. But there is another reason for humbling ourselves in service—the activity of the evil one (8, 9). It is he who would restrain us from doing it. Be watching out for him at such a time, resist him in the comfort of knowing that you are not alone in such experiences. Moreover, the conflict will not be for long, and glory follows (10).

Questions.

1. Name the four "inward" obligations of The Living Hope.

2. Define "spiritual" hospitality.

3. How is Peter sometimes designated, and why?

4. What motives should move us to serve one another?

5. Give a literal translation of 5:7.

SECOND EPISTLE OF PETER

FALLING FROM GRACE
—A WARNING

CHAPTER 1

Second Peter is the first of the New Testament books as to the canonicity of which there is any doubt. It was not mentioned by the earliest Christian writers, but this may be accounted for by the lateness of its appearance, and the fact that it was not addressed to any local church with an interest in and facility for making its existence known.

On the other hand there are points of genuineness, such as expressions similar to those in first Peter, similar views of prophecy, the writer's testimony to his presence at the transfiguration, etc., all of which substantiate the Petrine authorship. We cannot consider the subject at any length—enough to know that the book has been regarded as canonical by the whole church, with isolated exceptions, for sixteen or seventeen centuries at least.

Its Object.

Before analyzing the epistle let us consider its object which was to warn and to exhort (3:17, 18). And this warning was against falling from grace, while the exhortation was in the direction of growing in grace. A working outline will be found in considering:

1. The enforcement of this warning and exhortation (1:2-11).
2. The ground of it (1:12-21).
3. The occasion of it (2-3).

1. As to the enforcement notice three points:

(a) The source of growth, 2-4. This source is God Himself. Grace and peace are multiplied in us through the knowledge of Him (v. 2), but that is not all. His divine power grants unto us how many other things that pertain to the same end (v. 2)? And through what channel do they come (same verse)? By this knowledge of God we become possessed of certain things, what are they (4)? And through the possession of these promises of what do we come to partake? But what antecedently has become true of us? How does "the corruption that is in the world" control men so that they can not partake of the divine nature (same verse)?

(b) The lines of growth, 5-7. If we are to be preserved from falling from grace in what general directions should we be careful to grow in grace? We have obtained faith from God, in other words, and by this we have been declared righteous in a judicial sense, but what, now, are we to add to this faith, or "supply in it," to quote the Revised Version, in order to perfect assurance? The list of the virtues follows, of which one or two require a word of explanation. "Virtue," for example, is not chastity, but "Courage," perhaps moral courage to confess our faith before men. And "temperance" is not moderation in the use of intoxicating drinks merely, but in every line of conduct, self-restraint, in other words. Moreover, the word "charity" is to be interpreted by "love" as in 1 Corinthians 13.

(c) The need of growth, 8-11. The necessity for "diligence" in these matters is seen in what follows. It is the presence of these things in our lives that makes us fruitful in Christ, and bears testimony to the power of His cleansing blood (8, 9). Moreover, they produce the strength of assurance of our salvation (10), and secure that that salvation shall be a triumphant and glorious one (11).

Ground of the Warning.

Passing from the apostle's enforcement of his warning and exhortation to the ground of it, 12-21, we find it built upon the truth of the Gospel. And this is set before us along two lines of evidence:

(a) The testimony of Peter

himself 12-18. In introducing this he speaks of his object (to stir them up), his motive (his approaching decease), and his purpose (to prepare a record of these things, which, by the way, is supposed to be contained in the Gospel of Mark). But now, what is his testimony? That is, to what particular fact of Gospel history does he bear witness (16)? What kind of witness is it (same verse)? What did he see and hear? Do you remember who were with him? How does he interpret the transfiguration, that is, of what greater event does he speak of it as a foregleam?

(b) The testimony of the Old Testament prophets, 19-21. Verse 19 should read: "Wherefore we have the word of prophecy made more sure." It does not mean that the Old Testament prophets are more sure than the New, but that such words as his strengthen the prediction spoken before. How, then, should we regard the Old Testament prophecies (19)? What does he say of their origin (for so should "interpretation" be understood in verse 20)? And when he says those prophecies were not of any "private" origination, what does he mean, as gathered from verse 21? Does not this strongly corroborate Paul in 2 Timothy 3:16.

Questions.

1. What distinguishes this epistle in the canon?

2. What strong evidence is there to its canonicity?

3. State its object or purpose.

4. Give its outline.

5. How many questions in the text of the lesson have you answered satisfactorily?

OCCASION
OF THE WARNING

CHAPTERS 2-3

We now consider the last division which treats of the occasion for this warning and exhortation, chapters 2 and 3. In brief, this occasion was the incoming of false teachers in the church, 2:1;

whose success is predicted in verse 2; whose punishment is certain and dreadful, 3-9; and whose description follows in verses 10-22.

We shall not enter upon this description in detail, and, indeed, it presents many difficulties of interpretation. The presence of such teachers, in the visible church, is almost inconceivable, but we should recall what Christ said about wolves in sheeps' clothing. Their leading characteristics are carnality (10), presumption (10-12), reveling (13), and covetousness (14-16), but it is clear that the first-named played the largest part in the power exercised over their followers. Just what the features of this uncleanness were may come before us when we reach Jude, whose epistle contains the same picture of false teachers in about the same words.

Character of the False Teaching.

No portion of this epistle is more important than the last on which we now enter, and which, in connection with the description of the teachers describes their teaching. The latter focuses upon the second coming of Christ, chapter 3.

In the first place notice the second verse concerning the authority of the New Testament as compared with the Old, and how the apostle places his writings on a par with the prophets.

What period is being referred to (3)? Remember that "the last days" means the last days of the present age, not the end of the world. What is the subject of the scoffing marking the period spoken of (4)? Of what fact do the scoffers seem to be in practical ignorance (5, 6)? How will the next cosmic catastrophe differ from the last (7)? The reference in verse 7 is to the end of the world, but this will not be reached till a thousand years after the coming of the Lord. How does this fact seem to be alluded to in verse 8? For what reason is the coming of the Lord delayed (9)? To what period does verse 10 refer? We have seen (2 Thessalonians), the distinction between the coming of Christ for His church, and the introduction of "The Day of the Lord" which follows. This "day" begins and ends with judgment as Revelation reveals, although between the two series of judgments the millennium intervenes. We have been taught that the prophets see events in space rather than in time, often overlooking intervening occurrences between the objective points. In this way the church period is not alluded to in the Old Testament, while in the present instance Peter says noth-ing about the millennium. What application does he make of these words (11-12)? What hope is set before the believer (13)? With what warning and exhortation does he close (17, 18)?

Questions.

1. What was the occasion for the warning?

2. Name some characteristics of the false teachers.

3. What is meant by "the last days"?

4. When does "the Day of the Lord" begin and end?

5. How do the prophets see events?

FIRST EPISTLE OF JOHN

GOD IS LIGHT

CHAPTERS 1-2:28

First John is addressed to no particular church or individual, but it is thought that the apostle had in mind a cycle of churches like the seven of Asia (see Revelation 1). It is likely that the Christians to whom he wrote were of Gentile rather than Jewish origin, as judged by the few references to the Old Testament, and by such allusions as that in chapter 5:21.

The epistle was written later than the Gospel by the same author, as gathered from the circumstances that an acquaintance with its facts is pre-supposed, and also because the words of Christ are cited if known.

The occasion of its writing seems to have been the presence of false teachers, as we judge from passages, of which 2:18-26 and 4:1-6 are examples. And, indeed, we learn from the writers of church history that at a very early period there were three classes of heretics as they were called. (1) The Ebionites, who denied the Deity of Christ; (2) the Docetists, who denied His humanity; (3) the Cerinthians, who denied the union of the two natures, human and divine, prior to His baptism.

The Theme is stated to be "Fellowship with God" in chapter 1:3, 4, and the idea is presented to us not in a progression of thought, but after the manner of the law of recurrence, which we have come to recognize in other instances. Perhaps it might be said rather, that the apostle gives us three distinct cycles of thought, which form in their combination a beautiful picture of truth, and a cumulative application of the main line of instruction. For example, God is light (1:5), hence fellowship with God depends on our walking in the light. Again, God is righteous (2:29), hence fellowship with God depends on our

doing righteousness. And finally, God is love, (4:7, 8), hence fellowship with God depends on our possessing and manifesting love.

1. Introduction 1:1-4.

In the introduction three thoughts are set before us concerning the apostleship of Christ, which may be thus expressed:

The proofs of the apostleship, viz: to have seen and heard Christ, verse 1.

The character of the apostleship, viz: the declaration of Christ, verse 2.

The object of the apostleship, fellowship in Christ, verses 3, 4.

What peculiar expressions in the opening chapter of John's Gospel are recalled by the first verse? What bearing has this upon the statement that the Gospel was first written? Against which of the heresies, previously mentioned, do these words seem directed? How does the Revised Version translate verse 2, especially the phrase "that eternal life"? Against which of the heresies do these words, as given in the Revised Version, seem directed?

2. First Cycle of Thought 1:5-2: 28.

What is the first message that John declares to them (5)? If "God is light," how is fellowship to be maintained with Him, (6, 7)? If fellowship is to be maintained by walking in the light, how may we walk in the light?

1. By perceiving and confessing sin in the faith of Jesus Christ (1:8-2:2).

2. By keeping God's commandments (3, 8).

3. Especially the commandment of love to the brethren (9, 11).

4. This keeping of God's commandments is incompatible with the love of the world (15-17).

5. It is incompatible with fellowship of false teachers (18-28).

Notice how this last corroborates the remarks concerning the nature of the heresies in John's time. Notice the peculiar title ascribed to Christ in verse 20. How does this verse and verse 27 harmonize with John 15:6, and Acts 2:32, 33? What then is the unction believers have received from Christ?

Questions.

1. To what churches probably was this epistle addressed?

2. Why is its origin dated later than the fourth Gospel?

3. Name and define the three classes of heretics in mind.

4. State the theme and the manner of its treatment.

5. Give the main outline.

6. How may we walk in the light?

GOD IS RIGHTEOUS

Chapters 2:29-4:6

The second cycle centers around the thought that "God is righteous" (2-29), hence fellowship with God depends on doing righteousness.

Observe that in the working out of the proposition the apostle speaks of three things:

1. The motive for doing righteousness, viz: the hope we have through our sonship to God (3:1-10).

2. The test of doing righteousness, viz: love to the brethren (3:11-18).

3. The reward of doing righteousness, viz: assurance of salvation (3:19-4:6).

Referring more at length to the "motive," notice that our sonship to God includes likeness to Christ in His manifested glory (2). Notice that the evidence of the sonship is bound up with expectation of His coming, and the holiness of living it begets (3). Verses 3-8 continue the thought of Christ's holiness, and His work on the Cross to make it possible in our experience. Verse 9, has presented difficulty to some. "Whosoever is born of God," is taken by many to refer only to the new nature in the believer which does not sin. Others

interpret the word "commit" in the sense of practice (compare Galatians 5:21), (Revised Version). It is one thing to fall temporarily into sin as a consequence of sudden temptation, and another thing to practice it, i.e., to live in continual transgression. This no regenerated man does. The teaching of this verse should be balanced with that of 1:8, where the apostle is speaking to the same persons as in the present instance.

Referring to the "test" of doing righteousness, it is peculiar that brotherly love should be insisted on again as in the case of walking in the light. But it will be found to have an equally prominent place in the third cycle of thought, thus stamping this epistle as peculiarly the epistle of love. It speaks of God's love toward us and our love toward Him, but either side of that truth with John always runs into the corresponding one of love toward one another in Christ. Notice what hinders the flow of this love, verse 12. Notice its importance as demonstrating our spiritual condition, verse 14. Notice the spiritual application of the sixth commandment, verse 15. Notice the practical way this love should be demonstrated, verses 16-18.

Referring to the "reward" of righteousness as consisting in the assurance of salvation, notice the number of times and the different relations in which that word "know" is employed. This is the "assurance" epistle all the way through as well as the epistle of love, and it is more than a coincidence that these two things go together. See how assurance of salvation depends upon our having a good conscience and a warm heart in Christ (19-21). See how this assurance carries with it a corresponding assurance in prayer (22-24). See, again, that this is the evidence of the abiding life in Christ (24), and that just in the measure in which we are pleasing our Heavenly Father as Jesus did, will we receive the witness of the Holy Spirit to that fact as He did. Finally the

Christian who thus lives obediently has his assurance increased in the testimony to his overcoming of temptation. He will not be carried away by false doctrines or deceived by any anti-Christ (4:1-6).

Questions.

1. How is the thought of this lesson worked out?

2. How would you interpret 3:9?

3. What peculiar stamp is on this epistle?

4. What name might be given it from another point of view?

5. What lessons are here taught about assurance?

GOD IS LOVE

CHAPTERS 4: 7-5: 21

What is the third characteristic of God which John reveals (7, 8)? If, then, God is love, how is fellowship to be maintained with Him (same verses)? In the working out of the thought that fellowship with God is maintained by experiencing and exercising love, notice (1), how His love was particularly manifested toward us (9, 10), and (2), how our love toward Him should be manifested (11, 12). Third, notice how such love implies fellowship (13-16). Fourth, notice how it affects our spiritual life, begetting assurance, (17-18). Fifth, notice how its absence destroys fellowship (19-21). Sixth, notice how the experience and exercise of love is only another aspect of walking in the light and doing righteousness (5:1-4). Seventh, notice that the basis and source of this love, is faith in Christ (5-12). In conclusion, notice how many things we may thus know. Verses 13, 15, 18, 19, 20.

A simpler outline of this last division which some might prefer is: (a) the reason for love, God's love toward us (4:9-11); (b) the source of love, God's dwelling in us (4:12-16); (c) the rest or confidence of love, boldness in the day of judgment (4:17-19); (d) the fruit of love, loving the brethren (4:20-5:12).

The conclusion of the epistle verses 13-21, is easily to be interpreted in the light of what has preceded it.

Questions.

1. Can you name the seven divisions of the first treatment of this lesson?

2. Can you name the four divisions of the second treatment?

3. Have you considered all the things which the Christian may know?

4. Do you appreciate why John is called the apostle of love?

SECOND EPISTLE OF JOHN

The second epistle of John is addressed to whom? The word "lady" in the Greek is Kyria, which may be translated as a proper name, and perhaps in this case it should be so understood. Kyria was a common name among the Greeks and refers here, it may be, to some notable saint in the neighborhood of Ephesus, to which John ministered in his old age. The letter is brief, for the writer is soon to make a visit to this sister in Christ and to speak with her face to face (12).

. The Salutation, verses 1-4, is interesting for three or four things:

(a) The deep humility of the writer.

(b) The tender regard for the sister to whom he writes.

(c) The solicitude for the honor of Jesus Christ.

(d) The insight into the spiritual condition of this sister's household.

2. The burden message of the letter follows, 5-11. This burden is the old one of John—love. But love in the New Testament means not a passion, not an emotion, a life. An abiding principle influencing for righteousness, this is Christian love. Is not that what John says here (6)? And see how the idea is emphasized in verse 7. Not to love is not to hold to the truth in doctrine and to practice it in life. False teachers do not love. They may be amiable in their social relations, but they have not this Gospel love. They are deceivers, and love and deceit do not go together. And mark the central fact of that truth which constitutes love—the confession that Jesus Christ is come in the flesh. This strikes at the Jew's denial of Jesus, certainly, but also how can Christian Science, which denies the material body confess this? Changing the language again to conform to the Revised Version, we see that they are the deceivers and the anti-Christ in spirit who fail to confess that He "cometh in the flesh." It is

Christ's second coming John has in mind as truly as His first coming.

In the light of the above consider the warning in verse 8. There is danger of believers losing something which belongs to them. That something is "a full reward." Compare Luke 19:15-27; 1 Corinthians 3:11-15; 2 Peter 1:21; 1 Corinthians 3:11-15; 2 Peter 1. See Matthew 16-27; Revelation 22:12. Does not the comparison of these passages bear out verse 7 as rendered by the Revised Version?

What is it to transgress as given in verse 9? By the "doctrine of Christ" is not meant merely the things He taught while in the flesh, but the whole doctrine concerning Him, i. e., the whole of the Old and New Testaments. To deny the truth concerning Christ is to deny His first and His second coming, and He who denies this "hath not God." He may speak much of the "Father," but he only has the Father who has the Son. To have the One you must have the Other, (9).

Observe how strenuous we should be in maintaining this doctrine (v. 10). The command "receive him not into your house," is relative. It means not that we are to deny him meat and shelter altogether, if he be in need of them, but that we are not to fellowship him as a brother. Even our personal enemies we are to bless and pray for, if they hunger we are to feed them and if they thirst give them drink. But those who are the enemies of God by being enemies of His truth, we are to have nothing to do with in the capacity of fellow-Christians. We must not aid them in their plans or bid them God speed. How would such a course on our part involve us (11)?

The apostle closes with that allusion to his visit already referred to, and a greeting from Kyria's elect sister. Did this mean her sister in the flesh or only in the faith? And in this last case was it the apostle's wife?

Questions.

1. How may we translate "lady" and to whom may it refer?

2. Can you discover in the text the four points under the "Salutation"?

3. What is the message of this letter?

4. What is Christian love?

5. What is its central fact?

6. Who are spiritual anti-Christs?

7. Have you examined the parallel scriptures on the subject of "reward"?

8. What is meant by the "doctrine of Christ"?

9. Explain "receive him not into your house."

THIRD EPISTLE OF JOHN

Gaius is a name frequently alluded to by Paul, but whether this were the same individual as any of those is problematical. In any event he seems to have been a convert of John (v. 4). Another form of the name is Caius and this was a very common name indeed.

What distinction in spiritual things is ascribed to Gaius (2)? His soul was prospering even if his bodily health and his business were not, but the apostle is interested in other things as well. The Christian should be careful of his health, and it is compatible with a deep spiritual life that he should have a successful business.

As to the Christian character of Gaius, three particulars are named: (1) He possessed the truth (3). (2) He walked in the truth, i. e., his life and conduct measured up to the light he had received from God, (3, 4). (3) As walking in the truth he was "careful to maintain good works," especially in the distribution of his means (5,6). It is noticeable that his "faithfulness" in this regard is mentioned. It was not a spasmodic thing on his part, but a steady flow of grace through him. His breadth of disposition is also mentioned since his giving was not limited to those he knew but extended to those he did not know (5). Some recipients of his bounty are referred to in verse 6, and a journey mentioned toward the expense of which he was contributing (6). All this is very realistic, and brings the life of the church in the first century "up to date" as we sometimes say.

One or two facts are given concerning the recipients of Gaius' gifts equally honoring to them, (7). Look at the motive of their journey, " His Name's sake," and at the spirit actuating them "taking nothing of the Gentile," i.e., the heathen. Whatever the journey was, they might have been assisted in it pecuniarily by those who were not actuated by a love for His name, but their conscience would not permit them to receive such aid. How valuable this example. And what a close relationship it bears to the teaching of the second epistle about fellowshiping with heretics. How should such loyal and self-denying workers as these be treated in the church, and why (8)?

The Worldly Character of Diotrephes.

Here we have another type of the professing Christian in the worldly character of Diotrephes, 9-11.

What seems to have been his besetting sin (9)? How does this experience of John recall that of Paul in the churches of Corinth, Galatia and Thessalonica? In what manner did John intend to deal with him (10)? Does this recall anything similar in apostolic authority on Paul's part? How does verse 10 reveal the worldliness and insincerity of Diotrephes? What an awfully overbearing, autocratic, unholy man he must have been! How did he get into the church?

What advice is given Gaius in verse 11? How does this testify to the relation between faith and works? What opposite kind of example is set before him in verse 12? How many kinds of witnesses testify to the Christian character of Demetrius? One can not help wondering if this were the Demetrius of Acts 19. Such trophies of grace are by no means unusual, Paul was such a one.

Note the similarities in the conclusions of this epistle and the one previously considered (13, 14), suggesting that they may have been penned at the same time.

The Scofield Bible has an interesting note here, saying that "historically, this letter marks the beginning of that clerical assumption over the churches in which the primitive church order disappeared. It also reveals the believers' resource in such a day. John addresses this letter not to the church, but to a faithful man in the church for the comfort of those who were standing fast in the primitive simplicity. Second John conditions the personal walk of a Christian in a day of apostasy; and Third John the personal responsibility in such a day of the believer as a member of the local church."

Questions.

1. Analyze the Christian character of Gaius.

2. What two features marked his faithfulness?

3. Tell something of the character of the two other men named.

4. What epoch does this epistle mark?

5. Distinguish between second and third John.

EPISTLE OF JUDE

The writer of Jude, evidently not an apostle, calls himself a "servant of Jesus Christ and brother of James." Which James? There were two whose brother he might have been, the son of Alpheus and the brother of our Lord, and the general opinion is in favor of the last-named.

1. The first division is the salutation, 1, 2. Notice the Revised Version: "them that are called, beloved in God the Father, and kept for Jesus Christ." Why kept for Him? How much this suggests as to His coming glory and the part believers will take in it?

2. The object follows, 3, 4. What is that object as stated in verse 3? Notice that according to the Revised Version the faith delivered to the saints was delivered "once for all." "Faith" here is to be taken in the sense of that body of Christian doctrine which forms the substance of the truth concerning "our common salvation." It is used synonymously with "Gospel." This was delivered to the body of the church, at the beginning of its history as a complete revelation in itself (Revelation 22:18, 19). It is a sacred deposit to be preserved in its integrity, defended and earnestly contended for. The necessity for this defense is seen in verse 4. "Foreshadowed" in that verse should be "forewritten," i.e., the false teachers referred to had been predicted as coming in among the flock. Our Lord had spoken of them, and so had all His apostles. The nature and outcome of their teaching as suggested by "lasciviousness" is particularly noticeable.

False Teachers.

3. The third division deals with the false teachers, and we have first, a revelation of their punishment (5-7). From this their position as professed disciples would not save them any more than it saved the Israelites brought out of Egypt, when they afterward sinned against light (5); or the angels referred to in Peter's epistles and Genesis (6); or Sodom and Gomorrah (7). Do not fail to observe the class of sins prominent in these instances, especially the two last-named, and their relationship to "lasciviousness" already spoken of. While the erroneous teachings were intellectual, yet their power was augmented by carnality of the grossest kind.

4. The description of the teachers follows, (8-13). Observe in verse 8 that they not only defile the flesh but speak evil of dignitaries, by which may be meant both civil and ecclesiastical superiors. And there is a strange illustration in verse 9, that throws light on the burial of Moses recorded in Deuteronomy. Why that mystery? Why should God have buried Moses, and kept the place a secret? Why should Satan have desired possession of that body? Did his fore-knowledge of what should take place on the Mount of Transfiguration (Mt. Sinai) have aught to do with it? And further, shall we say with some, that Moses in the flesh is to be one of the two witnesses named in Revelation 11, and did Satan seek thus to frustrate God's purposes concerning the last days? And then the contention of Michael, how that brings to mind the teaching in Daniel concerning him as the prince that stands for Israel! What a bearing all this has on the teachings of the New Testament about the dominions, and principalities and powers of the air (see Ephesians 6).

Further analysis of these teachers is afforded in verse 11. With what three Old Testament individuals, each conspicuous for his self-willed and rebellious spirit, are they compared? How strange that such could have any standing in the Christian church were it not that we discover their successors at the present day. Read verse 12 in the Revised Version, "Spots in your feasts of charity," should be "hidden rocks in your love-feasts." These "love-feasts" were the Christian gatherings on the first day of the week for the "breaking of bread," and the presence of such would-be leaders in those assemblies suggested the perils of hidden rocks to mariners. What care was required to avoid disastrous contact with them. "Feeding themselves without fear," should be, "Shepherds that without fear feed themselves." It is characteristic of the heretical teacher that he is thinking of himself rather than the flock.

Six terse descriptions of these teachers may be given as follows: Visionary, 8, 9; Ignorant, 10, 11; Deceptive, 12, 13; Ungodly, 14, 15; Selfish, 16-18; Schismatic, 19.

5. The description of the teachers is followed by a reference to the fore-knowledge of them (14-16). Here is a quotation from Enoch in verse 14, on which we say a word. There is an apocryphal book in which it is found, but it is thought to have been of a later date than Jude, and that its author probably quoted from our epistle. How interesting to learn that Enoch, before the deluge, had his mind carried out in the Spirit to the Second Coming of Christ! And how perfectly his words agree with the later prophets, concerning that event!

The True Church in Contrast.

6. The reference to the false teachers gives way to a description of the true church in sharp contrast with the false (17-25).

It begins with a caution (17-19). To which of the apostles is he here referring, do you think? How does he describe these ungodly persons who have found their way into the visible Church? That word "sensual" is in the margin of the Revised Version, "natural" or "animal." It is a case of unregenerated Christians with whom the Church is still plentifully supplied.

The caution is followed by an exhortation (20, 21). "Build," "pray," "keep," "look," are the four corner posts defining the possessions of the Christian life. What is peculiar about the exhortation to pray? In Romans 8 we have revealed that the Holy Spirit prays in us, but here we are to pray in Him. Are these contradictory teachings? Is it not true that the Holy Spirit is our life, and also our spiritual atmosphere? In what are we to keep ourselves according to this exhortation? Does this mean God's love to us or our love to Him? How better can we keep ourselves in His love to us, and the consciousness of our love to Him than by building ourselves up on our most holy faith, and praying in the Holy Spirit? What do you suppose is meant by "looking for the mercy of our Lord Jesus Christ unto eternal life"? In the light of the previous teaching about the appearing of His glory, may it not refer to that?

The exhortation is followed by instruction concerning soul-winning (22, 23). The Greek text, especially in verse 23, is obscure, but the teaching calls for compassion on our part, and an effort to save the sinner while hating the sin.

7. The benediction and ascription follow. What two things is God able to do for believers in His Son? No wonder that we should ascribe unto Him through Jesus Christ "glory and majesty, dominion and power throughout all ages."

Supplemental.

Jude is particularly a Scripture for these times, and has been called "a picture of the last days," and "a preface to Revelation," as it shows the drift of the apostasy which makes the awful judgment of the book to be necessary.

R. V. Miller points out how it refers to all the more important articles of the Christian faith. (a), The Trinity, inasmuch as we have God the Father, (v. 1), Jesus Christ the Son, in several verses, and the Holy Spirit (v. 20); (b), the Deity of Christ, Who in half a dozen verses is called LORD; (c), the historicity of the Old Testament, whose miraculous events are used to illustrate the teaching and give point to the warnings as though they were actual occurrences (vv. 5-11); (d), the existence and power of a personal Satan against whom even the archangel himself dare not bring a railing accusation (v. 9); (e), the existence of angels and spirits (vv. 6, 7); (f), the certainty and fearfulness of future retribution (vv. 6, 7, 13); (g), the Second Coming of Christ (vv. 14, 15).

Questions.

1. How is the author of this epistle distinguished from some others?

2. Name the seven main divisions of it.

3. How is "Faith" (v. 3), to be understood?

4. What different ideas are suggested by the "mystery" in verse 9?

5. What was said in the lesson about verse 14?

6. Name the four corner posts of the Christian life?

7. What makes this epistle particularly applicable to, or useful in, these days?

8. What seven important articles of the Christian faith does it emphasize?

BOOK OF REVELATION

INTRODUCTORY
OR "THE THINGS WHICH THOU HAST SEEN"

Chapter 1

In this book we return to the atmosphere of the Old Testament, at least after the third chapter, at which point the apocalyptic part begins with a narration of events synchronizing with "the Day of the Lord."

The authorship is ascribed to John, who wrote the Gospel and three epistles bearing his name, and who at this time, about 95 A.D., had been banished by the Roman Emperor, to the Isle of Patmos in the Aegean Sea (1:9). The date is in dispute, some placing it as early as Nero, 64 or 65, but the preponderance of opinion is in favor of the later period of Domitian.

The opening chapter consists (1), of the Preface, verses 1-3, and a few questions will put us in possession of it. Whose revelation is it? Of course, the reference here is to Jesus Christ considered as the God-Man. Whence did He receive this revelation? For whom was it given to Him? And for what purpose with reference to them? To which of His servants was it representatively sent? And through what agency? What did this servant do with the revelation thus committed to him (verse 2)? "Things which must shortly come to pass" has puzzled some, and given rise to the opinion that the predictions have been fulfilled in the course of history from that time. However, while some of them have been fulfilled in the history of the seven churches of Asia, for example, the bulk of them are still future. "One day is with the Lord as a thousand years."

(2) The Salutation follows, 4-8. The seven churches in Asia were probably those over which John had particular charge. But it was a mistake to suppose that the readers were limited to those churches. To quote Alford, "The number seven itself can hardly have been chosen except as symbolical of universality, according to the writer's practice throughout the book."

Observe the allusion to the Trinity. "Him Which is, and Which was, and Which is to come," identifies God the Father. "The Seven Spirits before His Throne," God the Holy Ghost; "Jesus Christ the faithful witness," God the Son. Compare for the Seven Spirits, Isaiah 11:2-5.

(3) The salutation is followed by the Preparatory Vision John received, and which constituted his authority to write, 8-16. This vision was that of the Person of the glorified Christ. For the candlesticks, compare Rev. 1:20; Matt. 5:14-16; the clothing, Isa. 11:5, 61:10; Eph. 6:14; Rev. 19:8; the white head and hair, Dan. 7:9; Matt. 17:1, 2; Acts 22:6-8; 2 Peter 1:16-18; Rev. 22:5; the eyes of fire, 2 Tim. 1:7, 8; Heb. 12:29; the feet of brass, Prov. 1:24-28; Isa. 48:4; Luke 13:25-27; the voice of many waters, Dan. 10:6, Rev. 14:2, 3; 19:6; the seven stars, Dan. 12:3; Mal. 2:7; Rev. 1:20, 12:1; the two-edged sword, Eph. 6:17; Heb. 4:12; the keys, Isa. 22:20-22; Matt. 16:19; Luke 11:52; Rev. 3:7, 20:1; Matt. 28:18; John 20:22, 23; 1 Cor. 12:4, 8.

(4) The vision concludes with the general command to write, 17-20, in the terms of which (19) there is outlined the three major divisions of the book. "The things which thou hast seen," refers to the Patmos vision just considered; "the things which are," refers to the things then existing, i.e., the churches, and particularly the seven churches of Asia; "the things which shall be hereafter," or literally "after these," means, as we think, after the Church period ends. As the first division covers chapter one, so the second covers chapters two and three, and the third practically the rest of the book. The last division, as suggested by W. J. Erdman, falls into a series of six

sevens with five parenthetical passages making, with the church division, seven sevens. The six sevens are: (a) the seals, 4:1-8:1; (b) the trumpets, 8:2-9:19; (c) the personages, 12:1-14:20 (d) the vials, 15:1-16:21; (e) the dooms, 17:1-20:15; (f) the new things, 21:1-22:21.

Questions.

1. What peculiarity about the interpretation of this book is stated in the first paragraph of the lesson?

2. What is said about its date?

3. State the four main divisions of the chapter.

4. Have you examined its symbolism in the light of the parallel passages named?

5. Name the three major divisions of the book as indicated in verse 19?

6. Name the six sevens of the third division.

THE SEVEN CHURCHES, OR THE THINGS WHICH ARE

Chapters 2-3

No agreement exists as to the application of "angel" in the address to each of these churches, but as the word means "messenger," it may refer to those sent by the churches to interview the apostle at Patmos (cf. Phil. 4:18).

Of course, the seven churches existed at this time in Asia, yet the epistles have not only a local application to them, but apply representatively to the whole Church everywhere at that time.

Many also think they have an application prophetically to "the spiritual history of the Church at large from that day to the end of this age," when the true Church, which is the body of Christ, will be caught up to meet Him in the air. In this respect, they bear a close relation to the seven parables of Matt. 13 to which the student will refer. The apostasy in Christendom outlined in that chapter in Matthew, began in the apostolic days (2 Thess. 2), and

has been increasing ever since, and will culminate in the "man of sin" at the end of this age after the true Church has been translated. It is the course of this apostasy that is thought to be again outlined here prophetically in the epistles to the seven churches. One reason for this view is that we discover a gradual decline from the fervor of the first love of the Ephesian Church, or the Ephesian period of the Church, to the lukewarm, spewed-out-of-the-mouth condition of Laodicea.

Seven Periods in the Church.

The seven periods in the history of the Church as outlined in these epistles have been interpreted thus: The epistle to the church at Ephesus represents the spiritual condition of the first period of the Church universal from the ascension of Christ to the close of the first century, the apostolic era. The epistle to Smyrna represents the second period, or the martyr Church, from the death of John to the rise of Constantine, 100-311 A. D. The third Pergamos, from the state Church under Constantine to the rise of the papacy (Pope Gregory I), 311-590. The fourth, Thyatira, from the rise of the papacy to the reformation, 590-1517. The fifth, Sardis, the Protestant Churches from the Reformation to the rise of Methodism, 1517-1755. The sixth, Philadelphia, the Missionary period, 1755, to somewhere near the present time. The seventh, Laodicea, from the present time to the Second Coming of Christ.

"Nicolaitanes" (2:6-15), has been taken to mean an early heretical sect by that name, but the application is doubtful. The word comes from *nikao*, "to conquer," and *laos*, "the people" or "the laity," and may refer to the earliest notion of a priestly order of the "clergy," separating the equal priesthood of all believers into a few who were "priests," and the great majority who were not. In the earlier period represented by the epistle to Ephesus it was only "the deeds of the Nicolaitanes" which were referred to, but in the later period represented by Pergamos, the "deeds" had developed into a "doctrine." "The doctrine of Balaam" (2:14; 2 Pet. 2:5; Jude 11), was his "teaching Balak to corrupt the people who could not be cursed" (Num. 20:5, 23:8, 31:15, 16), by tempting them to defile themselves by marrying the heathen, and represents the union of the Church with the world which is spiritual adultery. "Satan's seat" is in the world 2:13, cf. with John 12:31, 14:30, 16:11). "That woman Jezebel" (2:20) brought idolatry into Israel, and suggests Romanism with its pagan ceremonies. "Sardis" stands for the Reformation period or Protestantism which grew out of it, in the sense that it is so largely profession without life. "Philadelphia" is the true church within the professing church, whose history overlaps that of Laodicea, or rather runs parallel with it for a while.

Little space is left to speak of the structure of the epistles, but quoting Archbishop Trench, it will be seen that there are certain forms fundamental to all of them; (1) an order to write, (2) a glorious title of the speaker, (3) an address to the Church, (4) a command to hear, (5) a promise to the faithful. It is further interesting that the title of the speaker, Christ, has in every instance two main features. First, it is taken from the imagery of the preceding vision, and secondly, it always seems to harmonize with the state or condition of the Church addressed.

Questions.

1. What may the term "Angel" mean in these epistles?

2. In what sense are the epistles to be regarded as prophetical?

3. Have you referred to Matthew 13?

4. How usually have been divided the seven periods in the history of the Church?

5. Give the interpretation of "Nicolaitanism," "Balaamism," and "Jezebelism."

6. Which two epistles find a realization in the present Church period?

7. Describe the literary form of the epistles.

THE SEVEN SEALS, OR THE THINGS, WHICH SHALL BE HEREAFTER

Chapters 4-8:1

It is assumed that the true Church is not upon the earth at the beginning of chapter 4, but that the translation of 1 Thess. 4:16-18 has taken place. Christendom is here, but the Church is with the Lord in the air. To some this may seem a bold assumption, but not to those who have pursued the study of the earlier books in this commentary. To them it will appear natural and proper that the Church should have been "caught up" before the judgments herein enumerated are poured forth. We cannot rehearse the proof of this, but it is significant that after chapter 3, the word "church" is not again found in this book. At the close of that chapter (v. 21), Christ appears seated with His Father on His Throne, "from thence expecting till his enemies be made His footstool" (Heb. 10:13). The call to John to "come up hither" (4:1), is also indicative of the fulfillment of 1 Thess. 4:16-18, and in a figure, set before us what will be true of the whole Church in that day.

The Throne, the Lamb and the Book.

Coming to the text we have in chapters 4-5, the vision of the Throne, the Lamb and the Book, which constitutes an "Introduction" to what follows. The vision of the Throne is limited to 4:1-3, the enthroned elders verses 4 and 5, and the four living creatures (R. V.) 6-8. It is commonly felt that the elders represent the glorified Church, but there is no agreement as to the interpretation of the living creatures. It is notable however, that in this chapter both the elders and living creatures worship the Lord because of *creation* (9-11), and that redemption is not named until the next chapter. The seven sealed book (5:1-4), is the revelation of the judgments to follow and seems even to be identical with the judgments themselves. This last thought is suggested by what follows, when Christ in His kingly character comes forward and opens the book (5-7). It is He only who prevails to open the book either in the sense of making its contents known or bringing its judgments to pass. His adoration follows on the part of the living creatures and the elders (8-10), the angels (11, 12), and the whole universe (12, 14). Redemption is here praised, for it is as Redeemer of men that He has obtained this prerogative of judge of men. Verse 9 should be read in the Revised Version, which does not include the living creatures in redemption but limits it to men.

Six Seals Opened.

The "Introduction" is followed by what Erdman calls the "Progression," or advance movement of the narrative (chapter 6), in which the judgments are seen actually to take place. "Come and see" in each case should be limited to "Come" (R. V.), for the words are not a command to the seer, but to the judgment. He is not called upon to observe what is about to come, but that which is about to come is commanded to "Come." The rider on the white horse (2) was identified with Christ in Synthetic Bible Studies, but the author now considers it more consistent to identify him with the "man of sin," and at that particular period in his career when, at the beginning of Daniel's seventieth week (Dan. 9:24), he takes the power into his hands as the head of the federated nations of the Roman Empire. As the result of his rule peace is taken from the earth as symbolized by the red horse (3, 4); famine follows the black horse (5, 6), and pestilence and death "over the fourth part of the earth" (7, 8). All this time there are faithful witnesses for Christ, who will not bow the knee to the impostor, and who suffer martyrdom in consequence (9-11). Their day of vengeance is coming, but not until their number is complete. The opening of the sixth seal brings this hour near (12-17). The student is requested to compare this chapter with Matt. 24, where the same period is covered prophetically, and the same events referred to.

Saved Remnants.

We now reach the first "parenthesis" spoken of in the first lesson, (chapter 7). There is no progression in this parenthetical part although it is both retrospective and prospective in its application. It tells of certain "sealed" ones, and others, who were in the great tribulation and came out of it, and in that respect it is prospective, and yet it points back to the fifth seal in which respect it is retrospection. In other words, according to the law of recurrence with which we became familiar in the Old Testament, chapter 7 gives in detail what verses 9-11 of chapter 6 gave in outline; it tells who the martyrs are and figuratively, how they are preserved. There appears to be a saved remnant of Jews (1-8), and also of Gentiles (9-17).

The Great Tribulation.

This is that period of unexampled trouble predicted in so many places in the Old Testament. It involves the whole earth (Rev. 3:10), and yet distinctively applies to the Jews who in a national capacity will at this time have returned to Palestine, though still unconverted so far as their acceptance of their Messiah is concerned (Jer. 30:7). Its duration is 3½ years, or the last half of Daniel's seventieth week (Dan. 9:24-27). The "man of sin" will be in power (Matt. 24:15; 2 Thess. 2:4) for Satan will have come down to earth having great wrath (Rev. 12:12, 13:4, 5, &c.) And yet it will be for some a time of salvation as chapter 7 shows, a salvation brought about by the suffering no doubt, and by the transcendent event of the Church's rapture which will have previously taken place. At the close of the tribulation Christ will come in glory with His saints, delivering Israel, judging the Gentile nations, destroying the "man of sin," binding Satan, and introducing His millennial reign on the earth.

Questions.

1. Where is the true Church supposed to be at the beginning of this lesson?

2. Give some reasons for believing this.

3. What do chapters 4 and 5 constitute?

4. What does the 7-sealed book represent?

5. What word describes chapter 6?

6. With what earlier chapter in the New Testament is this compared?

7. What word describes chapter 7?

8. Name the two classes of saved ones in the "Tribulation."

9. Define "The Great Tribulation."

10. What great event follows that period?

THE SEVEN TRUMPETS

CHAPTERS 8:2-11:19

We have here another illustration of the law of recurrence, for in these chapters we are going over the ground of the last, though certain features are being added which were not then revealed. In other words, it is still the "Tribulation Period."

1. Introduction, 8:2-5.

In the previous lesson the "Introduction" included the vision of "The Throne, the Lamb and the Book," while here it is the revelation of the angel and the incense. There is no satisfactory interpretation of this feature any more than of the "silence in heaven" revealed previously. Some would say that "the prayers of all saints" are those of the martyrs of the earlier chapter crying out for avenging, not for their own sakes but that the honor of God might be maintained in the face of His enemies. The "incense" is identified with the intercession of Christ on their behalf, and the answer is symbolized in what follows not only in verse 5, but all which results therefrom in the remainder of this chapter and the next.

2. Progression 8:6-9:21.

The first trumpet (8:7) symbolizes a judgment falling on the earth through the ordinary powers of nature. The "blood" may be caused by the destructive power of the large hailstones. The second trumpet (8, 9) symbolizes judgments resulting from extraordinary powers of nature, volcanic and marine. The third (10, 11), seems to point to suffering superinduced by superhuman agencies—"a great star from heaven." Is it identical with the allusion to Satan (12:7-9)? The fourth (12, 13) is suffering caused by the diminished influence of the heavenly bodies, while the fifth and sixth trumpets (9:1-21) again specifying superhuman agencies, indicate their tormenting power as particularly directed toward men. In the other instances while humanity felt the infliction yet it was indirect, whereas here it is direct.

3. Parenthesis 10-11, 14.

In chapter 10, the revelation of the "mighty angel" and the "little book" does not easily lend itself to any definite interpretation. Some identify the "angel" with our Lord Himself, and make the "little book" mean the supplemental revelation of the "beast" soon to follow (13) together with the whole story of the awful period of his reign. Chapter 11 is plainer. It refers to Jerusalem during the reign of the "beast" or "man of sin," "forty and two months" being equivalent to the last 3½ years of Daniel's 70th week already referred to. The "two witnesses testifying with supernatural power" during this time have been identified with Moses and Elijah returned to the earth in the flesh for that ministry.

Verse 6 strikingly parallels the illustrations of their earlier power, while the mysterious manner in which they were taken away from earth, the one buried by God's own hand and the other translated having never seen death, add their contribution to the probability of this application of the chapter.

4. Consummation 11:15-19.

Corresponds somewhat to the ending of the revelation of the seven seals (8:1); i.e., it seems to bring us up to the end or final climax, and yet to halt just short of it in order to retrace the ground for fuller detail.

Throughout these visions frequent allusions are made to the destructive forces of the heavens, "the power of the air," and also to conflicts of armies on the earth which suggests modern methods of warfare. Military airships stagger men not so much by their spectacle as by their slaughter. They seem to be faint gray linear objects silhouetted against the sky, but some of them carry torpedoes, and are able to pursue a battleship and send it to the bottom. Was Tennyson "also among the prophets," when he wrote:

"Men, my brothers, men the workers, ever reaping something new;

That which they have done but earnest of the things that they shall do;

"For I dipt into the future, far as human eye could see,

Saw the vision of the world, and all the wonder that would be;

"Saw the heavens filled with commerce, argosies of magic sails,

Pilots of the purple twilight, dropping down with costly bales;

"Heard the heavens fill with shouting, and there rained a ghastly dew

From the nations' airy navies, grappling in the central blue;

"Far along the world-wide whis-per of the sound wind rushing warm,

With the standards of the people plunging through the thunder storm.

"Till the war drum throbbed no longer, and the battle flags were furled

In the parliament of man, the federation of the world."

Questions.

1. What familiar law of rhetoric is illustrated in this lesson?

2. How do some interpret what we call the "Introduction"?

3. Interpret the six trumpets.

4. How do some interpret the "little book"?

5. Locate the forty and two months.

6. With whom are the two witnesses identified?

7. What modern invention of warfare is suggested by a part of the foregoing vision?

8. What modern poet is quoted?

THE SEVEN PERSONAGES

CHAPTERS 12-14

1. Introduction (The Woman and the Dragon) 12.

The seven personages of this division as identified by Erdman, include the woman, the child, the dragon, the archangel, the remnant (of Israel), the ten-horned beast, and the two-horned beast or false prophet, the first four being found in this chapter. The woman represents Israel it is believed, and the man-child to whom she gave birth, the Messiah. The dragon is Satan, whose ten horns represent the 10 kingdoms of the Roman Empire when in that day they shall be federated under the "beast" of the next chapter. The 7 heads are not so easily interpreted, though with Benjamin Wills Newton it may be thought that they stand for seven systems: commercial, industrial, social, military, educational, political, and ecclesiastical, which will contribute to the unity or federation just named.

The rule of the man-child refers to the millennial reign of Christ, and his being "caught up," to His ascension including in the thought the translation of the Church to be with Him as the body of which He is the Head. The "wilderness" is the Gentile nations among which the faithful remnant of Israel will be preserved during the tribulation, 1260 days. Verses 7-12 call for little comment as the event of which they speak synchronizes with the period of the Tribulation, and indeed accounts for it. Satan's enmity against Israel is revealed in verse 13, the aid she receives from some of the Gentile nations, verse 14, and his futile attempts at her destruction, verses 15, 16. When Satan sought to frustrate God in His plan for Israel in Egypt he "cast out of his mouth water as a flood," i.e., the Egyptian army, but "the earth opened her mouth and swallowed up the flood," and shall we say that the closing verses of chapter 12 point to an event not dissimilar from that of the Red Sea?

2. Progression (Tribulation period) 13.

The "sea" represents the Gentile nations, and the first "Beast," the last form of Gentile dominion in the earth. In the first three verses we have the ten-kingdom empire, but in 4-10 the emperor himself is designated, who is emphatically the "beast." The three animals, leopard, bear, and lion, recall Daniel 7 as symbols of the empires which preceded the Roman and all of whose characteristics entered into the qualities of that empire, and will be reproduced in the final form of Gentile rule (Scofield Bible). The "wounded" head which "was healed," the same authority refers to one of the ancient forms of government of the Empire, that of absolutism, which for a period ceased to exist and will be revived again at the end. But consistency demands that if the 7 heads be taken to represent 7 influential systems contributing to the federation of the empire under the "beast," then the

wounding of one head must be the temporary destruction of one of those systems, and its healing the restoration of it again to its former place. Newton regards this as the ecclesiastical system, and as pointing to the time when all religious influences will be suddenly swept away, while Satan has another system ready to be substituted for it, whose great high-priest is the second "beast" now to be described.

The second "beast" (13:17-18) is the last ecclesiastical head of the federated empire as the first "beast" is the last civil head. Many regard the second "beast" otherwise known as the "False Prophet," (Rev. 16:13), as the Anti-Christ, rather than the first "beast," and probably this is true. "For purposes of persecution he is permitted to exercise the power of the first or emperor-"beast." "666" is man's number in distinction from 7 which is God's number, and the reference to it is designed to comfort the remnant in that awful day, when they may take heart in the thought that powerful as he is, yet he is a man only and not God.

3. Parenthesis (The First Fruits and the Three Angels) 14:1-13.

The 144,000 on Mt. Zion are another picture of the saved remnant of Israel (see chapter 7). The mission of the first angel with "the everlasting gospel" is interpreted to mean that gospel which will be proclaimed at the end of the "Tribulation" immediately preceding the judgment of the nations (Matt. 25:31). As Scofield says, "It is neither the gospel of the kingdom nor the gospel of grace. Its burden is judgment, not salvation, and yet it is good news to Israel and others who, during the Tribulation have been saved (Ps. 96:2-13; Isa. 35:4-10; Luke 21-28; Rev. 7:9-14). The mission of the second angel will be seen in fulfillment in chapter 18, and that of the third in chapter 19.

4. Consummation (The Harvest and the Vintage) 14-20.

The "harvest" (14-16) is thought to refer to the judgment on the Gentile nations, while "the vine of the earth" is applied in the same way to Israel. For the first compare Matt. 25:31-46, and the second, Matt. 24:29-51.

Questions.

1. Name the seven "Personages" of this lesson.

2. Give in your own words an interpretation of the imagery of chapter 12.

3. Do the same with chapter 13.

4. Do the same with chapter 14.

5. What two views are given of the symbolism of the 7 heads?

THE SEVEN VIALS

CHAPTERS 15, 16

The law of recurrence finds a further illustration here for we are still in the "Tribulation" period, the latter half of Daniel's seventieth week, and are looking upon the features of that day of judgment.

1. The "Introduction" includes the whole of chapter 15, being the revelation of the "overcomers" and the seven angels. No one can read this without being struck by its likeness to the song of Moses after Israel's deliverance from Pharaoh at the Red Sea. (Ex. 15)

2. The "Progression" is set before us in the revelation of the six vials (16:1-12), which are doubtless literal plagues to be visited upon the followers of the "beast" and upon his throne, and which also suggest the story of Israel's deliverance from Egypt (Ex. 5-11).

3. The "Parenthesis" is the gathering up of the Kings (13-16). The drying up of the Euphrates may be taken literally, though it is difficult to say just who are meant by the "the kings of the east." Some regard the passage as paralleled by Ezekiel, chapters 38-39, which reveal the rising of Russia and her allies against the Roman federation sometime during the period, or approximate to the period, we are now considering. It is to be noted here that the great battle of verse 14 is not described, although its issue is announced (17-21), cf. also Zechariah 14:1-3.

4. The "Consummation" (17-21) synchronizes with the judgment on the city of Babylon—literal Babylon, rebuilt as the seat of the "beast" on the plain of Shinar, Isaiah 13-14.

Questions.

1. What law of rhetoric is again illustrated in this lesson?

2. What Old Testament parallel is suggested?

3. How may the six vials be interpreted?

4. What Old Testament prophecy is recalled by chapter 16:12?

5. Have you re-read the passage in Zechariah?

6. Have you reviewed our lesson on Isaiah 13-14?

THE SEVEN DOOMS

CHAPTERS 17-18

The seven dooms are those of Babylon, the beast, the false prophet, the kings, the dragon, gog, and the dead. This lesson will be limited to chapters 17 and 18, both of which speak of Babylon but in different ways, and to understand which, it is necessary to keep in mind that every city may be conceived of from two points of view, material and moral. The streets and parks, the buildings, the docks and market places, these are Chicago; but her politics and government, her commerce and industry, her educational and religious systems, these things which have made her what she is, constitute *Chicagoism*. The one is the city materially, and the other the city morally considered. This distinction is seen in Babylon and Babylonianism; chapter 15:5, revealing the doom of the city material, and chapter 17 that of the city moral.

1. Introduction (The Harlot and the Beast) 17.

The "Harlot" is Babylon from the moral side, i.e., Babylonianism, or in other words, the summing up in that figure of the prevailing worldly systems that enter into the final federation of the Gentile nations. The "waters" represent those nations, cf verses 1 and 18. The "beast" we have already identified as the federated Roman Empire, though sometimes the personal head of that empire himself, verses 3 and 8. The "mystery" is interpreted in the sense that the nations contribute to the supremacy of the "harlot," i.e., to Babylonianism, and benefit by it, and yet do not recognize it. "Drunken" is explained by the circumstance that the latitudinarianism, the breadth, the laxness of Babylonianism tolerates all schools and theories of religion inimical to God and the Bible like Romanism, Mohammedanism, Hinduism, etc., which have shed the blood of the saints in all the centuries. The "seven mountains" are related to the woman as the "seven heads" are to the beast, i.e., the systems of authority or power, the politics, government, commerce, industry, education, religion, etc., making the one totality. The "seven kings" is explained by Newton by the remark that God has allowed "executive power" in the prophetic earth to be exhibited in seven different forms, although there will be yet an eighth form before the end comes. By the "prophetic earth" is meant the nations clustering around the Mediterranean which, with their allies and dependencies, constitute the Roman Empire of the Caesars, and will constitute the federation at the end under the "beast." The history of this "executive power" commenced with Nimrod and concludes with the "beast," both of whom stand connected with Babel or Babylon. The whole of these seven forms of "executive power" include, "the native Monarchy of Nimrod, the theocracy of Israel, the despotism of Nebuchadnezzar; the aristocracy of Persia, the military monarchy of Alexander, the empire of the Caesars, and the constitutional monarchies of modern Europe. The sixth, that of the Caesars, was existent when this revelation was given ("one is," verse 10), the seventh is now in vogue, and the eighth (verse 11) will be that of the "beast." The teaching of verses 16 and 17 seems to be that the kings reigning over the ten kingdoms that will form the federation at the end, will find Babylonianism," i.e., the systems which control in their several kingdoms, to be a hard yoke upon them, especially so as these systems increase in influence with the increase of democracy which is always hateful to kings. It is to be rid of "Babylonianism" that they temporarily unite to "give their power and strength unto the "beast." As Newton says, "Gladly will they take refuge under the arm of one whom Satan strengthens for dominion, and join in destroying a system which has really made them its slaves." The *system* of Babylon will be destroyed (chapter 17), but the city itself with all its wealth of greatness will for a time continue, (chapter 18), the "beast" reigning over it until the hour of its dooms and his doom shall come together.

2. Progression (18), the Doom of the Material City.

But a pause should be made here to prove the application to a literal city of Babylon rebuilt on the plain of Shinar. This is necessary when so respected an authority as the Scofield Bible says, "The notion of a literal Babylon to be rebuilt on the site of ancient Babylon is in conflict with Isaiah 13:19-22." Those who have studied that chapter in this commentary will have seen reasons for the opposite view. The language of Isaiah chapters 13 and 14 seems to demand the rebuilding of Babylon for their fulfilment. But the reason the Scofield Bible holds this view, is partly explained by its interpretation of the preceding chapter. "Two Babylons are to be distinguished in the Revelation," it says, "ecclesiastical Babylon which is apostate Christendom, headed up under the papacy; and political Babylon, which is the beast's confederated empire, the last form of Gentile world-dominion. Ecclesiastical Babylon is 'the greatest harlot' and is destroyed by political Babylon." This commentary agrees that two Babylons are to be distinguished and that the Babylon of chapter 17 is "apostate Christendom." But it holds that "apostate Christendom" includes Protestantism as well as the papacy, and is in fact, the sum of the seven systems already indicated, one of which is ecclesiastical. It may be that the the "beast" comes into power, Protestantism will become effaced and the papacy be the only ecclesiastical system to be reckoned with, but as to this we have no light. "The language of Revelation 18," the Scofield Bible goes on to say, "seems beyond question to identify 'Babylon' the 'city' with 'Babylon' the ecclesiastical centre, viz: Rome"; but we do not see it that way, and are inclined to agree with another, that there will be "a certain logical conclusion of the history of the times of the Gentiles. The civilization and culture of the world will again become atheistic and man centered, and having described a circle, its cradle (Babylon) will become its grave."

In the study of chapter 18 one is impressed with the large place commerce is to hold in the greatness of that city. The merchants and ship masters are her chief mourners (compare Zech. 5:5-11).

Questions.

1. Name the seven "dooms."
2. In what two ways is "Babylon" to be conceived of?
3. Define the terms "Babylonianism," "Mystery," "Drunken," "Seven Mountains," and "Seven Kings."
4. What is meant by the "prophetic earth"?
5. Name the seven forms of executive power.

6. Why is "Babylonianism" destroyed by the "Beast"?
7. Have you reviewed the lesson on Isaiah 13 and 14?
8. Have you reviewed the lesson on Zechariah 5?

THE SEVEN DOOMS

CONTINUED

Chapters 19-20

1. Continuing the last lesson we begin this with what we have come to recognize as the "Parenthesis" (19:1-10), and which in this case is composed simply of four "allelujahs," two of which are retrospective and refer to the fall of Babylon, and two prospective touching on the marriage supper of the Lamb and the inauguration of the kingdom. The Lamb's "wife" spoken of in verse 7, is the bride (Rev. 21:9) or the Church, identified with the "heavenly Jerusalem" (Heb. 12:22, 23), and is to be distinguished from Israel, the adulterous and repudiated "wife" of Jehovah yet to be restored (Isa. 54:1-10; Hos. 2:1-7), who is identified with life on the earth (Hos. 2:23). "A forgiven and restored wife could not be called either a virgin (2 Cor. 11:2, 3) or a bride."—Scofield Bible.

2. The Consummation of this "seven" covers the remainder of the lesson (19, 11-20, 15), the first event being the coming of the Lord in glory (19:11-16). We have seen Him as already come for His Church which has been caught up to meet Him in the air, but this vision is that of His departure out of heaven *with* His Church and His holy angels preparatory to the judgment on the Gentile world-power headed up in the "beast" (Dan. 2:34, 35). "The day of the Lord," of which the Old Testament prophets speak, now begins. The second event in this period is the battle of Armageddon (17-19, cf. 16, 14). "Armageddon" refers to the hill and valley of Megiddo, west of the Jordan in the plain of Jezreel. At this place the Lord will deliver the Jewish remnant

beseiged by the Gentile world power under the "beast" (cf. 16: 13-16; Zechariah 12:1-9).

The third event is the doom of the "beast" and the "false prophet" (20). For the prophetic history of the "beast" cf. Dan. 7:24-26, 9:27; Matt. 24:15, and 2 Thess. 2:4-8. The "false prophet" has been previously referred to as the ecclesiastical head of the federated empire as the "beast" is the political head, and some would identify in him the Anti-Christ of 1 John 4, and other Scriptures. The fourth event is the doom of the kings (21). The fifth is the binding of Satan during the Millenium (20:1-3). The sixth, the first resurrection and the Millennial age (4-6). "The thrones and they that sat upon them," represent the raised and glorified saints in their capacity as judging and reigning (cf. Matt. 19:28, 1 Cor. 6:2; Rev. 3:21). "The souls of them that were beheaded" are the martyrs of the Tribulation period united to the Church in Millennial glory. The "thousand years" is the Millennial period intervening between the first and second resurrections (Luke 14:13, 14; Jno. 5:29; 1 Cor. 15:52).

The seventh event is the loosing of Satan at the close of the Millennium and the doom of Gog and Magog (7-9). Here Satan is again seen (this time in his own person) at the head of a final effort to overthrow the kingdom of God on earth. In the Millennial age sin still will be in the hearts of men except as they are regenerated, and Satan will find good soil to work in when his liberty is restored. The identity of "Gog and Magog" is not revealed, but their purpose is clearly indicated in verse 9. The eighth event is the doom of Satan (10) who, being cast into the lake of fire and brimstone, is not to be conceived of as then reigning in hell. This idea is borrowed from Milton but is not in the Bible. The ninth event is the doom of the unbelieving dead and the last judgment (11-15). The "dead" in this case excludes all the redeemed at least up until the translation of the Church, who have been in glory with Christ during the "thousand years." But they include all the wicked dead from the beginning of the race until the end of the world, for this is the last judgment.

Note the distinction between "books" and "another book." The wicked and unbelieving have always chosen to be justified by their deeds rather than by faith in Christ, and the "books" represent the record of those deeds. The outcome (15) shows the fallacy of their trust for the deeds of none were sufficient to justify. Only those "found written in the book of life" are saved.

There are three great judgments of mankind to be noted: (1) that of believers when Christ comes for His Church (2 Cor. 5:10) when not their salvation, but their rewards in glory are to be determined; (2) that of the living Gentile nations on the earth at the beginning of the Day of the Lord (Matt. 25:32), with which is closely connected the judgment of Israel (Ezek. 20:37); and (3) this last judgment with which the history of the present earth ends.

"The second death" and the "Lake of Fire" are identical terms (Rev. 20:14) and are used of the eternal state of the wicked. It is "second" relatively to the preceding death of the wicked in unbelief and rejection of God; their eternal state is one of eternal "death" (i.e., separation from God) in sin (John 8:21, 24). That the second death is not annihilation is shown by a comparison of Rev. 19:20 with Rev. 20:10, for after one thousand years in the lake of fire the beast and false prophet are still there, undestroyed." — Scofield Bible.

Questions.

1. Describe the "Allelujas."

2. Distinguish between the "wife" of the Lamb and the "wife" of Jehovah.

3. Name the nine events in their order under the head of the "Consummation."

4. Give the history of "Armageddon."

5. Describe and distinguish the last judgment.

6. Define the "second death."

7. What proves that it is not annihilation?

THE SEVEN NEW THINGS

CHAPTERS 21-22

According to Erdman, the seven "new things" are the new heaven, earth, peoples, city, temple, luminary, paradise.

1. The "Introduction" in this case covers the first two, the new heaven and the new earth (1-8). Following "Synthetic Bible Studies" observe the sequence of events suggested by verse 1: In the present time, we have the Church, in the Millennium will be the kingdom, and after that the new world where God shall be all in all (cf. I Cor. 15:23-28). Man's soul is redeemed by regeneration through the Holy Spirit now, his body shall be redeemed at the resurrection, and his dwelling-place at the creation of the new heaven and earth. "And there shall be no more sea." The sea is the type of perpetual unrest, and its absence after the metamorphosis of the earth answers to the unruffled state of solid peace which shall then prevail. A "river," and "water" are spoken of in the next chapter, but no sea.

In the descent of the holy city upon the earth as the tabernacle of God (2-8), are revealed some wondrous and precious things. Always distinguish between this New Jerusalem out of heaven, and that earthly Jerusalem in which Israel in the flesh shall dwell during the Millennium. The one will be done away with when the other comes. This new Jerusalem will be God's dwelling place with men in the new earth. It is the antitype of the tabernacle in the wilderness, and is also the same Greek word as that used of Christ's tabernacling among us (John 1:14). He was then seen in the weakness of the flesh, but at the new creation he shall be seen in the glory of his Godhead.

2. That which stands for the "Progression" in this instance is the revelation of the New Jerusalem (21:9-22:5). All the details of this city suggest glory, beauty, security and peace. In the Millennium, literal Israel in the flesh dwelling in Jerusalem, is the antitype of the Old Testament earthly theocracy; but in this, the eternal age, the heavenly Jerusalem is the antitype of the Church, composed of Jews and Gentiles. This idea seems to be suggested by the names of the twelve tribes and the twelve apostles written upon the gates and the foundations. The fact that no temple is seen in this city is remarkable, and suggests that the means of grace cease when the end of grace has come. Uninterrupted, immediate, direct communion with God and the Lamb will then be enjoyed. The student will be struck by the comparison evidently intended to be drawn between the picture in chapter 22:1-4, and the story of the garden of Eden and the expulsion of our first parents.

3. The "Consummation" is the epilog of the book (6-21), in which there is nothing more solemn than verse 11, which emphasizes the thought that "the punishment of sin is sin, just as the reward of holiness is holiness." "Eternal punishment is not so much an arbitrary law as a result necessarily following in the very nature of things as the fruit results from the bud." In this connection notice the allusion to the eternity of sin in verse 15. May God quicken us who know these things to do our duty in bearing witness to them, that some by all means may be saved. This duty is set before us in verse 17, and "He which testifieth these things saith, surely, I come, quickly. Amen. Even so, Come, Lord Jesus!"

Questions.

1. Name the seven "new things."

2. Give the sequence of events as outlined in 1 Cor. 15.23-28.

3. Interpret the reference to the "sea."

4. How would you distinguish between the earthly and the New Jerusalem?

5. Of what two things is the latter the antitype?

6. How is this suggested?

7. What significance may be attached to the absence of a temple?

8. What two awful things about sin are here taught?

INDEX

OF

Themes Receiving Special Attention, Texts Homiletically Treated, Scripture Passages Suggested for Bible Readings or Expository Discourses.